THE FIRST BOOK OF MOSES, C

EXODUS

EXODUS I
(Chapters 1-18)

THE
PREACHER'S
OUTLINE & SERMON
BIBLE®

THE FIRST BOOK OF MOSES, CALLED

EXODUS

EXODUS I
(Chapters 1-18)

THE PREACHER'S OUTLINE & SERMON BIBLE®

OLD TESTAMENT
_____
_____

KING JAMES VERSION

Leadership Ministries Worldwide
Chattanooga, TN

THE PREACHER'S OUTLINE & SERMON BIBLE® - EXODUS I

KING JAMES VERSION

Please address all requests for information or permission to:

Leadership Ministries Worldwide
Ph.# (800) 987-8790   E-Mail: info@lmw.org
Web: lmw.org

Library of Congress Catalog Card Number: 96-75921
International Standard Book Number: 978-1-57407-049-1

Printed in the United States of America

DEDICATED

To all the men and women of the world
who preach and teach the Gospel of
our Lord Jesus Christ and
to the Mercy and Grace of God

- Demonstrated to us in Christ Jesus our Lord.

  "In whom we have redemption through His blood, the forgiveness of sins, according to the riches of His grace." (Ep.1:7)

- Out of the mercy and grace of God, His Word has flowed. Let every person know that God will have mercy upon him, forgiving and using him to fulfill His glorious plan of salvation.

  "For God so loved the world, that he gave His only begotten Son, that whosoever believeth in Him should not perish, but have everlasting life. For God sent not his son into the world to condemn the world, but that the world through him might be saved." (Jn.3:16-17)

  "For this is good and acceptable in the sight of God our Saviour; who will have all men to be saved, and to come unto the knowledge of the truth." (1 Ti.2:3-4)

10/22

The Preacher's Outline & Sermon Bible®

is written for God's servants to use in their study, teaching, and preaching of God's Holy Word...

- to share the Word of God with the world.
- to help believers, both ministers and laypersons, in their understanding, preaching, and teaching of God's Word.
- to do everything we possibly can to lead men, women, boys, and girls to give their hearts and lives to Jesus Christ and to secure the eternal life that He offers.
- to do all we can to minister to the needy of the world.
- to give Jesus Christ His proper place, the place the Word gives Him. Therefore, no work of Leadership Ministries Worldwide will ever be personalized.

ACKNOWLEDGMENTS AND BIBLIOGRAPHY

Every child of God is precious to the Lord and deeply loved. And every child as a servant of the Lord touches the lives of those who come in contact with him or his ministry. The writing ministries of the following servants have touched this work, and we are grateful that God brought their writings our way. We hereby acknowledge their ministry to us, being fully aware that there are many others down through the years whose writings have touched our lives and who deserve mention, but whose names have faded from our memory. May our wonderful Lord continue to bless the ministries of these dear servants—and the ministries of us all—as we diligently labor to reach the world for Christ and to meet the desperate needs of those who suffer so much.

THE REFERENCE WORKS

Archer, Gleason L. *A Survey of Old Testament Introduction*. Chicago, IL: Moody Bible Institute of Chicago, 1974.

Brown, Francis. *The New Brown-Driver-Briggs-Gesenius Hebrew-English Lexicon*. Peabody, MA: Hendrickson Publishers, 1979.

Cruden's Complete Concordance of the Old & New Testament. Philadelphia, PA: The John C. Winston Co., 1930.

Baker's Dictionary of Theology. Everett F. Harrison, Editor-in-Chief. Grand Rapids, MI: Baker Book House, 1960.

Encyclopedia of Biblical Prophecy. J. Barton Payne. New York, NY: Harper & Row, Publishers, 1973.

Funk & Wagnalls Standard Desk Dictionary. Lippincott & Crowell, Publishers, 1980, Vol.2.

Geisler, Norman. *A Popular Survey of the Old Testament*. Grand Rapids, MI: Baker Book House, 1977.

Good News Bible. Old Testament: © American Bible Society, 1976. New Testament: © American Bible Society, 1966, 1971, 1976. Collins World.

Holy Bible, Pilgrim Edition. New York, NY: Oxford University Press, 1952.

Josephus, Flavius. *Complete Works*. Grand Rapids, MI: Kregel Publications, 1981.

Life Application® Bible. Wheaton, IL: Tyndale House Publishers, Inc., 1991.

Life Application® Study Bible. New International Version. Tyndale House Publishers, Inc.: Wheaton, IL 1991, and Zondervan Publishing House: Grand Rapids, MI, 1984.

Lindsell, Harold and Woodbridge, Charles J. *A Handbook of Christian Truth*. Westwood, NJ: Fleming H. Revell Company, A Division of Baker Book House, 1953.

Living Quotations For Christians. Edited by Sherwood Eliot Wirt and Kersten Beckstrom. New York, NY: Harper & Row, Publishers, 1974.

Lockyer, Herbert. *All the Books and Chapters of the Bible*. Grand Rapids, MI: Zondervan Publishing House, 1966.

———. *All the Men of the Bible*. Grand Rapids, MI: Zondervan Publishing House, 1958.

———. *The Women of the Bible*. Grand Rapids, MI: Zondervan Publishing House, 1967.

Martin, Alfred. *Survey of the Scriptures*, Part I, II, III. Chicago, IL: Moody Bible Institute of Chicago, 1961.

McDowell, Josh. *Evidence That Demands a Verdict*, Vol.1. San Bernardino, CA: Here's Life Publishers, Inc., 1979.

Miller, Madeleine S. & J. Lane. *Harper's Bible Dictionary*. New York, NY: Harper & Row Publishers, 1961.

New American Standard Bible, Reference Edition. La Habra, CA: The Lockman Foundation, 1975.

New International Version Study Bible. Grand Rapids, MI: Zondervan Bible Publishers, 1985.

Orr, William. *How We May Know That God Is*. Wheaton, IL: Van Kampen Press, n.d.

Owens, John Joseph. *Analytical Key to the Old Testament*, Vols.1, 2, 3. Grand Rapids, MI: Baker Book House, 1989.

Strong, James. *Strong's Exhaustive Concordance of the Bible*. Nashville, TN: Thomas Nelson, Inc., 1990.

Strong's Greek and Hebrew Dictionary as compiled by iExalt Software. Database NavPress Software, 1990-1993.

The Amplified Bible. Scripture taken from THE AMPLIFIED BIBLE, Old Testament copyright © 1965, 1987 by the Zondervan Publishing House. The Amplified New Testament copyright © 1958, 1987 by The Lockman Foundation. Used by permission.

The Holy Bible in Four Translations. Minneapolis, MN: Worldwide Publications. Copyright © The Iversen-Norman Associates: New York, NY, 1972.

The Interlinear Bible, Vols.1, 2, 3. Translated by Jay P. Green, Sr. Grand Rapids, MI: Baker Book House, 1976.

The International Standard Bible Encyclopaedia, Edited by James Orr. Grand Rapids, MI: Eerdmans Publishing Co., 1939.

The New Compact Bible Dictionary. Edited by T. Alton Bryant. Grand Rapids, MI: Zondervan Publishing House, 1967. Used by permission of Zondervan Publishing House.

The New Scofield Reference Bible. Edited by C.I. Scofield. New York, NY: Oxford University Press, 1967.

The New Thompson Chain Reference Bible. Indianapolis, IN: B.B. Kirkbride Bible Co., Inc., 1964.

The Open Bible. Nashville, TN: Thomas Nelson Publishers, 1975.

The Zondervan Pictorial Encyclopedia of the Bible, Vol.1. Merrill C. Tenney, Editor. Grand Rapids, MI: Zondervan Publishing House, 1982.

Theological Wordbook of the Old Testament. Edited by R. Laird Harris. Chicago, IL: Moody Bible Institute of Chicago, 1980.

Unger, Merrill F. & William White, Jr. *Nelson's Expository Dictionary of the Old Testament*. Nashville, TN: Thomas Nelson Publishers, 1980.

Vine, W.E., Merrill F. Unger, William White, Jr. *Vine's Complete Expository Dictionary of Old and New Testament Words*. Nashville, TN: Thomas Nelson Publishers, 1985.

Webster's Seventh New Collegiate Dictionary. Springfield, MA: G. & C. Merriam Company, Publishers, 1971.

Wilson, William. *Wilson's Old Testament Word Studies*. McLean, VA: MacDonald Publishing Company, n.d.

Wood, Leon. *A Survey of Israel's History*. Grand Rapids, MI: Zondervan Publishing House, 1982.

Young, Edward J. *An Introduction to the Old Testament*. Grand Rapids, MI: Eerdmans Publishing Co., 1964.

Young, Robert. *Young's Analytical Concordance to the Bible*. Grand Rapids, MI: Eerdmans Publishing Co., n.d.

ACKNOWLEDGMENTS AND BIBLIOGRAPHY

THE COMMENTARIES

Barclay, William. *The Old Law & The New Law*. Philadelphia, PA: The Westminster Press, 1972.

Barnes' Notes, Exodus to Esther. F.C. Cook, Editor. Grand Rapids, MI: Baker Book House, n.d.

Bush, George. *Exodus*. Minneapolis, MN: Klock & Klock Christian Publishers, Inc., 1981.

Childs, Brevard S. *The Book of Exodus*. Philadelphia, PA: The Westminster Press, 1974.

Cole, R. Alan. *Exodus*. "The Tyndale Old Testament Commentaries." Downers Grove, IL: Inter-Varsity Press, 1973.

Crockett, William Day. *A Harmony of Samuel, Kings, and Chronicles*. Grand Rapids, MI: Baker Book House, 1985.

Dunnam, Maxie. *The Preacher's Commentary on Exodus*. Nashville, TN: Word Publishing, 1987, 2003.

Durham, John I. *Understanding the Basic Themes of Exodus*. Dallas, TX: Word, Inc., 1990.

———. *Word Biblical Commentary, Exodus*. Waco, TX: Word, Inc., 1987.

Ellison, H.L. *Exodus*. Philadelphia, PA: The Westminster Press, 1982.

Fretheim, Terence E. *Exodus, Interpretation*. Louisville, KY: John Knox Press, 1991.

Gaebelein, Frank E. *The Expositor's Bible Commentary*, Vol.2. Grand Rapids, MI: Zondervan Publishing House, 1990.

Gill, John. *Gill's Commentary*, Vol.2. Grand Rapids, MI: Baker Book House, 1980.

Hayford, Jack W., Executive Editor. *Milestones to Maturity*. Nashville, TN: Thomas Nelson Publishers, 1994

Henry, Matthew. *Matthew Henry's Commentary*, 6 Vols. Old Tappan, NJ: Fleming H. Revell Co., n.d.

Heslop, W.G. *Extras from Exodus*. Grand Rapids, MI: Kregel Publications, 1931.

Huey, F.B. Jr. *A Study Guide Commentary, Exodus*. Grand Rapids, MI: Zondervan Publishing House, 1977.

Hyatt, J.P. *The New Century Bible Commentary, Exodus*. Grand Rapids, MI: Eerdmans Publishing Company, 1971.

Keil-Delitzsch. *Commentary on the Old Testament*, Vol.3. Grand Rapids, MI: Eerdmans Publishing Co., n.d.

Life Change Series, Exodus. Colorado Springs, CO: NavPress, 1989.

McGee, J. Vernon. *Thru the Bible*, Vol.2. Nashville, TN: Thomas Nelson Publishers, 1981.

Meyer, F.B. *Devotional Commentary on Exodus*. Grand Rapids, MI: Kregel Publications, 1978.

Napier, B. Davie. *Exodus*. "The Layman's Bible Commentary," Vol.3. Atlanta, GA: John Knox Press, 1963.

Pink, Arthur. *Gleanings in Exodus*. Chicago, IL: Moody Bible Institute of Chicago, Moody Press, n.d.

Reapsome, James. *Exodus*. Downers Grove, IL: InterVarsity Press, 1989.

Sarna, Nahum M. *Exploring Exodus*. New York, NY: Schocken Books Inc., 1986.

The Biblical Illustrator, Exodus. Edited by Joseph S. Exell. Grand Rapids, MI: Baker Book House, 1964.

The Interpreter's Bible, 12 Vols. New York, NY: Abingdon Press, 1956.

The Pulpit Commentary. 23 Vols. Edited by H.D.M. Spence & Joseph S. Exell. Grand Rapids, MI: Eerdmans Publishing Co., 1950.

Thomas, W.H. Griffith. *Through the Pentateuch Chapter by Chapter*. Grand Rapids, MI: Eerdmans Publishing Company, 1957.

Youngblood, Ronald F. *Exodus*. Chicago, IL: Moody Press, 1983.

———. *1 Samuel. 2 Samuel*. "The Expositor's Bible Commentary," Vol.3. Grand Rapids, MI: Zondervan Publishing House, 1990.

OTHER SOURCES

Illustrated Stedman's Medical Dictionary, 24th Edition. Baltimore, MD: Williams & Wilkins, 1982.

Knight, Walter B. *3,0000 Illustrations for Christian Service*. Grand Rapids, MI: Eerdmans Publishing Company, 1971,

Wilson, Grady. Pamphlet of a sermon preached on "The Hour of Decision." The Billy Graham Evangelistic Association, 1970.

ABBREVIATIONS

&	= and		O.T.	= Old Testament
Bc.	= because		p./pp.	= page/pages
Concl.	= conclusion		Pt.	= point
Cp.	= compare		Quest.	= question
Ct.	= contrast		Rel.	= religion
e.g.	= for example		Rgt.	= righteousness
f.	= following		Thru	= through
Illust.	= illustration		v./vv.	= verse/verses
N.T.	= New Testament		vs.	= versus

THE BOOKS OF THE OLD TESTAMENT

Book	Abbreviation	Chapters	Book	Abbreviation	Chapters
GENESIS	Gen. or Ge.	50	Ecclesiastes	Eccl. or Ec.	12
Exodus	Ex.	40	The Song of Solomon	S. of Sol. or Song	8
Leviticus	Lev. or Le.	27	Isaiah	Is.	66
Numbers	Num. or Nu.	36	Jeremiah	Jer. or Je.	52
Deuteronomy	Dt. or De.	34	Lamentations	Lam.	5
Joshua	Josh. or Jos.	24	Ezekiel	Ezk. or Eze.	48
Judges	Judg. or Jud.	21	Daniel	Dan. or Da.	12
Ruth	Ruth or Ru.	4	Hosea	Hos. or Ho.	14
1 Samuel	1 Sam. or 1 S.	31	Joel	Joel	3
2 Samuel	2 Sam. or 2 S.	24	Amos	Amos or Am.	9
1 Kings	1 Ki. or 1 K.	22	Obadiah	Obad. or Ob.	1
2 Kings	2 Ki. or 2 K.	25	Jonah	Jon. or Jona.	4
1 Chronicles	1 Chron. or 1 Chr.	29	Micah	Mic. or Mi.	7
2 Chronicles	2 Chron. or 2 Chr.	36	Nahum	Nah. or Na.	3
Ezra	Ezra or Ezr.	10	Habakkuk	Hab.	3
Nehemiah	Neh. or Ne.	13	Zephaniah	Zeph. or Zep.	3
Esther	Est.	10	Haggai	Hag.	2
Job	Job or Jb.	42	Zechariah	Zech. or Zec.	14
Psalms	Ps.	150	Malachi	Mal.	4
Proverbs	Pr.	31			

THE BOOKS OF THE NEW TESTAMENT

Book	Abbreviation	Chapters	Book	Abbreviation	Chapters
MATTHEW	Mt.	28	1 Timothy	1 Tim. or 1 Ti.	6
Mark	Mk.	16	2 Timothy	2 Tim. or 2 Ti.	4
Luke	Lk. or Lu.	24	Titus	Tit.	3
John	Jn.	21	Philemon	Phile. or Phm.	1
The Acts	Acts or Ac.	28	Hebrews	Heb. or He.	13
Romans	Ro.	16	James	Jas. or Js.	5
1 Corinthians	1 Cor. or 1 Co.	16	1 Peter	1 Pt. or 1 Pe.	5
2 Corinthians	2 Cor. or 2 Co.	13	2 Peter	2 Pt. or 2 Pe.	3
Galatians	Gal. or Ga.	6	1 John	1 Jn.	5
Ephesians	Eph. or Ep.	6	2 John	2 Jn.	1
Philippians	Ph.	4	3 John	3 Jn.	1
Colossians	Col.	4	Jude	Jude	1
1 Thessalonians	1 Th.	5	Revelation	Rev. or Re.	22
2 Thessalonians	2 Th.	3			

HOW TO USE
The Preacher's Outline & Sermon Bible®
Follow these easy steps to gain maximum benefit from The POSB.

1. **SUBJECT HEADING**

2. **MAJOR POINTS**

3. **SUBPOINTS**
   &
   SCRIPTURE

4. **COMMENTARY**

1 CORINTHIANS 13:1-13

CHAPTER 13

D. The Most Excellent Quality of Life: Love, Not Gifts, 13:1-13^DS1

1. The great importance of love
   a. Verdict 1: Tongues without love are meaningless
   b. Verdict 2: Gifts without love are nothing
      1) Prophecy is nothing
      2) Understanding all mysteries & knowledge are nothing
      3) Faith is nothing
   c. Verdict 3: Giving without love profits nothing
      1) Giving one's goods
      2) Giving one's life—martyrdom

2. The great acts of love

Though I speak with the tongues of men and of angels, and have not charity, I am become as sounding brass, or a tinkling cymbal.
2 And though I have the gift of prophecy, and understand all mysteries, and all knowledge; and though I have all faith, so that I could remove mountains, and have not charity, I am nothing.
3 And though I bestow all my goods to feed the poor, and though I give my body to be burned, and have not charity, it profiteth me nothing.
4 Charity suffereth long, and is kind; charity envieth not; charity vaunteth not itself, is not puffed up,
5 Doth not behave itself unseemly, seeketh not her own, is not easily provoked, thinketh no evil;

6 Rejoiceth not in iniquity, but rejoiceth in the truth;
7 Beareth all things, believeth all things, hopeth all things, endureth all things.
8 Charity never faileth: but whether there be prophecies, they shall fail; whether there be tongues, they shall cease; whether there be knowledge, it shall vanish away.
9 For we know in part, and we prophesy in part.
10 But when that which is perfect is come, then that which is in part shall be done away.
11 When I was a child, I spake as a child, I understood as a child, I thought as a child: but when I became a man, I put away childish things.
12 For now we see through a glass, darkly; but then face to face: now I know in part; but then shall I know even as also I am known.
13 And now abideth faith, hope, charity, these three; but the greatest of these is charity.

3. The great permanence of love
   a. It never fails, never ceases, never vanishes
   b. It is perfect & complete
   c. It is maturity—mature behavior
   d. It is the hope of being face-to-face with God—possessing perfect consciousness & knowledge

4. The great supremacy of love

DIVISION VII
THE QUESTIONS CONCERNING SPIRITUAL GIFTS, 12:1–14:40

D. The Most Excellent Quality of Life: Love, Not Gifts, 13:1-13

(13:1-13) **Introduction**: there is no question, what the world needs more than anything else is love. If people loved each other, really loved each other, there would be no more war, crime, abuse, injustice, poverty, hunger, starvation, homelessness, deprivation, or immorality. Love is the one ingredient that could revolutionize society. Love is the greatest quality of human life. Love is the supreme quality, the most excellent way for a man to live.
1. The great importance of love (vv.1-3).
2. The great acts of love (vv.4-7).
3. The great permanence of love (vv.8-12).
4. The great supremacy of love (v.13).

DEEPER STUDY # 1
(13:1-13) **Love**: throughout this passage, the word used for love or charity is the great word *agape*. (See DEEPER STUDY # 4, *Love*—Jn.21:15-17 for more discussion.) The meaning of *agape* love is more clearly seen by contrasting it with the various kinds of love. There are essentially four kinds of love. Whereas the English language has only the word *love* to describe all the affectionate experiences of men, the Greek language had a different word to describe each kind of love.
1. There is *passionate* love or *eros* love. This is the physical love between sexes; the patriotic love of a person for his nation; the ambition of a person for power, wealth, or fame. Briefly stated, *eros* love is the base love of a man that arises from his own inner passion. Sometimes *eros* love is focused upon good and other times it is focused upon bad. It should be noted that *eros* love is never used in the New Testament.
2. There is *affectionate* love or *storge* love. This is the kind of love that exists between parent and child and between loyal citizens and a trustworthy ruler. *Storge* love is also not used in the New Testament.
3. There is an *endearing* love, the love that cherishes. This is *phileo* love, the love of a husband and wife for each other, of a brother for a brother, of a friend for the dearest of friends. It is the love that cherishes, that holds someone or something ever so dear to one's heart.
4. There is *selfless and sacrificial* love or *agape* love. Agape love is the love of the mind, of the reason, of the will. It is the love that goes so far...
   - that it loves a person even if he does not deserve to be loved
   - that it actually loves the person who is utterly unworthy of being loved

---

1 Glance at the **Subject Heading**. Think about it for a moment.

2 Glance at the **Subject Heading** again, and then the **Major Points** (1, 2, 3, etc.). Do this several times, reviewing them together while quickly grasping the overall subject.

3 Glance at **both** the **Major Points** and **Subpoints** together while reading the **Scripture**. Do this slower than Step 2. Note how these points sit directly beside the related verse and simply restate what the Scripture is saying—in Outline form.

4 Next read the **Commentary**. Note that the *Major Point Numbers* in the Outline match those in the Commentary. A small raised number (**DS1, DS2, etc.**) at the end of a Subject Heading or Outline Point, directs you to a related **Deeper Study** in the Commentary.

Finally, read the **Thoughts** and **Support Scripture** (not shown).

As you read and re-read, pray that the Holy Spirit will bring to your attention exactly what you should preach and teach. May God bless you richly as you study and teach His Word.

The POSB contains everything you need for sermon preparation:

1. **The Subject Heading** describes the overall theme of the passage, and is located directly above the Scripture (keyed *alphabetically*).

2. **Major Points** are keyed with an outline *number* guiding you to related commentary. Note that the Commentary includes *"Thoughts"* (life application) and abundant Supporting Scriptures.

3. **Subpoints** explain and clarify the Scripture as needed.

4. **Commentary** is fully researched and developed for every point.

   • **Thoughts** (in bold) help apply the Scripture to real life.

   • **Deeper Studies** provide in-depth discussions of key words.

"Woe is unto me, if I preach not the gospel"
(1 Co.9:16)

TABLE OF CONTENTS
EXODUS

	PAGE
INTRODUCTION TO EXODUS	1
A GENERAL SURVEY OF EGYPTIAN HISTORY	8
TYPES, SYMBOLS, AND PICTURES IN EXODUS (Chs.1–18)	16
TIMELINE OF SUBJECTS, CHARACTERS, AND EVENTS IN EXODUS (Chs.1–18)	37
GENERAL OUTLINE OF EXODUS (Chs.1–18)	47
DIVISION I. ISRAEL AND EGYPT: THE OPPRESSION OF GOD'S PEOPLE BY A NATION THAT HAD REJECTED GOD, 1:1-22	49
DIVISION II. MOSES AND GOD: GOD RAISES UP A LEADER TO DELIVER HIS PEOPLE (ISRAEL), 2:1–7:7	71
DIVISION III. THE TEN PLAGUES AND EGYPT: GOD'S JUDGMENT UPON THOSE WHO REJECT HIM AND OPPRESS HIS PEOPLE, 7:8–11:10	141
DIVISION IV. THE PASSOVER AND THE TENTH PLAGUE: DELIVERANCE FROM GOD'S JUDGMENT—LIBERATED, SET FREE, 12:1–13:16	216
DIVISION V. THE RED SEA AND THE WILDERNESS WANDERINGS: THE BELIEVER'S TRIALS AS HE JOURNEYS TO THE PROMISED LAND, 13:17–18:27	262
OUTLINE & SUBJECT INDEX (Chs.1–18)	343
CHARTS - TABLES:	
Jacob's Family Tree	54
A General Survey of God's Call to His People	101
Names of God: Jehovah combined with other words	110
Family Tree of Levi, Moses, and Aaron	138
The God of History	139
The Ten Plagues: Practical Purposes; Items Under God's Control; Effects of the Plagues	143
List of men who attempted to be God and failed	155
God's Power Over the Body and Health	186
Significant Events in the Hebrew Calendar	230
MAPS:	
Map of Rameses and Pithom	66
Map of Midian	83
Map of Mt. Horeb or Mt. Sinai	94
Map of the Nile River	158
Map of Goshen	175
Map of Succoth and Etham	272
Map of Rephidim	320

EXODUS

INTRODUCTION

I. AUTHOR

Moses, the great lawgiver and deliverer of Israel. Moses was the great leader who led Israel from Egyptian bondage and through the *wilderness wanderings*.

1. The internal evidence of Scripture—Scripture itself—strongly points to Moses being the author of *Exodus*. The force of this claim can be clearly seen by simply glancing down through the following Scriptures.

a. The Old Testament points toward Moses being the author.

> "And the LORD said unto Moses, Write this *for* a memorial in a book, and rehearse *it* in the ears of Joshua: for I will utterly put out the remembrance of Amalek from under heaven" (Ex.17:14).
>
> "And Moses wrote all the words of the LORD, and rose up early in the morning, and builded an altar under the hill, and twelve pillars, according to the twelve tribes of Israel" (Ex.24:4).
>
> "And he took the book of the covenant, and read in the audience of the people: and they said, All that the LORD hath said will we do, and be obedient" (Ex.24:7).
>
> "And the LORD said unto Moses, Write thou these words: for after the tenor of these words I have made a covenant with thee and with Israel" (Ex.34:27).
>
> "These *are* the journeys of the children of Israel, which went forth out of the land of Egypt with their armies under the hand of Moses and Aaron. And Moses wrote their goings out according to their journeys by the commandment of the LORD: and these *are* their journeys according to their goings out" (Nu.33:1-2).
>
> "And Moses wrote this law, and delivered it unto the priests the sons of Levi, which bare the ark of the covenant of the LORD, and unto all the elders of Israel" (De.31:9).
>
> "Only be thou strong and very courageous, that thou mayest observe to do according to all the law, which Moses my servant commanded thee: turn not from it *to* the right hand or *to* the left, that thou mayest prosper whithersoever thou goest. This book of the law shall not depart out of thy mouth; but thou shalt meditate therein day and night, that thou mayest observe to do according to all that is written therein: for then thou shalt make thy way prosperous, and then thou shalt have good success" (Jos.1:7-8).
>
> "As Moses the servant of the LORD commanded the children of Israel, as it is written in the book of the law of Moses, an altar of whole stones, over which no man hath lift up *any* iron: and they offered thereon burnt offerings unto the LORD, and sacrificed peace of-ferings" (Jos.8:31).

b. The New Testament points toward Moses being the author.

> "For Moses said, Honour thy father and thy mother; and, Whoso curseth father or mother, let him die the death" (Mk.7:10).
>
> "And as touching the dead, that they rise: have ye not read in the book of Moses, how in the bush God spake unto him, saying, I [am] the God of Abraham, and the God of Isaac, and the God of Jacob?" (Mk.12:26).
>
> "And when the days of her purification according to the law of Moses were accom-plished, they brought him to Jerusalem, to present him to the Lord; (As it is written in the law of the Lord, Every male that openeth the womb shall be called holy to the Lord)" (Lu.2:22-23).

c. Jesus Christ Himself said that Moses was the author.

> "And they said, Moses suffered to write a bill of divorcement, and to put her away. And Jesus answered and said unto them, For the hardness of your heart he wrote you this precept" (Mk.10:4-5).
>
> "And he said unto them, These [are] the words which I spake unto you, while I was yet with you, that all things must be fulfilled, which were written in the law of Moses, and [in] the prophets, and [in] the psalms, concerning me" (Lu.24:44).
>
> "For had ye believed Moses, ye would have believed me: for he wrote of me. But if ye believe not his writings, how shall ye believe my words?" (Jn.5:46-47).
>
> "Did not Moses give you the law, and [yet] none of you keepeth the law? Why go ye about to kill me?" (Jn.7:19).

2. The external evidence also strongly points to Moses being the author of *Exodus*.
    a. Tradition—both Jewish and Christian tradition—has been unanimous in holding that Moses is the author of *Exodus*. In fact, tradition is strong, very strong, that Moses wrote the entire Pentateuch (*Genesis, Exodus, Leviticus, Numbers, Deuteronomy*).
    b. Archeology also points to Moses being the author. The author certainly lived during the day when *Exodus* was written. What shows us this? The facts we find in the Pentateuch, facts describing such matters as...

    - customs
    - conduct
    - geography
    - history
    - events
    - places
    - names

    F.B. Huey says this:

    > *Archaeological discoveries have confirmed the accuracy of customs, events, and names that are found in the Pentateuch and suggest that the author was not writing hundreds of years after the event.*[1]

3. The qualifications of Moses point to his being the author of *Exodus*.
    a. Moses had the education to write *Exodus*. He was well educated in "all the wisdom of the Egyptians" (Ac.7:22). Moreover, he was obviously well prepared by God to take both the written and oral testimony of his forefathers and write Exodus. (See *Introduction*, Author—*Genesis* for more discussion.)
    b. Moses was well acquainted with all that happened in the Book of *Exodus*. He knew all about Egypt, Midian, the desert, and the Sinai Peninsula. He knew all about the customs, conduct, geography, events, places, and people. He knew because he was there.
    c. Moses had the time to write *Exodus*. He lived and walked through the desert with the Israelites for forty years, forty long years. In forming the slaves into a nation of people, he was bound to know the importance of recording their history for future generations.
    d. Moses was God's appointed deliverer, the founding father of the nation Israel. Moses was a man of destiny, a man appointed by God to take a worn out body of slaves and form them into a nation of people. In building the nation, he was bound to record the events and history of the Israelites.
        Just think for a moment: being the great deliverer of Israel, it would have been most unusual—so unusual it would have been foolish—for him not to record the events and history of what was happening. In fact, keep in mind, he was building an impoverished body of people into a nation. He knew this. It would be must unreasonable to think Moses was not recording the events for posterity, to help give structure—building blocks, a foundation—to the nation
        In addition to all the above, if we believe that God inspired (breathed) the Holy Scriptures, one fact comes to the forefront: God would have led men from the earliest days of human history to record His plan of redemption. Therefore to the believer, there is no question: God appointed men from the very beginning of human history, appointed them to write the Holy Scriptures. And as they wrote, God inspired (God breathed) the words of Scripture (2 Ti.3:16).

As seen, the evidence is strong: Moses wrote the great Book of *Exodus*. No other person has ever been suggested that can rival Moses. It would be difficult to reject all the evidence that points to Moses and suggest that some *unknown, nameless* person wrote *Exodus*. The only reasonable and honest conclusion is to say what Scripture indicates: Moses wrote *Exodus*. (See *Introduction—Genesis* for more discussion.)

II. DATE
Probably some time between 1446–1406 B.C.
1. Moses lived 120 years (De.34:7).
2. Moses spent 40 years in Egypt (Ac.7:22-23).
3. Moses spent 40 years in Midian (Ex.2:15).
4. Moses spent 40 years leading Israel through the wilderness experiences (De.8:2f).

Now, we know with some accuracy when Moses lived:

> **"And it came to pass in the four hundred and eightieth year after the children of Israel were come out of the land of Egypt, in the fourth year of Solomon's reign over Israel, in the month Zif, which is the second month, that he began to build the house of the LORD"** (1 K.6:1).

The fourth year of Solomon's reign was about 966 B.C.; therefore, Moses led Israel out of Egypt around 1446 B.C. (480 years before Solomon's 4th year as king.[2] Based upon this information, Moses' life would be dated as follows:
⇒ Moses in Egypt 1526–1486 B.C.
⇒ Moses in Midian 1486–1446 B.C.
⇒ Moses leading Israel through the wilderness 1446–1406 B.C.

[1] F.B. Huey. *Exodus*. (Grand Rapids, MI: Zondervan Publishing House, 1977), p.8.
[2] *New International Version Study Bible*. (Grand Rapids, MI: Zondervan Bible Publishers, 1985). pp.2, 84.

Moses had access to the records and writings of Israel, and he personally led Israel through their wilderness wanderings. Moses unquestionably wrote at least four books of the Pentateuch during this period: Exodus, Leviticus, Numbers, and Deuteronomy). Genesis was either written during the same period of wilderness wandering or during Moses' latter years in Egypt or during his forty years in Midian. Apparently, he did what many great men have done down through history, he kept a diary of the events and compiled his notes into the various books as he found time. Remember, as the future prince of Egypt, Moses would have been taught the importance of writing and recording history.

Note two other significant points:

1. Moses was spiritually mature during the wilderness wanderings. He had the spiritual maturity necessary for the Holy Spirit to inspire him to write Exodus.

2. It was during the wilderness wanderings that God dealt with Moses time and again face to face (so to speak). God is the real Author of the Holy Scriptures. Therefore in the final analysis, the name of a human author has little if any bearing upon the value of the Scripture. Knowing the name of the human author is of secondary importance.

III. TO WHOM WRITTEN

Israel in particular and the human race in general.

1. Exodus was written to give Israel a record of its history and law and to instruct the people how they were to live, serve, and worship God.

2. Exodus was written to all people of all generations...
   - to give us an example and warning about how not to live

   "Now all these things happened unto them for examples: and they are written for our admonition [warning], upon whom the ends of the world are come" (1 Co.10:11).

   - to teach us so that through the Scripture we might be encouraged and have great hope

   "For whatsoever things were written aforetime were written for our learning, that we through patience and comfort of the scriptures might have hope" (Ro.15:4).

IV. PURPOSE

There are at least three purposes for the Book of *Exodus*.

1. The *historical purpose*: to give the Israelites a permanent record of their history and law and a record of how they were to serve and worship God. Historically, Exodus was written...
   a. To teach Israel their God-given purpose, the very reason God had chosen them to be His people (Ex.1:1-22).
      - To teach Israel that there was only one living and true God, one God who had created and purposed all things (Is.43:10-13).
      - To teach Israel its roots, that they had actually been chosen by God Himself through Abraham, appointed to be *the chosen line* of God's people.
      - To teach Israel that *the promised seed*, the Savior, was to be sent into the world through them. They were *the chosen line* through whom God was going to save the world. Salvation—*the promised seed*—was to come through Israel.
      - To teach Israel that they were to receive *the promised land*, the land of Canaan, and that God would be faithful to His Word and give them *the promised land*.

   b. To always remind Israel of their glorious deliverance from slavery to Egypt, glorious deliverance by the mighty hand of God (Ex.2:1–13:16).
   c. To teach Israel the great laws upon which their nation was to be built and governed (Ex.19:1–40:38).
   d. To teach Israel how they must believe and follow God...
      - in facing and conquering the trials and enemies of life
      - in seeking after the promised land (Ex.13:17–18:27)

   e. To teach Israel how they were to serve and worship God (Ex.19:1–40:38).
2. The doctrinal or spiritual purpose:
   a. To teach that the great promise of God, the promise of the *promised seed*, did take place: a great nation of people were born of Abraham's seed, the people who were to give birth to the *promised seed and Savior*, the Lord Jesus Christ (Ex.1:6-7).
   b. To teach the wonderful nature of God, the great doctrines of...
      - God's love, mercy, and grace (Ex.3:7-10; 6:5-9)
      - God's election, predestination, foreordination, and foreknowledge (Ex.6:6-9)
      - God's power and sovereignty (Ex.1:1–18:27)
      - God's justice and judgment (Ex.7:8-14:31; 17:8-16)
      - God's faithfulness (Ex.1:1-40:38)
      - God's salvation and redemption (Ex.1:1–40:38)
      - God's holiness (Ex.3:1-10; 19:1–40:38)
      - God's care, guidance, provision, and protection (Ex.1:1–40:38)

c. To teach that salvation is based solely upon the blood of the lamb: that a person must hide behind the blood of the lamb...
  • to be delivered from judgment
  • to begin a *new life*
  • to be given the hope of the promised land (a symbol of heaven) (Ex.12:1–13:16; see He.11:13-16, 24-29)

d. To teach the law of God and to make a covenant—an agreement—with man to keep His law (Ex.19:1–40:38).
e. To teach the terrible depravity of man, the true condition of man's heart...
  • that man is a sinner, a transgressor of God's law
  • that man breaks God's heart time and again, no matter how good God is to him (Ex.1:1–40:38)

f. To teach the desperate need of man for a mediator: that man desperately needs a mediator to approach God for him (Ex.1:1–40:38).
g. To teach the service and worship of God: to spell out how man is to serve and worship God (Ex.1:1–40:38).
h. To teach the absolute necessity of the Priesthood, that man needs a High Priest, a Mediator, an Intercessor, to represent him before God (Ex.1:1–40:38).

3. The *Christological or Christ-centered purpose*: to teach that certain things point to Jesus Christ as the Savior of the world:
  a. That the great deliverer Moses pictures the need of man for an even greater Deliverer, a Deliverer who can save man from the world (Egypt) and its enslavements and from the judgment to come.

  > **"The Lord thy God will raise up unto thee a Prophet [Deliverer] from the midst of thee, of thy brethren, like unto me; unto him ye shall hearken" (De.18:15).**

  b. That the Passover lamb pictures the need of man for the Lamb of God who takes away the sin of the world.

  > **"The next day John seeth Jesus coming unto him, and saith, Behold the Lamb of God, which taketh away the sin of the world" (Jn.1:29).**

  c. That the shed blood of the lamb without blemish pictures the need for man to escape the judgment of God by hiding behind the blood of the perfect Lamb of God, the Lord Jesus Christ.

  > **"For if the blood of bulls and of goats, and the ashes of an heifer sprinkling the unclean, sanctifieth to the purifying of the flesh: How much more shall the blood of Christ, who through the eternal Spirit offered himself without spot to God, purge your conscience from dead works to serve the living God?" (He.9:13-14; see Ro.5:8-9).**

  d. That the manna, the bread from heaven, pictures the Lord Jesus Christ who is the Bread of Life (Jn.6:32-33; 6:48-51; 6:58).

  > **"And Jesus said unto them, I am the bread of life: he that cometh to me shall never hunger; and he that believeth on me shall never thirst" (Jn.6:35).**

  e. That the law of God and man's inability to obey God's law in all its points (perfection) pictures the great need of man for an advocate, an intercessor, a mediator. Jesus Christ is our advocate, and He is also the propitiation (the sacrifice) for our sins.

  > **"My little children, these things write I unto you, that ye sin not. And if any man sin, we have an advocate with the Father, Jesus Christ the righteous: And he is the propitiation for our sins: and not for ours only, but also for the sins of the whole world" (1 Jn.2:1-2; see 1 Ti.2:5; He.8:6; 9:15, 24; 12:24).**

  f. That the priesthood of Israel and the high priest, Aaron, pictures the need of man for a perfect mediator, a perfect High Priest, who can approach God for man. The perfect High Priest is the Lord Jesus Christ.

  > **"Wherefore he is able also to save them to the uttermost that come unto God by him, seeing he ever liveth to make intercession for them. For such an high priest became us, who is holy, harmless, undefiled, separate from sinners, and made higher than the heavens; Who needeth not daily, as those high priests, to offer up sacrifice, first for his own sins, and then for the people's: for this he did once, when he offered up himself" (He.7:25-27; see He.2:17; 4:14-15; 9:11).**

g. That the tabernacle—"God's royal tent" (NIV), God's "portable temple" (Geisler)—pictures that man can enter God's holy presence only as God dictates, only through a prepared High Priest and Mediator, the Lord Jesus Christ.

> **"Now of the things which we have spoken this is the sum: We have such an high priest, who is set on the right hand of the throne of the Majesty in the heavens; A minister of the sanctuary, and of the true tabernacle, which the Lord pitched, and not man"** (He.8:1-2; see He.9:11; 2:17; 4:14-15; 7:25-27).

V. SPECIAL FEATURES

1. *Exodus* is "The Great Book of Israel's Exodus." The word *Exodus* means *departure, going out, exiting out, a road out,* or *a way out.* The word *Exodus* is the Latin word translated from the Greek Bible *exodos.* The exodus (deliverance, departure) of Israel is the greatest event in all the Old Testament, and it points to the greatest event in the New Testament, the cross of Christ.

2. *Exodus* is "The Great Book of Continuation." It continues the story of Genesis, the first book of the Bible. In fact, note Ex.1:6-7, where a period of about 400 years is covered. Two brief verses cover the whole history of the Israelites from Joseph to Moses. The point is this: Exodus picks up where Genesis left off. Exodus continues the *great history of redemption* that God began to write in Genesis. Exodus is one of the most important books in all the Word of God.

3. *Exodus* is "The Great Book of Hebrew History." Nowhere in Scripture can the reader find such a detailed record of Israel's history. From sensing the pain and suffering of enslavement over to rejoicing for their great deliverance from Pharaoh's grasp, the reader is given an inside look at how the Israelites experienced life as the people of God. Being God's elect meant the Israelites needed to keep God's Law, and they needed to know how to approach and worship Him. The major events in the history of the Hebrew people are herein covered: their slavery, deliverance, wilderness experiences, receiving the Law and the instructions to build the Tabernacle.

4. *Exodus* is "The Great Book of Salvation, Redemption, and Deliverance." God is seen...
   - saving His people from Egyptian slavery (Ex.1:1-11:10).
   - redeeming His people from the judgment of death through the Passover Lamb (Ex.12:1-13:16).
   - delivering His people through the trials of the wilderness wanderings: delivering them through six terrible trials as they journeyed toward the promised land (Ex.13:17-18:27).

5. *Exodus* is "The Great Book of God's Power and Sovereignty." God is the *Lord of History.* He is sovereign over history: the nations of this world and the affairs of men are ruled over by God.
   - It was God's sovereign power that chose one man, Abraham, to give birth to a whole new race of people, a race that was to be God's witness to the world.
   - It was God's sovereign power that caused Abraham's family of seventy plus people to be enslaved so they could multiply into a population of over two million. If they had not been enslaved, they would most likely have scattered and never stayed together as one race of people, not all two plus million.
   - It was God's sovereign power that launched the plagues of judgment upon Egypt and rescued the Israelites from slavery.
   - It was God's sovereign power that protected and provided for His people during their wilderness wanderings.
   - It was God's sovereign power that gave the law and the worship instructions to Israel and began to mold them into a nation.

6. *Exodus* is "The Great Book of Hope." For over four-hundred years, Egypt had become Israel's home. When they first came to Egypt, they came at the invitation of Pharaoh and lived in Goshen. Now, another Pharaoh who did not know nor remember Joseph ruled them with an iron fist. The *promised land* seemed to be only a distant dream, void of any reality. For the Israelites, life had become hopeless. But God still had a plan, a covenant, a promise to keep. In a land where hope was non-existent, hope took the form of a baby who floated down the Nile River in an ark. That baby grew up to be God's vessel of hope. As an adult, Moses became the physical embodiment of Israel's hope. Moses' leadership provided the basis for hope in:
   a. God's great faithfulness and deliverance (Ex.1:1-22).
   b. God's ability to send a deliverer (Ex.2:1-7:7).
   c. God's power over Pharaoh's power (Ex.7:8-11:10).
   d. God passing over them in judgment (the great Passover) (Ex.12:1-13:16).
   e. God's supernatural guidance by day and by night (Ex.13:17-22).
   f. God's provision of food and water (Ex.13:16-18:27).
   g. God's protection from their enemies (Ex.17:8-16).
   h. God's promise to take them to a special place, the *promised land* (Ex.3:8).

7. *Exodus* is "The Great Book of Liberty and Freedom." The reader sees how an entire race of slaves were set free: how they were given the glorious rights of all men, the right to life, liberty, and justice for all. The reader sees how God set His impoverished people free and formed them into a nation.

8. *Exodus* is "The Great Book Covering a Nation's Birth." The birth of Israel occurs in Exodus. God is seen taking a family of seventy people and causing them to multiply into a population of over two million, all within a period of about 430 years. And most of the growth took place while they were brutally enslaved by Egypt. Exodus shows God taking this body of impoverished slaves, delivering them and forming them into a great nation of people, a nation governed by the laws given by God Himself.

9. *Exodus* is "The Great Book of Law." The laws that were to take an impoverished group of slaves and form them into a nation are given in Exodus. Moreover, the great law that God gave to govern all men, the *Ten Commandments*, is covered in Exodus. Exodus covers...
- the Ten Commandments (Ex.20:1-26)
- the Moral or Civil Law of Israel (Ex.21:1-23:19)

10. *Exodus* is "The Great Book of the Mosaic Covenant." God lays down in Exodus the law by which Israel is to live and the Ten Commandments which are to govern all men. And God formulates the agreement that is to be signed and sealed within the heart of man.

> **"Now therefore, if ye will obey my voice indeed, and keep my covenant, then ye shall be a peculiar treasure unto me above all people: for all the earth is mine: And ye shall be unto me a kingdom of priests, and an holy nation. These are the words which thou shalt speak unto the children of Israel" (Ex.19:5-6).**
> **"But ye are a chosen generation, a royal priesthood, an holy nation, a peculiar people; that ye should show forth the praises of him who hath called you out of darkness into his marvellous light: Which in time past were not a people, but are now the people of God: which had not obtained mercy [through Christ], but now have obtained mercy" (1 Pe.2:9-10).**

11. *Exodus* is "The Great Book Demonstrating God's Judgment." In launching the ten plagues of judgment upon Egypt, God demonstrated for all generations a terrifying fact: a day of justice is coming. God is going to judge the ungodliness and unrighteousness of men.

12. *Exodus* is "The Great Book of *Christian Experience*" or "The Great Book of the *Believer's Pilgrimage*." Exodus covers Israel's deliverance from bondage through the power of God and the blood of the Passover lamb. It also covers the beginning of Israel's journey through the *wilderness wanderings*. This is...
- a picture of the believer being delivered by the blood of the Lord Jesus Christ, the Lamb of God.
- a picture of the believer as he journeys through the wilderness of this world on his way to the promised land of heaven.

13. *Exodus* is "The Great Book of the Wilderness Wanderings." Once the Israelites were delivered from Egypt, the people began a new life...
- a new life journeying away from their old life as slaves to Egypt (symbolizing the world).
- a new life journeying to the promised land of God.

This is what is known as the *wilderness wanderings* of Israel, the new life Israel had as free people, the new life of marching through the wilderness of this world to the promised land of God.

14. *Exodus* is "The Great Book of God's Care, Guidance, Provision, and Protection." From the opening to the ending page, God is seen looking after and taking care of His people. In the pages of Exodus, He demonstrates and proves...
- His care
- His guidance
- His provision
- His protection

15. *Exodus* is "The Great Book of Conquest and Victory." God is seen conquering the terrible enemies of Israel including...
- the Egyptian army that entrapped them at the Red Sea.
- the Amalekites who secretly attacked and slaughtered the stragglers: the maimed, the sick, the aged, the children.
- the impossible trials and obstacles that confronted them.

God triumphed over all the enemies of His people. God gave victory to the Israelites.

16. *Exodus* is "The Great Book of Worship." Explicit instructions on how God wanted His people to worship are given through the model of the Tabernacle. With these blueprints, God charged Moses to follow the instructions exactly as God had revealed. And this Moses did. Moses prepared a place where men could approach and worship God exactly as God dictated.

17. *Exodus* is "The Great Book of Family Life." Beginning with the first chapter of Exodus, the record of Israel's family tree introduces the important role of the family. It is significant to note that the building block for any vibrant civilization is the family unit: fathers, mothers, sons, daughters, grandparents, aunts, uncles, nephews, and nieces. In the book of Exodus, great detail is given to emphasize the family:
a. Jacob's family and extended family were seventy in number, not counting Joseph (Ex.1:5).
b. The names of Jacob's sons are listed (Ex.1:2-5).
c. Joseph's generation died, all the family members who first lived in Egypt (Ex.1:6).
d. Jacob's children, the children of Israel, rapidly grew into a large population (Ex.1:7)
e. The children of Israel were considered a threat to the stability of the new Pharaoh's regime (Ex.1:8-11).
f. Every member of the Israelite family became a slave, without exception (Ex.1:11-14).
g. The midwives took a moral stand for the unborn male babies. They refused to obey Pharaoh's evil instructions to kill the children (Ex.1:15-22).

h. Moses was born in a home where the mother was a courageous believer, a woman who risked her life in order to protect her son (Ex.2:1-3).

i. In God's sovereignty, Pharaoh's daughter adopted Moses and allowed his mother to assist in raising him (Ex.2:5-10).

j. Moses met a young woman (Zipporah) in Midian after escaping from Pharaoh, and he married her (Ex.2:21).

k. Moses' father-in-law was Jethro, the priest of Midian (Ex.3:1).

l. Moses had two sons, Gershom and Eliezer (Ex.2:22; 18:4).

m. Moses had a brother (Aaron) and a sister (Miriam) (Ex.4:14; 15:20).

n. The Passover meal was to be celebrated by each family; it was to be family-centered (Ex.12:3-4).

18. *Exodus* is "The Great Book of Transparency." It is a book that does not hide the failures of its main characters. Remember, it was:

a. Moses who killed an Egyptian (Ex.2:12).

b. Israel who wrongly placed their trust in Egypt (see outline—Ex.2:23).

c. Moses who was a reluctant prophet, offering arguments and excuses against serving God (Ex.3:11–4:17).

d. Moses' wife, Zipporah, who objected to circumcising their son (Ex.4:25-26).

e. Moses who had to be chastised by God almost to the point of death, chastised because he failed to circumcise his son according to the covenant (Ex.4:24).

f. The leaders of Israel who blamed Moses and Aaron for their troubles (Ex.5:20-21).

g. Moses who questioned God for allowing evil to fall upon His people (Ex.5:22).

h. Moses who questioned God's wisdom in sending him to deliver the Israelites (Ex.5:22).

i. Moses who blamed himself for bringing trouble upon Israel (Ex.5:23).

j. Israel who complained, grumbled, and murmured against Moses at Marah (Ex.15:22-27).

k. Israel who sinned by grumbling and failing to believe God (Ex.16:1-36).

l. Israel who trusted more in Moses than they did in God (Ex.17:1-7).

m. Israel who built and then worshipped the golden calf (Ex.32:1-35).

19. *Exodus* is "The Great Book of Theological Themes" (see Purpose, pt.2).

20. *Exodus* is "The Great Book of Types, Symbols, and Pictures." A vast wealth of Biblical types, symbols, and pictures can be drawn from the pages of *Exodus*. There are many historical facts that have a practical meaning for today's believer. (See Types Chart, VII.—*Introduction*.)

VI.   A GENERAL SURVEY OF EGYPTIAN HISTORY

Egypt, mighty Egypt, has been one of the greatest and most fascinating civilizations in the history of the world. Egypt has risen to the forefront as an important hub of Western culture. With origins dating back even before recorded history, a study of Egyptian history is an important task for the serious Bible student. As one of the leading nations of the ancient world, Egypt led the way as the rest of the world watched with amazement...
- the power of the nation becoming greater and greater
- the modern culture that was exported to the entire known world
- the great feats of engineering that built entire cities and the awe-inspiring pyramids
- the creative use of art that painted a description of life in Egypt
- the ground-breaking scientific discoveries that demonstrated an unlimited thirst for knowledge
- the creation of the solar-based calendar that accounted for a year of 365 days.
- the role that religion and cults played in the lives of the Egyptian people

Hundreds, even thousands, of books have been written about the Egyptian people. And more books will be written about Egypt and its history as long as civilization stands. Since our purpose is to look to the One Living God who makes and orchestrates history, our task will be to examine the history of Egypt as *His* story—for even Egypt is under the rule of the Sovereign Majesty of the universe, the Lord Jesus Christ.

"The Lord hath prepared his throne in the heavens; and his kingdom ruleth over all"
(Ps.103:19).

Our presentation of Egyptian history will focus on the following issues:
⇒ The specific period of history as it relates to the time preceding and up to Exodus.
- The central figures during each period of history
- The major contribution made during each period of history

⇒ The relationship with the Old Testament, especially as Egypt related to the Patriarchs.
⇒ The relationship with the New Testament.
⇒ The relationship with the Prophets and the end times.

What kind of nation was Egypt thousands of years ago? As we look back into time, we will discover a nation, a land and a people who were in many ways just like us: mortal, human, and locked into a narrow space called time.

A.   THE SPECIFIC PERIODS OF HISTORY
(Dates beyond the first period of Egyptian history are not being
given because there is such a variation of opinion among
historians, opinions that vary thousands of years and
dates that cannot be precisely agreed upon.)

1. PRE-HISTORY (Approx.6,000–4,000+ B.C.)
   - *The Central Figure*: the Nile River
   - *The Major Contribution*: The Nile River Valley was a fertile source of food and water that attracted the first settlers to Egypt.

2. THE FIRST AND SECOND DYNASTIES
   - *The Major Contribution*: A time when the ancient Egyptians began to develop politically. History records at least 17 kings ruled Egypt during this period of history.

3. THE OLD KINGDOM: THE THIRD THROUGH THE SIXTH DYNASTIES: THE GOLDEN AGE
   - *The Major Contribution*: Religion began to play a major role in how the Egyptians governed. It was during this period of time when the pharaohs ruled a theocracy. They claimed to be divine kings who had absolute rule.
   - *The Third Dynasty*: Cultural growth
   - *The Fourth Dynasty*: The pyramids, the arts and sciences, and the solar calendar based on a 365 day year.
   - *The Fifth Dynasty*: Continued military and economic strength. An increased bureaucracy began to sap the strength from the king.
   - *The Sixth Dynasty*: Central authority began to dissolve into smaller but more politically powerful districts.

4. THE FIRST INTERMEDIATE PERIOD: THE SEVENTH THROUGH THE TWELFTH DYNASTIES
   - *The Seventh Dynasty*: This was the beginning of the First Intermediate period; its influence to rule was weak. What power it did have was centered in the Memphis area.
   - *The Eighth Dynasty*: Like the previous dynasty, the eighth dynasty held little or no power. Its center of influence was also in Memphis.

A GENERAL SURVEY OF EGYPTIAN HISTORY

- *The Ninth Dynasty*: They controlled the area of Heracleopolis as well as the Nile Delta (including Memphis).
- *The Tenth Dynasty*: They maintained the territorial gains of the Ninth Dynasty.
- *The Eleventh Dynasty*: They controlled the south of Egypt. This dynasty overlapped the final days of the Tenth Dynasty and became the first dynasty of the Middle Kingdom.
- *The Twelfth Dynasty*: The reign of Amenemhet I made great strides in bringing national unity to the scattered centers of power. It was during this dynasty that Amon (also known by Ammon or Amen), the Egyptian god, was elevated over the other spectrum of deities.

5. THE SECOND INTERMEDIATE PERIOD: THE THIRTEENTH THROUGH THE SEVENTEENTH DYNASTIES
- *The Thirteenth Dynasty*: This period of rule was unstable. More than 60 different rulers tried their hand at government. Not one ruler stood out as a strong leader for his people. Eventually, their power was challenged by two different groups: the up-and-coming fourteenth dynasty and the Hyksos invaders from Palestine.
- *The Fourteenth Dynasty*: Much like the previous dynasty, the rule of the fourteenth dynasty was marked by division and upheaval.
- *The Fifteenth Dynasty*: The Hyksos, the invaders from Palestine, ruled a portion of Egypt. Their shadow of influence reached from the eastern Nile delta to the northern part of the country.
- *The Sixteenth Dynasty*: As the Hyksos ruled Egypt, during the same time period the sixteenth dynasty controlled parts of the Nile delta and portions of the middle of Egypt.
- *The Seventeenth Dynasty*: In the south of Egypt, the Theban or seventeenth dynasty united Egypt after conquering the Hyksos.

6. THE NEW KINGDOM: THE EIGHTEENTH DYNASTY
- Founded by the ruler who defeated the Hyksos people, Ahmose I. He united the country of Egypt once again. It was during his reign that the role of women was increased, especially those of royal stock.
- The boundaries of Egypt were expanded to include Nubia and Palestine.
- The god Amon received the greatest attention at the expense of other deities.
- During the eighteenth dynasty, a woman (Hatshepsut) ruled as pharaoh alongside her young son (Thutmose III)—the rightful ruler of Egypt. After Thutmose III grew up and gained sole control of Egypt, he conquered more lands (the break-away regions of Syria and Palestine).
- After several other rulers had come and gone, the military projection of power had dulled. What was once taken forcefully from other people was negotiated in the arena of diplomacy.
- The last of the eighteenth dynasty rulers was Tutankhamen. His famous tomb was discovered undisturbed in 1922.

7. THE RAMESSIDE PERIOD: THE NINETEENTH DYNASTY
- The delta capital was Pi-Ramesse.
- A downward slide in the government remained in progress during this period. Egypt had become a shell of what had been a seedbed for mighty rulers.

B. EGYPT'S RELATIONSHIP WITH THE OLD TESTAMENT

Egypt is an integral part of the Old Testament. We must remember that the Bible was not written in a vacuum. The great stories of the Bible were not removed from the world in which they occurred. God's use of Egypt played an important role as the setting for what God was doing in *His* story.

1. Egypt's relationship with **ABRAM**:
a. He traveled to Egypt because of a horrible famine in the land.

> **And there was a famine in the land: and Abram went down into Egypt to sojourn there; for the famine *was* grievous in the land. And it came to pass, when he was come near to enter into Egypt, that he said unto Sarai his wife, Behold now, I know that thou *art* a fair woman to look upon" (Ge.12:10-11).**

b. He deceived the Egyptians about his relationship with his wife Sarah.

> **And it came to pass, that, when Abram was come into Egypt, the Egyptians beheld the woman that she *was* very fair" (Ge.12:14).**

c. He left Egypt and returned to Palestine with his family.

> **"And Abram went up out of Egypt, he, and his wife, and all that he had, and Lot with him, into the south" (Ge.13:1).**
> **"And Lot lifted up his eyes, and beheld all the plain of Jordan, that it *was* well watered every where, before the LORD destroyed Sodom and Gomorrah, *even* as the garden of the LORD, like the land of Egypt, as thou comest unto Zoar" (Ge.13:10).**

d. He received the promise from God that sets the boundaries of the Promised Land which reached all the way down to Egypt.

> **"In the same day the LORD made a covenant with Abram, saying, Unto thy seed have I given this land, from the river of Egypt unto the great river, the river Euphrates" (Ge.15:18).**

e. He saw his son, Ishmael, marry an Egyptian woman.

> **"And he [Ishmael] dwelt in the wilderness of Paran: and his mother [Hagar] took him a wife out of the land of Egypt" (Ge.21:21).**

2. Egypt's relationship with **JOSEPH**:
a. He was sold into slavery and taken to Egypt.

> **"Then there passed by Midianites merchantmen; and they drew and lifted up Joseph out of the pit, and sold Joseph to the Ishmeelites for twenty *pieces* of silver: and they brought Joseph into Egypt" (Ge.37:28).**
> **"And Joseph was brought down to Egypt; and Potiphar, an officer of Pharaoh, captain of the guard, an Egyptian, bought him of the hands of the Ishmeelites, which had brought him down thither" (Ge.39:1).**

b. He was sentenced to prison in Egypt because of the false accusations by Potiphar's wife.

> **"And it came to pass, when his master heard the words of his wife, which she spake unto him, saying, After this manner did thy servant to me; that his wrath was kindled. And Joseph's master took him, and put him into the prison, a place where the king's prisoners *were* bound: and he was there in the prison" (Ge.39:19-20).**

c. He was given the ability to interpret the dream of the king of Egypt.

> **"And it came to pass in the morning that his spirit was troubled; and he sent and called for all the magicians of Egypt, and all the wise men thereof: and Pharaoh told them his dream; but *there was* none that could interpret them unto Pharaoh" (Ge.41:8).**
> **"Then Pharaoh sent and called Joseph, and they brought him hastily out of the dungeon: and he shaved *himself,* and changed his raiment, and came in unto Pharaoh. And Pharaoh said unto Joseph, I have dreamed a dream, and *there is* none that can interpret it: and I have heard say of thee, *that* thou canst understand a dream to interpret it. And Joseph answered Pharaoh, saying, *It is* not in me: God shall give Pharaoh an answer of peace" (Ge.41:14-16).**

d. He was made the prime minister, the second in command in all of Egypt.

> **"Now therefore let Pharaoh look out a man discreet and wise, and set him over the land of Egypt. Let Pharaoh do *this,* and let him appoint officers over the land, and take up the fifth part of the land of Egypt in the seven plenteous years" (Ge.41:33-34).**
> **"And Pharaoh said unto Joseph, See, I have set thee over all the land of Egypt" (Ge.41:41).**
> **"And he made him to ride in the second chariot which he had; and they cried before him, Bow the knee: and he made him *ruler* over all the land of Egypt. And Pharaoh said unto Joseph, I *am* Pharaoh, and without thee shall no man lift up his hand or foot in all the land of Egypt. And Pharaoh called Joseph's name Zaphnath-paaneah; and he gave him to wife Asenath the daughter of Poti-pherah priest of On. And Joseph went out over *all* the land of Egypt. And Joseph *was* thirty years old when he stood before Pharaoh king of Egypt. And Joseph went out from the presence of Pharaoh, and went throughout all the land of Egypt" (Ge.41:43-46).**

e. He was able to plan for the famine that was to come, saving Egypt and the surrounding nations from starvation.

> **"And the seven years of plenteousness, that was in the land of Egypt, were ended. And the seven years of dearth began to come, according as Joseph had said: and the dearth was in all lands; but in all the land of Egypt there was bread. And when all the land of Egypt was famished, the people cried to Pharaoh for bread: and Pharaoh said unto all the Egyptians, Go unto Joseph; what he saith to you, do. And the famine was over all the face of the earth: and Joseph opened all the storehouses, and sold unto the Egyptians; and the famine waxed sore in the land of Egypt. And all countries came into Egypt to Joseph for to buy *corn;* because that the famine was so sore in all lands. Now when Jacob saw that there was corn in Egypt, Jacob said unto his sons, Why do ye look one upon**

another? And he said, Behold, I have heard that there is corn in Egypt: get you down thither, and buy for us from thence; that we may live, and not die. And Joseph's ten brethren went down to buy corn in Egypt" (Ge.41:53-42:3).

f. He was able to save and reunite his family.

"And it came to pass, when they had eaten up the corn which they had brought out of Egypt, their father said unto them, Go again, buy us a little food" (Ge.43:2).
"And Joseph said unto his brethren, Come near to me, I pray you. And they came near. And he said, I *am* Joseph your brother, whom ye sold into Egypt" (Ge.45:4).
"So now *it was* not you *that* sent me hither, but God: and he hath made me a father to Pharaoh, and lord of all his house, and a ruler throughout all the land of Egypt. Haste ye, and go up to my father, and say unto him, Thus saith thy son Joseph, God hath made me lord of all Egypt: come down unto me, tarry not" (Ge.45:8-9).
"And take your father and your households, and come unto me: and I will give you the good of the land of Egypt, and ye shall eat the fat of the land. Now thou art commanded, this do ye; take you wagons out of the land of Egypt for your little ones, and for your wives, and bring your father, and come. Also regard not your stuff; for the good of all the land of Egypt *is* yours" (Ge.45:18-20).

g. He was able to start his own family, a wife and two children, in Egypt.

"And unto Joseph in the land of Egypt were born Manasseh and Ephraim, which Asenath the daughter of Poti-pherah priest of On bare unto him" (Ge.46:20).

h. He was able to see God's great hand of sovereignty in Egypt.

"But as for you, ye thought evil against me; *but* God meant it unto good, to bring to pass, as *it is* this day, to save much people alive" (Ge.50:20).

i. He died at the age of one-hundred and ten in Egypt.

"And Joseph dwelt in Egypt, he, and his father's house: and Joseph lived an hundred and ten years" (Ge.50:22).
"So Joseph died, *being* an hundred and ten years old: and they embalmed him, and he was put in a coffin in Egypt" (Ge.50:26).

3. Egypt's relationship with **MOSES**:
  a. Moses was born and raised in Egypt.

"And the woman conceived, and bare a son: and when she saw him that he *was a* goodly *child,* she hid him three months. And when she could not longer hide him, she took for him an ark of bulrushes, and daubed it with slime and with pitch, and put the child therein; and she laid *it* in the flags by the river's brink" (Ex.2:2-3)
"And the child grew, and she brought him unto Pharaoh's daughter, and he became her son. And she called his name Moses: and she said, Because I drew him out of the water" (Ex.2:10).

  b. Moses committed murder in Egypt.

"And it came to pass in those days, when Moses was grown, that he went out unto his brethren, and looked on their burdens: and he spied an Egyptian smiting an Hebrew, one of his brethren. And he looked this way and that way, and when he saw that *there was* no man, he slew the Egyptian, and hid him in the sand. And when he went out the second day, behold, two men of the Hebrews strove together: and he said to him that did the wrong, Wherefore smitest thou thy fellow? And he said, Who made thee a prince and a judge over us? intendest thou to kill me, as thou killedst the Egyptian? And Moses feared, and said, Surely this thing is known" (Ex.2:11-14).

  c. Moses, fleeing for his life, had to leave Egypt.

"Now when Pharaoh heard this thing, he sought to slay Moses. But Moses fled from the face of Pharaoh, and dwelt in the land of Midian: and he sat down by a well" (Ex.2:15).

  d. Moses was sent back to Egypt by God to deliver His people Israel.

"Come now therefore, and I will send thee unto Pharaoh, that thou mayest bring forth my people the children of Israel out of Egypt" (Ex.3:10).

e. Moses led God's people out of Egypt through the Red Sea.

> "And Moses stretched out his hand over the sea; and the LORD caused the sea to go *back* by a strong east wind all that night, and made the sea dry *land,* and the waters were divided. And the children of Israel went into the midst of the sea upon the dry *ground:* and the waters *were* a wall unto them on their right hand, and on their left" (Ex.14:21-22).

f. Moses saw Egypt's great army drown in the angry waters of the Red Sea.

> "And the LORD said unto Moses, Stretch out thine hand over the sea, that the waters may come again upon the Egyptians, upon their chariots, and upon their horsemen. And Moses stretched forth his hand over the sea, and the sea returned to his strength when the morning appeared; and the Egyptians fled against it; and the LORD overthrew the Egyptians in the midst of the sea. And the waters returned, and covered the chariots, and the horsemen, *and* all the host of Pharaoh that came into the sea after them; there remained not so much as one of them" (Ex.14:26-28).

C. EGYPT'S RELATIONSHIP WITH THE NEW TESTAMENT

Egypt's great power and glory had crumbled by the time of Christ. The days when the pharaohs ruled with an iron fist were replaced by another iron fist, the terrible fist of Caesar, the emperor of the Roman Empire. In spite of significant changes in the political landscape, the history of Egypt still made an impact on the New Testament.

1. Egypt's relationship with **JESUS**:
   a. Jesus was taken to Egypt by his parents in order to protect Him from Herod.

> "And when they were departed, behold, the angel of the Lord appeareth to Joseph in a dream, saying, Arise, and take the young child and his mother, and flee into Egypt, and be thou there until I bring thee word: for Herod will seek the young child to destroy him" (Mt.2:13).

   b. Jesus' father received a dream while living in Egypt, a dream that proclaimed the death of Herod.

> "But when Herod was dead, behold, an angel of the Lord appeareth in a dream to Joseph in Egypt" (Mt.2:19).

2. Egypt's relationship with the day of **PENTECOST**:

Jews from all over Europe and the Middle East, including Egypt, were eye-witnesses to the power of the Holy Spirit's coming upon the disciples who were waiting in the upper room.

> "Phrygia, and Pamphylia, in Egypt, and in the parts of Libya about Cyrene, and strangers of Rome, Jews and proselytes" [were all in Jerusalem during Pentecost] (Ac.2:10).

3. Egypt's relationship with **STEPHEN**:

Before he was stoned, Stephen's speech to the Sandhedrin was laced with references to Israel's experiences with Egypt.

> "And the patriarchs, moved with envy, sold Joseph into Egypt: but God was with him, And delivered him out of all his afflictions, and gave him favour and wisdom in the sight of Pharaoh king of Egypt; and he made him governor over Egypt and all his house. Now there came a dearth over all the land of Egypt and Chanaan, and great affliction: and our fathers found no sustenance. But when Jacob heard that there was corn in Egypt, he sent out our fathers first" (Ac.7:9-12).
> "So Jacob went down into Egypt, and died, he, and our fathers" (Ac.7:15).
> "But when the time of the promise drew nigh, which God had sworn to Abraham, the people grew and multiplied in Egypt" (Ac.7:17).
> "I have seen, I have seen the affliction of my people which is in Egypt, and I have heard their groaning, and am come down to deliver them. And now come, I will send thee into Egypt" (Ac.7:34).
> "He brought them out, after that he had showed wonders and signs in the land of Egypt, and in the Red sea, and in the wilderness forty years" (Ac.7:36).
> "To whom our fathers would not obey, but thrust *him* from them, and in their hearts turned back again into Egypt, Saying unto Aaron, Make us gods to go before us: for *as for* this Moses, which brought us out of the land of Egypt, we wot not what is become of him" (Ac.7:39-40).

4. Egypt's relationship with **PAUL**:

Paul's sermon to the Israelites and God-fearing Gentiles began with the time Israel spent in Egypt.

> **"The God of this people of Israel chose our fathers, and exalted the people when they dwelt as strangers in the land of Egypt, and with an high arm brought he them out of it" (Ac.13:17).**

5. Egypt's relationship with **THE WRITER OF HEBREWS**:
   a. The memories of Egypt are cast as a warning to the Jewish converts who were already well-versed in the history of their faith.

> **"For some, when they had heard, did provoke: howbeit not all that came out of Egypt by Moses" (He.3:16).**
> **"Not according to the covenant that I made with their fathers in the day when I took them by the hand to lead them out of the land of Egypt; because they continued not in my covenant, and I regarded them not, saith the Lord" (He.8:9).**

   b. The life of Moses is remembered as a man who was willing to forsake the riches of Egypt for the reproach of Christ.

> **"Esteeming the reproach of Christ greater riches than the treasures in Egypt: for he had respect unto the recompence of the reward. By faith he forsook Egypt, not fearing the wrath of the king: for he endured, as seeing him who is invisible" (He.11:26-27).**

D. EGYPT'S RELATIONSHIP WITH THE PROPHETS OF GOD AND THE END TIMES

What kind of plan does God have for Egypt? Think for a moment. Think about all the negative feelings that rise up through the gateway of recorded history. Remember:
   ⇒ the terrible evil of rebellion and rejection of God by the Egyptians.
   ⇒ the brutal, savage enslavement of people.
   ⇒ the gross perversion of idolatry in Egypt.
   ⇒ the very cruel way that God's people were treated by the Egyptians.
   ⇒ the hard heart of Pharaoh, the man who destroyed the lives of many of his countrymen.
   ⇒ the very symbol of Egypt, a picture of the world and all of its entrapments.

The truth be known, why bother with a nation that is beyond all hope...or are *they*?

1. There will be a remnant in Egypt, a remnant of people who love the Lord:

> **"And it shall come to pass in that day, *that* the Lord shall set his hand again the second time to recover the remnant of his people, which shall be left, from Assyria, and from Egypt, and from Pathros, and from Cush, and from Elam, and from Shinar, and from Hamath, and from the islands of the sea" (Is.11:11).**

2. Egypt will be dealt with by God just as all nations will be. God will judge them harshly:
   a. God will judge the idolatry and all the false worship in Egypt.

> **"The burden of Egypt. Behold, the LORD rideth upon a swift cloud, and shall come into Egypt: and the idols of Egypt shall be moved at his presence, and the heart of Egypt shall melt in the midst of it" (Is.19:1)**
> **"And the spirit of Egypt shall fail in the midst thereof; and I will destroy the counsel thereof: and they shall seek to the idols, and to the charmers, and to them that have familiar spirits, and to the wizards" (Is.19:3).**

   b. God will judge the self-proclaimed wisemen of Egypt.

> **"Where *are* they? where *are* thy wise *men?* and let them tell thee now, and let them know what the LORD of hosts hath purposed upon Egypt. The princes of Zoan are become fools, the princes of Noph are deceived; they have also seduced Egypt, *even they that are* the stay of the tribes thereof. The LORD hath mingled a perverse spirit in the midst thereof: and they have caused Egypt to err in every work thereof, as a drunken *man* staggereth in his vomit Neither shall there be *any* work for Egypt, which the head or tail, branch or rush, may do. In that day shall Egypt be like unto women: and it shall be afraid and fear because of the shaking of the hand of the LORD of hosts, which he shaketh over it" (Is.19:12-16).**

c. God will use Judah to grip Egypt with fear.

> And the land of Judah shall be a terror unto Egypt, every one that maketh mention thereof shall be afraid in himself, because of the counsel of the LORD of hosts, which he hath determined against it" (Is.19:17).

3. God will have a witness in Egypt.
   a. God will call the Egyptians His people.

> "In that day shall five cities in the land of Egypt speak the language of Canaan, and swear to the LORD of hosts; one shall be called, The city of destruction. In that day shall there be an altar to the LORD in the midst of the land of Egypt, and a pillar at the border thereof to the LORD. And it shall be for a sign and for a witness unto the LORD of hosts in the land of Egypt: for they shall cry unto the LORD because of the oppressors, and he shall send them a saviour, and a great one, and he shall deliver them. And the LORD shall be known to Egypt, and the Egyptians shall know the LORD in that day, and shall do sacrifice and oblation; yea, they shall vow a vow unto the LORD, and perform *it*. And the LORD shall smite Egypt: he shall smite and heal *it*: and they shall return *even* to the LORD, and he shall be intreated of them, and shall heal them. In that day shall there be a highway out of Egypt to Assyria, and the Assyrian shall come into Egypt, and the Egyptian into Assyria, and the Egyptians shall serve with the Assyrians. In that day shall Israel be the third with Egypt and with Assyria, *even* a blessing in the midst of the land: Whom the LORD of hosts shall bless, saying, Blessed *be* Egypt my people, and Assyria the work of my hands, and Israel mine inheritance" (Is.19:18-25).

b. God will receive worship from the Israelites who are living in Egypt.

> "And it shall come to pass in that day, *that* the LORD shall beat off from the channel of the river unto the stream of Egypt, and ye shall be gathered one by one, O ye children of Israel. And it shall come to pass in that day, *that* the great trumpet shall be blown, and they shall come which were ready to perish in the land of Assyria, and the outcasts in the land of Egypt, and shall worship the LORD in the holy mount at Jerusalem" (Is.27:12-13).

c. God will not permit His people to gain strength through an alliance with Egypt.

> "That walk to go down into Egypt, and have not asked at my mouth; to strengthen themselves in the strength of Pharaoh, and to trust in the shadow of Egypt! Therefore shall the strength of Pharaoh be your shame, and the trust in the shadow of Egypt *your* confusion" (Is.30:2-3).
>
> "Woe to them that go down to Egypt for help; and stay on horses, and trust in chariots, because *they are* many; and in horsemen, because they are very strong; but they look not unto the Holy One of Israel, neither seek the LORD!" (Is.31:1).
>
> "Lo, thou trustest in the staff of this broken reed, on Egypt; whereon if a man lean, it will go into his hand, and pierce it: so *is* Pharaoh king of Egypt to all that trust in him" (Is.36:6).
>
> "How then wilt thou turn away the face of one captain of the least of my master's servants, and put thy trust on Egypt for chariots and for horsemen?" (Is.36:9).

God has a plan, a very good plan, for the peoples of the earth. When we get to heaven, we will see Egyptians as well as people from all nations of the earth at the feet of Jesus Christ. Listen to the heart of God, a God who loves people, a glorious Savior…

- who loves the world

> "For God so loved the world, that he gave his only begotten Son, that whosoever believeth in him should not perish, but have everlasting life" (Jn.3:16).

- who does not wish that any should perish, but come to repentance

> "But, beloved, be not ignorant of this one thing, that one day *is* with the Lord as a thousand years, and a thousand years as one day. The Lord is not slack concerning his promise, as some men count slackness; but is longsuffering to us-ward, not willing that any should perish, but that all should come to repentance" (2 Pe.3:8-9).

- who will receive passionate worship from believers from *every* nation, tribe, and tongue

> "After this I beheld, and, lo, a great multitude, which no man could number, of all nations, and kindreds, and people, and tongues, stood before the throne, and before the Lamb, clothed with white robes, and palms in their hands; And cried with a loud voice, saying, Salvation to our God which sitteth upon the throne, and unto the Lamb. And all the angels

stood round about the throne, and *about* the elders and the four beasts, and fell before the throne on their faces, and worshipped God, Saying, Amen: Blessing, and glory, and wisdom, and thanksgiving, and honour, and power, and might, *be* unto our God for ever and ever. Amen" (Re.7:9-12).

What a glorious time that will be. Every Christian believer from every period of history will be bowing to worship the Lord Jesus Christ. Christ and Christ alone is the Alpha and the Omega—the Beginning and the End of history. While there is still time, may God give us the grace to work in *His* story in a way that many will be brought into His Kingdom. "Thy Kingdom come. Thy will be done, on earth as it is in heaven." Amen.

VII. TYPES, SYMBOLS, AND PICTURES
THE BOOK OF EXODUS

(PART I – Exodus 1:1–18:27)

What is a biblical type or symbol? Simply put, a *biblical type* is a *foreshadowing* of what was to come at a later time in history. Through a person, place or thing a biblical type points toward a New Testament fulfillment.

In addition to Biblical types, there are what we may call *Biblical pictures*. A biblical picture is a lesson that we can see in the Scriptures without distorting the truth. The study of biblical types and pictures is a valuable study in that it helps us apply the truth of the Scripture to our lives. Scripture itself tells us this:

> **"Now all these things happened unto them for examples: and they are written for our admonition, upon whom the ends of the world are come" (1 Co.10:11)**
> **"For whatsoever things were written aforetime were written for our learning, that we through patience and comfort of the scriptures might have hope" (Ro.15:4).**

GENERAL OUTLINE

PERSON/PLACE/THING	SCRIPTURE, OUTLINE AND DISCUSSION
(1) The Children of Israel (Ex.1:1)	Ex.1:1-7; 1:6-7 (D.S.#2)
(2) Egypt (Ex.1:8)	Ex.1:8-22
(3) Pharaoh (Ex.1:8)	Ex.1:11-14 (D.S.#2)
(4) Taskmasters (Ex.1:11)	Ex.1:11-14
(5) Moses' Basket [ark] (Ex.2:3)	Ex.2:3-4; 2:3 (D.S.#1)
(6) Gershom, Moses' Eldest Son (Ex.2:22)	Ex.2:15-22 (pt.5)
(7) Moses (Ex.3:1f)	Ex.3:1f
(8) The Burning Bush (Ex.3:2-5)	Ex.3:1-10
(9) Moses' Staff [or Rod] (Ex.4:2-5)	Ex.4:1-9 (pt.2)
(10) Moses' Leprous Hand (Ex.4:6-8)	Ex.4:1-9 (pt.2); 4:6-7 (D.S.#2)
(11) Aaron (Ex.4:14-16)	Ex.4:13-17; 4:27-31; 6:13-7:7
(12) Circumcision (Ex.4:24-26)	Ex.4:24-26
(13) The Ten Plagues (Ex.7:8-11:10)	Ex.7:8-11:10
(14) Egyptian Magicians (Ex.7:11)	Ex.7:10-13
(15) The Passover Feast (Ex.12:1-13; 12:21-28)	Ex.12:1-13:16; 12:1-13; 12:21-28
(16) The Passover Lamb "without blemish [defect]" (Ex.12:5)	Ex.12:5
(17) The Slaughter of the Lamb (Ex.12:7, 13; 12:21-23)	Ex.12:1-13:16; 12:6-11 (pt.1); 12:12-13
(18) The Blood from the Lamb (Ex.12:7, 13: 12-21-23)	Ex.12:1-13:16; 12:6-11 (pt.2); 12:12-13
(19) The Bitter Herbs (Ex.12:8)	Ex.12:6-11 (pt.3)
(20) The Roasting and Eating of the Passover Lamb (Ex.12:9-11)	Ex.12:6-11 (pt.4)
(21) Leaven (Ex.12:14-20)	Ex.12:1-13:16 (pt.7); 12:14-20; 12:34-41 (pt.4)
(22) Unleavened Bread (Ex.12:14-20)	Ex.12:1-13:16 (pt.7); 12:14-20; 12:34-41 (pt.4)
(23) No Broken Bones on the Lamb (Ex.12:46)	Ex.12:42-51 (pt.1)
(24) The Dedication of the Firstborn (Ex.13:2)	Ex.13:1-16
(25) The Wilderness Wanderings [Journey] (Ex.13:17-18:27)	Ex.13:17-18:27
(26) The Pillar of Cloud and Fire (Ex.13:21)	Ex.13:20-22; 16:10
(27) The Red Sea (Ex.14:13-31)	Ex.14:1-31; 14:16-18
(28) Pharaoh's Defeat (Ex.14:13-31)	Ex.14:1-31
(29) The Bitter Waters at Marah (Ex.15:22-27)	Ex.15:22-27; 15:26
(30) Manna (Ex.16:1-36)	Ex.16:1-36; 16:31
(31) The Rock at Rephidim (Ex.17:6)	Ex.17:5-6; 17:6
(32) Meribah (Ex.17:7)	Ex.17:1-7
(33) Massah (Ex.17:7)	Ex.17:1-7
(34) The Stone that Moses Sat Upon (Ex.17:12)	Ex.17:10-12 (pt.4)
(35) Jehovah Nissi: The LORD is my Banner (Ex.17:15-16)	Ex.17:13-16; 17:15
(36) Eliezer, Moses' Youngest Son (Ex.18:4)	Ex.18:1-8 (pt.3)

TYPES, SYMBOLS, AND PICTURES
THE BOOK OF EXODUS
(PART I – Exodus 1:1–18:27)

Again, we need to stress what a *biblical type* or *symbol* is. Simply put, a *biblical type* is a *foreshadowing* of what was to come at a later time in history. Through a person, place, or thing, a *biblical type* points toward a New Testament fulfillment.

In addition to *biblical types*, there are what we may call *biblical pictures*. A *biblical picture* is a lesson that we can see in the Scriptures without distorting the truth. The study of *biblical types* and *pictures* is a valuable study in that it helps us apply the truth of the Scripture to our lives. Scripture itself tells us this:

"Now all these things happened unto them for ensamples: and they are written for our admonition, upon whom the ends of the world are come" (1 Co.10:11)

"For whatsoever things were written aforetime were written for our learning, that we through patience and comfort of the scriptures might have hope" (Ro.15:4).

Historical Term	Type or Picture (Scriptural Basis for Each)	Life Application for Today's Believer	Biblical Application
(1) *The Children of Israel* (Ex.1:1)	*The people of God* "Now these are the names of the children of Israel, which came into Egypt; every man and his household came with Jacob" (Ex.1:1). "And thy seed [Jacob's] shall be as the dust of the earth, and thou shalt spread abroad to the west, and to the east, and to the north, and to the south: and in thee and in thy seed shall all the families of the earth be blessed" (Ge.28:14).	The Christian believer is spiritual Israel—the true people of God... • who are now a new creation in Christ Jesus • who are walking in the peace and mercy of God • who are the true *Israel of God*, the true believers who follow after God	*"For in Christ Jesus neither circumcision availeth anything, nor uncircumcision, but a new creature. And as many as walk according to this rule, peace be on them, and mercy, and upon the Israel of God" (Ga.6:15-16). (see Ga. 3:7, 26,29)* *"For he is not a Jew, which is one outwardly; neither is that circumcision, which is outward in the flesh: But he is a Jew, which is one inwardly; and circumcision is that of the heart, in the spirit, and not in the letter; whose praise is not of men, but of God" (Ro.2:28-29).*
(2) *Egypt* (Ex.1:8)	*A picture of the world* "Now there arose up a new king over Egypt, which knew not Joseph" (Ex.1:8). "I am the LORD thy God, which brought thee out of the land of Egypt [the world], from the house of bondage" (De.5:6).	The world (Egypt) opposes and enslaves God's people, enslaves them to the bondages of sin and death.	*"Love not the world, neither the things that are in the world. If any man love the world, the love of the Father is not in him. For all that is in the world, the lust of the flesh, and the lust of the eyes, and the pride of life, is not of the Father, but is of the world" (1 Jn.2:15-16).* *"Jesus answered them, Verily, verily, I say unto you, Whosoever committeth sin is the servant of sin" (Jn.8:34).* *"Know ye not, that to whom ye yield yourselves servants to obey, his servants ye are to whom ye obey; whether of sin unto death, or of obedience unto righteousness? But God be thanked, that ye were the servants of sin, but ye have obeyed from the heart that form of doctrine which was delivered you" (Ro.6:16-17).* *"His own iniquities shall take the wicked himself, and he shall be holden with the cords of his sins" (Pr.5:22). (see Ro.7:14-15)*

Historical Term	Type or Picture (Scriptural Basis for Each)	Life Application for Today's Believer	Biblical Application
(3) *Pharaoh* (Ex.1:8)	*A picture of Satan* "And Pharaoh said, Who *is* the LORD, that I should obey his voice to let Israel go? I know not the LORD, neither will I let Israel [God's people] go" (Ex.5:2). "For thou [Satan] hast said in thine heart, I will ascend into heaven, I will exalt my throne above the stars of God: I will sit also upon the mount of the congregation, in the sides of the north: I will ascend above the heights of the clouds; I will be like the most High" (Is.14:13-14).	Satan seeks to keep men in bondage, eternal bondage.	"Now is the judgment of this world: now shall the prince of this world be cast out" (Jn.12:31). "In whom the god of this world [Satan] hath blinded the minds of them which believe not, lest the light of the glorious gospel of Christ, who is the image of God, should shine unto them" (2 Co.4:4). "Wherein in time past ye walked according to the course of this world, according to the prince of the power of the air, the spirit that now worketh in the children of disobedience" (Ep.2:2). "And that they may recover themselves out of the snare of the devil, who are taken captive by him at his will" (2 Ti.2:26). "Forasmuch then as the children are partakers of flesh and blood, he also himself likewise took part of the same; that through death he might destroy him that had the power of death, that is, the devil" (He.2:14). "He that committeth sin is of the devil; for the devil sinneth from the beginning. For this purpose the Son of God was manifested, that he might destroy the works of the devil" (1 Jn.3:8). (see Jb.1:12; Lu.4:6; Ac.26:18; 1 Pe.5:8)
(4) *Taskmasters* (Ex.1:11)	*A picture of evil men persecuting God's people* "Therefore they [the Egyptians] did set over them taskmasters to afflict them with their burdens. And they built for Pharaoh treasure cities, Pithom and Raamses" (Ex.1:11).	Evil men will always persecute God's people through… • ridicule • harassment • poking fun • scorn • abuse • murder	"Blessed are ye, when men shall revile you, and persecute you, and shall say all manner of evil against you falsely, for my sake" (Mt.5:11; see Mt.24:9; Ph.1:29; 1 Th.3:3; 1 Pe.4:12-13; 4:16; Ps.119:86). "And ye shall be hated of all [men] for my name's sake: but he that endureth to the end shall be saved" (Mt.10:22). "And they stirred up the people, and the elders, and the scribes, and came upon him [Stephen], and caught him, and brought him to the council" (Ac.6:12). "Yea, and all that will live godly in Christ Jesus shall suffer persecution" (2 Ti.3:12).

Historical Term	Type or Picture (Scriptural Basis for Each)	Life Application for Today's Believer	Biblical Application
(5) *Moses' Basket [ark]* (Ex.2:3)	*Salvation: Safety and security. The ark saved baby Moses from death.* "And when she could no longer hide him, she took for him an ark of bulrushes, and daubed it with slime and with pitch, and put the child therein; and she laid *it* in the flags by the river's brink" (Ex.2:3). "And the flood was forty days upon the earth; and the waters increased, and bare up the ark, and it was lift up above the earth" (Gen.7:17). "And every living substance was destroyed which was upon the face of the ground, both man, and cattle, and the creeping things, and the fowl of the heaven; and they were destroyed from the earth: and Noah only remained *alive,* and they that *were* with him in the ark" (Ge.7:23).	Jesus Christ is our ark: our salvation from judgment • our safety and security from the attacks of the world, its evil and its persecutors	*"For God so loved the world, that he gave his only begotten Son, that whosoever believeth in him should not perish, but have everlasting life" (Jn.3:16).* *"He that believeth on him is not condemned: but he that believeth not is condemned already, because he hath not believed in the name of the only begotten Son of God" (Jn.3:18; see Jn.5:24).* *"I am the door: by me if any man enter in, he shall be saved, and shall go in and out, and find pasture" (Jn.10:9).* *"I pray not that thou shouldest take them out of the world, but that thou shouldest keep them from the evil" (Jn.17:15)* *"For the wages of sin is death; but the gift of God is eternal life through Jesus Christ our Lord" (Ro.6:23).* *"For whosoever shall call upon the name of the Lord shall be saved" (Ro.10:13).*
(6) *Gershom, Moses' Eldest Son* (Ex.2:22)	*The name "Gershom" means: A stranger in a strange land* "And she bare *him* a son, and he called his name Gershom: for he said, I have been a stranger in a strange land" (Ex.2:22). "And I have also established my covenant with them, to give them the land of Canaan, the land of their pilgrimage, wherein they were strangers" (Ex.6:4). "These all died in faith, not having received the promises, but having seen them afar off, and were persuaded of *them,* and embraced *them,* and confessed that they were strangers and pilgrims on the earth" (He.11:13).	Believers are strangers in this world, followers of Christ… • who have been given the eternal inheritance of God Himself, the promised land of heaven • who are now marching to the promised land of heaven • who are only pilgrims on the journey through the wilderness (trials) of this world • who long to be home in heaven with Christ	*"For our conversation [citizenship] is in heaven; from whence also we look for the Saviour, the Lord Jesus Christ" (Ph.3:20).* *"These all died in faith, not having received the promises, but having seen them afar off, and were persuaded of them, and embraced them, and confessed that they were strangers and pilgrims on the earth" (He.11:13; see He.11:13-16; 1 Jn.2:15).* *"Dearly beloved, I beseech you as strangers and pilgrims, abstain from fleshly lusts, which war against the sou" (1 Pe.2:11).* *"I am a stranger in the earth: hide not thy commandments from me" (Ps.119:19).*

Historical Term	Type or Picture (Scriptural Basis for Each)	Life Application for Today's Believer	Biblical Application
(7) *Moses* (Ex.3:1f)	• *Moses was saved during childhood (Ex.2:1-10).*	• *Jesus Christ was saved during childhood).*	*"When he arose, he took the young child and his mother by night, and departed into Egypt: And was there until the death of Herod: that it might be fulfilled which was spoken of the Lord by the prophet, saying, Out of Egypt have I called my son" (Mt.2:14-15).*
	• *Moses struggled with Pharaoh (a symbol of Satan) (Ex.7:11).*	• *Jesus Christ struggled with Satan.*	*"Then was Jesus led up of the Spirit into the wilderness to be tempted of the devil" (Mt.4:1).*
	• *Moses fasted 40 days (Ex.34:28).*	• *Jesus Christ fasted 40 days.*	*"And when he had fasted forty days and forty nights, he was afterward an hungred" (Mt.4:2).*
	• *Moses was used by God to control the Sea (Ex.14:21).*	• *Jesus Christ controlled the Sea.*	*"And he saith unto them, Why are ye fearful, O ye of little faith? Then he arose, and rebuked the winds and the sea; and there was a great calm" (Mt.8:26).*
	• *Moses fed a multitude (Ex.16:15).*	• *Jesus Christ fed a multitude.*	*"And they did all eat, and were filled: and they took up of the fragments that remained twelve baskets full. And they that had eaten were about five thousand men, beside women and children" (Mt.14:20-21).*
	• *Moses' face glowed with God's glory (Ex.34:35).*	• *Jesus Christ's face glowed with God's glory.*	*"And was transfigured before them: and his face did shine as the sun, and his raiment was white as the light" (Mt.17:2).*
	• *Moses suffered the complaints and fault-finding of people (Ex.15:24).*	• *Jesus Christ suffered the complaints and fault-finding of people.*	*"And when they saw some of his disciples eat bread with defiled, that is to say, with unwashen, hands, they found fault" (Mk.7:2).*
	• *Moses suffered the opposition of his own family (Nu.12:1).*	• *Jesus Christ suffered the opposition of his own family.*	*"For neither did his brethren believe in him" (Jn.7:5).*
	• *Moses was an intercessor. (He offered up the prayer of intercession for his people) (Ex.32:31-32).*	• *Jesus Christ was an intercessor. (He offered up the prayer of intercession for his people.)*	*"I pray for them: I pray not for the world, but for them which thou hast given me; for they are thine" (Jn.17:9).*
	• *Moses had seventy helpers (Nu.11:16-17).*	• *Jesus Christ had seventy helpers.*	*"After these things the Lord appointed other seventy also, and sent them two and two before his face into every city and place, whither he himself would come" (Lu.10:1).*
	• *Moses established ordinances, memorials (Ex.12:14).*	• *Jesus Christ established ordinances, memorials.*	*"And he took bread, and gave thanks, and brake [it], and gave unto them, saying, This is my body which is given for you: this do in remembrance of me" (Lu.22:19).*

Historical Term	Type or Picture (Scriptural Basis for Each)	Life Application for Today's Believer	Biblical Application
(7) *Moses (continued)* (Ex.3:1f)	• *Moses reappeared after death (Mt.17:3).*	• *Jesus Christ reappeared after death.*	*"To whom also he showed himself alive after his passion by many infallible proofs, being seen of them forty days, and speaking of the things pertaining to the kingdom of God" (Ac.1:3).*

Note: the comparison between Moses and Christ is taken from *The Thompson Chain Reference Bible*, Cyclopedia Index. (Indianapolis, IN: B.B. Kirkbride Bible Co., Inc., 1964), p.95, # 2421.

Historical Term	Type or Picture (Scriptural Basis for Each)	Life Application for Today's Believer	Biblical Application
(8) *The Burning Bush* (Ex.3:2, 5)	*A picture of the glory, presence and holiness of God* "And the angel of the LORD appeared unto him in a flame of fire out of the midst of a bush: and he looked, and, behold, the bush burned with fire, and the bush *was* not consumed....And he said, Draw not nigh hither: put off thy shoes from off thy feet, for the place whereon thou standest is holy ground" (Ex.3:2, 5). "For I am the LORD that bringeth you up out of the land of Egypt, to be your God: ye shall therefore be holy, for I am holy" (Le.11:45). (see Le.19:2; 1 Chr.16:29)	The glory, presence, and holiness of God are available to every believer... • who seeks deeper experiences with God • who longs to know God more and more • who draws closer and closer to God • who loves God without any reservation	*"I beseech you therefore, brethren, by the mercies of God, that ye present your bodies a living sacrifice, holy, acceptable unto God, which is your reasonable service. And be not conformed to this world: but be ye transformed by the renewing of your mind, that ye may prove what is that good, and acceptable, and perfect, will of God"* (Ro.12:1-2). *"Having therefore these promises, dearly beloved, let us cleanse ourselves from all filthiness of the flesh and spirit, perfecting holiness in the fear of God"* (2 Co.7:1). *"But as he which hath called you is holy, so be ye holy in all manner of conversation [behavior, conduct]; Because it is written, Be ye holy; for I am holy"* (1 Pe.1:15-16). *(see 1 Chr.16:29; Is.6:1-3, 5; Ro.11:33; 2 Co.3:18)*
(9) *Moses' Staff [or Rod]* (Ex.4:2-5)	*God's power...* • *over Pharaoh: symbolizes the evil rulers of this world and Satan* • *over Egypt: symbolizes the world and its enslavements* "And the LORD said unto him, What *is* that in thine hand? And he said, A rod. And he said, Cast it on the ground. And he cast it on the ground, and it became a serpent; and Moses fled from before it. And the LORD said unto Moses, Put forth thine hand, and take it by the tail. And he put forth his hand, and caught it, and it became a rod in his hand: That they may believe that the LORD God of their fathers, the God of Abraham, the God of Isaac, and the God of Jacob, hath appeared unto thee" (Ex.4:2-5; see Ps.2:9).	God's power rules over both the physical and the spiritual world... • all the principalities, powers, and rulers of this world • all the wicked forces in the spiritual world	*"[That you may know] what is the exceeding greatness of his power to us-ward who believe, according to the working of his [God's] mighty power, Which he wrought in Christ, when he raised him from the dead, and set him at his own right hand in the heavenly places, Far above all principality, and power, and might, and dominion, and every name that is named, not only in this world, but also in that which is to come: And hath put all things under his feet"* (Ep.1:19-22). *"Put on the whole armour of God, that ye may be able to stand against the wiles of the devil. For we wrestle not against flesh and blood, but against principalities, against powers, against the rulers of the darkness of this world, against spiritual wickedness in high places"* (Ep.6:11-12; see Col.2:15).

Historical Term	Type or Picture (Scriptural Basis for Each)	Life Application for Today's Believer	Biblical Application
(10) *Moses' Leprous Hand* (Ex.4:6-8)	*God's power...* • *over health* • *over disease* • *over life* • *over sin* • *over death* **"And the LORD said furthermore unto him, Put now thine hand into thy bosom. And he put his hand into his bosom: and when he took it out, behold, his hand *was* leprous as snow. And he said, Put thine hand into thy bosom again. And he put his hand into his bosom again; and plucked it out of his bosom, and, behold, it was turned again as his other flesh"** (Ex.4:6-7. See outline and notes—Ex.9:8-12).	Jesus Christ has complete control over our bodies and our lives. His power will... • heal or strengthen the sick • comfort all who cry out to Him • forgive the sin of all who ask Him • save all who call upon Him, save them for all eternity	*"The Spirit of the Lord [is] upon me, because he hath anointed me to preach the gospel to the poor; he hath sent me to heal the brokenhearted, to preach deliverance to the captives, and recovering of sight to the blind, to set at liberty them that are bruised"* (Lu.4:18). *"And the Lord shall deliver me from every evil work, and will preserve me unto his heavenly kingdom: to whom be glory for ever and ever"* (2 Ti.4:18). *"But I am poor and needy; yet the LORD thinketh upon me: thou art my help and my deliverer; make no tarrying, O my God"* (Ps.40:17). *"In him was life; and the life was the light of men. That was the true Light, which lighteth every man that cometh into the world"* (Jn.1:4, 9). *"For whosoever shall call upon the name of the Lord shall be saved"* (Ro.10:13). see. Ex.15:26; De.7:15; Ps. 41:4; Ps.147:3; Is.46:4; Is. 53:5; Je.30:17; Jn.3:16; 10:10)
(11) *Aaron* (Ex.4:14-16)	*A picture of a spokesman or ambassador* **"And he [Aaron] shall be thy spokesman unto the people: and he shall be, *even* he shall be to thee instead of a mouth, and thou shalt be to him instead of God"** (Ex.4:16). **"And the LORD said unto Moses, See, I have made thee a god to Pharaoh: and Aaron thy brother shall be thy prophet. Thou shalt speak all that I command thee: and Aaron thy brother shall speak unto Pharaoh, that he send the children of Israel out of his land"** (Ex.7:1-2).	A faithful ambassador carries with him... • the authority of the One (Christ) who sent him • the message of the One (Christ) who sent him • the will of the One (Christ) who sent him	*"Also I heard the voice of the LORD, saying, Whom shall I send, and who will go for us? Then said I, Here am I; send me"* (Is.6:8). *"Now then we are ambassadors for Christ, as though God did beseech you by us: we pray you in Christ's stead, be ye reconciled to God"* (2 Co.5:20). *"Ye have not chosen me, but I have chosen you, and ordained you, that ye should go and bring forth fruit, and [that] your fruit should remain: that whatsoever ye shall ask of the Father in my name, he may give it you"* (Jn.15:16). *"Feed the flock of God which is among you, taking the oversight thereof, not by constraint, but willingly; not for filthy lucre, but of a ready mind; Neither as being LORD over God's heritage, but being ensamples to the flock"* (1 Pe.5:2-3). (see Ac.20:28; 1 Ti.1:12; 1 Co.2:1-5)

Historical Term	Type or Picture (Scriptural Basis for Each)	Life Application for Today's Believer	Biblical Application
(12) *Circumcision* (Ex.4:24-26)	*A sign of God's covenant with man* "**This** *is* **my covenant, which ye shall keep, between me and you and thy seed after thee; Every man child among you shall be circumcised**" (Ge.17:10). "**And he gave him the covenant of circumcision: and so Abraham begat Isaac, and circumcised him the eighth day; and Isaac begat Jacob; and Jacob begat the twelve patriarchs**" (Ac.7:8). "**Circumcise therefore the foreskin of your heart, and be no more stiffnecked**" (De.10:16). (see De.30:6; Je.4:4)	Since the coming of Christ, circumcision... <ul><li>is no longer an outward sign</li><li>places no confidence in the flesh</li><li>takes place in the heart of believers</li></ul>	"*For we are the circumcision, which worship God in the spirit, and rejoice in Christ Jesus, and have no confidence in the flesh*" (Ph.3:3). "*In whom [Christ] also ye are circumcised with the circumcision made without hands, in putting off the body of the sins of the flesh by the circumcision of Christ*" (Col.2:11). "*For circumcision verily profiteth, if thou keep the law: but if thou be a breaker of the law, thy circumcision is made uncircumcision*" (Ro.2:25). "*But he is a Jew, which is one inwardly; and circumcision is that of the heart, in the spirit, and not in the letter; whose praise is not of men, but of God*" (Ro.2:29).
(13) *The Ten Plagues* (Ex.7:8-11:10)	*A picture of God's judgment upon all who reject Him and oppress people, upon the ungodly and unrighteous in the world.* "**But Pharaoh shall not hearken unto you, that I may lay my hand upon Egypt, and bring forth mine armies,** *and* **my people the children of Israel, out of the land of Egypt by great judgments**" (Ex.7:4).	God's judgment is going to fall upon all... <ul><li>who resist and deny Him</li><li>who worship other gods</li><li>who oppress and hurt people</li><li>who are ungodly and unrighteous</li><li>who reject the truth</li></ul>	"*And as it is appointed unto men once to die, but after this the judgment*" (He.9:27). "*Now the works of the flesh are manifest, which are these; Adultery, fornication, uncleanness, lasciviousness, Idolatry, witchcraft, hatred, variance, emulations, wrath, strife, seditions, heresies, Envyings, murders, drunkenness, revellings, and such like: of the which I tell you before, as I have also told you in time past, that they which do such things shall not inherit the kingdom of God*" (Ga.5:19-21). "*For the Son of man shall come in the glory of his Father with his angels; and then he shall reward every man according to his works*" (Mt.16:27). "*The Lord knoweth how to deliver the godly out of temptations, and to reserve the unjust unto the day of judgment to be punished*" (2 Pe.2:9). (see Mt.12:36; 25:31-32; Ro.1:18, 29-32; 2:5; 2 Pe.3:7; Jude 14-15; Re.21:8)

Historical Term	Type or Picture (Scriptural Basis for Each)	Life Application for Today's Believer	Biblical Application
(14) *Egyptian Magicians* (Ex.7:11)	*A picture of false messengers* "Then Pharaoh also called the wise men and the sorcerers: now the magicians of Egypt, they also did in like manner with their enchantments" (Ex.7:11-12). "Now as Jannes and Jambres [two of the magicians] withstood Moses, so do these also resist the truth: men of corrupt minds, reprobate concerning the faith" (2 Ti. 3:8). see Ex.7:1; 8:7; 9:11. (See note—2 Ti.3:6-9).	The false messenger deceives people… • by claiming to be God's messenger (2 Co. 11:13-15). • by perverting the meaning of God's Word (Gal.1:6-10) • by seducing people to reject God's truth (2 Ti.4:3-4) • by denying the LORD who died for them (2 Pe.2:1; 1 Jn.4:1-3)	"Beware of false prophets, which come to you in sheep's clothing, but inwardly they are ravening wolves" (Mt.7:15). "For such are false apostles, deceitful workers, transforming themselves into the apostles of Christ. And no marvel; for Satan himself is transformed into an angel of light. Therefore it is no great thing if his ministers also be transformed as the ministers of righteousness; whose end shall be according to their works" (2 Co.11:13-15). "Beloved, believe not every spirit, but try the spir-its whether they are of God: because many false prophets are gone out into the world. Hereby know ye the Spirit of God: Every spirit that confesseth that Jesus Christ is come in the flesh is of God: And every spirit that confesseth not that Jesus Christ is come in the flesh is not of God" (1 Jn.4:1-3). (see Pr.6:19; 12:17; Mt.24:11; Gal. 1:6-10; 1 Ti.6:3-5; 2 Ti. 4:3-4; 2 Pe.2:1; Is.56:10-12; Je.23:2; 50:6; Eze.34:2-3)
(15) *The Passover Feast* (Ex.12:1-13; 12:21-27)	*Salvation: Deliverance from God's judgment. God's judgment passes over all who hide behind the blood of the Passover Lamb.* "And it shall come to pass, when your children shall say unto you, What mean ye by this service? That ye shall say, It is the sacrifice of the LORD'S passover, who passed over the houses of the children of Israel in Egypt, when he smote the Egyptians, and delivered our houses" (Ex.12:26-27).	God's judgment passes over all who hide behind the blood of Jesus Christ, the Lamb of God. The Son of God Himself, the Lord Jesus Christ, has delivered the believer from eternal judgment.	"Through faith he [Moses] kept the passover, and the sprinkling of blood, lest he that destroyed the firstborn should touch them" (He.11:28). "The next day John seeth Jesus coming unto him, and saith, Behold the Lamb of God, which taketh away the sin of the world" (Jn.1:29). "Purge out therefore the old leaven, that ye may be a new lump, as ye are unleavened. For even Christ our passover is sacrificed for us" (1 Co.5:7). "He that believeth on the Son hath everlasting life: and he that believeth not the Son shall not see life; but the wrath of God abideth on him" (Jn.3:36). "But God commendeth his love toward us, in that, while we were yet sinners, Christ died for us. Much more then, being now justified by his blood, we shall be saved from wrath through him" (Ro.5:8-9).

TYPES, SYMBOLS, AND PICTURES
THE BOOK OF EXODUS

Historical Term	Type or Picture (Scriptural Basis for Each)	Life Application for Today's Believer	Biblical Application
(16) *The Passover Lamb "without blemish [defect or imperfection]"* (Ex.12:5)	*Purity and perfection* "Your lamb shall be without blemish [defect], a male of the first year: ye shall take *it* out from the sheep, or from the goats" (Ex.12:5).	Jesus Christ is the Passover Lamb who lived a pure, sinless, and perfect life	*"For he hath made him to be sin for us, who knew no sin; that we might be made the righteousness of God in him"* (2 Co.5:21). *"The next day John seeth Jesus coming unto him, and saith, Behold the Lamb of God, which taketh away the sin of the world"* (Jn.1:29). *"And being made perfect, he became the author of eternal salvation unto all them that obey him"* (He.5:9). *"Forasmuch as ye know that ye were not redeemed with corruptible things, as silver and gold, from your vain conversation received by tradition from your fathers; But with the precious blood of Christ, as of a lamb without blemish and without spot"* (1 Pe.1:18-19). (see He.4:15; 7:26; 9:14; 2:22)
(17) *The Slaughter of the Lamb* (Ex.12:7, 13; 12:21-23)	*Substitutionary atonement: The lamb had to die for the believer: its blood had to be smeared on the doorposts to save the believer.* "And they shall take of the blood, and strike *it* on the two side posts and on the upper door post of the houses, wherein they shall eat it....And the blood shall be to you for a token upon the houses where ye are: and when I see the blood, I will pass over you, and the plague shall not be upon you to destroy you, when I smite the land of Egypt" (Ex.12:7, 13).	Jesus Christ, the Lamb of God, died for man. He gave His life for man. The life, the very death and blood, of Jesus Christ was offered upon the cross as a substitute for the believer. Scripture declares this glorious truth, the truth of the *substitutionary death* of Jesus Christ.	*"But he was wounded for our transgressions, he was bruised for our iniquities: the chastisement of our peace was upon him; and with his stripes we are healed....He was oppressed, and he was afflicted, yet he opened not his mouth: he is brought as a lamb to the slaughter, and as a sheep before her shearers is dumb, so he openeth not his mouth"* (Is.53:5, 7). *"But God commendeth his love toward us, in that, while we were yet sinners, Christ died for us"* (Ro.5:8). *"For Christ also hath once suffered for sins, the just for the unjust, that he might bring us to God, being put to death in the flesh, but quickened by the Spirit"* (1 Pe.3:18). *"Who his own self bare our sins in his own body on the tree, that we, being dead to sins, should live unto righteousness: by whose stripes ye were healed"* (1 Pe.2:24). (see Ro.3:25; 1 Co.5:7; Gal.3:13; He.2:9; 10:4; 13:11-12; 1 Jn.2:2)

Historical Term	Type or Picture (Scriptural Basis for Each)	Life Application for Today's Believer	Biblical Application
(18) *The Blood from the Lamb* (Ex.12:7, 13; 12:21-23)	*The forgiveness of sin: The blood of the lamb smeared on the doorposts...* • hid the believer with all his weaknesses and sins behind the blood. • made the believer acceptable to God. **"And they shall take of the blood, and strike *it* on the two side posts and on the upper door post of the houses, wherein they shall eat it....And the blood shall be to you for a token upon the houses where ye are: and when I see the blood, I will pass over you, and the plague shall not be upon you to destroy you, when I smite the land of Egypt" (Ex.12:7, 13; see Ex.12:21-23).**	The shed blood of Jesus Christ... • provides forgiveness of sin • makes the believer acceptable to God • delivers the believer from the wrath of God, the judgment to come	*"The next day John seeth Jesus coming unto him, and saith, Behold the Lamb of God, which taketh away the sin of the world"* (Jn.1:29). *"In whom we have redemption through his blood, the forgiveness of sins, according to the riches of his grace"* (Ep.1:7). *"For this is my blood of the new testament, which is shed for many for the remission of sins"* (Mt.26:28). *"And ye know that he was manifested to take away our sins; and in him is no sin"* (1 Jn.3:5). *"Unto him that loved us, and washed us from our sins in his own blood"* (Re.1:5). (see Jn.3:16; Jn.3:17-18; Ac.5:31; Ro.5:9; Gal.1:4; Ga.3:13; He.9:22; 9:26-28; 1 Pe.3:18; Re.1:5; Is.53:5)
(19) *The Bitter Herbs* (Ex.12:8)	*The bitter days of Israel's slavery [to sin]* **"And they shall eat the flesh in that night, roast with fire, and unleavened bread; *and* with bitter *herbs* they shall eat it"** (Ex.12:8).	Slavery is sin, the height of evil. To suffer the cruel bondage of slavery is to suffer the most brutal evil imaginable. There is no joy—only bitterness—in being a slave to such an evil. This is a clear picture of man's slavery to sin. Sin is a cruel master: it enslaves people to such bondages as... • the lust of the flesh • the lust of the eyes • the pride of life But there is glorious news. Jesus Christ has broken the power of sin. Jesus Christ can take a person and set him free from the lethal bondage of sin.	*"Jesus answered them, Verily, verily, I say unto you, Whosoever committeth sin is the servant of sin"* (Jn.8:34). *"For I know that in me (that is, in my flesh,) dwelleth no good thing: for to will is present with me; but how to perform that which is good I find not. For the good that I would I do not: but the evil which I would not, that I do. Now if I do that I would not, it is no more I that do it, but sin that dwelleth in me"* (Ro.7:18-20). *"Who gave himself for our sins, that he might deliver us from this present evil world, according to the will of God and our Father"* (Ga.1:4). *"Stand fast therefore in the liberty wherewith Christ hath made us free, and be not entangled again with the yoke of bondage"* (Ga.5:1). *"For ye have not received the spirit of bondage again to fear; but ye have received the Spirit of adoption, whereby we cry, Abba, Father"* (Ro.8:15). (see Ro.7:14-25; 8:1-2)

Historical Term	Type or Picture (Scriptural Basis for Each)	Life Application for Today's Believer	Biblical Application
(20) *The Roasting and Eating of the Passover Lamb* (Ex.12:9-11)	*Identifying with the lamb's death* "Eat not of it raw, nor sodden at all with water, but roast *with* fire; his head with his legs, and with the purtenance thereof. And ye shall let nothing of it remain until the morning; and that which remaineth of it until the morning ye shall burn with fire. And thus shall ye eat it; *with* your loins girded, your shoes on your feet, and your staff in your hand; and ye shall eat it in haste: it *is* the LORD's passover" (Ex.12:9-11).	The believer cannot partake in Christ's death from afar—it is a personal decision... • to partake of Christ by believing in Christ • to partake of Christ by living a life that dies to self and lives for Christ	"For God so loved the world, that he gave his only begotten Son, that whosoever believeth in him should not perish, but have everlasting life" (Jn.3:16). "Moreover, brethren, I declare unto you the gospel which I preached unto you, which also ye have received, and wherein ye stand; By which also ye are saved, if ye keep in memory what I preached unto you, unless ye have believed in vain. For I delivered unto you first of all that which I also received, how that Christ died for our sins according to the scriptures" (1 Co.15:1-3). "And he said to [them] all, If any [man] will come after me, let him deny himself, and take up his cross daily, and follow me" (Lu.9:23). "And that he died for all, that they which live should not henceforth live unto themselves, but unto him which died for them, and rose again" (2 Co.5:15). (see. Jn.5:25; Ro.10:9-10; Ga.2:20; Tit.2:14)
(21) *Leaven* (Ex.12:14-20)	*Evil* "Seven days shall ye eat unleavened bread; even the first day ye shall put away leaven [evil] out of your houses: for whosoever eateth leavened bread from the first day until the seventh day, that soul shall be cut off from Israel" (Ex.12:15; see Ex.12:19-20; Ex.12:39).	The believer must take personal responsibility for purging the evil out of his life... • by getting rid of all sin (Col.3:8-9).by getting rid of the sin that so easily entangles him (He.12:1).by abstaining even from the appearance of evil (1 Th.5:22) • by constantly searching his heart for unconfessed sin (Ps.139;23-24) • by never making peace with sin, by making it a despised habit, a hated foe, a defeated enemy	"Then Jesus said unto them, Take heed and beware of the leaven [evil] of the Pharisees and of the Sadducees" (Mt.16:6). "Your glorying is not good. Know ye not that a little leaven leaveneth the whole lump? Purge out therefore the old leaven, that ye may be a new lump, as ye are unleavened. For even Christ our passover is sacrificed for us: Therefore let us keep the feast, not with old leaven, neither with the leaven of malice and wickedness; but with the unleavened bread of sincerity and truth" (1 Co.5:6-8). "Abstain from all appearance of evil" (1 Th.5:22). "Now these things were our examples, to the intent we should not lust after evil things, as they also lusted" (1 Co.10:6). (see Ro.12:9; Ga.5:9; Col.3:8-10; He.12:1; 1 Pe.-3:11; 1 Jn.1:9; Ps.51:1-13; 139:23-24)

Historical Term	Type or Picture (Scriptural Basis for Each)	Life Application for Today's Believer	Biblical Application
(22) *Unleavened Bread* (Ex.12:14-20)	In fleeing Egypt, the Israelite did not have time to allow the leaven (yeast) to ferment in the bread. He had to take unleavened bread. (1) This is a picture of urgency, haste, readiness: the believer must be immediately ready to leave Egypt (the world) and quickly begin the march to the promised land. (2) This is a picture of the believer's *new life of righteousness*: the believer must leave his *old life* in Egypt and begin his march to the promised land. **"And ye shall observe *the feast of* unleavened bread; for in this selfsame day have I brought your armies out of the land of Egypt: therefore shall ye observe this day in your generations by an ordinance for ever" (Ex.12:17).**	There is the urgent need for a person... • to rush away from the world, to be immediately converted and to quickly begin his march to the promised land of heaven • to leave his *old life* behind and to begin his *new life of righteousness*	*"Behold, now is the accepted time; behold, now is the day of salvation"* (2 Co.6:2). *"Christ was raised up from the dead by the glory of the Father, even so we also should walk in newness of life"* (Ro.6:4). *"Therefore if any man be in Christ, he is a new creature: old things are passed away; behold, all things are become new"* (2 Co.5:17). *"But now ye also put off all these; anger, wrath, malice, blasphemy, filthy communication out of your mouth. Lie not one to another, seeing that ye have put off the old man with his deeds; And have put on the new man, which is renewed in knowledge after the image of him that created him"* (Col.3:8-10). (see 2 Co.6:17-18; Mt. 24:44; 25:13; He.2:3; Ep.4:24; Col.3:8-10)
(23) *No Broken Bones on the Lamb* (Ex.12:46)	*A picture of unity: The parts of the lamb were not to be divided: the lamb was to remain a unified body. The family members were not to be divided: the family was to be hid behind the blood of the lamb as one body, as one unified family.* **"In one house shall it be eaten; thou shalt not carry forth ought of the flesh abroad out of the house; neither shall ye break a bone thereof" (Ex.12:46).**	Jesus Christ died without a single bone being broken. Not a part was dismembered. All parts of His body remained unified. Jesus Christ is the Head of one body (the church), a body... • that has many members • that has different gifts • that has been called to serve the Lamb of God in unity, without division	*"For these things were done, that the scripture should be fulfilled, A bone of him shall not be broken"* (Jn.19:36). *"Now ye are the body of Christ, and members in particular. And God hath set some in the church, first apostles, secondarily prophets, thirdly teachers, after that miracles, then gifts of healings, helps, governments, diversities of tongues"* (1 Co.12:27-28). *"But now hath God set the members every one of them in the body, as it hath pleased him....That there should be no schism in the body; but that the members should have the same care one for another"* (1 Co.12:18, 25). *"I in them, and thou in me, that they may be made perfect in one; and that the world may know that thou hast sent me, and hast loved them, as thou hast loved me"* (Jn.17:23). (see Ro.12:4-5; 1 Co.12:12-13; Ep.1:23; 4:11-12; Col.1:24; Ac.2:1; 1:14; 2:42-47)

Historical Term	Type or Picture (Scriptural Basis for Each)	Life Application for Today's Believer	Biblical Application
(24) *The Dedication of the Firstborn* (Ex.13:2)	*Sanctification: Setting apart a life for God* **"Sanctify unto me all the firstborn, whatsoever openeth the womb among the children of Israel, *both of man and of beast: it is mine*" (Ex.13:2).**	God demands that we be sanctified (holy) completely and totally set apart to God. We must be constantly reminded... • that Jesus Christ is our sanctification (1 Co.1:30) • that Jesus Christ sanctifies us through His blood (He.13:12) • that we are chosen by God through the sanctifying work of the Holy Spirit (1 Pe.1:2) • that Jesus Christ gave Himself for the church, that He might sanctify it (Ep.5:26) • that we are sanctified through the truth, through God's Word (Jn.17:17) • that we are to be sanctified [holy] vessels, fit for God to use (2 Ti.2:21) • that God's will is for us to live sanctified, pure, and holy lives (Lu. 1:74; 2 Co.7:10; 1 Th.4:3)	*"But of him are ye in Christ Jesus, who of God is made unto us wisdom, and righteousness, and sanctification, and redemption"* (1 Co.1:30). *"Wherefore Jesus also, that he might sanctify the people with his own blood, suffered without the gate"* (He.13:12). *"Sanctify them through thy truth: thy word is truth"* (Jn.17:17). *"If a man therefore purge himself from these, he shall be a vessel unto honour, sanctified, and meet for the master's use, and prepared unto every good work"* (2 Ti.2:21). *"For this is the will of God, even your sanctification, that ye should abstain from fornication"* (1 Th. 4:3). (see Pr.3:9-10; Mt.6:33; 1 Pe.1:2; Ep.5:26)
(25) *The Wilderness Wanderings (Journey)* (Ex.13:16-18:27)	*The pilgrimage (journey, wanderings) of the believer...* • *as he turns away from Egypt (the world) and leaves behind his old life.* • *as he turns to begin his new life by marching to the promised land.* • *as he marches through the wilderness [trials] of this world and conquers all that the wilderness throws against him.* **"But God led the people about, through the way of the wilderness of the Red sea: and the children of Israel went up harnessed [marching in military rank] out of the land of Egypt" (Ex.13:17-18).** (see Nu.14:33; De.8:2-3, 5-6; 32:10)	Once a person has been saved—turned to God from the world (Egypt), turned away from his old life—he begins his *new life* (in Christ). He immediately begins to march to the promised land of heaven. His new life is the *pilgrim-age* of the Christian believer: a march through the *wilderness* of this world, through all that the wilderness throws up against him... • trials • temptations • problems • difficulties • obstacles • accidents • sufferings • death	*"Now all these things happened unto them for ensamples: and they are written for our admonition, upon whom the ends of the world are come"* (1 Co.10:11). *"And, behold, I am with thee, and will keep thee in all places whither thou goest, and will bring thee again into this land; for I will not leave thee, until I have done that which I have spoken to thee of"* (Ge.28:15). *"When thou passest through the waters, I will be with thee; and through the rivers, they shall not overflow thee: when thou walkest through the fire, thou shalt not be burned; neither shall the flame kindle upon thee"* (Is.43:2). *"There hath no temptation taken you but such as is common to man: but God is faithful, who will not suffer you to be tempted above that ye are able; but will with the temptation also make a way to escape, that ye may be able to bear it"* (1 Co.10:13). (see Mt.4:1-11; Lu.4:1-13; 2 S.22:2; Je.1:8; He.2:14-15)

Historical Term	Type or Picture (Scriptural Basis for Each)	Life Application for Today's Believer	Biblical Application
(26) *The Pillar of Cloud and Fire* (Ex.13:21)	*A picture of God's awesome presence and guidance. This cloud was...* • *a source of light* • *a source for direction* • *a source of protection* • *a picture of baptism* **"And the LORD went before them by day in a pillar of a cloud, to lead them the way; and by night in a pillar of fire, to give them light; to go by day and night: He took not away the pillar of the cloud by day, nor the pillar of fire by night, from before the people"** (Ex.13:21-22; see Ex.14:19-20).	God has promised His presence, guidance, and protection as we journey through the wilderness of this world, journey to the promised land of heaven. God's presence and guidance... • will guide us with His counsel (Ps.73:24) • will show us the exact way to go (Is.42:16) • will protect and deliver us (Ps.34:7; see Ps. 91:4) • will be with us through all—no matter what (Ge.28:15; Ex. 33:14) • will lead us to the green pastures and still waters (Ps.23:2)	*"Thou wilt show me the path of life: in thy presence is fullness of joy; at thy right hand there are pleasures for evermore"* (Ps.16:11). *"Thy word is a lamp unto my feet, and a light unto my path"* (Ps.119:105). *"I will instruct thee and teach thee in the way which thou shalt go: I will guide thee with mine eye"* (Ps.32:8). *"He maketh me to lie down in green pastures: he leadeth me beside the still waters"* (Ps.23:2). *"For this God is our God for ever and ever: he will be our guide even unto death"* (Ps.48:14). *"Thou shalt guide me with thy counsel, and afterward receive me to glory"* (Ps.73:24).
(27) *The Red Sea* (Ex.14:13-31)	*A picture of deliverance through the greatest trials and obstacles* **"And Moses said unto the people, Fear ye not, stand still, and see the salvation of the LORD, which he will show to you to day: for the Egyptians whom ye have seen to day, ye shall see them again no more for ever"** (Ex.14:13). **"And Moses stretched out his hand over the sea; and the LORD caused the sea to go back by a strong east wind all that night, and made the sea dry land, and the waters were divided. And the children of Israel went into the midst of the sea upon the dry ground: and the waters were a wall unto them on their right hand, and on their left"** (Ex.14:21-22). **"And Moses stretched forth his hand over the sea...And the waters returned, and covered the chariots, and the horsemen, and all the host of Pharaoh that came into the sea after them; there remained not so much as one of them"** (Ex.14:26-28).	God promises to deliver us through all the trials and temptations of life, no matter how... • difficult • terrorizing • frightening • fearful • impossible	*"But I am poor and needy; yet the LORD thinketh upon me: thou art my help and my deliverer; make no tarrying, O my God"* (Ps.40:17). *"Fear thou not; for I am with thee: be not dismayed; for I am thy God: I will strengthen thee; yea, I will help thee; yea, I will uphold thee with the right hand of my righteousness"* (Is.41:10). *"And the Lord shall deliver me from every evil work, and will preserve me unto his heavenly kingdom: to whom be glory for ever and ever"* (2 Ti.4:18). *"Who delivered us from so great a death, and doth deliver: in whom we trust that he will yet deliver us"* (2 Co.1:10). *"Fear not: for I have redeemed thee, I have called thee by thy name; thou art mine. When thou passest through the waters, I will be with thee; and through the rivers, they shall not overflow thee: when thou walkest through the fire, thou shalt not be burned; neither shall the flame kindle upon thee"* (Is.43:1-2). *(see Jn.16:13; 1 Co.10:13; He.2:14-15; 13:5-6; 2 Pe.2:9; Is.30:21; Ps.48:14; 73:24; Ge.28:15; Ex.33:14; De.20:1; Ps.91:3; Is.46:4; Je.1:8)*

Historical Term	Type or Picture (Scriptural Basis for Each)	Life Application for Today's Believer	Biblical Application
(28) *Pharaoh's Defeat* (Ex.14:13-31)	*A Picture of God's complete and total victory over enemies* **"And the waters returned, and covered the chariots, and the horsemen,** *and* **all the host of Pharaoh that came into the sea after them; there remained not so much as one of them" (Ex.14:28).**	Jesus Christ—through His death and resurrection—has conquered all the evil forces of the physical world and of the spiritual world. He now rules... • over the principalities and powers and rulers of this dark world • over the wicked forces of the spiritual world (Satan and his wicked angels) (Remember: Pharaoh symbolizes Satan.)	*"Now is the judgment of this world: now shall the prince of this world be cast out" (Jn.12:31).* *"[The power of God] which he wrought in Christ, when he raised him from the dead, and set him at his own right hand in the heavenly places, Far above all principality, and power, and might, and dominion, and every name that is named, not only in this world, but also in that which is to come: And hath put all things under his feet, and gave him to be the head over all things to the church" (Ep.1:20-22).* *"And having spoiled principalities and powers [upon the cross], he made a show of them openly, triumphing over them in it" (Col.2:15).* *(see Ps.7:11; 2:8-9; Jn.16:11; Col.1:16-17; He.2:14-15; 2 Pe.2:4, 6, 9; Re.20:10; 21:8)*
(29) *The Bitter Waters at Marah* (Ex.15:22-26)	*Bitter trials of life* **"And when they came to Marah, they could not drink of the waters of Marah, for they were bitter: therefore the name of it was called Marah. And the people murmured against Moses, saying, What shall we drink? And he cried unto the LORD; and the LORD showed him a tree, which when he had cast into the waters, the waters were made sweet: there he made for them a statute and an ordinance, and there he proved them" (Ex.15:23-25).**	God will take the bitter experiences of our lives and sweeten them. He will purify and clean up the bitter experiences of life. Just imagine all the trouble, problems, difficulties, trials, and temptations of life... • God will take the bitterness out of them all. • God will enable us to bear them all. • God will strengthen us to conquer and walk through them all—victoriously and triumphantly.	*"Many are the afflictions of the righteous: but the LORD delivereth him out of them all" (Ps.34:19).* *"The LORD will strengthen him upon the bed of languishing: thou wilt make all his bed in his sickness" (Ps.41:3).* *"Surely he shall deliver thee from the snare of the fowler, and from the noisome pestilence" (Ps.91:3).* *"Fear thou not; for I am with thee: be not dismayed; for I am thy God: I will strengthen thee; yea, I will help thee; yea, I will uphold thee with the right hand of my righteousness" (Is.41:10).* *"And we know that all things work together for good to them that love God, to them who are the called according to his purpose" (Ro.8:28).* *"And I will walk among you, and will be your God, and ye shall be my people" (Le.26:12).*

TYPES, SYMBOLS, AND PICTURES
THE BOOK OF EXODUS

Historical Term	Type or Picture (Scriptural Basis for Each)	Life Application for Today's Believer	Biblical Application
(30) *Manna* (Ex.16:1-36)	*God's provision: the Bread from Heaven* "Then said the LORD unto Moses, Behold, I will rain bread from heaven for you; and the people shall go out and gather a certain rate every day, that I may prove them, whether they will walk in my law, or no" (Ex.16:4).	The LORD Jesus Christ is the Bread from Heaven—the Bread of Life—a life that sustains the believer both now and forever.	"Then Jesus said unto them, Verily, verily, I say unto you, Moses gave you not that bread from heaven; but my Father giveth you the true bread from heaven" (Jn.6:32-33). "And Jesus said unto them, I am the bread of life: he that cometh to me shall never hunger; and he that believeth on me shall never thirst" (Jn.6:35). "I am that bread of life. Your fathers did eat manna in the wilderness, and are dead. This is the bread which cometh down from heaven, that a man may eat thereof, and not die. I am the living bread which came down from heaven: if any man eat of this bread, he shall live for ever: and the bread that I will give is my flesh, which I will give for the life of the world" (Jn.6:48-51;see Jn.6:58).
(31) *The Rock at Rephidim* (Ex.17:6)	*God's Provision of Water* "Behold, I will stand before thee there upon the rock in Horeb; and thou shalt smite the rock, and there shall come water out of it, that the people may drink. And Moses did so in the sight of the elders of Israel" (Ex.17:6). "Therefore with joy shall ye draw water out of the wells of salvation" (Is. 12:3).	Jesus Christ is our Rock, the rock of our salvation… • who provides the water that saves and gives us life • who supports us during the storms of life • who is the chief cornerstone that determines the fate of us all • who is the only foundation upon which we can build and base our lives	"And did all drink the same spiritual drink: for they drank of that spiritual Rock that followed them: and that Rock was Christ" (1 Co.10:4;see Is.53:4-5). "Jesus answered and said unto her, Whosoever drinketh of this water shall thirst again: But whosoever drinketh of the water that I shall give him shall never thirst; but the water that I shall give him shall be in him a well of water springing up into everlasting life" (Jn.4:13-14). "Wherefore also it is contained in the scripture, Behold, I lay in Sion a chief corner stone, elect, precious: and he that believeth on him shall not be confounded. Unto you therefore which believe he is precious: but unto them which be disobedient, the stone which the builders disallowed, the same is made the head of the corner, And a stone of stumbling, and a rock of offence, even to them which stumble at the word, being disobedient: whereunto also they were appointed" (1 Pe.2:6-8; see 1 Co.3:11).

Historical Term	Type or Picture (Scriptural Basis for Each)	Life Application for To-day's Believer	Biblical Application
(32) *Meribah* (Ex.17:7)	*Argument, contention, and strife: Complaining against God and His servants* **"And the people thirst-ed there for water; and the people murmured against Moses, and said, Where-fore is this that thou hast brought us up out of Egypt, to kill us and our children and our cattle with thirst?...And he called the name of the place Massah, and Meri-bah, because of the chid-ing of the children of Isra-el, and because they tempted the LORD, saying, Is the LORD among us, or not?" (Ex.17:3, 7).**	Carnal (fleshly) believers complain, murmur, and grumble. They complain against God and His serv-ants. They are like a spiritu-al cancer that spreads and infects the whole body of believers.	*"Neither murmur ye, as some of them also mur-mured, and were destroyed of the destroyer" (1 Co.10:10).* *"Do all things without murmurings and disput-ings" (Ph.2:14).* *"Jesus therefore answer-ed and said unto them, Murmur not among your-selves" (Jn.6:43).* *"If any man among you seem to be religious, and bridleth not his tongue, but deceiveth his own heart, this man's religion is vain" (Js.1:26).* *(see Ex.16:8; Ps.52:2; 106:24-25; 120:2; Js.3:5-8; 1 Pe.3:10; Jude 14-16)*
(33) *Massah* (Ex.17:7)	*The name "Massah" means testing: Doubting and ques-tioning God* **"And he called the name of the place Massah, and Meribah, because of the chiding of the children of Israel, and because they tempted the LORD, saying, Is the LORD among us, or not?" (Ex.17:7).**	God is not to be doubted nor questioned. How can the creature question the LORD God... • who is the great Crea-tor and Sustainer of the universe • who is the Sovereign LORD and Majesty of all • who is the Giver of every good and perfect gift, the Father of Light, who never changes • who is the only living and true God	*"Take heed, brethren, lest there be in any of you an evil heart of unbelief, in departing from the living God" (He.3:12).* *"Because of unbelief they [Israel] were broken off, and thou standest by faith. Be not highminded, but fear: For if God spared not the natural branches, take heed lest he also spare not thee" (Ro.11:20-21).* *"Then he said unto them, O fools, and slow of heart to believe all that the prophets have spoken" (Lu.24:25).* *"Art thou the Christ? tell us. And he said unto them, If I tell you, ye will not be-lieve" (Lu.22:67).* *"But though he had done so many miracles before them, yet they believed not on him" (Jn.12:37).* *"And he did not many mighty works there be-cause of their unbelief" (Mt.13:58).* *"He staggered not at the promise of God through unbelief; but was strong in faith, giving glory to God; And being fully persuaded that, what he had prom-ised, he was able also to perform" (Ro.4:20-21).* *(see 2 Th.3:3; 1 Ti.1:13; 2 Ti.2:13; He.3:19; He.10:23)*

	Historical Term	Type or Picture (Scriptural Basis for Each)	Life Application for Today's Believer	Biblical Application
(34)	*The Stone that Moses Sat Upon* (Ex.17:12)	*A picture of support and salvation* "But Moses' hands *were* heavy; and they took a stone, and put *it* under him, and he sat thereon; and Aaron and Hur stayed up his hands, the one on the one side, and the other on the other side; and his hands were steady until the going down of the sun" (Ex.17:12). I waited patiently for the LORD; and he inclined unto me, and heard my cry. He brought me up also out of an horrible pit, out of the miry clay, and set my feet upon a rock, *and* established my goings" (Ps.40:1-2).	Jesus Christ is the Rock of our lives, the Rock that undergirds us as we walk through the wilderness of this world. Jesus Christ is the Rock of... • our salvation • our support • our security • our foundation	"He only is my rock and my salvation; he is my defence; I shall not be greatly moved" (Ps.62:2). "The stone which the builders refused is become the head stone [Jesus Christ] of the corner" (Ps.118:22). "And [you] are built upon the foundation of the apostles and prophets, Jesus Christ himself being the chief corner stone" (Eph.2:20). "For who is God save the LORD? or who is a rock save our God? It is God that girdeth me with strength, and maketh my way perfect" (Ps.18:31-32). "But the LORD is my defence; and my God is the rock of my refuge" (Ps.94:22). (see 1 S.2:2; 2 S.22:47; De.32:4; Ps.28:1; 62:2; 1 Pe.2:6-9
(35)	*Jehovah Nissi: The LORD Is my Banner* (Ex.17:15-16)	*God's name is the banner of the believer. His name is the emblem, the symbol, the identifying sign of the believer.* "And Moses built an altar, and called the name of it Jehovah-nissi [the LORD is my banner]: For he said, Because the LORD hath sworn *that* the LORD *will have* war with Amalek from generation to generation" (Ex.17:15-16). "Some *trust* in chariots, and some in horses: but we will remember the name of the LORD our God" (Ps.20:7).	The Name of the Lord Jesus Christ is the Banner. His name is the emblem, the symbol, the identifying sign—of the believer. The name of the LORD is what the believer carries with him as he journeys through the wilderness of this world. The name of the LORD is his banner (his power), his witness, as he marches to the promised land of heaven.	"Wherefore God also hath highly exalted him, and given him a name which is above every name: That at the name of Jesus every knee should bow, of things in heaven, and things in earth, and things under the earth; And that every tongue should confess that Jesus Christ is Lord, to the glory of God the Father" (Ph.2:9-11). "But these are written, that ye might believe that Jesus is the Christ, the Son of God; and that believing ye might have life through his name" (Jn.20:31). "Because he hath set his love upon me, therefore will I deliver him: I will set him on high because he hath known my name" (Ps.91:14). "Our help is in the name of the LORD, who made heaven and earth" (Ps.124:8). "The name of the LORD is a strong tower: the righteous runneth into it, and is safe" (Pr.18:10). (see Ne.9:5-6; Ps.113:1-5)

Historical Term	Type or Picture (Scriptural Basis for Each)	Life Application for Today's Believer	Biblical Application
(36) *Eliezer, Moses' Youngest Son* (Ex.18:4)	*God is my helper* **"And the name of the other** *was* **Eliezer; for the God of my father,** *said he, was* **mine help, and delivered me from the sword of Pharaoh"** (Ex.18:4).	God is our helper. He helps us when we are… • weak • needy • poor • helpless • distressed • fearful • criticized • condemned • attacked • lonely • empty • lost • overlooked • ignored	*"But I am poor and needy; yet the* LORD *thinketh upon me: thou art my help and my deliverer; make no tarrying, O my God"* (Ps. 40:17). *"Fear thou not; for I am with thee: be not dismayed; for I am thy God: I will strengthen thee; yea, I will help thee; yea, I will uphold thee with the right hand of my righteousness"* (Is.41:10). *"So that we may boldly say, The Lord is my helper, and I will not fear what man shall do unto me"* (He.13:6).

VIII. TIMELINE OF SUBJECTS, CHARACTERS, & EVENTS

DIVISION I. ISRAEL AND EGYPT: THE OPPRESSION OF GOD'S PEOPLE BY A NATION THAT REJECTED GOD (Exodus 1:1-22)		
THE EVENT	THE SCRIPTURE	PRACTICAL APPLICATION
The Past Deliverance of Israel	Exodus 1:1-7	The Picture of God's Deliverance & God's Faithfulness
The Enslavement of Israel by Egypt	Exodus 1:8-22	How God's People Overcome Oppression

"Now there arose up a new king over Egypt, which knew not Joseph" (Ex.1:8).

DIVISION II. MOSES AND GOD: GOD RAISES UP A LEADER TO DELIVER HIS PEOPLE (Exodus 2:1-7:7)		
THE EVENT	THE SCRIPTURE	PRACTICAL APPLICATION
The Birth of Moses	Exodus 2:1-10	The Picture of a Believing, Courageous Mother
The First Significant Events of Moses' Life	Exodus 2:11-25	Experiences that Change a Person's Life

"And there went a man of the house of Levi, and took to wife a daughter of Levi. And the woman conceived, and bare a son: and when she saw him that he was a goodly child, she hid him three months" (Ex.2:1).

EXODUS CHRONOLOGY OF MAIN CHARACTERS AND EVENTS		
	Chapter 1	Chapter 2
JOSEPH	*Joseph died, 1:1-7, esp. 6*	
PHARAOH (The new Pharaoh)	*Did not know Joseph, 1:8-22, esp.8*	
FIRST MENTION OF ISRAEL'S BONDAGE	*Slaves in Egypt, 1:8-22*	
THE BIRTH OF MOSES		*Birth & protection, 2:1-25*
THE CALL OF MOSES		
MOSES' EXCUSES		
MOSES' SURRENDER TO GOD'S WILL		
MOSES' FIRST CONFRONTATION WITH PHARAOH (The second Pharaoh mentioned)		
GOD'S ENCOURAGEMENT & MESSAGE TO MOSES		
THE TEN PLAGUES		
THE PASSOVER		
THE EXODUS BEGINS		
ISRAEL'S FIRST CRISIS IN THE WILDERNESS		
MOSES' GREAT SONG OF PRAISE TO GOD		
ISRAEL'S SECOND CRISIS IN THE WILDERNESS		
ISRAEL'S THIRD CRISIS IN THE WILDERNESS		
ISRAEL'S FOURTH CRISIS IN THE WILDERNESS		
ISRAEL'S FIFTH CRISIS IN THE WILDERNESS		
ISRAEL'S SIXTH CRISIS IN THE WILDERNESS		

DIVISION II. MOSES AND GOD: GOD RAISES UP A LEADER TO DELIVER HIS PEOPLE (continued) (Exodus 2:1-7:7)		
THE EVENT	THE SCRIPTURE	PRACTICAL APPLICATION
The Call of Moses	Exodus 3:1-10	A Study of God's Call & Commission to Service
The Excuses of Moses	Exodus 3:11-4:17	A Reluctant Prophet—Arguments Against Serving God
The Surrender of Moses to God's Call	Exodus 4:18-31	The Fruit of Obedience

"And he said, Draw not nigh hither: put off thy shoes from off thy feet, for the place whereon thou standest is holy ground" (Ex. 3:5).

EXODUS CHRONOLOGY OF MAIN CHARACTERS AND EVENTS

	Chapter 3	Chapter 4
JOSEPH		
PHARAOH (The first Pharaoh mentioned)		
FIRST MENTION OF ISRAEL'S BONDAGE		
THE BIRTH OF MOSES		
THE CALL OF MOSES	*The burning bush, 3:1-10*	
MOSES' EXCUSES	*Saying no to God, 3:11-4:17*	
MOSES' SURRENDER TO GOD'S WILL		*Finally, obedience, 4:18-31*
MOSES' FIRST CONFRONTATION WITH PHARAOH (The second Pharaoh mentioned)		
GOD'S ENCOURAGEMENT & MESSAGE TO MOSES		
THE TEN PLAGUES		
THE PASSOVER		
THE EXODUS BEGINS		
ISRAEL'S FIRST CRISIS IN THE WILDERNESS		
MOSES' GREAT SONG OF PRAISE TO GOD		
ISRAEL'S SECOND CRISIS IN THE WILDERNESS		
ISRAEL'S THIRD CRISIS IN THE WILDERNESS		
ISRAEL'S FOURTH CRISIS IN THE WILDERNESS		
ISRAEL'S FIFTH CRISIS IN THE WILDERNESS		
ISRAEL'S SIXTH CRISIS IN THE WILDERNESS		

DIVISION II. MOSES AND GOD: GOD RAISES UP A LEADER TO DELIVER HIS PEOPLE (continued) (Exodus 2:1-7:7)		
THE EVENT	THE SCRIPTURE	PRACTICAL APPLICATION
The First Confrontation of Moses with Pharaoh	Exodus 5:1-23	Opposing God's Will for His People, Freedom of Life & Worship
The Great Encouragement & Message Given to Moses	Exodus 6:1-7:7	Deliverance & Freedom

"Go in, speak unto Pharaoh king of Egypt, that he let the children of Israel go out of his land" (Ex. 6:11).

EXODUS CHRONOLOGY OF MAIN CHARACTERS AND EVENTS

	Chapter 5	Chapter 6
JOSEPH		
PHARAOH (The first Pharaoh mentioned)		
FIRST MENTION OF ISRAEL'S BONDAGE		
THE BIRTH OF MOSES		
THE CALL OF MOSES		
MOSES' EXCUSES		
MOSES' SURRENDER TO GOD'S WILL		
MOSES' FIRST CONFRONTATION WITH PHARAOH (The second Pharaoh mentioned)	*"Let my people go!"... "No!" 5:1-23*	
GOD'S ENCOURAGEMENT & MESSAGE TO MOSES		*Discouragement overcome, 6:1-7:7*
THE TEN PLAGUES		
THE PASSOVER		
THE EXODUS BEGINS		
ISRAEL'S FIRST CRISIS IN THE WILDERNESS		
MOSES' GREAT SONG OF PRAISE TO GOD		
ISRAEL'S SECOND CRISIS IN THE WILDERNESS		
ISRAEL'S THIRD CRISIS IN THE WILDERNESS		
ISRAEL'S FOURTH CRISIS IN THE WILDERNESS		
ISRAEL'S FIFTH CRISIS IN THE WILDERNESS		
ISRAEL'S SIXTH CRISIS IN THE WILDERNESS		

DIVISION III. THE TEN PLAGUES & EGYPT: GOD'S JUDGMENT UPON THOSE WHO REJECT HIM & OPPRESS HIS PEOPLE (Exodus 7:8-11:10)		
THE EVENT	**THE SCRIPTURE**	**PRACTICAL APPLICATION**
The Credentials of God's Servant	Exodus 7:8-13	Proof that a Person is God's Servant
The First Plague—Water Changed to Blood	Exodus 7:14-25	Proof that God is the LORD, the God of Redemption, the Only Living & True God
The Second Plague—Frogs Every-where	Exodus 8:1-15	Proof that God has No Equal, that No One is Like the LORD our God
The Third Plague—Lice or Gnats In-fest the Land	Exodus 8:16-19	Proof that the Finger (Power) of God Controls All Things, Even the Very Dust of the Ground
The Fourth Plague—Flies Swarm Over the Land	Exodus 8:20-32	Proof that the LORD is the Redeemer (the Savior), the Only Living & True God, in Every Land & in Every Place
The Fifth Plague—A Severe Disease Struck & Killed All Livestock in the Field	Exodus 9:1-7	Proof that the Hand of God Controls the Animal Life of the World
The Sixth Plague—Festering Boils Afflicted Man & Animal	Exodus 9:8-12	Proof that God has Power Over Body & Health
The Seventh Plague—A Catastrophic Hail & Thunderstorm	Exodus 9:13-35	Proof that the Earth is the LORD's
The Eighth Plague—Locusts Swarmed Over the Land	Exodus 10:1-20	Proof that the LORD is the Great Redeemer of Mankind
The Ninth Plague—Darkness Covered the Land	Exodus 10:21-29	Proof that God has Power Over the Light & Darkness of the Earth
The Tenth Plague—Death of the Firstborn Announced	Exodus 11:1-10	Proof that God is the God of True Believers

"And the LORD said unto Moses, Yet will I bring one plague more upon Pharaoh, and upon Egypt; afterwards he will let you go hence: when he shall let you go, he shall surely thrust you out hence altogether" (Ex.11:1).

EXODUS CHRONOLOGY OF MAIN CHARACTERS AND EVENTS

	Chapters 7-11
JOSEPH	
PHARAOH (The first Pharaoh mentioned)	
FIRST MENTION OF ISRAEL'S BONDAGE	
THE BIRTH OF MOSES	
THE CALL OF MOSES	
MOSES' EXCUSES	
MOSES' SURRENDER TO GOD'S WILL	
MOSES' FIRST CONFRONTATION WITH PHARAOH (The second Pharaoh mentioned)	
GOD'S ENCOURAGEMENT & MESSAGE TO MOSES	
THE TEN PLAGUES	*Judgment! 7:8-11:10*
THE PASSOVER	
THE EXODUS BEGINS	
ISRAEL'S FIRST CRISIS IN THE WILDERNESS	
MOSES' GREAT SONG OF PRAISE TO GOD	
ISRAEL'S SECOND CRISIS IN THE WILDERNESS	
ISRAEL'S THIRD CRISIS IN THE WILDERNESS	
ISRAEL'S FOURTH CRISIS IN THE WILDERNESS	
ISRAEL'S FIFTH CRISIS IN THE WILDERNESS	
ISRAEL'S SIXTH CRISIS IN THE WILDERNESS	

DIVISION IV. THE PASSOVER & TENTH PLAGUE: DELIVERANCE FROM GOD'S JUDGMENT—LIBERATED, SET FREE (Exodus 12:1-13:16)		
THE EVENT	THE SCRIPTURE	PRACTICAL APPLICATION
The Institution of the Passover	Exodus 12:1-13	The Two Basic Essentials for Redemption
The Feast of Unleavened Bread, the Second Essential for Redemption—Unleavened Bread	Exodus 12:14-20	Putting All Leaven, All Evil, Out of One's Life
The Tenth Plague, the Death of the Firstborn & the Passover	Exodus 12:21-51	Deliverance From God's Judgment— Liberated, Set Free
The Dedication of the Firstborn	Exodus 13:1-16	Remembering God's Great Deliverance

"And the blood shall be to you for a token upon the houses where ye are: and when I see the blood, I will pass over you, and the plague shall not be upon you to destroy you, when I smite the land of Egypt" (Ex. 12:13).

EXODUS CHRONOLOGY OF MAIN CHARACTERS AND EVENTS		
	Chapter 12	Chapter 13
JOSEPH		
PHARAOH (The first Pharaoh mentioned)		
FIRST MENTION OF ISRAEL'S BONDAGE		
THE BIRTH OF MOSES		
THE CALL OF MOSES		
MOSES' EXCUSES		
MOSES' SURRENDER TO GOD'S WILL		
MOSES' FIRST CONFRONTATION WITH PHARAOH (The second Pharaoh mentioned)		
GOD'S ENCOURAGEMENT & MESSAGE TO MOSES		
THE TEN PLAGUES		
THE PASSOVER	*Deliverance, 12:1-13:16*	
THE EXODUS BEGINS		*Free at last!, 13:17-22*
ISRAEL'S FIRST CRISIS IN THE WILDERNESS		
MOSES' GREAT SONG OF PRAISE TO GOD		
ISRAEL'S SECOND CRISIS IN THE WILDERNESS		
ISRAEL'S THIRD CRISIS IN THE WILDERNESS		
ISRAEL'S FOURTH CRISIS IN THE WILDERNESS		
ISRAEL'S FIFTH CRISIS IN THE WILDERNESS		
ISRAEL'S SIXTH CRISIS IN THE WILDERNESS		

DIVISION V. THE CROSSING OF THE RED SEA & THE WILDERNESS WANDERINGS (Exodus 13:17-18:27)		
THE EVENT	**THE SCRIPTURE**	**PRACTICAL APPLICATION**
Beginning the Wilderness Journey	Exodus 13:17-22	God's Guidance by Day & Night
The First Crisis of Israel in the Wilderness: Crossing of the Red Sea	Exodus 14:1-31	God's Great Deliverance
Moses' Great Song of Praise	Exodus 15:1-21	Praising God For His Great Deliverance
The Second Crisis of Israel In the Wilderness, Thirst— Bitter Water at Marah	Exodus 15:22-27	The First Great Sin of Israel, That of Complaining, Grumbling & Murmuring

"And Moses said unto the people, Fear ye not, stand still, and see the salvation of the LORD, which he will show to you to day: for the Egyptians whom ye have seen to day, ye shall see them again no more for ever" (Ex. 14:13).

EXODUS CHRONOLOGY OF MAIN CHARACTERS AND EVENTS		
	Chapter 14	**Chapter 15**
JOSEPH		
PHARAOH (The first Pharaoh mentioned)		
FIRST MENTION OF ISRAEL'S BONDAGE		
THE BIRTH OF MOSES		
THE CALL OF MOSES		
MOSES' EXCUSES		
MOSES' SURRENDER TO GOD'S WILL		
MOSES' FIRST CONFRONTATION WITH PHARAOH (The second Pharaoh mentioned)		
GOD'S ENCOURAGEMENT & MESSAGE TO MOSES		
THE TEN PLAGUES		
THE PASSOVER		
THE EXODUS BEGINS		
ISRAEL'S FIRST CRISIS IN THE WILDERNESS	*Crossing the Red Sea; Salvation, 14:1-31*	
MOSES' GREAT SONG OF PRAISE TO GOD		*Thanksgiving, 15:1-21*
ISRAEL'S SECOND CRISIS IN THE WILDERNESS		*Bitter water, 15:22-27*
ISRAEL'S THIRD CRISIS IN THE WILDERNESS		
ISRAEL'S FOURTH CRISIS IN THE WILDERNESS		
ISRAEL'S FIFTH CRISIS IN THE WILDERNESS		
ISRAEL'S SIXTH CRISIS IN THE WILDERNESS		

DIVISION V. THE CROSSING OF THE RED SEA & THE WILDERNESS WANDERINGS (Exodus 13:17-18:27) (continued)		
THE EVENT	THE SCRIPTURE	PRACTICAL APPLICATION
The Third Crisis of Israel In the Wilderness—Hunger	Exodus 16:1-36	The Two Great Sins of Israel, That of Grumbling & Disobedience (Unbelief)
The Fourth Crisis of Israel In the Wilderness—Thirst	Exodus 17:1-7	God's Provision of Water
The Fifth Crisis of Israel In the Wilderness—Warfare	Exodus 17:8-16	Victory Through Prevailing Prayer

And Moses built an altar, and called the name of it Jehovah-nissi [the LORD is my Banner]" (Ex. 17:15).

EXODUS CHRONOLOGY OF MAIN CHARACTERS AND EVENTS		
	Chapter 16	Chapter 17
JOSEPH		
PHARAOH (The first Pharaoh mentioned)		
FIRST MENTION OF ISRAEL'S BONDAGE		
THE BIRTH OF MOSES		
THE CALL OF MOSES		
MOSES' EXCUSES		
MOSES' SURRENDER TO GOD'S WILL		
MOSES' FIRST CONFRONTATION WITH PHARAOH (The second Pharaoh mentioned)		
GOD'S ENCOURAGEMENT & MESSAGE TO MOSES		
THE TEN PLAGUES		
THE PASSOVER		
THE EXODUS BEGINS		
ISRAEL'S FIRST CRISIS IN THE WILDERNESS		
MOSES' GREAT SONG OF PRAISE TO GOD		
ISRAEL'S SECOND CRISIS IN THE WILDERNESS		
ISRAEL'S THIRD CRISIS IN THE WILDERNESS	*Hunger, 16:1-36*	
ISRAEL'S FOURTH CRISIS IN THE WILDERNESS		*Thirst, 17:1-7*
ISRAEL'S FIFTH CRISIS IN THE WILDERNESS		*Warfare, 17:8-16*
ISRAEL'S SIXTH CRISIS IN THE WILDERNESS		

DIVISION V. THE CROSSING OF THE RED SEA & THE WILDERNESS WANDERINGS (Exodus 13:17-18:27) (continued)		
THE EVENT	**THE SCRIPTURE**	**PRACTICAL APPLICATION**
The Sixth Crisis of Israel in the Wilderness—Marital Separation and Overwork: Helping Others	Exodus 18:1-27	Lack of Organization, Marital Separation, and Overwork

"And Moses' father in law said unto him, The thing that thou doest is not good. Thou wilt surely wear away, both thou, and this people that is with thee: for this thing is too heavy for thee; thou art not able to perform it thyself alone" (Ex.18:17-18).

EXODUS CHRONOLOGY OF MAIN CHARACTERS AND EVENTS	
	Chapter 18
JOSEPH	
PHARAOH (The first Pharaoh mentioned)	
FIRST MENTION OF ISRAEL'S BONDAGE	
THE BIRTH OF MOSES	
THE CALL OF MOSES	
MOSES' EXCUSES	
MOSES' SURRENDER TO GOD'S WILL	
MOSES' FIRST CONFRONTATION WITH PHARAOH (The second Pharaoh mentioned)	
GOD'S ENCOURAGEMENT & MESSAGE TO MOSES	
THE TEN PLAGUES	
THE PASSOVER	
THE EXODUS BEGINS	
ISRAEL'S FIRST CRISIS IN THE WILDERNESS	
MOSES' GREAT SONG OF PRAISE TO GOD	
ISRAEL'S SECOND CRISIS IN THE WILDERNESS	
ISRAEL'S THIRD CRISIS IN THE WILDERNESS	
ISRAEL'S FOURTH CRISIS IN THE WILDERNESS	
ISRAEL'S FIFTH CRISIS IN THE WILDERNESS	
ISRAEL'S SIXTH CRISIS IN THE WILDERNESS	*Marital separation & overwork, 18:1-27*

A BRIEF CHRONOLOGY OF THE MAIN CHARACTERS AND EVENTS OF EXODUS

PART I
(Chapters 1-18)

	Chapter 1	Chapter 2
JOSEPH	*Joseph died, 1:6*	
PHARAOH (The first Pharaoh mentioned)	*Did not know Joseph, 1:8*	
FIRST MENTION OF ISRAEL'S BONDAGE	*Slaves in Egypt, 1:8-22*	
THE BIRTH OF MOSES		*Birth & protection, 2:1-25*
	Chapter 3	**Chapter 4**
THE CALL OF MOSES	*The burning bush, 3:1-10*	
MOSES' EXCUSES	*Saying no to God: Finally, obedience, 3:11-4:17*	
MOSES' SURRENDER TO GOD'S WILL		*He finally obeys, 4:18-31*
	Chapter 5	**Chapter 6**
MOSES' FIRST CONFRONTATION WITH PHARAOH (The second Pharaoh mentioned)	*"Let my people go!"... "No!" 5:1-23*	
GOD'S ENCOURAGEMENT & MESSAGE TO MOSES		*Discouragement overcome, 6:1-7:7*
	Chapters 7-11	
THE TEN PLAGUES	*Judgment! 7:8-11:10*	
	Chapter 12	**Chapter 13**
THE PASSOVER	*Deliverance, 12:1-13:16*	
THE EXODUS BEGINS		*Free at last!, 13:17-22*
	Chapter 14	**Chapter 15**
ISRAEL'S FIRST CRISIS IN THE WILDERNESS	*Crossing the Red Sea; Salvation, 14:1-31*	
MOSES' GREAT SONG OF PRAISE TO GOD		*Thanksgiving, 15:1-21*
ISRAEL'S SECOND CRISIS IN THE WILDERNESS		*Bitter water, 15:22-27*
	Chapter 16	**Chapter 17**
ISRAEL'S THIRD CRISIS IN THE WILDERNESS	*Hunger, 16:1-36*	
ISRAEL'S FOURTH CRISIS IN THE WILDERNESS		*Thirst, 17:1-7*
ISRAEL'S FIFTH CRISIS IN THE WILDERNESS		*Warfare, 17:8-16*
	Chapter 18	
ISRAEL'S SIXTH CRISIS IN THE WILDERNESS	*Marital separation & overwork, 18:1-27*	

OUTLINE OF EXODUS

Part I

(Chapters 1–18)

THE PREACHER'S OUTLINE AND SERMON BIBLE® is *unique*. It differs from all other Study Bibles and Sermon Resource Materials in that every Passage and Subject is outlined right beside the Scripture. When you choose any *Subject* below and turn to the reference, you have not only the Scripture but also an outline of the Scripture and Subject *already prepared for you—verse by verse*.

For a quick example, choose one of the subjects below and turn over to the Scripture; you will find this to be a marvelous help for more organized and streamlined study.

In addition, every point of the Scripture and Subject is *fully developed in a Commentary with supporting Scripture* at the end of each point. Again, this arrangement makes sermon preparation much simpler and more efficient.

Note something else: the Subjects of *Exodus* have titles that are both Biblical and *practical*. The practical titles are often more appealing to people. This *benefit* is clearly seen for use on billboards, bulletins, church newsletters, etc.

A suggestion: for the *quickest* overview of *Exodus*, first read *all the Division titles* (I, II, III, etc.), then come back and read the individual outline titles.

OUTLINE OF EXODUS

Part I

(Chapters 1–18)

I. **ISRAEL AND EGYPT: THE OPPRESSION OF GOD'S PEOPLE BY A NATION THAT HAD REJECTED GOD, 1:1-22**
    A. The Past Deliverance of Israel: The Picture of God's Deliverance and God's Faithfulness, 1:1-7
    B. The Enslavement of Israel By Egypt: How God's People Overcome Oppression, 1:8-22

II. **MOSES AND GOD: GOD RAISES UP A LEADER TO DELIVER HIS PEOPLE (ISRAEL), 2:1–7:7**
    A. The Birth of Moses: The Picture of a Believing, Courageous Mother, 2:1-10
    B. The First Significant Events of Moses' Life: Experiences That Change a Person's Life, 2:11-25
    C. The Call of Moses: A Study of God's Call to Service, 3:1-10
    D. The Excuses of Moses: A Reluctant Prophet—Arguments Against Serving God, 3:11–4:17
    E. The Surrender of Moses to God's Call: The Fruit of Obedience, 4:18-31
    F. The First Confrontation of Moses with Pharaoh: Opposing God's Will for His People, the Right of Man to Live and Worship God in Freedom, 5:1-23
    G. The Great Encouragement and Message Given to Moses: Deliverance and Freedom, 6:1–7:7

III. **THE TEN PLAGUES AND EGYPT: GOD'S JUDGMENT UPON THOSE WHO REJECT HIM AND OPPRESS HIS PEOPLE, 7:8–11:10**
    A. The Credentials of God's Servant: Proof That a Person Is God's Servant, 7:8-13
    B. The First Plague—Water Changed to Blood: Proof that God Is the LORD, the God of Salvation, the Only Living and True God, 7:14-25
    C. The Second Plague—Frogs Everywhere: Proof That God Has No Equal, That No One Is Like the LORD Our God, 8:1-15
    D. The Third Plague—Lice or Gnats Infested the Land: Proof That the Finger (Power) of God Controls All Things, Even the Very Dust of the Ground, 8:16-19
    E. The Fourth Plague—Flies Swarmed Over the Land: Proof that the LORD Is the Savior in Every Land and in Every Place, 8:20-32
    F. The Fifth Plague—A Severe Disease Struck and Killed All Livestock in the Field: Proof That the Hand of God Controls the Animal Life of the World, 9:1-7
    G. The Sixth Plague—Festering Boils Afflicted Man and Animal: Proof that God Has Power Over Body and Health, 9:8-12
    H. The Seventh Plague—A Catastrophic Hail and Thunderstorm: Proof That the Earth Is the LORD's, 9:13-35
    I. The Eighth Plague—Locusts Swarmed Over the Land: Proof That the LORD Is the Great Savior of Mankind, 10:1-20
    J. The Ninth Plague—Darkness Covered the Land: Proof That God Has Power Over the Light and Darkness of the Earth, 10:21-29
    K. The Tenth Plague—Death of the Firstborn Announced: Proof That God Is the God of True Believers, 11:1-10

OUTLINE OF EXODUS

IV.   **THE PASSOVER AND THE TENTH PLAGUE: DELIVERANCE FROM GOD'S JUDGMENT— LIBERATED, SET FREE, 12:1–13:16**
- A.   The Passover: The First Basic Essential for Redemption—an Unblemished Lamb, 12:1-13
- B.   The Feast of Unleavened Bread: The Second Basic Essential for Redemption—Putting All Leaven, All Evil, Out of One's Life, 12:14-20
- C.   The Tenth Plague, the Death of the Firstborn and the Passover: Deliverance from God's Judgment— Liberated, Set Free, 12:21-51
- D.   The Dedication of the Firstborn: Remembering God's Great Deliverance, 13:1-16

V.   **THE RED SEA AND THE WILDERNESS WANDERINGS: THE BELIEVER'S TRIALS AS HE JOURNEYS TO THE PROMISED LAND, 13:17–18:27**
- A.   Beginning the Wilderness Journey: God's Guidance by Day and By Night, 13:17-22
- B.   The First Crisis of Israel in the Wilderness—Crossing the Red Sea: God's Great Deliverance, 14:1-31
- C.   Moses' Great Song of Praise: Praising God for His Great Deliverance, 15:1-21
- D.   The Second Crisis of Israel in the Wilderness, Bitter Water at Marah: Bitter Experiences Made Sweet and Pure, 15:22-27
- E.   The Third Crisis of Israel in the Wilderness—Hunger: The Two Great Sins of Israel, That of Grumbling and Disobedience (Unbelief), 16:1-36
- F.   The Fourth Crisis of Israel in the Wilderness—Thirst: God's Provision of Water, 17:1-7
- G.   The Fifth Crisis of Israel in the Wilderness—Warfare: Victory Through Prevailing Prayer, 17:8-16
- H.   The Sixth Crisis of Israel in the Wilderness—Marital Separation and Overwork: Helping Others, 18:1-27

DIVISION I

ISRAEL AND EGYPT: THE OPPRESSION OF GOD'S PEOPLE BY A NATION THAT HAD REJECTED GOD, 1:1-22

(1:1-22) **DIVISION OVERVIEW—Israel**: Exodus is the great book of deliverance, of salvation, and of redemption. Exodus clearly pictures and proclaims that God...
- delivers us
- saves us
- redeems us

God's great deliverance is pictured for us in the experiences of Israel. Israel was a *new people* created by God in ages past to be His witnesses, the people of God who were to bear witness to the only living and true God. Israel is the focus of the Book of Exodus.

Throughout Exodus, it is helpful to remember this fact: Israel was a whole *new race* of people, a race created by God to carry on the godly line of believers and eventually to bear the promised seed, the Savior of the world. What had happened was this.

From the very beginning of human history, man had sinned and brought death upon the human race. But to counteract sin and death, God had promised to send a Savior (the promised seed) through the godly line of Adam and his son Seth. Time and again God had to intervene to keep the godly line of believers pure. This He did right up to *The Great Flood*. At that time God chose Noah, and later the line of his son Shem, to carry on the godly line of people. God kept His promise and kept the hope of the promised seed and Savior alive.

But even after The Great Flood, the human race, just as it had always done, continued to deteriorate into utter depravity (Gen.11:1-32). Thus God had to once again intervene in human history. This He did by calling Abraham to father a whole *new race* of people, a people who were to carry on the godly line and give birth to the promised seed and Savior of the world, the Lord Jesus Christ. As stated above, that *new race* of people was Israel.

Note this: God had at least five purposes for creating a *new race* of people through Abraham. Note that the same five purposes are true of both Israel as a nation and believers as the new nation and people of God. (See note, pt.3—Ge.12:3; also see notes—Jn.4:22; Ro.4:1-25; and Lu.1:68 for more discussion.)

1. God wanted a people who would love and serve God supremely. His followers were to be a people who would give Him their first loyalty.

   "**And I will establish my covenant between me and thee and thy seed after thee in their generations for an everlasting covenant, to be a God unto thee, and to thy seed after thee**" (Ge.17:7).

   "**And now, Israel, what doth the LORD thy God require of thee, but to fear the LORD thy God, to walk in all his ways, and to love him, and to serve the LORD thy God with all thy heart and with all thy soul**" (De.10:12; see De.6:5; Is.43:10; Mt.22:37).

2. God wanted a people who would be His missionary force to the world. His followers were to be a people who would be a dynamic witness to all other nations that God and God alone is the only living and true God.

   "**Ye are my witnesses, saith the LORD, and my servant whom I have chosen: that ye may know and believe me, and understand that I am he: before me there was no God formed, neither shall there be after me. I, even I, am the LORD; and beside me there is no saviour**" (Is.43:10-11).

   "**Men and brethren, children of the stock of Abraham, and whosoever among you feareth God, to you is the word of this salvation....For so hath the Lord commanded us, saying, I have set thee to be a light of the Gentiles, that thou shouldest be for salvation unto the ends of the earth**" (Ac.13:26, 47; see Ge.12:3; 22:18).

3. God wanted a people through whom He could send His Son to the world. His followers were to be a people through whom He could send the promised seed, the Savior and Messiah of the world, the Lord Jesus Christ.

   "**And in thy seed shall all the nations of the earth be blessed; because thou hast obeyed my voice**" (Ge.22:18).

   "**Now to Abraham and his seed were the promises made. He saith not, And to seeds, as of many; but as of one, And to thy seed, which is Christ**" (Ga.3:16; see Ge.3:15; Jn.4:22. See notes—Ex.1:6-7.)

4. God wanted a people through whom He could give His written Word, the Holy Bible, to the world.

> **"Who are Israelites; to whom pertaineth the adoption, and the glory, and the covenants, and the giving of the law, and the service of God, and the promises; whose are the fathers, and of whom as concerning the flesh Christ came, who is over all, God blessed for ever" (Ro.9:4-5).**
>
> **"God, who at sundry times and in divers manners spake in time past unto the fathers by the prophets" (He.1:1).**
>
> **"For the prophecy came not in old time by the will of man: but holy men of God spake as they were moved by the Holy Ghost" (2 Pe.1:19-21; see 2 Ti.3:16; 1 Pe.1:10-11).**

5. God wanted a people through whom He could demonstrate the truth about life and salvation to the world. Note that all three of these truths were demonstrated throughout the history of Israel. (See notes—Ep.1:3; 1:7; 2:8-9; 2:11-18.)

    a. God wanted to demonstrate that *life and salvation are not of this world*, not of the physical and material world. Israel was always seeking the physical and material blessings of this earth, and most Israelites trusted the physical rituals of religion to save them and to identify them as the people of God (physical rituals such as circumcision and ceremonies). But the world is passing away: it possesses a seed of corruption and does not last; it is not permanent and eternal. The world desperately needs to acknowledge and learn this fact. Thus God used Israel to demonstrate this fact to the world, that life and salvation are not of this world, not of the physical and material world. (See notes—Mt.8:17; 1 Co.15:50; 2 Pe.1:4.)

    > **"Now this I say, brethren, that flesh and blood cannot inherit the kingdom of God; neither doth corruption inherit incorruption" (1 Co.15:50).**
    >
    > **"But the day of the Lord will come as a thief in the night; in the which the heavens shall pass away with a great noise, and the elements shall melt with fervent heat, the earth also and the works that are therein shall be burned up" (2 Pe.3:10).**
    >
    > **"Love not the world, neither the things that are in the world. If any man love the world, the love of the Father is not in him. For all that is in the world, the lust of the flesh, and the lust of the eyes, and the pride of life, is not of the Father, but is of the world. And the world passeth away, and the lust thereof: but he that doeth the will of God abideth for ever" (1 Jn.2:15-17; see Ps.102:25-26; Is.24:4; 34:4; 51:6; 2 Co.4:18; Re.21:1).**

    b. God wanted to demonstrate that *life and salvation are spiritual and eternal*. Again, Israel's constant search for physical and material blessings—the people's neglect of the spiritual and eternal—demonstrated this. What was needed for life and salvation was not the physical and material blessings of the earth, and not a religion of form and ritual. What was needed was a permanent and incorruptible seed: a new creature, a new man, was necessary in order to provide salvation and life for man. The world needed to know that whatever God did, He did permanently and perfectly. Thus life and salvation are not to be of this earth, of physical and material elements (which last only for a few short years). Life is of the spirit, of another dimension of being entirely, the spiritual dimension. The spiritual dimension is the real world where God Himself and His heavenly host and the departed believers live—all in perfection and for eternity. Life is forever and permanent, and it is either lived with God or apart from God. (See note—Ep.1:3.)

    > **"Being born again, not of corruptible seed, but of incorruptible, by the word of God, which liveth and abideth for ever" (1 Pe.1:23).**
    >
    > **"Therefore if any man be in Christ, he is a new creature: old things are passed away; behold all things are become new" (2 Co.5:17).**
    >
    > **"And that ye put on the new man, which after God is created in righteousness and true holiness" (Ep.4:24; see Jn.3:3, 5, 16).**

    c. God wanted to demonstrate that *life and salvation are secured by faith and by faith alone*, not by works and self-righteousness. The religious rules, rituals, and ceremonies of Israel could not save the people. Good works and religious service can never make a person perfect, and perfection is essential to live in God's presence. Thus no man is saved by works and self-righteousness. He is saved...
    *   by trusting in the righteousness and perfection of the promised seed, the Savior, the Lord Jesus Christ.
    *   by trusting that the righteousness and perfection of the promised Savior covers him and makes him acceptable to God.
    *   by trusting that God accepts him in the righteousness and perfection of the promised Savior, that God actually counts his faith in the Savior as righteousness.

    All of these are just different ways of saying the same thing: man is saved by the grace of God through faith—no other way. He is saved only by grace and by faith. God demonstrated this through the history of Israel. (See note—Ep.2:8-10. Also see outline and notes—Ro.9:1-5.)

    > **"For by grace are ye saved through faith; and that not of yourselves: it is the gift of God: not of works, lest any man should boast" (Ep.2:8-9).**
    >
    > **"Not by works of righteousness which we have done, but according to his mercy he saved us, by the washing of regeneration, and renewing of the Holy Ghost" (Tit.3:5).**

As stated, Israel was a whole new race of people, the descendents of Abraham. God had created Israel to carry on the godly line of believers and to eventually bear the promised seed, the Savior and Messiah of the world. The first great Book of the Bible, Genesis, covered the birth and early beginnings of Israel.

Now, the second great Book of the Bible, Exodus, begins with Israel in Egypt. Remember that Egypt is a picture, a type, a symbol of worldliness. Egypt was a society that had reached the summit of prosperity, technology, and pleasure; but the people had rejected the only living and true God (Jehovah) and created their own gods to follow. Israel, the new race of people who believed in the true God, sat right in the midst of Egypt; and Egypt was oppressing and enslaving Israel. The people of God were being persecuted by the world. Israel needed God's help. The people who believed in the true God (true believers) needed God to intervene on their behalf. The believers of that day needed God to deliver them from the persecution and oppression of the Egyptians. Thus the great subject of Exodus—the great need for deliverance, salvation, and redemption—jumps right out at the reader in the very first chapter of this great book of the Bible.

ISRAEL AND EGYPT: THE OPPRESSION OF GOD'S PEOPLE BY A NATION THAT HAD REJECTED GOD, 1:1-22

A. The Past Deliverance of Israel: The Picture of God's Deliverance and God's Faithfulness, 1:1-7

B. The Enslavement of Israel by Egypt: How God's People Overcome Oppression, 1:8-22

EXODUS

	CHAPTER 1	2 Reuben, Simeon, Levi, and Judah,	b. Leah's sons: Reuben through Zebulun
	I. ISRAEL & EGYPT: THE OPPRESSION OF GOD'S PEOPLE BY A NATION THAT HAD REJECTED GOD, 1:1-22	3 Issachar, Zebulun, and Benjamin,	c. Rachel's son: Benjamin
		4 Dan, and Naphtali, Gad, and Asher.	d. Bilhah's two sons
		5 And all the souls that came out of the loins of Jacob were seventy souls: for Joseph was in Egypt already.	e. Zilpah's two sons
	A. The Past Deliverance of Israel: The Picture of God's Deliverance & God's Faithfulness, 1:1-7		f. Seventy descendents altogether, not counting Joseph; he was already in Egypt
		6 And Joseph died, and all his brethren, and all that generation.	**2. God's faithfulness**
1. God's deliverance[DS1]		7 And the children of Israel were fruitful, and increased abundantly, and multiplied, and waxed exceeding mighty; and the land was filled with them.	a. God kept fulfilling His promise to His people down through the generations: To give the promised seed, to create a great nation of people (believers)[DS2]
a. God had led His people, Israel, down into Egypt 400 years earlier (Ac.7:6)	Now these are the names of the children of Israel, which came into Egypt; every man and his household came with Jacob.		b. God caused Israel's population to multiply

DIVISION I

ISRAEL AND EGYPT: THE OPPRESSION OF GOD'S PEOPLE BY A NATION THAT HAD REJECTED GOD, 1:1-22

A.   The Past Deliverance of Israel: The Picture of God's Deliverance and God's Faithfulness, 1:1-7

(1:1-7) **Introduction**: the very first passage of Exodus deals with the great theme of Exodus: deliverance. God had delivered Israel in the past. Therefore, the implication is clear: God will deliver Israel in the future. No matter what the trouble may be, no matter how terrifying and hopeless, no matter how helpless the circumstances may seem—God will deliver Israel again, deliver them just as He had delivered them in the past.

God always saves His people. He has always saved them when they were in trouble. Therefore, the implication for us is clear: God will always save and deliver us. God cares and will help us no matter what the circumstances are…

- disease
- sickness
- suffering
- death
- loneliness
- emptiness
- hunger
- thirst
- broken heart
- backsliding
- loss of spouse
- imprisonment
- unemployment
- poverty

Even if the situation is terrifying and hopeless—even if we are helpless—God will deliver and save us through the circumstances. He will even work the terrifying circumstances out for our good. This is the promise of God to His people, to those who truly love and follow Him (Ro.8:28). God will deliver us; He will save us. This is the assurance of this introductory passage of Exodus. The great subject is: *The Past Deliverance of Israel: The Picture of God's Deliverance and God's Faithfulness,* 1:1-7.

1. God's deliverance (vv.1-5).
2. God's faithfulness (vv.6-7).

[1]   (1:1-5) **Deliverance—Israel**: God had delivered and saved His people, Israel, some 400 years earlier. He had led them, every member of Jacob's household, down into Egypt (Ac.7:6). This event is covered in Ge.46:1-27 (see esp. vv.2-4). Why had God led Israel into Egypt?

Because Israel was not behaving like the chosen seed (people) of God. The family of Jacob was about to lose its godly identity. They were not living clean lives; they were not protecting the purity of the godly family. This is seen in two facts.

a. There was moral decay within the family. The sons were living immoral, violent, and lawless lives (Ge.34:1-31; 37:1-36; 38:1-30).

b. The family was being immersed in the worldliness of their environment. They were following the life-style of the people who lived around them, of unbelievers, of the Canaanites. The family was surrounded by Canaanites who lived ungodly lives, and the family was young and small in number (seventy people). Tragically, they became attracted by the bright lights and the immoral and ungodly practices of their neighbors. They were adopting and becoming submerged under the Canaanite way of life. Through intermingling and intermarriage, they faced the threat of becoming a part of the Canaanite people. They could have easily lost their distinctive identity as the people of God. Israel—Jacob and his sons—was about to become lost as a separate nation.

Therefore, God set out to save and preserve His people in order to fulfill His purposes for them. God made three moves.

First, God took one of the sons of Jacob and set him up as the ruler of Egypt. The son was Joseph, who ruled Egypt as second only to Pharaoh himself. (See note—Ge.41:37-44 for more discussion.)

Second, God caused the entire family to move away from the worldly temptation and influence of the Canaanites. He used a famine to drive them down into Egypt (Ge.41:56f).

Third, God placed the family beside the Egyptians, a people who considered them an abomination, totally unacceptable, a people who would have nothing to do with them (Ge.46:34). Thus the chance of intermingling and intermarriage was much, much less. Thereby, Israel would keep to itself and keep its godly identity. The people would be isolated, forced to live in the district of Goshen, forced to lived off by themselves and keep the godly line of descendents pure.

Now, note two significant facts about God's past deliverance of Israel.

1. God had delivered Israel down to the Egyptian district of Goshen, delivered them about four hundred years before the events of Exodus began (Ac.7:6; see Ge.15:13-14). Israel was in Egypt for about 430 years (Ex.12:40-41).

2. Every member of Jacob's family went down into Egypt, seventy descendents in all (vv.2-5).
- Leah's six sons had twenty-five sons and two grandsons which made a total of *thirty-three people*
- Rachel's two sons had twelve sons which equaled *fourteen people*
- Bilhah's two sons had five sons which totaled *seven people*
- Zilpah's two sons had eleven sons and one daughter and two grandsons totaling *sixteen persons*
- Thus the total of the sons and grandsons and of the one daughter is seventy persons

The point to see is this: God delivered His people Israel down to Egypt. He saved the people of God—seventy persons—those who truly believed Him and who sincerely followed the only living and true God.

Thought 1. God always delivers and saves His people, any of us who truly believe Him and who sincerely follow Him as the only living and true God. God always delivers us no matter…
- how bad the circumstances
- how terrible the sin and shame
- how severe the pain
- how frightening the news

God cares for us. God will deliver and save us from the very depths of sin and death, no matter how terrible they may be. But this is not all: God will also deliver us *through* all the crises and trials of life no matter how painful they may be.

"And he said, The LORD is my rock, and my fortress, and my deliverer" (2 S.22:2).

"But I am poor and needy; yet the Lord thinketh upon me: thou art my help and my deliverer; make no tarrying, O my God" (Ps.40:17).

"For thou hast delivered my soul from death, mine eyes from tears, and my feet from falling. I will walk before the LORD in the land of the living" (Ps.116:8-9).

"Fear thou not; for I am with thee: be not dismayed; for I am thy God: I will strengthen thee; yea, I will help thee; yea, I will uphold thee with the right hand of my righteousness" (Is.41:10).

"And even to your old age I am he; and even to hoar (gray) hairs will I carry you: I have made, and I will bear; even I will carry, and will deliver you" (Is.46:4).

"For the Son of man is come to seek and to save that which was lost" (Lu.19:10).

"For God so loved the world, that he gave his only begotten Son, that whosoever believeth in him should not perish, but have everlasting life" (Jn.3:16).

"There hath no temptation taken you but such as is common to man: but God is faithful, who will not suffer you to be tempted above that ye are able; but will with the temptation also make a way to escape, that ye may be able to bear it" (1 Co.10:13).

"And the Lord shall deliver me from every evil work, and will preserve me unto his heavenly kingdom: to whom be glory for ever and ever. Amen" (2 Ti.4:18).

"Forasmuch then as the children are partakers of flesh and blood, he also himself likewise took part of the same; that through death he might destroy him that had the power of death, that is, the devil; and deliver them who through fear of death were all their lifetime subject to bondage" (He.2:14-15).

Thought 2. To the natural mind, Egypt would be the last place a person would choose as a place of refuge. Nevertheless it was God's place. How often we miss God's will because we give in to the ways of the world instead of following the way of God. Far, far too many of us have left the way of God and become immersed in the worldliness of our environment and suffered moral decay. God's way is *always*, without exception, the best way.

"As for God, his way is perfect: the word of the LORD is tried: he is a buckler to all those that trust in him" (Ps.18:30).

"The LORD is righteous in all his ways, and holy in all his works" (Ps.145:17).

"That the LORD thy God may show us the way wherein we may walk, and the thing that we may do" (Je.42:3).

"Who is wise, and he shall understand these things? prudent, and he shall know them? for the ways of the LORD are right, and the just shall walk in them: but the transgressors shall fall therein" (Ho.14:9).

"His ways are everlasting" (Ha.3:6).

"Because strait [is] the gate, and narrow [is] the way, which leadeth unto life, and few there be that find it" (Mt.7:14).

"O the depth of the riches both of the wisdom and knowledge of God! how unsearchable are his judgments, and his ways past finding out!" (Ro.11:33).

"And they sing the song of Moses the servant of God, and the song of the Lamb, saying, Great and marvellous are thy works, Lord God Almighty; just and true are thy ways, thou King of saints" (Re.15:3).

DEEPER STUDY # 1
(1:1-5) Genealogy, of Jacob—Family Tree—Jacob, Sons of:

JACOB'S FAMILY TREE
(See also Genesis 29:31-30:24)

Child's Name	Meaning of Name	Mother of Child	Mother's Perspective
Reuben	"See, a son"	Leah	Felt God had blessed her with a child, thus Jacob would now love her
Simeon	"Hearing"	Leah	Felt God knew she was neglected and had heard her prayer
Levi	"Attached"	Leah	Felt Jacob would now become attached to her
Judah	"Praise"	Leah	Felt she owed God praise for what He had done
Dan	"Judging, vindication"	Bilhah (Rachel's maid)	(Rachel) felt God had heard and vindicated her to be worthy of children
Naphtali	"Wrestling"	Bilhah	(Rachel) felt God caused her to prevail against Leah for Jacob's attention
Gad	"Good luck"	Zilpah (Leah's maid)	(Leah) felt the child was good fortune
Asher	"Happy"	Zilpah	(Leah) felt people would call her blessed, happy
Issachar	"Reward"	Leah	Felt God had given her wages, a good reward
Zebulun	"Honor" or "Dwelling"	Leah	Felt God had given a good gift, thus Jacob would now favor and dwell more with her
Dinah	"Judgment" or "Vindication"	Leah	Felt God had judged, vindicated her love for Jacob
Joseph	"May God add"	Rachel	Felt God had removed her reproach by giving another child
Benjamin • Named Benonoi (by Rachel) • Named Benjamin (by Jacob)	"Son of my sorrow" "Son of the right hand"	Rachel	Rachel died during childbirth (Ge.35:16-20)

2 (1:6-7) **God, Faithfulness of—Seed, The Promised**: God proved faithful and kept fulfilling His promise down through the generations. What promise? The promise of the promised seed, the promise to create a great nation of people (believers).

a. Keep in mind why God had appointed Israel to be a great nation of people: God wanted…
- a people through whom He could send the very special promised seed, meaning *the Savior of the world, the Lord Jesus Christ*
- a people through whom He could send *God's Holy Word* to the world
- a people who would bear a *strong witness* to the only living and true God
- a people who would *love and worship God supremely*
- a people through whom He could demonstrate *the great truth about life and salvation* to the world, mainly the truth that a person becomes acceptable to God (saved, justified) by faith and not by his own works and righteousness. (See *Division I—Ex.1:1-22* for more discussion.)

Israel had its beginning long, long ago. God confronted Abraham and made a great promise to him: if Abraham would believe God—truly believe and follow God—then God would cause a great nation of people to be born through his seed. Abraham believed God and God began to fulfill His promise. (See outlines and notes—Gen.12:1; 12:1-3; 12:4-9 for more discussion.)

The present passage—the great multiplication of Israel—is a dramatic picture of God's fulfilling His great promise to Abraham. Note how clearly God was fulfilling His promise to Abraham; note how often God had given His promise.

⇒ Note God's great promise to Abraham:

"Now the LORD had said unto Abram, Get thee out of thy country, and from thy kindred, and from thy father's house, unto a land that I will show thee: and I will make of thee a great nation…." (Ge.12:1-2).

⇒ Note God's great promise to Isaac, Abraham's son:

"And the LORD appeared unto him, and said, Go not down into Egypt; dwell in the land which I shall tell thee of: sojourn in this land, and I will be with thee, and will bless thee; for unto thee, and unto thy seed, I will give all these countries, and I will perform the oath which I sware unto Abraham thy father; and I will make thy seed to multiply as the stars of heaven, and will give unto thy seed all these countries; and in thy seed shall all the nations of the earth be blessed; because that Abraham obeyed my voice, and kept my charge, my commandments, my statutes, and my laws" (Ge.26:2-5).

⇒ Note God's great promise to Jacob, Abraham's grandson:

"And God spake unto Israel in the visions of the night, and said, Jacob, Jacob. And he said, Here am I. And he said, I am God, the God of thy father: fear not to go down into Egypt; for I will there make of thee a great nation" (Ge.46:2-3).

⇒ Note here in Exodus how clearly and dramatically God was fulfilling His great promise.

"And the children of Israel were fruitful, and increased abundantly, and multiplied, and waxed exceeding mighty; and the land was filled with them" (Ex.1:7).

b. Note the enormous population growth, how graphically it is pictured. The growth and population of Israel…
- "was fruitful"
- "increased abundantly" (KJV) or "greatly" (NASB)
- "multiplied" (KJV)
- became "exceeding mighty" (KJV) or "exceedingly numerous" (NIV)

As stated above, this was the fulfillment of God's promise to Abraham. But it was also the fulfillment of God's promise to man since the beginning of the creation. Note His promise:
1) God's promise to Adam.

"And God blessed them, and God said unto them, Be fruitful, and multiply, and replenish the earth, and subdue it: and have dominion over the fish of the sea, and over the fowl of the air, and over every living thing that moveth upon the earth" (Ge.1:28).

2) God's promise to Noah.

"Bring forth with thee every living thing that is with thee, of all flesh, both of fowl, and of cattle, and of every creeping thing that creepeth upon the earth; that they may breed abundantly in the earth, and be fruitful, and multiply upon the earth" (Ge.8:17).

"And God blessed Noah and his sons, and said unto them, Be fruitful, and multiply, and replenish the earth….And you, be ye fruitful, and multiply; bring forth abundantly in the earth, and multiply therein" (Ge.9:1, 7).

3) God's promise to Abraham.

> "Now the LORD had said unto Abram, Get thee out of thy country, and from thy kindred, and from thy father's house, unto a land that I will show thee: And I will make of thee a great nation, and I will bless thee, and make thy name great; and thou shalt be a blessing: And I will bless them that bless thee, and curse him that curseth thee: and in thee shall all families of the earth be blessed" (Ge.12:1-3).
> "And I will make my covenant between me and thee, and will multiply thee exceedingly. And Abram fell on his face: and God talked with him, saying, As for me, behold, my covenant is with thee, and thou shalt be a father of many nations. Neither shall thy name any more be called Abram, but thy name shall be Abraham; for a father of many nations have I made thee. And I will make thee exceeding fruitful, and I will make nations of thee, and kings shall come out of thee" (Ge.17:2-6).
> "That in blessing I will bless thee, and in multiplying I will multiply thy seed as the stars of the heaven, and as the sand which is upon the sea shore; and thy seed shall possess the gate of his enemies" (Ge.22:17).

4) God's promise to Isaac.

> "And I will make thy seed to multiply as the stars of heaven, and will give unto thy seed all these countries; and in thy seed shall all the nations of the earth be blessed" (Ge.26:4).

5) God's promise to Jacob.

> "And God Almighty bless thee, and make thee fruitful, and multiply thee, that thou mayest be a multitude of people" (Ge.28:3).
> "And thy seed shall be as the dust of the earth, and thou shalt spread abroad to the west, and to the east, and to the north, and to the south: and in thee and in thy seed shall all the families of the earth be blessed" (Ge.28:14).
> "And God said unto him, I am God Almighty: be fruitful and multiply; a nation and a company of nations shall be of thee, and kings shall come out of thy loins" (Ge.35:11).
> "And said unto me, Behold, I will make thee fruitful, and multiply thee, and I will make of thee a multitude of people; and will give this land to thy seed after thee for an everlasting possession" (Ge.48:4).

The point to see is God's faithfulness. God was faithful to His promise. He was fulfilling His promise, gloriously fulfilling it. He was causing the promised seed, the descendents of Israel, to grow into a great and mighty nation that was to soon number more than two million people (Nu.1:46; Ps.105:24; De.26:5). Israel was becoming a great people, a people...

- who were to believe and follow God
- who were to be His great witnesses upon earth

Thought 1. God is faithful, always faithful. God keeps His Word and fulfills His promises. We can trust Him. He will keep every promise He has ever made.

(1) God promised to send the promised seed to the world. By promised seed He meant the Savior, the Lord Jesus Christ. This He did.

> "Now to Abraham and his seed were the promises made. He saith not, And to seeds, as of many; but as of one, And to thy seed, which is Christ" (Ga.3:16).
> "For unto you is born this day in the city of David a Saviour, which is Christ the Lord" (Lu.2:11).
> "For God so loved the world, that he gave his only begotten Son, that whosoever believeth in him should not perish, but have everlasting life" (Jn.3:16).

(2) God has promised to forgive our sins if we confess and repent (turn away from sin to God). This He does.

> "Then Peter said unto them, Repent, and be baptized every one of you in the name of Jesus Christ for the remission of sins, and ye shall receive the gift of the Holy Ghost" (Ac.2:38).
> "Repent ye therefore, and be converted, that your sins may be blotted out, when the times of refreshing shall come from the presence of the Lord" (Ac.3:19).
> "If my people, which are called by my name, shall humble themselves, and pray, and seek my face, and turn from their wicked ways; then will I hear from heaven, and will forgive their sin, and will heal their land" (2 Chr.7:14).
> "Let the wicked forsake his way, and the unrighteous man his thoughts: and let him return unto the LORD, and he will have mercy upon him; and to our God, for he will abundantly pardon" (Is.55:7).
> "If we confess our sins, he is faithful and just to forgive us our sins, and to cleanse us from all unrighteousness" (1 Jn.1:9).

56

(3) God promised to give eternal life to true believers and to make absolutely sure that they receive it. This He does.

"For God so loved the world, that he gave his only begotten Son, that whosoever believeth in him should not perish, but have everlasting life" (Jn.3:16).

"Verily, verily, I say unto you, He that heareth my word, and believeth on him that sent me, hath everlasting life, and shall not come into condemnation; but is passed from death unto life" (Jn.5:24).

"And I give unto them eternal life; and they shall never perish, neither shall any [person or being] pluck them out of my hand. My Father, which gave [them] me, is greater than all; and no [person or being] is able to pluck [them] out of my Father's hand" (Jn.10:28-29).

"For he that soweth to his flesh shall of the flesh reap corruption; but he that soweth to the Spirit shall of the Spirit reap life everlasting" (Ga.6:8).

"Being confident of this very thing, that he which hath begun a good work in you will perform it until the day of Jesus Christ" (Ph.1:6).

"I know whom I have believed, and am persuaded that he is able to keep that which I have committed unto him against that day" (2 Ti.1:12).

"And the Lord shall deliver me from every evil work, and will preserve me unto his heavenly kingdom: to whom be glory for ever and ever" (2 Ti.4:18).

"[Believers] who are kept by the power of God through faith unto salvation ready to be revealed in the last time" (1 Pe.1:5).

"Now unto him that is able to keep you from falling, and to present you faultless before the presence of his glory with exceeding joy, to the only wise God our Saviour, be glory and majesty, dominion and power, both now and ever" (Jude 24-25).

(4) God has promised to be with believers through all the trials, problems, and terrible circumstances of life. This He never fails to do.

"Lo, I am with you alway, [even] unto the end of the world" (Mt.28:20).

"Let your conversation [conduct, behavior] be without covetousness; and be content with such things as ye have: for he hath said, I will never leave thee, nor forsake thee. So that we may boldly say, The Lord is my helper, and I will not fear what man shall do unto me" (He.13:5-6).

"And he said, My presence shall go with thee, and I will give thee rest" (Ex.33:14).

"For in the time of trouble he shall hide me in his pavilion: in the secret of his tabernacle shall he hide me; he shall set me up upon a rock" (Ps.27:5).

"Thou shalt hide them in the secret of thy presence from the pride of man: thou shalt keep them secretly in a pavilion from the strife of tongues" (Ps.31:20).

"Thou art my hiding place; thou shalt preserve me from trouble; thou shalt compass me about with songs of deliverance" (Ps.32:7

"But I *am* poor and needy; *yet* the Lord thinketh upon me: thou *art* my help and my deliverer; make no tarrying, O my God" (Ps.40:17).

"God is our refuge and strength, a very present help in trouble" (Ps.46:1).

"Be merciful unto me, O God, be merciful unto me: for my soul trusteth in thee: yea, in the shadow of thy wings will I make my refuge, until these calamities be overpast" (Ps.57:1).

"Fear thou not; for I am with thee: be not dismayed; for I am thy God: I will strengthen thee; yea, I will help thee; yea, I will uphold thee with the right hand of my righteousness" (Is.41:10).

"When thou passest through the waters, I will be with thee; and through the rivers, they shall not overflow thee: when thou walkest through the fire, thou shalt not be burned; neither shall the flame kindle upon thee" (Is.43:2).

DEEPER STUDY # 2

(1:6-7) **Seed, The Promised—Israel—Covenant, The Abrahamic—Abraham**: God promised to give Abram the promised seed, to make him the father of a great nation and race of people. God meant this both literally and spiritually. Note these facts:

1. God meant the promised seed to be *a physical and literal people*. Abram was to give birth to a new race of people: the Jews, the nation of Israel.

   a. Note the Old Testament references.

"And I will make thy seed as the dust of the earth: so that if a man can number the dust of the earth, then shall thy seed also be numbered" (Ge.13:16).

"And he brought him forth abroad, and said, Look now toward heaven, and tell the stars, if thou be able to number them: and he said unto him, So shall thy seed be" (Ge.15:5).

"As for me, behold, my covenant is with thee, and thou shalt be a father of many nations. Neither shall thy name any more be called Abram, but thy name shall be Abraham; for a father of many nations have I made thee. And I will make thee exceeding fruitful, and I will make nations of thee, and kings shall come out of thee. And I will establish my covenant between me and thee and thy seed after thee in their generations for an everlasting covenant, to be a God unto thee, and to thy seed after thee" (Ge.17:4-7).

"And God said unto Abraham, As for Sarai thy wife, thou shalt not call her name Sarai, but Sarah shall her name be. And I will bless her, and give thee a son also of her: yea, I will bless her, and she shall be a mother of nations; kings of people shall be of her" (Ge.17:15-16).

"And the LORD said, Shall I hide from Abraham that thing which I do; seeing that Abraham shall surely become a great and mighty nation, and all the nations of the earth shall be blessed in him?" (Ge.18:17-18).

"That in blessing I will bless thee, and in multiplying I will multiply thy seed as the stars of the heaven, and as the sand which is upon the sea shore; and thy seed shall possess the gate of his enemies" (Ge.22:17).

"And the LORD said unto her [Rebekah, Abram's daughter-in-law], Two nations are in thy womb, and two manner of people shall be separated from thy bowels; and the one people shall be stronger than the other people: and the elder shall serve the younger" (Ge.25:23).

"And I will make thy seed to multiply as the stars of heaven, and will give unto thy seed all these countries; and in thy seed shall all the nations of the earth be blessed" (Ge.26:4, the promise is confirmed with Isaac, Abram's son).

"And thy seed shall be as the dust of the earth, and thou shalt spread abroad to the west, and to the east, and to the north, and to the south: and in thee and in thy seed shall all the families of the earth be blessed" (Ge.28:14, the promise is confirmed with Jacob, Abram's grandson).

"And God said unto him, I am God Almighty: be fruitful and multiply; a nation and a company of nations shall be of thee, and kings shall come out of thy loins" (Ge.35:11, the promise is again confirmed with Jacob, Abram's grandson).

"And he said, I am God, the God of thy father: fear not to go down into Egypt; for I will there make of thee a great nation" (Ge.46:3, the promise is again confirmed with Jacob, Abram's grandson).

b. Note the New Testament references.

"Ye [the children of Israel] are the children of the prophets, and of the covenant which God made with our fathers, saying unto Abraham, And in thy seed shall all the kindreds of the earth be blessed" (Ac.3:25).

"And God spake on this wise, That his [Abraham's] seed should sojourn in a strange land [Egypt]; and that they should bring them into bondage, and entreat them evil four hundred years" (Ac.7:6).

"Who are Israelites; to whom pertaineth the adoption, and the glory, and the covenants, and the giving of the law, and the service of God, and the promises" (Ro.9:4).

"Through faith also Sarah [Abram's wife] herself received strength to conceive seed, and was delivered of a child when she was past age, because she judged him faithful who had promised. Therefore sprang there even of one, and him as good as dead, so many as the stars of the sky in multitude, and as the sand which is by the sea shore innumerable" (He.11:11-12).

2. God meant the promised seed to be *a spiritual people*. Abram was to give birth to a new race of spiritual people: the people of faith, true and genuine believers who would follow after God and His promises. Believers of all nations are counted as *children of Abraham*. Note how clearly Scripture states this fact:

"And he [Abraham] received the sign of circumcision, a seal of the righteousness of the faith which he had yet being uncircumcised: that he might be the father of all them that believe, though they be not circumcised; that righteousness might be imputed unto them also" (Ro.4:11).

"For the promise, that he should be the heir of the world, was not to Abraham, or to his seed, through the law, but through the righteousness of faith. For if they which are of the law be heirs, faith is made void, and the promise made of none effect" (Ro.4:13-14).

"Therefore it [the promise] is of faith, that it might be by grace; to the end the promise might be sure to all the seed; not to that only which is of the law, but to that also which is of the faith of Abraham; who is the father of us all" (Ro.4:16).

"Now it was not written for his [Abraham's] sake alone, that it was imputed to him; but for us also, to whom it shall be imputed, if we believe on him [God] that raised up Jesus our Lord from the dead; who was delivered for our offences, and was raised again for our justification" (Ro.4:23-25).

"Know ye therefore that they which are of faith, the same are the children of Abraham" (Ga.3:7).

"And the scripture, foreseeing that God would justify the heathen through faith, preached before the gospel unto Abraham, saying, In thee shall all nations be blessed" (Ga.3:8).

"So then they which be of faith are blessed with faithful Abraham [counted as his children, the children of faith]" (Ga.3:9).

"That the blessing of Abraham might come on the Gentiles through Jesus Christ; that we might receive the promise of the Spirit through faith" (Ga.3:14).

"For ye are all the children of God by faith in Christ Jesus....And if ye be Christ's, then are ye Abraham's seed, and heirs according to the promise" (Ga.3:26, 29).

"And as many as walk according to this rule, peace be on them, and mercy, and upon the Israel of God" (Ga.6:16).

The promised seed was a spiritual promise as well as a literal promise. This double meaning must always be kept in mind when reading or studying *the promised seed* given to Abram.

⇒ Note the Old Testament references above (the first point), the promise that Abram's seed would number as the stars of the sky and as the grains of sand by the seashore (Ge.13:16; 15:5). Literally, this could never be fulfilled if it referred only to one physical nation of people upon earth. There must, therefore, be a double reference. The promise must refer to all believers of *all nations* down through all centuries and millenniums of human history. And history must last a long time, continue on and on so that more and more people can trust Christ and become followers of God and His promise. (What a challenge to get out and bear witness to our Lord and Savior Jesus Christ!)

⇒ Note all the Scriptures above (the second point): spiritually, Abram was to be the father of all who believe the promises of God. He was the first person since The Great Flood and Noah—within the new world—to believe and commit his life to the promises of God. Therefore, Abram was to be the father of all those who followed him in believing the promises. All who walk in the steps of the faith of Abram are counted as his children, as the children of faith, and are to spiritually receive the very same promises made to Abram (Ro.4:11-12. See notes—Ro.4:11-12; 4:13 for more discussion.)

TYPES, SYMBOLS, AND PICTURES
(Exodus 1:1-7)

Historical Term	Type or Picture (Scriptural Basis for Each)	Life Application for Today's Believer	Biblical Application
The Children of Israel (Ex. 1:1)	*The people of God* **"Now these are the names of the children of Israel, which came into Egypt; every man and his household came with Jacob"** (Ex.1:1). **"And thy seed [Jacob's] shall be as the dust of the earth, and thou shalt spread abroad to the west, and to the east, and to the north, and to the south: and in thee and in thy seed shall all the families of the earth be blessed"** (Ge.28:14).	The Christian believer is spiritual Israel—the true people of God... • who are now a new creation in Christ Jesus • who are walking in the peace and mercy of God • who are the true *Israel of God*, the true believers who follow after God	*"For in Christ Jesus neither circumcision availeth anything, nor uncircumcision, but a new creature. And as many as walk according to this rule, peace be on them, and mercy, and upon the Israel of God"* **(Ga.6:15-16).** *(see Ga.3:7, 26,29)* *"For he is not a Jew, which is one outwardly; neither is that circumcision, which is outward in the flesh: But he is a Jew, which is one inwardly; and circumcision is that of the heart, in the spirit, and not in the letter; whose praise is not of men, but of God"* **(Ro.2:28-29).**

1. The causes of oppression
- a. Ignorance: The new king knew nothing about Joseph[DS1]
- b. Fear of people (Israel)
  1) Their numbers & strength
  2) Their joining forces with some enemy
- c. Fear of loss: That Israel's labor & economic power would be lost

2. The first oppression, that of persecution: But it was overcome by God's purpose & promise[DS2]
- a. The persecution: Enslavement & a forced labor for the state
- b. Overcoming the persecution: God caused the people to multiply even more—all in fulfillment of His purpose & promise (vv.6-7)
- c. The reaction of the persecutors against God's people: Forced a more ruthless labor & made life very bitter
  1) In construction
  2) In agriculture

3. The second oppression, a plot

B. The Enslavement of Israel By Egypt: How God's People Overcome Oppression, 1:8-22

8 Now there arose up a new king over Egypt, which knew not Joseph.
9 And he said unto his people, Behold, the people of the children of Israel are more and mightier than we:
10 Come on, let us deal wisely with them; lest they multiply, and it come to pass, that, when there falleth out any war, they join also unto our enemies, and fight against us, and so get them up out of the land.
11 Therefore they did set over them taskmasters to afflict them with their burdens. And they built for Pharaoh treasure cities, Pithom and Raamses.
12 But the more they afflicted them, the more they multiplied and grew. And they were grieved because of the children of Israel.
13 And the Egyptians made the children of Israel to serve with rigour:
14 And they made their lives bitter with hard bondage, in morter, and in brick, and in all manner of service in the field: all their service, wherein they made them serve, was with rigour.
15 And the king of Egypt spake to the Hebrew midwives, of which the name of the one was Shiphrah, and the name of the other Puah:
16 And he said, When ye do the office of a midwife to the Hebrew women, and see them upon the stools; if it be a son, then ye shall kill him: but if it be a daughter, then she shall live.
17 But the midwives feared God, and did not as the king of Egypt commanded them, but saved the men children alive.
18 And the king of Egypt called for the midwives, and said unto them, Why have ye done this thing, and have saved the men children alive?
19 And the midwives said unto Pharaoh, Because the Hebrew women are not as the Egyptian women; for they are lively, and are delivered ere the midwives come in unto them.
20 Therefore God dealt well with the midwives: and the people multiplied, and waxed very mighty.
21 And it came to pass, because the midwives feared God, that he made them houses.
22 And Pharaoh charged all his people, saying, Every son that is born ye shall cast into the river, and every daughter ye shall save alive.

of deception: But it was overcome by some people (midwives) who feared God more than man
- a. The persecution: The king ordered the two supervising midwives to have all baby boys killed at birth—while still on the delivery stool—to kill them without their mothers knowing it
- b. Overcoming the persecution: The midwives feared God more than they feared the king: They let the boys live
- c. The king called for the midwives & questioned their action
  1) Why had they not carried out his orders
  2) They avoided a direct answer, giving a true fact about women who are physically fit: Hebrew women were vigorous & delivered before the midwives reached them
- d. God blessed the midwives & continued to bless Israel
  1) He multiplied Israel
  2)
  3) He gave the midwives families of their own

4. The third oppression, a murderous law: But it was overcome by a mother who believed God (see Ex.2:1-25 to see how the persecution was overcome)

DIVISION I

ISRAEL AND EGYPT: THE OPPRESSION OF GOD'S PEOPLE BY A NATION THAT HAD REJECTED GOD, 1:1-22

B. The Enslavement of Israel By Egypt: How God's People Overcome Oppression, 1:8-22

(1:8-22) **Introduction**: the world rejects God and persecutes believers. If a person is a true believer—if a person sincerely seeks to follow and bear testimony to Christ—he will be persecuted by the world. Persecution is inevitable; it is a sure thing. And the persecution can range from being mildly shunned or ridiculed over to being physically enslaved, abused, or even killed for one's faith.

This is the subject of this tragic passage of Scripture. It covers the persecution and enslavement of Israel. It tells how Israel lost its position of privilege and comfort in Egypt and became the subject of a terrible, ruthless oppression. It tells us why Egypt began to persecute and enslave Israel. And it tells how Israel overcame the oppression. Note how Egypt is a picture of the world throughout this passage, the world that ridicules and persecutes God's people, those who truly seek to follow God and to live righteous lives.

This is a passage that needs to be studied by the nations of the world as well as by individuals, for it shows why people and nations persecute others. It also assures believers that God will always deliver us from persecution and enslavement—if we will just hold on to our faith, just persevere in following after Him. As stated, this subject is important for the nations of the earth as well as for individuals. This passage covers: *The Enslavement of Israel by Egypt: How God's People Overcome Oppression*, 1:8-22.

1. The causes of oppression (vv.8-10).
2. The first oppression, that of enslavement: but it was overcome by God's purpose and promise (vv.11-14).
3. The second oppression, a plot of deception: but it was overcome by some people (midwives) who feared God more than man (vv.15-21).
4. The third oppression, a murderous law: but it was overcome by a mother who believed God (v.22).

1 (1:8-10) **Oppression—Persecution—Slavery**: the causes of oppression. Why do people and nations persecute and enslave others? There are primarily three reasons and all three can be seen in Egypt's enslavement of Israel.

a. There was ignorance: the new king knew nothing about Joseph, and he knew nothing about God, not the only true and living God. No nation (or person) who enslaves others knows God, not in a personal way (v.8). Pharaoh was ignorant of history or else he paid little or no attention to history. He was ignorant of the great contribution Joseph had made to Egypt. Joseph had literally saved Egypt and the surrounding world from starvation and helped establish Egypt as one of the greatest nations upon earth (see outline and notes—Ge. chs.41–47). The king was also ignorant of Joseph's people, Israel…

- ignorant of who they were
- ignorant of why and how they had migrated to Egypt
- ignorant of the great contribution they had made to Egypt's labor force and to the growth and economy of Egypt down through the years—all as a free people living in the Egyptian district of Goshen. (See outline and notes—Ge.47:1-6. Also see Ge.47:27.)
- ignorant of the great value and dignity of human life
- ignorant of God, ignorant of the only true and living God

Simply stated, the new king was ignorant of people, that they are basically spiritual beings with the fundamental need to be free. He failed to see that people need to use their own personal initiative in providing for themselves and their families and in building their own lives and society. He was ignorant of one of the most basic facts of human nature: that people produce far more when they are free and allowed to use their own personal initiative.

Thought 1. People, both believers and unbelievers, often find themselves in situations like the Israelites were in. A new king who does not 'know Joseph' takes over and we suffer because of his power. The new king may be…
- a supervisor or company owner who holds authority over us and mistreats us or jeopardizes our jobs
- a spouse who misuses his or her authority and becomes unsupporting, distant, dominating, or threatening
- a king or government official who abuses his power and restricts our freedom and, in some cases, enslaves us

Millions of lives are tragically affected every day because of situations like these. The answer to oppression and persecution is God, believing and trusting God. God delivers all who truly believe and trust Him—all true believers.

"Many are the afflictions of the righteous: but the LORD delivereth him out of them all" (Ps.34:19).
"The LORD will strengthen him upon the bed of languishing: thou wilt make all his bed in his sickness" (Ps.41:3).
"Call upon me in the day of trouble: I will deliver thee, and thou shalt glorify me" (Ps.50:15).
"Though I walk in the midst of trouble, thou wilt revive me: thou shalt stretch forth thine hand against the wrath of mine enemies, and thy right hand shall save me" (Ps.138:7).
"When thou passest through the waters, I will be with thee; and through the rivers, they shall not overflow thee: when thou walkest through the fire, thou shalt not be burned; neither shall the flame kindle upon thee" (Is.43:2).
"Let not your heart be troubled: ye believe in God, believe also in me. In my Father's house are many mansions: if [it were] not [so], I would have told you. I go to prepare a place for you" (Jn.14:1-2).
"And we know that all things work together for good to them that love God, to them who are the called according to his purpose" (Ro.8:28).
"For our light affliction, which is but for a moment, worketh for us a far more exceeding and eternal weight of glory" (2 Co.4:17).

Thought 2. Leaders of nations, businesses, and groups need to remember this basic fact about human nature: man is a spiritual being with the need to be free. God created man as a spiritual being, created him with the highest dignity and honor possible, created him in the very image of God Himself. Therefore, man is driven to use his own personal initiative to worship, work, and play. He must, therefore, be allowed to live in freedom, to live and share his life with others: his life of faith, work, and play. (See note—Gen.1:26 for more discussion.)

"So God created man in his own image, in the image of God created he him; male and female created he them" (Ge.1:27).
"And the LORD God formed man of the dust of the ground, and breathed into his nostrils the breath of life; and man became a living soul" (Ge.2:7).
"The Spirit of the Lord GOD is upon me; because the LORD hath anointed me to preach good tidings unto the meek; he hath sent me to bind up the brokenhearted, to proclaim liberty to the captives, and the opening of the prison to them that are bound" (Is.61:1).
"Therefore all things whatsoever ye would that men should do to you, do ye even so to them: for this is the law and the prophets" (Mt.7:12).
"The Spirit of the Lord [is] upon me, because he hath anointed me to preach the gospel to the poor; he hath sent me to heal the brokenhearted, to preach deliverance to the captives, and recovering of sight to the blind, to set at liberty them that are bruised" (Lu.4:18).
"And as ye would that men should do to you, do ye also to them likewise" (Lu.6:31).
"Bear ye one another's burdens, and so fulfil the law of Christ" (Ga.6:2).

b. There was the fear of people (Israel) (v.9). The new king feared that the people were a threat to his nation and their way of life. The king feared their numbers and strength:

⇒ Israel's population was exploding, growing by leaps and bounds.
⇒ They were becoming a mighty force of people just by their sheer numbers.
⇒ The king feared their joining forces with some enemy and attacking Egypt.
⇒ The Israelites were different from the Egyptians, different in appearance, life-style, and religion.

The point is this: it is the fear of people—feeling that they are a threat or different in some way—that causes people to persecute other people. This was one of the reasons why Egypt persecuted Israel.

Thought 1. People often persecute believers because they fear believers. They feel that believers are a threat to their way of life; therefore they must stop believers and shut them up. Think for a moment...

• Believers preach and teach love, but most people want the right to dislike others when they wish. They want the right to reject love and to shun, ignore, get upset and be angry with others they do not like. They want the right to even hate and retaliate against others when others mistreat them.

• Believers preach and teach righteousness, that God demands righteousness from us all. God demands purity, modest dress, sexual morality, clean speech, no cursing, controlled thoughts, a disciplined life, and honesty. But many people in the world want to live, look, speak, and do exactly what they want when they want. Most people want the right to do their own thing. Therefore, they stand against true believers, those who live and teach true righteousness. Righteousness is a threat to their way of life.

• Believers preach and teach unselfishness and sacrificial giving. Believers stress the desperate needs of people, their need to be loved, befriended, cared for, looked after, fed, clothed, housed, ministered to, and above all, their need to hear the gospel of the Lord Jesus Christ. This demands our time, talents, and money—the sacrificial giving of all that we are and have. Most people do not want to hear the message of unselfish, sacrificial giving. They want the possessions of this world, as much as they can get. Therefore, they stand against true believers, those who teach unselfishness and sacrificial giving. Sacrificial giving is a threat to their way of life.

On and on the list could go, but the application to us is clear. The people of the world fear true believers because they are a threat to their way of life. Therefore, some people will always shun, neglect, ignore, ridicule, and threaten believers. People will even try to silence and take away the rights of believers; and sometimes, if needed, even abuse, enslave, and kill them.

"But beware of men: for they will deliver you up to the councils, and they will scourge you in their synagogues" (Mt.10:17).

"Then shall they deliver you up to be afflicted, and shall kill you: and ye shall be hated of all nations for my name's sake" (Mt.24:9).

"Remember the word that I said unto you, The servant is not greater than his lord. If they have persecuted me, they will also persecute you; if they have kept my saying, they will keep yours also" (Jn.15:20).

"For unto you it is given in the behalf of Christ, not only to believe on him, but also to suffer for his sake" (Ph.1:29).

"That no man should be moved by these afflictions: for yourselves know that we are appointed thereunto" (1 Th.3:3).

"Yea, and all that will live godly in Christ Jesus shall suffer persecution" (2 Ti.3:12).

"Beloved, think it not strange concerning the fiery trial which is to try you, as though some strange thing happened unto you: But rejoice, inasmuch as ye are partakers of Christ's sufferings; that, when his glory shall be revealed, ye may be glad also with exceeding joy. If ye be reproached for the name of Christ, happy are ye; for the spirit of glory and of God resteth upon you: on their part he is evil spoken of, but on your part he is glorified" (1 Pe.4:12-14).

"Yet if any man suffer as a Christian, let him not be ashamed; but let him glorify God on this behalf" (1 Pe.4:16).

"And one of the elders answered, saying unto me, What are these which are arrayed in white robes? and whence came they? And I said unto him, Sir, thou knowest. And he said to me, These are they which came out of great tribulation, and have washed their robes, and made them white in the blood of the Lamb" (Re.7:13-14).

"And God shall wipe away all tears from their eyes; and there shall be no more death, neither sorrow, nor crying, neither shall there be any more pain: for the former things are passed away" (Re.21:4).

"All thy commandments are faithful: they persecute me wrongfully; help thou me" (Ps.119:86).

c. There was the fear of loss, the loss of position and power, of possessions and wealth. The king feared that Israel might leave the land of Egypt. If they did, then Israel's labor and economic power would be lost to Egypt. The loss of Israel's wealth and trade would be a devastating blow to Egypt. The population of Israel was about two million at this time. The loss of two million people—of their labor and trade—would wreck the economy of any small nation. Pharaoh had to make absolutely sure that Israel's labor and trade was not lost to Egypt.

Thought 1. The world, both men and women, seek…
- position and power
- possessions and wealth

The position and power sought after may be one's standing in the family, business community, town, city, state, or nation. The possessions and wealth sought after can be the simple comforts of home, a good job, just enough to live comfortably, a successful business or farm, or millions and billions of dollars.

There is nothing wrong with position and power. The positions of responsibility within all organizations have to be held and looked after by someone. And there is nothing wrong with possessions and wealth. Some of us have to be wealthy enough to venture out and build the businesses that provide the jobs for the rest of us. However, when greed, covetousness, and lusting for more kick in and we begin to hoard wealth while others suffer, this is wrong. To allow hunger, starvation, homelessness, disease, ignorance, and worst of all, death without Christ to continue—this is wrong. Pharaoh went so far as to persecute and enslave Israel in order to protect his wealth and the wealth of his people.

Persecution, enslavement, and hoarding wealth are all wrong. Scripture declares that all greed and covetousness will be judged, condemned severely. Moreover, Jesus Christ Himself declared that a covetous and greedy person shall not inherit eternal life.

"For the wicked boasteth of his heart's desire, and blesseth the covetous, whom the LORD abhorreth" (Ps.10:3).

"Woe to them that devise iniquity, and work evil upon their beds! when the morning is light, they practice it, because it is in the power of their hand. And they covet fields, and take them by violence; and houses, and take them away: so they oppress a man and his house, even a man and his heritage. Therefore thus saith the LORD; Behold, against this family do I devise an evil, from which ye shall not remove your necks; neither shall ye go haughtily: for this time is evil" (Mi.2:1-3).

"Jesus said unto him, If thou wilt be perfect, go [and] sell that thou hast, and give to the poor, and thou shalt have treasure in heaven: and come [and] follow me. But when the young man heard that saying, he went away sorrowful: for he had great possessions. Then said Jesus unto his disciples, Verily I say unto you, That a rich man shall hardly enter into the kingdom of heaven. And again I say unto you, It is easier for a camel to go through the eye of a needle, than for a rich man to enter into the kingdom of God" (Mt.19:21-24).

"And he said unto them, Take heed, and beware of covetousness: for a man's life consisteth not in the abundance of the things which he possesseth" (Lu.12:15).

"And I will say to my soul, Soul, thou hast much goods laid up for many years; take thine ease, eat, drink, [and] be merry. But God said unto him, [Thou] fool, this night thy soul shall be required of thee: then whose shall those things be, which thou hast provided?" (Lu.12:19-20).

"Mortify therefore your members which are upon the earth; fornication, uncleanness, inordinate affection, evil concupiscence, and covetousness, which is idolatry: For which things' sake the wrath of God cometh on the children of disobedience" (Col.3:5-6).

"But fornication, and all uncleanness, or covetousness, let it not be once named among you, as becometh saints….For this ye know, that no whoremonger, nor unclean person, nor covetous man, who is an idolater, hath any inheritance in the kingdom of Christ and of God" (Ep.5:3, 5).

"Charge them that are rich in this world, that they be not highminded, nor trust in uncertain riches, but in the living God, who giveth us richly all things to enjoy" (1 Ti.6:17).

DEEPER STUDY # 1

(1:8) **Pharaoh—King**: Who was the new king who ruled over Egypt and enslaved Israel? Scripture does not say. In fact, the Bible never gives the name of any Egyptian king during this period of Israel's history. Scripture only refers to Pharaoh, and Pharaoh is not a personal name; it is the official title of the Egyptian king. Thus the exact dating of the events that happened in Egypt between Exodus and Ruth cannot be determined. Just who the new king was is not known; however, there seem to be two major positions that have some weight supporting them.

1. The new king who enslaved Israel could have been the Egyptian ruler who overthrew the Hyksos dynasty. The Hyksos people were foreigners who invaded and conquered Egypt somewhere around 1730 B.C. They ruled until about 1550 B.C., a period of about 180 years. At that time, the Egyptians rose up and overthrew the Hyksos king and took their nation back from the foreign rulers. Two facts need to be noted about this position.

   a. The Hyksos people were a Semitic people, that is, they were of the same racial family as the Israelites. This has led some interpreters to say that a Hyksos king would more readily accept Joseph and his people (Israel). Remember, the Egyptians detested shepherds (Ge.46:34). Thus, this position feels that it was probably a Hyksos king who exalted Joseph to be governor of Egypt and who brought his family, Jacob and his sons, to live in Egypt. Thus it is thought more reasonable to conclude that the Hyksos kings welcomed Israel and some Egyptian Pharaoh enslaved them.

   b. Moreover, the word *new* in the Hebrew does not mean just another king, but a new kind, a different kind of king. Therefore, this position holds that the new king was the Egyptian ruler—a king of a different nationality—who overthrew the Hyksos king. In answer to this position, note the prediction given to Abraham by God: Israel was to be enslaved and afflicted for 400 years (Ge.15:13). (Remember the Hyksos dynasty lasted about 180 years.)

The point is this: if it was a Hyksos king who exalted Joseph and accepted Israel in Egypt, then the Israelites most likely lived in peace for a hundred years or more. This just does not seem to match the prediction of four hundred years of enslavement and affliction (Ge.15:13). Moreover, it would take the Egyptian people themselves decades to forget what Joseph had done for the nation.

It is difficult to imagine an Egyptian rising to the throne and enslaving Israel, for either he or some official in his cabinet would certainly know something about one of the great rulers and significant events in their recent history. However, this would not be true if the new king was an invader from another nation. He would know little if anything about Egyptian rulers of past history.

For these reasons, this position seems to be weaker than the next suggestion.

2. The new king could have been the Hyksos king who invaded and conquered Egypt. The facts supporting this position would be these:

   a. The new Hyksos king, as a foreign invader, would more likely have no way of knowing about Joseph and the history of Egypt.

   b. God told Abraham that his seed would be enslaved and afflicted for 400 years (Ge.15:13). Note that Scripture actually says that Israel will be afflicted for hundreds of years, four hundred to be exact. At the very least, this suggests a long period of bondage for Israel—hundreds of years—not just a few years or decades at the end of their stay in Egypt.

   c. The Hyksos dynasty ruled for about 180 years which means that Israel was enslaved all this time.

   d. The new Egyptian king who overthrew the Hyksos foreigners would most likely continue to subject and enslave all foreigners including Israel. Thus Israel's enslavement would continue on beyond the 180 years of the Hyksos oppression, continue for more than another 220 years or so.

   Note how this fact allows the Hyksos invasion to take place soon after Joseph's rule and death (about seventy years). Israel was in Egypt for about 430 years (Ex.12:40). Deduct Joseph's rule of 70 years and the enslavement could have been close to 360 years. This comes much closer to God's prediction of Israel being enslaved for 400 years (Ge.15:13).

   e. The exodus of Israel from Egypt lends support to this position. Two Scriptures give a hint about the date of *the Exodus*.

   "Now the sojourning of the children of Israel, who dwelt in Egypt, was four hundred and thirty years" (Ex.12:40).

   "And it came to pass in the four hundred and eightieth year after the children of Israel were come out of the land of Egypt, in the fourth year of Solomon's reign over Israel, in the month Zif, which is the second month, that he began to build the house of the LORD" (1 K.6:1).

   Solomon's' reign can be somewhat accurately fixed as about 970–930 B.C. Thus the fourth year of his reign was 966 B.C. If the exodus took place 480 years earlier, this means that Israel left Egypt about 1446 B.C. What all this means is this:

   ⇒ These two verses suggest that Israel's stay in Egypt was somewhere close to 1876-1446 B.C. (430 years, Ex.12:40).

   ⇒ If the affliction of Israel was to be close to 400 years, then the Hyksos kings have to be included in the ruling dynasties who enslaved Israel. Why? Because they ruled Egypt for close to 180 years while Israel was in Egypt (about 1730-1550 B.C.).

   Thus the new king, who knew nothing about Joseph and Israel, was probably the Hyksos king who first conquered Egypt somewhere around 1703 B.C. This suggests the following timetable.

   ⇒ About 1876 B.C., Israel entered Egypt.

   ⇒ About 1730 B.C., Israel was enslaved and oppressed by a Hyksos king who attacked and conquered Egypt.

   ⇒ About 1575-1550 B.C., the Egyptians overthrew the Hyksos dynasty and regained their country but continued to hold Israel as slaves.

   ⇒ About 1446 B.C., the great exodus of Israel took place; Israel was freed. They had suffered affliction for about 284 years. (For additional information, see Walter C. Kaiser, Jr. *Exodus*, The Expositor's Bible Commentary, Vol.2, pp.304-305. Also, note the chronology of *The Preacher's Outline & Sermon Bible*, where Israel's enslavement, exodus, and conquest of Canaan took place between 1800–1050 B.C., *Genesis*, Vol.1, Old Testament Chronology, p.13.)

   Just keep this fact in mind: when looking at events in ancient history, it is impossible to determine the exact dates of said events with absolute accuracy.

2 (1:11-14) **Oppression—Persecution**: the first oppression launched by the new king was that of persecution and enslavement. But note, it was overcome by God's purpose and promise.

a. The Egyptians launched a brutal persecution against Israel. They enslaved Israel and set slave-masters over the people, forcing them to labor for the state. The Egyptians wanted...

   • to stop Israel's population growth
   • to break their spirits and keep them from bearing children
   • to cause a number of them to die from hard work and harsh treatment, thereby shortening their days on earth

The people were enslaved and no doubt oppressed, mistreated, abused, and beaten. They were forced to build two storage cities for Egypt, the cities of Pithom and Rameses. These were apparently used for the storage of military arms and supplies and for farm and government products.

The point to see is that a deliberate attempt was being made to cut the population growth of Israel. And the method chosen was vicious and cruel, that of enslavement, of being abused, beaten, and slowly killed off until the population was controllable. Israel's freedom was not only restricted, it was lost. The people were enslaved and forced to work for the government. Pictures of the slave-masters have been found on wall paintings. They are seen standing over slaves, armed with "heavy whips."[1]

b. But the people overcame the persecution. How? By multiplying and bearing more and more children. In fact, the more the people were persecuted, the more they grew. How was this possible when the Egyptians were inflicting so much suffering upon the people? When they were actually trying to wear the people out, trying to make them so tired that they would not have the strength to conceive children? There is only one answer: God. God's great promise to send *the promised seed* through Israel had to be fulfilled. No man, not even the great Pharaohs and rulers of the earth, can stop God from fulfilling His promises to His people. Therefore, God gave the people of Israel the strength to conceive and bear children. God caused the people to multiply despite their exhaustion and suffering. (See notes—Ex.1:6-7; Ge.12:1; 12:1-3; 12:4-9 for more discussion.)

c. The reaction of the persecutors against God's people was fierce. The Egyptians forced a more ruthless labor upon the people; they made life even more bitter for the Israelites. The Egyptians became more and more vicious and evil; they inflicted harsh, animal-like work upon the people.

⇒ In the field of construction, the people were forced to make brick and mortar and to build whole cities for the Egyptian government.

⇒ In the field of agriculture, they were obviously forced to plant, tend, harvest, clear new fields, and dig and construct irrigation canals. Note the word *rigor* or *ruthless* (beparek). It means a fierce, back-breaking, crushing labor, a labor so harsh that it literally breaks the body down.

The Egyptians were determined to control Israel's population growth. Pharaoh was willing to launch any evil in order to keep the people as slaves to serve his desires.

Thought 1. The promises of God are irrevocable. He had promised *the promised seed* to Abraham, the birth of a great nation of people. This passage shows how God poured out His grace upon Israel, how He fulfilled His promise, how He caused a great nation of people to be born of the seed of Abraham. Whatever God promises us, He will do. No matter what confronts us—no matter how terrible or painful—God will be with us and help us. He will fulfill—carry out, complete—exactly what He has promised.

"And he said, My presence shall go with thee, and I will give thee rest" (Ex.33:14).

"But I am poor and needy; yet the Lord thinketh upon me: thou art my help and my deliverer; make no tarrying, O my God" (Ps.40:17).

"Fear thou not; for I am with thee: be not dismayed; for I am thy God: I will strengthen thee; yea, I will help thee; yea, I will uphold thee with the right hand of my righteousness" (Is.41:10).

"When thou passest through the waters, I will be with thee; and through the rivers, they shall not overflow thee: when thou walkest through the fire, thou shalt not be burned; neither shall the flame kindle upon thee" (Is.43:2).

"So that we may boldly say, The Lord is my helper, and I will not fear what man shall do unto me" (He.13:6).

DEEPER STUDY # 2

(1:11-14) **Pharaoh—Satan—Symbol - Type**: the Pharaoh of ancient Egypt is a picture, a type, a symbol of the evil prince of this world, Satan himself. Note these facts pictured in this particular passage.

1. Pharaoh was the prince of Egypt; Satan is the prince of this world.

"Now is the judgment of this world: now shall the prince of this world be cast out" (Jn.12:31).

"Hereafter I will not talk much with you: for the prince of this world cometh, and hath nothing in me" (Jn.14:30).

"Of judgment, because the prince of this world is judged" (Jn.16:11).

2. Pharaoh oppressed people; Satan also oppresses God's people.

"And as he was yet a coming, the devil threw him down, and tare him. And Jesus rebuked the unclean spirit, and healed the child, and delivered him again to his father" (Lu.9:42).

"And supper being ended, the devil having now put into the heart of Judas Iscariot, Simon's son, to betray him" (Jn.13:2).

"In whom the god of this world hath blinded the minds of them which believe not, lest the light of the glorious gospel of Christ, who is the image of God, should shine unto them" (2 Co.4:4).

"Wherein in time past ye walked according to the course of this world, according to the prince of the power of the air, the spirit that now worketh in the children of disobedience" (Ep.2:2).

---

[1] Frank E. Gaebelein, Editor. *The Expositor's Bible Commentary,* Vol.2 (Grand Rapids, MI: Zondervan Publishing House, 1990), p.304.

3. Pharaoh held the people of Egypt under his rule; Satan holds the people of the world under his rule.

> "And the devil said unto him, All this power will I give thee, and the glory of them: for that is delivered unto me; and to whomsoever I will I give it" (Lu.4:6).
> "To open their eyes, and to turn them from darkness to light, and from the power of Satan unto God, that they may receive forgiveness of sins, and inheritance among them which are sanctified by faith that is in me" (Ac.26:18).
> "For we wrestle not against flesh and blood, but against principalities, against powers, against the rulers of the darkness of this world, against spiritual wickedness in high places" (Ep.6:12).
> "Who hath delivered us from the power of darkness [Satan], and hath translated us into the kingdom of his dear Son" (Col.1:13).
> "Forasmuch then as the children are partakers of flesh and blood, he also himself likewise took part of the same; that through death he might destroy him that had the power of death, that is, the devil" (He.2:14).

4. Pharaoh enslaved people to do his will; Satan enslaves people to do his will, that is, to sin.

> "Then was Jesus led up of the Spirit into the wilderness to be tempted of the devil" (Mt.4:1).
> "But now being made free from sin, and become servants to God, ye have your fruit unto holiness, and the end everlasting life" (Ro.6:22).
> "Wherein in time past ye walked according to the course of this world, according to the prince of the power of the air, the spirit that now worketh in the children of disobedience" (Ep.2:2).
> "He that committeth sin is of the devil; for the devil sinneth from the beginning. For this purpose the Son of God was manifested, that he might destroy the works of the devil" (1 Jn.3:8).

DEEPER STUDY #3
(1:11) **Pithom** (See **Cities; Map, of Egypt**): a city built by the Israelites while they were enslaved in Egypt. This is the only time Pithom is mentioned in the Bible.

DEEPER STUDY #4
(1:11) **Rameses** (See **Cities; Map, of Egypt**): was the capital city of Pharaoh's Egypt. Moses, who was found as a baby floating in the Nile River in a basket, was found by Pharaoh's daughter and brought to Rameses. The enslaved Israelites were forced to build this city for Pharaoh.

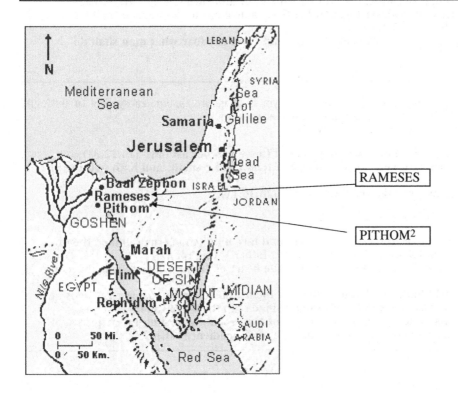

3 (1:15-21) **Oppression—Persecution—Fear, of God; Of Men**: the second oppression launched by the new king was a plot of deception. But it was overcome by the believers who feared God more than man.

a. The king plotted a terrible evil, a horrendous persecution. He ordered the two supervising midwives to actually see that all baby boys were killed at birth while they were still on the delivery stool, to kill them without their mothers knowing it (vv.15-16). Obviously, the mothers were to be deceived into thinking that some complication had set in that killed the boys.

The two midwives were obviously supervisors over all the midwives. Remember, Israel's population was around two million at this time. Note that their names are given: *Shiphrah*, which means beauty; and *Puah*, which means splendor.

b. How was the deceptive plot—the persecution—overcome? By the fear of God (v.17). The midwives very simply feared God more than they feared the king. Consequently, they refused to obey the king. They let the boys live.

c. The king was no doubt furious. He called for the midwives and questioned their actions (vv.18-19).
⇒ Why had they not carried out his orders (v.18)?
⇒ They avoided a direct answer, but they gave what was obviously a true answer: Hebrew women were more vigorous in giving birth than Egyptian women. They gave birth before the midwives could reach them. Remember: the Hebrew women were slaves, which means they worked hard and were physically strong.

This answer was acceptable to Pharaoh, for he did not strike out against the midwives. They were neither imprisoned nor executed. Rather, they were free to leave and continue on with their lives and work as midwives.

d. Note that God blessed the midwives and continued to bless Israel (vv.20-21). He kept on multiplying the people (v.20), and He gave the midwives families of their own (v.21).

Thought 1. What a strong testimony and courage these women demonstrated! To fear God more than man, even in the face of persecution and the threat of imprisonment and death.

Who do we fear the most, men or God? When the world ridicules, mocks, accuses, threatens, imprisons, and attacks us, do we fear the world so much...
• that we give in and go along with the world?
• that we deny Christ?
• that we become discouraged and defeated and give up?

Who do we honestly fear the most: men or God? We must always remember the warning—the strong warning—of Scripture.

"**And fear not them which kill the body, but are not able to kill the soul: but rather fear him which is able to destroy both soul and body in hell**" (Mt.10:28).
"**Seeing it is a righteous thing with God to recompense tribulation to them that trouble you; and to you who are troubled rest with us, when the Lord Jesus shall be revealed from heaven with his mighty angels, in flaming fire taking vengeance on them that know not God, and that obey not the gospel of our Lord Jesus Christ: who shall be punished with everlasting destruction from the presence of the Lord, and from the glory of his power**" (2 Th.1:6-9).
"**For we know him that hath said, Vengeance belongeth unto me, I will recompense, saith the Lord. And again, The Lord shall judge his people. It is a fearful thing to fall into the hands of the living God**" (He.10:30-31).
"**And if ye call on the Father, who without respect of persons judgeth according to every man's work, pass the time of your sojourning here in fear**" (1 Pe.1:17).
"**I, even I, am he that comforteth you: who art thou, that thou shouldest be afraid of a man that shall die, and of the son of man which shall be made as grass**" (Is.51:12).

4 (1:22) **Oppression—Persecution**: the third oppression launched by the new king was a murderous law. But it was overcome by a courageous mother who believed God. Pharaoh was furious. He had launched every evil he could conceive. But no matter what he plotted, Pharaoh's evil plans were overcome. He was left with only one other option: the law of the land. Thus he passed a murderous law: all baby boys born to Israel were to be drowned. Who were the executioners to be? All the Egyptians. Pharaoh ordered *all his people* to drown all the baby boys they saw born to Israelite women, to drown them in the Nile River.

How was this murderous law overcome? By a courageous mother who believed God. This courageous mother was the mother of Moses himself. What she did is so important that it is necessary to take a whole study to cover her great faith. She and her faith are the subject of the next outline. (See outline and notes—Ex.2:1-10 for discussion.)

For now, the point to see is the evil and ferocious persecution against God's people launched by Pharaoh.
⇒ He had enslaved the people of Israel, creating the most horrible conditions possible for life and inflicting upon them the most vicious, cruel pain possible. He was determined to brutally crush the spirit of Israel, to stop their population growth, and to hold them forever as the slaves of Egypt.
⇒ He had also launched a murderous plot among the midwives to kill all baby boys at birth.

But note, God overcame the persecution. God touched the heart of a believer, and she refused to obey the murderous law of Pharaoh. She refused to kill her baby boy. She courageously stood against the murderous law, and most likely, she stood against the well-intentioned advice of friends who would have counseled her to obey the law lest she herself be arrested and perhaps executed. She boldly took a stand and she set out to save her newborn son, a son who was eventually to become the great deliverer of Israel (see outline and notes—Ex.2:1-10).

Thought 1. God met the needs of His people. He raised up the mother of Moses to bring forth the great deliverer of Israel. He always meets our needs, no matter how terrible the circumstance, trial, temptation, or suffering.

"**Surely he shall deliver thee from the snare of the fowler, and from the noisome pestilence**" (Ps.91:3).

"**Be not afraid of their faces: for I am with thee to deliver thee, saith the LORD**" (Je.1:8).

"**There hath no temptation taken you but such as is common to man: but God is faithful, who will not suffer you to be tempted above that ye are able; but will with the temptation also make a way to escape, that ye may be able to bear it**" (1 Co.10:13).

"**And the Lord shall deliver me from every evil work, and will preserve me unto his heavenly kingdom: to whom be glory for ever and ever. Amen**" (2 Ti.4:18).

"**Forasmuch then as the children are partakers of flesh and blood, he also himself likewise took part of the same; that through death he might destroy him that had the power of death, that is, the devil; and deliver them who through fear of death were all their lifetime subject to bondage**" (He.2:14-15).

"**The Lord knoweth how to deliver the godly out of temptations, and to reserve the unjust unto the day of judgment to be punished**" (2 Pe.2:9).

Thought 2. "Who deserves to live?" This is a question that each generation, each civilization, and each person must face. During Pharaoh's time, he made a choice about who should live and who should die, and he based his decision upon pure economic and political factors. Perceiving that male Hebrew babies were a direct threat to his rule, he made the devilish edict: kill all male babies of the Israelites. At first the charge was directed to the mid-wives, but eventually Pharaoh charged all his people to kill the Hebrew babies.

The point is this: the people chosen to die in that day and time were the male babies of the Israelites. The same spirit of murder poisons the culture of every generation. The value of human life within a culture becomes relative. The self-centered people of society place little or no value on…

- the unwanted and unplanned baby
- the handicapped child
- the sick who require expensive care
- the older person who can no longer contribute economically
- the people who proclaim the true teachings of Jesus Christ and the Holy Scriptures

The sanctity of life is under lethal attack. As the flood of public opinion swells, the believer must fight with all his might to stay above the evil tide. Will you stand up for life?

"**Only be thou strong and very courageous, that thou mayest observe to do according to all the law, which Moses my servant commanded thee: turn not from it *to* the right hand or *to* the left, that thou mayest prosper whithersoever thou goest**" (Jos.1:7).

"**So God created man in his own image, in the image of God created he him; male and female created he them**" (Ge.1:27).

"**This is the book of the generations of Adam. In the day that God created man, in the likeness of God made he him**" (Ge.5:1)

"**Did not he that made me in the womb make him? and did not one fashion us in the womb?**" (Jb.31:15).

"**Thy hands have made me and fashioned me: give me understanding, that I may learn thy commandments**" (Ps.119:73).

"**For thou hast possessed my reins: thou hast covered me in my mother's womb. I will praise thee; for I am fearfully and wonderfully made: marvellous are thy works; and that my soul knoweth right well. My substance was not hid from thee, when I was made in secret, and curiously wrought in the lowest parts of the earth. Thine eyes did see my substance, yet being unperfect; and in thy book all my members were written, which in continuance were fashioned, when as yet there was none of them. How precious also are thy thoughts unto me, O God! how great is the sum of them! If I should count them, they are more in number than the sand: when I awake, I am still with thee**" (Ps.139:13-18).

"**As thou knowest not what is the way of the spirit, nor how the bones do grow in the womb of her that is with child: even so thou knowest not the works of God who maketh all**" (Ec.11:5).

"**Then the word of the LORD came unto me, saying, Before I formed thee in the belly I knew thee; and before thou camest forth out of the womb I sanctified thee, and I ordained thee a prophet unto the nations**" (Je.1:4-5).

"**Now the birth of Jesus Christ was on this wise: When as his mother Mary was espoused to Joseph, before they came together, she was found with child of the Holy Ghost. Then Joseph her husband, being a just man, and not willing to make her a publick example, was minded to put her away privily. But while he thought on these things, behold, the angel of the Lord appeared unto him in a dream, saying, Joseph, thou son of David, fear not to take unto thee Mary thy wife: for that which is conceived in her is of the Holy Ghost**" (Mt.1:18-20).

"**For ye are bought with a price: therefore glorify God in your body, and in your spirit, which are God's**" (1 Co.6:20).

TYPES, SYMBOLS, AND PICTURES
(Exodus 1:8-22)

Historical Term	Type or Picture (Scriptural Basis for Each)	Life Application for Today's Believer	Biblical Application
Egypt (Ex.1:8)	*A picture of the world* "Now there arose up a new king over Egypt, which knew not Joseph" (Ex.1:8). "I am the LORD thy God, which brought thee out of the land of Egypt [the world], from the house of bondage" (De.5:6).	The world (Egypt) opposes and enslaves God's people, enslaves them to the bondages of sin and death.	*"Love not the world, neither the things that are in the world. If any man love the world, the love of the Father is not in him. For all that is in the world, the lust of the flesh, and the lust of the eyes, and the pride of life, is not of the Father, but is of the world" (1 Jn.2:15-16).* *"Jesus answered them, Verily, verily, I say unto you, Whosoever committeth sin is the servant of sin" (Jn.8:34).* *"Know ye not, that to whom ye yield yourselves servants to obey, his servants ye are to whom ye obey; whether of sin unto death, or of obedience unto righteousness? But God be thanked, that ye were the servants of sin, but ye have obeyed from the heart that form of doctrine which was delivered you" (Ro.6:16-17).* *"His own iniquities shall take the wicked himself, and he shall be holden with the cords of his sins" (Pr.5:22).* *(see Ro.7:14-15)*
Pharaoh (Ex.1:8)	*A picture of Satan* "And Pharaoh said, Who is the LORD, that I should obey his voice to let Israel go? I know not the LORD, neither will I let Israel [God's people] go" (Ex.5:2). "For thou [Satan] hast said in thine heart, I will ascend into heaven, I will exalt my throne above the stars of God: I will sit also upon the mount of the congregation, in the sides of the north: I will ascend above the heights of the clouds; I will be like the most High" (Is.14:13-14).	Satan seeks to keep men in bondage, eternal bondage	*"Now is the judgment of this world: now shall the prince of this world be cast out" (Jn.12:31).* *"In whom the god of this world [Satan] hath blinded the minds of them which believe not, lest the light of the glorious gospel of Christ, who is the image of God, should shine unto them" (2 Co.4:4).* *"Wherein in time past ye walked according to the course of this world, according to the prince of the power of the air, the spirit that now worketh in the children of disobedience" (Ep.2:2).* *"And that they may recover themselves out of the snare of the devil, who are taken captive by him at his will" (2 Ti.2:26).* *"Forasmuch then as the children are partakers of flesh and blood, he also himself likewise took part of the same; that through*

TYPES, SYMBOLS, AND PICTURES
(Exodus 1:8-22)

Historical Term	Type or Picture (Scriptural Basis for Each)	Life Application for Today's Believer	Biblical Application
Pharaoh (continued) (Ex.1:8)			*death he might destroy him that had the power of death, that is, the devil"* (He.2:14). *"He that committeth sin is of the devil; for the devil sinneth from the beginning. For this purpose the Son of God was manifested, that he might destroy the works of the devil"* (1 Jn.3:8). *(see Jb.1:12; Lu. 4:6; Ac.26:18; 1 Pe. 5:8)*
Taskmasters (Ex.1:11)	*A picture of evil men persecuting God's people* **"Therefore they [the Egyptians] did set over them taskmasters to afflict them with their burdens. And they built for Pharaoh treasure cities, Pithom and Raamses"** (Ex.1:11).	Evil men will always persecute God's people through... • ridicule • harassment • poking fun • scorn • abuse • murder	*"Blessed are ye, when men shall revile you, and persecute you, and shall say all manner of evil against you falsely, for my sake"* (Mt.5:11; see Mt.24:9; Ph.1:29; 1 Th.3:3; 1 Pt.4:12-13; 4:16; Ps.119:86). *"And ye shall be hated of all [men] for my name's sake: but he that endureth to the end shall be saved"* (Mt.10:22). *"And they stirred up the people, and the elders, and the scribes, and came upon him [Stephen], and caught him, and brought him to the council"* (Ac.6:12). *"Yea, and all that will live godly in Christ Jesus shall suffer persecution"* (2 Ti.3:12).

DIVISION II

MOSES AND GOD: GOD RAISES UP A LEADER TO DELIVER HIS PEOPLE (ISRAEL), 2:1–7:7

(2:1–7:7) **DIVISION OVERVIEW—Moses**: the story of Moses now begins. God raised up Moses…

- to deliver Israel from slavery (Chs.3–11)
- to lead Israel to the promised land, guiding them through the Red Sea and through the wilderness wanderings (Chs.12–18)
- to give the Law and the Ten Commandments to Israel and to the world at large; to establish Israel as a nation governed by law (Chs.19–24)
- to plan and draw the blueprint for the tabernacle, Israel's house of worship, and to establish the priesthood and religion of Israel (Chs.25–31)
- to proclaim the Word of God to Israel and to intercede for God's forgiveness when the people sinned and went astray (Chs.32–34)
- to construct the tabernacle and lead the people to obey God in all they did (Chs.35–40)

Never has one man done so much for so many as has Moses, except of course for Jesus Christ. Moses was chosen by God to single-handedly save Israel. God was to use Israel to give to the world the two greatest gifts possible: both the Word of God and the Savior, the Lord Jesus Christ. Moses believed God, and he knew God. He had a close, personal relationship with God: he walked and talked with God. His fellowship with God was probably as close as a man can experience. He obviously had what we might call *an unbroken communion and fellowship with God*, the very thing for which we all should long. The magnitude of his life and walk with God can be seen in his farewell speeches to his dear people, the people of Israel. These are recorded for us in the great book of *Deuteronomy*. But for now, our focus is to be upon the early years of Moses. The great subject of this section of Scripture is: "MOSES AND GOD: GOD RAISES UP A LEADER TO DELIVER HIS PEOPLE (ISRAEL)," 2:1–7:7

MOSES AND GOD: GOD RAISES UP A LEADER TO DELIVER HIS PEOPLE (ISRAEL), 2:1–7:7

A. The Birth of Moses: The Picture of a Believing, Courageous Mother, 2:1-10

B. The First Significant Events of Moses' Life: Experiences That Change a Person's Life, 2:11-25

C. The Call of Moses: A Study of God's Call to Service, 3:1-10

D. The Excuses of Moses: A Reluctant Prophet—Arguments Against Serving God, 3:11–4:17

E. The Surrender of Moses to God's Call: The Fruit of Obedience, 4:18-31

F. The First Confrontation of Moses with Pharaoh: Opposing God's Will for His People, the Right of Man to Live and Worship God in Freedom, 5:1-23

G. The Great Encouragement and Message Given to Moses: Deliverance and Freedom, 6:1–7:7

	CHAPTER 2 **II. MOSES & GOD: GOD RAISES UP A LEADER TO DELIVER HIS PEOPLE (ISRAEL), 2:1–7:7** **A. The Birth of Moses: The Picture of a Believing, Courageous Mother, 2:1-10**	self at the river; and her maidens walked along by the river's side; and when she saw the ark among the flags, she sent her maid to fetch it.	a. Pharaoh's daughter discovered the ark-like basket
1. She was a Hebrew, of Levi's tribe: A slave of the lowest rank & position imaginable **2. She was a courageous, righteous woman** a. She bore a son b. She did the righteous thing: Hid him for three months **3. She had great wisdom: She planned ahead & trusted God completely** a. She made a watertight, ark-like basket[DS1] b. She put Moses in the basket & hid him among the reeds of the Nile River: Trusting God to save him c. She had Moses watched over by his older sister **4. She witnessed the sovereign, guiding hand of God**	**A**nd there went a man of the house of Levi, and took to wife a daughter of Levi. 2 And the woman conceived, and bare a son: and when she saw him that he was a goodly child, she hid him three months. 3 And when she could not longer hide him, she took for him an ark of bulrushes, and daubed it with slime and with pitch, and put the child therein; and she laid it in the flags by the river's brink. 4 And his sister stood afar off, to wit what would be done to him. 5 And the daughter of Pharaoh came down to wash her-	6 And when she had opened it, she saw the child: and, behold, the babe wept. And she had compassion on him, and said, This is one of the Hebrews' children. 7 Then said his sister to Pharaoh's daughter, Shall I go and call to thee a nurse of the Hebrew women, that she may nurse the child for thee? 8 And Pharaoh's daughter said to her, Go. And the maid went and called the child's mother. 9 And Pharaoh's daughter said unto her, Take this child away, and nurse it for me, and I will give thee thy wages. And the woman took the child, and nursed it. 10 And the child grew, and she brought him unto Pharaoh's daughter, and he became her son. And she called his name Moses: and she said, Because I drew him out of the water.	b. She opened the basket & was moved with compassion for the crying baby c. Moses' sister demonstrated courage: Walked up & suggested that Pharaoh's daughter have a Hebrew woman nurse the child d. Pharaoh's daughter agreed (under God's sovereign, guiding hand) **5. She had her faith rewarded** a. She was employed to nurse the child b. She saw God work all things out for good: Her son Moses was not only saved, but adopted by the daughter of Pharaoh himself (under God's sovereign, guiding hand)

DIVISION II

MOSES AND GOD: GOD RAISES UP A LEADER TO DELIVER HIS PEOPLE (ISRAEL), 2:1–7:7

A. The Birth of Moses: The Picture of a Believing, Courageous Mother, 2:1-10

(2:1-10) **Introduction—Mothers, Godly**: this passage covers the birth of Moses, but it focuses upon the mother of Moses. It tells us how she saved Moses from being killed by the king, how she trusted God to take care of her baby boy. Moses' mother was a godly mother, a young woman who trusted God with all her heart. When we survey the pages of human history, godly mothers are few and far between. Mothers who truly believe God—who have the courage to stand up for God and His demand for righteousness and purity—are hard to find upon the face of this earth. Nevertheless, godly mothers do exist. Here and there a few godly mothers can be found. There are some mothers within every generation who have given all they are to God, who are totally committed to follow after the righteousness and purity demanded by God.

This is the subject of the present Scripture: *The Birth of Moses: The Picture of a Believing, Courageous Mother*, 2:1-10.

1. She was a Hebrew, of Levi's tribe: a slave of the lowest social rank and position imaginable (v.1).
2. She was a courageous, righteous woman (v.2).
3. She was a woman of great wisdom: she planned ahead and trusted God completely (vv.3-4).
4. She witnessed the sovereign, guiding hand of God (vv.5-8).
5. She had her faith rewarded (vv.9-10).

1 (2:1) **Mothers**: Moses' mother was a Hebrew, of Levi's tribe, a slave of the lowest social rank and position imaginable. Remember, Israel had probably been enslaved for a century or more. The parents of Moses were therefore slaves when they married. This meant that both mother and father...

- worked as slave-laborers, as beasts of burden
- were abused and yelled at, probably cursed and beaten at the whim of slave-masters
- were poor, even poverty-stricken
- lived in a small, poorly furnished house or shanty
- had few, if any, possessions to call their own
- had no opportunity to do what they wanted
- could not better themselves

Moses' mother had no social standing within society, no decent clothes, no possessions, no rank, no position. She was a slave. She worked in the brickyards or in the fields or as the servant of some wealthy Egyptian. Yet God was to use this humble mother, this enslaved woman, beyond imagination. She was to give birth to one of the greatest men who has ever lived.

Thought 1. Moses' mother is a great example to us. No matter how lowly or far down we are, God will use us. God will use us no matter how lowly our...

- past
- present
- social standing
- position

- education
- rank
- achievement
- finances

- abilities
- heritage
- possessions
- appearance

If we will only do what Moses' mother did—believe God and follow after God—God will accept us and use us to bless the lives of many throughout the world. God always uses the lowly who truly trust and follow after Him, uses them to confound and humble those who exalt themselves.

"For ye see your calling, brethren, how that not many wise men after the flesh, not many mighty, not many noble, are called: but God hath chosen the foolish things of the world to confound the wise; and God hath chosen the weak things of the world to confound the things which are mighty; and base things of the world, and things which are despised, hath God chosen, yea, and things which are not, to bring to nought things that are: that no flesh should glory in his presence" (1 Co.1:26-29).

"Out of the mouth of babes and sucklings hast thou ordained strength because of thine enemies, that thou mightest still the enemy and the avenger" (Ps.8:2).

"Then drew near unto him all the publicans and sinners for to hear him. And the Pharisees and scribes murmured, saying, This man receiveth sinners, and eateth with them. And he spake this parable unto them, saying, What man of you, having an hundred sheep, if he lose one of them, doth not leave the ninety and nine in the wilderness, and go after that which is lost, until he find it? And when he hath found [it], he layeth [it] on his shoulders, rejoicing. And when he cometh home, he calleth together [his] friends and neighbours, saying unto them, Rejoice with me; for I have found my sheep which was lost. I say unto you, that likewise joy shall be in heaven over one sinner that repenteth, more than over ninety and nine just persons, which need no repentance" (Lu.15:1-7).

2 (2:2) **Mothers—Moses, Birth**: Moses' mother was a courageous, righteous woman. At some point, she became pregnant and bore Moses. This was her third child.

⇒ *Miriam*, Moses' only sister, was obviously a young lady when Moses was born, probably somewhere around thirteen to sixteen years old (Ex.2:4-8; 15:20; Nu.26:59).

⇒ *Aaron*, Moses' only brother, was three years older than Moses (Ex.7:7).

Note that the king's law to drown all newborn boys was not in effect at Aaron's birth. As stated, he was a three-year old boy, alive and well, when Moses was born. The law was obviously passed right before the birth of Moses.

Picture for a moment the uneasiness of Moses' parents when his mother discovered that she was pregnant. Just imagine their concern, anxiety, fear, uncertainty—wondering what would happen if the child was a boy. What would they do? What could they do? Month after month—for nine long months—they would have prayed and wondered, trying their best to figure out what they would do if the child was a boy.

Then, finally, the day came, and their worst fears became a reality: a baby boy, Moses, was born. Note what his mother did: she did the courageous, righteous thing. She hid the child for three months. Why? What would make her risk her own life to save her child's life? The same thing that has driven many mothers to save their child's life when the child was threatened:

⇒ love
⇒ duty
⇒ responsibility

⇒ righteousness
⇒ justice
⇒ the sanctity of life

But note the phrase "goodly child" (A.V.) or "fine child" (NIV). This can refer to Moses' physical appearance, meaning that he was a beautiful child (see Ge.39:6). But it can also mean "fair in the sight of God." In fact, the Greek actually says this in Acts 7:20: "[Moses] was fair in the sight of God" (en asteios to theo). This would seem to be the true meaning of the statement in Exodus.

The point is this: Moses' mother was a courageous, righteous woman. When she looked at Moses, God gave her a sense that her child was special. He was a gift, a very special gift from God. His life was important to God; therefore, she had to be courageous and do the righteous thing: she had to save her child's life. God's purpose for the child was far more important than even her love. Thus, she wanted to save the child not only because she loved him, but also because he was a special gift from God. Therefore, she hid the child for three months. Day after day and week after week—three long months—she hid the child from the authorities and neighbors, from everyone who might be a threat, lest someone report the child's presence. She hid the child at the risk of her own life. Moses' mother was a godly woman, a courageous and righteous woman.

Thought 1. What are we to do when the law of the state stands opposed to the law of God? Moses' mother is a strong example for us: quietly and humbly, just as she did, we are to be courageous and righteous: we are to obey God. We are to do the courageous and righteous thing—always.

"O that there were such an heart in them, that they would fear me, and keep all my commandments always, that it might be well with them, and with their children for ever!" (De.5:29).

"Not every one that saith unto me, Lord, Lord, shall enter into the kingdom of heaven; but he that doeth the will of my Father which is in heaven" (Mt.7:21).

"Then Peter and the other apostles answered and said, We ought to obey God rather than men" (Ac.5:29).

"Blessed are they that do his commandments, that they may have right to the tree of life, and may enter in through the gates into the city" (Re.22:14).

Thought 2. How many parents see their children as Moses' mother did? How many see them as a gift from God, as very special and important to God? What a different world this would be if parents followed the example of Moses' mother:

⇒ If parents loved their children, truly loved them.
⇒ If parents saw their children as *gifts* from God, as very special and important to God.
⇒ If parents protected their children, protected them even at the risk of their own lives.
⇒ If parents committed their children to God, committed their welfare and care into the hands of God.
⇒ If parents led their children to trust God, to trust His promises.
⇒ If parents taught their children the Word of God and prayed with them (see note—Ex.2:9-10 for more discussion).

Note what Scripture declares about children. Two significant declarations are made.
(1) Children are the gift of God.

"And he lifted up his eyes, and saw the women and the children; and said, Who are those with thee? And he said, The children which God hath graciously given thy servant" (Ge.33:5).

"And Joseph said unto his father, They are my sons, whom God hath given me in this place. And he said, Bring them, I pray thee, unto me, and I will bless them" (Ge.48:9).

"And I took your father Abraham from the other side of the flood, and led him throughout all the land of Canaan, and multiplied his seed, and gave him Isaac" (Jos.24:3).

"He maketh the barren woman to keep house, and to be a joyful mother of children. Praise ye the LORD" (Ps.113:9).

"Lo, children are an heritage of the LORD: and the fruit of the womb is his reward" (Ps.127:3).

"Behold, I and the children whom the LORD hath given me are for signs and for wonders in Israel from the LORD of hosts, which dwelleth in mount Zion" (Is.8:18).

(2) Children must be taught the Word of God and the promises of God. They must be taught to follow after God.

"Only take heed to thyself, and keep thy soul diligently, lest thou forget the things which thine eyes have seen, and lest they depart from thy heart all the days of thy life: but teach them thy sons, and thy sons' sons" (De.4:9).

"And thou shalt teach them [God's Words] diligently unto thy children, and shalt talk of them when thou sittest in thine house, and when thou walkest by the way, and when thou liest down, and when thou risest up" (De.6:7).

"Train up a child in the way he should go: and when he is old, he will not depart from it" (Pr.22:6).

"Whom shall he teach knowledge? and whom shall he make to understand doctrine? them that are weaned from the milk, and drawn from the breasts" (Is.28:9).

"And, ye fathers, provoke not your children to wrath: but bring them up in the nurture and admonition of the Lord" (Ep.6:4).

3 (2:3-4) **Mothers—Moses—Trust**: Moses' mother was a woman of great wisdom, a woman who planned ahead and trusted God completely. The day came when the baby Moses could no longer be hidden in the house. Why? Scripture does not say. But there were bound to be periodic patrols down the streets to keep the slaves under control. This always happens when any people are being kept in subjection. There also must have been periodic house-to-house searches, just to make sure no newborn children were being hidden.

Babies cry; thus there was great danger that Moses' crying might be heard by a patrolling guard or that he might be discovered by some guard searching their family's house. There was even the possibility that some neighbor, hoping to receive a reward or to be favored by the Egyptians, could snitch on the child.

The day came when Moses could no longer be hidden. His mother had to do something. What could she do to save her child? She had to be wise—work out the wisest plan she could—and she had to trust God, completely trust Him to use her plan and save her child. This she did.

⇒ She made a watertight ark-like basket (v.3).
⇒ She put Moses in the basket and placed the basket among the reeds of the Nile River. No doubt, she knew right where Pharaoh's daughter (and probably other Egyptian officials) bathed and swam. She knew that Moses could be saved from the king's death threat only if some Egyptian official could find him, have compassion, and keep the child as his or her own. Thus when she placed the ark-like basket in the Nile River, she was trusting God to cause some Egyptian authority to find the baby and save him (v.3).
⇒ She then had the oldest child, Miriam, stand some distance away, keeping watch over the child (v.4).

The point to see is the great wisdom and faith of Moses' mother. She did all she could and she trusted God, trusted Him to use her efforts and bless them. She laid the best plans she could and carried them out. And in the midst of her plans, she trusted God to work everything out: to save her child. The faith of Moses' mother was so great that she is listed in *The Great Hall of Faith* in Hebrews:

> **"By faith Moses, when he was born, was hid three months of his parents, because they saw he was a proper child; and they were not afraid of the king's commandment" (He.11:23).**

Thought 1. Great wisdom and great faith are two qualities needed by us all. Situations beyond our control will someday arise, situations such as...

- oppression
- loss
- sickness
- accident
- death
- bankruptcy
- hunger and thirst
- loneliness
- emptiness
- failure
- temptation
- sin

(1) When situations beyond our control strike us, we need to lay the wisest plans we can and carry them on.

> **"And we know that all things work together for good to them that love God, to them who are the called according to his purpose" (Ro.8:28).**
> **"Work out your own salvation [deliverance] with fear and trembling" (Ph.2:12).**
> **"If any of you lack wisdom, let him ask of God, that giveth to all men liberally, and upbraideth not [does not find fault]; and it shall be given him" (Js.1:5).**

(2) When situations beyond our control strike us, we need to trust God, trust Him completely, trust Him to work the situation out for us.

> **"The LORD redeemeth the soul of his servants: and none of them that trust in him shall be desolate" (Ps.34:22).**
> **"Trust in the LORD, and do good; so shalt thou dwell in the land, and verily thou shalt be fed" (Ps.37:3).**
> **"Commit thy way unto the LORD; trust also in him; and he shall bring it to pass" (Ps.37:5).**
> **"It is better to trust in the LORD than to put confidence in man" (Ps.118:8).**
> **"They that trust in the LORD shall be as mount Zion, which cannot be removed, but abideth for ever" (Ps.125:1).**
> **"Trust in the LORD with all thine heart; and lean not unto thine own understanding. In all thy ways acknowledge him, and he shall direct thy paths" (Pr.3:5-6).**
> **"Thou wilt keep him in perfect peace, whose mind is stayed on thee: because he trusteth in thee. Trust ye in the LORD for ever: for in the LORD JEHOVAH is everlasting strength" (Is.26:3-4).**

Thought 2. How many questions and what kinds of questions flooded the tender heart of Moses' mother? One can only imagine the things that could have entered her mind. Questions like:

⇒ "God, why did our precious baby have to be a boy?"
⇒ "Why did our family have to live in such a dangerous place like Egypt?"
⇒ "How did we wind up with such an evil ruler like Pharaoh?"
⇒ "How long can we keep hiding our baby before someone finds out and reports us?"
⇒ "What can I do to save my baby?"

In the safety of the heart, the believer has a sanctuary where the hard questions of life can be asked of God. It is through prayer...

- that God answers our most perplexing questions
- that God meets our deepest needs
- that God shows us what to do

Prayer is where faith grows, where life's impossibilities become God's solutions.

> **"How long wilt thou forget me, O Lord? for ever? how long wilt thou hide thy face from me? How long shall I take counsel in my soul, having sorrow in my heart daily? how long shall mine enemy be exalted over me?" (Ps.13:1-2).**
> **"He shall call upon me, and I will answer him: I will be with him in trouble; I will deliver him, and honour him" (Ps.91:15).**
> **"And it shall come to pass, that before they call, I will answer; and while they are yet speaking, I will hear" (Is.65:24).**
> **"And ye shall seek me, and find me, when ye shall search for me with all your heart" (Je.29:13).**
> **"O Lord, how long shall I cry, and thou wilt not hear! even cry out unto thee of violence, and thou wilt not save! Why dost thou show me iniquity, and cause me to behold grievance? for spoiling and violence are before me: and there are that raise up strife and contention" (Hab.1:2-3).**
> **"Although the fig tree shall not blossom, neither shall fruit be in the vines; the labour of the olive shall fail, and the fields shall yield no meat; the flock shall be cut off from the fold, and there shall be no herd in the stalls: Yet I will rejoice in the Lord, I will joy in the God of my salvation.**

The LORD God is my strength, and he will make my feet like hinds' *feet*, and he will make me to walk upon mine high places" (Hab.3:17-19).

"Ask, and it shall be given you; seek, and ye shall find; knock, and it shall be opened unto you" (Mt.7:7).

"If ye abide in me, and my words abide in you, ye shall ask what ye will, and it shall be done unto you" (Jn.15:7).

"Hitherto have ye asked nothing in my name: ask, and ye shall receive, that your joy may be full" (Jn.16:24).

DEEPER STUDY # 1

(2:3) **Ark** (Tebah): the Hebrew word used for the small ark-like basket is the same word used for Noah's ark. In fact, these are the only two times that the word is used in the Bible. This fact suggests the following picture or type:

⇒ The ark was a place of salvation—safety and security—for Moses, just as it was for Noah. (See outline and note—Ge.7:13-16 for more discussion.)

⇒ Christ is the believer's ark, the believer's salvation from judgment, the believer's safety and security.

"And, behold, I am with thee, and will keep thee in all places whither thou goest, and will bring thee again into this land; for I will not leave thee, until I have done that which I have spoken to thee of" (Ge.28:15).

"But the salvation of the righteous is of the LORD: he is their strength in the time of trouble" (Ps.37:39).

"For the Son of man is come to seek and to save that which was lost" (Lu.19:10).

"For God so loved the world, that he gave his only begotten Son, that whosoever believeth in him should not perish, but have everlasting life. For God sent not his Son into the world to condemn the world; but that the world through him might be saved" (Jn.3:16-17).

"Being confident of this very thing, that he which hath begun a good work in you will perform it until the day of Jesus Christ" (Ph.1:6).

"For there is one God, and one mediator between God and men, the man Christ Jesus" (1 Ti.2:5).

"I know whom I have believed, and am persuaded that he is able to keep that which I have committed unto him against that day" (2 Ti.1:12).

"Wherefore he is able also to save them to the uttermost that come unto God by him, seeing he ever liveth to make intercession for them" (He.7:25).

"Who are kept by the power of God through faith unto salvation ready to be revealed in the last time" (1 Pe.1:5).

"Now unto him that is able to keep you from falling, and to present you faultless before the presence of his glory with exceeding joy, To the only wise God our Saviour, be glory and majesty, dominion and power, both now and ever. Amen" (Jude 24-25).

---

4 (2:5-8) **Mothers—Moses—God, Sovereignty of**: Moses' mother was a woman who witnessed the sovereign, guiding hand of God. The plan of Moses' mother worked.

⇒ Pharaoh's daughter discovered the ark-like basket (v.5). She came down to the river and began to bathe. At some point, she noticed the basket floating among the reeds and asked one of her servants to wade in and get it.

⇒ When Pharaoh's daughter opened the basket, the baby immediately began to cry. This touched her heart and she was moved with compassion for the crying child (v.6). Note: she knew that the child was a Hebrew baby.

⇒ At that very moment, Moses' sister demonstrated great courage: she walked up and suggested that Pharaoh's daughter have a Hebrew woman nurse the child for her (v.7). Would Pharaoh's daughter have kept Moses if Miriam had not made the suggestion to the princess? We cannot know, not for sure, but the compassion she felt combined with Miriam's suggestion stirred her to act.

⇒ Pharaoh's daughter agreed with the suggestion: she instructed Miriam to go and find a Hebrew woman to nurse the baby boy for her (v.8). Miriam went and brought her own mother (Moses' mother) to the princess.

The point to see is God's sovereignty—His guiding hand—through this entire event. God's Spirit was hovering all around the small basket and the little baby lying in it. Note how everything worked out for good:

⇒ The reeds held the basket close to shore and kept it from floating downstream with the current.

⇒ No crocodile or passing dogs came along to threaten the child.

⇒ Pharaoh's daughter herself came to bathe, not some other high-ranking official. The very person who was most likely to feel compassion for a small baby came along, the daughter of Pharaoh himself.

⇒ Pharaoh's daughter glanced in the right direction to see the basket.

⇒ The baby began to cry at just the right moment, right when Pharaoh's daughter lifted the lid to the basket.

⇒ The arousal of *deep compassion*—a compassion deep enough to later convince her father, the king, to let her keep the child—was stirred at the very moment needed.

⇒ Courage was stirred within Moses' sister, who was just a young girl, courage enough to walk up to Pharaoh's daughter and suggest that she keep the baby as her own child.

Moses' mother had prayed and trusted God to save her child and to use him in God's service. And God was doing just that. God was looking after and taking care of the baby. Moses' mother was witnessing the sovereign, guiding hand of

God. She was experiencing just how God works all things out for good to those who truly love and follow after Him (Ro.8:28). God is sovereign; God possesses all power. He can do anything.

"And we know that all things work together for good to them that love God, to them who are the called according to his purpose" (Ro.8:28).
"With men this is impossible; but with God all things are possible" (Ro.16:27).
"Jesus said unto him, If thou canst believe, all things [are] possible to him that believeth" (Mk.9:23).
"Therefore I say unto you, Whatsoever things ye desire, when ye pray, believe that ye receive [them], and ye shall have [them]" (Mk.11:24).
"And all things, whatsoever ye shall ask in prayer, believing, ye shall receive" (Mt.21:22).
"For with God nothing shall be impossible" (Lu.1:37).
"I know that thou canst do every thing, and that no thought can be withholden from thee" (Jb.42:2).
"God hath spoken once; twice have I heard this; that power belongeth unto God" (Ps.62:11).
"But our God is in the heavens: he hath done whatsoever he hath pleased" (Ps.115:3).
"Yea, before the day was I am he; and there is none that can deliver out of my hand: I will work, and who shall let [hinder] it?" (Is.43:13).

5 (2:9-10) **Faith—Rewards**: Moses' mother had her faith rewarded. The most that she could have hoped for now happened.

a. She was employed to nurse Moses (v.9). When Miriam brought her mother to Pharaoh's daughter, the princess hired her to look after Moses. Note that Moses' mother was even paid wages to care for her child. It was during the early years of Moses' life, sitting at the knee of his mother and father, that he was most likely taught to trust God and to believe the great promises of God to Israel. No doubt, having been his nurse, she was allowed to maintain a relationship with him throughout his years in the palace of Pharaoh. She also would have continued to instruct Moses when they were visiting one another. There is a possibility that she was kept in the palace serving Pharaoh's daughter throughout Moses' years in Egypt.

b. Moses' mother saw God work all things out for good: her son was not only saved, but he was adopted by the daughter of Pharaoh himself (under God's sovereign, guiding hand). When Moses reached a certain age, his mother took him to the princess, and Moses became the son of Pharaoh's daughter.

Note that it was Pharaoh's daughter who named the child *Moses*. The name *Moses* (Moseh) means "I drew him out of the water." Note how God took the evil plan of Pharaoh, twisted it, and worked it out for good. God caused Pharaoh to give food, shelter, and clothing to the very child who was to take the lead in freeing the Israelite slaves, the very thing Pharaoh was trying to prevent.

Thought 1. Moses' mother had her faith rewarded. Our faith will also be rewarded if we will only trust God. God will twist events and work all things out for our good if we will just love Him and follow after Him.

"And we know that all things work together for good to them that love God, to them who are the called according to his purpose" (Ro.8:28).
"Forasmuch then as the children are partakers of flesh and blood, he also himself likewise took part of the same; that through death he might destroy him that had the power of death, that is, the devil; and deliver them who through fear of death were all their lifetime subject to bondage" (He.2:14-15).
"And he said, The LORD is my rock, and my fortress, and my deliverer" (2 S.22:2).
"The LORD is my strength and my shield; my heart trusted in him, and I am helped: therefore my heart greatly rejoiceth; and with my song will I praise him" (Ps.28:7).
"But I am poor and needy; yet the Lord thinketh upon me: thou art my help and my deliverer; make no tarrying, O my God" (Ps.40:17).
"Surely he shall deliver thee from the snare of the fowler, and from the noisome pestilence" (Ps.91:3).
"Fear thou not; for I am with thee: be not dismayed; for I am thy God: I will strengthen thee; yea, I will help thee; yea, I will uphold thee with the right hand of my righteousness" (Is.41:10).
"Be not afraid of their faces: for I am with thee to deliver thee, saith the LORD" (Je.1:8).
"There hath no temptation taken you but such as is common to man: but God is faithful, who will not suffer you to be tempted above that ye are able; but will with the temptation also make a way to escape, that ye may be able to bear it" (1 Co.10:13).
"And the Lord shall deliver me from every evil work, and will preserve me unto his heavenly kingdom: to whom be glory for ever and ever. Amen" (2 Ti.4:18).
"But without faith it is impossible to please him: for he that cometh to God must believe that he is, and that he is a rewarder of them that diligently seek him" (He.11:6).
"The Lord knoweth how to deliver the godly out of temptations, and to reserve the unjust unto the day of judgment to be punished" (2 Pe.2:9).

TYPES, SYMBOLS, AND PICTURES
(Exodus 2:1-10)

Historical Term	Type or Picture (Scriptural Basis for Each)	Life Application for Today's Believer	Biblical Application
Moses' Basket [ark] (Ex.2:3)	*Salvation: Safety & security. The ark saved baby Moses from death.* **"And when she could no longer hide him, she took for him an ark of bulrushes, and daubed it with slime and with pitch, and put the child therein; and she laid** *it* **in the flags by the river's brink" (Ex.2:3).** **"And the flood was forty days upon the earth; and the waters increased, and bare up the ark, and it was lift up above the earth" (Ge.7:17).** **"And every living substance was destroyed which was upon the face of the ground, both man, and cattle, and the creeping things, and the fowl of the heaven; and they were destroyed from the earth: and Noah only remained** *alive,* **and they that** *were* **with him in the ark" (Ge.7:23).**	Jesus Christ is our ark: • our salvation from judgment • our safety and security from the attacks of the world, its evil and its persecutors	*"For God so loved the world, that he gave his only begotten Son, that whosoever believeth in him should not perish, but have everlasting life" (Jn.3:16).* *"He that believeth on him is not condemned: but he that believeth not is condemned already, because he hath not believed in the name of the only begotten Son of God" (Jn.3:18; see Jn.5:24).* *"I am the door: by me if any man enter in, he shall be saved, and shall go in and out, and find pasture" (Jn.10:9).* *"I pray not that thou shouldest take them out of the world, but that thou shouldest keep them from the evil" (Jn.17:15)* (see Ro.6:23; 10:13)

B. The First Significant Events of Moses' Life: Experiences That Change a Person's Life, 2:11-25

1. **Moses' visit to his own people: The stirring of compassion & purpose, a spirit that identified with his people**
2. **Moses' murder of an Egyptian: The reaction of a carnal, fleshly spirit**
   a. He saw an Egyptian beating a Hebrew brother
   b. He reacted in the flesh: Killed the Egyptian & hid him in the sand
3. **Moses' attempt to settle a dispute between two Hebrew brothers: The discovery that others knew about his sin**
   a. He tried to make peace, to reconcile them
   b. He reaped the results of a carnal, fleshly spirit: A ruined testimony; his help was rejected
   c. He experienced fear—tormenting fear
   d. He experienced separation, alienation: Had to flee for his life
4. **Moses' flight to Midian: A time for preparation & growth**
   a. He grew by living in Midian, learning hardship & poverty
   b. He grew by standing up for justice & for the oppressed
      1) He fled to Midian & sat down by a well (v.15)
      2) Seven daughters of a local priest came to water their

11 And it came to pass in those days, when Moses was grown, that he went out unto his brethren, and looked on their burdens: and he spied an Egyptian smiting an Hebrew, one of his brethren.
12 And he looked this way and that way, and when he saw that there was no man, he slew the Egyptian, and hid him in the sand.
13 And when he went out the second day, behold, two men of the Hebrews strove together: and he said to him that did the wrong, Wherefore smitest thou thy fellow?
14 And he said, Who made thee a prince and a judge over us? intendest thou to kill me, as thou killedst the Egyptian? And Moses feared, and said, Surely this thing is known.
15 Now when Pharaoh heard this thing, he sought to slay Moses. But Moses fled from the face of Pharaoh, and dwelt in the land of Midian: and he sat down by a well.
16 Now the priest of Midian had seven daughters: and they came and drew water, and filled the troughs to water their father's flock.
17 And the shepherds came

and drove them away: but Moses stood up and helped them, and watered their flock.
18 And when they came to Reuel their father, he said, How is it that ye are come so soon to day?
19 And they said, An Egyptian delivered us out of the hand of the shepherds, and also drew water enough for us, and watered the flock.
20 And he said unto his daughters, And where is he? why is it that ye have left the man? call him, that he may eat bread.
21 And Moses was content to dwell with the man: and he gave Moses Zipporah his daughter.
22 And she bare him a son, and he called his name Gershom: for he said, I have been a stranger in a strange land.
23 And it came to pass in process of time, that the king of Egypt died: and the children of Israel sighed by reason of the bondage, and they cried, and their cry came up unto God by reason of the bondage.
24 And God heard their groaning, and God remembered his covenant with Abraham, with Isaac, and with Jacob.
25 And God looked upon the children of Israel, and God had respect unto them.

   father's flocks (v.16)
   3) Some shepherds came up & drove the daughters away
   4) Moses stood up & rescued the oppressed ladies
   5) The girls returned to their father, Reuel, & he asked why they had returned so early
   6) They shared how the Egyptian (Moses) had rescued them from the shepherds & had even watered their flocks for them
   7) Their father rebuked them for leaving the Egyptian (their deliverer) at the well & sent them to invite him to eat
   c. He grew by committing himself to serve & to work for others
   d. He grew by making a commitment to marriage
   e. He grew by declaring his faith in the promised land: Named his son Gershom, which means he was a stranger, away from Israel & the promised land
5. **Moses' people—Israel—& their terrible suffering: Shows how God prepared Israel for deliverance**
   a. The king died
   b. The Israelites suffered & groaned: Egypt no longer meant comfort & plenty for them
   c. The response of God
      1) God heard their cry
      2) God remembered His covenant[DS1]
      3) God looked upon the people (had compassion for them)
      4) God knew, took notice, was concerned

DIVISION II

MOSES AND GOD: GOD RAISES UP A LEADER TO DELIVER HIS PEOPLE (ISRAEL), 2:1-7:7

B. The First Significant Events of Moses' Life: Experiences That Change a Person's Life, 2:11-25

(2:11-25) **Introduction—Moses**: nothing is known about Moses from birth to age forty. In fact, there is only one verse that even mentions those years:

> **"And when he was full forty years old, it came into his heart to visit his brethren the children of Israel" (Ac.7:23).**

Think about this fact for a moment: not a single event was recorded about the first forty years of Moses' life. Apparently, there was nothing in those forty years that God wanted us to know about.

This is significant: it tells us that the events now recorded in this passage are of critical importance. They are the very first events of Moses' adult life that God wanted us to know about. Why? Because they are the experiences that changed Moses' life. This is the subject of this important passage of Scripture: *The First Significant Events of Moses' Life: Experiences That Change a Person's Life,* 2:11-25.

1. Moses' visit to his own people: the stirring of compassion and purpose, a spirit that identified with his people (v.11).
2. Moses' murder of an Egyptian: the reaction of a carnal, fleshly spirit (vv.11-12).
3. Moses' attempt to settle a dispute between two Hebrew brothers: the discovery that others knew about his sin (vv.13-15).
4. Moses' flight to Midian: a time for preparation and growth (vv.15-22).
5. Moses' people—Israel—and their terrible suffering: shows how God prepared Israel for deliverance (vv.23-25).

1 (2:11) **Moses—Compassion—Sympathy—Identifying With Others**: there was the first experience, Moses' visit to his own people. This visit changed Moses' life: it stirred within Moses a spirit of purpose, mission, and compassion, a spirit that felt for and identified with his people.

Note when Moses went out to visit his people: when he had grown up (v.11). Acts says that he was forty years old (Ac.7:23). Does this mean that Moses had never before gone out to visit Israel? That since he had been carried to the palace, he had never seen his brother Aaron nor his sister Miriam nor his mother who had nursed and cared for him as a baby? That he had gone thirty some years and never visited them? Not likely, although Scripture does not specifically say. But when Pharaoh's daughter found Moses as a baby, she knew that Moses was a Hebrew child, and she had a Hebrew woman nurse the baby. That woman, unknown to the princess, was Moses' very own mother. Thus, Moses knew that he was a Hebrew from the very first. During the years of his early nursing and training at the knee of his mother, she no doubt taught Moses his great heritage and the great promises of God to Israel. Most likely, having been his childhood nurse, she was allowed to maintain a relationship with Moses throughout his life in the court of Pharaoh. She was perhaps even kept in the palace serving Pharaoh's daughter through the remaining years of her life.

But we know nothing about Moses' life during the forty years of his life in Pharaoh's court—nothing until now, until this visit to his people at age forty. As stated, this was the first event that Moses recorded, the first event that God wanted us to know about. Why? There could be only one reason: this event reveals a great change in the heart and life of Moses, reveals a great change that was taking place in his heart toward his people, Israel. Four significant facts show us this.

a. Moses went out to visit Israel when he had *grown up*. The word *grown* seems to mean more than just years, more than just chronological age. By *grown* is meant maturity, full development. Moses now had a heart that was mature and fully developed, that had a sense of purpose and mission in life.

b. The words "*went out*" are emphatic. This suggests that Moses was going out to visit his people with some sense of mission and purpose, with a heart that had been stirred and was set on helping his people.

c. When Moses finally stood before his people, he looked, watched, and studied their plight. The word "*looked*" or "*watched*" (wayyak) means to look at with sympathy, with deep feelings and emotions, to identify with. The idea seems to be that Moses had gone there to investigate the sufferings of his people, that he stood there deliberately looking the situation over. He watched them toil at their hard labor, and he saw the heavy burdens that were weighing them down. The impact was dynamic: he was moved, touched with the deepest emotions and feelings possible. His heart reached out in compassion for them. Moses felt for his people and identified with them.

d. The New Testament tells us that this was exactly what happened to Moses.

> **"And when he was full forty years old, it came into his heart to visit his brethren the children of Israel" (Ac.7:23).**

The thought that he needed to visit his people, Israel, "entered his mind" (ASV) and "he decided" (NIV) to visit them. During his forty years as a prince of Egypt, Moses had no doubt often seen his people suffer under the weight of slavery, laboring in the shops and in the construction and farming industries of Egypt. He had seen them abused, whipped, lashed, and mistreated. Thus the whole point of this particular event is to show that something different was happening to Moses. God had apparently moved the heart of Moses, aroused feelings of compassion toward the Israelites. God stirred Moses to make a special visit to investigate the sufferings of his people and to make plans to help them. Thus this particular visit reveals that Moses had a spirit that was gripped with a sense of purpose, mission, and compassion. He had a spirit that was actually identifying with his people and their terrible suffering and that was set on figuring out how to help them.

> **Thought 1**. A sense of compassion can change our lives. Most if not all of us occasionally sense compassion for others. If we would just allow compassion to grip us as it did Moses, then most of the desperate needs of people could be met, the needs of the...

• orphans	• prisoners	• diseased	• empty	• lost
• widows	• brokenhearted	• suffering	• thirsty	• sinful
• widowers	• backslidden	• hungry	• alienated	• discriminated against
• lonely	• dying	• poor	• unforgiven	

> When we first feel the movement of compassion for others, if we will only reach out and help, eventually we will become compassionate people. Our hearts and lives will be changed. Showing compassion and helping others will become one of the major purposes of our lives.
> ⇒ Many of us will give ourselves as never before to our work in order to earn more so that we can help the needy.
> ⇒ Others of us will sacrifice as never before.
> ⇒ Others will personally go to the needy all around the earth to help them.

> Compassion can make us far more useful and helpful individuals. A compassionate person makes a greater contribution to society than the uncompassionate, a greater contribution to friends, neighbors, communities, cities, nations, and the world. A compassionate person meets the desperate needs of the world. The experience of feeling compassion for others, of identifying with them (if acted upon), can change our lives. It can even change the world.

> **"I have showed you all things, how that so laboring ye ought to support the weak, and to remember the words of the Lord Jesus, how he said, It is more blessed to give than to receive" (Ac.20:35).**
> **"We then that are strong ought to bear the infirmities of the weak, and not to please ourselves" (Ro.15:1).**
> **"Bear ye one another's burdens, and so fulfil the law of Christ" (Ga.6:2).**

"Put on therefore, as the elect of God, holy and beloved, bowels of mercies, kindness, humbleness of mind, meekness, longsuffering" (Col.3:12).

"Remember them that are in bonds, as bound with them; and them which suffer adversity, as being yourselves also in the body" (He.13:3).

"Pure religion and undefiled before God and the Father is this, To visit the fatherless and widows in their affliction, and to keep himself unspotted from the world" (Js.1:27).

2 (2:11-12) **Carnal—Fleshly—Murder**: there was the second experience, Moses' murder of an Egyptian. Moses actually allowed his carnal, fleshly nature to take hold of him and he committed murder. What happened was this.

Moses stood there watching his people make mortar and brick and suffering beyond measure under the driving demands and threats of the taskmasters. All of a sudden, off to the side, he saw an Egyptian taskmaster beating one of the Hebrew slaves (v.11). The slave was helpless against the anger and cutting lashes of the taskmaster. The sight of such an inhuman scene angered Moses to no end, and he reacted in the flesh (v.12).

⇒ He looked all around, glancing this way and that.
⇒ He saw that no one was close by the Egyptian who was beating the Hebrew slave.
⇒ Moses walked over to the Egyptian and killed him and hid him in the sand.

Was Moses justified in rescuing the Hebrew slave and in killing the Egyptian? Not likely. He acted on impulse, in anger and wrath, becoming enraged. He failed to discipline and control his emotions. Note that he looked all about to make sure no one was around and that he buried the murdered Egyptian in the sand to keep him from being discovered. Moses apparently knew he was wrong. He had given in to his carnal, fleshly nature and had lashed out in anger. And this experience of anger—giving in to his carnal, fleshly nature—was to bring a tormenting fear into Moses' life, a fear that was to cause a radical change in Moses' life. This will be seen in the next points.

Thought 1. A carnal, fleshly act often brings a radical (bad, terrible) change to our lives. Our lives—relationships, marriage, employment, and all other areas of life—can be changed by one carnal, fleshly act:
⇒ adultery ⇒ cheating ⇒ drunkenness
⇒ stealing ⇒ gossiping ⇒ taking drugs
⇒ lying ⇒ laziness

God warns us against giving in to the flesh, against living a carnal, fleshly life.

"For they that are after the flesh do mind the things of the flesh; but they that are after the Spirit the things of the Spirit. For to be carnally minded is death; but to be spiritually minded is life and peace" (Ro.8:5-6).

"But put ye on the Lord Jesus Christ, and make not provision for the flesh, to fulfil the lusts thereof" (Ro.13:14).

"Now the works of the flesh are manifest, which are these; Adultery, fornication, uncleanness, lasciviousness, idolatry, witchcraft, hatred, variance, emulations, wrath, strife, seditions, heresies, envyings, murders, drunkenness, revellings, and such like: of the which I tell you before, as I have also told you in time past, that they which do such things shall not inherit the kingdom of God" (Ga.5:19-21).

"Mortify therefore your members which are upon the earth; fornication, uncleanness, inordinate affection, evil concupiscence, and covetousness, which is idolatry" (Col.3:5).

"Dearly beloved, I beseech you as strangers and pilgrims, abstain from fleshly lusts, which war against the soul" (1 Pe.2:11).

"That he no longer should live the rest of his time in the flesh to the lusts of men, but to the will of God" (1 Pe.4:2).

3 (2:13-15) **Sin, Discovered; Known**: there was the third experience, Moses' attempt to settle a dispute between two Hebrew brothers. Moses discovered that his sin was known, that others knew he had murdered the Egyptian.

a. On the very next day Moses saw two Hebrew men fighting, and he tried to stop the fight and make peace between them (v.13). He asked the man who started the fight, "Why are you hitting your neighbor?"

b. Now note what happened: Moses reaped the results of his carnal, fleshly nature (vv.13-15). He reaped three tragic consequences.

1) Moses reaped a ruined testimony: his help was rejected (v.14). What Moses had done was commendable: he had tried to stop the fight and make peace between the two Hebrew neighbors. But the man who started the fight turned and fired two stinging questions at Moses.
⇒ *"Who made you a ruler and judge over us?"*
⇒ *"Are you planning to kill me as you killed the Egyptian?"*

Moses' sin was known. His testimony was ruined; his help was rejected. Whatever hope he had for helping his people was now lost, all because of his carnal, fleshly nature.

2) Moreover, fear struck Moses' heart like a bolt of lightning, a tormenting fear (v.14). His sin was now known: it was public knowledge. Moses would no longer be able to face his people, not without embarrassment and shame, and, perhaps, ridicule and accusations against him. Moses also knew that Pharaoh would hear about the murder. His heart was filled with a flood of fear. For the longest time, he would have to live in fear, all because of giving in to his carnal, fleshly nature.

3) But more than this, Moses' sin reaped a life of separation and alienation from his family and people (v.15). Moses lost everything. When Pharaoh heard about the murder, one of the things Moses feared happened. Moses had to flee for his life, for Pharaoh sought to have him arrested and executed. Moses was forced to flee and leave behind everything he held dear: his family, his royal position and authority, his people, Israel, and any hope he had of helping them.

c. Now, note what the New Testament says about Moses during these days when he visited his people.

> **"By faith Moses, when he was come to years, refused to be called the son of Pharaoh's daughter; choosing rather to suffer affliction with the people of God, than to enjoy the pleasures of sin for a season; esteeming the reproach of Christ greater riches than the treasures in Egypt: for he had respect unto the recompense of the reward" (He.11:24-26).**

When did Moses refuse the court or throne of Pharaoh and choose to identify himself with his own people, Israel? Josephus says that Pharaoh had only one daughter and that she had no children of her own, only Moses, who was her adopted son. Thus Moses was most likely appointed to rule Egypt after Pharaoh's death.[1] Moses held a high position in Egypt as the son of Pharaoh's daughter. He had great authority, honor, and wealth. But at some point he refused the life of royalty and perhaps the throne itself. He turned away from it all and chose to identify with his own people. When? Scripture does not say. But events given here in Exodus seem to point toward Moses' decision being made during these days. He perhaps had just refused the throne or else turned away from the life of royalty when he went out to visit his people, Israel (v.11). This may be the reason Pharaoh was so angry with Moses, angry enough to have him arrested and killed for murdering an Egyptian. Pharaoh himself was the law: what he said was done. Thus it was not uncommon for members of the royal family to injure common people and for Pharaoh to forgive and pardon them. Obviously, something had happened between Pharaoh and Moses for Pharaoh to seek Moses' life. As stated, the fractured relationship may have been due either to Moses' rejection of the throne or of the royal family.

The point to see is that Moses was now reaping the results of his sin, of his carnal, fleshly nature. He had murdered an Egyptian and hid him in the sand, trying to keep his sin secret. But the sin had been discovered, and he was now fleeing for his life. He was flooded with the tormented fear of being caught and executed.

Thought 1. When secret sins become known, it can drastically change our lives. Tragic consequences often happen.
(1) Sin ruins our testimony.

> **"Even as I have seen, they that plow iniquity, and sow wickedness, reap the same" (Jb.4:8).**
> **"Teaching us that, denying ungodliness and worldly lusts, we should live soberly, righteously, and godly, in this present world; looking for that blessed hope, and the glorious appearing of the great God and our Saviour Jesus Christ; who gave himself for us, that he might redeem us from all iniquity, and purify unto himself a peculiar people, zealous of good works. These things speak, and exhort, and rebuke with all authority. Let no man despise thee" (Tit.2:12-15).**
> **"Let us lay aside every weight, and the sin which doth so easily beset us, and let us run with patience the race that is set before us" (He.12:1).**
> **"But sanctify [set apart] the Lord God in your hearts: and be ready always to give an answer to every man that asketh you a reason of the hope that is in you with meekness and fear" (1 Pe.3:15).**

(2) Sin causes fear, a tormenting fear. When people know about our sin, we often fear facing them. We fear embarrassment, shame, ridicule, and accusations.

> **"In the morning thou [the sinner, the disobedient] shalt say, Would God it were even! and at even thou shalt say, Would God it were morning! for the fear of thine heart wherewith thou shalt fear, and for the sight of thine eyes which thou shalt see" (De.28:67).**
> **"O my God, I am ashamed and blush to lift up my face to thee, my God: for our iniquities are increased over our head, and our trespass is grown up unto the heavens" (Ezr.9:6).**
> **"My confusion is continually before me, and the shame of my face hath covered me" (Ps.44:15).**
> **"And I will bring an everlasting reproach upon you, and a perpetual shame, which shall not be forgotten" (Je.23:40).**
> **"Ye have sinned against the LORD: and be sure your sin will find you out" (Nu.32:23).**
> **"Whose hatred is covered by deceit, his wickedness shall be showed before the whole congregation" (Pr.26:26).**
> **"For there is nothing covered, that shall not be revealed; neither hid, that shall not be known" (Lu.12:2).**
> **"For it is a shame even to speak of those things which are done of them in secret" (Ep.5:12).**

(3) Sin causes loss of family, friends, possessions, job, heath, life, and a host of other losses. Sin often separates and alienates us from those we love the most.

> **"Be not deceived; God is not mocked: for whatsoever a man soweth, that shall he also reap. For he that soweth to his flesh shall of the flesh reap corruption; but he that soweth to the Spirit shall of the Spirit reap life everlasting" (Ga.6:7-8).**

1 Flavius Josephus. *Antiquities of the Jews.* "Complete Works." (Grand Rapids, MI: Kregel Publications, 1981), Book 2, Chapter IX, 7, p.57.

"He that covereth his sins shall not prosper: but whoso confesseth and forsaketh them shall have mercy" (Pr.28:13).

"Your iniquities have turned away these things, and your sins have withholden good things from you" (Je.5:25).

"And not many days after the younger son gathered all together, and took his journey into a far country, and there wasted his substance with riotous living. And when he had spent all, there arose a mighty famine in that land; and he began to be in want. And he went and joined himself to a citizen of that country; and he sent him into his fields to feed swine. And he would fain have filled his belly with the husks that the swine did eat: and no man gave unto him [all friends had forsaken him]" (Lu.15:13-16).

"Follow peace with all men, and holiness, without which no man shall see the Lord: looking diligently lest any man fail of the grace of God; lest any root of bitterness springing up trouble you, and thereby many be defiled; lest there be any fornicator, or profane person, as Esau, who for one morsel of meat sold his birthright. For ye know how that afterward, when he would have inherited the blessing, he was rejected: for he found no place of repentance, though he sought it carefully with tears" (He.12:14-17).

4 (2:15-22) **Commitment—Reuel—Jethro—Midian**: there was the fourth experience, Moses' flight to Midian. His years in Midian were to be a time of preparation for Moses, a period of great growth both mentally and spiritually. His character and spiritual commitment were to grow enormously during these years. At least five areas of growth can be gleaned from these eight verses.

a. Moses' character grew by living in Midian, a hard, harsh, and impoverished place. Note that Moses *chose* to live in Midian (v.15). Midian was located somewhere in Arabia, which was south of Palestine. The best information places Midian in the northwest corner of Arabia, along the eastern shore of the Red Sea, near Aqaba. There is also the possibility that some Midianites settled in the Sinai peninsula area.[2] Both Arabia and the Sinai were desert, wilderness areas with only scattered resources of water, fertile soil, and pasture land. Life was rough and hard in such a place. In Midian, Moses, the prince from Egypt, was to learn...

- the geographical terrain of the desert wilderness
- the harsh environment of the desert with its scattered water holes and food supply
- the strength needed to face poverty by living in a harsh land
- the sufferings of people who lived in a poor, harsh environment

All of this would help to prepare Moses to lead his people, Israel—an entire nation of people—through the wilderness wanderings.

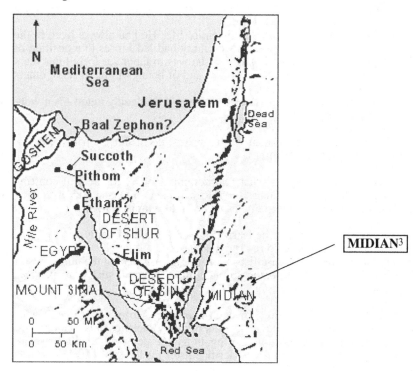

b. Moses' character grew by standing up for justice and for the oppressed (vv.15-20). Remember, Moses had already demonstrated a strong sense of justice. He had already taken at least two strong stands for the oppressed of this world:

First, he had taken a stand for the oppressed Israelite who was being beaten by an Egyptian. True, he had gone too far in killing the Egyptian; nevertheless, it was his sense of justice that aroused him to defend the oppressed Israelite (vv.11-12).

---

2 F.B. Huey, Jr. *Exodus*, p.25.
3 Map from *Life Application® Bible*. Used by permission.

Second, he had taken a stand for the oppressed Israelite who had been drawn into a fight by a neighbor, a fellow Israelite (vv.13-14). Again, Moses' sense of justice and compassion for the oppressed is seen in this second incident.

Now, for a third time, his great sense of justice and compassion for the oppressed is seen. Moses' character was, no doubt, developed time and again throughout the years by being stirred to stand up for justice and for the oppressed. Note this particular story.

⇒ Moses had just arrived in the land of Midian and sat down by a well to rest (v.15).
⇒ Sometime later, seven daughters of a local priest came up to the well to water their father's flocks (v.16).
⇒ As soon as they had begun to fill the troughs with water, some other shepherds came along and drove the girls away (v.17).
⇒ But Moses stood up and rescued the girls and finished watering their flocks himself (v.17).
⇒ The shepherds' oppression of the girls was obviously a daily attack, for note that Moses' help enabled the girls to return home early (v.18). In fact, they were so far ahead of schedule that their father actually asked why they were returning home so early.
⇒ In reply, they simply related what had happened: an Egyptian had rescued them from the shepherds and had even watered their flocks for them (v.19). Note that Moses' appearance, language, and behavior pointed toward him being an Egyptian. He had been so trained and immersed in Egyptian society that he had become an Egyptian in appearance—not in heart, but in appearance.
⇒ Upon hearing how Moses had defended his daughters, Reuel, the father, rebuked his daughters for having left the Egyptian at the well. He immediately sent them back to invite Moses to dinner (v.20).

The point to note is Moses' sense of justice, his defense of the oppressed daughters against the shepherds. Moses' character was being shaped with a great sense of justice and compassion for the oppressed of this world. These two traits—a sense of justice and compassion for the oppressed—would be desperately needed as Moses faced the problems of the future.

⇒ He would have to insist upon justice from Pharaoh when he began to demand that Pharaoh free Israel from slavery.
⇒ He would also have to insist that the people live by the laws of justice when he began to mold Israel into a nation governed by law.

c. Moses' character grew by committing himself to serve and work for others (v.21). The father's name was Reuel (v.18) or Jethro (Ge.3:1). It was common for people of ages past to have two names, one name being a personal name and the other an official name or title. Remember that Reuel was a priest of Midian. Perhaps Reuel was the official name for the priest of Midian (v.16). The name Reuel means *friend, companion of God.*

Note that the father invited Moses to live with him, to be a member of his household. This obviously meant that Moses was to serve and work for the father. Moses agreed, and he settled down in Midian becoming an employee—a shepherd—working for Reuel or Jethro (v.21).

Remember, Moses had never served nor worked at hard labor for anyone in his entire life. He had always lived in the court of Pharaoh, lived a life of luxury, softness, and plenty. But now, God's sovereignty had led Moses to a position of serving and laboring for others. He was to learn what hard, laborious work was, and he was to labor for forty long years serving as an employee and shepherd for Reuel. The two traits of being a hard worker and of being willing to serve others were now to be molded into the character of Moses.

d. Moses' character grew by making a commitment to marriage (v.21). True marriage—a true godly union—is a wonderful thing, and a godly union teaches a person two great traits:

⇒ the trait of *agape love*, of sacrificial love, of self-denial and unselfishness.
⇒ the trait of commitment, of committing oneself to a person no matter what arises, no matter the trials, circumstances, difficulties, trouble, suffering, or failures and shortcomings.

A person who truly commits himself to enter a godly marriage learns what real commitment is, for he will confront every conceivable trial and problem imaginable during the long years of marriage. He will have to persist and persevere, ever learning what true love really is. The great traits of *agape love*, of godly sacrifice and commitment, will be molded into his character.

No doubt, Moses learned agape love through the years of his marriage: he learned the great traits of godly sacrifice and commitment. He learned more and more what it meant to love a person, to really give oneself…

• to the point of sacrifice, of caring so much that he would act unselfishly for the sake of helping the other person
• to the point of commitment, of really being committed to a person so much that he would stick with them no matter how difficult the situation might seem

The point is this: God in His sovereignty led Moses to marry Zipporah. Through marriage, Moses was to learn what God wants all married persons to learn: the great lesson of *agape love*, the great traits of godly sacrifice and commitment. Moses' love for Israel and his commitment to Israel were to be tested time and again by the people's rebellious spirit. Thus his heart had to be filled with *agape love*, with a spirit that was willing to sacrifice itself for the sake of others and to commit itself to others no matter what happened.

e. Moses' character grew by declaring his faith in the promised land. This is seen in the naming of his son (v.22). Moses named his first son "Gershom," which means *stranger, alien, sojourner,* or *expulsion.* Note why Moses named his son Gershom: because Moses was a stranger in a strange land. He was an alien, a sojourner in a land that was not his. Where was Moses' land? Why was Moses not claiming Midian as his home? Had he not settled there? Married there? And now was he not having children there? Moses was to live in Midian for forty years. What did Moses mean when he said that he was only a stranger in a strange land (Midian)? He would not be referring to Egypt, for Moses was not an Egyptian, and his people were enslaved by the Egyptians. Moses certainly would not be claiming Egypt as his home.

There could be only one land to which Moses was referring: the *promised land*, the land of Canaan, which was a symbol and picture of the promised land of heaven. Moses' heart was upon the promised land of God. And he was declaring his faith in the *promised land*, both the promised land of Canaan and the promised land of heaven. (See DEEPER STUDY # 1—Ex.2:24; note 2—Ge.12:1 for more discussion.) The New Testament declares that the great leaders of the Bible believed in the promised land of heaven as well as the promised land of Canaan. They believed in a *heavenly country* and a *heavenly city*. Their real home was not this earth, not a worldly country or city. Their real home was a heavenly home—a heavenly country and city that are eternal—that Abraham and all believers are to inherit. Note how clearly Scripture declares this fact:

> **"By faith Abraham, when he was called to go out into a place which he should after receive for an inheritance, obeyed; and he went out, not knowing whither he went. By faith he sojourned in the land of promise, as in a strange country, dwelling in tabernacles with Isaac and Jacob, the heirs with him of the same promise: for he looked for a city which hath foundations, whose builder and maker is God" (He.11:8-10).**

> **"These all died in faith, not having received the promises, but having seen them afar off, and were persuaded of them, and embraced them, and confessed that they were strangers and pilgrims on the earth. For they that say such things declare plainly that they seek a country. And truly, if they had been mindful of that country from whence they came out, they might have had opportunity to have returned. But now they desire a better country, that is, an heavenly: wherefore God is not ashamed to be called their God: for he hath prepared for them a city" (He.11:13-16. Note v.15: it clearly states that Abraham's mind was on the heavenly and eternal country. If it had not been, he would have returned to his former home. He would have never wandered about, suffering the hardships he bore. We might add, neither would have Moses.)**

> **"But ye are come unto mount Sion, and unto the city of the living God, the heavenly Jerusalem, and to an innumerable company of angels" (He.12:22).**

> **"For here have we no continuing city [a perfect, heavenly city], but we seek one to come" (He.13:14).**

> **"For the promise, that he should be the heir of the world [the new heavens and earth], was not to Abraham, or to his seed, through the law, but through the righteousness of faith" (Ro.4:13; see 2 Pe.3:10-13).**

5 (2:23-25) **Israel—Hebrews—God**: there was the fifth experience, Moses' people and their terrible suffering and God's response to the cries of His people. About forty years passed between verses 22 and 23, between Moses' flight to Midian and the response of God to the cries of His people.

a. The king of Egypt died (v.23). This was obviously the same king who had sought to arrest and execute Moses. The very fact that his death is mentioned suggests that he was the same king (see Ex.2:15; 4:19). Moses was now free to return to Egypt. Legally and politically, he could now return to Egypt without being arrested.

b. The Israelites suffered and groaned under the heavy weight of their enslavement (v.23). Remember, the Israelites were suffering severe, inhuman oppression:

⇒ being forced to labor for the state.
⇒ being worked ruthlessly, given backbreaking, crushing tasks to do.
⇒ being viciously mistreated, abused, beaten, and slowly killed off in order to control the population growth.

The people just *groaned* under the bitterness of their enslavement. The idea is that of misery, anguish, and pain, of crying out in desperation, of groaning under the heaviest affliction.[4] When Joseph was ruling Egypt, the people were comfortable and had plenty of food and everything else, living a life of ease. But not now: Egypt no longer meant comfort, plenty, and ease. Egypt meant enslavement, a life of hard labor and harsh treatment.

Now, note this fact: many of the Israelites had forsaken God and begun to worship the false gods of the Egyptians. Obviously, the days of plenty, comfort, and ease after Joseph's death made the Israelites spiritually soft. They became more interested in the things of the world than in the promises of God. Many became carnal and fleshly, forsaking God and worshipping the false gods of Egypt. Scripture actually says that this is the reason God allowed the Israelites to be enslaved and to suffer so much in Egypt, that the bondage and suffering were part of the discipline and chastisement of God. Allowing the people to suffer was God's way of awakening the people to turn back to Him.

> **"Then said I unto them, Cast ye away every man the abominations of his eyes, and defile not yourselves with the idols of Egypt: I am the LORD your God. But they rebelled against me, and would not hearken unto me: they did not every man cast away the abominations of their eyes, neither did they forsake the idols of Egypt: then I said, I will pour out my fury upon them to accomplish my anger against them in the midst of the land of Egypt" (Eze.20:7-8).**

God's sovereign plan had worked. The anguish and pain of their bitter affliction had broken the people. In desperation they cried out to God, to the only living and true God. And note what happened: their cry reached heaven; their cry went up to God.

c. The response of God is expressed by four verbs of strong action (vv.24-25). God was stirred; He moved and acted; God made four responses to the painful, desperate cry of the people.

---

4 William Wilson. *Wilson's Old Testament Word Studies*. (McLean, VA: MacDonald Publishing Company, no date given), p.202.

1) God *heard* the groaning of the people, heard the groaning of their misery, desperation, anguish, and pain. The true God, the only living God, never turns a deaf ear to a person who turns to Him. God always hears the cries of people who truly cry out to Him for help. God heard the people's groaning; He heard their cry for help.

2) God *remembered* His covenant with Israel, the covenant He had made with Abraham, Isaac, and Jacob (v.24). What was that covenant? It was the Abrahamic covenant, which included three great promises (see outline and notes—Ge.12:1-3; 17:6-8; 26:1-6; 28:12-15; Deeper Study # 2—Ex.1:6-7; Deeper Study # 1—Ex.2:24 for more discussion):

⇒ There was the promise of the promised seed or descendants. God promised that He would cause a great nation of people to be born through the seed of Abraham, Isaac, and Jacob. (See outline and notes—Ge.12:2-3; Deeper Study # 2—Ex.1:6-7 for more discussion.)

⇒ There was the promise of the promised seed, which also referred to one seed or one descendant. God promised that He would send the Savior of the world through the seed or descendants of Israel (see outline and note—Ge.12:3; Deeper Study # 2—Ex.1:6-7 for more discussion).

⇒ There was the promise of the promised land. The promised land referred both to the land of Canaan and to the land of heaven. (See Deeper Study # 1—Ex.2:24; note—Ge.12:1 for more discussion.)

The point is this: the people had been broken and were turning back to God, crying out for His help. And God heard their cry and remembered the great covenant promises He had made to the fathers of Israel. This does not mean that God had forgotten His covenant promise. God never forgets. When Scripture speaks of God *remembering*, it means that God is actively thinking about the covenant He had made with Abraham, Isaac, and Jacob. God was actively thinking about the great promises He had made, the promises of the promised land and the promised seed (meaning both the great nation of people and the Savior of the world).

3) God *looked* upon the people, meaning that He had compassion for them (v.25).

4) God *"had respect* unto them" (KJV), "was concerned for them" (NIV), "took notice of them" (NAS). The Hebrew word is *wayyeda*, which literally means "He knew," knew experientially, knew feeling for them. God knew all about the pain and anguish of the people; He knew all about the terrible affliction they were suffering.

The point is this: the people were broken and repentant. They had learned that "the way of transgressors is hard" (Pr.13:15). They knew the bitterness and terrible consequence of sin. They were now ready to turn away from the false worship of Egypt and ready to turn back to God, to the only living and true God. This they did: they cried out in desperation for God to help. Now both Moses and Israel had been prepared, prepared spiritually and mentally for God to deliver His people out of Egypt. Now God could begin anew to fulfill His great promises to His people...

• the promise of the promised land
• the promise of the promised seed, meaning both the seed of a great nation of people and the seed of the Savior

Thought 1. God hears the cries of His people when they cry out to Him for help. God, the only true and living God, never turns a deaf ear to any person who sincerely turns to Him for help.

"But if from thence thou shalt seek the LORD thy God, thou shalt find him, if thou seek him with all thy heart and with all thy soul" (De.4:29).

"The eyes of the LORD are upon the righteous, and his ears are open unto their cry" (Ps.34:15).

"This poor man cried, and the LORD heard him, and saved him out of all his troubles" (Ps.34:6).

"From the end of the earth will I cry unto thee, when my heart is overwhelmed: lead me to the rock that is higher than I" (Ps.61:2).

"He shall call upon me, and I will answer him: I will be with him in trouble; I will deliver him, and honor him" (Ps.91:15).

"Then shalt thou call, and the LORD shall answer; thou shalt cry, and he shall say, Here I am. If thou take away from the midst of thee the yoke, the putting forth of the finger, and speaking vanity" (Is.58:9).

"And it shall come to pass, that before they call, I will answer; and while they are yet speaking, I will hear" (Is.65:24).

"They shall call on my name, and I will hear them: I will say, It is my people: and they shall say, The LORD is my God" (Zec.13:9).

DEEPER STUDY # 1

(2:24) **Land, Promised—Canaan—Covenant—Heaven—Inheritance—Rest, Spiritual**: God promised that He would give Abram *the promised land* of Canaan. God actually promised land to Abram. But note:

⇒ The land was only promised: it lay out in the future; it was not to be immediately possessed. The land was just what believers have called it for centuries, *the promised land*. It was to be the great hope of Abram. This is the reason the land of Canaan is referred to as *the promised land*.

All Abram had to go on was the promise of God, on what God had said. Abram had to step out in faith and believe God's Word—His promise—about *the promised land*. Note several facts about this great promise to Abram.

1. *The promised land* definitely refers to Palestine, the land of Israel. This is clearly stated by God time and again.
   a. Note God's promise to Abram.

"And Abram passed through the land unto the place of Sichem, unto the plain of Moreh. And the Canaanite was then in the land. And the LORD appeared unto Abram, and said, Unto thy seed

---

will I give this land: and there builded he an altar unto the LORD, who appeared unto him" (Ge.12:6-7).

"And the LORD said unto Abram, after that Lot was separated from him, Lift up now thine eyes, and look from the place where thou art northward, and southward, and eastward, and westward: for all the land which thou seest, to thee will I give it, and to thy seed for ever....Arise, walk through the land in the length of it and in the breadth of it: for I will give it unto thee" (Ge.13:14-15, 17).

"And he said unto him, I am the LORD that brought thee out of Ur of the Chaldees, to give thee this land to inherit it....In the same day the LORD made a covenant with Abram, saying, Unto thy seed have I given this land, from the river of Egypt unto the great river, the river Euphrates: the Kenites, and the Kenizzites, and the Kadmonites, and the Hittites, and the Periozzites, and the Rephaims, and the Amorites, and the Canaanites, and the Girgashites, and the Jebusites" (Ge.15:7, 18-21).

"And I will give unto thee, and to thy seed after thee, the land wherein thou art a stranger, all the land of Canaan, for an everlasting possession: and I will be their God" (Ge.17:8).

b. Note God's promise to Abram's son, Isaac.

"Sojourn in this land, and I will be with thee, and will bless thee; for unto thee, and unto thy seed, I will give all these countries, and I will perform the oath which I sware unto Abraham thy father" (Ge.26:3).

c. Note God's promise to Abram's grandson, Jacob.

"And, behold, the LORD stood above it, and said, I am the LORD God of Abraham thy father, and the God of Isaac: the land whereon thou liest, to thee will I give it, and to thy seed" (Ge.28:13).

"And the land which I gave Abraham and Isaac, to thee I will give it, and to thy seed after thee will I give the land" (Ge.35:12).

2. *The promised land* definitely refers to heaven. The promised land of Canaan is a symbol (a type, a picture, an illustration) of heaven, of God's promise to the believer that he will inherit heaven, the new heavens and earth. Note two facts:
   a. God's promised land refers to *the whole world*. It is *the whole world* that Abram and believers are to *inherit*.

"For the promise, that he should be the heir of the world, was not to Abraham, or to his seed, through the law, but through the righteousness of faith" (Ro.4:13).

The inheritance of the whole world could only refer to the *new heavens and earth*—the new universe—that God is going to recreate in the end time. It could not refer to a corruptible universe that is deteriorating, wasting away, and running down, that would eventually cease to exist millions of years from now—cease to exist just by the natural process of time. (See outlines and notes—2 Pe.3:1-18 for more discussion.)

"But the day of the Lord will come as a thief in the night; in the which the heavens shall pass away with a great noise, and the elements shall melt with fervent heat, the earth also and the works that are therein shall be burned up. Seeing then that all these things shall be dissolved, what manner of persons ought ye to be in all holy conversation and godliness. Looking for and hasting unto the coming of the day of God, wherein the heavens being on fire shall be dissolved, and the elements shall melt with fervent heat? Nevertheless we, according to his promise, look for new heavens and a new earth, wherein dwelleth righteousness" (2 Pe.3:10-13).

"And I saw a new heaven and a new earth: for the first heaven and the first earth were passed away; and there was no more sea. And I John saw the holy city, new Jerusalem [the capital of the new universe], coming down from God out of heaven, prepared as a bride adorned for her husband. And I heard a great voice out of heaven saying, Behold, the tabernacle of God is with men, and he will dwell with them, and they shall be his people, and God himself shall be with them, and be their God. And God shall wipe away all tears from their eyes; and there shall be no more death, neither sorrow, nor crying, neither shall there be any more pain: for the former things are passed away" (Re.21:1-4).

"Of old hast thou laid the foundation of the earth: and the heavens are the work of thy hands. They shall perish, but thou shalt endure: yea, all of them shall wax old like a garment; as a vesture shalt thou change them, and they shall be changed: but thou art the same, and thy years shall have no end" (Ps.102:25-27).

"And all the host of heaven shall be dissolved, and the heavens shall be rolled together as a scroll: and all their host shall fall down, as the leaf falleth off from the vine, and as a falling fig from the fig tree" (Is.34:4).

"Lift up your eyes to the heavens, and look upon the earth beneath: for the heavens shall vanish away like smoke, and the earth shall wax old like a garment, and they that dwell therein shall die in like manner: but my salvation shall be for ever, and my righteousness shall not be abolished" (Is.51:6).

"For, behold, I create new heavens and a new earth: and the former shall not be remembered, nor come into mind" (Is.65:17).

"For as the new heavens and the new earth, which I will make, shall remain before me, saith the LORD, so shall your seed and your name remain" (Is.66:22).

b. God's promised land refers to *a heavenly country* and *a heavenly city*. It is a heavenly home—a heavenly country and city that are eternal—that Abram and believers are to inherit. Note how clearly Scripture states this:

"By faith Abraham, when he was called to go out into a place which he should after receive for an inheritance, obeyed; and he went out, not knowing whither he went. By faith he sojourned in the land of promise, as in a strange country, dwelling in tabernacles with Isaac and Jacob, the heirs with him of the same promise: for he looked for a city which hath foundations, whose builder and maker is God....These all died in faith, not having received the promises, but having seen them afar off, and were persuaded of them, and embraced them, and confessed that they were strangers and pilgrims on the earth. For they that say such things declare plainly that they seek a country. And truly, if they had been mindful of that country from whence they came out, they might have had opportunity to have returned. But now they desire a better country, that is, an heavenly: wherefore God is not ashamed to be called their God: for he hath prepared for them a city" (He.11:8-10, 13-16).

"But ye are come unto mount Sion, and unto the city of the living God, the heavenly Jerusalem, and to an innumerable company of angels" (He.12:22).

"For here have we no continuing city [a perfect heavenly city], but we seek one to come" (He.13:14).

"And I John saw the holy city, new Jerusalem, coming down from God out of heaven, prepared as a bride adorned for her husband. And I heard a great voice out of heaven, saying, Behold, the tabernacle of God is with men, and he will dwell with them, and they shall be his people, and God himself shall be with them, and be their God. And God shall wipe away all tears from their eyes; and there shall be no more death, neither sorrow, nor crying, neither shall there be any more pain: for the former things are passed away" (Re.21:2-4).

"And he carried me away in the spirit to a great and high mountain, and showed me that great city, the holy Jerusalem, descending out of heaven from God" (Re.21:10).

3. *The promised land* represented many things to Abram.
   a. The promised land was the assurance of *a personal inheritance*: the possession of a new country, of his own property with all its good land, wealth, and rights. Abram believed that he would live in a new city within his own land and country—all given by God Himself. And the land was to be forever, for it was promised by the eternal God Himself.
   Note this, for it is important: Abram's hope was for a permanent, eternal city and country. True, he was physically journeying all throughout the promised land of Canaan, believing that God was going to give him and his seed (descendents) the land of Canaan. But while he was journeying, his hope was for the permanent, eternal city and country of God. Abram knew that God's promised land referred to the heavenly as well as to the earthly land. Note how clearly Scripture states this:

⇒ "For all the land which thou seest, to thee will I give it, and to thy seed for ever" (Ge.13:15).

God's promise included the eternal, permanent possession of the promised land, and Abram knew this.

⇒ "By faith he sojourned in the land of promise, as in a strange country, dwelling in tabernacles with Isaac and Jacob, the heirs with him of the same promise: for he looked for a city which hath foundations, whose builder and maker is God" (He.11:9-10).

This refers to the heavenly Jerusalem, the capital of the new heavens and earth (see He.12:22; 13:14. See pt.2 above. Also see note—Re.21:2.)

⇒ "These all died in faith, not having received the promises, but having seen them afar off, and were persuaded of them, and embraced them, and confessed that they were strangers and pilgrims on the earth. For they that say such things declare plainly that they seek a country. And truly, if they had been mindful of that country from whence they came out, they might have had opportunity to have returned. But now they desire a better country, that is, an heavenly: wherefore God is not ashamed to be called their God: for he hath prepared for them a city" (He.11:13-16).

Note v.15: it clearly states that Abram's mind was on the heavenly and eternal country. If it had not been, he would have returned to his former home. He would have never wandered about, suffering the hardships he bore.

Thought 1. Note how the promise given to Abram parallels the promise given to the believer. Abram was to inherit *the promised land* if he turned away from the world and followed God. We are to inherit *the promised land of heaven* if we turn away from the world and follow God. *The promised land* is a symbol, a type, a picture of heaven.

(1) The promise given to Abram.

> "And I will give unto thee, and to thy seed after thee, the land wherein thou art a stranger, all the land of Canaan, for an everlasting possession; and I will be their God" (Ge.17:8).

(2) The promise given to the believer.

> "In my Father's house are many mansions: if it were not so, I would have told you. I go to prepare a place for you. And if I go and prepare a place for you, I will come again, and receive you unto myself; that where I am, there ye may be also" (Jn.14:2-3).
> "For we know that if our earthly house of this tabernacle were dissolved, we have a building of God, an house not made with hands, eternal in the heavens" (2 Co.5:1).
> "For our conversation [citizenship] is in heaven; from whence also we look for the Saviour, the Lord Jesus Christ: who shall change our vile body, that it may be fashioned like unto his glorious body, according to the working whereby he is able even to subdue all things unto himself" (Ph.3:20-21).
> "By faith Abraham, when he was called to go out into a place which he should after receive for an inheritance, obeyed; and he went out, not knowing whither he went. By faith he sojourned in the land of promise, as in a strange country, dwelling in tabernacles with Isaac and Jacob, the heirs with him of the same promise: for he looked for a city which hath foundations, whose builder and maker is God" (He.11:8-10).
> "These all died in faith, not having received the promises, but having seen them afar off, and were persuaded of them, and embraced them, and confessed that they were strangers and pilgrims on the earth. For they that say such things declare plainly that they seek a country. And truly, if they had been mindful of that country from whence they came out, they might have had opportunity to have returned. But now they desire a better country, that is, an heavenly: wherefore God is not ashamed to be called their God: for he hath prepared for them a city" (He.11:13-16).
> "Blessed be the God and Father of our Lord Jesus Christ, which according to his abundant mercy hath begotten us again unto a lively hope by the resurrection of Jesus Christ from the dead, to an inheritance incorruptible, and undefiled, and that fadeth not away, reserved in heaven for you, who are kept by the power of God through faith unto salvation ready to be revealed in the last time" (1 Pe.1:3-5).
> "Blessed are they that do his commandments, that they may have right to the tree of life, and may enter in through the gates into the city [New Jerusalem]" (Re.22:14).

b. The promised land was the assurance of *conquest and rest, of spiritual victory and spiritual rest*. The promised land was to bring a God-given peace and security, freedom and liberty, deliverance and salvation to Abram. The promised land meant victory and rest to Abram, a God-given victory and rest...
- from having to wander about
- from never being settled
- from restlessness
- from being exposed to all kinds of trials, dangers, threats, attacks, slavery, and bondage that comes from having no settled home within this world, from having no place that is given and protected by God Himself

To Abram, the promised land was the assurance of victory and rest, the conquest and triumph over all enemies, a victory and rest that was to be given by God Himself.

Thought 1. Note how the spiritual victory and rest promised to Abram represents the spiritual rest promised to the believer (see note—He.4:1 for more discussion).
(1) The promise given to Abram.

> "And I will make of thee a great nation, and I will bless thee, and make thy name great; and thou shalt be a blessing: and I will bless them that bless thee, and curse him that curseth thee: and in thee shall all families of the earth be blessed" (Ge.12:2-3).
> "After these things the word of the LORD came unto Abram in a vision, saying, Fear not, Abram: I am thy shield, and thy exceeding great reward" (Ge.15:1).
> "That in blessing I will bless thee, and in multiplying I will multiply thy seed as the stars of the heaven, and as the sand which is upon the sea shore; and thy seed shall possess the gate of his enemies; and in thy seed shall all the nations of the earth be blessed; because thou hast obeyed my voice" (Ge.22:17-18).

(2) The promise given to the believer.

> "Take my yoke upon you, and learn of me; for I am meek and lowly in heart: and ye shall find rest unto your souls" (Mt.11:29).
> "And I heard a voice from heaven saying unto me, Write, Blessed are the dead which die in the Lord from henceforth: yea, saith the Spirit, that they may rest from their labours; and their works do follow them" (Re.14:13).
> "Let us therefore fear, lest, a promise being left us of entering into his rest, any of you should seem to come short of it. For unto us was the gospel preached, as well as unto them: but the word

preached did not profit them, not being mixed with faith in them that heard it. For we which have believed do enter into rest" (He.4:1-3).

"Let us labour therefore to enter into that rest, lest any man fall after the same example of unbelief" (He.4:11).

"And he said, My presence shall go with thee, and I will give thee rest" (Ex.33:14).

"And I said, Oh that I had wings like a dove! for then would I fly away, and be at rest" (Ps.55:6).

"Return unto thy rest, O my soul; for the LORD hath dealt bountifully with thee" (Ps.116:7).

"To whom he said, This is the rest wherewith ye may cause the weary to rest; and this is the refreshing: yet they would not hear" (Is.28:12).

c. The promised land was the assurance of *God's own presence*, that is, of God's love, care, provision, and protection. Abram was bound to know this: if God were going to give him the promised land, then God must love and care for him. God would therefore provide and protect him no matter what lay ahead. God—His strong presence—would be with him through all the trials and struggles of life.

Thought 1. Abram's assurance of God's presence symbolizes the believer's experience. The believer can be assured of God's presence: of God's love, care, provision, and protection.

(1) The promise given to Abram.

"And I will give unto thee, and to thy seed after thee, the land wherein thou art a stranger, all the land of Canaan, for an everlasting possession; and I will be their God" (Ge.17:8).

"And, behold, I am with thee, and will keep thee in all places whither thou goest, and will bring thee again into this land; for I will not leave thee, until I have done that which I have spoken to thee of" (Ge.28:15).

(2) The promise given to the believer.

"When thou goest out to battle against thine enemies, and seest horses, and chariots, and a people more than thou, be not afraid of them: for the LORD thy God is with thee, which brought thee up out of the land of Egypt" (De.20:1).

"When thou passest through the waters, I will be with thee; and through the rivers, they shall not overflow thee: when thou walkest through the fire, thou shalt not be burned; neither shall the flame kindle upon thee" (Is.43:2).

"But seek ye first the kingdom of God, and his righteousness; and all these things shall be added unto you" (Mt.6:33).

"Lo, I am with you alway, even unto the end of the world" (Mt.28:20).

"Let your conversation be without covetousness; and be content with such things as ye have: for he hath said, I will never leave thee, nor forsake thee" (He.13:5).

TYPES, SYMBOLS, AND PICTURES
(Exodus 2:11-25)

Historical Term	Type or Picture (Scriptural Basis for Each)	Life Application for Today's Believer	Biblical Application
Gershom, Moses' Eldest Son (Ex.2:22)	*The name "Gershom" means: A stranger in a strange land* "And she bare *him* a son, and he called his name Gershom: for he said, I have been a stranger in a strange land" (Ex.2:22). "And I have also established my covenant with them, to give them the land of Canaan, the land of their pilgrimage, wherein they were strangers" (Ex.6:4). "These all died in faith, not having received the promises, but having seen them afar off, and were persuaded of *them*, and embraced *them*, and confessed that they were strangers and pilgrims on the earth" (He.11:13).	Believers are strangers in this world, followers of Christ... • who have been given the eternal inheritance of God Himself, the promised land of heaven • who are now marching to the promised land of heaven • who are only pilgrims on the journey through the wilderness (trials) of this world • who long to be home in heaven with Christ	*"For our conversation [citizenship] is in heaven; from whence also we look for the Saviour, the Lord Jesus Christ" (Ph.3:20).* *"These all died in faith, not having received the promises, but having seen them afar off, and were persuaded of them, and embraced them, and confessed that they were strangers and pilgrims on the earth" (He.11:13; see He.11:13-16; 1 Pe.2:11; 1 Jn.2:15).* *"I am a stranger in the earth: hide not thy commandments from me" (Ps.119:19).*

CHAPTER 3

C. The Call of Moses: A Study of God's Call To Service, 3:1-10

1. The kind of man God called

a. Moses was a shepherd: This suggests he had a heart that could shepherd people

b. Moses was a hard-working man: Tended the flock in the desert (a desolate place) at Mt. Horeb[DS1]

c. Moses was a man of faith, a man who would believe the miracles, the impossible acts of God: The angel of the LORD appeared to Moses as blazing fire from within a bush

d. Moses was a man who would stop & seek the meaning of things: He stopped to seek the meaning of the burning bush

2. The call of God itself

a. God's call was to a seeking man

b. God's call was a personal call
1) God called Moses by name
2) Moses' response: "Here am I"

c. God's call was a holy call
1) Symbolized in God's instructions for Moses to remove his sandals
2) The reason: God is holy

d. God's call was a call from the

Now Moses kept the flock of Jethro his father in law, the priest of Midian: and he led the flock to the backside of the desert, and came to the mountain of God, even to Horeb.

2 And the angel of the LORD appeared unto him in a flame of fire out of the midst of a bush: and he looked, and, behold, the bush burned with fire, and the bush was not consumed.

3 And Moses said, I will now turn aside, and see this great sight, why the bush is not burnt.

4 And when the LORD saw that he turned aside to see, God called unto him out of the midst of the bush, and said, Moses, Moses. And he said, Here am I.

5 And he said, Draw not nigh hither: put off thy shoes from off thy feet, for the place whereon thou standest is holy ground.

6 Moreover he said, I am the God of thy father, the God of Abraham, the God of Isaac, and the God of Jacob. And Moses hid his face; for he was afraid to look upon God.

7 And the LORD said, I have surely seen the affliction of my people which are in Egypt, and have heard their cry by reason of their taskmasters; for I know their sorrows;

8 And I am come down to deliver them out of the hand of the Egyptians, and to bring them up out of that land unto a good land and a large, unto a land flowing with milk and honey; unto the place of the Canaanites, and the Hittites, and the Amorites, and the Perizzites, and the Hivites, and the Jebusites.

9 Now therefore, behold, the cry of the children of Israel is come unto me: and I have also seen the oppression wherewith the Egyptians oppress them.

10 Come now therefore, and I will send thee unto Pharaoh, that thou mayest bring forth my people the children of Israel out of Egypt.

only living and true God, the God who fulfills His promises to people
1) God declared the fact: He is (not *was*) the God of Abraham, Isaac, & Jacob
2) Moses' response

3. The reasons for God's call

a. God was deeply concerned about His people's suffering
1) God saw their affliction
2) God heard their cries
3) God knew about their suffering & was deeply concerned

b. God came down to deliver His people (Israel) from their suffering: He wanted to deliver them

c. God wanted to give the promised land to His people (a symbol of heaven)[DS2]
1) He wanted to give a fruitful land to them
2) He wanted to give a spacious land to them

4. The expected response to God's call[DS3]

a. Moses was to behold God's vision & compassion for His people

b. Moses was to go as God's messenger to deliver God's people from their enslavement

DIVISION II

MOSES AND GOD: GOD RAISES UP A LEADER TO DELIVER HIS PEOPLE (ISRAEL), 2:1–7:7

C. The Call of Moses: A Study of God's Call To Service, 3:1-10

(3:1-10) **Introduction**: God calls people to serve Him. Just think who it is that calls us to serve Him: the LORD Himself, the great God and Savior who created the universe and sustains everything throughout the universe. It is the sovereign LORD and Majesty of all—God Himself—who actually stoops down and offers us the wonderful privilege of serving Him. This should excite us. It should stir us to seek God's call, to seek God's hand upon our lives.

To all who are seeking God, to all who want to serve God, to all who want God's call upon their lives, this Scripture shows us how we can receive God's call: *The Call of Moses: A Study of God's Call to Service*, 3:1-10.

1. The kind of man God called (vv.1-3).
2. The call of God itself (vv.4-6).
3. The reasons why God called Moses (vv.7-8).
4. The expected response to God's call (vv.9-10).

1 (3:1-3) **Call, of God—Moses**: first, what kind of person does God call? Moses shows us. Remember, Moses had been the prince of Egypt. Consequently, a disappointed Pharaoh was seeking Moses' life and Moses was forced to flee down into Midian. In that distant but safe land, Moses met and agreed to work for Jethro, the priest of Midian. But note: all this had happened *forty years* before the present Scripture. God's call to Moses took place after Moses' flight from Egypt and settlement in Midian. In recording the significant events of his life, Moses says nothing about this second forty year period of his life. They are silent, unknown years.

But now, forty years later, a significant event occurs: God calls Moses, calls him to a heroic task. Note the kind of man Moses was, the kind of person God called.

a. Moses was a shepherd, which suggests that he had a heart that could shepherd people. When the call of God came to Moses, he was tending the flocks of Jethro, his father-in-law. The Hebrew has the idea of continuous action; that is, tending the flocks was his job. Moses was a shepherd by occupation. The work of a shepherd was...

- to feed and water the sheep
- to guide the sheep
- to seek and save the sheep who got lost
- to protect the sheep
- to keep the sheep separate from the goats (see outline and notes—Jn.10:2-3 for more discussion)

It took a person with a very special heart to be a shepherd. His heart had to be both tough and tender, hard and compassionate, disciplined and soft. In addition to this, the shepherd had to spend a great deal of time alone out in the countryside. While alone, he could, of course, just allow his mind to waste time and wander about from thought to thought or else he could utilize the time to develop his thought processes and to draw near God. The shepherd always had the opportunity to use his time to become a man of great devotion and prayer.

Obviously, Moses had spent forty years doing just this: developing the heart of a true shepherd and utilizing the hours alone to draw closer and closer to God. Now God was ready to call him to be the shepherd of God's people.

Thought 1. God's call does not come to a particular profession. It comes to a particular heart—to a heroic heart, to a heart that is willing to tackle a heroic task. God's call comes to a heart that is willing to shepherd people, a heart that is both...

- tough and tender
- hard and compassionate
- disciplined and soft

(1) God's call comes to a person who does not waste time, but who uses his time wisely; to a person who utilizes his time to develop his thought processes and to draw near God; to a person who becomes an individual of devotion and prayer.

(2) God's call comes to a person who is willing to feed and guide people, to seek and save people, and to protect and keep people for God.

"**And I will give you pastors according to mine heart, which shall feed you with knowledge and understanding**" (Je.3:15).

"**And I will set up shepherds over them which shall feed them: and they shall fear no more, nor be dismayed, neither shall they be lacking, saith the LORD**" (Je.23:4).

"**And I will set up one shepherd over them, and he shall feed them, even my servant David; he shall feed them, and he shall be their shepherd**" (Eze.34:23).

"**He saith unto him the third time, Simon, [son] of Jonas, lovest thou me? Peter was grieved because he said unto him the third time, Lovest thou me? And he said unto him, Lord, thou knowest all things; thou knowest that I love thee. Jesus saith unto him, Feed my sheep**" (Jn.21:17).

"**Take heed therefore unto yourselves, and to all the flock, over the which the Holy Ghost hath made you overseers, to feed the church of God, which he hath purchased with his own blood**" (Ac.20:28).

"**Feed the flock of God which is among you, taking the oversight thereof, not by constraint, but willingly; not for filthy lucre, but of a ready mind**" (1 Pe.5:2).

b. Moses was a hard-working, industrious man (v.1). Note where he was when God's call came to him: he was tending the flock at the far side of the desert. He was a common laborer, working for his father-in-law Jethro. As pointed out, the job Jethro had given him was hard, that of being a shepherd. A shepherd's job demanded long hours, seven days a week. His work sometimes demanded that he be far away from home, away from his family and, no doubt, away for weeks at a time. The work was also lonely and dangerous.

The point to see is that Moses was a hard, industrious worker. He was not lazy nor slothful. He worked at a job and in a place that few people would, and he worked longer hours and more days than most people would. Thus when God looked at Moses, He saw a hard-working, industrious man.

Thought 1. God does not call lazy, slothful people. A lazy person will not work, not long, hard hours. Neither will a lazy person finish a task, not often. God needs people who will work long and hard at any task, people who will finish the task no matter how difficult it may be.

Again, the person God calls is a hard-working, industrious person. God does not call the lazy, slothful person.

"**The soul of the sluggard desireth, and hath nothing: but the soul of the diligent shall be made fat**" (Pr.13:4).

"**The way of the slothful man is as an hedge of thorns: but the way of the righteous [diligent] is made plain**" (Pr.15:19).

"**Not slothful in business; fervent in spirit; serving the Lord**" (Ro.12:11).

"**For we hear that there are some which walk among you disorderly, working not at all, but are busybodies. Now them that are such we command and exhort by our Lord Jesus Christ, that with quietness they work, and eat their own bread**" (2 Th.3:11-12).

"**That ye be not slothful, but followers of them who through faith and patience inherit the promises**" (He.6:12).

c. Moses was a man of faith, a man who believed the miracles of God, the impossible acts of God (v.2). The person God uses must be a person of faith, a person who believes God. Note what now happened.

EXODUS 3:1-10

The angel of the LORD appeared to Moses (v.2). He appeared as a blazing fire within a bush, a flame of fire that did not burn out nor consume the bush. Who was this? God Himself or some angelic messenger (angel means messenger) that God sent? Note these facts:

⇒ God's voice called out to Moses from within the burning bush (v.4).
⇒ God identified Himself as the God of Abraham, Isaac, and Jacob (v.6).
⇒ The LORD continued to speak to Moses from within the burning bush. In fact, the LORD alone spoke from verse four to the end of this passage, verse ten.

In light of these facts, the messenger seems to be the LORD God Himself, more particularly, the second person of the Godhead, the Lord Jesus Christ. (See note—Ge.16:7 for more discussion.) Note that the LORD appeared as a blazing fire from within the bush, a flame of fire that just kept on burning and did not consume the bush (v.2). God has often used fire to symbolize and represent His presence (Ex.13:21; 19:18; 24:17; Jdg.13:20; 1 K.18:24, 38; 2 Chr.7:1-3; Eze.1:4-28; Da.7:9-10; He.12:29).

Arthur W. Pink points out that the Hebrew word here for *bush* (sen-eh) is used only one other time, in De.33:16.

"And for the precious things of the earth and fulness thereof, and for the good will of him that dwelt in the bush: let the blessing come upon the head of Joseph, and upon the top of the head of him that was separated from his brethren" (De. 33:16).

In this verse, the Hebrew word for "dwelt" is *shaw-kan* or *shakan*. This was, then, the Shekinah glory, the very presence of God Himself shining and blazing forth in the bush.[1] (See DEEPER STUDY # 2, *Shekinah Glory*—Ex.16:10. Also see notes—Ro.9:4; Mt.17:5-8 for more discussion.)

The point to see is this: God Himself was meeting Moses. He was manifesting and revealing Himself, meeting Moses in a very special way. Moses needed a deep, intense, unforgettable experience with God. He needed an experience with God that he would never forget as he launched out for God. Moses needed to see the glory of God…

• before he could undertake the mission of God
• before he could minister and serve in the power of God

Thought 1. Every believer should seek deeper experiences with God, to know God more and more, to draw closer to Him.

(1) We should seek to experience more and more of the glory of God, God's glory manifested in Jesus Christ, our Lord and Savior.

"But we all, with open face beholding as in a glass the glory of the Lord, are changed into the same image from glory to glory, even as by the Spirit of the Lord" (2 Co.3:18).

"For God, who commanded the light to shine out of darkness, hath shined in our hearts, to give the light of the knowledge of the glory of God in the face of Jesus Christ. But we have this treasure in earthen vessels, that the excellency of the power may be of God, and not of us" (2 Co.4:6-7).

"God….Hath in these last days spoken unto us by his Son, whom he hath appointed heir of all things, by whom also he made the worlds; who being the brightness of his glory, and the express image of his person, and upholding all things by the word of his power, when he had by himself purged our sins, sat down on the right hand of the Majesty on high" (He.1:1-3).

(2) Once we have truly seen the glory of God, we will then minister and bear witness in the power of God. The shepherds who saw the glory of God when Jesus Christ was born into the world are a dynamic example of this truth.

"And there were in the same country shepherds abiding in the field, keeping watch over their flock by night. And, lo, the angel of the Lord came upon them, and the glory of the Lord shone round about them: and they were sore afraid. And the angel said unto them, Fear not: for, behold, I bring you good tidings of great joy, which shall be to all people. For unto you is born this day in the city of David a Saviour, which is Christ the Lord. And this shall be a sign unto you; Ye shall find the babe wrapped in swaddling clothes, lying in a manger. And suddenly there was with the angel a multitude of the heavenly host praising God, and saying, glory to God in the highest, and on earth peace, good will toward men. And it came to pass, as the angels were gone away from them into heaven, the shepherds said one to another, Let us now go even unto Bethlehem, and see this thing which is come to pass, which the Lord hath made known unto us. And they came with haste, and found Mary, and Joseph, and the babe lying in a manger. And when they had seen it, they made known abroad the saying which was told them concerning this child" (Lu.2:8-17).

"To wit, that God was in Christ, reconciling the world unto himself, not imputing their trespasses unto them; and hath committed unto us the word of reconciliation. Now then we are ambassadors for Christ, as though God did beseech *you* by us: we pray *you* in Christ's stead, be ye reconciled to God" (2 Co.5:19-20).

---

[1] Arthur W. Pink. *Gleanings in Exodus*. (Chicago, IL: Moody Bible Institute of Chicago, Moody Press, no date given), p.23

Thought 2. Two other examples of men who saw the glory of God are:
⇒ Isaiah (Is.6:1f)
⇒ Paul the apostle (Ac.9:3f)

d. Moses was a man who would stop and seek the meaning of things (v.3). Note that he stopped, turned aside, and went over to see the unusual sight, just why the blazing fire did not burn out nor consume the bush. Just think what would have happened if Moses had not stopped and gone over to see the unusual sight: he would have…
• missed the blessing of God
• missed this deep experience with God
• missed the call of God upon his life

Thought 1. Many people are not interested in the meaning of things, not enough to stop and study the real meaning lying behind things, especially the meaning of God and of spiritual things. Many people ignore God and the things of God. They are…
• just too busy and too wrapped up in the affairs of life
• just interested in the pleasures and possessions of this world

Most people are not like Moses: they just are not willing to stop and to seek the meaning of spiritual things. The LORD was appearing to Moses and Moses stopped and sought the meaning of the LORD's appearance. The LORD has appeared to us; He has come to earth. We must stop and seek the meaning of His coming. The person who truly seeks the LORD will find Him.

> "But if from thence thou shalt seek the LORD thy God, thou shalt find him, if thou seek him with all thy heart and with all thy soul" (De.4:29).
> "Seek ye the LORD while he may be found, call ye upon him while he is near" (Is.55:6).
> "And ye shall seek me, and find me, when ye shall search for me with all your heart" (Je.29:13).
> "And I say unto you, Ask, and it shall be given you; seek, and ye shall find; knock, and it shall be opened unto you. For every one that asketh receiveth; and he that seeketh findeth; and to him that knocketh it shall be opened" (Lu.11:9-10).
> "That they should seek the Lord, if haply they might feel after him, and find him, though he be not far from every one of us" (Ac.17:27).

DEEPER STUDY # 1

(3:1) **Mt. Horeb—Mt. Sinai**: Horeb means *desert* or *desolation*. Mt. Horeb and Mt. Sinai are either the same mountain or within the same mountain range. Both names seem to be used interchangeably throughout Scripture. Note that the mountain is called "the mountain of God." Mt. Sinai or Horeb is the mountain…
• where God called Moses to deliver His people from slavery (Ex.3:1f)
• where God gave the law to Moses and His people (Ex.19:1f)
• where Moses struck the rock and God caused water to flow out from the rock (Ex.17:6)
• where the people repented and gave offerings to God (Ex.33:6)
• where Elijah fled from Jezebel (1 K.19:8)

MT. HOREB or MT. SINAI[2]

---

2 Map from *Life Application*® *Bible*. Used by permission.

2 (3:4-6) **Call, of God—Moses—God, Holy**: second, there was the call of God itself. God's call to Moses shows us exactly what is involved when God calls a person. It shows us the factors included in God's call.

a. God's call was to a seeking man. Note when God called Moses: when Moses stopped and sought the meaning of the burning bush (v.4). Then and only then did God call out to Moses. What would have happened if Moses had ignored the bush and concluded that it was not worth the effort to seek to understand it? Most likely God would not have called him.

But Moses did stop and seek to understand the burning bush. God's call was to a seeking man, a man who sought to understand the truth and meaning of things.

Thought 1. The person who seeks to know the truth and meaning of things, and is open to God, will be met by God. God will meet and call the seeking person. The Bible clearly says that any person who seeks God, who seeks to know and understand God, will find God.

> "But if from thence thou shalt seek the LORD thy God, thou shalt find him, if thou seek him with all thy heart and with all thy soul" (De.4:29).
> "I love them that love me; and those that seek me early shall find me" (Pr.8:17).
> "And ye shall seek me, and find me, when ye shall search for me with all your heart" (Je.29:13).
> "For thus saith the LORD unto the house of Israel, Seek ye me, and ye shall live" (Am.5:4).
> "And I say unto you, Ask, and it shall be given you; seek, and ye shall find; knock, and it shall be opened unto you. For every one that asketh receiveth; and he that seeketh findeth; and to him that knocketh it shall be opened" (Lu.11:9-10).

b. God's call was a personal call (v.4). God called Moses by name. Note Moses' response: "Here am I."

Thought 1. Two points of application.
(1) God's call to us is personal. He knows us by name, every one of us.

> "I know thee by name, and thou hast also found grace in my sight" (Ex.33:12).
> "But know that the LORD hath set apart him that is godly for himself: the LORD will hear when I call unto him" (Ps.4:3).
> "Fear not: for I have redeemed thee, I have called thee by thy name; thou art mine" (Is.43:1).

(2) We must always respond positively to God's call: "Here am I." We must obey God: go and do exactly what He wants.
- Abraham responded, "Here I am."

> "And it came to pass after these things, that God did tempt Abraham, and said unto him, Abraham: and he said, Behold, here I am" (Ge.22:1).

- Samuel responded, "Here am I."

> "That the LORD called Samuel: and he answered, Here am I" (1 S.3:4).

- Isaiah responded, "Here am I."

> "Also I heard the voice of the Lord, saying, Whom shall I send, and who will go for us? Then said I, Here am I; send me" (Is.6:8).

- Paul responded, "Here am I."

> "And he trembling and astonished said, Lord, what wilt thou have me to do [Here am I]? And the Lord said unto him, Arise, and go into the city, and it shall be told thee what thou must do" (Ac.9:6).

c. God's call was a holy call (v.5). God stopped Moses dead in his tracks. He told Moses to come no closer and to take off his shoes. Why? Because the ground where he stood was holy ground. Note that the ground was not holy *in and of* itself; it was holy because God was there. God was making a very special manifestation of Himself and using the ground for a specific purpose, that of calling a man to be God's servant, God's messenger.

When God told Moses to take off his shoes, He was teaching Moses a necessary lesson, a lesson that every person must learn: God is holy. Holy means to be separate and distinct, different—entirely different—from mortal man. It means that God is pure, righteous, moral, just, and eternal—perfectly so, in every detail of His being.

God is holy. Therefore, when mortal man enters God's presence, he must be prepared: man must be respectful, reverent, and submissive.

Thought 1. God is not a *chummy friend* to man. Neither is He *the man upstairs*. Nor is He a *grandfather-type* person who allows us to behave like we want and gives us what we want.

God is holy—different, completely set apart from this universe—ruling and reigning as the Supreme LORD and Majesty of the universe. Therefore, we must enter His holy presence prepared: we must be respectful, reverent, and submissive.

"Who is like unto thee, O LORD, among the gods? who is like thee, glorious in holiness, fearful in praises, doing wonders?" (Ex.15:11).

"For I am the LORD your God: ye shall therefore sanctify yourselves, and ye shall be holy; for I am holy: neither shall ye defile yourselves with any manner of creeping thing that creepeth upon the earth" (Le.11:44).

"Exalt the LORD our God, and worship at his holy hill; for the LORD our God is holy" (Ps.99:9).

"And one cried unto another, and said, Holy, holy, holy, is the LORD of hosts: the whole earth is full of his glory" (Is.6:3).

"Because it is written, Be ye holy; for I am holy" (1 Pe.1:16).

"Who shall not fear thee, O Lord, and glorify thy name? for thou only art holy: for all nations shall come and worship before thee; for thy judgments are made manifest" (Re.15:4).

d. God's call was a call from the only living and true God, the only God who can truly fulfill His promises to man (v.6). God declared an amazing thing to Moses. Note exactly what He said: "I am the God of your father, the God of Abraham, the God of Isaac, and the God of Jacob." God did not declare that He *was* the God of Moses' forefathers; He declared that He *is* their God. Present, active tense. Jesus Christ Himself referred to this passage saying that God was proving His existence and the reality of life hereafter. God was proving:

⇒ that He is the living and true God.
⇒ that believers are living and are actively engaged with God when they leave this earth.
⇒ that believers really do enter the promised land of heaven.

God *is* the God of Abraham, Isaac, and Jacob. They had long ago died and had been gone for more than four hundred years, yet they were still alive, living with God and serving Him.

Now, note exactly what God was declaring to Moses: "I am [present, active tense] the God of your father, the God of Abraham, the God of Isaac, and the God of Jacob" (v.6).

⇒ He is the only living and true God.
⇒ He is the God of Moses' forefathers, the very God whom they believed and served.
⇒ He is the God who had made the promises to Moses' forefathers, the promise of the promised land and of the promised seed, meaning both a great nation of people and the Savior Himself.
⇒ He is the God with whom Moses' forefathers were living, the God who had fulfilled His promises to give the promised land of heaven, eternal life, to them.

Note Moses' response to such a wonderful revelation: he hid his face, for he was afraid to look at God (v.6).

Thought 1. God's call was bound to strengthen Moses' faith. Just think what Moses had learned from this revelation: God is; God actually exists.

⇒ The promised land of heaven, eternal life, is true.
⇒ Believers—all believers who have gone on before—are living and will forever live in God's presence.
⇒ God fulfills His promises. He fulfilled His promises to Abraham, Isaac, and Jacob. Therefore, He will fulfill His promises to us.

"Know therefore that the LORD thy God, he is God, the faithful God, which keepeth covenant and mercy with them that love him and keep his commandments to a thousand generations" (De.7:9).

"Blessed be the LORD, that hath given rest unto his people Israel, according to all that he promised: there hath not failed one word of all his good promise, which he promised by the hand of Moses his servant" (1 K.8:56).

"Thy mercy, O LORD, is in the heavens; and thy faithfulness reacheth unto the clouds" (Ps.36:5).

"God is faithful, by whom ye were called unto the fellowship of his Son Jesus Christ our Lord" (1 Co.1:9).

"But the Lord is faithful, who shall stablish you, and keep you from evil" (2 Th.3:3).

"I know whom I have believed, and am persuaded that he is able to keep that which I have committed unto him against that day" (2 Ti.1:12).

"Let us hold fast the profession of our faith without wavering; for he is faithful that promised" (He.10:23).

3 (3:7-8) **Call, of God**: third, there were the reasons why God called Moses. God called Moses for three very specific reasons, reasons that are true of every God-given call.

a. God was deeply concerned about the suffering of His people (v.7). His concern is graphically pictured:
1) God saw the affliction and misery of His people (v.7). Note how forcefully the fact is stated: "I have surely [indeed] seen the affliction of my people" (v.7). This is the first time God ever called Israel "my people."
2) God heard the cries of His people (v.7). The taskmasters no doubt were cursing, abusing, beating, and forcing the people to work beyond utter exhaustion. The people moaned and groaned under the oppressive affliction. They had no hope but God, and they could do nothing but cry out to God. This they did, and the most wonderful thing was now happening: God heard their cries and was now acting to meet their need.
3) God knew about their sorrow and suffering and was deeply concerned for them (v.7).

Thought 1. Two lessons are clearly seen in this point.
(1) God always sees our suffering and misery, and He always hears our cries. God knows all about our sorrows and is deeply concerned for us. The very reason God calls us to serve Him is because…

- He sees the affliction and misery of people
- He hears their cries for help
- He knows all about their sorrows and is deeply concerned for them

"But I am poor and needy; yet the Lord thinketh upon me: thou art my help and my deliverer; make no tarrying, O my God" (Ps.40:17).

"Fear thou not; for I am with thee: be not dismayed; for I am thy God: I will strengthen thee; yea, I will help thee; yea, I will uphold thee with the right hand of my righteousness" (Is.41:10).

"When thou passest through the waters, I will be with thee; and through the rivers, they shall not overflow thee: when thou walkest through the fire, thou shalt not be burned; neither shall the flame kindle upon thee" (Is.43:2).

"And even to your old age I am he; and even to hoar [gray] hairs will I carry you: I have made, and I will bear; even I will carry, and will deliver you" (Is.46:4).

"Casting all your care upon him; for he careth for you" (1 Pe.5:7).

(2) God also wants us to see, hear, and be concerned for His people, for those who suffer in this world.

"I have showed you all things, how that so labouring ye ought to support the weak, and to remember the words of the Lord Jesus, how he said, It is more blessed to give than to receive" (Ac.20:35).

"We then that are strong ought to bear the infirmities of the weak, and not to please ourselves" (Ro.15:1).

"Bear ye one another's burdens, and so fulfil the law of Christ" (Ga.6:2).

"Put on therefore, as the elect of God, holy and beloved, bowels of mercies, kindness, humbleness of mind, meekness, longsuffering" (Col.3:12).

"Remember them that are in bonds, as bound with them; and them which suffer adversity, as being yourselves also in the body" (He.13:3).

b. God came down to deliver His people from their suffering (v.8). He wanted to deliver them from their enslavement, from the enslaving hand of their enemy (Egypt). Note the picture: God came down as the God of deliverance to do the work of redemption. God came down to save His people, to deliver them from the bondage of the evil prince and of the evil enslavers of Egypt.

Thought 1. This should give us great assurance, great confidence, great security—God has the power to deliver us.
(1) God is able to deliver us from all our suffering.
(2) God is able to deliver us from the enslavement of any thing, person, nation, or power, whether the power be physical or spiritual. Throughout Scripture, ancient Egypt is a symbol of the world and its worldly ways; and Pharaoh is a symbol of the evil prince, Satan himself. God is able to deliver us from Satan and the world and from the enslavements of this world. No matter how enslaved some power may hold us, whether physical or spiritual power, God is able to deliver us.

"And he said, The LORD is my rock, and my fortress, and my deliverer" (2 S.22:2).

"Surely he shall deliver thee from the snare of the fowler, and from the noisome pestilence" (Ps.91:3).

"Be not afraid of their faces: for I am with thee to deliver thee, saith the LORD" (Je.1:8).

"He delivereth and rescueth, and he worketh signs and wonders in heaven and in earth, who hath delivered Daniel from the power of the lions" (Da.6:27).

"There hath no temptation taken you but such as is common to man: but God is faithful, who will not suffer you to be tempted above that ye are able; but will with the temptation also make a way to escape, that ye may be able to bear it" (1 Co.10:13).

"And the Lord shall deliver me from every evil work, and will preserve me unto his heavenly kingdom: to whom be glory for ever and ever. Amen" (2 Ti.4:18).

"Forasmuch then as the children are partakers of flesh and blood, he also himself likewise took part of the same; that through death he might destroy him that had the power of death, that is, the devil; and deliver them who through fear of death were all their lifetime subject to bondage" (He.2:14-15).

"The Lord knoweth how to deliver the godly out of temptations, and to reserve the unjust unto the day of judgment to be punished" (2 Pe.2:9).

Thought 2. Note two significant facts about redemption.
(1) God is our Redeemer.

"For I know that my redeemer liveth, and that he shall stand at the latter day upon the earth" (Jb.19:25).

"And he shall redeem Israel from all his iniquities" (Ps.130:8).

"For their redeemer is mighty; he shall plead their cause with thee" (Pr.23:11).

"Thus saith the LORD, thy redeemer, and he that formed thee from the womb, I am the LORD that maketh all things; that stretcheth forth the heavens alone; that spreadeth abroad the earth by myself" (Is.44:24).

"As for our redeemer, the LORD of hosts is his name, the Holy One of Israel" (Is.47:4).

"And the Redeemer shall come to Zion, and unto them that turn from transgression in Jacob, saith the LORD" (Is.59:20).

"Into thine hand I commit my spirit: thou hast redeemed me, O LORD God of truth" (Ps.31:5).

"He sent redemption unto his people: he hath commanded his covenant for ever: holy and reverend is his name" (Ps.111:9).

"Let Israel hope in the LORD: for with the LORD there is mercy, and with him is plenteous redemption" (Ps.130:7).

"But now thus saith the LORD that created thee, O Jacob, and he that formed thee, O Israel, Fear not: for I have redeemed thee, I have called thee by thy name; thou art mine" (Is.43:1).

"Blessed be the Lord God of Israel; for he hath visited and redeemed his people" (Lu.1:68).

"And she coming in that instant gave thanks likewise unto the Lord, and spake of him (Jesus Christ) to all them that looked for redemption in Jerusalem" (Lu.2:38).

(2) God redeems us through His Son, the Lord Jesus Christ. It is Christ who saves and delivers us from the power of Satan and from the enslavements of this world. Jesus Christ can deliver us out of shame, brokenness, loneliness, routineness, immorality, drugs, alcohol, pornography, stealing, abuse, crime, and any other enslaving power. Jesus Christ is the Redeemer and Savior of man. Jesus Christ can deliver us...

- from sin to righteousness
- from death to life
- from hell to heaven
- from emptiness to fulness
- from loneliness to friendship
- from darkness to light
- from no direction to purpose
- from meaninglessness to significance

"Being justified freely by his grace through the redemption that is in Christ Jesus" (Ro.3:24).

"But of him are ye in Christ Jesus, who of God is made unto us wisdom, and righteousness, and sanctification, and redemption" (1 Co.1:30).

"Christ hath redeemed us from the curse of the law, being made a curse for us: for it is written, Cursed is every one that hangeth on a tree" (Ga.3:13).

"In whom we have redemption through his blood, even the forgiveness of sins" (Col.1:14).

"Who gave himself for us, that he might redeem us from all iniquity, and purify unto himself a peculiar people, zealous of good works" (Tit.2:14).

"Neither by the blood of goats and calves, but by his own blood he entered in once into the holy place, having obtained eternal redemption for us" (He.9:12).

"Forasmuch as ye know that ye were not redeemed with corruptible things, as silver and gold, from your vain conversation received by tradition from your fathers" (1 Pe.1:18).

"And they sung a new song, saying, Thou art worthy to take the book, and to open the seals thereof: for thou wast slain, and hast redeemed us to God by thy blood out of every kindred, and tongue, and people, and nation" (Re.5:9).

c. God wanted to give the promised land to His people (v.8). Remember, the promised land of Cannan was a symbol of the promised land of heaven (see note—Ge.12:1). Note exactly what God said: not only was He going to deliver His people from their enslavement, but He was also going to lead them into the promised land. He said two things about the land:

⇒ It was a land "flowing with milk and honey" (v.8). This is a picture of plenty, fruitfulness, fertility, and abundance. The promised land was a land that just flourished with the best of everything, a land where full provision was available to meet all the physical needs of God's people. The term is used throughout Scripture (Ex.3:17; 13:5).

⇒ It was a land that was spacious, a land so spacious that six nations were then living there (v.8). The idea is that the land was large enough to take care of everyone. It was a land where everyone would have plenty of space and would live in peace with one another (v.8).

Thought 1. God not only redeems us *from* something, He redeems us *to* something. He redeems us from Satan and the world and redeems us to Himself and to heaven. The land of Canaan promised to Israel is a picture of the promised land of heaven.

(1) Heaven is a place that is flowing with milk and honey, a place where all our needs are abundantly met.

"But as it is written, Eye hath not seen, nor ear heard, neither have entered into the heart of man, the things which God hath prepared for them that love him" (1 Co.2:9).

"And I saw a new heaven and a new earth: for the first heaven and the first earth were passed away....And I John saw the holy city, new Jerusalem [the capital of the new heavens and earth], coming down from God out of heaven, prepared as a bride adorned for her husband. And I heard a great voice out of heaven saying, Behold, the tabernacle [holy presence] of God is with men, and he will dwell with them, and they shall be his people, and God himself shall be with them, and be their God. And God shall wipe away all tears from their eyes; and there shall be no more death, neither

"And he showed me a pure river of water of life, clear as crystal, proceeding out of the throne of God and of the Lamb. In the midst of the street of it, and on either side of the river, was there the tree of life, which bare twelve manner of fruits, and yielded her fruit every month [an abundance of harvest and food]: and the leaves of the tree were for the healing of the nations. And there shall be no more curse: but the throne of God and of the Lamb shall be in it; and his servants shall serve him: and they shall see his face; and his name shall be in their foreheads. And there shall be no night there; and they need no candle, neither light of the sun; for the Lord God giveth them light: and they shall reign for ever and ever" (Re.22:1-5).

(2) Heaven is spacious: there is room in heaven for all who will believe God.

"For God so loved the world, that he gave his only begotten Son, that whosoever believeth in him should not perish, but have everlasting life" (Jn.3:16).

"Let not your heart be troubled: ye believe in God, believe also in me. In my Father's house are many mansions: if [it were] not [so], I would have told you. I go to prepare a place for you. And if I go and prepare a place for you, I will come again, and receive you unto myself; that where I am, [there] ye may be also" (Jn.14:1-3).

"For we know that if our earthly house of this tabernacle were dissolved, we have a building of God, an house not made with hands, eternal in the heavens" (2 Co.5:1).

"By faith Abraham, when he was called to go out into a place which he should after receive for an inheritance, obeyed; and he went out, not knowing whither he went. By faith he sojourned in the land of promise, as in a strange country, dwelling in tabernacles with Isaac and Jacob, the heirs with him of the same promise: for he looked for a city which hath foundations, whose builder and maker is God" (He.11:8-10).

"These all died in faith, not having received the promises, but having seen them afar off, and were persuaded of them, and embraced them, and confessed that they were strangers and pilgrims on the earth. For they that say such things declare plainly that they seek a country. And truly, if they had been mindful of that country from whence they came out, they might have had opportunity to have returned. But now they desire a better country, that is, an heavenly: wherefore God is not ashamed to be called their God: for he hath prepared for them a city" (He.11:13-16).

"Blessed be the God and Father of our Lord Jesus Christ, which according to his abundant mercy hath begotten us again unto a lively hope by the resurrection of Jesus Christ from the dead, to an inheritance incorruptible, and undefiled, and that fadeth not away, reserved in heaven for you" (1 Pe.1:3-4).

"But the day of the Lord will come as a thief in the night; in the which the heavens shall pass away with a great noise, and the elements shall melt with fervent heat, the earth also and the works that are therein shall be burned up. Seeing then that all these things shall be dissolved, what manner of persons ought ye to be in all holy conversation and godliness, Looking for and hasting unto the coming of the day of God, wherein the heavens being on fire shall be dissolved, and the elements shall melt with fervent heat? Nevertheless we, according to his promise, look for new heavens and a new earth, wherein dwelleth righteousness" (2 Pe.3:10-13).

DEEPER STUDY # 2
(3:8) **Canaanites—Israel—Land, Promised—Spiritual Struggle—Separation—Compromise—Religion, False—Warfare—Worldliness**: the land that God had promised the Israelites was not void of people. Before Israel could fully possess the land flowing with milk and honey, they would have to deal with a variety of foes.

⇒ The *Canaanites* were direct descendents from Canaan (Ge.10:15-18). From the sons of Canaan came a variety of different people: the Hittites, the Amorites, the Perizzites, the Hivites, and the Jebusites.

⇒ The *religion* of the Canaanites focused on a variety of deities, but gave greatest emphasis to El (who was also known as Baal). Over time, Israel would find itself neglecting the command of God to destroy every Canaanite influence. They would fail to worship God alone. They would allow the false religion of the Canaanites to seep into their lives. This neglect would later prove to be a fatal error.

⇒ The *materialistic* and *immoral* lifestyle of the Canaanites became very appealing to the Israelites. Instead of Israel pulling up the Canaanite culture, the Canaanites pulled the Israelites down into their culture. The Israelites allowed the poison of worldliness to pollute their lives with lust, with the lust for the things of this world: they lusted after the men and women of Canaan and they lusted after the material possessions of the Canaanites. It was a poison that numbed their desire to live a moral life before God and man.

Thought 1. We face a daily struggle...
• in seeking to live a life of separation, a life of morality and righteousness
• in seeking to resist people and things that try to turn us away from God
• in seeking to not compromise Biblical convictions in an ever-changing moral climate
• in seeking to resist the temptation to run in the 'rat race' of seeking material possessions
• in seeking to avoid the pitfalls of idolatry
• in seeking to live for the truth
• in seeking to walk about acknowledging and praising God

4 (3:9-10) **Call, of God**: there was the expected response to God's call. God expected two responses from Moses, the same two responses He expects from every person He calls to serve Him.

a. Moses was to behold—see, grasp, lay hold of—God's vision and compassion for His people (v.9). Note that God was repeating what He had just said in verse seven: the cry of His people had reached Him and He saw their terrible suffering. Why repeat this fact? Obviously, the sufferings of the people had deeply touched God. But more than this, God wanted to drive the point home to Moses' heart. God wanted to touch Moses' heart with the sufferings of His people. God wanted Moses' heart broken with compassion. Moses needed to grasp the great vision of God for His people. Then and only then would Moses obey God's call.

b. Moses was to go as God's messenger to deliver God's people from their enslavement (v.10). This is the great call of Moses, the great commission that God gave to Moses. Note these facts:

1) It was God who was sending Moses (v.10). Moses was not appointing himself to be God's spokesman; he had no authority to do such a thing. Moses was being appointed, chosen, sent, and commissioned by God Himself. God and God alone has the authority to call and commission people to represent Him.

Thought 1. How many pulpits have been filled by people who were not truly called by God? Who looked upon the ministry only as a profession? Only as a way to make some money or a decent living? How many people have chosen the ministry only because it seemed to be the best way to serve people and to make a commendable contribution to society?

"Beware of false prophets, which come to you in sheep's clothing, but inwardly they are ravening wolves" (Mt.7:15).

"But in vain they do worship me, teaching [for] doctrines the commandments of men" (Mt.15:9).

"For we are not as many, which corrupt the word of God: but as of sincerity, but as of God, in the sight of God speak we in Christ" (2 Co.2:17).

"But have renounced the hidden things of dishonesty, not walking in craftiness, nor handling the word of God deceitfully; but by manifestation of the truth commending ourselves to every man's conscience in the sight of God" (2 Co.4:2).

"Now the Spirit speaketh expressly, that in the latter times some shall depart from the faith, giving heed to seducing spirits, and doctrines of devils; speaking lies in hypocrisy; having their conscience seared with a hot iron" (1 Ti.4:1-2).

"But there were false prophets also among the people, even as there shall be false teachers among you, who privily shall bring in damnable heresies, even denying the Lord that bought them, and bring upon themselves swift destruction" (2 Pe.2:1).

2) Moses' call and commission was to rescue people, to deliver them from their enslavement (v.10).

Thought 1. When God calls us, He expects us to respond, to accept His call.
(1) God expects us to grasp His vision and compassion for people.
(2) God expects us to go forth as His messengers, to go forth and deliver people from their enslavement to the worldly ways of this earth. God expects us to lead sinners...
- from sin to righteousness
- from bondage to liberty
- from death to life
- from suffering to health
- from hunger to fulness
- from loneliness to friendship
- from division to reconciliation
- from hate to love
- from war to peace
- from prejudice to acceptance

"Even as the Son of man came not to be ministered unto, but to minister, and to give his life a ransom for many" (Mt.20:28).

"Go ye therefore, and teach all nations, baptizing them in the name of the Father, and of the Son, and of the Holy Ghost: teaching them to observe all things whatsoever I have commanded you: and, lo, I am with you alway, [even] unto the end of the world. Amen" (Mt.28:19-20).

"And he said unto them, Go ye into all the world, and preach the gospel to every creature" (Mk.16:15).

"Ye have not chosen me, but I have chosen you, and ordained you, that ye should go and bring forth fruit, and [that] your fruit should remain: that whatsoever ye shall ask of the Father in my name, he may give it you" (Jn.15:16).

"But ye shall receive power, after that the Holy Ghost is come upon you: and ye shall be witnesses unto me both in Jerusalem, and in all Judaea, and in Samaria, and unto the uttermost part of the earth" (Ac.1:8).

"But the Lord said unto him, Go thy way: for he is a chosen vessel unto me, to bear my name before the Gentiles, and kings, and the children of Israel" (Ac.9:15).

"And he said, The God of our fathers hath chosen thee, that thou shouldest know his will, and see that Just One, and shouldest hear the voice of his mouth. For thou shalt be his witness unto all men of what thou hast seen and heard" (Ac.22:14-15).

"That which we have seen and heard declare we unto you, that ye also may have fellowship with us: and truly our fellowship is with the Father, and with his Son Jesus Christ" (1 Jn.1:3).

DEEPER STUDY # 3

(3:9-10) **Call, of God—Chart, of Persons God Called**: when God calls a person, two things occur: God calls and the person responds. The believer can learn much from a simple study which focuses on the call of some Old Testament Bible characters.

A GENERAL SURVEY OF GOD'S CALL TO HIS PEOPLE

The Person	The Reference	The Call	The Response
Adam	Ge.2:15-17	To cultivate the garden and keep it while staying away from the tree of the knowledge of good and evil.	Adam disobeyed God and ate the fruit from the forbidden tree.
Noah	Ge.6:14-22	To make an ark that would save Noah, his family, and two of every living creature.	Noah did all that God commanded him to do.
Abraham	Ge.12:1-4	To leave... • his country • his relatives • his father's household ...and seek the promised land of God.	Abram left and did exactly what the LORD demanded.
Moses	Ex.3:1-10	To enter Pharaoh's Egypt and deliver Israel from its bondage.	After giving God a list of excuses, Moses finally surrendered to God's call to free Israel.
Joshua	Jos.1:1-9	To lead Israel into the Promised Land.	Embracing God's challenge to be "strong and courageous," Joshua led the people into the Promised Land.
Gideon	Jdg.6:11-24	To deliver Israel from the hand of Midian.	Midian was subdued before the sons of Israel (Jud.8:28).
Samuel	1 S.3:1-14	To replace the corrupt priestly leadership of Eli's house.	During a time when a word from the LORD was rare, Samuel not only heard the LORD ("Here I am"), but he also shared that word with Eli.
Saul	1 S.9:15-16	[Given to Saul through Samuel] • To be a captain or prince (NASV) over Israel • To deliver Israel from the Philistines.	Saul reigned as king for 32 years (1 S.13:1).
David	1 S.16:7-13	To become Israel's king.	Even though David's call to be king came during his youth, God was maturing him for the task: from a shepherd boy to a king. After Saul, David became Israel's next king.
Solomon	1 K.2:1-4	[David's charge to his son] • To be strong, like a man • To keep the charge of the LORD God • To walk in God's ways • To keep God's statutes, judgments, and His testimonies.	Solomon's kingdom was "established greatly" (1 K.2:12).

The Person	The Reference	The Call	The Response
Isaiah	Is.6:1-8	To be sent by God to preach to His rebellious people.	Isaiah responded with this great confession: "Here am I; send me."
Ezekiel	Eze.2:1-10	To be a prophet in the midst of God's people, the rebellious nation of Israel that was in captivity.	Ezekiel, a man who was filled with the Spirit of God, obeyed the LORD and prophesied to those in Babylon.
Jeremiah	Je.1:4-19	To turn his world up-side down by pronouncing God's judgment upon Judah.	Known as the "weeping prophet," Jeremiah faithfully proclaimed the Word of the LORD.

TYPES, SYMBOLS, AND PICTURES
(Exodus 3:1-10)

Historical Term	Type or Picture (Scriptural Basis for Each)	Life Application for Today's Believer	Biblical Application
Moses (Ex.3:1f) Moses (continued) (Ex.3:1f)	• Moses was saved during childhood (Ex.2:1-10).	• Jesus Christ was saved during childhood).	"When he arose, he took the young child and his mother by night, and departed into Egypt: And was there until the death of Herod: that it might be fulfilled which was spoken of the Lord by the prophet, saying, Out of Egypt have I called my son" (Mt.2:14-15).
	• Moses struggled with Pharaoh (a symbol of Satan) (Ex.7:11).	• Jesus Christ struggled with Satan.	"Then was Jesus led up of the Spirit into the wilderness to be tempted of the devil" (Mt.4:1).
	• Moses fasted 40 days (Ex.34:28).	• Jesus Christ fasted 40 days.	"And when he had fasted forty days and forty nights, he was afterward an hungred" (Mt.4:2).
	• Moses was used by God to control the Sea (Ex.14:21).	• Jesus Christ controlled the Sea.	"And he saith unto them, Why are ye fearful, O ye of little faith? Then he arose, and rebuked the winds and the sea; and there was a great calm" (Mt.8:26).
	• Moses fed a multitude (Ex.16:15).	• Jesus Christ fed a multitude.	"And they did all eat, and were filled: and they took up of the fragments that remained twelve baskets full. And they that had eaten were about five thousand men, beside women and children" (Mt.14:20-21).
	• Moses' face glowed with God's glory (Ex.34:35).	• Jesus Christ's face glowed with God's glory.	"And was transfigured before them: and his face did shine as the sun, and his raiment was white as the light" (Mt.17:2).
	• Moses suffered the complaints & fault-finding of people (Ex.15:24).	• Jesus Christ suffered the complaints & fault-finding of people.	"And when they saw some of his disciples eat bread with defiled, that is to say, with unwashen, hands, they found fault" (Mk.7:2).
	• Moses suffered the opposition of his own family (Nu.12:1).	• Jesus Christ suffered the opposition of his own family.	"For neither did his brethren believe in him" (Jn.7:5).
	• Moses was an intercessor. (He offered up the prayer of intercession for his people) (Ex.32:31-32).	• Jesus Christ was an intercessor. (He offered up the prayer of intercession for his people.)	"I pray for them: I pray not for the world, but for them which thou hast given me; for they are thine" (Jn.17:9).

TYPES, SYMBOLS, AND PICTURES
(Exodus 3:1-10)

Historical Term	Type or Picture (Scriptural Basis for Each)	Life Application for Today's Believer	Biblical Application
	• Moses had seventy helpers (Nu.11:16-17).	• Jesus Christ had seventy helpers.	"After these things the Lord appointed other seventy also, and sent them two and two before his face into every city and place, whither he himself would come" (Lu.10:1).
	• Moses established ordinances, memorials (Ex.12:14).	• Jesus Christ established ordinances, memorials.	"And he took bread, and gave thanks, and brake [it], and gave unto them, saying, This is my body which is given for you: this do in remembrance of me" (Lu.22:19).
	• Moses reappeared after death (Mt.17:3).	• Jesus Christ reappeared after death.	"To whom also he showed himself alive after his passion by many infallible proofs, being seen of them forty days, and speaking of the things pertaining to the kingdom of God" (Ac.1:3).
The Burning Bush (Ex. 3:2, 5)	A picture of the glory, presence and holiness of God "And the angel of the LORD appeared unto him in a flame of fire out of the midst of a bush: and he looked, and, behold, the bush burned with fire, and the bush *was* not consumed....And he said, Draw not nigh hither: put off thy shoes from off thy feet, for the place whereon thou standest is holy ground" (Ex.3:2, 5). "For I am the LORD that bringeth you up out of the land of Egypt, to be your God: ye shall therefore be holy, for I am holy" (Le.11:45). (see Le.19:2; 1 Chr.16:29)	The glory, presence, and holiness of God are available to every believer… • who seeks deeper experiences with God • who longs to know God more and more • who draws closer and closer to God • who loves God without any reservation	"I beseech you therefore, brethren, by the mercies of God, that ye present your bodies a living sacrifice, holy, acceptable unto God, which is your reasonable service. And be not conformed to this world: but be ye transformed by the renewing of your mind, that ye may prove what is that good, and acceptable, and perfect, will of God" (Ro.12:1-2). "Having therefore these promises, dearly beloved, let us cleanse ourselves from all filthiness of the flesh and spirit, perfecting holiness in the fear of God" (2 Co.7:1). "But as he which hath called you is holy, so be ye holy in all manner of conversation [behavior, conduct]; Because it is written, Be ye holy; for I am holy" (1 Pe.1:15-16). (see 1 Chr.16:29; Is.6:1-3, 5; Ro.11:33; 2 Co.3:18)

Note: the comparison between Moses and Christ is taken from *The Thompson Chain Reference Bible*, Cyclopedia Index. (Indianapolis, IN: B.B. Kirkbride Bible Co., Inc., 1964), p.95, # 2421.

1. Argument 1: He felt incapable, unqualified
- a. Moses' excuse: Who am I to take on such a task?
  - 1) To go before Pharaoh
  - 2) To deliver a captive people
- b. God's reply: A demand for faith—to believe God's promise
  - 1) The promise of God's presence: "I will be with you"
  - 2) The promise of a sign: Israel would worship God upon the very mountain where Moses stood

2. Argument 2: He felt the people were ignorant of God & would be skeptical of God's power to truly help them
- a. Moses' excuse: He felt the people would question his call & question just who God is, question His power to save & deliver them
- b. God's reply: Moses was to declare several facts to Israel
  - 1) God's name: "I AM THAT I AM"—it was He who sent Moses[DS1]
  - 2) God's identity, the Lord God: He is the same God as the God of Abraham, the God of Isaac, & the God of Jacob—it was He who sent Moses
  - 3) God's memorial: His name, the Lord God, is His memorial, the name to be known & remembered forever
  - 4) God's concern & care for His people, Israel

  - 5) God's past promise of deliverance: God promised 400 years before to bring Israel out from Egypt to the promised land (Ge.15:13-14; 50:24)

  - 6) God's promise to His servant Moses: The people would listen & accept his leadership
  - 7) God's instructions to the elders (leaders): Moses &

D. The Excuses of Moses: A Reluctant Prophet— Arguments Against Serving God, 3:11–4:17

11 And Moses said unto God, Who am I, that I should go unto Pharaoh, and that I should bring forth the children of Israel out of Egypt?
12 And he said, Certainly I will be with thee; and this shall be a token unto thee, that I have sent thee: When thou hast brought forth the people out of Egypt, ye shall serve God upon this mountain.
13 And Moses said unto God, Behold, when I come unto the children of Israel, and shall say unto them, The God of your fathers hath sent me unto you; and they shall say to me, What is his name? what shall I say unto them?
14 And God said unto Moses, I AM THAT I AM: and he said, Thus shalt thou say unto the children of Israel, I AM hath sent me unto you.
15 And God said moreover unto Moses, Thus shalt thou say unto the children of Israel, The LORD God of your fathers, the God of Abraham, the God of Isaac, and the God of Jacob, hath sent me unto you: this is my name for ever, and this is my memorial unto all generations.
16 Go, and gather the elders of Israel together, and say unto them, The LORD God of your fathers, the God of Abraham, of Isaac, and of Jacob, appeared unto me, saying, I have surely visited you, and seen that which is done to you in Egypt:
17 And I have said, I will bring you up out of the affliction of Egypt unto the land of the Canaanites, and the Hittites, and the Amorites, and the Perizzites, and the Hivites, and the Jebusites, unto a land flowing with milk and honey.
18 And they shall hearken to thy voice: and thou shalt come, thou and the elders of Israel, unto the king of Egypt, and ye shall say unto him, The Lord God of the

Hebrews hath met with us: and now let us go, we beseech thee, three days' journey into the wilderness, that we may sacrifice to the Lord our God.
19 And I am sure that the king of Egypt will not let you go, no, not by a mighty hand.
20 And I will stretch out my hand, and smite Egypt with all my wonders which I will do in the midst thereof: and after that he will let you go.
21 And I will give this people favour in the sight of the Egyptians: and it shall come to pass, that, when ye go, ye shall not go empty:
22 But every woman shall borrow of her neighbour, and of her that sojourneth in her house, jewels of silver, and jewels of gold, and raiment: and ye shall put them upon your sons, and upon your daughters; and ye shall spoil the Egyptians.

CHAPTER 4

And Moses answered and said, But, behold, they will not believe me, nor hearken unto my voice: for they will say, The LORD hath not appeared unto thee.
2 And the LORD said unto him, What is that in thine hand? And he said, A rod.
3 And he said, Cast it on the ground. And he cast it on the ground, and it became a serpent; and Moses fled from before it.
4 And the LORD said unto Moses, Put forth thine hand, and take it by the tail. And he put forth his hand, and caught it, and it became a rod in his hand:
5 That they may believe that the LORD God of their fathers, the God of Abraham, the God of Isaac, and the God of Jacob, hath appeared unto thee.
6 And the LORD said furthermore unto him, Put now thine hand into thy bosom. And he put his hand into his bosom: and when he took it out, behold, his hand was leprous as snow.
7 And he said, Put thine hand into thy bosom again.

the elders were to approach Pharaoh & declare that God had appeared to them & demanded that they travel for some three days away from Egypt & worship God
- 8) God's prediction & forewarning: The king of Egypt would reject their request
- 9) God's judgment & His assurance of deliverance: His hand of judgment would force the king to free Israel
- 10) God's power: His power to cause the Egyptians to favor His people & to rectify their injustices against His people: When freed by Egypt, they were to ask the Egyptians for silver, gold, and clothes

3. Argument 3: He felt that people would not believe him
- a. Moses' excuse: He feared personal rejection, that the people would deny his call & mission
- b. God's reply: God would give the people three signs

  - 1) Sign 1: Moses' staff would be turned into a snake when cast to the ground & turned back into a rod when picked up—a symbol of God's power over Pharaoh & Egypt (Pharaoh wore the emblem of a serpent on his crown, see 7:10-13)

  - 2) God's purpose: To stir belief in God & in God's messenger

  - 3) Sign 2: Moses' hand would be afflicted with leprosy when placed inside his cloak & restored when placed back into his cloak—a symbol of God's power over health & disease, life & death[DS2]

	And he put his hand into his bosom again; and plucked it out of his bosom, and, behold, it was turned again as his other flesh.	12 Now therefore go, and I will be with thy mouth, and teach thee what thou shalt say.	2) Assured His servant Moses: He would help Moses to speak & teach him what to say
4) God's purpose for the second sign: To stir belief if the people did not believe the first sign*DS3*	8 And it shall come to pass, if they will not believe thee, neither hearken to the voice of the first sign, that they will believe the voice of the latter sign.	13 And he said, O my Lord, send, I pray thee, by the hand of him whom thou wilt send.	5. Argument 5: He did not want to go; he refused, asking God to send someone else
5) Sign 3: Water taken from the Nile would be turned into blood when poured upon the ground	9 And it shall come to pass, if they will not believe also these two signs, neither hearken unto thy voice, that thou shalt take of the water of the river, and pour it upon the dry land: and the water which thou takest out of the river shall become blood upon the dry land.	14 And the anger of the LORD was kindled against Moses, and he said, Is not Aaron the Levite thy brother? I know that he can speak well. And also, behold, he cometh forth to meet thee: and when he seeth thee, he will be glad in his heart.	a. Moses' rejection: An unwilling, unbelieving heart b. God's reply: Spoken in righteous anger 1) God would give Moses a helper—his brother Aaron—to be the spokesman
6) God's purpose for the third sign: To stir belief (v.9)			2) Aaron was, in fact, on his way to visit Moses: Aaron would accept & rejoice in Moses & his call
		15 And thou shalt speak unto him, and put words in his mouth: and I will be with thy mouth, and with his mouth, and will teach you what ye shall do.	3) Moses was to share God's Word with Aaron: God would help both Moses & Aaron to speak, teaching both what to do
4. Argument 4: He felt he was not eloquent, not a gifted speaker*DS4* a. Moses' excuse: He was slow of speech & tongue	10 And Moses said unto the LORD, O my Lord, I am not eloquent, neither heretofore, nor since thou hast spoken unto thy servant: but I am slow of speech, and of a slow tongue.	16 And he shall be thy spokesman unto the people: and he shall be, even he shall be to thee instead of a mouth, and thou shalt be to him instead of God.	4) Aaron was to be the spokesman to the people, the very mouth of Moses to the people, & Moses was to be as God's spokesman to Aaron
b. God's reply 1) Questioned His servant Moses: Is it not God who gives speech, hearing, & sight to man?	11 And the LORD said unto him, Who hath made man's mouth? or who maketh the dumb, or deaf, or the seeing, or the blind? have not I the LORD?	17 And thou shalt take this rod in thine hand, wherewith thou shalt do signs.	5) Moses was also to take the staff in his hand: To perform miracles with it

DIVISION II

MOSES AND GOD: GOD RAISES UP A LEADER TO DELIVER HIS PEOPLE (ISRAEL), 2:1–7:7

D. The Excuses of Moses: A Reluctant Prophet—Arguments Against Serving God, 3:11–4:17

(3:11–4:17) **Introduction—Call, of God**: one of the greatest calls ever given to man was given to Moses. God Himself called Moses, called him to go and deliver God's people out of slavery and into the promised land. This we saw in the former passage (Ex.3:1-10). Now we come to the shocking response of Moses: he fought against the call of God. He thought up every excuse he could against going. He did not want to go, and he objected to going. As Scripture says, he had no intention of going (Ex.4:13). Moses was set on living life like he wanted not like God wanted, set on doing his thing not God's thing. Moses had made up his mind to reject God's call.

How many of us have rejected God's call? How many of us have been called to preach or teach or serve in some administrative capacity in the church? Or as a missionary or evangelist? How many of us have been called to establish a business or set up some estate in order to support taking the gospel to the world? Yet, we have refused. We have used excuse after excuse for not doing what God has called us to do. Who among us has made…

- some excuse for not going?
- some excuse for not preaching or teaching?
- some excuse for not supporting the sending of the gospel around the world?

With bold honesty, Scripture tells us that Moses fought against God's call upon his life. Moses thought up every excuse he could. This is the shocking subject we now study: *The Excuses of Moses: A Reluctant Prophet—Arguments Against Serving God,* 3:11–4:17.

1. Argument 1: he felt incapable, unqualified (3:11-12).
2. Argument 2: he felt the people were ignorant of God and would be skeptical of God's power to truly help them (3:13-22).
3. Argument 3: he felt that people would not believe him (4:1-9).
4. Argument 4: he felt he was not eloquent, not a gifted speaker (4:10-12).
5. Argument 5: he just did not want to go; he refused, asking God to send someone else (4:13-17).

1 **(3:11-12) Excuses—Humility—Insufficiency—Call, of God—Service—Ministry**: the first argument: Moses felt incapable and unqualified for the task.
  a. Note Moses' excuse: "Who am I, that I should go?" (v.11). God was telling Moses...
    • that he should go before the king
    • that he should go and deliver Israel out of Egypt, out of captivity and slavery

Moses was no doubt expressing both humility and fear to God. He was only a simple shepherd, only a simple man. For forty years he had worked as a shepherd in Midian, a desert-like land far removed from the centers of government and affairs of state. Who was he—a simple man, a simple shepherd—to go before the king of Egypt and make demands? Who was he to go to the people of Israel and proclaim that God was going to deliver them from slavery, from the land of Egypt into the promised land? Moses felt incapable, unqualified, inadequate: "Who am I, that I should go?" (v.11).
  b. But note God's reply to this argument. God made two great promises (v.12).
    1) There was the promise of God's presence: "I will be with you" (v.12). God's very own presence would be with Moses. This meant that God Himself would equip Moses.
      ⇒ God would give whatever inner strength and ability was needed.
      ⇒ God would arouse the confidence, assurance, and faith needed to do the task.
      ⇒ God would lead, guide, and work things out.

Thought 1. The great promise of God's presence has been given time and again throughout Scripture. God will be with us as we go forth serving and bearing witness for Him.
  • God promised to be with Isaac

    "**And, behold, I am with thee, and will keep thee in all places whither thou goest, and will bring thee again into this land; for I will not leave thee, until I have done that which I have spoken to thee of**" (Ge.28:15).

  • God promised to be with Joshua

    "**There shall not any man be able to stand before thee all the days of thy life: as I was with Moses, so I will be with thee: I will not fail thee, nor forsake thee**" (Jos.1:5).
    "**And the LORD said unto Joshua, This day will I begin to magnify thee in the sight of all Israel, that they may know that, as I was with Moses, so I will be with thee**" (Jos.3:7).
    "**And he gave Joshua the son of Nun a charge, and said, Be strong and of a good courage: for thou shalt bring the children of Israel into the land which I sware unto them: and I will be with thee**" (De.31:23).

  • God promised to be with Jeremiah

    "**Be not afraid of their faces: for I am with thee to deliver thee, saith the LORD**" (Je.1:8).

  • God promised to be with Israel

    "**Then spoke Haggai the LORD's messenger in the LORD's message unto the people, saying, I am with you, saith the LORD**" (Hag.1:13).

  • God promised to be with all believers who bear witness for Christ.

    "**Go ye therefore, and teach all nations, baptizing them in the name of the Father, and of the Son, and of the Holy Ghost: teaching them to observe all things whatsoever I have commanded you: and, lo, I am with you alway, [even] unto the end of the world. Amen**" (Mt.28:19-20).

    2) There was the promise of a successful mission: the people would be delivered (v.12). Moses would bring Israel out of Egypt, and they would worship God on the very mountain where Moses then knelt before God. Note that this was to be a sign to Moses, a sign that he was indeed called by God and appointed to be the great deliverer of Israel. But note that this was a future sign, a sign that Moses had to believe. God was demanding that Moses believe Him, believe...
      • that God was calling him
      • that God would be with him
      • that God would give him a successful mission

    This should have been enough for Moses, but it was not. Moses still did not want to serve God. He just wanted to live as he wished, to do his own thing in life. Thus he had more excuses to argue against God's call.

Thought 1. No person is qualified to serve God. No person is capable, adequate, sufficient—not in his or her own strength, not to serve God. When God calls us, we often sense our inadequacy and our insufficiency. We often feel incapable, as though we do not have what it takes, as though there is no way we can undertake the task God has called us to do. But God is faithful to us just as He was faithful to Moses. God makes the very same promises to us:

9351939595279

(1) "I will be with you" (v.12). He will give us whatever inner strength and ability is needed. And He will lead, guide, and work things out for us.

> "When thou goest out to battle against thine enemies, and seest horses, and chariots, and a people more than thou, be not afraid of them: for the LORD thy God is with thee, which brought thee up out of the land of Egypt" (De.20:1).
> "And he said, My presence shall go with thee, and I will give thee rest" (Ex.33:14).
> "When thou passest through the waters, I will be with thee; and through the rivers, they shall not overflow thee: when thou walkest through the fire, thou shalt not be burned; neither shall the flame kindle upon thee" (Is.43:2).
> "Go ye therefore, and teach all nations, baptizing them in the name of the Father, and of the Son, and of the Holy Ghost: teaching them to observe all things whatsoever I have commanded you: and, lo, I am with you alway, [even] unto the end of the world. Amen" (Mt.28:19-20).
> "Let your conversation [conduct, behavior] be without covetousness; and be content with such things as ye have: for he hath said, I will never leave thee, nor forsake thee" (He.13:5).

(2) God will use us to deliver people out of Egypt (the world) and into the promised land of heaven. God promises that we will worship and serve Him in the very mountain of God, in heaven itself (v.12).

> "All the ends of the world shall remember and turn unto the LORD: and all the kindreds of the nations shall worship before thee. For the kingdom is the LORD's: and he is the governor among the nations" (Ps.22:27-28).
> "And it shall come to pass, that from one new moon to another, and from one sabbath to another, shall all flesh come to worship before me, saith the LORD" (Is.66:23).
> "Wherefore God also hath highly exalted him, and given him a name which is above every name: that at the name of Jesus every knee should bow, of things in heaven, and things in earth, and things under the earth; and that every tongue should confess that Jesus Christ is Lord, to the glory of God the Father" (Ph.2:9-11).
> "And every creature which is in heaven, and on the earth, and under the earth, and such as are in the sea, and all that are in them, heard I saying, Blessing, and honour, and glory, and power, be unto him that sitteth upon the throne, and unto the Lamb for ever and ever" (Re.5:13).
> "Who shall not fear thee, O Lord, and glorify thy name? for thou only art holy: for all nations shall come and worship before thee; for thy judgments are made manifest" (Re.15:4).

2 (3:13-22) **Excuse—Call, of God**: the second argument: Moses felt that the people were ignorant of God, that they were skeptics and would question God's power to save and deliver them.

a. Note Moses' excuse: when Moses went to the people declaring that he had been sent by God to deliver them, he knew that the people were going to ask him a pointed question:
⇒ What god was it that had sent him?
⇒ What god actually had the power to save and deliver them from their terrible circumstances?
⇒ What was his name?

Keep in mind two facts about Israel:
⇒ First, many Israelites were like innumerable people in every nation: they turned away from God to the false religions of the world. Many were worshipping the false gods of Egypt, and were to continue worshipping them even after God delivered and saved them. Joshua tells us this:

> "Now therefore fear the LORD, and serve him in sincerity and in truth: and put away the gods which your fathers served on the other side of the flood, and in Egypt; and serve ye the LORD" (Jos.24:14). (See note—Ex.2:23-25 for more discussion.)

⇒ Second, the people of Israel had been enslaved and tortured for almost 400 years and, in their minds, no god had ever shown any interest in them, not enough to hear their cries for help, not enough to save and deliver them.

Moses obviously knew these two facts. He just felt there was no chance the people were going to accept him, not a man who suddenly appeared upon the scene declaring that God had sent him to deliver and save them. The people would be skeptical, questioning, asking…
• What god are you talking about—what is his name?
• What god has the power to save and deliver us—what is his name?

Thought 1. We live in a world of unbelief and skepticism. People are ignorant of God, and they question God's existence and power to save and deliver man. This fact should not stir us to reject God's call; rather, it should stir us to declare God's power to save and deliver people. People need God; they need to be delivered and saved from the enslavement and death of this world. Therefore, we must declare the power of God to save and deliver them.

"For the Son of man is come to seek and to save that which was lost" (Lu.19:10).

"Then said Jesus to them again, Peace [be] unto you: as [my] Father hath sent me, even so send I you [to seek and save the lost]" (Jn.20:21).

"For the grace of God that bringeth salvation hath appeared to all men, Teaching us that, denying ungodliness and worldly lusts, we should live soberly, righteously, and godly, in this present world; Looking for that blessed hope, and the glorious appearing of the great God and our Saviour Jesus Christ; Who gave himself for us, that he might redeem us from all iniquity, and purify unto himself a peculiar people, zealous of good works. These things speak, and exhort, and rebuke with all authority. Let no man despise thee" (Tit.2:11-15).

b. Now, what was God's reply to this argument, the argument that uses people's ignorance and skepticism as an excuse for not serving God (vv.13-22)? God told Moses to declare ten things to Israel. The outline points show these clearly.

1) Moses was to declare God's name to the people: "I AM WHO I AM"—it was He who sent Moses (v.14. See DEEPER STUDY # 1—Ex.3:14-15 for more discussion.)

Thought 1. We must declare the name of God to the people of our generation. God is the great "I AM," the only living and true God, the only God who truly exists, the only God we are to worship and serve.

2) Moses was to declare God's identity to the people: the LORD God is His name. He is the same God who is the God of Abraham, Isaac, and Jacob—it was He who sent Moses (v.15). This point would remind the people of the great promises that God had made to their forefathers...
   • the promise of the promised land (see note—Ge.12:1).
   • the promise of the promised seed, meaning both the seed of a great nation of people and the one particular seed, the Messiah and Savior of the world (see notes—Ge.12:2-3; 12:3; DEEPER STUDY # 2—Ex.1:6-7).

Thought 1. The LORD God is the God of our forefathers. He is the very God who has promised the Savior and heaven to us, the very God who sent the Savior to the world and who took our forefathers into heaven when they passed from this world into heaven. This we must declare to the people of our generation.

3) Moses was to declare God's memorial to the people: His name—the LORD God—is His memorial, the name by which He is to be remembered forever (v.15).

4) Moses was to gather the elders of Israel together and declare God's concern and care for His people: God saw what was being done to them; He saw their suffering (v.16).

Thought 1. God is concerned and cares for us even as He did for Israel. God sees exactly what is happening to us, all our trials and sufferings.

5) Moses was to declare God's past promise of deliverance to the elders: God had promised 400 years before to bring Israel out from Egypt and into the promised land, a land that flowed with milk and honey (v.17, see Ge.15:13-14; 50:24). Note the number of nations occupying the promised land. This pointed toward the land being spacious, large enough to take care of the Israelites and to give them an abundance of provision. God had given this great promise to Abraham, and Joseph had reviewed the promise with the people of Israel some 300 years earlier. The elders—at least some of them, most likely the true believers—would remember the great promise of deliverance. Great joy and hope would therefore flood their hearts when Moses declared that *the great day of deliverance* had come.

Thought 1. God has promised to deliver us from the enslavements of this world, including the terrible enslavements of sin and death. Moreover, God has promised to deliver us into the promised land of heaven, the perfect land that flows with milk and honey.

6) Moses was to declare God's promise to him, God's appointed servant: the promise that the elders and people would listen and accept his leadership (v.18). Note how positive this point was to be. It was bound to stir the elders to listen and accept Moses as God's messenger and prophet.

Thought 1. Once we accept God's call to follow Him, God will stir the family of true believers (at least some of them) to accept us. Together, as the family of God, we all serve and bear testimony for God. We bear testimony to a lost and dying world.

7) Moses was to declare God's instructions to the elders (leaders): Moses and the elders were to go to Pharaoh and declare that God had appeared to them and demanded sacrifice, apparently at Mount Sinai, some three days away from Egypt (v.18).

Remember, the people of ancient history were very religious. The right of worship—the right to worship as a person wished—was often respected. Thus this request of Moses and the elders, which may seem unreasonable to us, was not necessarily an unreasonable request for that day and time. Even today, various religious holidays that require travel to certain religious sites are practiced by the religions of the world.

Thought 1. We must approach the leaders of the world and request the right, the freedom, to worship "the LORD our God." We must declare God's revelation to man, that God has appeared to His people and demanded that they worship Him as "the LORD God."

8) Moses was to declare God's prediction and forewarning to the elders: the king would reject their request (v.19). God was telling Moses and the elders not to be discouraged by the king's rejection. God knew all about the rejections ahead of time. They were all a part of God's great plan for both Israel and Egypt.

Thought 1. We will sometimes be rejected and persecuted by the world. But we must never allow rejection to discourage us. God knows, and He is in control of the situation.

9) Moses was to declare God's judgment and His assurance of deliverance: God was going to act in judgment and force the king to free Israel (v.20). The phrase "stretch out my hand and smite [strike]" is an act of judgment. God was going to judge the terrible sins of Egypt against His people while He was freeing Israel. Note that this was a prediction of the coming plagues to fall upon Egypt.

Thought 1. We must declare God's coming judgment and deliverance. God is going to judge the world for its sins and deliver the godly for their faith in Him.

10) Moses was to declare God's power: His power to cause the Egyptians to favor His people and to rectify their injustices against His people. When God's people were freed by Egypt, they were to ask the Egyptians for silver, gold, and clothes (vv.21-22). The Egyptians had, no doubt, stolen most of the possessions and valuables of the Israelites when they enslaved them. As slaves, the Israelites would not even have enough food to eat, much less the right to earn a living. They had no right to work for money to purchase clothing and possessions in order to live a reasonable and comfortable life. Thus God was to rectify the injustices of the Egyptians. He was going to strike so much fear in the Egyptians that they would give His people whatever they asked and more, give them whatever it took to get rid of them lest more judgment fall upon Egypt (Ex.12:33-36).

Thought 1. God has the power to stir the people of the world to favor believers, and He has the power to rectify the injustices of the world against His people. We must, therefore, be constantly praying for God to stop the persecution of His people around the world. We must ask God to stir the world to grant the right to live and worship in freedom.

DEEPER STUDY # 1

(3:14-15) **God—LORD (Hebrew, YAHWEH or English, JEHOVAH)—Chart—God, Name - Titles of**: the word Jehovah or Yahweh comes from the verb "to be"; thus it means simply "I AM"—"I AM who I AM." This means that God is...

- the Self-Existent One
- the God who exists (who alone exists and who can never cease to exist)
- the Eternal One
- the Perfect One
- the Absolute One
- the Uncaused One

The Pulpit Commentary says this: "The idea expressed by the name is...that of real, perfect, unconditional, independent existence."[1] (See notes—Ge.1:1; 14:18-20; 15:2; 17:1; 21:33; 22:14; Ex.3:14-15; 4:10-11; 1 S.1:3.)

There are two wonderful facts about the name Jehovah. (See note 4—Ge.2:4; note 2, pt.3—Ge.2:7 for more discussion.)

1. Jehovah is the God who is personal and who reveals Himself. Jehovah is the personal name of God, the name that shows that God is the God of revelation.

a. It is the name God chose for Himself when He revealed Himself to Moses (Ex.3:14).

b. It is the name by which Adam and others of his day knew God (Ge.4:26, see Ge.2:4). It can accurately be assumed that God had revealed His name (Jehovah) to Adam personally.

c. It is the name which Christ claimed for Himself when He revealed Himself as God (Jn.8:58, see 8:24, 28).

2. Jehovah is the God who establishes a personal relationship with man—caring and looking after every need which man may have. He is man's special guardian, completely dependable and utterly trustworthy. He can be relied upon totally.

a. Jehovah is the redemptive name of God. God is the LORD (Jehovah, Yahweh), the God of redemption, salvation, and deliverance. It was Jehovah Elohim who sought after man when man first sinned (Ge.3:9-13). Jehovah is the Holy One, necessitating redemption (Le.11:44-45; 19:1-2; 20:26; Hab.1:12-13). Jehovah shall judge sin, necessitating redemption even more (Ge.6:5-7; Ex.34:6-7; De.32:36-42). Jehovah is merciful and forgiving and He shall redeem many (Ex.34:6-7, see Ge.3:21; 8:20-21).

b. Jehovah is the covenant or redemptive name of God (Ex.19:3; 20:1-2; Je.31:34). Jehovah is the God of redemption, salvation, and deliverance.

The word Jehovah is sometimes combined with other words in the Old Testament. These combined words paint a revealing picture of God's redemptive dealings with man.

---

1 *Exodus.* "The Pulpit Commentary," Vol.1, Edited by H.D.M. Spence & Joseph S. Exell. (Grand Rapids, MI: Eerdmans Publishing Co., 1950), p.57.

NAMES OF GOD	SCRIPTURE REFERENCE	ENGLISH MEANING
Jehovah-Jireh	Ge.22:14	"Jehovah will provide" or "The LORD who has already seen the provision." He provides the needed sacrifice (Ge.22:14-15).
Jehovah-Ropheka or Rapha	Ex.15:26	"Jehovah who heals you."
Jehovah-Nissii	Ex.17:15	"Jehovah is my banner." Victory over one's enemies (physical or spiritual) is wholly due to "the LORD our banner."
Jehovah-Meqaaddeshkem	Ex.31:13	"Jehovah who sanctifies you."
Jehovah-Shalom	Jdg.6:24	"Jehovah is Peace."
Jehovah-Hoseenu	Ps.99:5, 8, 9	"Jehovah, the LORD our God."
Jehovah-Tsabaoth	1 S.1:3	"Jehovah of hosts."
Jehovah-Elyon	Ps.7:17	"Jehovah Most High."
Jehovah-Roi	Ps.23:1	"Jehovah, my shepherd."
Jehovah-Elohay	Zec.14:5	"Jehovah, the LORD my God."
Jehovah-Tsidkenu	Je.23:6; 33:16	"Jehovah is our righteousness."
Jehovah-Shammah	Eze. 48:35; see Is.60:14-22; 62:2; Re.21:2	"Jehovah is there." "He is there" in the future as well as there now, in the present.
Jehovah-Elohim	Ge.2:4-25	"Jehovah the eternal creator."
Adonai-Jehovah	Ge.15:2, 8	"Jehovah the Sovereign LORD, our Master."
Jehovah-Hoseenu or Eloheenu	Ps.99:5, 8, 9	"Jehovah, the LORD our God."
Jehovah-Eloheka	Ex.20:2, 5, 7	"Jehovah, the LORD your God"

[3] (4:1-9) **Excuse—Call, of God**: the third argument: Moses felt the people would not believe him.

a. Note Moses' excuse: what he feared was personal rejection...
   • that the people would deny his call and mission
   • that they would not believe the LORD had appeared to him
   • that the message of deliverance and freedom from slavery was not of God

There is a problem with this argument: the duty of the prophet is to obey God, not to argue against the call of God and question the response of people. No prophet is ever to shrink back from the call of God, and certainly not because he fears a negative response from the people. Drawing people to Himself—arousing faith within their hearts—is God's work, not the prophet's. The prophet's duty is to surrender to God's call and go—go and proclaim the message of God.

But not Moses: he was still fighting against the call of God, still arguing, still making up every excuse he could. He still wanted to live like he wanted, to do his own thing. He did not want to give up the comfortable life he had.

Thought 1. It is God who quickens the gospel to hearts and arouses faith within people to believe and trust Jesus Christ. The duty of God's servants is simply to go and proclaim the gospel.

"So then faith cometh by hearing, and hearing by the word of God" (Ro.10:17).
"And you hath he quickened [made us alive], who were dead in trespasses and sins" (Ep.2:1).
"But God, who is rich in mercy, for his great love wherewith he loved us, Even when we were dead in sins, hath quickened us [made us alive] together with Christ, (by grace ye are saved)" (Ep.2:4-5).

b. But note God's reply. As always, God had a ready answer for this feeble excuse. God would give signs—miraculous signs—to prove His prophet and His message of deliverance, signs that would prove beyond a doubt that Moses and his message were of God. Three particular signs were given to Moses.

1) The first sign: Moses' staff would be turned into a snake when cast to the ground and turned back into a rod when picked up (v.2). God gave Moses a personal demonstration of this sign.

Picture the scene: Moses often saw snakes out in the desert as a shepherd. But here he is arguing with God, so God tells him to cast his rod (staff) to the ground. As soon as it hits the ground, it is turned into a snake, no doubt a poisonous snake. Note that Moses did just what we would do: jumped back and ran away.

The scene was probably humorous, especially when God told Moses to pick up the serpent by its tail. A snake is picked up by its neck, right behind the head, seldom by its tail, so that it cannot swing around and bite its handler. But here was God telling Moses to pick up the snake by its tail. We can only wonder what Moses was thinking, having stood there arguing with God. Nevertheless, he quickly reached over, snatched up the snake, and it was immediately turned back into a rod.

Now, why this sign? Why did God choose to demonstrate His power over a shepherd's rod and a serpent? To symbolize His power and authority over Pharaoh and his government. The snake was the animal chosen by Egypt to symbolize its authority and power just as nations today choose animals as the emblems of their authority and power (for example: the eagle chosen by America and the bear chosen by Russia). Pharaoh actually wore the emblem of a snake on his crown to symbolize the authority of Egyptian rule.[2] God was giving a clear picture of His sovereignty, power, authority, and dominion over the nations of the world—even over the greatest of nations, Egypt, and its great ruler, Pharaoh himself. God could take rods and turn them into the feared serpents of this earth; similarly, He could take the feared serpents of this earth and turn them into rods. Egypt and its authority existed only as God willed and allowed.

This sign would, of course, help convince the people that Moses was truly sent of God. God clearly states that this was His purpose for giving the signs to Moses: to stir the people to believe that Moses and his message of deliverance were true (v.5, 8). God was able to deliver them from their enslavement.

> **Thought 1**. God holds the reigns of power over all nations and all people. Therefore, God can deliver us, and He can use us to deliver people.
>
> > "Both riches and honour come of thee, and thou reignest over all; and in thine hand is power and might; and in thine hand it is to make great, and to give strength unto all" (1 Chr.29:12).
> > "And [Jehosaphat] said, O LORD God of our fathers, art not thou God in heaven? and rulest not thou over all the kingdoms of the heathen? and in thine hand is there not power and might, so that none is able to withstand thee?" (2 Chr.20:6).
> > "But our God is in the heavens: he hath done whatsoever he hath pleased" (Ps.115:3).
> > "The king's heart is in the hand of the LORD, as the rivers of water: he turneth it whithersoever he will" (Pr.21:1).
> > "To the only wise God our Saviour, be glory and majesty, dominion and power, both now and ever. Amen" (Jude 1:25).
> > "And I heard as it were the voice of a great multitude, and as the voice of many waters, and as the voice of mighty thunderings, saying, Alleluia: for the Lord God omnipotent reigneth" (Re.19:6).
> > "Who shall change our vile body, that it may be fashioned like unto his glorious body, according to the working whereby he is able even to subdue all things unto himself" (Ph.3:21).

2) The second sign: Moses' hand would be afflicted with leprosy when placed into his cloak and taken out, and restored when put back into his cloak (vv.6-7). This sign was a symbol of God's great power over health and disease, life and death. Leprosy was one of, if not *the* most, feared diseases in the ancient world.

Note God's purpose for this second sign: to stir belief if the people did not believe the first sign (v.4). When the people saw Moses' hand turned to leprosy, they would be asking themselves, "If God could strike a man with leprosy—within a second's time—what could He do to the person who rejected His messenger and message of deliverance?" A demonstration of God's power to control health and disease, life and death would be a strong sign to stir belief. (See DEEPER STUDY # 2—Ex.4:6-7 for more discussion.)

> **Thought 1**. God has the power to control health and disease, life and death. This stands as a warning to us: we must hear the call of God; we must obey and serve God.
>
> > "And said, If thou wilt diligently hearken to the voice of the LORD thy God, and wilt do that which is right in his sight, and wilt give ear to his commandments, and keep all his statutes, I will put none of these diseases upon thee, which I have brought upon the Egyptians: for I am the LORD that healeth thee" (Ex.15:26).
> > "And the LORD will take away from thee all sickness, and will put none of the evil diseases of Egypt, which thou knowest, upon thee; but will lay them upon all them that hate thee" (De.7:15).

---

2 Ronald F. Youngblood. *Exodus*. (Chicago, IL: Moody Press, 1983), p.35.

"My son, attend to my words; incline thine ear unto my sayings. Let them not depart from thine eyes; keep them in the midst of thine heart. For they are life unto those that find them, and health to all their flesh" (Pr.4:20-22).

"Therefore also will I make thee sick in smiting thee, in making thee desolate because of thy sins" (Mi.6:13).

"For this cause many are weak and sickly among you, and many sleep. For if we would judge ourselves, we should not be judged" (1 Co.11:30-31).

3) The third sign: Moses was to take water from the Nile River and pour it upon the ground. As the water hit the ground, God would turn it into blood (v.9).

The Nile was the life of Egypt, providing the water necessary for both drinking and agriculture. Simply put, the Nile was the very source of the necessities of life, of food and water for the Egyptians. By turning the water of the Nile into blood, God was demonstrating...

- that He held the power over the basic necessities of life
- that He was the ultimate Source and Provision of the necessities of life
- that He was the Bread and Water of life
- that God, not the king, controlled the food and water supply of the land

"Therefore take no thought, saying, What shall we eat? or, What shall we drink? or, Wherewithal shall we be clothed?...But seek ye first the kingdom of God, and his righteousness; and all these things shall be added unto you" (Mt.6:31, 33).

"And ye shall serve the LORD your God, and he shall bless thy bread, and thy water; and I will take sickness away from the midst of thee" (Ex.23:25).

DEEPER STUDY # 2

(4:6-7) **Leprosy—Plagues—Diseases**: this dreaded skin condition is well-documented throughout the Bible (the term is used 37 times in the KJV). It was a plague which had no human cure; a disease which demanded social isolation for its victims. Unless God intervened, a long, drawn-out life of suffering left the victims of leprosy pleading for death. (See note 3—Lu.5:12 for more discussion. Also see DEEPER STUDY # 1—Ex.9:10)

"When a man shall have in the skin of his flesh a rising, a scab, or a bright spot, and it be in the skin of his flesh *like* the plague of leprosy; then he shall be brought unto Aaron the priest, or unto one of his sons the priests: And the priest shall look on the plague in the skin of the flesh: and *when* the hair in the plague is turned white, and the plague in sight *be* deeper than the skin of his flesh, it *is* a plague of leprosy: and the priest shall look on him, and pronounce him unclean" (Le.13:2-3).

"Then the priest shall come and look, and, behold, *if* the plague be spread in the house, it *is* a fretting leprosy in the house: it is unclean" (Le.14:44).

"And it came to pass, when he was in a certain city, behold a man full of leprosy: who seeing Jesus fell on *his* face, and besought him, saying, Lord, if thou wilt, thou canst make me clean. And he put forth *his* hand, and touched him, saying, I will: be thou clean. And immediately the leprosy departed from him" (Lu.5:12-13).

Thought 1. Leprosy is a picture, a type, a symbol of sin in the Bible. Leprosy caused pain and shame for those who lived in Bible days, and unforgiven sin causes pain and shame for the believer today.

- Unforgiven sin has no human cure

"For all have sinned, and come short of the glory of God" (Ro.3:23).

- Unforgiven sin causes a break in fellowship between God and His people

"Moreover if thy brother shall trespass against thee, go and tell him his fault between thee and him alone: if he shall hear thee, thou hast gained thy brother. But if he will not hear *thee, then* take with thee one or two more, that in the mouth of two or three witnesses every word may be established. And if he shall neglect to hear them, tell *it* unto the church: but if he neglect to hear the church, let him be unto thee as an heathen man and a publican" (Mt.18:15-17).

- Unforgiven sin leads to a slow, painful death that will have no end, lasting eternally.

"Then shall he say also unto them on the left hand, Depart from me, ye cursed, into everlasting fire, prepared for the devil and his angels....And these shall go away into everlasting punishment: but the righteous into life eternal" (Mt. 25:41, 46).

"And beside all this, between us and you there is a great gulf fixed: so that they which would pass from hence to you cannot; neither can they pass to us, that *would come* from thence" (Lu. 16:26).

"And to you who are troubled rest with us, when the Lord Jesus shall be revealed from heaven with his mighty angels, In flaming fire taking vengeance on them that know not God, and that obey not the gospel of our Lord Jesus Christ" (2 Th.1:7-8).

"The Lord knoweth how to deliver the godly out of temptations, and to reserve the unjust unto the day of judgment to be punished" (2 Pe.2:9).

"But the heavens and the earth, which are now, by the same word are kept in store, reserved unto fire against the day of judgment and perdition of ungodly men" (2 Pe.3:7).

"And Enoch also, the seventh from Adam, prophesied of these, saying, Behold, the Lord cometh with ten thousands of his saints, To execute judgment upon all, and to convince all that are ungodly among them of all their ungodly deeds which they have ungodly committed, and of all their hard speeches which ungodly sinners have spoken against him" (Jude 14-15).

"And I saw a great white throne, and him that sat on it, from whose face the earth and the heaven fled away; and there was found no place for them. And I saw the dead, small and great, stand before God; and the books were opened: and another book was opened, which is the book of life: and the dead were judged out of those things which were written in the books, according to their works. And the sea gave up the dead which were in it; and death and hell delivered up the dead which were in them: and they were judged every man according to their works. And death and hell were cast into the lake of fire. This is the second death. And whosoever was not found written in the book of life was cast into the lake of fire" (Re.20:11-15).

DEEPER STUDY # 3

(4:8) **Signs**: a sign is a miraculous event given by God to men for a specific purpose. God uses signs for these purposes.

1. God uses signs to demonstrate His power, that He is truly God, the Supreme LORD and Majesty of the universe, sovereign and omnipotent, ruling and reigning over all.

"And I will establish my covenant with you; neither shall all flesh be cut off any more by the waters of a flood; neither shall there any more be a flood to destroy the earth. And God said, This is the token of the covenant which I make between me and you and every living creature that is with you, for perpetual generations: I do set my bow in the cloud, and it shall be for a token [sign] of a covenant between me and the earth. And it shall come to pass, when I bring a cloud over the earth, that the bow shall be seen in the cloud: and I will remember my covenant, which is between me and you and every living creature of all flesh; and the waters shall no more become a flood to destroy all flesh. And the bow shall be in the cloud; and I will look upon it, that I may remember the everlasting covenant between God and every living creature of all flesh that is upon the earth" (Ge.9:11-16).

2. God uses signs to give assurance and confidence to His followers.

"And Gideon said unto God, If thou wilt save Israel by mine hand, as thou hast said, behold, I will put a fleece of wool in the floor; and if the dew be on the fleece only, and it be dry upon all the earth beside, then shall I know that thou wilt save Israel by mine hand, as thou hast said. And it was so: for he rose up early on the morrow, and thrust the fleece together, and wringed the dew out of the fleece, a bowl full of water. And Gideon said unto God, Let not thine anger be hot against me, and I will speak but this once: let me prove, I pray thee, but this once with the fleece; let it now be dry only upon the fleece, and upon all the ground let there be dew. And God did so that night: for it was dry upon the fleece only, and there was dew on all the ground" (Jdg.6:36-40).

3. God uses signs to stir repentance and belief.

"And before they were laid down, she came up unto them upon the roof; and she [Rahab] said unto the men, I know that the Lord hath given you the land, and that your terror is fallen upon us, and that all the inhabitants of the land faint because of you. For we have heard how the Lord dried up the water of the Red sea for you, when ye came out of Egypt; and what ye did unto the two kings of the Amorites, that were on the other side Jordan, Sihon and Og, whom ye utterly destroyed. And as soon as we had heard these things, our hearts did melt, neither did there remain any more courage in any man, because of you: for the Lord your God, he is God in heaven above, and in earth beneath. Now therefore, I pray you, swear unto me by the Lord, since I have showed you kindness, that ye will also show kindness unto my father's house, and give me a true token [sign]: and that ye will save alive my father, and my mother, and my brethren, and my sisters, and all that they have, and deliver our lives from death" (Jos.2:8-13).

"That they may believe that the Lord God of their fathers, the God of Abraham, the God of Isaac, and the God of Jacob, hath appeared unto thee....And it shall come to pass, if they will not believe thee, neither hearken to the voice of the first sign, that they will believe the voice of the latter sign" (Ex.4:5, 8).

"Then began he to upbraid the cities wherein most of his mighty works were done, because they repented not" (Mt.11:20).

"But if I do, though ye believe not me, believe the works: that ye may know, and believe, that the Father [is] in me, and I in him" (Jn.10:38).

4. God uses signs as a warning.

"And the Lord said unto Moses, Bring Aaron's rod again before the testimony, to be kept for a token [sign] against the rebels; and thou shalt quite take away their murmurings from me, that they die not" (Nu.17:10).

5. God uses signs to seal and strengthen the faith of His people.

"And I gave them my statutes, and showed them my judgments, which if a man do, he shall even live in them. Moreover also I gave them my sabbaths, to be a sign between me and them, that they might know that I am the Lord that sanctify them" (Eze.20:11-12).

6. God uses signs to point to the fulfillment of His Word and promises.

"Therefore the Lord himself shall give you a sign; Behold, a virgin shall conceive, and bear a son, and shall call his name Immanuel" (Is.7:14).

"And there were in the same country shepherds abiding in the field, keeping watch over their flock by night. And, lo, the angel of the Lord came upon them, and the glory of the Lord shone round about them: and they were sore afraid. And the angel said unto them, Fear not: for, behold, I bring you good tidings of great joy, which shall be to all people. For unto you is born this day in the city of David a Saviour, which is Christ the Lord. And this shall be a sign unto you; Ye shall find the babe wrapped in swaddling clothes, lying in a manger" (Lu.2:8-12).

"And as he sat upon the mount of Olives, the disciples came unto him privately, saying, Tell us, when shall these things be? and what [shall be] the sign of thy coming, and of the end of the world?...And then shall appear the sign of the Son of man in heaven: and then shall all the tribes of the earth mourn, and they shall see the Son of man coming in the clouds of heaven with power and great glory" (Mt.24:3, 30).

4 (4:10-12) **Excuse—Call, of God—Speech**: the fourth argument: Moses felt he was not eloquent, not a gifted speaker.

a. What did Moses mean by this excuse? He tells us: he was "slow of speech and tongue." That is…
- He was not fluent, not skillful with words, not expressive, not persuasive
- He did not have a good, forceful, persuasive speech or delivery
- He was not smooth-talking nor silver-tongued
- He did not speak with ease and was nervous when speaking. He was ill at ease even when speaking to individuals, much less to groups of people. Words did not come easily nor readily to him, no matter whom he was talking with. (Moses told God to note that he was slow speaking—even to Him.)
- He was perhaps tongue-tied, or had a stuttering problem or some other speech impediment (see Ex.6:12, 30)

Now note: this was not the only point Moses made about his slow, uneasy speech. He adds that he was not eloquent nor fluent and had never been, and that he was not even speaking with ease standing there talking with God. The implication was this: if he could not speak easily with God, how could he with others?

b. What is God's reply to the person who argues this excuse? He questions and gives a great promise to His servant. Is it not God who gives speech to man and who causes man to hear and see? The answer is clear: Yes. Then go. God will help you speak, and teach you exactly what to say.

"For the Holy Ghost shall teach you in the same hour what ye ought to say" (Lu.12:12).

"But the Comforter, [which is] the Holy Ghost, whom the Father will send in my name, he shall teach you all things, and bring all things to your remembrance, whatsoever I have said unto you" (Jn.14:26).

"Howbeit when he, the Spirit of truth, is come, he will guide you into all truth: for he shall not speak of himself; but whatsoever he shall hear, [that] shall he speak: and he will show you things to come" (Jn.16:13).

"And I, brethren, when I came to you, came not with excellency of speech or of wisdom, declaring unto you the testimony of God" (1 Co.2:1).

"Which things also we speak, not in the words which man's wisdom teacheth, but which the Holy Ghost teacheth; comparing spiritual things with spiritual" (1 Co.2:13).

"The Spirit of the Lord spoke by me, and his word was in my tongue" (2 S.23:2).

"For this God is our God for ever and ever: he will be our guide even unto death" (Ps.48:14).

"Thou shalt guide me with thy counsel, and afterward receive me to glory" (Ps.73:24).

"The Lord GOD hath given me the tongue of the learned, that I should know how to speak a word in season to him that is weary: he wakeneth morning by morning, he wakeneth mine ear to hear as the learned" (Is.50:4).

"And I have put my words in thy mouth, and I have covered thee in the shadow of mine hand, that I may plant the heavens, and lay the foundations of the earth, and say unto Zion, Thou art my people" (Is.51:16).

"Then the Lord put forth his hand, and touched my mouth. And the Lord said unto me, Behold, I have put my words in thy mouth" (Je.1:9).

"Wherefore thus saith the Lord God of hosts, Because ye speak this word, behold, I will make my words in thy mouth fire, and this people wood, and it shall devour them" (Je.5:14).

"Son of man, I have made thee a watchman unto the house of Israel: therefore hear the word at my mouth, and give them warning from me" (Eze.3:17).

DEEPER STUDY # 4

(4:10-11) **God, LORD (capital letters) and Lord (small letters)**: the word *LORD* (capital letters) is the Hebrew word *Yahweh* or the English word *Jehovah*. In the King James Bible, when the word *Jehovah* is translated *LORD*, it is printed in capital letters. This is to distinguish it from *Adonai* which is also translated Lord, but always printed with small letters.

Note two important facts about the names used for God throughout the Old Testament.

1. Men were careful in the way they approached and addressed God in the Old Testament. This passage clearly illustrates this fact.

> "Moses said unto the LORD (Jehovah), O my Lord (Adonai)....And the LORD (Jehovah) said unto him...." (Ex.4:10-11).

Each name painted a different picture of God's nature and expressed just what the person wanted or needed to say. The different pictures or meanings of the names are given below and in various other footnotes.

2. God revealed a new name for Himself when man needed a fresh experience with God. Each name was revealed at the needed time. God obviously knows what is needed in each believer's experience and when it is needed. Thus at the exact time when a new revelation of His nature was needed, God revealed that part of His nature. He revealed more about Himself—a new trait, a new characteristic, a new truth. And man's need was met personally or socially.

Another way to say this is to say that the revelation of God's name was progressive, i.e., it was progressive revelation. Very simply stated, the Old Testament believers grew in their knowledge of God as they walked through life and gained experience with God. They grew step by step (the same as all believers have always grown) and God revealed Himself to man truth by truth, part by part. He lifted the veil of His nature fold by fold (He.1:1 [polumeros, "in many parts"]. See Ep.3:10, God's manifold wisdom, i.e., His richly, variegated or many-colored and diversified wisdom—a wisdom of many parts.)

There are three basic names for God used in the Bible. In this particular footnote, only a brief statement is given about each name. A complete discussion of each name is given in the notes to which one is referred. (For a complete list, see notes—Ge.1:1; 14:19; 15:2; 17:1; 21:33; 22:14; Ex.3:14-15; 4:10-11; 1 S.1:3.)

1. There is the name *El, Elah, Elohim*. Elohim is primarily used when God is addressed in general, as the God of all men and the God of creation. Elohim is the God of omnipotent, unlimited, and absolute power (see note 6—Ge.1:1).

2. There is the name *Jehovah* or *Yahweh*. Jehovah is almost always used when God is addressed as the God of His people, the people with whom He has made a covenant. (Jehovah means that God is The Great Redeemer and Savior, The Sustainer and Provider, The Source, Provision, and Supplier of all.) The name Jehovah points to God as the God of Revelation and Redemption. Jehovah (Yahweh) has always been considered to be the most precious and hallowed name for God among His people (see DEEPER STUDY # 2—Ex.3:14-15).

3. There is the name *Adon* or *Adonai*. Adonai means Master or Lord. It is used to address both God and men (see note—Ge.15:2).

---

5 (4:13-17) **Excuse—Call, of God**: the fifth argument: Moses just did not want to go; he refused and asked God to send someone else. The picture of Moses now seen is sad and heart-breaking.

a. Moses rejected God's call. He had run out of excuses, so he now had to admit the truth: he just did not want to go. Look at the scene: he actually begged God to send someone else. "O Lord, please send someone else" (NIV). The Hebrew literally says "please send the message by the hand of whomever you will" (v.3). The Hebrew often uses the word *hand* (yad) to express instrumentality, agency, channel, or means. For example:

> "The LORD warned Israel and Judah through [literally, 'spoken by the hand of'] all his prophets" (2 K.17:13, see Ex.9:35).[3]

The point is this: Moses wanted God to call someone else, to send His message by the hand of someone else. He did not want to go; he wanted to live like he wanted, to do his own thing with his life. He was rejecting God's call...

- refusing to do what God wanted
- refusing to be God's messenger
- refusing to go forth
- refusing to declare the glorious message of salvation and deliverance to Israel

b. What was God's response? Anger. Righteous anger. Moses would be allowed to say no more. God would still act in mercy toward Moses, but God meant business. Moses was to go and proclaim the glorious deliverance that was coming. There were to be no more arguments, no more excuses. Note that Moses was allowed to say nothing else. God alone now spoke. God said five things, and these five things concluded God's great call to Moses.

---

[3] Frank E. Gaebelein, Editor. *The Expositor's Bible Commentary*, Vol.2, p.329-330.

1) God promised to give Moses a helper, his brother Aaron, to be the spokesman (v.14). Note that God refers to Aaron as *the Levite*. Moses, too, was from the tribe of Levi, so it is unlikely that God was informing Moses that Aaron was a member of the tribe of Levi. Why then did God refer to Aaron as the Levite? He was probably giving a hint of things to come. Aaron and his sons, all the men of the tribe of Levi, were to become God's spokesmen and messengers—His priests—to Israel. Aaron was to be God's first messenger and spokesman to the people; therefore, God began immediately to refer to Aaron as Aaron the Levite. The Levites were soon after to become God's mediators—His spokesmen, His messengers, His priests and ministers to Israel.

2) God also told Moses that Aaron was on his way to visit him. Moreover, Aaron would accept and rejoice in Moses and his call by God (v.14).

3) God then instructed Moses as to the kind of relationship he was to have with Aaron. Moses was always to share God's Word with Aaron. God would help both of them speak and would teach them both what to do (v.15).

4) Aaron was to be the spokesman to the people, the very mouth of Moses to the people; and Moses was to be as God to Aaron (that is, as God's spokesman to Aaron) (v.16).

5) Moses was also to take the rod in his hand with him: to perform miraculous signs with it (v.17).

Thought 1. Rejecting God's call is serious business. Note that God chose Aaron to replace Moses in a significant area, that of being God's spokesman and messenger to the people. Moses lost the great privilege of being God's spokesman to the people—all because he had rejected God's call for so long. He also lost the wonderful privilege of being the father, the first of God's priests, the very first of God's messengers and spokesmen to Israel. All because he had argued so much against God's call.

"Son of man, I have made thee a watchman unto the house of Israel: therefore hear the word at my mouth, and give them warning from me" (Eze.3:17).

"But if the watchman see the sword come, and blow not the trumpet, and the people be not warned; if the sword come, and take any person from among them, he is taken away in his iniquity; but his blood will I require at the watchman's hand" (Eze.33:6).

"Go ye therefore, and teach all nations, baptizing them in the name of the Father, and of the Son, and of the Holy Ghost: teaching them to observe all things whatsoever I have commanded you: and, lo, I am with you alway, [even] unto the end of the world. Amen" (Mt.28:19-20).

"Wherefore I put thee in remembrance that thou stir up the gift of God, which is in thee by the putting on of my hands…. Be not thou therefore ashamed of the testimony of our Lord, nor of me his prisoner: but be thou partaker of the afflictions of the gospel according to the power of God" (2 Ti.1:6, 8).

"No man that warreth entangleth himself with the affairs of this life; that he may please him who hath chosen him to be a soldier" (2 Ti.2:4).

"I charge thee therefore before God, and the Lord Jesus Christ, who shall judge the quick [living] and the dead at his appearing and his kingdom; preach the word; be instant in season, out of season; reprove, rebuke, exhort with all longsuffering and doctrine" (2 Ti.4:1-2).

"Demas hath forsaken me, having loved this present world" (2 Ti.4:10).

TYPES, SYMBOLS, AND PICTURES
(Exodus 3:11–4:17)

Historical Term	Type or Picture (Scriptural Basis for Each)	Life Application for Today's Believer	Biblical Application
Moses' Staff [or Rod] (Ex.4:2-5)	*God's power…* • *over Pharaoh: Symbolizes the evil rulers of this world and Satan* • *over Egypt: Symbolizes the world and its enslavements* "And the LORD said unto him, What *is* that in thine hand? And he said, A rod. And he said, Cast it on the ground. And he cast it on the ground, and it became a serpent; and Moses fled from before it. And the LORD said unto Moses, Put forth thine hand, and take it by the tail. And he put forth his hand, and caught it, and it became a rod in	God's power rules over both the physical and the spiritual world… • all the principalities, powers, and rulers of this world • all the wicked forces in the spiritual world	*"[That you may know] what is the exceeding greatness of his power to us-ward who believe, according to the working of his [God's] mighty power, Which he wrought in Christ, when he raised him from the dead, and set him at his own right hand in the heavenly places, Far above all principality, and power, and might, and dominion, and every name that is named, not only in this world, but also in that which is to come: And hath put all things under his feet" (Ep.1:19-22).* *"Put on the whole armour of God, that ye may be able to stand against the wiles of the devil. For we*

116

TYPES, SYMBOLS, AND PICTURES
(Exodus 3:11–4:17)

Historical Term	Type or Picture (Scriptural Basis for Each)	Life Application for Today's Believer	Biblical Application
	his hand: That they may believe that the LORD God of their fathers, the God of Abraham, the God of Isaac, and the God of Jacob, hath appeared unto thee" (Ex.4:2-5; see Ps.2:9).		*wrestle not against flesh and blood, but against principalities, against powers, against the rulers of the darkness of this world, against spiritual wickedness in high places" (Ep.6:11-12; see Col.2:15).*
Moses' Leprous Hand (Ex.4:6-8)	*God's power...* • *over health* • *over disease* • *over life* • *over sin* • *over death* **"And the LORD said furthermore unto him, Put now thine hand into thy bosom. And he put his hand into his bosom: and when he took it out, behold, his hand** *was* **leprous as snow. And he said, Put thine hand into thy bosom again. And he put his hand into his bosom again; and plucked it out of his bosom, and, behold, it was turned again as his other flesh" (Ex.4:6-7. See outline and notes—Ex.9:8-12).**	Jesus Christ has complete control over our bodies and our lives. His power will... • heal or strengthen the sick • comfort all who cry out to Him • forgive the sin of all who ask Him • save all who call upon Him, save them for all eternity	*"The Spirit of the Lord [is] upon me, because he hath anointed me to preach the gospel to the poor; he hath sent me to heal the brokenhearted, to preach deliverance to the captives, and recovering of sight to the blind, to set at liberty them that are bruised" (Lu.4:18).* *"And the Lord shall deliver me from every evil work, and will preserve me unto his heavenly kingdom: to whom be glory for ever and ever" (2 Ti.4:18).* *"But I am poor and needy; yet the Lord thinketh upon me: thou art my help and my deliverer; make no tarrying, O my God" (Ps.40:17).* *"In him was life; and the life was the light of men. That was the true Light, which lighteth every man that cometh into the world" (Jn.1:4, 9).* *"For whosoever shall call upon the name of the Lord shall be saved" (Ro.10:13).* *(see Ex.15:26; De.7:15; Ps.41:4; Ps.147:3; Is.46:4; Is.53:5; Je.30:17; Jn.3:16; 10:10)*
Aaron (Ex.4:14-16)	*A picture of a spokesman or ambassador* **"And he [Aaron] shall be thy spokesman unto the people: and he shall be,** *even* **he shall be to thee instead of a mouth, and thou shalt be to him instead of God" (Ex.4:16).** **"And the Lord said unto Moses, See, I have made thee a god to Pharaoh: and Aaron thy brother shall be thy prophet. Thou shalt speak all that I command thee: and Aaron thy brother shall speak unto Pharaoh, that he send the children of Israel out of his land" (Ex.7:1-2).**	A faithful ambassador carries with him... • the authority of the One (Christ) who sent him • the message of the One (Christ) who sent him • the will of the One (Christ) who sent him	*"Also I heard the voice of the Lord, saying, Whom shall I send, and who will go for us? Then said I, Here am I; send me" (Is.6:8).* *"Now then we are ambassadors for Christ, as though God did beseech you by us: we pray you in Christ's stead, be ye reconciled to God" (2 Co.5:20).* *"Ye have not chosen me, but I have chosen you, and ordained you, that ye should go and bring forth fruit, and [that] your fruit should remain: that whatsoever ye shall ask of the Father in my name, he may give it you" (Jn.15:16).* *"Feed the flock of God which is among you, taking the oversight thereof, not*

TYPES, SYMBOLS, AND PICTURES
(Exodus 3:11–4:17)

Historical Term	Type or Picture (Scriptural Basis for Each)	Life Application for Today's Believer	Biblical Application
Aaron (continued) (Ex.4:14-16)			*by constraint, but willingly; not for filthy lucre, but of a ready mind; Neither as being lords over God's heritage, but being ensamples to the flock"* (1 Pe.5:2-3). *(see Ac.20:28; 1 Ti.1:12; 1 Co.2:1-5)*

1. Obedience, then God's assurance

a. Moses' obedience: He asked permission to return to Egypt—to see if his family was still living
   1) He did not boastfully mention God's call
   2) Jethro granted permission
b. God's assurance: The way was prepared; all who sought his life were now dead

2. Obedience, then God's guidance

a. Moses' obedience
   1) He made a permanent move to Egypt: Moved his family
   2) He took the rod of God: Just as God had instructed (v.17)
b. God's direction: His guidance & instruction
   1) Go to Pharaoh: Perform all the miracles
   2) But know: Pharaoh's heart will be hardened; he will not let the people go^DS1
   3) Declare the LORD's Word
   • Israel is my son, my firstborn
   • Let my son go: That he may serve me
   • If you refuse, God will slay your firstborn son

E. The Surrender of Moses to God's Call: The Fruit of Obedience, 4:18-31

18 And Moses went and returned to Jethro his father in law, and said unto him, Let me go, I pray thee, and return unto my brethren which are in Egypt, and see whether they be yet alive. And Jethro said to Moses, Go in peace.
19 And the LORD said unto Moses in Midian, Go, return into Egypt: for all the men are dead which sought thy life.
20 And Moses took his wife and his sons, and set them upon an ass, and he returned to the land of Egypt: and Moses took the rod of God in his hand.
21 And the LORD said unto Moses, When thou goest to return into Egypt, see that thou do all those wonders before Pharaoh, which I have put in thine hand: but I will harden his heart, that he shall not let the people go.
22 And thou shalt say unto Pharaoh, Thus saith the LORD, Israel is my son, even my firstborn:
23 And I say unto thee, Let my son go, that he may serve me: and if thou refuse to let him go, behold, I will slay thy son, even thy firstborn.

24 And it came to pass by the way in the inn, that the LORD met him, and sought to kill him.
25 Then Zipporah took a sharp stone, and cut off the foreskin of her son, and cast it at his feet, and said, Surely a bloody husband art thou to me.
26 So he let him go: then she said, A bloody husband thou art, because of the circumcision.
27 And the LORD said to Aaron, Go into the wilderness to meet Moses. And he went, and met him in the mount of God, and kissed him.
28 And Moses told Aaron all the words of the LORD who had sent him, and all the signs which he had commanded him.
29 And Moses and Aaron went and gathered together all the elders of the children of Israel:
30 And Aaron spake all the words which the LORD had spoken unto Moses, and did the signs in the sight of the people.
31 And the people believed: and when they heard that the LORD had visited the children of Israel, and that he had looked upon their affliction, then they bowed their heads and worshipped.

3. Obedience, then God's hand of chastisement was removed

a. God chastised Moses: Was about to kill him
b. The reason: Moses' wife had apparently objected to circumcision & Moses had given in to his wife, disobeyed God & not circumcised his son
c. Moses' wife circumcised their son, but in disgust
d. God removed His hand of chastisement & saved Moses

4. Obedience, then God fulfilled His promise

a. Aaron's call & obedience
   1) God called Aaron: He obeyed God & went to meet Moses
   2) Moses shared with Aaron: Shared God's call & the miraculous signs given him to do
b. Moses' & Aaron's obedience: They gathered together all the elders of Israel
   1) Aaron shared what God had told Moses
   2) Moses performed the miraculous signs
c. God's promise was fulfilled—just as God had promised: The people believed & bowed down & worshipped (see vv.5, 8)

DIVISION II

MOSES AND GOD: GOD RAISES UP A LEADER TO DELIVER HIS PEOPLE (ISRAEL), 2:1–7:7

E. The Surrender of Moses to God's Call: The Fruit of Obedience, 4:18-31

(4:18-31) **Introduction**: God had just met Moses at the burning bush. The great call of Moses had just taken place. God wanted Moses to be His messenger, to go and deliver His people from slavery. But Moses did not want to go. He did not want to live a life of service and witness, a life obligated to God. He wanted to be free to live life like he wanted, to do his own thing. Standing there before God, Moses made up excuse after excuse, arguing against God's call. In fact, he argued so long and so much that he angered God. In righteous anger, God insisted that Moses go. Moses was to be God's messenger. No excuse, no argument was valid. Moses was to surrender to God's call: he was to go and proclaim God's glorious message of deliverance and freedom. What happened? The present passage tells us: *The Surrender of Moses to God's Call: The Fruit of Obedience,* 4:18-31.

1. Obedience, then God's assurance (vv.18-19).
2. Obedience, then God's guidance (vv.20-23).
3. Obedience, then God's hand of chastisement was removed (vv.24-26).
4. Obedience, then God fulfilled His promise (vv.27-31).

1 (4:18-19) **Obedience—Courtesy**: first, there was obedience, then God's assurance was given.

a. Moses obeyed God, surrendered to God's call (v.18). He left the desert and went home to take care of business matters. He began to lay plans to return to Egypt. He had worked for his father-in-law, Jethro, for forty years, so he had to handle whatever business arrangements existed between them. He could not just leave Jethro hanging without making arrangements for a replacement. Moreover, Jethro was the head of the family: the father of Moses' wife and the grandfather of Moses' sons.

The point to note is that Moses was kind and respectful to his wife's father; he did not just pick up and leave. He did not ignore the effect of his leaving upon his wife's family. He asked permission of Jethro; he made arrangements before he left.

Thought 1. God's call demands first loyalty, even before family. But we must always be loving, kind, and respectful to our families when we are called to be away from them. And we must help them understand God's call as well as we can.

"He that loveth father or mother more than me is not worthy of me: and he that loveth son or daughter more than me is not worthy of me. And he that taketh not his cross, and followeth after me, is not worthy of me" (Mt.10:37-38).

"And he said to [them] all, If any [man] will come after me, let him deny himself, and take up his cross daily, and follow me" (Lu.9:23).

Note another fact as well: Moses did not boastfully mention God's call. He did not act super-spiritual. Think of the great experience he had just had with God, yet he was ever so quiet and humble about the experience.

"Whosoever therefore shall humble himself as this little child, the same is greatest in the kingdom of heaven" (Mt.18:4).

"For I say, through the grace given unto me, to every man that is among you, not to think of himself more highly than he ought to think; but to think soberly, according as God hath dealt to every man the measure of faith" (Ro.12:3).

"Let nothing be done through strife or vainglory; but in lowliness of mind let each esteem other better than themselves. Look not every man on his own things, but every man also on the things of others" (Ph.2:3-4).

"Likewise, ye younger, submit yourselves unto the elder. Yea, all of you be subject one to another, and be clothed with humility: for God resisteth the proud, and giveth grace to the humble" (1 Pe.5:5).

b. Once Moses obeyed God, after he had begun to make arrangements to go to Egypt, God gave Moses great assurance. God gave Moses the assurance of safety, security, and protection (v.19). God told Moses that the men who had sought to kill him were now dead. The coast was clear. There was no reason to fear. Remember, Moses had been a wanted man in Egypt. He had killed an Egyptian official forty years earlier, and Pharaoh had put the order out: arrest and execute Moses. Just as it would with any of us, fear had arisen within Moses as he went about making arrangements to return to Egypt.

But God is faithful: here He was giving assurance to Moses. His dear messenger was surrendering to His God-given call. Despite the execution order that hung over his head, Moses was obeying God. He was surrendering to God's call and going forth to deliver God's people. Thus God met Moses to give him assurance: his enemies were all dead. There was no need to fear; he would be safe as he returned to Egypt.

Thought 1. The first fruit of obedience is God's assurance. When we surrender to God's call, surrender to do His will, it is then that God's assurance sweeps over our souls. God assures us; He will take care of us when we obey Him. He will bless us with great assurance and care.

"Now therefore, if ye will obey my voice indeed, and keep my covenant, then ye shall be a peculiar treasure unto me above all people: for all the earth is mine" (Ex.19:5).

"When thou art in tribulation, and all these things are come upon thee, even in the latter days, if thou turn to the LORD thy God, and shalt be obedient unto his voice; (for the LORD thy God is a merciful God;) he will not forsake thee, neither destroy thee, nor forget the covenant of thy fathers which he sware unto them" (De.4:30-31).

"O that there were such an heart in them, that they would fear me, and keep all my commandments always, that it might be well with them, and with their children for ever!" (De.5:29).

"And if thou wilt walk in my ways, to keep my statutes and my commandments, as thy father David did walk, then I will lengthen thy days" (1 K.3:14).

"Go ye therefore, and teach all nations, baptizing them in the name of the Father, and of the Son, and of the Holy Ghost: Teaching them to observe all things whatsoever I have commanded you: and, lo, I am with you alway, [even] unto the end of the world" (Mt.28:19-20).

"He that hath my commandments, and keepeth them, he it is that loveth me: and he that loveth me shall be loved of my Father, and I will love him, and will manifest myself to him" (Jn.14:21).

"Ye have not chosen me, but I have chosen you, and ordained you, that ye should go and bring forth fruit, and [that] your fruit should remain: that whatsoever ye shall ask of the Father in my name, he may give it you" (Jn.15:16).

"But whoso looketh into the perfect law of liberty, and continueth therein, he being not a forgetful hearer, but a doer of the work, this man shall be blessed in his deed" (Js.1:25).

"Blessed are they that do his commandments, that they may have right to the tree of life, and may enter in through the gates into the city" (Re.22:14).

2 (4:20-23) **Obedience—Guidance**: second, there was obedience, then God's guidance and direction were given.

a. Moses was obedient to God, fully obedient (v.20). Note that he set out to make a permanent move to Egypt: he took his family with him which included his wife and two sons. Note also that he took the rod of God just as God had instructed him (see Ex.4:17).

b. Again, Moses' obedience bore fruit. As Moses continued to obey God, God continued to meet his need. God now met a very special need of Moses, the need for guidance and direction (vv.21-23). He needed to know exactly what to do when he reached Egypt and appeared before Pharaoh. And he needed to know before he reached Egypt so that he would have time to meditate and plan the meeting. This need God now met, and how God's heart must have been flooded with joy. For His servant was now obeying Him, obeying despite all the excuses he had against surrendering and obeying. God's servant was now obedient; therefore, God was now able to meet His dear servant and give him guidance and direction. God told Moses to do three things when he reached Egypt.

1) Moses was to go to Pharaoh and perform all the miracles God had given him the power to do (v.21).
2) Moses was, however, to know one thing: God was going to harden Pharaoh's heart so that he would not let the people go (v.21). God was making sure that Moses was not caught by surprise nor discouraged when Pharaoh rejected his message and refused to free God's people (see DEEPER STUDY # 1—Ex.4:21 for more discussion).
3) Moses was to proclaim the Word of God. He was to declare three points to Pharaoh:
⇒ First, Israel was "God's son, even His firstborn" (v.22). This is the first time God referred to Israel as His Son and His firstborn. F.B. Huey says:

> "In this statement Israel was brought into the closest, most loving and honored relationship that could be realized in the ancient Near East. The eldest son was given a place of special honor and respect.
> • "He received a double portion of the family inheritance (Deut.21:17).
> • "The law of redemption applied to him in a special way (Exod.13:11-15).
> • "He was looked upon as the one who would succeed his father as head of the family or clan.
> • "He was given preferential status (Ge.43:33), authority (Ge.27:37), and responsibility (Ge.37:22).
> • "As his birthright, he had claims on the family blessing (Ge.27:1-4, 35-37)."[1]

⇒ Second, Pharaoh was to free Israel so that Israel could serve and live for God (v.23).
⇒ Third, if Pharaoh refused, God would slay the firstborn son of Pharaoh (v.23).

Thought 1. There is a strong lesson for us in this point: if we do not obey and surrender to God's call, then God cannot guide and direct our lives. Why? Because He would be indulging and giving license to disobedience, rebellion, and sin. But when we obey and surrender to God's call, then God can guide and direct our lives. This He promises.

"**Lead me in thy truth, and teach me: for thou art the God of my salvation; on thee do I wait all the day**" (Ps.25:5).
"**The meek will he guide in judgment: and the meek will he teach his way**" (Ps.25:9).
"**For this God is our God for ever and ever: he will be our guide even unto death**" (Ps.48:14).
"**Thou shalt guide me with thy counsel, and afterward receive me to glory**" (Ps.73:24).
"**Teach me to do thy will; for thou art my God: thy spirit is good; lead me into the land of uprightness**" (Ps.143:10).
"**And thine ears shall hear a word behind thee, saying, This is the way, walk ye in it, when ye turn to the right hand, and when ye turn to the left**" (Is.30:21).
"**[Christ came] to give light to them that sit in darkness and in the shadow of death, to guide our feet into the way of peace**" (Lu.1:79).
"**Howbeit when he, the Spirit of truth, is come, he will guide you into all truth: for he shall not speak of himself; but whatsoever he shall hear, [that] shall he speak: and he will show you things to come**" (Jn.16:13).

DEEPER STUDY # 1
(4:21) **Judgment, Judicial—Hard - Hardness—Hearts, Harden**: God hardened Pharaoh's heart. What does this mean? Note these facts:
a. God is said to harden Pharaoh's heart ten different times in *Exodus* (Ex.4:21; 7:3; 9:12; 10:1, 20, 27; 11:10; 14:4, 8, 17).
b. Pharaoh is said to harden his own heart ten different times (Ex.7:13, 14, 22; 8:15, 19, 32; 9:7, 34, 35; 13:15).
c. Three different words are translated *hardened* in the passages dealing with Pharaoh.
⇒ There is the Hebrew word *chazaq* which means to be strong or braced or tightened. Thus the idea is that of being strongly against, or braced against or stubborn—to be set against God (Ex.4:21; 7:13, 22; 8:19; 9:12, 35; 10:20, 27; 11:10; 14:4, 8).
⇒ There is the Hebrew word *kabed* which means to be heavy, weighty, or hard. The idea is that of being dull and unresponsive to God's Spirit (Ex.7:14; 8:15, 32; 9:7, 34; 10:1. See 1 S.6:6.)
⇒ There is the Hebrew word *qashah* which means to be sharp, severe, cruel, hard. The idea is that of being obstinate (Ex.7:3).

---

[1] F.B. Huey Jr. *Exodus*, pp.34-35. The points are set apart for clarity.

d. Pharaoh hardened his heart long before God is said to have hardened Pharaoh's heart.
⇒ Pharaoh hardened his heart against the first miraculous sign performed by Moses, that of turning his rod into a snake (Ex.7:10-13, esp. 13).
⇒ Pharaoh hardened his heart against God as a result of the first five plagues. Scripture says that beginning with the sixth sign, God began to harden Pharaoh's heart. (Pharaoh hardened his heart in Ex.7:22; 8:15, 19, 32; 9:7. God began to harden Pharaoh's heart in Ex.9:12.)

e. Note that here in verse 21 the order of the hardening seems to be given. God told Moses to go to Pharaoh and perform the miraculous signs, and then Pharaoh would harden his heart. This would indicate that the hardening of heart would take place after the miraculous signs. Thus the order of events would be:
⇒ the miraculous signs.
⇒ the response of Pharaoh: he hardened his heart against the signs.
⇒ the justice and judgment of God: He hardened Pharaoh's heart.

This is what is known as the *judicial judgment of God* or the *righteous judgment of God:* the judgment that is just and righteous, a judgment that is due, that has to be executed by God who is both righteous and loving. Remember…
• If God is love, He has to execute justice. Love demands that a person be treated justly and fairly, that he be treated with honesty, honor, and decency
• If God is righteous, He has to execute justice. Righteousness demands that a person pay for his transgressions and violations of God's law, that he pay for the penalty for his unrighteous and unlawful acts

Thus Pharaoh's heart was hardened because his heart deserved to be hardened. Pharaoh had…
• worshipped false gods and idols all his life
• lived an ungodly and unrighteous life
• treated others unjustly and unfairly: he brutalized and enslaved people
• rejected the pleas of God time and again, and even rejected the plagues and warnings of God, as God's messenger (Moses) proclaimed the message of God

Pharaoh's heart was hard because he had made it hard through the years, made it hard by the decisions he had made. Time and again he had made decision after decision to do wrong, so much so that he now found it easy to do wrong. His conscience and inner knowledge of righteousness had become hardened, more and more encrusted and rock-like.
The Pulpit Commentary says this:

Men, it is said, harden their own hearts against God; God does not actively interfere to harden the heart of anyone….A supernatural hardening of Pharaoh's heart is not to be thought of. But among the natural punishments which God has attached to sin, would seem to be the hardening of the entire nature of the man who sins.
⇒ *If men "do not like to retain God in their knowledge, God gives them up to a reprobate mind" (Ro.1:28).*
⇒ *If they resist the Spirit, he "takes his holy Spirit from them" (Ps.51:11).*
⇒ *If they sin against light he withdraws the light.*
⇒ *If they stifle their natural affections of kindness, compassion and the like, it is a law of his providence that those affections shall wither and decay.*

This seems to be the "hardening of the heart" here intended—not an abnormal and miraculous interference with the soul of Pharaoh, but the natural effect upon his soul…[because] of those acts which he wilfully and wrongfully committed.[2]

Alexander Maclaren makes these statements:

⇒ *"God hardens no man's heart who has not first hardened it himself."*
⇒ *"Was not the accumulation of plagues, intended as they were to soften, a cause of hardening?"*
⇒ *"Does not the gospel, if rejected, harden, making conscience and wills less susceptible?"*
⇒ *"The same fire softens wax and hardens clay."*
⇒ *"Whosoever is not brought near is driven farther off by the influences which God brings to bear on us."*[3]

Maxie Dunnam gives an excellent application for this discussion:

This is serious business. It is soul business with eternal consequences….To refuse the gospel call upon our lives at any level is to lay another brick in our wall of resistance to God's grace. That's the reason little decisions—responses to what appear to be minor calls—are important. Our obedience to the everyday calls of God is the discipline that equips us to respond faithfully when the big calls come.
What are those everyday calls?
• *to repent; as soon as you sense some sin in your life, repent, come to Christ, be genuinely sorry, beg His forgiveness.*
• *to give a cup of cold water in Jesus' name.*
• *to speak up for that colleague or neighbor who is being maligned by gossip.*

---

2 *Exodus.* "The Pulpit Commentary," Vol.1, p.103. The statements are set apart for clarity.
3 Alexander Maclaren. *Expositions of Holy Scripture*, 11 Vols. (Grand Rapids, MI: Eerdmans Publishing Company, 1952-59), Vol.1, p.37. The statements are set apart for clarity.

- to tithe your income as God has called each one of us to do.
- "to witness for Christ every time the opportunity arises.
- "to live holy lives; to be recognized as set apart, refusing to participate in the immorality that is rampant in our time—cheating, infidelity, deceit, fornication, lying.

God's call comes to us in some form every day. Every day we have the opportunity to respond to Him. Though it may not be noticeable to us, refusing these calls will gradually harden our hearts.[4]

(See DEEPER STUDY # 1—Ex.10:1. See outlines and notes—Mt.13:13-15; Jn.12:39-41; Ro.1:24; 11:7-10 for more discussion.)

3 (4:24-26) **Obedience—Chastisement—Circumcision**: third, there was obedience, then God's hand of chastisement was removed. What now happened to Moses stands as a warning to all believers and servants of God.

a. Moses was obeying God and was on his way to Egypt when God's hand of chastisement fell upon him (v.24). Why? Because he was deliberately disobeying God in a particular area of his life, a critical area.

What happened was this: Moses and his family had stopped and set up camp for the night. Then suddenly Moses became very sick and was about to die. Note what Scripture says was happening: God had met Moses and was about to slay him (v.24). This means that God was chastising and correcting Moses, and the chastisement was severe: Moses was about to die. Here he was surrendering to God's call to go and proclaim the glorious message of deliverance, yet God began to severely chastise him. What could Moses be doing that was so bad? What was it that he was not surrendering to God, that he was holding back and refusing to correct? What was Moses doing that displeased God so much that God would stop using Moses and take him on home to heaven?

b. Scripture tells us: Moses' wife had apparently objected to circumcision, bitterly objected to it. She caused so much strife that Moses just gave in to his wife. He put his wife and her objections before God. In order to keep peace in the home, he gave in to his wife. He chose to avoid the fussing and arguing of his wife instead of obeying God. He disobeyed God and did not circumcise his son (v.25). Remember three critical facts about circumcision.

First, circumcision was *the sign* of the covenant between God and man. God had given circumcision to teach His people to have no confidence in the flesh. The cutting away of the flesh was the picture (the symbol and sign) that the true believer was not to place his trust in the flesh. He was to put his trust in God. (Ph.3:3; Col.2:11-12). Remember this fact: When God made this covenant with Abraham, he was the least likely to become a father of many nations (Ge.17:4-6). Given his failure to have children with Sarah, G.E. Farley notes:

> [Abraham's] circumcision may have meant symbolically: I am yielding my powers of procreation, my stake in the future to Yahweh. I am becoming totally dependent upon Him. If I have descendants enough to be a great nation it will be Yahweh's doing, not my own. One can imagine that this was the supreme sacrifice for the ancient patriarch.[5]

Second, circumcision was the sign that a man trusted God, that he was a true follower of God, that he was a true believer in the great promises of God:

⇒ The promise of the promised land (see note—Ex.1:1-22; 1:6-7; 2:23-25. For detailed discussion see note—Ge.12:1.)
⇒ The promise of the promised seed, including both the seed of a great nation of people and the one particular seed, the Savior and Messiah of the world. (See notes—Ex.1:1-22; 1:6-7; 2:23-25. For detailed discussion see notes—Ge.12:2-3; 12:3.)

These promises are of critical importance to both God and man. They are the very basis of God's great covenant with man: the promise of heaven and the promise of the Savior, God's very own Son. It is God's Son who makes it possible for man to enter heaven and to live forever with God.

Third, God Himself stressed the critical importance of circumcision. Note Ge.17:10-14 where God commanded Abraham to circumcise every male child on the eighth day after birth. This was to be the sign that the father and his family were true believers and followers of God and His great promises. The critical importance of circumcision is also seen in God's other commandment to Abraham: any uncircumcised male was to be *cut off* and *separated* from the people; he was not a believer and follower of God. He had broken the covenant of God (Ge.17:10-14).

⇒ How then could Moses lead the people unless he himself obeyed God?
⇒ How could Moses teach the covenant to people if he refused to circumcise his own son?
⇒ How could Moses teach people to love and obey God unless he loved and obeyed God?
⇒ How could Moses teach people to put God first if he put his wife first?
⇒ How could Moses be the servant and messenger of God if he was unwilling to obey God in the very basic sign of God's great covenant?

On and on the questions go, but the point is made: God had to correct Moses. God had to chastise Moses so that Moses would do what he needed to do: obey God and circumcise his son. The very man whom God was choosing to be the great lawgiver to the world, Moses himself, had to be corrected by God, severely chastened. He was disobeying God in one of the most basic commandments of God, that of bearing the sign of the covenant, circumcision.

c. Note that Moses' wife circumcised their son, but she apparently did it in anger, disgust, and with a rebellious spirit (v.25). She was obviously against circumcision so much that she took the foreskin and threw it at Moses' feet as he lay

4 Maxie Dunnam. *Mastering the Old Testament, Vol.2, Exodus.* (Dallas, TX: Word Publishing, 1987), pp.82-83. The statements are set apart for clarity.
5 Merrill C. Tenney, Editor. *The Zondervan Pictorial Encyclopedia of the Bible,* Vol.1. (Grand Rapids, MI: Zondervan Publishing House, 1982), p.866.

there in bed dying. She angrily cried out: "You are a husband of blood to me." She was in rebellion against God, bitter rebellion.

    d. God then removed His hand of chastisement and saved Moses (v.26). Moses recovered his health and resumed his journey to Egypt. Note: Moses apparently sent his wife and children back home after this, back to her father, Jethro.
- Her bitter rebellion against God almost cost Moses his life
- Her rebellion would have been a devastating hindrance to the purpose of God and to the ministry of Moses. (See note—Ex.18:1-8 for more discussion.)

Thought 1. We must obey God in all areas of our lives. We must not hold anything back; we must surrender everything we are and have to God. If not, then God has no choice: He must correct and chastise us. God must discipline us when we disobey and go astray. God must do all He can to keep us from sin and the terrible results of sin. God must keep us from harming and hurting ourselves, from destroying our lives, our testimony, and our witness for Him. God must chastise us, make us sit up, take notice, and correct ourselves before we go too far.

    "Thou shalt also consider in thine heart, that, as a man chasteneth his son, so the LORD thy God chasteneth thee" (De.8:5).
    "Blessed is the man whom thou chastenest, O LORD, and teachest him out of thy law" (Ps.94:12).
    "My son, despise not the chastening of the LORD; neither be weary of his correction: for whom the LORD loveth he correcteth; even as a father the son in whom he delighteth" (Pr.3:11-12).
    "Every branch in me that beareth not fruit he taketh away: and every [branch] that beareth fruit, he purgeth it, that it may bring forth more fruit" (Jn.15:2).
    "And ye have forgotten the exhortation which speaketh unto you as unto children, My son, despise not thou the chastening of the Lord, nor faint when thou art rebuked of him: for whom the Lord loveth he chasteneth, and scourgeth every son whom he receiveth If ye endure chastening, God dealeth with you as with sons; for what son is he whom the father chasteneth not?" (He.12:5-7).
    "As many as I love, I rebuke and chasten: be zealous therefore, and repent" (Re.3:19).

4   (4:27-31) **Obedience**: fourth, there was obedience, then God fulfilled His promise. While God was calling and dealing with Moses, a wonderful thing was happening to his brother Aaron. God was working in Aaron's heart as well, calling and preparing him to serve right by the side of Moses—all as God had promised Moses.

    a. Note Aaron's call and obedience: God called him to go into the wilderness and meet Moses (vv.27-28). This he did: he met up with Moses at the Mount of God itself, Mt. Sinai. The reunion must have been glorious. They kissed each other and, no doubt, Aaron shared all that had happened to the family during the 40 year absence of Moses. Then Moses shared with Aaron, shared God's call and the power God had given him to work signs and miracles before the people. After the reunion, Moses and Aaron journeyed to Egypt together.

    b. When they reached Egypt, they obeyed God: they gathered together all the elders of Israel (vv.30-31).
      ⇒ Aaron shared what God had told Moses. Remember: God had appointed him to be the spokesman for Moses (see vv.14-16).
      ⇒ Moses performed the miracles (see Ex.4:3-9). Remember: God had commissioned Moses to perform the signs. Because of this the personal pronoun *he* should probably be inserted before "did the signs" to indicate that they were performed by Moses and not Aaron.[6]

    c. God's wonderful promise to Moses was fulfilled: the people believed and they bowed down, worshipping God (v.31). The message that God cared for them and was deeply concerned about their suffering stirred a great hope within the people. Picture the scene:
      ⇒ There stood Moses, the great former prince of Egypt, who had been in exile for over forty years. And there stood Aaron, his brother, by his side, one of their leaders whom they deeply respected and had known for so many years.
      ⇒ There was the great message of deliverance that had just been proclaimed to them by Aaron, the message from the LORD God, the Great I AM Himself.
      ⇒ There were the extraordinary miracles just performed by Moses before their very eyes.

    All this aroused within their hearts the deepest emotions imaginable: they were about to be freed, freed by the power of God Himself. Joy, hope, and expectancy flooded their hearts. A deep sense of God's care and love flowed through their bodies. A spirit of thankfulness and praise to God gripped their souls. Thus, they fell to their knees and worshipped God. In the words of George Bush:

    All conspired to produce in their breasts the deepest emotions of wonder and joy; a strong confidence in God; and an assurance that he was indeed about to show them mercy. In testimony of this...the whole assembly bowed their heads and worshipped.[7]

    Thought 1. When we obey God, God fulfills His promises—always. First obedience; then fulfillment. Obedience always bears fruit, the fruit of God's presence, love, and blessing.

---

6 George Bush. *Exodus*. (Minneapolis, MN: Klock & Klock Christian Publishers, Inc., 1981), p.71.
7 Ibid., p.71.

"Now therefore, if ye will obey my voice indeed, and keep my covenant, then ye shall be a peculiar treasure unto me above all people: for all the earth is mine" (Ex.19:5).

"And ye shall serve the Lord your God, and he shall bless thy bread, and thy water; and I will take sickness away from the midst of thee" (Ex.23:25).

"O that there were such an heart in them, that they would fear me, and keep all my commandments always, that it might be well with them, and with their children forever!" (De.5:29).

"This book of the law shall not depart out of thy mouth; but thou shalt meditate therein day and night, that thou mayest observe to do according to all that is written therein: for then thou shalt make thy way prosperous, and then thou shalt have good success" (Jos. 1:8).

"And if thou wilt walk in my ways, to keep my statutes and my commandments, as thy father David did walk, then I will lengthen thy days" (1 K.3:14).

"But seek ye first the kingdom of God, and his righteousness; and all these things shall be added unto you" (Mt.6:33).

"Not every one that saith unto me, Lord, Lord, shall enter into the kingdom of heaven; but he that doeth the will of my Father which is in heaven" (Mt.7:21).

"He that hath my commandments, and keepeth them, he it is that loveth me: and he that loveth me shall be loved of my Father, and I will love him, and will manifest myself to him" (Jn.14:21).

"Jesus answered and said unto him, If a man love me, he will keep my words: and my Father will love him, and we will come unto him, and make our abode with him" (Jn.14:23).

"If ye keep my commandments, ye shall abide in my love; even as I have kept my Father's commandments, and abide in his love" (Jn.15:10).

"Ye are my friends, if ye do whatsoever I command you" (Jn.15:14).

"Blessed are they that do his commandments, that they may have right to the tree of life, and may enter in through the gates into the city" (Re.22:14).

TYPES, SYMBOLS, AND PICTURES
(Exodus 4:18-31)

Historical Term	Type or Picture (Scriptural Basis for Each)	Life Application for Today's Believer	Biblical Application
Circumcision (Ex.4:24-26)	*A sign of God's covenant with man* **"This *is* my covenant, which ye shall keep, between me and you and thy seed after thee; Every man child among you shall be circumcised" (Ge.17:10).** **"And he gave him the covenant of circumcision: and so Abraham begat Isaac, and circumcised him the eighth day; and Isaac begat Jacob; and Jacob begat the twelve patriarchs" (Ac.7:8).** **"Circumcise therefore the foreskin of your heart, and be no more stiffnecked" (De.10:16).** (see De.30:6; Je.4:4)	Since the coming of Christ, circumcision... • is no longer an outward sign • places no confidence in the flesh • takes place in the heart of believers	*"For we are the circumcision, which worship God in the spirit, and rejoice in Christ Jesus, and have no confidence in the flesh" (Ph.3:3).* *"In whom [Christ] also ye are circumcised with the circumcision made without hands, in putting off the body of the sins of the flesh by the circumcision of Christ" (Col.2:11).* *"For circumcision verily profiteth, if thou keep the law: but if thou be a breaker of the law, thy circumcision is made uncircumcision" (Ro.2:25).* *"But he is a Jew, which is one inwardly; and circumcision is that of the heart, in the spirit, and not in the letter; whose praise is not of men, but of God" (Ro.2:29).*

CHAPTER 5

F. The First Confrontation of Moses with Pharaoh: Opposing God's Will for His People, The Right of Man to Live & Worship God in Freedom, 5:1-23

1. The declaration of God's will
  a. God's will: Freedom, liberty
  b. God's purpose: That His people might live, worship, & serve Him in freedom & liberty

2. The rejection of God's will
  a. Because Pharaoh was ignorant of God
    1) He refused to obey God: Would not free the people
    2) The messengers of God warned Pharaoh: He must free God's people or else face the judgment of God, some terrible plagues or foreign invaders
  b. Because Pharaoh accused God's messengers of disturbing the peace, of interfering with the people's work & lives
  c. Because Pharaoh was mean-spirited & ruthless: He instructed the slave-drivers to oppress God's people more & more
    1) By no longer supplying straw for the bricks, but forcing them to gather their own straw
    2) By forcing them to produce the same quota of bricks per day despite the extra labor required to gather the straw
    3) By making the work so hard that the people would not have time to listen to the messengers of God
  d. Because Pharaoh thought God's messengers were liars
  e. Because Pharaoh misused his authority & power
    1) God's people were made to gather their own straw

And afterward Moses and Aaron went in, and told Pharaoh, Thus saith the LORD God of Israel, Let my people go, that they may hold a feast unto me in the wilderness.
2 And Pharaoh said, Who is the LORD, that I should obey his voice to let Israel go? I know not the LORD, neither will I let Israel go.
3 And they said, The God of the Hebrews hath met with us: let us go, we pray thee, three days' journey into the desert, and sacrifice unto the LORD our God; lest he fall upon us with pestilence, or with the sword.
4 And the king of Egypt said unto them, Wherefore do ye, Moses and Aaron, let the people from their works? get you unto your burdens.
5 And Pharaoh said, Behold, the people of the land now are many, and ye make them rest from their burdens.
6 And Pharaoh commanded the same day the taskmasters of the people, and their officers, saying,
7 Ye shall no more give the people straw to make brick, as heretofore: let them go and gather straw for themselves.
8 And the tale of the bricks, which they did make heretofore, ye shall lay upon them; ye shall not diminish ought thereof: for they be idle; therefore they cry, saying, Let us go and sacrifice to our God.
9 Let there more work be laid upon the men, that they may labour therein; and let them not regard vain words.
10 And the taskmasters of the people went out, and their officers, and they spake to the people, saying, Thus saith Pharaoh, I will not give you straw.
11 Go ye, get you straw where ye can find it: yet not ought of your work shall be diminished.
12 So the people were scattered abroad throughout all the land of Egypt to gather stubble instead of straw.
13 And the taskmasters hasted them, saying, Fulfil your works, your daily tasks, as when there was straw.
14 And the officers of the children of Israel, which Pharaoh's taskmasters had set over them, were beaten, and demanded, Wherefore have ye not fulfilled your task in making brick both yesterday and to day, as heretofore?
15 Then the officers of the children of Israel came and cried unto Pharaoh, saying, Wherefore dealest thou thus with thy servants?
16 There is no straw given unto thy servants, and they say to us, Make brick: and, behold, thy servants are beaten; but the fault is in thine own people.
17 But he said, Ye are idle, ye are idle: therefore ye say, Let us go and do sacrifice to the LORD.
18 Go therefore now, and work; for there shall no straw be given you, yet shall ye deliver the tale of bricks.
19 And the officers of the children of Israel did see that they were in evil case, after it was said, Ye shall not minish ought from your bricks of your daily task.
20 And they met Moses and Aaron, who stood in the way, as they came forth from Pharaoh:
21 And they said unto them, The LORD look upon you, and judge; because ye have made our savour to be abhorred in the eyes of Pharaoh, and in the eyes of his servants, to put a sword in their hand to slay us.
22 And Moses returned unto the LORD, and said, Lord, wherefore hast thou so evil entreated this people? why is it that thou hast sent me?
23 For since I came to Pharaoh to speak in thy name, he hath done evil to this people; neither hast thou delivered thy people at all.

    & maintain their work level & quota of bricks
    2) God's people were scattered all over Egypt to gather stubble (were displaced, separated from families)
    3) The slave-drivers continually pressed God's people to fill their daily quota
    4) The Israelite foremen were beaten because the people failed to meet the set quotas

3. The rejection of an appeal for justice: The rejection of reason, understanding & compassion
  a. The appeal for justice: The justice of reason, understanding, & compassion
  b. The reaction of Pharaoh
    1) Made a false accusation: God's people were lazy & had no need to worship
    2) Showed a spirit of injustice, unreasonableness, & lack of compassion: The "no straw" policy & quota stood
  c. The effect upon the foremen: A spirit of hopelessness & helplessness

4. The cry of the messenger of God: He cried out to God in behalf of God's people
  a. Moses met the representatives of God's people & listened to their complaints & needs
  b. Moses got alone with God & cried out in prayer
    1) Asked why God allowed such trouble
    2) Asked why God had sent him
    3) Blamed himself for bringing trouble upon the people & cried out, "Deliver them—as you promised"

DIVISION II

MOSES AND GOD: GOD RAISES UP A LEADER TO DELIVER HIS PEOPLE (ISRAEL), 2:1–7:7

F. The First Confrontation of Moses with Pharaoh: Opposing God's Will for His People, The Right of Man to Live and Worship God in Freedom, 5:1-23

(5:1-23) **Introduction**: freedom, liberty, and justice for all is God's will for man. Man's heart cries out for freedom, the freedom to live and worship as he chooses. Yet, there have always been those persons who oppose God's will, who seek power over the lives of others, who want...

- their egos boosted by forcing their wills and ways upon others
- their wealth increased by the forced and cheap labor of others
- their names and fame known through the conquest of others

This is the subject now to be studied: *The First Confrontation of Moses with Pharaoh: Opposing God's Will for His People, The Right of Man to Live and Worship God in Freedom, 5:1-23.*

1. The declaration of God's will (v.1).
2. The rejection of God's will (vv.2-14).
3. The rejection of an appeal for justice: the rejection of reason, understanding, and compassion (vv.15-19).
4. The cry of the messenger of God: he cried out to God in behalf of God's people (vv.20-23).

1 (5:1) **Freedom—Liberty—Will, of God**: there was the declaration of God's will: that God's people be freed, set at liberty so they could worship and serve God.

Picture the scene within the royal palace and court of Egypt. There sat the great king Pharaoh upon his throne. And there before him stood Moses, a simple shepherd, and Aaron, a slave. Pharaoh was most likely the most powerful man upon earth. The elders of Israel were probably also with Moses and Aaron, for God had told Moses to take them with him (Ex.3:18). Pharaoh would no doubt have granted an interview to the elders of the nation, thinking that some official business needed to be discussed. Whatever the case, there stood a group of slaves before the great king of Egypt, and for what purpose? To demand that he free God's people so they could make a religious pilgrimage to worship and serve God out in the wilderness.

> **Thought 1**. The point to see is this: God's will for His people—yea, for all people—is to have liberty, freedom, and justice. God wanted Israel freed just as He wants all enslaved people freed. God wants no people enslaved, and no people upon earth should ever be enslaved. God created people to live in freedom, to be free to work and play, but primarily to be free to worship and serve Him in all they do. Therefore, God wanted Israel freed, and God wants us to be free no matter who we are—as stated, so that we can live in freedom, worshipping and serving Him in all that we do.
>
> > "The rich and poor meet together: the LORD is the maker of them all" (Pr.22:2).
> > "The Spirit of the Lord GOD is upon me; because the LORD hath anointed me to preach good tidings unto the meek; he hath sent me to bind up the brokenhearted, to proclaim liberty to the captives, and the opening of the prison to them that are bound" (Is.61:1).
> > "But be not ye called Rabbi: for one is your Master, [even] Christ; and all ye are brethren" (Mt.23:8).
> > "And he said unto them, Ye know how that it is an unlawful thing for a man that is a Jew to keep company, or come unto one of another nation; but God hath showed me that I should not call any man common or unclean" (Ac.10:28).
> > "For there is no difference between the Jew and the Greek: for the same Lord over all is rich unto all that call upon him" (Ro.10:12).
> > "There is neither Jew nor Greek, there is neither bond nor free, there is neither male nor female: for ye are all one in Christ Jesus" (Ga.3:28).
> > "For, brethren, ye have been called unto liberty; only use not liberty for an occasion to the flesh, but by love serve one another" (Ga.5:13).
> > "As free, and not using your liberty for a cloke of maliciousness, but as the servants of God" (1 Pe.2:16).

2 (5:2-14) **Will, of God—Liberty—Freedom—Persecution—Oppression**: there was the rejection of God's will. The whole scene was ridiculous to Pharaoh, an affront to his position, a misuse of his time and authority. His response was sharp, cynical, and severe. His response shows exactly how he felt about such a ridiculous request. No doubt, his thoughts ran something like this: "Imagine! A group of slaves appearing before me demanding that I free them to go on a religious pilgrimage. Do they take me for a fool? And the audacity, trying to strike fear in me by claiming that their God sent them with such a ridiculous request. I'll teach them a lesson they will never forget."

Now, why did Pharaoh not take the request of Moses and Aaron seriously? Why did he enslave God's people, mistreat them so unjustly? Why did he not believe in the only living and true God? Why did he not rule Egypt with liberty, freedom, and justice for all peoples, including God's people? There were five reasons, and the same five reasons are the very reasons so many persons mistreat and persecute God's people today.

a. Pharaoh was ignorant of God—of the only living and true God—and he did not fear God (v.2).
   1) His response to the request for freedom was immediate, crisp, and cynical. He declared in no uncertain terms: he did not know the LORD; he would not let Israel go.

   Thought 1. The world does not know God; therefore, the world will often persecute believers. A person who truly knows God will never persecute other believers, nor will he persecute anyone else. He knows that all men are the offspring of God

   > "But all these things will they do unto you for my name's sake, because they know not him that sent me" (Jn.15:21).
   > "And these things will they do unto you, because they have not known the Father, nor me" (Jn.16:3).
   > "Forasmuch then as we are the offspring of God, we ought not to think that the Godhead is like unto gold, or silver, or stone, graven by art and man's device. And the times of this ignorance God winked at; but now commandeth all men every where to repent: Because he hath appointed a day, in the which he will judge the world in righteousness by that man whom he hath ordained; whereof he hath given assurance unto all men, in that he hath raised him from the dead" (Ac.17:29-31).
   > "[Unbelievers] having the understanding darkened, being alienated from the life of God through the ignorance that is in them, because of the blindness of their heart" (Ep.4:18).
   > "Yea, the stork in the heaven knoweth her appointed times; and the turtle and the crane and the swallow observe the time of their coming; but my people know not the judgment of the LORD" (Je.8:7).
   > "For they know not to do right, saith the LORD, who store up violence and robbery in their palaces" (Am.3:10).

   2) At that point, the messengers of God warned Pharaoh: God had truly revealed Himself to them. He demanded that Israel be freed to worship and serve Him. Pharaoh must free them or else the judgment of God would fall upon him and the Egyptians (vv.3). Note what they suggested: that God might send upon the Egyptians some form of disease or some foreign invader across the eastern border where Israel lived.
   This angered Pharaoh beyond measure. What now happened shows this.

   Thought 1. The judgment of God will fall upon all who persecute and enslave God's people.

   > "Seeing it is a righteous thing with God to recompense tribulation to them that trouble you; and to you who are troubled rest with us, when the Lord Jesus shall be revealed from heaven with his mighty angels, in flaming fire taking vengeance on them that know not God, and that obey not the gospel of our Lord Jesus Christ: who shall be punished with everlasting destruction from the presence of the Lord, and from the glory of his power; when he shall come to be glorified in his saints, and to be admired in all them that believe (because our testimony among you was believed) in that day" (2 Th.1:6-10).
   > "Vengeance is mine; I will repay, saith the Lord" (Ro.12:19).
   > "Cursed be he that perverteth the judgment of the stranger, fatherless, and widow. And all the people shall say, Amen" (De.27:19).
   > "Woe unto them that decree unrighteous decrees, and that write grievousness which they have prescribed" (Is.10:1).

b. Pharaoh accused God's messengers (Moses and Aaron) with disturbing the peace, accused them of interfering with the people's work (vv.4-5). He demanded that they get back to work, for these messengers were hindering the work. Keep in mind that the work produced by Israel was enormous, for the people had grown to an estimated two million plus population.
c. Pharaoh was mean-spirited, hard-hearted, malicious, and ruthless. He reacted, instructing the slave-drivers to oppress God's people more and more (vv.6-8).
   1) Pharaoh no longer supplied straw for the bricks, but instead forced the people to gather their own straw (v.7). This took an enormous amount of labor and time, labor and time that had previously been used to make brick.
   2) Pharaoh forced the people to produce the same quota of bricks per day despite the extra labor necessary to gather the straw (v.8).
d. Pharaoh dismissed the message of God's messengers as a lie (v.9ᵇ).

   Thought 1. How many people today believe that the message of God's preachers and teachers is a lie, that the message of God's Word is...
   • false?
   • empty?
   • meaningless?
   • useless?
   • a waste of time?
   • of no value in the real world?

"But they mocked the messengers of God, and despised his words, and misused his prophets, until the wrath of the LORD arose against his people, till there was no remedy" (2 Chr.36:16).

"The fear of the LORD is the beginning of knowledge: but fools despise [godly] wisdom and instruction" (Pr.1:7).

"And say, How have I hated [godly] instruction, and my heart despised reproof" (Pr.5:12).

"Wherefore thus saith the Holy One of Israel, Because ye despise this word, and trust in oppression and perverseness, and stay thereon: therefore this iniquity shall be to you as a breach ready to fall, swelling out in a high wall, whose breaking cometh suddenly at an instant" (Is.30:12-13).

"Yea, they made their hearts as an adamant stone, lest they should hear the law, and the words which the LORD of hosts hath sent in his spirit by the former prophets: therefore came a great wrath from the LORD of hosts" (Zec.7:12).

"He that heareth you heareth me; and he that despiseth you despiseth me; and he that despiseth me despiseth him that sent me" (Lu.10:16; see vv.10-16).

e. Pharaoh misused his authority and power: he made the oppression of God's people the law of the land, "Thus says Pharaoh, the king...." (vv.10-14). He sent the slave-masters to carry out his orders:
⇒ The slave-masters made the people gather their own straw, yet the people had to maintain their work level and quota of bricks (v.11).
⇒ God's people were scattered all over Egypt to gather stubble to use for straw (v.11). This meant that many were displaced and separated from their families.
⇒ The slave-drivers continually pressed God's people to fill their daily quota (v.13).
⇒ The Israelite foremen were beaten because the people failed to meet the set quotas (v.14).

Thought 1. One of the great problems within society is the misuse of authority and power. Authority can range from the authority of a king over to the authority of a supervisor who is over just one person. God is clear about the authority or rule a person holds: the person must not misuse his authority or rule.

"How long will ye judge unjustly, and accept the persons of the wicked?" (Ps.82:2).

"He that oppresseth the poor reproacheth his Maker: but he that honoureth him hath mercy on the poor" (Pr.14:31).

"If thou seest the oppression of the poor, and violent perverting of judgment and justice in a province, marvel not at the matter: for he that is higher than the highest regardeth; and there be higher than they" (Ec.5:8).

"Then I consulted with myself, and I rebuked the nobles, and the rulers, and said unto them, Ye exact usury [excess, loans and interest, taxes], every one of his brother. And I set a great assembly against them" (Ne.5:7).

"The LORD will enter into judgment with the ancients of his people, and the princes thereof: for ye have eaten up the vineyard; the spoil of the poor is in your houses" (Is.3:14).

"Woe unto them that decree unrighteous decrees, and that write grievousness which they have prescribed" (Is.10:1).

"Son of man, say unto the prince of Tyrus, Thus saith the Lord GOD; Because thine heart is lifted up, and thou hast said, I am a God, I sit in the seat of God, in the midst of the seas; yet thou art a man, and not God, though thou set thine heart as the heart of God....Therefore thus saith the Lord GOD; Because thou hast set thine heart as the heart of God; behold, therefore I will bring strangers upon thee, the terrible of the nations: and they shall draw their swords against the beauty of thy wisdom, and they shall defile thy brightness. They shall bring thee down to the pit, and thou shalt die the deaths of them that are slain in the midst of the seas" (Eze.28:2, 6-8).

3 (5:15-19) **Will, of God—Freedom—Justice**: there was the rejection of an appeal for justice, the rejection of reason, understanding, and compassion. What now happened shows just how hard-hearted and malicious Pharaoh was.
a. The Israelite foremen appealed to Pharaoh for justice: that he be reasonable and understanding, showing some compassion for God's people (vv.15-16). There were obviously thousands of foremen overseeing the work of the Israelite slaves. Keep in mind that all the people—both males and females—would be forced to work, beginning somewhere around ten to twelve years old, perhaps even younger. This meant there were over one million Israelite slaves at work for the Egyptians. Thus, the foremen who requested an audience with Pharaoh were a representative group appointed to represent the whole corps of Israelite foremen.
b. The reaction of Pharaoh was twofold.
⇒ He made a sarcastic and false accusation: God's people were lazy and had no need to worship (v.17).
⇒ He demonstrated a spirit of injustice, unreasonableness, and lack of compassion (v.18).

c. The effect upon the foremen was exactly what would be expected by such a reaction from Pharaoh: they were overwhelmed with a spirit of hopelessness and helplessness (v.19). They could expect only more severe abuse, oppression, and brutality.

Thought 1. All who are in authority are to supervise and rule with justice: to be reasonable, understanding, and compassionate as they oversee the work of people.

"That which is altogether just shalt thou follow, that thou mayest live, and inherit the land [symbol of heaven] which the LORD thy God giveth thee" (De.16:20).

"The God of Israel said, the Rock of Israel spake to me, He that ruleth over men must be just, ruling in the fear of God" (2 S.23:3).

"And said to the judges, Take heed what ye do: for ye judge not for man, but for the LORD, who is with you in the judgment" (2 Chr.19:6).

"Be wise now therefore, O ye kings: be instructed, ye judges of the earth. Serve the LORD with fear, and rejoice with trembling" (Ps.2:10-11).

"Defend the poor and fatherless: do justice to the afflicted and needy" (Ps.82:3).

"Mercy and truth preserve the king: and his throne is upholden by mercy" (Pr.20:28).

"To do justice and judgment is more acceptable to the LORD than sacrifice" (Pr.21:3).

"The king that faithfully judgeth the poor, his throne shall be established for ever" (Pr.29:14).

"Thus saith the LORD, Keep ye judgment, and do justice: for my salvation is near to come, and my righteousness to be revealed" (Is.56:1).

"He that is faithful in that which is least is faithful also in much: and he that is unjust in the least is unjust also in much" (Lu.16:10).

"Render therefore to all their dues: tribute to whom tribute is due; custom to whom custom; fear to whom fear; honour to whom honour" (Ro.13:7).

"Masters [rulers], give unto your servants that which is just and equal; knowing that ye also have a Master in heaven" (Col.4:1).

4 (5:20-23) **Prayer—Ministering**: the cry of the messenger of God. He cried out to God in behalf of God's people.

a. Moses, along with Aaron, went out to meet the foremen representatives, anxiously hoping for a favorable response from Pharaoh (v.21). What happened shocked Moses. The foremen bitterly blamed Moses and Aaron for the brutal and savage abuse being heaped upon them. Nevertheless, as a true minister of God, Moses stood there and listened to their complaints and needs.

In no uncertain terms, the foremen told Moses that he was personally to blame, that he had made them stink in the nostrils of Pharaoh and his officials, that Pharaoh might take up the sword and kill them at any moment (v.21).

b. Having his own people viciously attack him disturbed Moses to no end. He was obviously crushed, in a state of shock. He did all he could do: he got alone with God and cried out to Him in prayer (v.22). He asked why God had allowed such trouble to fall upon the people. And note, he questioned his own call to the ministry: Why had God called him?

Moses was blaming himself for having brought such trouble upon the people. He was in despair, questioning and wondering what was going on, why God was allowing such trouble when He had promised to deliver the people. Then, as always with God's dear servants, Moses cried out to God: "You have not delivered your people, not as You promised. Deliver them" (v.23).

Thought 1. All ministers—yea all believers—are to do just what Moses did:
(1) Listen to the complaints and needs of people when they face difficulty.
(2) Get alone with God, crying out in prayer for God to deliver His people from their trouble.

"This poor man cried, and the LORD heard him, and saved him out of all his troubles" (Ps.34:6).

"Hear my cry, O God; attend unto my prayer. From the end of the earth will I cry unto thee, when my heart is overwhelmed: lead me to the rock that is higher than I. For thou hast been a shelter for me, and a strong tower from the enemy" (Ps.61:1-3).

"When thou art in tribulation, and all these things are come upon thee, even in the latter days, if thou turn to the LORD thy God, and shalt be obedient unto his voice; (For the LORD thy God is a merciful God;) he will not forsake thee, neither destroy thee, nor forget the covenant of thy fathers which he sware unto them" (De.4:30-31).

"He shall call upon me, and I will answer him: I will be with him in trouble; I will deliver him, and honour him" (Ps.91:15).

"And I say unto you, Ask, and it shall be given you; seek, and ye shall find; knock, and it shall be opened unto you" (Lu.11:9).

CHAPTER 6

G. The Great Encouragement & Message Given to Moses: Deliverance & Freedom, 6:1–7:7

1. God's great encouragement to His messenger

a. God promised to raise His mighty hand against the king: To free His people

b. God revealed His new name: The LORD (Jehovah, Yahweh), the God of redemption & deliverance

c. God reviewed His covenant: His great promise to give the promised land to His people

d. God shared His concern for the sufferings of His people: He heard their cries & remembered His covenant

2. God's great encouragement to His people

a. God is the LORD (Jehovah, Yahweh)

b. God will deliver His people: From slavery & suffering

c. God will redeem His people: With great power, with mighty acts of judgment

d. God will adopt His people

  1) God's promise: I will be your God & you will be my people

  2) God's purpose: That they might know that He is the Lord, their great Deliverer

e. God will lead His people to the promised land

f. God is the LORD (able to do all He says)

g. God's messenger proclaimed God's message, but the people refused to listen

3. God's great message to the king

a. The message: Deliverance & freedom

Then the LORD said unto Moses, Now shalt thou see what I will do to Pharaoh: for with a strong hand shall he let them go, and with a strong hand shall he drive them out of his land.

2 And God spake unto Moses, and said unto him, I am the LORD:

3 And I appeared unto Abraham, unto Isaac, and unto Jacob, by the name of God Almighty, but by my name JEHOVAH was I not known to them.

4 And I have also established my covenant with them, to give them the land of Canaan, the land of their pilgrimage, wherein they were strangers.

5 And I have also heard the groaning of the children of Israel, whom the Egyptians keep in bondage; and I have remembered my covenant.

6 Wherefore say unto the children of Israel, I am the LORD, and I will bring you out from under the burdens of the Egyptians, and I will rid you out of their bondage, and I will redeem you with a stretched out arm, and with great judgments:

7 And I will take you to me for a people, and I will be to you a God: and ye shall know that I am the LORD your God, which bringeth you out from under the burdens of the Egyptians.

8 And I will bring you in unto the land, concerning the which I did swear to give it to Abraham, to Isaac, and to Jacob; and I will give it you for an heritage: I am the LORD.

9 And Moses spake so unto the children of Israel: but they hearkened not unto Moses for anguish of spirit, and for cruel bondage.

10 And the LORD spake unto Moses, saying,

11 Go in, speak unto Pharaoh king of Egypt, that he let the children of Israel go out of his land.

12 And Moses spake before the LORD, saying, Behold, the children of Israel have not hearkened unto me; how then shall Pharaoh hear me, who am of uncircumcised lips?

13 And the LORD spake unto Moses and unto Aaron, and gave them a charge unto the children of Israel, and unto Pharaoh king of Egypt, to bring the children of Israel out of the land of Egypt.

14 These be the heads of their fathers' houses: The sons of Reuben the first-born of Israel; Hanoch, and Pallu, Hezron, and Carmi: these be the families of Reuben.

15 And the sons of Simeon; Jemuel, and Jamin, and Ohad, and Jachin, and Zohar, and Shaul the son of a Canaanitish woman: these are the families of Simeon.

16 And these are the names of the sons of Levi according to their generations; Gershon, and Kohath, and Merari: and the years of the life of Levi were an hundred thirty and seven years.

17 The sons of Gershon; Libni, and Shimi, according to their families.

18 And the sons of Kohath; Amram, and Izhar, and Hebron, and Uzziel: and the years of the life of Kohath were an hundred thirty and three years.

19 And the sons of Merari; Mahali and Mushi: these are the families of Levi according to their generations.

20 And Amram took him Jochebed his father's sister to wife; and she bare him Aaron and Moses: and the years of the life of Amram were an hundred and thirty and seven years.

21 And the sons of Izhar; Korah, and Nepheg, and Zichri.

22 And the sons of Uzziel; Mishael, and Elzaphan, and Zithri.

23 And Aaron took him Elisheba, daughter of Amminadab, sister of Naashon, to wife; and she bare him Nadab, and Abihu, Eleazar, and Ithamar.

24 And the sons of Korah; Assir, and Elkanah, and

b. The uneasiness of God's messenger

4. God's great messengers & their family tree: Chosen by God's grace alone[DS1]

a. The heads of Moses' & Aaron's ancestors: Saved by God's grace

  1) Reuben & his sons & clans

  2) Simeon & his sons & clans

  3) Levi & his sons & clans

b. The family tree of Levi, the family of Levi's descendents

	Abiasaph: these are the families of the Korhites. 25 And Eleazar Aaron's son took him one of the daughters of Putiel to wife; and she bare him Phinehas: these are the heads of the fathers of the Levites according to their families. 26 These are that Aaron and Moses, to whom the LORD said, Bring out the children of Israel from the land of Egypt according to their armies. 27 These are they which spake to Pharaoh king of Egypt, to bring out the children of Israel from Egypt: these are that Moses and Aaron.	**CHAPTER 7** And the LORD said unto Moses, See, I have made thee a god to Pharaoh: and Aaron thy brother shall be thy prophet. 2 Thou shalt speak all that I command thee: and Aaron thy brother shall speak unto Pharaoh, that he send the children of Israel out of his land. 3 And I will harden Pharaoh's heart, and multiply my signs and my wonders in the land of Egypt.	c. God's assurance 1) Moses was to be God's messenger 2) Aaron was to be the spokesman for Moses 3) God would harden Pharaoh's heart & multiply His miraculous signs in Egypt
c. The call of God was given to this same Aaron & Moses: They were the ones who proclaimed God's great message of deliverance to Pharaoh		4 But Pharaoh shall not hearken unto you, that I may lay my hand upon Egypt, and bring forth mine armies, and my people the children of Israel, out of the land of Egypt by great judgments. 5 And the Egyptians shall know that I am the LORD, when I stretch forth mine hand upon Egypt, and bring out the children of Israel from among them.	4) God was going to bring mighty acts of judgment upon Egypt: All to deliver & free His people 5) God's purpose: So that the Egyptians would know that He is The LORD (Jehovah, the Great Redeemer & Deliverer)[DS2]
5. God's great message to be proclaimed only by God-called men: Moses' call reinforced a. God's call to Moses: To go to Pharaoh with the message of God b. Moses' arguments against God's call	28 And it came to pass on the day when the LORD spake unto Moses in the land of Egypt, 29 That the LORD spake unto Moses, saying, I am the LORD: speak thou unto Pharaoh king of Egypt all that I say unto thee. 30 And Moses said before the LORD, Behold, I am of uncircumcised lips, and how shall Pharaoh hearken unto me?	6 And Moses and Aaron did as the LORD commanded them, so did they. 7 And Moses was fourscore years old, and Aaron fourscore and three years old, when they spake unto Pharaoh.	6. Moses & Aaron obeyed God a. Moses was 80 years old b. Aaron was 83 years old

DIVISION II

MOSES AND GOD: GOD RAISES UP A LEADER TO DELIVER HIS PEOPLE (ISRAEL), 2:1–7:7

G. The Great Encouragement and Message Given to Moses: Deliverance and Freedom, 6:1–7:7

(6:1–7:7) **Introduction**: Moses was desperate. The people had just repudiated him, for Pharaoh had begun to persecute the enslaved Israelites more severely than ever before. The increased oppression was due to Pharaoh's reaction against Moses, against his demand that Pharaoh free the people to serve and worship God. Before Moses' demand, their task had been to make the brick for Egyptian construction projects, and the Egyptians had always furnished the straw necessary to make the brick. But now, since Moses' demand, Pharaoh was forcing the Israelites to gather their own straw. Moreover, he was insisting that they produce the same daily quota of brick. This was utterly impossible. The result was tragic: the Egyptian slave-drivers were working the people beyond exhaustion, threatening, cursing, beating, abusing, and no doubt killing some.

Consequently, the people blamed Moses and wanted him out of their lives. They rejected and repudiated him; they wanted nothing to do with him, not anymore. In their minds, Moses had brought nothing but trouble to them, severe trouble that could even cause a holocaust: the king was so angry that he could take up the sword and slaughter them (see Ex.5:21).

Moses was crushed, broken, desperate. What could he do? There was only one thing, the very same thing that we have to do when we face crushing problems. Moses got alone with God and poured out his soul. This we saw in the last passage (Ex.5:22-23). Now, we come to God's answer to Moses. This great passage shows how God helped Moses and met his need. It shows how God will help us and meet our need. This is: *The Great Encouragement and Message Given to Moses: Deliverance and Freedom, 6:1-7:7*.

1. God's personal encouragement to His messenger (vv.1-5).
2. God's personal encouragement to His people (vv.6-9).
3. God's great message to the king (vv.10-12).
4. God's great messengers and their family tree: chosen by God's grace alone (vv.13-27).
5. God's great message is to be proclaimed only by God-called men: God recalled Moses (vv.28–7:5).
6. Moses and Aaron obeyed God (vv.6-7).

1 (6:1-5) **Encouragement—Covenant—Jehovah (Yahweh)**: there was God's personal encouragement to His messenger, Moses. God encouraged Moses by doing four things.

a. God promised to raise His mighty hand against Pharaoh and force Pharaoh to free the people (v.1). God had already made this promise to His messenger at the burning bush (Ex.3:10). But as with all of us, Moses needed to be reassured of God's promise time and again. He needed to be reminded of God's great promise, that He would force the terrible enslaver to free the people of God.

Thought 1. The LORD will deliver us by His mighty hand. He will deliver us from all our enemies, whether seen or unseen, visible or invisible, physical or spiritual.

"And the Lord shall deliver me from every evil work, and will preserve me unto his heavenly kingdom: to whom be glory for ever and ever" (2 Ti.4:18).
"The Lord knoweth how to deliver the godly out of temptations [trials], and to reserve the unjust unto the day of judgment to be punished" (2 Pe.2:9).
"Be not afraid of their faces: for I am with thee to deliver thee, saith the LORD" (Je.1:8).
"And he said, The LORD is my rock, and my fortress, and my deliverer" (2 S.22:2).

b. God assured Moses: I am the LORD (Jehovah, Yahweh). The basic meaning of LORD is Savior, Redeemer, and Deliverer. The LORD was able to redeem and deliver the people of God (vv.2-3). This was a very special revelation being made to Moses, a very special experience that God was giving to His dear messenger who was so crushed, broken, and desperate.

⇒ The great patriarchs—Abraham, Isaac, and Jacob—had *experienced* God as God Almighty (El Shaddai) not as Jehovah. (See note—Ge.17:1 for more discussion.) They had known God as Jehovah, known that He was the great Redeemer and Deliverer, but they had never witnessed the deliverance of God's people. They had the great promises of God, but they had never experienced the fulfillment of those promises. (See note, Jehovah—Ge.2:4 for more discussion.)

But now, Moses and Israel were to see the very meaning of God's name fulfilled. They were to be the eye-witnesses of God's name exploding across the pages of human history: they were to see the LORD (Jehovah, Yahweh) redeem and deliver His people in the *great Exodus* from Egypt. God's name as LORD (Jehovah, Yahweh), as the great Redeemer and Deliverer, was to be fulfilled in the redemption and deliverance of Israel from slavery to freedom.

Note: the name Jehovah or Yahweh is used some 162 times in Genesis. People address God as Jehovah or Yahweh in at least 34 of these times. Even Abraham addressed God as Yahweh Yireh in the experience of offering up Isaac as a sacrifice to God (Ge.22:24). In fact, from the very beginning of human history, people called upon the name of Jehovah or Yahweh (Ge.4:26).[1]

Note also that God declared His name four times in giving this great encouragement to Moses: "I am the LORD" (vv.2, 6, 7, 8). He is able to do anything and all things, even redeem and deliver His people from slavery and set them free.

c. God reviewed His covenant with Moses, reviewed His great promise to give the promised land to His people (v.4. See note, pt.3—Ex.2:23-25; see DEEPER STUDY # 1—Ex.2:24; see note—Gen.12:1ᶜ for detailed discussion on the promised land.)

d. God shared His compassion and concern for the sufferings of His people: He heard their cries and remembered His covenant with them (v.5).

Thought 1. God cares for His people, for all of us, just as He cared for Moses and Israel. No matter how crushed, broken, and desperate we may become, God is concerned. He has great compassion for us, and He will help meet our need. No matter what our problem, sin, or shame is, God longs to help us. God is the LORD, our great Redeemer and Deliverer. He will redeem and deliver us from all our troubles and enslavements to this world.

"The LORD is my strength and my shield; my heart trusted in him, and I am helped: therefore my heart greatly rejoiceth; and with my song will I praise him" (Ps.28:7).
"But I am poor and needy; yet the LORD thinketh upon me: thou art my help and my deliverer; make no tarrying, O my God" (Ps.40:17).
"Fear thou not; for I am with thee: be not dismayed; for I am thy God: I will strengthen thee; yea, I will help thee; yea, I will uphold thee with the right hand of my righteousness" (Is.41:10).
"There hath no temptation [trial] taken you but such as is common to man: but God is faithful, who will not suffer you to be tempted above that ye are able; but will with the temptation [trial] also make a way to escape, that ye may be able to bear it" (1 Co.10:13).
"And the Lord shall deliver me from every evil work, and will preserve me unto his heavenly kingdom: to whom be glory for ever and ever" (2 Ti.4:18).
"Let Israel hope in the LORD: for with the LORD there is mercy, and with him is plenteous redemption. And he shall redeem Israel from all his iniquities" (Ps.130:7-8).
"Fear not, thou worm Jacob, and ye men of Israel; I will help thee, saith the LORD, and thy redeemer, the Holy One of Israel" (Is.41:14).
"And even to your old age I am he; and even to hoar [gray] hairs will I carry you: I have made, and I will bear; even I will carry, and will deliver you" (Is.46:4).

---

[1] Frank E. Gaebelein, Editor. *Expositor's Bible Commentary*, Vol.2, p.340-341.

2 (6:6-9) **Encouragement—Deliverance—God, Name of—Jehovah—Yahweh—Adoption**: there was God's personal encouragement to His people. God gave Moses the very message of encouragement He wanted proclaimed to the people. Note how glorious and personal, how joyful and hopeful God's message was. God declared five wonderful facts, facts that are true for us even as for believers of all generations.

a. God is the LORD (Jehovah, Yahweh), the great Redeemer and Deliverer of His people, the God who fulfills the covenant of His great promises (v.6). The very meaning of God's name, the LORD (Jehovah, Yahweh), was now ready to be fulfilled. God was now going to redeem and deliver His dear people.

Now note how God proclaims seven "I wills" in the next three proclamations (pts.2-4).

b. God will deliver His people (v.6).
⇒ I will bring you out: from your burdens.
⇒ I will free you: from slavery.
⇒ I will redeem you: with power and with mighty acts of judgment.

"And he said, The LORD is my rock, and my fortress, and my deliverer" (2 S.22:2).
"Be not afraid of their faces: for I am with thee to deliver thee, saith the LORD" (Je.1:8).
"He delivereth and rescueth, and he worketh signs and wonders in heaven and in earth, who hath delivered Daniel from the power of the lions" (Da.6:27).
"Who delivered us from so great a death, and doth deliver: in whom we trust that he will yet deliver us" (2 Co.1:10).

c. God will adopt His people (v.7).
⇒ I will take you to be my own people.
⇒ I will be your God.
⇒ God's purpose: that His people might know that He is the LORD, their great Deliverer from all burdens.

"For thou art an holy people unto the LORD thy God, and the LORD hath chosen thee to be a peculiar people unto himself, above all the nations that are upon the earth" (De.14:2).
"Doubtless thou art our father, though Abraham be ignorant of us, and Israel acknowledge us not: thou, O LORD, art our father, our redeemer; thy name is from everlasting" (Is.63:16).
"But as many as received him, to them gave he power to become the sons of God, even to them that believe on his name" (Jn.1:12).
"The Spirit itself beareth witness with our spirit, that we are the children of God" (Ro.8:16).
"Wherefore come out from among them, and be ye separate, saith the Lord, and touch not the unclean thing; and I will receive you, and will be a Father unto you, and ye shall be my sons and daughters, saith the Lord Almighty" (2 Co.6:17-18).

d. God will lead His people to the promised land (v.8).
⇒ I will bring you to the land, the promised land.
⇒ I will give the land to you.

Thought 1. Remember the promised land of Canaan is a symbol, a type, a picture of the promised land of heaven, of the new heavens and earth (see note—Ge.12:1ᶜ for detailed discussion).

"By faith Abraham, when he was called to go out into a place which he should after receive for an inheritance, obeyed; and he went out, not knowing whither he went. By faith he sojourned in the land of promise, as in a strange country, dwelling in tabernacles with Isaac and Jacob, the heirs with him of the same promise: for he looked for a city which hath foundations, whose builder and maker is God" (He.11:8-10).
"But now they desire a better country, that is, an heavenly: wherefore God is not ashamed to be called their God: for he hath prepared for them a city" (He.13:16).
"But the day of the Lord will come as a thief in the night; in the which the heavens shall pass away with a great noise, and the elements shall melt with fervent heat, the earth also and the works that are therein shall be burned up. Seeing then that all these things shall be dissolved, what manner of persons ought ye to be in all holy conversation and godliness, looking for and hasting unto the coming of the day of God, wherein the heavens being on fire shall be dissolved, and the elements shall melt with fervent heat? Nevertheless we, according to his promise, look for new heavens and a new earth, wherein dwelleth righteousness." (2 Pe.3:10-13).
"For, behold, I create new heavens and a new earth: and the former shall not be remembered, nor come into mind" (Is.65:17).

Again, glance at the above three points and note the seven "I wills" promised by God. What a glorious promise and encouragement this should be to all believers.

e. God is the LORD (Jehovah, Yahweh) (v.8ᶜ). Again, the point is restated because of its importance: God is the great Redeemer and Deliverer of His people, and the time has now come for the very meaning of His name to be fulfilled. The time has now come for Him to redeem and deliver His people from their sufferings.

f. Note that Moses took God's message of encouragement to the people, but they did not listen to him. The idea of being freed was just too incredible, too far-fetched. Their oppression was so cruel and brutal, their suffering so painful, they were just consumed with discouragement. Their minds were so exhausted with the pain of suffering, they could no longer think long enough to hear any message, no matter how hopeful and encouraging it might be. If they were to be delivered, it would not be because of their attention upon God, but because of God's mercy being poured out upon them.

Thought 1. God is able and ready to meet our desperate needs, no matter how crushed and down we may be. No matter how exhausted we may be from suffering and from failing, God will have mercy upon us. He will deliver us if we will only cry out to Him.

"Many are the afflictions of the righteous: but the Lord delivereth him out of them all. He keepeth all his bones: not one of them is broken" (Ps.34:19-20).

"And call upon me in the day of trouble: I will deliver thee, and thou shalt glorify me" (Ps.50:15).

"Though I walk in the midst of trouble, thou wilt revive me: thou shalt stretch forth thine hand against the wrath of mine enemies, and thy right hand shall save me" (Ps.138:7).

"When thou passest through the waters, I will be with thee; and through the rivers, they shall not overflow thee: when thou walkest through the fire, thou shalt not be burned; neither shall the flame kindle upon thee" (Is.43:2).

"And he said unto me, My grace is sufficient for thee: for my strength is made perfect in weakness. Most gladly therefore will I rather glory in my infirmities, that the power of Christ may rest upon me" (2 Co.12:9).

"And God shall wipe away all tears from their eyes; and there shall be no more death, neither sorrow, nor crying, neither shall there be any more pain: for the former things are passed away" (Re.21:4).

3 (6:10-12) **Message**: there was God's great message to the king. After Moses proclaimed God's message of encouragement to the people, God told Moses to go, to deliver God's message to the king. Remember, Moses had already delivered one message to Pharaoh and the result was a cruel, brutal reaction (see Ex.4:21-23; 5:1-23). Now Moses was to go to Pharaoh a second time and declare once again God's message to him, the message of deliverance and freedom (v.11). The king was to free God's people, let them go to worship and serve God.

But note Moses' uneasiness (v.12). His first message to Pharaoh had aroused the anger of the king and caused him to react with a savage vengeance. Pharaoh had afflicted the people with heavier work quotas, demanding that they work to the point of exhaustion—all under the watchful eye of cruel slave-drivers. The result: the Israelites turned against Moses, blaming him and insisting that he leave and get out of their sight.

Moses had been crushed: he was bewildered by the reaction of the Israelites and the king. He had expected God to free Israel immediately; he had expected Pharaoh to release the people after hearing God's message. Thus Moses questioned God: Since Pharaoh rejected the first message and the people refused to listen to him, why would Pharaoh now listen to him? What was going to make Pharaoh change his mind? He, Moses, could not, for he was incapable. He could not even present a message clearly and forcefully. He spoke with faltering lips. (See note—Ex.4:10-12 for more discussion.)

Note that God did not answer Moses. The charge had been given. God's servant was to go forth and do as God instructed.

Thought 1. The messenger of God is to obey God, no matter his handicap or lack of ability. The messenger may not be eloquent nor have a forceful voice or delivery. He may not be at ease in preaching or teaching. He may even be handicapped in that he stutters or has some other speech impediment. Nevertheless, if God has truly called the person, the person must obey God: he must go and proclaim the message of God; he must reach out and minister to people.

"And whosoever will be chief among you, let him be your servant: Even as the Son of man came not to be ministered unto, but to minister, and to give his life a ransom for many" (Mt.20:27-28).

"Then said Jesus to them again, Peace [be] unto you: as [my] Father hath sent me, even so send I you" (Jn.20:21; see Mt.20:27-28 above).

"But God hath chosen the foolish things of the world to confound the wise; and God hath chosen the weak things of the world to confound the things which are mighty; and base things of the world, and things which are despised, hath God chosen, yea, and things which are not, to bring to nought things that are: That no flesh should glory in his presence" (1 Co.1:27-29).

"And I, brethren, when I came to you, came not with excellency of speech or of wisdom, declaring unto you the testimony of God. For I determined not to know any thing among you, save Jesus Christ, and him crucified. And I was with you in weakness, and in fear, and in much trembling. And my speech and my preaching was not with enticing words of man's wisdom, but in demonstration of the Spirit and of power: That your faith should not stand in the wisdom of men, but in the power of God" (1 Co.2:1-5).

"And I thank Christ Jesus our Lord, who hath enabled me, for that he counted me faithful, putting me into the ministry" (1 Ti.1:12).

4 (6:13-27) **Moses, Family Tree—Aaron, Family Tree**: there were God's great messengers and their family tree: they were chosen by God's grace alone. God's message is to be proclaimed only by men who are truly of God's people and truly chosen by God's grace alone. The family tree (genealogy) of Moses and Aaron is now given. Note, the fact is stated that Moses and Aaron were the chosen servants of God (v.13). Three significant points are given.

135

a. The proof that they were true Israelites, truly of God's people, is then given. The family tree of Moses and Aaron is listed (vv.14-16). But note, in giving the family history, only three sons of Jacob are listed:

⇒ Reuben
⇒ Simeon
⇒ Levi

Why stop with Levi? Because Levi was the family head, the father of the tribe of Levi, the tribe into which Moses and Aaron were born (see DEEPER STUDY # 1—Ex.6:13-27). Moses and Aaron were the messengers chosen by God to lead The Great Exodus of God's people from Egypt. The purpose of the present genealogy is to show that they were legitimate messengers, true messengers who were of God's chosen people, Israel. The genealogy needed to go no further than Levi.

Note another fact as well: everything mentioned about the family tree of Moses points to the grace of God, not to ancestors of great moral character, nor of natural ability, nor of political leadership.

⇒ *Reuben* committed incest with his mother's servant (Bilhah, his father's concubine). (See notes—Ge.35:22; 49:3-4 for discussion.)
⇒ *Simeon* and *Levi* were gripped by a spirit of revenge and slaughtered all the males of Shechem, a small town. (See notes—Ge.34:25-29; 49:5-7 for more discussion.)

All three of these men were later converted. In fact, they were all led by Joseph himself to confess their sin and faith in the LORD and in His great covenant promises to Israel (the promise of the promised land and of the promised seed). (See note—Ge.44:14-17 for more discussion.)

The point is this: the ancestors of Moses were not chosen by God because of their own personal morality and righteousness. They were members of God's people because of the grace of God, because the day came when they confessed their terrible sin and repented, trusting God and His covenant promises. They were saved only by the grace of God through faith (see Ep.2:8-9).

Thus it was with Moses. He was not saved and chosen by God because of godly ancestors or parents: he was saved and chosen by God because of the grace of God. Moses believed in the LORD and in the covenant promises of God; therefore, God had mercy upon him and showered His grace upon him. Moses was chosen by the grace of God and by the grace of God alone.

Note one other fact about the family tree of Moses. Keep in mind the great privileges and responsibilities placed by the ancient world upon the firstborn son. Upon the father's death, he received the birthright of the father with all his rights, privileges, and responsibilities. He also received two thirds of the inheritance. This was the law of the land. Thus when a younger son received any part of the birthright or any additional inheritance, it was a gift, a gift freely given. It was an act of grace. (See notes—Gen.25:31; 48:17-18 for more discussion.) Now note these facts about Moses and Aaron:

⇒ They were not from the tribe of the firstborn, Reuben, but from the tribe of Levi, the third son (vv.14, 16, 20). (See DEEPER STUDY # 1—Ex.6:13-27 for more discussion.)
⇒ They were not from Levi's oldest son, but from Kohath, Levi's second son (vv.16-19).
⇒ Moses was not even the oldest son of his father, Amram, but the second son (v.20).

The point is well made: Moses was not chosen by God because he was the firstborn son. He did not merit God's call because he was born of the privileged class. He was chosen by God's grace and by God's grace alone. (See DEEPER STUDY # 1—Ex.6:13-27 for Moses' ancestors and family tree.)

b. Note that the family tree of Levi is given in some detail. This was for the purpose stated above: to show that the priesthood was truly of God's people. The priests (Levites) were truly chosen by the grace of God, chosen to be His messengers and ministers to Israel. The priests were with Israel from the first: they helped in the founding and building of the nation.

c. Note: the fact that Moses and Aaron were messengers of God is so important it is repeated. Moses and Aaron were the servants chosen by God to proclaim His message of deliverance and freedom to Pharaoh (vv.26-27).

DEEPER STUDY # 1

(6:13-27) **Chart—Table—Genealogy—Family Tree—Moses—Aaron—Levi—Levites, Tribe of**: this chart gives the family tree of Moses and Aaron. It gives the ancestors of these two great servants of God. (Because of the length of this Deeper Study, it is placed at the end of the commentary to keep from breaking the flow of a person's study. Please see DEEPER STUDY # 1 at the conclusion of the commentary.)

---

5 (6:28-7:5) **Call, of God—Message, of God**: God's great message is to be proclaimed only by God-called men: God reinforced Moses' call, gave him a second call. Why did God give Moses a second call? Why was it necessary for God to again confront Moses and tell him what to do? Because of the awesome task God had given Moses to do. Moses was as all of us would be: crushed, broken, and desperate. Pharaoh had severely reacted against God's message. The king was reacting with a vengeance, oppressing God's people beyond measure:

⇒ forcing more and more laborious work out of them
⇒ having them lashed and beaten when they failed to meet impossible daily quotas
⇒ having the weak and sick killed so they would not have to be fed and kept up

Who was to be blamed for Pharaoh's vengeful reaction? The people accused Moses. They blamed and repudiated him. It was this that had crushed and broken Moses. He feared returning to Pharaoh, feared that he might arouse the wrath of Pharaoh even more. This was the reason God had to give Moses a second call. God had to reinforce—spell out in no uncertain terms—what His dear servant was to do. God knew that Moses needed to be lifted up and assured, that he needed to be encouraged, that he needed to have his God-given call reinforced. Thus God met His dear servant, met him face to face, and recalled him to the ministry. Note four facts.

a. God's second call to Moses was given in Egypt (v.28). God told Moses that he was to go to Pharaoh with the message of God Himself, that he was to go and declare all that God gave him to say.

b. But note: Moses again argued against God's call, argued just as he had at God's first call (v.30). Moses questioned God, speaking with faltering lips. Since he was not eloquent and Pharaoh had rejected him before, why would Pharaoh listen to him now? (See notes—Ex.4:10-12; 6:10-12 for more discussion.)

c. God answered Moses by giving him great assurance (Ex.7:1-5). God told Moses five things.

1) Moses was to be God's messenger: he was to be as God to Pharaoh, that is, he was to be endued with the very power and authority of God Himself (v.1).

2) Moses was not to be alone; he was to have a fellow-servant: Aaron was to be his spokesman (vv.1-2). In fact, Aaron would be the one actually doing the speaking. This fact would have encouraged Moses to no end. Knowing that we do not stand alone, that we have a companion in the ministry, always encourages us.

3) Now note: God told Moses a fact that he needed to remember: God was going to harden Pharaoh's heart. Why? So that He could multiply His miraculous signs in Egypt (v.3).

4) God restated the fact: the king would not listen to the message; consequently, God was going to lay His mighty hand of judgment upon Egypt—all to deliver and free His people (v.4).

5) God told Moses His purpose: that the Egyptians might know that God is the LORD (Jehovah, Yahweh), the Great Redeemer and Deliverer (v.5).

6 (7:6-7) **Obedience—Elderly**: note that Moses and Aaron obeyed God (vv.6-7). Moses was 80 years old and Aaron 83 years old when they were called to serve God and declare the message of deliverance and freedom to Pharaoh and the people (vv.6-7). Imagine! Two aged men being called to stand toe-to-toe against the most powerful nation upon earth.

Thought 1. What a lesson for us! We are never too old to serve God.

"And even to your old age I am he; and even to hoar [gray] hairs will I carry you: I have made, and I will bear; even I will carry, and will deliver you" (Is.46:4).

Thought 2. God meets the needs of His dear servants and people, no matter what the needs are. If we need to be encouraged to serve God, God will encourage us. God will call us to serve Him time and again if needed. God does not want us crushed and broken; does not want us refusing to serve and bear witness for Him day by day. God wants us declaring the glorious gospel of deliverance and freedom to the world, a world lost in sin and shame and doomed to death.

"Come, and let us return unto the Lord: for he hath torn, and he will heal us; he hath smitten, and he will bind us up" (Ho.6:1).

"When thou passest through the waters, I will be with thee; and through the rivers, they shall not overflow thee: when thou walkest through the fire, thou shalt not be burned; neither shall the flame kindle upon thee" (Is.43:2).

"Also I heard the voice of the LORD, saying, Whom shall I send, and who will go for us? Then said I, Here am I; send me" (Is.6:8).

"Go ye therefore into the highways, and as many as ye shall find, bid to the marriage" (Mt.22:9).

"But rise, and stand upon thy feet: for I have appeared unto thee [Paul] for this purpose, to make thee a minister and a witness both of these things which thou hast seen, and of those things in the which I will appear unto thee" (Ac.26:16).

"And we know that all things work together for good to them that love God, to them who are the called according to his purpose" (Ro.8:28).

"And he said unto me, My grace is sufficient for thee: for my strength is made perfect in weakness. Most gladly therefore will I rather glory in my infirmities, that the power of Christ may rest upon me" (2 Co.12:9).

DEEPER STUDY # 1
(6:13-27) **Chart—Table—Genealogy—Family Tree—Moses—Aaron—Levi—Levites, Tribe of**: this chart gives the family tree of Levi, Moses, and Aaron. It gives the ancestors of these two great servants of God.

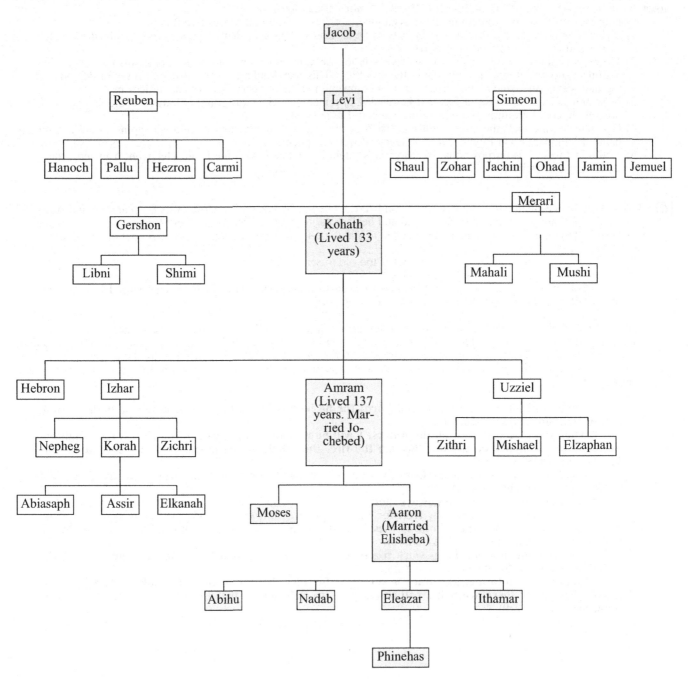

(Please see next page for DEEPER STUDY # 2)

DEEPER STUDY # 2
(7:5) **History—God, Sovereignty**: throughout history, God has chosen to become directly involved in the affairs of this world. God does not rule and reign from afar off. It is God's very nature that compels Him to become involved in the lives and affairs of men. God is both loving and just; He executes both compassion and justice, both mercy and judgment upon men and nations. The present passage is a stirring example of God's passion for personal involvement in history.

THE GOD OF HISTORY

God's Involvement (The Cause)	The Effect	The Scripture from Exodus
⇒ Now shalt thou see what I will do to Pharaoh	• for with a strong hand shall he let them [the Israelites] go, and with a strong hand shall he drive them out of his land (justice, mercy)	**6:1** Then the LORD said unto Moses, Now shalt thou see what I will do to Pharaoh: for with a strong hand shall he let them go, and with a strong hand shall he drive them out of his land.
⇒ I *am* the LORD	• And God spake unto Moses (love)	**6:2** And God spake unto Moses, and said unto him, I *am* the LORD:
⇒ And I appeared	• unto Abraham, unto Isaac, and unto Jacob, by *the name of* God Almighty, but by my name JEHOVAH was I not known to them (love, mercy)	**6:3** And I appeared unto Abraham, unto Isaac, and unto Jacob, by *the name of* God Almighty, but by my name JEHOVAH was I not known to them.
⇒ And I have also established my covenant with them	• to give them the land of Canaan, the land of their pilgrimage, wherein they were strangers (love, mercy)	**6:4** And I have also established my covenant with them, to give them the land of Canaan, the land of their pilgrimage, wherein they were strangers.
⇒ And I have also heard the groaning of the children of Israel	• and I have remembered my covenant (compassion, mercy)	**6:5** And I have also heard the groaning of the children of Israel, whom the Egyptians keep in bondage; and I have remembered my covenant.
⇒ I *am* the LORD	• I will bring you out from under the burdens of the Egyptians • I will rid you out of their bondage • I will redeem you with a stretched out arm (compassion, mercy) • and with great judgments (justice, judgment)	**6:6** Wherefore say unto the children of Israel, I *am* the LORD, and I will bring you out from under the burdens of the Egyptians, and I will rid you out of their bondage, and I will redeem you with a stretched out arm, and with great judgments:

God's Involvement (The Cause)	The Effect	The Scripture from Exodus
⇒ I will take you to me for a people, and I will be to you a God	• ye shall know that I *am* the LORD your God, which bringeth you out from under the burdens of the Egyptians (love, compassion)	**6:7 And I will take you to me for a people, and I will be to you a God: and ye shall know that I *am* the LORD your God, which bringeth you out from under the burdens of the Egyptians.**
⇒ I *am* the LORD	• I will bring you in unto the land, concerning the which I did swear to give it to Abraham, to Isaac, and to Jacob • I will give it you for an heritage (love, mercy)	**6:8 And I will bring you in unto the land, concerning the which I did swear to give it to Abraham, to Isaac, and to Jacob; and I will give it you for an heritage: I *am* the LORD.**
⇒ I *am* the LORD	• speak thou unto Pharaoh king of Egypt all that I say unto thee (justice, judgment)	**6:29 That the LORD spake unto Moses, saying, I *am* the LORD: speak thou unto Pharaoh king of Egypt all that I say unto thee.**
⇒ I will harden Pharaoh's heart	• multiply my signs and my wonders in the land of Egypt. (justice, judgment)	**7:3 And I will harden Pharaoh's heart, and multiply my signs and my wonders in the land of Egypt.**
⇒ I will lay my hand upon Egypt	• But Pharaoh shall not hearken unto you, that I may lay my hand upon Egypt, and bring forth mine armies, *and* my people the children of Israel, out of the land of Egypt by great judgments (justice, judgment)	**7:4 But Pharaoh shall not hearken unto you, that I may lay my hand upon Egypt, and bring forth mine armies, *and* my people the children of Israel, out of the land of Egypt by great judgments.**
⇒ I *am* the LORD	• the Egyptians shall know that I *am* the LORD when I stretch forth mine hand upon Egypt, and bring out the children of Israel from among them (justice, judgment)	**7:5 And the Egyptians shall know that I *am* the LORD, when I stretch forth mine hand upon Egypt, and bring out the children of Israel from among them.**

DIVISION III

THE TEN PLAGUES AND EGYPT: GOD'S JUDGMENT UPON THOSE WHO REJECT HIM AND OPPRESS HIS PEOPLE, 7:8–11:10

(7:8–11:10) **DIVISION OVERVIEW—Plagues, The Ten**: the call of God had been given. The servant of God had proclaimed God's message of deliverance and freedom to the most powerful ruler upon earth, the king of Egypt. "Let God's people go—free them so they can live in freedom and serve God."

What had been the response? Anger, wrath, retaliation. The king had accused Moses of disturbing the peace and arousing the people. But more than this, in madness he had increased the work load upon the enslaved people. But even more than this, he had brutally oppressed, abused, whipped, and scourged the people beyond measure. He literally drove them into the ground, rejecting all appeals for understanding and reason. Obviously, as with all enslaved people who are savagely oppressed, the strong were weakened, and the sick and aged died by the thousands. An atrocity, a holocaust beyond imagination, was being launched against God's people. Pharaoh seemed ready to draw the sword to slay the whole nation (Ex.5:21). The people were helpless and hopeless against the maddening rage of Pharaoh. And why? All because of the evil that lurked within the hearts of the Egyptians, the evil of enslavement, the evil of oppressing God's people, the evil of greed, of covetousness, of wanting cheap labor.

Now the day of judgment and the day of redemption were drawing near, God's judgment upon Egypt and God's redemption of His people. God was ready to execute justice: ready to judge the Egyptians for their terrible sin, ready to force Pharaoh to free Israel. God was going to unleash a series of *ten plagues* upon Egypt. The ten plagues would touch every Egyptian household; not a single Egyptian would be left untouched. In the end, Pharaoh would free Israel; in fact, he would demand that they get out of Egypt.

Now, several points need to be noted about the plagues before we look at them in detail.

1. All the plagues were severe: they posed a serious threat to the very survival of Egypt as a nation. If the plagues had continued and never been stopped, the land would have been devastated. The life of every living thing would have perished or else been forced to move elsewhere. It was the mercy of God that stopped the plagues and gave the Egyptians a chance to repent. They were given opportunity after opportunity to turn from their terrible sins, opportunity after opportunity to turn back to the living and true God.

2. There was perhaps a severe increase in the intensity (suffering) of each plague. Some commentators say so. However, the severity of each plague was terrible, catastrophic, and devastating. Any one of the plagues, if never stopped, would have devastated Egypt beyond repair.

3. The purposes of the plagues need to be understood. Scripture itself tells us that the plagues had several purposes.

    a. God used the plagues to teach the world this one thing: the LORD (Jehovah, Yahweh) is the God of redemption, of salvation, and of deliverance. He is the only living and true God, the Sovereign Lord and Majesty of the universe, the God who controls all nature and all history.

> "And the Egyptians shall know that I am the LORD, when I stretch forth mine hand upon Egypt, and bring out the children of Israel from among them" (Ex.7:5).
>
> "For I will at this time send all my plagues upon thine heart, and upon thy servants, and upon thy people; that thou mayest know that there is none like me in all the earth. For now I will stretch out my hand, that I may smite thee and thy people with pestilence; and thou shalt be cut off from the earth" (Ex.9.14-15).
>
> "And that thou mayest tell in the ears of thy son, and of thy son's son, what things I have wrought in Egypt, and my signs which I have done among them; that ye may know how that I am the LORD" (Ex.10:2).
>
> "Now I know that the LORD is greater than all gods: for in the thing wherein they dealt proudly he was above them" (Ex.18:11).

    b. God used the plagues to demonstrate His omnipotent, almighty power to all the earth and to proclaim His name.

> "And in very deed for this cause have I raised thee up, for to show in thee my power; and that my name may be declared throughout all the earth" (Ex.9:16).
>
> "Then the magicians said unto Pharaoh, This is the finger [power] of God: and Pharaoh's heart was hardened, and he hearkened not unto them; as the LORD had said" (Ex.8:19).
>
> "Did ever people hear the voice of God speaking out of the midst of the fire, as thou hast heard, and live? Or hath God assayed [ever tried] to go and take him a nation from the midst of another nation, by temptations [trials], by signs, and by wonders, and by war, and by a mighty hand, and by a stretched out arm, and by great terrors, according to all that the LORD your God did for you in Egypt before your eyes?" (De.4:33-34).

c. God used the plagues to force Pharaoh and the Egyptians to free Israel.

> **"But Pharaoh shall not hearken unto you, that I may lay my hand upon Egypt, and bring forth mine armies, and my people the children of Israel, out of the land of Egypt by great judgments"** (Ex.7:4).
> **"And Jethro said, Blessed be the LORD, who hath delivered you out of the hand of the Egyptians, and out of the hand of Pharaoh, who hath delivered the people from under the hand of the Egyptians"** (Ex.18:10).

d. God used the plagues to show the great distinctive between Israel and Egypt, the great difference between those who followed Him and those who did not. Those who followed God (true believers) were His chosen people and under His protective care. God actually protected the land of Goshen from the plagues. (Remember: the Israelites lived in Goshen.)

> **"And I will sever [separate, divide] in that day the land of Goshen, in which my people dwell, that no swarms of flies shall be there; to the end thou mayest know that I am the LORD in the midst of the earth. And I will put a division between my people and thy people: to morrow shall this sign be"** (Ex.8:22-23).
> **"But against any of the children of Israel shall not a dog move his tongue, against man or beast: that ye may know how that the LORD doth put a difference between the Egyptians and Israel"** (Ex.11:7).
> **"That ye shall say, It is the sacrifice of the LORD'S passover, who passed over the houses of the children of Israel in Egypt, when he smote the Egyptians, and delivered our houses. And the people bowed the head and worshipped"** (Ex.12:27).

e. God used the plagues to judge the Egyptians for their terrible sins, for worshipping false gods, for enslaving and brutalizing people. Ages before, the Egyptians had rejected the only true and living God and they had continued to reject Him down through the centuries. Now they were rejecting Him even during the ten plagues. They were a hard-hearted, stiff-necked, and prideful people, an idolatrous people who worshipped everything ranging from man himself over to birds, four-footed animals, and creeping things (Ro.1:18-34).
   In addition, the Egyptians were gripped...
* by the lust for pleasure, comfort, and ease
* by the lust for more and more wealth and possessions

It was this enslaving lust that caused them to enslave and brutalize others: all so they could line their pockets and live a life of luxury based upon cheap slave-labor.

This was the reason God judged Egypt, the reason He sent the ten plagues upon Pharaoh and his people. The judgment of God fell upon them because they had rejected God and given themselves over to the pleasures and possessions of this world. Maxie Dunnam has an excellent statement on the judgment of God that is well worth quoting in its entirety.

> *There can be no covering up or diminishing the reality of divine judgment. The fact is set forth on page after page of Bible history. God judged Adam and Eve, expelling them from the garden and pronouncing curses on their future earthly life. God judged the corrupt world of Noah's day, sending a flood to destroy humankind. God judged Sodom and Gomorrah, engulfing them in a volcanic catastrophe (Ge.19:24). And God judged Pharaoh and the Egyptians just as He had foretold He would (Ge.15:14), unleashing against them the terrors of the ten plagues.*
> *There are "big judgments" about which we all know. Apart from these, the pages of the Bible are literally filled with judgment. Those who don't study the Bible seriously nonchalantly suggest that when you leave the Old Testament and come to the New, the theme of divine judgment fades almost to nothing. That isn't so. Even a cursory reading of the New Testament reveals God's action as judge. In fact, the entire New Testament is overshadowed by the certainty of a coming day of universal judgment which was set forth by Jesus Himself. It's not easy to forget that picture, the powerful imagery of it—the sheep separated from the goats, the righteous on the right hand of God and the unrighteous o the left, the righteous invited into the presence of the Lord, the unrighteous condemned to eternal punishment where there is "weeping and gnashing of teeth" (Matt.8:12).*
> *The picture in the New Testament is that the world's Savior, Jesus Christ, is also the world's judge. Listen to Jesus Himself:*

> > *"'For the Father judges no one, but has committed all judgment to the Son, that all should honor the Son just as they honor the Father. He who does not honor the Son does not honor the Father who sent Him.*
> > *"'Most assuredly, I say to you, he who hears My word and believes in Him who sent Me has everlasting life, and shall not come into judgment, but has passed from death into life. Most assuredly, I say to you, the hour is coming, and now is, when the dead will hear the voice of the Son of God; and those who hear will live. For as the Father has life in Himself, so He has granted the Son to have life in Himself, and has given Him authority to execute judgment also, because He is the Son of Man. Do not marvel at this; for the hour is coming in which all who are*

in the graves will hear His voice and come forth—those who have done good, to the resurrection of life, and those who have done evil, to the resurrection of condemnation.'

John 5:22-29

There is no way to cover up or diminish the reality of divine judgment.[1]

"But Pharaoh shall not hearken unto you, that I may lay my hand upon Egypt, and bring forth mine armies, and my people the children of Israel, out of the land of Egypt by great judgments" (Ex.7:4).

"And that thou mayest tell in the ears of thy son, and of thy son's son, what things I have wrought in Egypt, and my signs which I have done among them; that ye may know how that I am the LORD" (Ex.10:2).

"Then Pharaoh called for Moses and Aaron in haste; and he said, I have sinned against the LORD your God, and against you" (Ex.10:16).

"For I will pass through the land of Egypt this night, and will smite all the firstborn in the land of Egypt, both man and beast; and against all the gods of Egypt I will execute judgment: I am the LORD" (Ex.12:12).

"Now I know that the LORD is greater than all gods: for in the thing wherein they dealt proudly he was above them" (Ex.18:11).

4. God had very specific purpose in launching each plague upon Egypt.

THE TEN PLAGUES AND EGYPT: GOD'S JUDGMENT UPON THOSE WHO REJECT HIM AND OPPRESS HIS PEOPLE (Exodus 7:8-11:10)

The Plague	The Scripture	The Practical Purpose of the Plague
The First Plague—Water Changed to Blood	Exodus 7:14-25	Proof that God is the LORD, the God of Redemption, the Only Living and True God
The Second Plague—Frogs Everywhere	Exodus 8:1-15	Proof That God Has No Equal, That No One Is Like the LORD Our God
The Third Plague—Lice or Gnats Infested the Land	Exodus 8:16-19	Proof That the Finger (Power) of God Controls All Things, Even the Very Dust of the Ground
The Fourth Plague—Flies Swarmed Over the Land	Exodus 8:20-32	Proof That the LORD is the Redeemer (the Savior), the Only Living and True God, In Every Land and In Every Place
The Fifth Plague—A Severe Disease Struck & Killed All Livestock in the Field	Exodus 9:1-7	Proof that the Hand of God Controls the Animal Life of the World
The Sixth Plague—Festering Boils Afflicted Man and Animal	Exodus 9:8-12	Proof that God has Power Over Body and Health
The Seventh Plague—A Severe Hail & Thunderstorm	Exodus 9:13-35	Proof that the Earth is the LORD's
The Eighth Plague—Locusts Swarmed Over the Land	Exodus 10:1-20	Proof That the LORD is the Great Savior of Mankind
The Ninth Plague—Darkness Covered the Land	Exodus 10:21-29	Proof That God Has Power Over the Light & Darkness of the Earth
The Tenth Plague—Death of the Firstborn Announced	Exodus 11:1-10	Proof That God is the God of True Believers

---

[1] Maxie Dunnam. *Mastering the Old Testament, Volume 2, Exodus*, p.137-138.

5. The ten plagues clearly demonstrated how all things within the universe are under God's control, that He is beyond all question the only living and true God.

Plague	Item Under God's Control	Effect of the Plagues	King's Response
1. Nile River turned to blood (7:14-24)	Water supply (7:17-18)	Contamination of water supply; disease	Heart became hard (7:22)
2. Frogs (8:1-15)	Personal property: Frogs swarmed over all the property of man (8:3-4)	Property ruined; threat of disease	Hardened his heart & would not listen (8:15)
3. Lice, gnats, fleas, or mosquitoes (8:16-19)	Personal comfort (8:18)	Discomfort of body; threat of disease	Heart was hard & would not listen (8:19)
4. Flies or beetles (8:20-32)	Land & all possessions (8:21, 24)	Pollution & uncleanness; threat of disease	Hardened his heart (8:32)
5. Livestock plague or disease (9:1-7)	Animal life (9:3, 5)	Death of livestock; threat of disease	Heart was hardened (9:7)
6. Festering Boils (9:8-12)	Health & well-being (9:9-11)	Inability to stand, work, move about	LORD hardened his heart (9:12)
7. Hail & lightning (9:13-35)	The heavens (sky) & one's personal security (9:18, 23-25)	Destruction of property & exposed livestock	Heart was hard (9:35)
8. Locusts (10:1-20)	Vegetation, food supply (10:4-6)	Destruction of food supply	LORD hardened his heart (10:20)
9. Darkness (10:21-29)	Light (10:21-22)	Darkness—inability to see, move about, or work	LORD hardened his heart (10:27)
10. Death of firstborn of man & animal (11:1-10)	Life & death (11:5)	Death	Freed God's people

6. Each plague seemed to be launched against a particular god of Egypt. God proved beyond doubt that He is the only living and true God.

Plague	The Egyptian God Mocked
1. Nile River turned to blood (7:14-24)	Nilus or Hopi, the god of the Nile River & of water who controlled the waters of the earth.
2. Frogs (8:1-15)	Ptha, the frog-headed god, & Hekt, the goddess of reproduction. Frogs were believed to be extremely fruitful in reproduction. Therefore the spirit that enabled such fruitful reproduction, that gave or created life, was worshipped as a frog-headed idol.
3. Lice, gnats, fleas, or mosquitoes (8:16-19)	Seb, god of the earth: this idol was worshipped in the hope that he would bless the earth by making it productive and by protecting the earth & the land of Egypt from natural catastrophes (8:16-19)
4. Flies or beetles (8:20-32)	Khephera, the beetle or sacred god. The Dake Bible says the god was Beelzebub, god of the flies: he was worshipped in the hope that he would help the disease-infested flies go away (*Dake's Bible*, p.72).
5. Livestock plague or disease (9:1-7)	Hathor and Apis, the sacred cattle gods at Memphis. They were worshipped as gods of reproduction and fertility, as gods who could protect from plagues, diseases, and accidents.
6. Festering Boils (9:8-12)	Typhon, the evil-eye god: worshipped in the hope of averting plagues
7. Hail and lightning (9:13-35)	Iris, the water god, and Osiris, the fire and lightning god, and Shu, the god of the atmosphere: all worshipped in the hope that they would control nature & provide protection against storms and natural catastrophes
8. Locusts (10:1-20)	Seraphis, the insect god: worshipped in the hope of being protected from locusts
9. Darkness (10:21-29)	Ra, the sun god: worshipped to protect against any natural disaster from the sun & to provide warmth, light, & fruitfulness
10. Death of firstborn of man and animal (11:1-10)	Ptah, the god of life. This plague may have been attacking all the gods of Egypt, demonstrating clearly that the LORD (Jehovah, Yahweh) is the only God of redemption and salvation, the only true and living God.

7. Other Scriptures refer to the plagues.

    a. Moses declared to Israel (obviously time and again) that God had brought the plagues upon Egypt to show that He alone is God, that there is no other God. The LORD and the LORD alone is the God of redemption and salvation.

> **"Or hath God assayed [ever tried] to go and take him a nation from the midst of another nation, by temptations, by signs, and by wonders, and by war, and by a mighty hand, and by a stretched out arm, and by great terrors, according to all that the LORD your God did for you in Egypt before your eyes? Unto thee it was showed, that thou mightest know that the LORD he is God; there is none else beside him" (De.4:34-35).**

    b. The Psalmist challenges people to learn from Israel's history, to learn from the plagues that God cast upon Egypt. We must make sure that we never forget the judgment of God's power.

> **"They remembered not his hand, nor the day when he delivered them from the enemy. How he had wrought his signs in Egypt, and his wonders in the field of Zoan: And had turned their rivers into blood; and their floods, that they could not drink. He sent divers sorts of flies among them, which devoured them; and frogms, which destroyed them. He gave also their increase unto the caterpillar, and their labour unto the locust. He destroyed their vines with hail, and their sycamore trees with frost. He gave up their cattle also to the hail, and their flocks to hot thunderbolts. He cast upon them the fierceness of his anger, wrath, and indignation, and trouble, by sending evil angels among them. He made a way to his anger; he spared not their soul from death, but gave their life over to the pestilence; And smote all the firstborn in Egypt; the chief of their strength in the tabernacles of Ham" (Ps.78:42-51).**

    c. The Psalmist also challenges people to remember the great works of God, to remember the judgments of the plagues.

> **"Remember his marvelous works that he hath done; his wonders, and the judgments of his mouth....He sent darkness, and made it dark; and they rebelled not against his word. He turned their waters into blood, and slew their fish. Their land brought forth frogs in abundance, in the chambers of their kings. He spake, and there came divers sorts of flies, and lice in all their coasts. He gave them hail for rain, and flaming fire in their land. He smote their vines also and their fig trees; and brake the trees of their coasts. He spake, and the locusts came, and caterpillars, and that without number, And did eat up all the herbs in their land, and devoured the fruit of their ground. He smote also all the firstborn in their land, the chief of all their strength" (Ps.105:5, 28-36).**

    d. The Psalmist says that God demonstrated His greatness in the tenth plague, demonstrated His greatness in a very special way. By slaying the firstborn of Egypt, He proved beyond question that He is above all gods.

> **"For I know that the LORD is great, and that our Lord is above all gods....Who smote the firstborn of Egypt, both of man and beast" (Ps.135:5, 8).**

    e. The Psalmist says that God even demonstrated His mercy by striking down the firstborn of Egypt. He should therefore be praised for His mercy. God's mercy was demonstrated...
- in that He used the killing of the firstborn to free His people from the holocaust of Egyptian atrocities and enslavement
- in that He judged Egypt for its savage and ruthless evil

> **"O give thanks unto the LORD; for he is good: for his mercy endureth for ever....To him that smote Egypt in their firstborn: for his mercy endureth for ever" (Ps.136:1, 10).**

    f. The prophet Jeremiah declared that the power of God was demonstrated in the great wonders He worked in Egypt:

> **"Ah Lord GOD! behold, thou hast made the heaven and the earth by thy great power and stretched out arm, and there is nothing too hard for thee....Which hast set signs and wonders in the land of Egypt, even unto this day, and in Israel, and among other men" (Je.32:17, 20).**

    g. Scripture says that the faith of Moses led Israel to keep the Passover and that the sprinkling of the blood saved the firstborn of Israel from the plague.

> **"Through faith he kept the passover, and the sprinkling of blood, lest he that destroyed the firstborn should touch them" (He.11:28).**

    h. Scripture says that in the last days of world history, God is going to pour some cosmic plagues out upon the earth. Some of the plagues resemble the plagues that fell upon Egypt. (See outlines and notes—Re. Chs. 8-9, 15-16 for discussion.)

146

THE TEN PLAGUES AND EGYPT: GOD'S JUDGMENT UPON THOSE WHO REJECT HIM AND OPPRESS HIS PEOPLE, 7:8–11:10

A. The Credentials of God's Servant: Proof That a Person Is God's Servant, 7:8-13

B. The First Plague—Water Changed to Blood: Proof that God Is the LORD, the God of Salvation, the Only Living and True God, 7:14-25

C. The Second Plague—Frogs Everywhere: Proof That God Has No Equal, That No One Is Like the LORD Our God, 8:1-15

D. The Third Plague—Lice or Gnats Infested the Land: Proof That the Finger (Power) of God Controls All Things, Even the Very Dust of the Ground, 8:16-19

E. The Fourth Plague—Flies Swarmed Over the Land: Proof that the LORD Is the Savior in Every Land and in Every Place, 8:20-32

F. The Fifth Plague—A Severe Disease Struck and Killed All Livestock in the Field: Proof That the Hand of God Controls the Animal Life of the World, 9:1-7

G. The Sixth Plague—Festering Boils Afflicted Man and Animal: Proof that God Has Power Over Body and Health, 9:8-12

H. The Seventh Plague—A Catastrophic Hail and Thunderstorm: Proof That the Earth Is the LORD's, 9:13-35

I. The Eighth Plague—Locusts Swarmed Over the Land: Proof That the LORD Is the Great Savior of Mankind, 10:1-20

J. The Ninth Plague—Darkness Covered the Land: Proof That God Has Power Over the Light and Darkness of the Earth, 10:21-29

K. The Tenth Plague—Death of the Firstborn Announced: Proof That God is the God of True Believers, 11:1-10

	III. THE TEN PLAGUES & EGYPT: GOD'S JUDGMENT UPON THOSE WHO REJECT HIM & OPPRESS HIS PEOPLE, 7:8–11:10
	
	 A. The Credentials of God's Servant: Proof That a Person Is God's Servant, 7:8-13
		a serpent.
		 10 And Moses and Aaron went in unto Pharaoh, and they did so as the LORD had commanded: and Aaron cast down his rod before Pharaoh, and before his servants, and it became a serpent.
		 11 Then Pharaoh also called the wise men and the sorcerers: now the magicians of Egypt, they also did in like manner with their enchantments.
			& it would turn to a serpent
			 2. Credential 2: Obedience to God
			   a. Moses & Aaron went to Pharaoh
			   b. They did exactly what God had instructed
			 3. Credential 3: God's power, His supreme power
			   a. God's power: Turned the rod into a snake
			   b. The king countered with his own display of power: His magicians seemingly duplicated the sign

1. Credential 1: The knowledge of God, of His Word & His instructions
   a. God informed Moses: The king would challenge him, demand proof that his message was from God
   b. God instructed Moses: To cast the rod before Pharaoh,
	8 And the LORD spake unto Moses and unto Aaron, saying,
	 9 When Pharaoh shall speak unto you, saying, Show a miracle for you: then thou shalt say unto Aaron, Take thy rod, and cast it before Pharaoh, and it shall become
		12 For they cast down every man his rod, and they became serpents: but Aaron's rod swallowed up their rods.
		 13 And he hardened Pharaoh's heart, that he hearkened not unto them; as the LORD had said.
			c. God's supreme power: He empowered Aaron's rod to swallow up the rods of Pharaoh's magicians
			   d. The tragic response to the credentials of God's servant: Pharaoh's heart was hard & he would not listen

DIVISION III

THE TEN PLAGUES AND EGYPT: GOD'S JUDGMENT UPON THOSE WHO REJECT HIM AND OPPRESS HIS PEOPLE, 7:8–11:10

A. The Credentials of God's Servant: Proof That a Person Is God's Servant, 7:8-13

(7:8-13) **Introduction**: God loves the world, and He loved the Egyptian people of Moses' day. God did not want a single Egyptian to perish without knowing Him. But God knew the hearts of Pharaoh and the Egyptians. He knew that their hearts were hard against Him, that they had rejected Him in ages past and had turned to the worship of self-made gods. God also knew that they had enslaved His people, that they were a vicious, brutal, cruel, and savage people who abused others in order to get free labor and to satisfy their own personal greed and desires.

God had to execute justice: the Egyptians had to be judged for their evil. This God was now ready to do. The hand of His retribution and vengeance, of God's judgment, was now ready to fall upon Pharaoh and the Egyptians. But God still loved the Egyptians and wanted to give them every opportunity to repent, to turn back to the only living and true God.

This is what this present passage is all about. God wanted to give the king of Egypt one last chance to repent and to free God's people, one last warning before God launched His judgment, His plagues upon the nation.

What did God do to warn Pharaoh? God sent Moses to present his credentials to Pharaoh, to prove that he and his message were truly from God. This passage covers the second confrontation of Moses with Pharaoh. In the first meeting, Moses only presented the message of God to Pharaoh. Now, he presented his credentials: he proved that God had sent him. This is the subject of this passage, *The Credentials of God's Servant: Proof That a Person Is God's Servant,* 7:8-13.

1. Credential 1: the knowledge of God, of His Word and His instructions (vv.8-9).
2. Credential 2: obedience to God (v.10).
3. Credential 2: God's power, His supreme power (vv.10-13).

1 (7:8-9) **Servant, of God—Minister**: the first credential of God's servant is basic: it is knowing God, His Word and His instructions. When a person claims that he is from God, that God has called him to preach and teach God's Word, we need to know one basic fact: does the person know God and know God's Word? Has God truly spoken to him and commissioned him to proclaim God's Word?

Note that God spoke to Moses and Aaron; He gave them His Word (v.8). God was commissioning His servants to go to Pharaoh and proclaim His message of freedom and liberty, that the king was to let God's people go. But just as any king would, Pharaoh was going to challenge God's servants, demand proof that their message was truly from God. He was going to ask for some miracle, some sign to validate their claim. In asking for a sign, Pharaoh's tone was probably skeptical and somewhat mocking. He just did not expect the miracle to be truly performed.

Now note, God's Word does not include just the commissioning of His servants to go forth; His Word includes instructions, clear-cut guidance. God told His servants exactly what to do to handle the skepticism and mockery. God instructed His servants to cast their rod before Pharaoh, and it would miraculously turn to a serpent (tannin). Some scholars say that the Hebrew word used here usually refers to larger reptiles such as crocodiles or some large sea animal (see Ge.1:21; De.32:33; Je.51:34; Eze.29:3). However, it also means snake or serpent.

Note: this act of God involved no judgment; it only demonstrated God's power. It gave Pharaoh one last chance before the judgment of God began to fall. Pharaoh, with sarcasm and ridicule, wanted to know the credentials of God's servant. God gave him their credentials: God gave them His Word and His instructions. God told His servants exactly what to say and to do as they stood before Pharaoh.

Thought 1. The first credential of God's messenger is this one basic fact: he knows God and knows God's Word.
(1) He knows God.

"Ye are my witnesses, saith the LORD, and my servant whom I have chosen: that ye may know and believe me, and understand that I am he: before me there was no God formed, neither shall there be after me" (Is.43:10).

"But let him that glorieth glory in this, that he understandeth and knoweth me, that I am the LORD which exercise lovingkindness, judgment, and righteousness, in the earth: for in these things I delight, saith the LORD" (Je.9:24).

"Then said Jesus to those Jews [to any believer] which believed on him, If ye continue in my word, [then] are ye my disciples indeed" (Jn.8:31).

"I know whom I have believed, and am persuaded that he is able to keep that which I have committed unto him against that day" (2 Ti.1:12).

(2) He knows God's Word.

"Neither have I gone back from the commandment of his lips; I have esteemed the words of his mouth more than my necessary food" (Jb.23:12).

"Wherewithal shall a young man cleanse his way? by taking heed thereto according to thy word" (Ps.119:9).

"Thy word have I hid in mine heart, that I might not sin against thee" (Ps.119:11).

"Thy words were found, and I did eat them; and thy word was unto me the joy and rejoicing of mine heart: for I am called by thy name, O LORD God of hosts" (Je.15:16).

"But these are written [the Holy Scriptures], that ye might believe that Jesus is the Christ, the Son of God; and that believing ye might have life through his name" (Jn.20:31).

"For I am not ashamed of the gospel of Christ: for it is the power of God unto salvation to every one that believeth; to the Jew first, and also to the Greek" (Ro.1:16).

"But as we were allowed of God to be put in trust with the gospel, even so we speak; not as pleasing men, but God, which trieth our hearts" (1 Th.2:4).

"According to the glorious gospel of the blessed God, which was committed to my trust. And I thank Christ Jesus our Lord, who hath enabled me, for that he counted me faithful, putting me into the ministry" (1 Ti.1:11-12).

"Study to show thyself approved unto God, a workman that needeth not to be ashamed, rightly dividing the word of truth" (2 Ti.2:15).

"All scripture is given by inspiration of God, and is profitable for doctrine, for reproof, for correction, for instruction in righteousness" (2 Ti.3:16).

"But [God] hath in due times manifested his word through preaching, which is committed unto me according to the commandment of God our Saviour" (Tit.1:3).

"For the word of God is quick, and powerful, and sharper than any twoedged sword, piercing even to the dividing asunder of soul and spirit, and of the joints and marrow, and is a discerner of the thoughts and intents of the heart" (He.4:12).

2 (7:10) **Obedience**: the second credential of God's servant is crucial: it is obedience to God. When God gives His Word to a person, He expects obedience. God had given His Word to His messengers. He had commissioned and instructed them, telling them exactly what to do. Thus He expected obedience; He expected them to do exactly what He had commissioned them to do. And note: Moses and Aaron obeyed God. They went to Pharaoh and did exactly what God had said.

Thought 1. When God tells us what to do, He expects obedience. He expects us to do exactly...
• what He has instructed us to do
• what He has commanded us to do

(1) God has commissioned and instructed us to go and proclaim His Word to a world lost in sin and darkness. This was what God was commissioning Moses and Aaron to do, and it is what He has commissioned us to do.

"Go ye therefore, and teach all nations, baptizing them in the name of the Father, and of the Son, and of the Holy Ghost: Teaching them to observe all things whatsoever I have commanded you: and, lo, I am with you alway, [even] unto the end of the world" (Mt.28:19-20).

"And he said unto them, Go ye into all the world, and preach the gospel to every creature" (Mk.16:15).

"But ye shall receive power, after that the Holy Ghost is come upon you: and ye shall be witnesses unto me both in Jerusalem, and in all Judaea, and in Samaria, and unto the uttermost part of the earth" (Ac.1:8).

"And he said, The God of our fathers hath chosen thee, that thou shouldest know his will, and see that Just One, and shouldest hear the voice of his mouth. For thou shalt be his witness unto all men of what thou hast seen and heard" (Ac.22:14-15).

"These things speak, and exhort, and rebuke with all authority. Let no man despise thee" (Tit.2:15).

"But sanctify the Lord God in your hearts: and be ready always to give an answer to every man that asketh you a reason of the hope that is in you with meekness and fear" (1 Pe.3:15).

(2) God expects us to obey Him, to do exactly what He commands and says.

> **"Now therefore, if ye will obey my voice indeed, and keep my covenant, then ye shall be a peculiar treasure unto me above all people: for all the earth is mine" (Ex.19:5).**

⇒ Noah obeyed the LORD.

> **"Thus did Noah; according to all that God commanded him, so did he" (Ge.6:22).**

⇒ Joshua obeyed the LORD.

> **"As the LORD commanded Moses his servant, so did Moses command Joshua, and so did Joshua; he left nothing undone of all that the LORD commanded Moses" (Jos.11:15).**

⇒ Hezekiah obeyed the LORD.

> **"For he clave to the LORD, and departed not from following him, but kept his commandments, which the LORD commanded Moses" (2 K.18:6).**

⇒ Paul obeyed the LORD.

> **"Whereupon, O king Agrippa, I was not disobedient unto the heavenly vision" (Ac.26:19).**

⇒ Christ obeyed the Father.

> **"But that the world may know that I love the Father; and as the Father gave me commandment, even so I do. Arise, let us go hence" (Jn.14:31).**
> **"Though he were a Son, yet learned he obedience by the things which he suffered" (He.5:8).**

⇒ We are to obey the LORD

> **"Now therefore, if ye will obey my voice indeed, and keep my covenant, then ye shall be a peculiar treasure unto me above all people: for all the earth is mine" (Ex.19:5).**
> **"This day the LORD thy God hath commanded thee to do these statutes and judgments: thou shalt therefore keep and do them with all thine heart, and with all thy soul" (De.26:16).**
> **"Not every one that saith unto me, Lord, Lord, shall enter into the kingdom of heaven; but he that doeth the will of my Father which is in heaven" (Mt.7:21).**
> **"Jesus answered and said unto him, If a man love me, he will keep my words: and my Father will love him, and we will come unto him, and make our abode with him" (Jn.14:23).**
> **"Then Peter and the other apostles answered and said, We ought to obey God rather than men" (Ac.5:29).**

---

3 (7:10-13) **Power, of God—Credentials, of God's Servant—Minister—Messenger**: the third credential of God's servant is absolutely essential: it is God's power, His supreme authority. What now happened was interesting.

a. God's power was demonstrated right *before* Pharaoh and his officials (v.10b). God turned the rod of Moses into a snake.

b. But note: the king countered with his own display of power. He wanted to prove that Moses was nothing more than a magician, that there was no living and true God who was empowering Moses to do such a feat. Thus, he called together all the officials of his court:

⇒ The *wise men* (hakamim): they were the educated and trained politicians of that day.
⇒ The *sorcerers* (kashshap): they practiced witchcraft, the occult, and the casting of spells upon people.
⇒ The *magicians* (hartummim) they used trickery and the occult to perform feats. The word is used in the Old Testament only to refer to sorcery.[1]

These advisors seemingly duplicated the sign. The two officials or magicians of Pharaoh's court are named in the New Testament by Paul: they were Jannes and Jambres (2 Ti.3:8). Paul refers to them as two false teachers who resisted the Word of God.

How did Pharaoh's magicians perform this feat, that of turning their rods into snakes? How did they duplicate exactly what Moses and Aaron did?

⇒ Did they use illusion, some slight of hand or deceptive appearance? It is possible to immobilize snakes by putting pressure on a nerve in their neck. This is called *catalepsy*. Were the magicians holding stiff, immobile snakes that appeared to be rods, immobile snakes that jolted out of their stiff stupor when thrown to the floor before Pharaoh? Some commentators think so.

⇒ Did the magicians perform the miracle through demonic power? The commentators who feel that a real conflict was taking place between the power of God and Satan tend to hold this position. Satan and his demonic spirits can seemingly duplicate miracles and signs, works that can come close to deceiving even the true followers of God.

---

1 Frank E. Gaebelein, Editor. *The Expositor's Bible Commentary*, Vol.2, p.347.

"For there shall arise false Christs, and false prophets, and shall show great signs and wonders; insomuch that, if [it were] possible, they shall deceive the very elect" (Mt.24:24).

c. However, God's power proved supreme. Aaron's rod swallowed up the rods of Pharaoh's magicians. This act demonstrated two striking facts to Pharaoh and his officials.

   1) God's power was supreme: the snake was the symbol of power in Egypt. In fact, it was the very symbol of Pharaoh's power: he wore the insignia of a metal snake in his crown.[2] Thus, when the rod of God swallowed the snakes produced by the magicians, God demonstrated beyond question His supreme power. God's power was stronger than the power of the greatest ruler upon earth, far stronger, strong enough to swallow Pharaoh's power.

   2) God had truly sent Moses. Pharaoh was bound to get the message: Moses did possess the credentials of God, the credentials of a far greater power than the religious leaders of Egypt. Pharaoh needed, therefore, to heed the warning of God and His messenger. But would he?

d. Tragically, no. Pharaoh's heart was hard, and he would not listen to God's messengers.

Thought 1. One of the greatest credentials of God's servants is the power of God.

(1) God holds supreme power over all things, including the nations and rulers of this earth. Thus He is able to deliver us when a man, a government, a supervisor, a spouse, a fellow-worker or anyone else causes trouble for us.

    "Both riches and honour come of thee, and thou reignest over all; and in thine hand is power and might; and in thine hand it is to make great, and to give strength unto all" (1 Chr.29:12).
    "But if thou wilt go, do it, be strong for the battle: God shall make thee fall before the enemy: for God hath power to help, and to cast down" (2 Chr.25:8).
    "He divideth the sea with his power, and by his understanding he smiteth through the proud" (Jb.26:12).
    "God hath spoken once; twice have I heard this; that power belongeth unto God" (Ps.62:11).
    "But our God is in the heavens: he hath done whatsoever he hath pleased" (Ps.115:3).
    "Yea, before the day was I am he; and there is none that can deliver out of my hand: I will work, and who shall let it?" (Is.43:13).
    "Let every soul be subject unto the higher powers. For there is no power but of God: the powers that be are ordained of God" (Ro.13:1).

(2) God demonstrates His power in the lives of His followers, the power to conquer all the terrible trials and evils of this earth. Thus, when the servant of God proclaims the message of God, we must not be as Pharaoh was: hardhearted. We must be soft-hearted, tender, and receptive to God's Word. If we heed the message of God, He will then give the power to conquer and triumph in life.

    "Fear thou not; for I am with thee: be not dismayed; for I am thy God: I will strengthen thee; yea, I will help thee; yea, I will uphold thee with the right hand of my righteousness" (Is.41:10).
    "And my speech and my preaching was not with enticing words of man's wisdom, but in demonstration of the Spirit and of power: That your faith should not stand in the wisdom of men, but in the power of God" (1 Co.2:4-5).
    "There hath no temptation taken you but such as is common to man: but God is faithful, who will not suffer you to be tempted above that ye are able; but will with the temptation also make a way to escape [His power], that ye may be able to bear it" (1 Co.10:13).
    "And [that you may know] what is the exceeding greatness of his power to us-ward who believe, according to the working of his mighty power" (Ep.1:19).
    "That he would grant you, according to the riches of his glory, to be strengthened with might by his Spirit in the inner man" (Ep.3:16).
    "Now unto him that is able to do exceeding abundantly above all that we ask or think, according to the power that worketh in us" (Ep.3:20).
    "Strengthened with all might, according to his glorious power, unto all patience and longsuffering with joyfulness" (Col.1:11).
    "For God hath not given us the spirit of fear; but of power, and of love, and of a sound mind" (2 Ti.1:7).

TYPES, SYMBOLS, AND PICTURES
(Exodus 7:8-13)

Historical Term	Type or Picture (Scriptural Basis for Each)	Life Application for Today's Believer	Biblical Application
The Ten Plagues (Ex.7:8-11:10)	*A picture of God's judgment upon all who reject Him and oppress people, upon the ungodly and unrighteous in the world.*	God's judgment is going to fall upon all... • who resist and deny Him • who worship other gods	*"And as it is appointed unto men once to die, but after this the judgment" (He.9:27).* *"Now the works of the flesh are manifest, which*

---

[2] Ronald F. Youngblood. *Exodus.* (Chicago, IL: Moody Press, 1983), p.35.

TYPES, SYMBOLS, AND PICTURES
(Exodus 7:8-13)

Historical Term	Type or Picture (Scriptural Basis for Each)	Life Application for Today's Believer	Biblical Application
	"But Pharaoh shall not hearken unto you, that I may lay my hand upon Egypt, and bring forth mine armies, *and* my people the children of Israel, out of the land of Egypt by great judgments" (Ex.7:4).	• who oppress and hurt people • who are ungodly and unrighteous • who reject the truth	*are these; Adultery, fornication, uncleanness, lasciviousness, Idolatry, witchcraft, hatred, variance, emulations, wrath, strife, seditions, heresies, Envyings, murders, drunkenness, revellings, and such like: of the which I tell you before, as I have also told you in time past, that they which do such things shall not inherit the kingdom of God" (Ga.5:19-21).* *"For the Son of man shall come in the glory of his Father with his angels; and then he shall reward every man according to his works" (Mt.16:27).* *"The Lord knoweth how to deliver the godly out of temptations, and to reserve the unjust unto the day of judgment to be punished" (2 Pe.2:9).* *(see Mt.12:36; 25:31-32; Ro.1:18, 29-32; 2:5; 2 Pe. 3:7; Jude 14-15; Re.21:8)*
Egyptian Magicians (Ex. 7:11)	*A picture of false messengers* **"Then Pharaoh also called the wise men and the sorcerers: now the magicians of Egypt, they also did in like manner with their enchantments" (Ex. 7:11-12).** **"Now as Jannes and Jambres [two of the magicians] withstood Moses, so do these also resist the truth: men of corrupt minds, reprobate concerning the faith" (2 Ti.3:8).** see Ex.7:1; 8:7; 9:11. (See note—2 Ti.3:6-9).	The false messenger deceives people… • by claiming to be God's messenger (2 Co. 11:13-15) • by perverting the meaning of God's Word (Ga.1:6-10) • by seducing people to reject God's truth (2 Ti.4:3-4) • by denying the Lord who died for them (2 Pe.2:1; 1 Jn.4:1-3)	*"Beware of false prophets, which come to you in sheep's clothing, but inwardly they are ravening wolves" (Mt.7:15).* *"For such are false apostles, deceitful workers, transforming themselves into the apostles of Christ. And no marvel; for Satan himself is transformed into an angel of light. Therefore it is no great thing if his ministers also be transformed as the ministers of righteousness; whose end shall be according to their works" (2 Co.11:13-15).* *"Beloved, believe not every spirit, but try the spirits whether they are of God: because many false prophets are gone out into the world. Hereby know ye the Spirit of God: Every spirit that confesseth that Jesus Christ is come in the flesh is of God: And every spirit that confesseth not that Jesus Christ is come in the flesh is not of God" (1 Jn.4:1-3).* *(see Pr.6:19; 12:17; Mt.24:11; Ga.1:6-10; 1 Ti.6:3-5; 2 Ti. 4:3-4; 2 Pe.2:1; Is.56:10-12; Je.23:2; 50:6; Eze.34:2-3)*

	B. The First Plague—Water Changed to Blood: Proof that God is the LORD, the God of Salvation, the Only Living & True God, 7:14-25	Egypt, upon their streams, upon their rivers, and upon their ponds, and upon all their pools of water, that they may become blood; and that there may be blood throughout all the land of Egypt, both in vessels of wood, and in vessels of stone.	

1. The tragic situation that caused the judgment: Pharaoh's heart was hard against God—he refused to free God's people	14 And the LORD said unto Moses, Pharaoh's heart is hardened, he refuseth to let the people go.	20 And Moses and Aaron did so, as the LORD commanded; and he lifted up the rod, and smote the waters that were in the river, in the sight of Pharaoh, and in the sight of his servants; and all the waters that were in the river were turned to blood.	**5. The day of judgment arrived**
			a. Moses & Aaron obeyed God
			  1) Lifted up the rod & struck the waters of the Nile
			  2) In the very presence of Pharaoh & his servants

2. The declaration of God's Word, His will
a. Moses was to intercept Pharaoh in the morning when he went out to the bank of the river
b. Moses was to take his rod (staff) with him
c. Moses was to proclaim God's Word, His will: Let God's people go—free them to serve & worship God
d. Moses was to charge Pharaoh with refusing to listen to God's Word & demand, with rejection & rebellion against God
	15 Get thee unto Pharaoh in the morning; lo, he goeth out unto the water; and thou shalt stand by the river's brink against he come; and the rod which was turned to a serpent shalt thou take in thine hand.
	16 And thou shalt say unto him, The LORD God of the Hebrews hath sent me unto thee, saying, Let my people go, that they may serve me in the wilderness: and, behold, hitherto thou wouldest not hear.
		21 And the fish that was in the river died; and the river stank, and the Egyptians could not drink of the water of the river; and there was blood throughout all the land of Egypt.	b. The judgment fell
			  1) The Nile river turned to blood
			  2) The fish died
			  3) The water stunk
			  4) The people could not drink the water
			  5) The blood was in all the water

3. The purpose of the judgment: To prove that God is the LORD, the God of salvation, redemption & deliverance, the only living and true God **4. The warning & pronouncement of judgment** a. God's judgment: The Nile[DS1] waters will be turned into blood b. The results: The water will be polluted, will stink, will be unfit to drink, & fish will die c. The great reach of the judgment: Was to include the streams, canals, & ponds or reservoirs	17 Thus saith the LORD, In this thou shalt know that I am the LORD: behold, I will smite with the rod that is in mine hand upon the waters which are in the river, and they shall be turned to blood. 18 And the fish that is in the river shall die, and the river shall stink; and the Egyptians shall loathe to drink of the water of the river. 19 And the LORD spake unto Moses, Say unto Aaron, Take thy rod, and stretch out thine hand upon the waters of	22 And the magicians of Egypt did so with their enchantments: and Pharaoh's heart was hardened, neither did he hearken unto them; as the LORD had said. 23 And Pharaoh turned and went into his house, neither did he set his heart to this also. 24 And all the Egyptians digged round about the river for water to drink; for they could not drink of the water of the river. 25 And seven days were fulfilled, after that the LORD had smitten the river.	**6. The response to God's judgment** a. The false messengers (magicians) imitated the miracle: Used their secret arts b. Pharaoh's heart became harder: He returned to the palace & refused to heed the judgment c. The people: Dug wells for water

DIVISION III

THE TEN PLAGUES AND EGYPT: GOD'S JUDGMENT UPON THOSE WHO REJECT HIM AND OPPRESS HIS PEOPLE, 7:8–11:10

B. The First Plague—Water Changed to Blood: Proof that God is the LORD, the God of Salvation, the Only Living and True God, 7:14-25

(7:14-25) **Introduction—Gods, False**: there are many gods, but only one true and living God. Throughout the ages, man's imagination has run wild with images of God. Consequently, man has created gods within his own mind and often formed idols made out of wood, metal, and stone. People even worship the sun, moon, and stars of the sky, studying what they call the Zodiac, hoping to determine what destiny the stars hold for their lives. Some men even worship themselves, despite their imperfect, depraved, dying flesh and minds. Just imagine! How foolish—how terribly unthinking, dishonest, and deceptive—we can be; and far too often we are.

This was Pharaoh and the Egyptians. They worshipped false gods—many gods. But they were also guilty of another terrible evil, that of enslaving and mistreating people, even entire races of people. Thus the hand of God's judgment was ready to fall upon Egypt and its people. For generations God had been patient, giving the people of Egypt time to repent and acknowledge Him as the living and true God. But neither the rulers nor the people ever repented. They continued on in their false, idolatrous religions and evil ways. They had even enslaved the only people upon earth who were following the true and living God: they had enslaved Israel, the very people created by God to bear the promised seed, the Savior of the world, the Lord Jesus Christ.

God had no choice. Through Moses, He had warned the ruler of Egypt, Pharaoh himself: "Let my people go—free them." But the king had refused. Thus God had to judge and chastise Egypt in order to free His people so they could fulfill God's great promises upon earth: the promises of the promised land and of the promised seed. (See DEEPER STUDY # 2—Ex.1:6-7; DEEPER STUDY # 1—Ex.2:24; outline and notes—Ge.12:1-3 for more discussion.)

The hand of God's judgment was now ready to fall. God was ready to bring the plagues of judgment upon Egypt. This passage covers, *The First Plague—Water Changed to Blood: Proof that God is the LORD, the God of Salvation, the Only Living and True God,* 7:14-25.

1. The tragic situation that caused the judgment: Pharaoh's heart was hard against God—he refused to free God's people (v.14).
2. The declaration of God's Word, His will (vv.15-16).
3. The purpose of the judgment: to prove that God is the LORD, the God of salvation, redemption, and deliverance, the only living and true God (v.17).
4. The warning and pronouncement of judgment (vv.17-19).
5. The day of judgment arrived (vv.20-21).
6. The response to God's judgment (vv.22-25).

1 (7:14) **Heart, Hard—Hard—Pharaoh**: there was the tragic situation that caused the judgment: Pharaoh's heart was hard against God—he refused to free God's people. God had already sent His messenger to Pharaoh on two different occasions, once to appeal to him and a second time to warn him. But Pharaoh had hardened his heart and refused to listen. He flatly refused to repent, refused to free God's people to worship and serve God. He was stiff-necked, obstinate, hard, rock-hard, unyielding. It was this—hardness of heart against God, an unyielding heart—that brought the judgment of the plagues upon Pharaoh and his people.

Thought 1. The very thing that brings the judgment and chastisement of God upon us is hardness of heart, an unyielding heart against God.

"**Happy is the man that feareth alway: but he that hardeneth his heart shall fall into mischief [trouble, judgment]**" (Pr.28:14).

"**He, that being often reproved hardeneth his neck, shall suddenly be destroyed, and that without remedy**" (Pr.29:1).

"**If ye will not hear, and if ye will not lay it to heart, to give glory unto my name, saith the LORD of hosts, I will even send a curse upon you, and I will curse your blessings: yea, I have cursed them already, because ye do not lay it to heart**" (Mal.2:2).

"**Or despisest thou the riches of his goodness and forbearance and longsuffering; not knowing that the goodness of God leadeth thee to repentance? But after thy hardness and impenitent heart treasurest up unto thyself wrath against the day of wrath and revelation of the righteous judgment of God; who will render to every man according to his deeds**" (Ro.2:4-6).

2 (7:15-16) **Liberty—Freedom**: there was the declaration of God's Word, His will.

a. God told Moses to intercept Pharaoh in the morning when he went out to the bank of the Nile River (v.15). Why would Pharaoh be going out to the Nile River in the morning?
  ⇒ To bathe?
  ⇒ To take a morning walk?
  ⇒ To see if the Nile River was rising, indicating that the flood season was about to begin?
  ⇒ To have morning devotions, worshipping the Nile River, the god Hapi or Nilus? (Remember the Nile River was worshipped and thought to be sacred, just as the Ganges is worshipped and thought to be sacred by the Hindus.) (See DIVISION OVERVIEW, note 6—Ex.7:8-11:10 for more discussion.)

b. Moses was to take his rod (staff) with him (v.15). Remember, the rod was a symbol of God's power and authority.

c. Moses was to proclaim God's Word, His will: "Let God's people go—free them to serve and worship God" (v.16). Keep in mind the terrible oppression of God's people. They were suffering unbelievable brutality and savagery: the Egyptians had enslaved them. God's will is for no people to be oppressed, for there to be no enslavement upon earth. But in particular, God objects to the oppression of His people, of those who truly believe and follow after Him. This was the very thing God was after in Moses' day, the freedom and liberty of His people (Israel). This was the message Moses was to proclaim: Pharaoh and Egypt were to let God's people go—free them, set them at liberty—so they could live in freedom and worship and serve Him.

d. Moses was to charge Pharaoh with refusing to listen to God's Word and demand, with rejection and rebellion against God (v.16).

Thought 1. There should be no slavery, no oppression of any people or race, not even of a single person. Oppression and slavery are evil: they stand opposed—diametrically opposed—to God's holy Word and will. Governments, rulers, lawmakers, and oppressors of God's people must hear and heed. God's Word is clear: God loudly proclaims for all to hear, "Let my people go! Free them to live, serve, and worship me." God's will is for people to love one another not oppress one another. God wants us to love one another and to treat our neighbors as we want to be treated.

"**But the stranger that dwelleth with you shall be unto you as one born among you, and thou shalt love him as thyself; for ye were strangers in the land of Egypt: I am the LORD your God**" (Le.19:34).

"**...proclaim liberty throughout all the land unto all the inhabitants thereof....**" (Le.25:10).

"Love ye therefore the stranger: for ye were strangers in the land of Egypt" (De.10:19).

"But I say unto you, Love your enemies, bless them that curse you, do good to them that hate you, and pray for them which despitefully use you, and persecute you" (Mt.5:44).

"And the second [great commandment is] like unto it, Thou shalt love thy neighbour as thyself" (Mt.22:39).

"And the second [is] like, namely this, Thou shalt love thy neighbour as thyself. There is none other commandment greater than these" (Mk.12:31).

"This is my commandment, That ye love one another, as I have loved you" (Jn.15:12).

"Let love be without dissimulation [hypocrisy]. Abhor that which is evil; cleave to that which is good" (Ro.12:9).

"Therefore if thine enemy hunger, feed him; if he thirst, give him drink: for in so doing thou shalt heap coals of fire on his head" (Ro.12:20).

"Love worketh no ill to his neighbour: therefore love is the fulfilling of the law" (Ro.13:10).

"For all the law is fulfilled in one word, even in this; Thou shalt love thy neighbour as thyself" (Ga.5:14).

"If ye fulfil the royal law according to the scripture, Thou shalt love thy neighbour as thyself, ye do well" (Js.2:8).

3 (7:17) **Pharaoh—Judgment:** the purpose of the judgment was to prove that God is the LORD, the God of salvation, redemption, and deliverance, the only living and true God. Pharaoh worshipped false gods, but even more than this, Pharaoh himself was considered a god in Egypt. He held supreme power over the land and people. Pharaoh even thought of himself as a god, as the molder and maker of Egypt and its people. He no doubt felt what so many people feel about themselves today, that he determined his own fate and the fate of his people: their lives, comfort, welfare, and destiny.

Pharaoh had earlier declared, "I do not know the Lord" (Ex.5:2). Now God was going to help Pharaoh know *the Lord*—just who God is. Pharaoh was to learn that neither he nor any other idol were true gods. They were nothing in the face of God Himself, nothing but the mere creations of man's imaginations. God was going to prove...

*   that He and He alone is the LORD, the God of redemption, the only God who can truly save and deliver man
*   that He and He alone is the only living and true God

"As the hart panteth after the water brooks, so panteth my soul after thee, O God. My soul thirsteth for God, for the living God: when shall I come and appear before God?" (Ps.42:1-2).

"My soul longeth, yea, even fainteth for the courts of the LORD: my heart and my flesh crieth out for the living God" (Ps.84:2).

"I [Darius] make a decree, That in every dominion of my kingdom men tremble and fear before the God of Daniel: for he is the living God, and stedfast for ever, and his kingdom that which shall not be destroyed, and his dominion shall be even unto the end" (Da.6:26).

"And [Paul and Barnabas] saying, Sirs, why do ye these things? We also are men of like passions with you, and preach unto you that ye should turn from these vanities unto the living God, which made heaven, and earth, and the sea, and all things that are therein" (Ac.14:15).

"For they themselves show of us what manner of entering in we had unto you, and how ye turned to God from idols to serve the living and true God" (1 Th.1:9).

"It is a fearful thing to fall into the hands of the living God" (He.10:31).

Thought 1. The earth is filled with the remains of men who thought they could...
*   fill the role of God in their lives
*   mold and make their own lives
*   blaze their own path in life
*   determine their own destiny and fate
*   set their own future and success

In the strongest of terms, history reveals their failure, the utter futility of their efforts to rule over life. Following is a partial list of some men who attempted to be God, and failed.

⇒ Adam	• Ate of the forbidden fruit tree in an attempt to be like God.	"For God doth know that in the day ye eat thereof, then your eyes shall be opened, and ye shall be as gods, knowing good and evil" (Ge.3:5).
⇒ Pharaoh	• Did not know Moses' God: he was not interested in knowing the only living and true God.	"And Pharaoh said, Who *is* the LORD, that I should obey his voice to let Israel go? I know not the LORD, neither will I let Israel go" (Ex.5:2).
⇒ Nebuchadnezzar	• Demanded that his own image be worshipped, worshipped by the three Hebrew slaves: Shadrach, Meshach and Abednego.	"Now if ye be ready that at what time ye hear the sound of the cornet, flute, harp, sackbut, psaltery, and dulcimer, and all kinds of musick, ye fall down and worship the image which I have made; *well:* but if ye worship not, ye shall be cast the same hour into the midst of a burning fiery furnace; and who *is* that God that shall deliver you out of my hands?" (Da.3:15).

| ⇒ Herod | • Sought the worship and honor of men, the worship and honor that belonged to God alone. | "And upon a set day Herod, arrayed in royal apparel, sat upon his throne, and made an oration unto them. And the people gave a shout, *saying, It is* the voice of a god, and not of a man. And immediately the angel of the Lord smote him, because he gave not God the glory: and he was eaten of worms, and gave up the ghost" (Ac.12:21-23). |

Have men who are outside the record of Scripture fared any better than these Biblical characters? No!

1) *Alexander the Great*, the Greek ruler who conquered the great Persian Empire, placed himself in the lofty position of God. Just before he died in 323 B.C., Alexander ordered every Greek city to worship him as a god. After he died of a fever, people for the most part annulled his command and went about their lives—obeying the dictates of other gods.

2) *Nero*, the fifth emperor of Rome, watched as Rome burned in 64 A.D. Many scholars believe that Nero placed blame for the fire on the Christian community in Rome. Jealous for their worship, he sought to destroy them, to cruelly persecute them. Four years later, Nero fled Rome as an enemy of the Roman Senate. Life for Nero ended in 68 A.D. when he committed suicide.

3) *Adolph Hitler*, the evil leader of the German Third Reich, commanded blind devotion to him and to his cause. Forming a society that had no room for Christians, Jews, or minorities, Hitler boasted,

> *Nothing will prevent me from tearing up Christianity, root and branch...We are not out against a hundred-to-one different kinds of Christianity, but against Christianity itself. All people who profess creeds...are traitors to the people. Even those Christians who really want to serve the people...we have to suppress. I myself am a heathen to the core.*[1]

There were many Aryans, the "super-race" of men, who sold their souls to Hitler. The Nazi swastika replaced the cross of Christ as millions swore their allegiance to Hitler, even unto death. After many more millions of those who refused to worship Hitler were slaughtered, Hitler took his own life before he could be captured by the Allied troops in 1945. With his suicide, Hitler's kingdom died along with him.

4) *Voltaire* (Francois Marie Arouet de Voltaire, 1694-1778), a French writer and thinker, was a leader during the Enlightenment period of history. He was a vocal opponent of Christian thought. His writings denounced the supernatural, religion, and the power of the clergy. Stoked by an arrogant lack of fear of God, he set his life's course in order to destroy Christianity. Obviously, he failed as Walter B. Knight notes:

> =*One day Voltaire said to a friend, "It took twelve ignorant fishermen to establish Christianity; I will show the world how one Frenchman can destroy it." Setting to his task, he openly ridiculed Sir Isaac Newton. One day Newton made a prophecy based on Dan. 12:4 and Nahum 2:4 when he said, "Man will some day be able to travel at the tremendous speed of 40 miles an hour." Voltaire replied with, "See what a fool Christianity makes of an otherwise brilliant man, such as Sir Isaac Newton! Doesn't he know that if man traveled 40 miles an hour, he would suffocate and his heart would stop?"*
> *Twenty-five years after Voltaire died, his home was purchased by the Geneva Bible Society and became a Bible storage building, and his printing press was used to print an entire edition of the Bible.*[2]

When Voltaire died, the nurse who stood by his bed said, *"I never want to see another infidel die."*[3]

5) *Thomas Hobbes* (1588-1679), a well known English philosopher and infidel, was a humorist. He set man up to be his own god. As he lay dying, he screamed out, *"I'm taking a fearful leap out into the dark."*[4]

6) Robert Ingersoll (1833-1899) was a staunch unbeliever and agnostic. He had a strong distaste for the LORD and for belief in a personal God. He believed that man himself was most likely the only true god, the only person who really determined the fate and destiny of the world. He said as he stood by his brother's grave, *"The curtain falls, will it ever rise again?"*[5]

[1] Walter B. Knight. *3,000 Illustrations for Christian Service* (Grand Rapids, MI: Eerdmans Publishing Co., 1971), p. 23.

[2] ibid., p. 24.

[3] Grady Wilson. Pamphlet of a sermon preached on "The Hour of Decision," no. 192. (The Billy Graham Evangelistic Association, 1970), p.2.

[4] ibid., p.2.

[5] Grady Wilson. Pamphlet of a sermon preached on "The Hour of Decision," no. 192. (The Billy Graham Evangelistic Association, 1970), p.2.

"I *am* the LORD thy God, which have brought thee out of the land of Egypt, out of the house of bondage. Thou shalt have no other gods before me. Thou shalt not make unto thee any graven image, or any likeness of any thing that is in heaven above, or that is in the earth beneath, or that is in the water under the earth: Thou shalt not bow down thyself to them, nor serve them: for I the Lord thy God am a jealous God, visiting the iniquity of the fathers upon the children unto the third and fourth generation of them that hate me" (Ex.20:2-5).

"And it shall be, if thou do at all forget the Lord thy God, and walk after other gods, and serve them, and worship them, I testify against you this day that ye shall surely perish" (De.8:19).

"Lord, how are they increased that trouble me! many are they that rise up against me. Many there be which say of my soul, There is no help for him in God" (Ps.3:1-2).

"The fool hath said in his heart, There is no God. They are corrupt, they have done abominable works, there is none that doeth good" (Ps.14:1).

"The fear of the Lord is the beginning of wisdom: and the knowledge of the holy is understanding" (Pr.9:10).

"There is a way that seemeth right unto a man, but the end thereof are the ways of death" (Pr.16:25).

"Then Paul stood in the midst of Mars' hill, and said, Ye men of Athens, I perceive that in all things ye are too superstitious. For as I passed by, and beheld your devotions, I found an altar with this inscription, TO THE UNKNOWN GOD. Whom therefore ye ignorantly worship, him declare I unto you" (Ac.17:22-23).

---

4 (7:17-19) **Judgment—Nile River**: there was the warning and pronouncement of judgment. Note the description of the judgment that was coming, that was to fall upon the ungodliness and unrighteousness of people who rejected God and oppressed people:

⇒ The Nile waters would be turned into blood.
⇒ The water would be polluted and unusable.
⇒ The fish would die and the water would stink.
⇒ The water would not be fit to drink.
⇒ The great reach of the judgment was to include all the waters of Egypt: the streams, canals, and the ponds or reservoirs.

Was the water turned into real blood? Some commentators say no, that God caused a natural disaster to happen that discolored the water to look like blood. It is felt that a red sediment flowed down from Ethiopia into the Nile that turned the water red, that God caused such heavy rains and flooding that an enormous tonnage of the sediment flowed down into the Nile. Moreover, the flooding washed a fish-killing algae down the river, enough algae to kill the oxygen level of the river that caused the fish to die.

Other commentators feel that God turned the water into actual blood. They feel that this is the only adequate explanation that covers the events that followed the flooding.

Whatever the case, the turning of the Nile into blood was done at God's bidding and timing. Whatever changes took place in the water of the Nile, the changes killed the fish, made the water stink, and made the water undrinkable. God caused the water to become contaminated, and whatever contaminated the water was red, just like blood, if not blood itself. It killed the fish and caused the river to stink and to be undrinkable.

Thought 1. God has given warning after warning: we shall be judged for the sins we have committed. Every one of us shall give an account to God. We shall stand before God and be judged for the things we have done on this earth. One fact is unquestionable, absolutely certain: statistically, one hundred percent of us shall die. We shall die and face God in judgment.

"I the LORD search the heart, I try the reins, even to give every man according to his ways, and according to the fruit of his doings" (Je.17:10).

"And as it is appointed unto men once to die, but after this the judgment" (He.9:27).

"For the Son of man shall come in the glory of his Father with his angels; and then he shall reward every man according to his works" (Mt.16:27).

"For we must all appear before the judgment seat of Christ; that every one may receive the things done in his body, according to that he hath done, whether it be good or bad" (2 Co.5:10).

"And if ye call on the Father, who without respect of persons judgeth according to every man's work, pass the time of your sojourning here in fear" (1 Pe.1:17).

"And I saw the dead, small and great, stand before God; and the books were opened: and another book was opened, which is the book of life: and the dead were judged out of those things which were written in the books, according to their works" (Re.20:12).

"And, behold, I come quickly; and my reward is with me, to give every man according as his work shall be" (Re.22:12).

DEEPER STUDY # 1

(7:17-19) River, Nile: this mighty river has a celebrated and noteworthy history that has impacted Egyptian life for thousands of years. The mighty Nile begins above Lake Victoria in the middle of the African continent at some point close to the equator. It stretches all the way to the Mediterranean Sea for a total of over 4,000 miles. The Nile flows through majestic mountains, through the arid desert of Egypt, and through tropical marshlands in the delta. Note these facts about the Nile River:

⇒ The river is the longest river in the world.
⇒ The river's source is the Kagera River in the nation of Tanzania. The Kagera spills into Lake Victoria.
⇒ The river flows *northward*.
⇒ The river is not called "the Nile" in Exodus. It is called "The River."
⇒ The river often floods, and its flood-waters have made the delta in Northern Egypt one of the most fertile regions in the world.
⇒ The river was where Moses' mother placed him in an ark and where Pharaoh's daughter found him.
⇒ The bank of the river is where papyrus reed grows so plentifully and fruitfully. The papyrus reed was the ancient writer's source of paper.
⇒ The river is called "Sihor" in the KJV in Isaiah 23:3.
⇒ The river was where Pharaoh wanted to drown the Hebrew male babies (Ex.1:22).
⇒ The river was directly related to two of the plagues in Exodus...
  • The water turned into blood (see 7:14-25).
  • The frogs that swarmed Egypt (see 8:1-15).

THE NILE[6]

5 (7:20-21) **Judgment—Nile River**: there was the day of judgment which fell upon the Egyptians.

a. Moses and Aaron obeyed God: they did exactly what God had told them to do (v.20). They lifted up the rod and struck the waters of the Nile, and they did it in the very presence of Pharaoh and all his servants.

b. The judgment of God immediately fell upon the Nile River (vv.20-21).
⇒ The Nile River turned to blood.
⇒ The fish died.
⇒ The water stunk.
⇒ The people could not drink the water.
⇒ The blood was in all the water throughout Egypt.

The judgment was a frightening plague. Vast rolling streams of blood or of some blood-like material began to flow down through the river in full view of all onlookers. Word of the catastrophe must have spread like wildfire all throughout Egypt. The economy of Egypt was threatened. Think of the effect upon...
  • the fishing industry, with no fish to harvest and sell
  • the farming industry, with no water for irrigation and crops
  • the food and water supply for the people
  • the utter disruption of day-to-day life

_____

6 Map from *Life Application*® *Bible*. Used by permission.

First, note that this was a righteous and just judgment. The Egyptians were a brutal, savage, and hard-hearted people. Moreover, they had rejected the Creator of the universe, the only living and true God. They had lived the life of indulgence, luxury, and plenty, of comfort and ease. But now, they were to learn the hand of discipline and chastisement. God's judgment and justice were falling upon them for all the evil they had done. They had lived a life of worldly pleasure and worldly religion; now they were to live under the judgment of God. God was executing upon them the just measure of their sins and evil.

Second, God's purpose for this judgment was obviously achieved. Remember, the Nile was worshipped as a god, a god named Hopi or Nilus. The spirit of some god was thought to control the waters of the river. Consequently, the Egyptians prayed to the Nile, prayed for a good supply of water for drink, irrigation, and crops. Think of the impact when the God of Moses brought utter devastation to the god of the Nile: the thoughts of the Egyptians that their god was not as powerful as the God of Moses. The sight of rolling streams of blood flowing down through the Nile must have stricken the people with fright and horror. The attention of many Egyptians was soon beginning to focus upon the only living and true God. They were beginning to think more and more about the God of Moses, the God who had such power.

Thought 1. The day of judgment is coming: the hand of justice will fall upon the world. God is going to judge us, every one of us.

> **"When the Son of man shall come in his glory, and all the holy angels with him, then shall he sit upon the throne of his glory: And before him shall be gathered all nations: and he shall separate them one from another, as a shepherd divideth [his] sheep from the goats: And he shall set the sheep on his right hand, but the goats on the left" (Mt.25:31-33).**
> **"The Lord knoweth how to deliver the godly out of temptations, and to reserve the unjust unto the day of judgment to be punished" (2 Pe.2:9).**
> **"But the heavens and the earth, which are now, by the same word are kept in store, reserved unto fire against the day of judgment and perdition of ungodly men" (2 Pe.3:7).**
> **"And Enoch also, the seventh from Adam, prophesied of these, saying, Behold, the Lord cometh with ten thousands of his saints, To execute judgment upon all, and to convince all that are ungodly among them of all their ungodly deeds which they have ungodly committed, and of all their hard speeches which ungodly sinners have spoken against him" (Jude 14-15).**

6 (7:22-25) **Judgment—Heart, Hard—Miracles, Demonic**: there was the response to God's judgment.

a. The false messengers (magicians) imitated the miracle. They used their secret arts to turn some small quantity of water into what appeared to be blood (v.22). Where did the magicians get fresh water? From the wells being dug by the people (see v.24). How were the magicians able to turn fresh water into what appeared to be blood?

⇒ Did they use some enchantment, some chant and dance, and while they were dancing around, they threw some chemical into a small quantity of water that caused it to change into a blood-red color?
⇒ Did God allow Satan to imitate the same miracle through these false messengers and magicians?

Scripture does not say how the magicians duplicated the miracle. But Scripture does teach that Satan and his false messengers are especially strong in the power of deception. Remember: ever since Adam and Eve, Satan has deceived the whole human race and led them away from God, except for a few believers here and there. False messengers are clever and skillful. They lay their plans ever so carefully and are usually successful in carrying out their deceitful plans. The magicians and priests of Pharaoh had their very reputation at stake in the confrontation with God's messenger, Moses. They would leap at any chance they had to enhance and hold their position as one of the key officials of Pharaoh's court. Thus, when the "father of lies," Satan, suggested to their minds some clever method of imitating the miracle performed by Moses, they jumped at the idea and deceived the eyes of Pharaoh and the other onlookers standing there.

How do we know that the magical feat performed by the magicians was a deception? By this: if the magicians had possessed real godly power, they would have turned the bloody waters back into pure waters. This feat would have been a true miracle, and far more helpful and beneficial to the people of Egypt.

> **"Jesus answered them, Verily, verily, I say unto you, Whosoever committeth sin is the servant of sin" (Jn.8:34).**
> **"But if our gospel be hid, it is hid to them that are lost: In whom the god of this world hath blinded the minds of them which believe not, lest the light of the glorious gospel of Christ, who is the image of God, should shine unto them" (2 Co.4:3-4).**
> **"For such are false apostles, deceitful workers, transforming themselves into the apostles of Christ. And no marvel; for Satan himself is transformed into an angel of light. Therefore it is no great thing if his ministers also be transformed as the ministers of righteousness; whose end shall be according to their works" (2 Co.11:13-15).**
> **"Put on the whole armour of God, that ye may be able to stand against the wiles [strategies] of the devil. For we wrestle not against flesh and blood, but against principalities, against powers, against the rulers of the darkness of this world, against spiritual wickedness in high places" (Ep.6:11-12).**
> **"Be sober, be vigilant; because your adversary the devil, as a roaring lion, walketh about, seeking whom he may devour" (1 Pe.5:8).**

b. Pharaoh's heart became harder: he returned to the palace and refused to heed the judgment (vv.22-23). The magical or secret arts of the magicians gave Pharaoh an excuse for not heeding the judgment of God. He was hard, obstinate, and determined not to listen to the messengers of God. Tragically, he just was not going to let God's people go—not free them to live, worship, and serve God. He turned and went into his palace, refusing to learn from the lesson of this judgment.

c. The people dug wells for water (v.24). They were forced to dig for fresh water because all the waters throughout the land of Egypt had become contaminated. They were reaping the results of their sin and evil, the sin of idolatry and the evil of enslaving and brutalizing other people.

> **Thought 1**. We must absolutely guard ourselves against a hard heart. We must learn from this judgment that fell upon the ancient Egyptians. We must repent and turn from our evil ways, lest we too bring the judgment of God upon our heads.

> > "**Let the wicked forsake his way, and the unrighteous man his thoughts: and let him return unto the LORD, and he will have mercy upon him; and to our God, for he will abundantly pardon**" (Is.55:7).
> > "**Cast away from you all your transgressions, whereby ye have transgressed; and make you a new heart and a new spirit: for why will ye die?**" (Eze.18:31).
> > "**I tell you, Nay: but, except ye repent, ye shall all likewise perish**" (Lu.13:3).
> > "**Repent therefore of this thy wickedness, and pray God, if perhaps the thought of thine heart may be forgiven thee**" (Ac.8:22).

CHAPTER 8

C. The Second Plague—Frogs Everywhere: Proof That God Has No Equal, That No One Is Like the LORD Our God, 8:1-15

Outline	Scripture	Notes
1. The declaration of God's Word (given seven days after the first plague, 7:25): Let God's people go—free them to serve & worship God	And the LORD spake unto Moses, Go unto Pharaoh, and say unto him, Thus saith the LORD, Let my people go, that they may serve me.	brought up frogs upon the land of Egypt.	a. The false messengers (magicians) imitated the miracle
2. The warning & pronouncement of judgment	2 And if thou refuse to let them go, behold, I will smite all thy borders with frogs:	8 Then Pharaoh called for Moses and Aaron, and said, Intreat the LORD, that he may take away the frogs from me, and from my people; and I will let the people go, that they may do sacrifice unto the LORD.	b. Pharaoh cried for deliverance
a. The cause for judgment: Rejecting God—oppressing people	3 And the river shall bring forth frogs abundantly, which shall go up and come into thine house, and into thy bedchamber, and upon thy bed, and into the house of thy servants, and upon thy people, and into thine ovens, and into thy kneading-troughs:	9 And Moses said unto Pharaoh, Glory over me: when shall I intreat for thee, and for thy servants, and for thy people, to destroy the frogs from thee and thy houses, that they may remain in the river only?	1) Pharaoh called for the messengers of God: Asked for relief, that God take the frogs away
b. The judgment: The Nile will swarm with frogs			2) Promised to free God's people: To let them go & offer sacrifices to God
1) Vast numbers will be in homes, bedrooms, & beds			**5. The purpose for the judgment**
2) Vast numbers will be on people, in ovens, & in kneading-bowls		10 And he said, To morrow. And he said, Be it according to thy word: that thou mayest know that there is none like unto the LORD our God.	a. To challenge Pharaoh to test the power of God
3) Vast numbers will be on everyone: No person will escape	4 And the frogs shall come up both on thee, and upon thy people, and upon all thy servants.	11 And the frogs shall depart from thee, and from thy houses, and from thy servants, and from thy people; they shall remain in the river only.	1) Moses told Pharaoh to set the time for the frogs' removal (by setting the time, he would know their removal was not by chance)
			2) Pharaoh's quick response: Tomorrow
3. The day of judgment arrived	5 And the LORD spake unto Moses, Say unto Aaron, Stretch forth thine hand with thy rod over the streams, over the rivers, and over the ponds, and cause frogs to come up upon the land of Egypt.	12 And Moses and Aaron went out from Pharaoh: and Moses cried unto the LORD because of the frogs which he had brought against Pharaoh.	b. To prove that God has no equal, no one is like the LORD our God
a. The Lord gave the commandment to Moses: Instruct Aaron to execute the judgment			1) He is the LORD of all power, the LORD who executes justice
		13 And the LORD did according to the word of Moses; and the frogs died out of the houses, out of the villages, and out of the fields.	2) He is the LORD of mercy, deliverance, and salvation as well as the LORD of justice
b. Aaron obeyed: Stretched out his arms over the waters	6 And Aaron stretched out his hand over the waters of Egypt; and the frogs came up, and covered the land of Egypt.	14 And they gathered them together upon heaps: and the land stank.	**6. The deliverance from judgment**
			a. God's messenger interceded, cried out for deliverance
c. The judgment fell: Frogs covered the land			b. God heard His messenger, stopped the judgment
		15 But when Pharaoh saw that there was respite, he hardened his heart, and hearkened not unto them; as the LORD had said.	1) The frogs dropped dead right where they were
			2) The people stacked the frogs into heaps
			3) The odor filled the land
4. The response to the judgment: A cry for deliverance	7 And the magicians did so with their enchantments, and		**7. The sin of turning back: Once the judgment was removed, Pharaoh hardened his heart & refused to heed the warning**

DIVISION III

THE TEN PLAGUES AND EGYPT: GOD'S JUDGMENT UPON THOSE WHO REJECT HIM AND OPPRESS HIS PEOPLE, 7:8–11:10

C. The Second Plague—Frogs Everywhere: Proof That God Has No Equal, That No One Is Like the LORD Our God, 8:1-15

(8:1-15) **Introduction**: no one is like the LORD our God. He has no equal; He and He alone is the only living and true God.

Remember, Pharaoh was considered to be a god by the Egyptians. He even thought of himself as a god. He was as so many people are within every generation, so confident in the abilities and power of man that they exalt man to be god. Far, far too often, man exalts himself to be god.

⇒ Some people exalt the spirit of man (the combined spirit of all people) to be god. They suggest that the combined spirit of all people is all that is needed to develop society and meet the needs of people. A pointed question to ask against this position is this: What generation of people will experience the development of society that fully meets the needs of people? What generation of people will know no brutality, lawlessness, immorality, and know the peace, security, and the plenty of a "heaven on earth"?

⇒ Others suggest that each of us has a spirit that will be reincarnated into some other form of life at death. In this way we live on and on, from generation to generation, ever developing and progressing into a more and more perfect person. A pointed question to ask against this particular position is this: What about each person's desire to know completeness, fulfillment, and security while he is living upon this earth? What about our need to have the assurance of forgiveness of sins and of living forever in a perfect world? If man is reincarnated into some other form of life, what happens in the future when the earth and the universe wear down, as scientists tell us the universe is doing?

On and on the list of humanistic, man-made philosophies could be given, but the point is clear and dramatic: there is no person—no man and no spirit—like the LORD our God.

⇒ No one but the LORD can truly forgive sins.
⇒ No one but the LORD can give perfect assurance of living forever in the promised land of heaven.
⇒ No one but the LORD can fully satisfy and fulfill the longings and needs of the human heart and mind.
⇒ No one but the LORD can teach us "the depth of the riches both of the wisdom and knowledge of God" (Ro.11:33).
⇒ No one but the LORD could ever die for our sins, could ever pay the perfect price that would cover the punishment for our sins.
⇒ No one but the LORD could ever arise from the dead, conquering death.
⇒ No one but the LORD could ever give us victory day by day over all the trials and temptations of this life.

A world of facts could be declared about the LORD our God—all proclaiming His Person and work, that He has no equal. The LORD is the only living and true God. There is no one like God.

But note, the Egyptians had rejected God and turned to the evil ways of this sinful world, turned to idolatry and to the brutalizing and enslaving of people. Because of their evil, God's judgment had begun to fall upon the nation in a series of plagues. The first plague had just been launched, but the Egyptians still refused to heed God's call to repentance and mercy. They still refused to let God's people go—still refused to free God's people to live, worship, and serve God in liberty and justice for all. Now the second plague was about to be launched by God. This is: *The Second Plague—Frogs Everywhere: Proof That God Has No Equal, That No One Is Like the LORD Our God,* 8:1-15.

1. The declaration of God's Word (given seven days after the first plague, 7:25): let God's people go—free them to serve and worship God (v.1).
2. The warning and pronouncement of judgment: frogs everywhere (vv.2-4).
3. The day of judgment arrived (vv.5-6).
4. The response to the judgment: a cry for deliverance (vv.7-8).
5. The purpose for the judgment (vv.9-11).
6. The deliverance from judgment (vv.12-14).
7. The sin of turning back: once the judgment was removed, Pharaoh hardened his heart and refused to heed the warning (v.15).

1 (8:1) **Freedom—Liberty**: the declaration of God's Word (given seven days after the first plague, 7:25): let God's people go—free them to live and serve God. What now happened took place seven days after the first plague had fallen upon Egypt (7:25). This suggests that the ten plagues probably took place within a short period of time, one right after the other. By rolling in upon one another, the impact upon Pharaoh and his people would be forceful. They would be shaken to the core and know one fact beyond question: the LORD God proclaimed by Moses was the only living and true God, the LORD, the true Savior of man.

Now note the message proclaimed by Moses: let God's people go—free them to serve God. God's will is for people to live in freedom and liberty. The right of freedom is a God-given right...

• freedom of life
• freedom of work
• freedom of worship

Thought 1. No person, nation, government, or armed force is to deny people this God-given right. People are not to be enslaved; they are not to be oppressed. God did not create people to be abused, brutalized, and persecuted. God created man to live a life of love, work, service, and worship—all under His care and provision.

This was the message Moses was to declare to Pharaoh and the Egyptians. They were to let God's people go—free them to serve and live for Him.

"**The rich and poor meet together: the LORD is the maker of them all**" (Pr.22:2).

"**The Spirit of the Lord GOD is upon me; because the LORD hath anointed me to preach good tidings unto the meek; he hath sent me to bind up the brokenhearted, to proclaim liberty to the captives, and the opening of the prison to them that are bound**" (Is.61:1).

"**But be not ye called Rabbi: for one is your Master, [even] Christ; and all ye are brethren**" (Mt.23:8).

"**And he said unto them, Ye know how that it is an unlawful thing for a man that is a Jew to keep company, or come unto one of another nation; but God hath showed me that I should not call any man common or unclean**" (Ac.10:28).

"**For there is no difference between the Jew and the Greek: for the same Lord over all is rich unto all that call upon him**" (Ro.10:12).

"**There is neither Jew nor Greek, there is neither bond nor free, there is neither male nor female: for ye are all one in Christ Jesus**" (Ga.3:28).

"For, brethren, ye have been called unto liberty; only use not liberty for an occasion to the flesh, but by love serve one another" (Ga.5:13).

"As free, and not using your liberty for a cloke of maliciousness, but as the servants of God" (1 Pe.2:16).

2 (8:2-4) **Judgment—Plagues—Egypt**: the warning and pronouncement of judgment: frogs everywhere. Note that this was only the warning of judgment to come. Pharaoh was given time to repent and obey God: he was given time to free God's people.

a. There was one major cause for the judgment: Pharaoh rejected God and refused to stop the oppression of God's people. Under no circumstances was he going to give up the flow of wealth that Egypt received from the cheap labor of the Israelites. To free the Israelites would have collapsed the economy of Egypt. Most if not all the construction projects would be stopped dead in their tracks, and the agricultural industries of the nation would be ruined. Egypt would be devastated, and the Egyptian people would be forced to live sacrificially until they themselves could restructure their nation around their own labor force. There is no way Pharaoh was going to free the 2 million plus Israelites slaves. Human rights—the morality of slavery and oppression—had nothing to do with the situation: it was all an economic and financial matter, a matter of greed and power and comfort and ease for those in power.

This was the cause for the judgment: the Egyptians were not going to free God's people no matter what God said, no matter how many people were oppressed, no matter how much the human rights of the Israelites were violated. The Egyptians rejected God's will, His demand that His people be freed. The Egyptians continued to oppress God's people.

Thought 1. People are far more important than things. People are far more important than even the economy of nations. Money and economy should never be based upon the abuse of human rights, never be structured upon the oppression and enslavement of people. But tragically, people are often oppressed in order to financially fill the pockets of others. Far too often people are oppressed through...

- low wages
- unjust wages (cheating)
- illegitimate labor
- overwork
- prostitution
- gambling

- stealing
- lying
- abuse
- slavery
- unjust laws
- misuse of authority

All for the purpose of financial gain. This is not God's will. God condemns the oppression of people. Rejecting God's Word and will causes the judgment of God to fall upon us.

"Also thou shalt not oppress a stranger: for ye know the heart of a stranger, seeing ye were strangers in the land of Egypt" (Ex.23:9).

"Thou shalt not oppress an hired servant that is poor and needy, whether he be of thy brethren, or of thy strangers that are in thy land within thy gates" (De.24:14).

"The LORD shall cut off all flattering lips, and the tongue that speaketh proud things: Who have said, With our tongue will we prevail; our lips are our own: who is lord over us? For the oppression of the poor, for the sighing of the needy, now will I arise, saith the LORD; I will set him in safety from him that puffeth at him" (Ps.12:3-5).

"Trust not in oppression, and become not vain in robbery: if riches increase, set not your heart upon them" (Ps.62:10).

"Envy thou not the oppressor, and choose none of his ways. For the froward [perverse] is abomination to the LORD: but his secret is with the righteous" (Pr.3:31-32).

"He that oppresseth the poor reproacheth his Maker: but he that honoureth him hath mercy on the poor" (Pr.14:31).

"He that oppresseth the poor to increase his riches, and he that giveth to the rich, shall surely come to want" (Pr.22:16).

"If thou seest the oppression of the poor, and violent perverting of judgment and justice in a province, marvel not at the matter: for he that is higher than the highest regardeth; and there be higher than they" (Ec.5:8).

"And the word of the LORD came unto Zechariah, saying, Thus speaketh the LORD of hosts, saying, Execute true judgment, and show mercy and compassions every man to his brother: And oppress not the widow, nor the fatherless, the stranger, nor the poor; and let none of you imagine evil against his brother in your heart. But they refused to hearken, and pulled away the shoulder, and stopped their ears, that they should not hear. Yea, they made their hearts as an adamant stone, lest they should hear the law, and the words which the LORD of hosts hath sent in his spirit by the former prophets: therefore came a great wrath from the LORD of hosts. Therefore it is come to pass, that as he cried, and they would not hear; so they cried, and I would not hear, saith the LORD of hosts: But I scattered them with a whirlwind among all the nations whom they knew not. Thus the land was desolate after them, that no man passed through nor returned: for they laid the pleasant land desolate" (Zec.7:8-14).

b. Note the judgment that was to fall upon Egypt: the Nile River was to be swarmed with frogs (vv.2-4). Vast numbers of frogs were...
- to swarm in the homes, bedrooms, and even on the beds of the people
- to swarm on the people themselves, and in their ovens and kneading-bowls
- to swarm on all the people; not a single person was to escape the swarming frogs

What was to cause so many frogs to appear and to move away from their natural habitat, away from the Nile River and its canals?
⇒ Were the swarming frogs due to the contaminated water of the Nile? Remember this judgment fell just seven days after the waters of the Nile had been turned into blood (7:25).
⇒ Were the swarming frogs due to the flooding of the Nile during the rainy season? Were the swarming frogs forced to high ground by the flooding waters?
⇒ Were the swarming frogs due to an immediate, miraculous reproduction or creation of frogs by God?

Scripture does not say where so many frogs came from. But whatever their source, God caused the judgment of the swarming frogs. Note: this was a prediction, a warning of coming judgment, an event that had not yet happened. But the judgment was going to happen if Pharaoh did not repent and obey God. Thus—no matter the source of the frogs, no matter where they were to come from—God Himself was to cause the swarming frogs to come forth. The judgment of swarming frogs was to be launched by God, by the miraculous hand of God Himself.

Thought 1. God warns us, judgment is to fall if we reject Him and oppress people. The rejection of God, of His Word, will cause the judgment of God to fall upon us:

"The hand of our God is upon all them for good that seek him; but his power and his wrath is against all them that forsake him" (Ezr.8:22).
"Because I have called, and ye refused; I have stretched out my hand, and no man regarded; But ye have set at nought all my counsel, and would [have] none of my reproof: I also will laugh at your calamity; I will mock when your fear cometh; When your fear cometh as desolation, and your destruction cometh as a whirlwind; when distress and anguish cometh upon you" (Pr.1:24-27).
"And I will utter my judgments against them touching all their wickedness, who have forsaken me, and have burned incense unto other gods, and worshipped the works of their own hands" (Je.1:16).
"He therefore that despiseth, despiseth not man, but God, who hath also given unto us his holy Spirit" (1 Th.4:8).
"And [the unjust] shall receive the reward of unrighteousness, as they that count it pleasure to riot [party] in the day time. Spots they are and blemishes, sporting themselves with their own deceivings while they feast with you; Having eyes full of adultery, and that cannot cease from sin; beguiling unstable souls: an heart they have exercised with covetous practices; cursed children: Which have forsaken the right way, and are gone astray, following the way of Balaam the son of Bosor, who loved the wages of unrighteousness" (2 Pe.2:13-15).

3 (8:5-6) **Judgment**: the day of judgment arrived. The Lord gave the commandment to Moses: instruct Aaron to execute the judgment. Aaron obeyed; he stretched out his arms over the water and the judgment fell. Frogs covered the land of Egypt.
The judgment was a horrible plague. To many people, frogs are repulsive, distasteful, disgusting, filthy, even contemptible. Just imagine vast numbers of frogs swarming: millions of frogs, frogs even in a person's home, hopping all over the furniture and in the oven and upon the dishes and utensils—so many frogs that they were even hopping all over the people themselves. The sight was so repulsive and grossly offensive that some people were, no doubt, almost driven out of their minds.

Thought 1. The day of judgment is coming. The person who has rejected God and has oppressed people will face the awful plague of God's eternal wrath.

"For the wrath of God is revealed from heaven against all ungodliness and unrighteousness of men, who hold the truth in unrighteousness....And even as they did not like to retain God in their knowledge, God gave them over to a reprobate mind, to do those things which are not convenient; Being filled with all unrighteousness, fornication, wickedness, covetousness, maliciousness; full of envy, murder, debate, deceit, malignity; whisperers, backbiters, haters of God, despiteful, proud, boasters, inventors of evil things, disobedient to parents, Without understanding, covenantbreakers, without natural affection, implacable, unmerciful: Who knowing the judgment of God, that they which commit such things are worthy of death, not only do the same, but have pleasure in them that do them" (Ro.1:18, 28-32).
"But the heavens and the earth, which are now, by the same word are kept in store, reserved unto fire against the day of judgment and perdition of ungodly men" (2 Pe.3:7).
"And Enoch also, the seventh from Adam, prophesied of these, saying, Behold, the Lord cometh with ten thousands of his saints, To execute judgment upon all, and to convince all that are ungodly among them of all their ungodly deeds which they have ungodly committed, and of all their hard speeches which ungodly sinners have spoken against him" (Jude 14-15).

"And I saw a great white throne, and him that sat on it, from whose face the earth and the heaven fled away; and there was found no place for them. And I saw the dead, small and great, stand before God; and the books were opened: and another book was opened, which is the book of life: and the dead were judged out of those things which were written in the books, according to their works. And the sea gave up the dead which were in it; and death and hell delivered up the dead which were in them: and they were judged every man according to their works. And death and hell were cast into the lake of fire. This is the second death. And whosoever was not found written in the book of life was cast into the lake of fire" (Re.20:11-15).

"But the fearful, and unbelieving, and the abominable, and murderers, and whoremongers, and sorcerers, and idolaters, and all liars, shall have their part in the lake which burneth with fire and brimstone: which is the second death" (Re.21:8).

4 (8:7-8) **Hypocrisy—Magicians**: there was the response to the judgment: a cry for deliverance.

a. The false messengers (magicians) imitated the miracle (v.7). They used their secret arts to seemingly cause some frogs to flee to higher ground. But just as before, the magical feat was obviously a deception. How do we know this? If the magicians had possessed real godly power, they would have removed the frogs of God's judgment. This was what Pharaoh and the people really needed, not more frogs. (See note—Ex.7:22-25 for more discussion.)

b. Pharaoh cried for deliverance (v.8). The magic feat of the magicians had apparently not impressed Pharaoh. He had wanted them to remove the frogs of God's judgment from the land of Egypt, not cause more frogs to invade the land.

Pharaoh immediately called for the messengers of God and he asked for relief, that God take the frogs away. Note that he promised to free God's people, to let them go and offer sacrifice to their LORD. He had been defiant; now he was crying out for God's mercy. He had rejected God's Word; now he was ready to obey God's Word.

Thought 1. Terrible, severe trials flood in upon us throughout life. We all experience some terrible trial such as...

- accident
- disease
- suffering
- financial crisis
- broken heart
- loneliness
- emptiness
- loss of job
- death

There are times throughout life when most of us cry out for God's deliverance and mercy. We become keenly aware of our failures, shortcomings, or sins. We realize that no man can help us, not really, that only God can help us. Consequently we cry out for God's mercy and help, for His deliverance. This was the experience of Pharaoh, and it is sometimes our experience. What we must do is make sure that when we turn to God, we are making a true profession and not a false profession. A false profession will condemn us to the eternal judgment of God.

"And they remembered that God was their rock, and the high God their redeemer. Nevertheless they did flatter him with their mouth, and they lied unto him with their tongues" (Ps.78:35-36).

"Hear ye this, O house of Jacob, which are called by the name of Israel, and are come forth out of the waters of Judah, which swear by the name of the LORD, and make mention of the God of Israel, but not in truth, nor in righteousness" (Is.48:1).

"And they [false professors] come unto thee as the people cometh, and they sit before thee as my people, and they hear thy words, but they will not do them: for with their mouth they show much love, but their heart goeth after their covetousness" (Eze.33:31).

"Not every one that saith unto me, Lord, Lord, shall enter into the kingdom of heaven; but he that doeth the will of my Father which is in heaven. Many will say to me in that day, Lord, Lord, have we not prophesied in thy name? and in thy name have cast out devils? and in thy name done many wonderful works? And then will I profess unto them, I never knew you: depart from me, ye that work iniquity" (Mt.7:21-23).

"He answered and said unto them, Well hath Esaias prophesied of you hypocrites, as it is written, This people honoureth me with [their] lips, but their heart is far from me" (Mk.7:6).

"They profess that they know God; but in works they deny him, being abominable, and disobedient, and unto every good work reprobate" (Tit.1:16).

5 (8:9-11) **Judgment, Purpose of—Test - Testing—God, Person**: there were at least two purposes for this particular judgment falling upon Egypt.

a. There was the purpose of challenging Pharaoh to test the power of God (vv.9-10). Moses told Pharaoh to set the time for the frogs' removal. By setting the time, Pharaoh would know that their removal was not by chance, but by the hand of God Himself. Note Pharaoh's quick response: he wanted the frogs removed no later than tomorrow.

b. There was the purpose for the judgment: to prove that God has no equal, that no one is like the LORD our God (v.10). This great truth was being proven in two ways.

1) God had proven that He was the LORD of all power, the LORD who executes justice. He had executed judgment upon Egypt. He and He alone is omnipotent, possessing the right and power to judge men. God had proven that He had power over the reproduction of life. Remember, the Egyptians felt that the spirit of reproduction lived in the frog with unusual power; consequently, they worshipped frog-headed gods (Ptha and Hekt), asking for their blessing in reproduction and in bearing children. Thus, when God plagued Egypt with swarms of frogs, He

struck a devastating blow against this false worship of the Egyptians. He proved beyond doubt who really had the power to bless and control the reproduction process of man and animals: the LORD our God.

2) God was about to prove that He is truly the LORD God (Jehovah, Yahweh), the God of mercy, deliverance, and salvation. He will save all who cry out for deliverance and salvation. God had the power to remove as well as launch the hand of chastisement and judgment. Pharaoh needed to learn both lessons: God is merciful as well as just; God is the God of mercy as well as the God of judgment. Through Moses, God proclaimed that He has the power to remove as well as cause judgment. He was merciful; therefore, God would stop the hand of chastisement if a person would just cry out for mercy and deliverance.

> **"But he, being full of compassion, forgave their iniquity, and destroyed them not: yea, many a time turned he his anger away, and did not stir up all his wrath" (Ps.78:38).**
> **"It is of the LORD's mercies that we are not consumed, because his compassions fail not" (Lam.3:22).**
> **"Not by works of righteousness which we have done, but according to his mercy he saved us, by the washing of regeneration, and renewing of the Holy Ghost" (Tit.3:5).**

Thought 1. The LORD our God has no equal. No one is like the LORD our God. He is both just and merciful. He does execute chastisement and judgment upon the sinner, but He also will have mercy upon the sinner who cries out for deliverance and salvation.

> **"Who is like unto thee, O LORD, among the gods? who is like thee, glorious in holiness, fearful in praises, doing wonders?" (Ex.15:11).**
> **"Wherefore thou art great, O LORD God: for there is none like thee, neither is there any God beside thee, according to all that we have heard with our ears" (2 S.7:22).**
> **"And he said, LORD God of Israel, there is no God like thee, in heaven above, or on earth beneath, who keepest covenant and mercy with thy servants that walk before thee with all their heart" (1 K.8:23).**
> **"O LORD, there is none like thee, neither is there any God beside thee, according to all that we have heard with our ears" (1 Chr.17:20).**
> **"For who in the heaven can be compared unto the LORD? who among the sons of the mighty can be likened unto the LORD?" (Ps.89:6).**
> **"To whom then will ye liken God? or what likeness will ye compare unto him? The workman melteth a graven image, and the goldsmith spreadeth it over with gold, and casteth silver chains. He that is so impoverished that he hath no oblation chooseth a tree that will not rot; he seeketh unto him a cunning workman to prepare a graven image, that shall not be moved. For who in the heaven can be compared unto the LORD? who among the sons of the mighty can be likened unto the LORD? Have ye not known? have ye not heard? hath it not been told you from the beginning? have ye not understood from the foundations of the earth? It is he that sitteth upon the circle of the earth, and the inhabitants thereof are as grasshoppers; that stretcheth out the heavens as a curtain, and spreadeth them out as a tent to dwell in: That bringeth the princes to nothing; he maketh the judges of the earth as vanity" (Is.40:18-23).**
> **"And the scribe said unto him, Well, Master, thou hast said the truth: for there is one God; and there is none other but he" (Mk.12:32).**

6 (8:12-14) **Deliverance—Prayer—Intercession**: the deliverance from judgment was stunning. God's messenger, Moses, did just what every messenger should do when the hand of God's chastisement has fallen upon a people. He got alone and sought the face of God. He interceded for the people. He became an intercessor for the lost of the world, for the unbelieving Egyptians who were now crying out for God's mercy and deliverance.

Note what happened: God heard His messenger and immediately stopped the judgment. His hand of chastisement was removed:

⇒ The frogs dropped dead right where they were: in the homes, in the villages, out in the fields.
⇒ The people piled the frogs into heaps.
⇒ The land stunk; it reeked with the smell of death.

What exactly killed the frogs? Did God use some natural means like bacteria from the contaminated waters, canals, and springs that had been polluted from the Nile seven days earlier? Or did God just miraculously speak and the frogs died? Scripture does not say: it simply reports that God answered Moses' prayer and the frogs died.

Thought 1. Intercession—crying out for the lost souls of the world—is one of the dire needs facing our world today. Believers who will be prayer warriors, who will commit themselves to cry out for lost souls, are desperately needed.

The messengers of God, those who have truly been called of God, must take the lead in intercession. They must preach and teach, but more desperately, they must practice intercession. They, before all others, must get before God and cry out for the lost souls of this world.

> **"And Abraham drew near, and said, Wilt thou also destroy the righteous with the wicked? Peradventure there be fifty righteous within the city: wilt thou also destroy and not spare the place for the fifty righteous that are therein? That be far from thee to do after this manner, to slay the righteous**

with the wicked: and that the righteous should be as the wicked, that be far from thee: Shall not the Judge of all the earth do right? And the LORD said, If I find in Sodom fifty righteous within the city, then I will spare all the place for their sakes. And Abraham answered and said, Behold now, I have taken upon me to speak unto the Lord, which am but dust and ashes: Peradventure there shall lack five of the fifty righteous: wilt thou destroy all the city for lack of five? And he said, If I find there forty and five, I will not destroy it. And he spake unto him yet again, and said, Peradventure there shall be forty found there. And he said, I will not do it for forty's sake. And he said unto him, Oh let not the Lord be angry, and I will speak: Peradventure there shall thirty be found there. And he said, I will not do it, if I find thirty there. And he said, Behold now, I have taken upon me to speak unto the Lord: Peradventure there shall be twenty found there. And he said, I will not destroy it for twenty's sake. And he said, Oh let not the Lord be angry, and I will speak yet but this once: Peradventure ten shall be found there. And he said, I will not destroy it for ten's sake" (Ge.18:23-32).

"Thus I fell down [prayed, interceded] before the LORD forty days and forty nights, as I fell down at the first; because the LORD had said he would destroy you" (De.9:25).

"Seek the LORD and his strength, seek his face continually" (1 Chr.16:11).

"Ask, and it shall be given you; seek, and ye shall find; knock, and it shall be opened unto you" (Mt.7:7).

"For every one that asketh receiveth; and he that seeketh findeth; and to him that knocketh it shall be opened" (Lu.11:10).

"And he spake a parable unto them to this end, that men ought always to pray, and not to faint" (Lu.18:1).

"Praying always with all prayer and supplication in the Spirit, and watching thereunto with all perseverance and supplication for all saints" (Ep.6:18).

"Continue in prayer, and watch in the same with thanksgiving; Withal praying also for us, that God would open unto us a door of utterance, to speak the mystery of Christ, for which I am also in bonds" (Col.4:2-3).

"Pray without ceasing" (1 Th.5:17).

7 (8:15) **Turning Back—Forsaking God—Hard - Hardened—Heart, Hard**: there was the sin of turning back. Once the judgment was removed, Pharaoh hardened his heart and refused to heed the warning. This is a most tragic scene. God had been merciful and delivered Pharaoh and his people from the hand of chastisement and judgment. But Pharaoh shamefully abused the mercy of God.

⇒ The chastisement of God was forgotten.
⇒ The convictions wore off.
⇒ The promises made were unfulfilled.
⇒ The pain of the suffering faded.
⇒ The fear of judgment passed.
⇒ The heart became hard.

Tragically, Pharaoh turned his back upon God and the promise he had made. The price of following God was just too great to pay: he could not afford to free God's people. To obey God meant the loss of wealth, of cheap labor and financial gain—too great a price to pay in order to obey God.

Thought 1. How often we cry to God for deliverance from some terrible trial! And we make promises to God, promises to obey and do exactly what He commands.

But how many of us follow through with our promises? How many of us shamefully abuse the mercy and patience of God? How many of us truly repent and turn with renewed vigor and commitment to God?

⇒ Did the pain of suffering fade from our memories?
⇒ Did the convictions wear off?
⇒ Were the promises made forgotten?
⇒ Is what we felt at that moment gone forever?
⇒ Have our hearts become so hardened?

Behold, all souls are mine; as the soul of the father, so also the soul of the son is mine: the soul that sinneth, it shall die. (Eze.18:4)

"Now the parable is this: The seed is the word of God....And they came to him, and awoke him, saying, Master, master, we perish. Then he arose, and rebuked the wind and the raging of the water: and they ceased, and there was a calm. And he said unto them, Where is your faith? And they being afraid wondered, saying one to another, What manner of man is this! for he commandeth even the winds and water, and they obey him. And they arrived at the country of the Gadarenes, which is over against Galilee" (Lu.8:11:24-26).

"It is the spirit that quickeneth; the flesh profiteth nothing: the words that I speak unto you, [they] are spirit, and [they] are life. But there are some of you that believe not. For Jesus knew from the beginning who they were that believed not, and who should betray him" (Jn.6:63-64).

"For Demas hath forsaken me, having loved this present world" (2 Ti.4:10).

"They went out from us, but they were not of us; for if they had been of us, they would no doubt have continued with us: but they went out, that they might be made manifest that they were not all of us" (1 Jn.2:19).

	D. The Third Plague—Lice or Gnats Infested the Land: Proof That the Finger (Power) of God Controls All Things, Even the Very Dust of the Ground, 8:16-19	with his rod, and smote the dust of the earth, and it became lice in man, and in beast; all the dust of the land became lice throughout all the land of Egypt. 18 And the magicians did so with their enchantments to bring forth lice, but they could not: so there were lice upon man, and upon beast.	warning to Pharaoh 1) The dust became lice or gnats 2) The gnats came upon men & animals 3) All the dust became lice or gnats d. The false messengers attempted to duplicate the miracle: Used their secret arts, but they failed
1. The day of judgment arrived a. The LORD charged Moses 1) Instruct Aaron to execute judgment, to take his rod & touch the dust of the ground 2) The result: The dust was to become lice or gnats b. The obedience: This they did c. The judgment fell without any	16 And the LORD said unto Moses, Say unto Aaron, Stretch out thy rod, and smite the dust of the land, that it may become lice throughout all the land of Egypt. 17 And they did so; for Aaron stretched out his hand	19 Then the magicians said unto Pharaoh, This is the finger of God: and Pharaoh's heart was hardened, and he hearkened not unto them; as the LORD had said.	**2. The purpose of the judgment: To prove that the finger of God controls all things, even the minute dust of the ground** **3. The response to the judgment: Pharaoh's heart was hard—he would not listen**

DIVISION III

THE TEN PLAGUES AND EGYPT: GOD'S JUDGMENT UPON THOSE WHO REJECT HIM AND OPPRESS HIS PEOPLE, 7:8–11:10

D. The Third Plague—Lice or Gnats Infested the Land: Proof That the Finger (Power) of God Controls All Things, Even the Very Dust of the Ground, 8:16-19

(8:16-19) **Introduction**: the finger of God controls the dust of the ground. Dust is the most minute thing visible to the naked eye. The point is this: the finger of God controls all things within the universe, even the most minute things, the very building-blocks of matter and energy. The finger of God controls…

- all particles
- all forces
- all matter
- all atoms
- all protons
- all neutrons
- all cells

- all energy
- all electrical impulses
- all electrons
- all chemicals
- all gas
- all DNA
- all life, both animal and vegetable

Whatever the most minute particle or energy is that forms the very first building-block of existence or being, it is controlled by the finger of God. It was created by God, and it is under the control of God's finger. God's finger controls the very dust of the ground, and if it controls the most minute particle, then His finger controls all things.

This was a lesson that Pharaoh and the Egyptians needed to learn. There are not many gods…

- not one god who controls the weather
- not another god who controls the water and food supply of the earth
- not still another god who protects and looks after our welfare

There are not many gods. There is only one LORD God of the universe who saves, redeems, and delivers us, only one living and true God. It is His finger (power) and His finger alone that controls all things, even the very dust of the earth, the most minute things of the earth. His finger alone…

- can save, redeem, and deliver man
- can look after the very hairs of a person's head (as Jesus Christ said, Mt.10:30)

This was the lesson that God was now going to teach the Egyptians. And this is the lesson that we, too, need to learn: *The Third Plague—Lice or Gnats Infested the Land: Proof That the Finger (Power) of God Controls All Things, Even the Very Dust of the Ground,* 8:16-19.

1. The day of judgment arrived (vv.16-18).
2. The purpose of the judgment: to prove that the finger of God controls all things, even the minute dust of the ground (v.19).
3. The response to the judgment: Pharaoh's heart was hard—he would not listen (v.19).

1 (8:16-18) **Judgment—Miracles, Demonic—Sorcery**: the day of judgment arrived. And note, there was no warning of this particular plague. Pharaoh should have expected this judgment. The God who had the power to turn water into blood and cause a swarm of frogs to invade the land could cast any other judgment He wished upon Egypt. And the Lord was not going to let Egypt escape His judgment, not unless Pharaoh and his people did what He demanded: repent. They had to turn to God and forsake their sins, in particular the evil of idolatry and slavery. Egypt was going to suffer another judgment from God unless they freed God's people. This Pharaoh should have known; consequently, God gave no warning of the judgment about to be executed upon Egypt.

a. The LORD gave His charge to Moses (v.10). Moses was to instruct Aaron to execute judgment, to take his rod and touch the dust of the ground. The result was to be astounding: the dust would become a swarm of some insect, billions and billions of them (v.16). The entire land of Egypt would be infested with the horde of insects. What was the insect? The Hebrew is *kinnim,* and it is used only here in Exodus and in Psalm 105:31 (perhaps in Isaiah 51:6). The KJV translates the word here in Exodus as "lice," but most commentators seem to hold that the insect was actually *gnats.* The Hebrew word has been translated as mosquitoes, fleas, sand-flies, maggots, and gadflies.[1]

Whatever the insect was, it was sent by God. God caused billions and billions of the lice or gnats to swarm over the land. Where did they come from? Did God miraculously create the gnats out of nowhere? Or had He caused an enormous number of gnats to breed in the flooded fields of Egypt, to breed just for this particular time and judgment?

b. Note that the messengers of God did just as God had instructed (v.17). Aaron stretched out his hand with the rod and struck the dust of the ground.

c. Immediately the judgment fell (v.17).
⇒ The dust became lice or gnats.
⇒ The lice or gnats swarmed all over the people and the animals.
⇒ All the dust became lice or gnats. They were obviously so thick that no one could escape being attacked, bitten, and infected by them.

d. The false messengers (magicians) attempted to imitate the miracle (v.18). They used their secret arts, but to no avail: they failed. And note: Scripture says that after their failure, lice or gnats covered both man and animal. Does this mean that the magicians had also attempted to remove the plague of insects from the land? Apparently. But whatever the case, the false messengers were tragically unable to help the people. They were a defeated foe in the eyes of Pharaoh and the Egyptians. The false messengers could not stop the judgment of God, nor could they deliver the people from the judgment of God.

Thought 1. At least two significant lessons can be learned from this point.

(1)No man knows when the judgment of God is going to fall upon the earth. When the day of judgment comes, it will be unannounced.

"**Heaven and earth shall pass away, but my words shall not pass away. But of that day and hour knoweth no [man], no, not the angels of heaven, but my Father only**" (Mt.24:35-36).
"**And he said, Go thy way, Daniel: for the words [of the end time] are closed up and sealed till the time of the end**" (Da.12:9).
"**And no man in heaven, nor in earth, neither under the earth, was able to open the book [of the destiny of the world], neither to look thereon**" (Re.5:3).
"**And when the seven thunders had uttered their voices, I was about to write: and I heard a voice from heaven saying unto me, Seal up those things which the seven thunders [of judgment] uttered, and write them not**" (Re.10:4).

(2)The false messengers of this earth cannot stop the judgment of God, nor will they be able to deliver people from the judgment of God.

"**There is none that can deliver out of thine hand**" (Jb.10:7).
"**The Lord knoweth how to deliver the godly out of temptations, and to reserve the unjust unto the day of judgment to be punished**" (2 Pe.2:9).
"**But the heavens and the earth, which are now, by the same word are kept in store, reserved unto fire against the day of judgment and perdition of ungodly men**" (2 Pe.3:7).
"**And Enoch also, the seventh from Adam, prophesied of these [false teachers], saying, Behold, The Lord cometh with ten thousands of his saints, to execute judgment upon all, and to convince all that are ungodly among them of all their ungodly deeds which they have ungodly committed, and of all their hard speeches which ungodly sinners have spoken against him**" (Jude 14-15).
"**And I saw the dead, small and great, stand before God; and the books were opened: and another book was opened, which is the book of life: and the dead were judged out of those things which were written in the books, according to their works**" (Re.20:12).

---

[2] (8:19) **God, Power of—Finger, of God—Hand, of God**: the specific purpose of this judgment was to arouse people, to stir them to acknowledge that the finger of God controls all things, even the minute dust of the ground.

The scene was dramatic: the magicians had been humbled by the power of God. They had failed in their attempt to help the king and the people. Their only hope to save their position before Pharaoh was to lead Pharaoh to acknowledge the existence and the power of the LORD, the God of redemption who had the power to deliver His people. This they did; and note: they declared God to be all powerful. All God had to do to send a plague upon earth was to lift His finger. Neither the strength of His arm or hand was needed. Again, He was so powerful that all He needed was His finger. It was the finger of God that worked this miracle. (Note: the finger of God is a reference to the power of God.)

---

[1] F.B. Huey, *Exodus,* p.45.

Note this fact as well: one of the protecting gods of the Egyptians was the god of the earth (Leb or Set). People obviously prayed to this god for protection from natural disasters and for him to bless the ground so that it would bear fruitful crops. Thus, when Moses threw a hand full of dust into the air and God sent forth a dust-storm of lice or gnats, the truth was not lost on the Egyptians. The true God of the earth was the God of Moses. It was His finger (power), the finger of the LORD Himself (Jehovah, Yahweh), that was sovereign over the earth, not the Egyptian god (Set), nor any other earthly god worshipped by man.

Thought 1. The finger, the very power, of God Himself, controls all things, even the dust of the ground, even the most minute things of the universe. The finger of God controls the most basic elements and building-blocks of existence...

- all particles
- all forces
- all matter
- all energy
- all electrical impulses
- all atoms
- all protons
- all neutrons
- all electrons
- all chemicals
- all gas
- all DNA
- all cells
- all life, both animal and vegetation

(1) Whatever the most minute element or building-block of existence is, God's finger created it and controls it. This is exactly what Scripture declares.

"In the beginning God created the heaven and the earth" (Ge.1:1).

"Thou, even thou, art Lord alone; thou hast made heaven, the heaven of heavens, with all their host, the earth, and all things that are therein, the seas, and all that is therein, and thou preservest them all; and the host of heaven worshippeth thee" (Ne.9:6).

"When I consider thy heavens, the work of thy fingers, the moon and the stars, which thou hast ordained; What is man, that thou art mindful of him? and the son of man, that thou visitest him?" (Ps.8:3-4).

"Of old hast thou laid the foundation of the earth: and the heavens are the work of thy hands" (Ps.102:25).

"All things were made by him; and without him was not any thing made that was made" (Jn.1:3).

"And saying, Sirs, why do ye these things? We also are men of like passions with you, and preach unto you that ye should turn from these vanities unto the living God, which made heaven, and earth, and the sea, and all things that are therein" (Ac.14:15).

"But to us there is but one God, the Father, of whom are all things, and we in him; and one Lord Jesus Christ, by whom are all things, and we by him" (1 Co.8:6).

"And to make all men see what is the fellowship of the mystery, which from the beginning of the world hath been hid in God, who created all things by Jesus Christ" (Ep.3:9).

"For by him were all things created, that are in heaven, and that are in earth, visible and invisible, whether they be thrones, or dominions, or principalities, or powers: all things were created by him, and for him: And he is before all things, and by him all things consist" (Col.1:16-17).

"God, who at sundry times and in divers manners spake in time past unto the fathers by the prophets, Hath in these last days spoken unto us by his Son, whom he hath appointed heir of all things, by whom also he made the worlds" (He.1:1-2).

"Through faith we understand that the worlds were framed by the word of God, so that things which are seen were not made of things which do appear" (He.11:3).

(2) This means a most wonderful thing: the Lord has the power to redeem and save us, the power to look after even the most minute details and events of life.

"O love the Lord, all ye his saints: for the Lord preserveth the faithful, and plentifully rewardeth the proud doer" (Ps.31:23).

"For the Lord loveth judgment, and forsaketh not his saints; they are preserved for ever: but the seed of the wicked shall be cut off" (Ps.37:28).

"But I am poor and needy; yet the Lord thinketh upon me: thou art my help and my deliverer; make no tarrying, O my God" (Ps.40:17).

"Fear thou not; for I am with thee: be not dismayed; for I am thy God: I will strengthen thee; yea, I will help thee; yea, I will uphold thee with the right hand of my righteousness" (Is.41:10).

"And even to your old age I am he; and even to hoar [gray] hairs will I carry you: I have made, and I will bear; even I will carry, and will deliver you" (Is.46:4).

"Behold the fowls of the air: for they sow not, neither do they reap, nor gather into barns; yet your heavenly Father feedeth them. Are ye not much better than they?" (Mt.6:26).

"But seek ye first the kingdom of God, and his righteousness; and all these things [food, clothing, shelter] shall be added unto you" (Mt.6:33).

"But if I with the finger of God cast out devils, no doubt the kingdom of God is come upon you" (Lu.11:20).

"But even the very hairs of your head are all numbered. Fear not therefore: ye are of more value than many sparrows" (Lu.12:7).

"And the Lord shall deliver me from every evil work, and will preserve me unto his heavenly kingdom: to whom be glory for ever and ever" (2 Ti.4:18).

"Casting all your care upon him; for he careth for you" (1 Pe.5:7).

3 (8:19) **Heart, Hard—Hard - Hardened—Rejection—Stiff-necked—Stubborn**: the response to the judgment was tragic: Pharaoh's heart was hard; he would not listen. This was most tragic, for Pharaoh had just heard a strong testimony concerning God and His power. His own advisors had just declared that the judgment was due to the finger of God Himself. But Pharaoh refused to repent of his unbelief and hardness of heart. He shut his ears: he would not listen nor heed the witness to God.

Thought 1. How many of us have hard hearts? How many of us...

- have heard the message of God time and again?
- have been witnessed to time and again?
- have seen the finger of God at work time and again?
- have felt the chastisement of God time and again?
- have shut our ears time and again?
- have been warned time and again?
- have been counseled time and again?
- have refused to listen and heed time and again?
- have rejected God time and again?

"And the Lord said unto Samuel...they have not rejected thee, but they have rejected me, that I should not reign over them" (1 S.8:7).

"But they mocked the messengers of God, and despised his words, and misused his prophets, until the wrath of the Lord arose against his people, till there was no remedy" (2 Chr.36:16).

"But my people would not hearken to my voice; and Israel would none of me. So I gave them up unto their own hearts' lust: and they walked in their own counsels. Oh that my people had hearkened unto me, and Israel had walked in my ways!" (Ps.81:11-13).

"The fear of the Lord is the beginning of knowledge: but fools despise wisdom and instruction" (Pr.1:7).

"Because I have called, and ye refused; I have stretched out my hand, and no man regarded; But ye have set at nought all my counsel, and would none of my reproof: I also will laugh at your calamity; I will mock when your fear cometh; When your fear cometh as desolation, and your destruction cometh as a whirlwind; when distress and anguish cometh upon you. Then shall they call upon me, but I will not answer; they shall seek me early, but they shall not find me: For that they hated knowledge, and did not choose the fear of the Lord: They would none of my counsel: they despised all my reproof. Therefore shall they eat of the fruit of their own way, and be filled with their own devices." (Pr.1:24-31).

"To whom shall I speak, and give warning, that they may hear? behold, their ear is uncircumcised [closed], and they cannot hearken: behold, the word of the Lord is unto them a reproach; they have no delight in it" (Je.6:10).

"Yea, they made their hearts as an adamant stone, lest they should hear the law, and the words which the Lord of hosts hath sent in his spirit by the former prophets: therefore came a great wrath from the Lord of hosts" (Zec.7:12).

"He therefore that despiseth, despiseth not man, but God, who hath also given unto us his holy Spirit" (1 Th.4:7-8).

E. The Fourth Plague—Flies Swarmed Over the Land: Proof that the LORD Is the Savior in Every Land & in Every Place, 8:20-32

1. **The declaration of God's Word, His will**
   a. Moses was to go, intercept Pharaoh in the morning at the Nile river
   b. Moses was to proclaim God's Word & will: Let God's people go—free them to serve & worship God

2. **The warning & pronouncement of judgment**
   a. The cause for judgment: Rejecting God, oppressing people
   b. The judgment: Flies would swarm the land, covering everyone
      1) Filling the houses
      2) Flooding the ground

3. **The purpose of the judgment**
   a. To prove that the LORD is the Savior, the only living & true God in every land
   b. The proof: God protected His people
      1) God kept the flies out of Goshen, where Israel lived
      2) God made a distinction between His people & Pharaoh's people

4. **The day of judgment arrived: Dense swarms of flies filled the houses & lands—the land was blackened & ruined by the flies**

5. **The response to the judg-**

20 And the LORD said unto Moses, Rise up early in the morning, and stand before Pharaoh; lo, he cometh forth to the water; and say unto him, Thus saith the LORD, Let my people go, that they may serve me.
21 Else, if thou wilt not let my people go, behold, I will send swarms of flies upon thee, and upon thy servants, and upon thy people, and into thy houses: and the houses of the Egyptians shall be full of swarms of flies, and also the ground whereon they are.
22 And I will sever in that day the land of Goshen, in which my people dwell, that no swarms of flies shall be there; to the end thou mayest know that I am the LORD in the midst of the earth.
23 And I will put a division between my people and thy people: to morrow shall this sign be.
24 And the LORD did so; and there came a grievous swarm of flies into the house of Pharaoh, and into his servants' houses, and into all the land of Egypt: the land was corrupted by reason of the swarm of flies.
25 And Pharaoh called for Moses and for Aaron, and said, Go ye, sacrifice to your God in the land.
26 And Moses said, It is not meet so to do; for we shall sacrifice the abomination of the Egyptians to the LORD our God: lo, shall we sacrifice the abomination of the Egyptians before their eyes, and will they not stone us?
27 We will go three days' journey into the wilderness, and sacrifice to the LORD our God, as he shall command us.
28 And Pharaoh said, I will let you go, that ye may sacrifice to the LORD your God in the wilderness; only ye shall not go very far away: intreat for me.
29 And Moses said, Behold, I go out from thee, and I will intreat the LORD that the swarms of flies may depart from Pharaoh, from his servants, and from his people, to morrow: but let not Pharaoh deal deceitfully any more in not letting the people go to sacrifice to the LORD.
30 And Moses went out from Pharaoh, and intreated the LORD.
31 And the LORD did according to the word of Moses; and he removed the swarms of flies from Pharaoh, from his servants, and from his people; there remained not one.
32 And Pharaoh hardened his heart at this time also, neither would he let the people go.

ment: A cry for deliverance
   a. Pharaoh called for Moses & offered to compromise: To let Israel sacrifice to God, but only in Egypt
   b. Moses rejected the compromise
      1) Because the sacrifice of animals was offensive to the Egyptians: Could possibly cause an uprising against the Israelites
      2) Because the Israelites had to obey God: They had to go into the wilderness three days away
   c. Pharaoh gave in, but insisted Israel not try to escape
   d. Pharaoh begged for prayer & deliverance (while the flies were filling the room & swarming around his head)
   e. Moses promised deliverance: Assured Pharaoh of his prayers and of God's deliverance

   f. Moses warned Pharaoh against acting deceitfully, against making another false profession

6. **The deliverance from judgment**
   a. Moses prayed
   b. God delivered Egypt, removed His hand of judgment: The flies left; not a single one remained

7. **The sin of turning back: Pharaoh hardened his heart—would not free the people**

DIVISION III

THE TEN PLAGUES AND EGYPT: GOD'S JUDGMENT UPON THOSE WHO REJECT HIM AND OPPRESS HIS PEOPLE, 7:8–11:10

E.   The Fourth Plague—Flies Swarmed Over the Land: Proof that the LORD Is the Savior in Every Land and in Every Place, 8:20-32

(8:20-32) **Introduction—Idolatry—False Gods**: there is only one LORD, one Savior in all the universe who can redeem and deliver us. Who is he? Who can deliver us from the body of death? From the trials, sufferings, temptations, evil, and death of this world?

> **"Jesus saith unto him, I am the way, the truth, and the life: no man cometh unto the Father, but by me" (Jn.14:6).**
> **"I thank God through Jesus Christ our Lord" (Ro.7:25).**
> **"For there is one God, and one Mediator between God and men, the man Christ Jesus" (1 Ti.2:5).**

The Egyptians had long before rejected God and turned to the worship of the world and of self, the worship of man and of nature. The Egyptians were worshipping the imaginations of their own minds. They and all the other peoples of the world had their own gods. People in every nation felt there were many gods:

⇒ There were gods who favored one nation and gods who favored other nations.
⇒ There were gods who could deliver from one problem and other gods who could deliver from a second problem.

All over the world there was, just as there is today, the worship of many gods. People's imaginations ran wild with images of God, images that ran from man himself being his own god over to the images of four-footed beasts and creeping things being the gods who controlled human life (see Ro.1:18-32).

The idea that there was only one LORD, only one Savior and Redeemer who could deliver people, had long ago been rejected by the Egyptians. This was the great lesson the Egyptians now had to learn, the same lesson that so many people today need to learn: there is only one LORD, only one Savior, and He is the LORD in every land upon earth. The LORD alone is the true and living God—*everywhere*—in every tribe and every nation and every land upon earth. This passage covers this great subject: *The Fourth Plague—Flies Swarmed Over the Land: Proof that the LORD is the Savior (the Redeemer), the Only Living and True God, in Every Land and in Every Place,* 8:20-32.

1. The declaration of God's Word, His will (v.20).
2. The warning and pronouncement of judgment (v.21).
3. The purpose of the judgment (vv.22-23).
4. The day of judgment arrived: dense swarms of flies filled the houses and lands—the land was blackened and ruined by the flies (v.24).
5. The response to the judgment: a cry for deliverance (vv.25-29).
6. The deliverance (vv.30-31).
7. The sin of turning back: Pharaoh hardened his heart—would not free the people (v.32).

[1] (8:20) **Freedom—Liberty**: there was the declaration of God's Word, His will. Moses was to get up early in the morning and intercept Pharaoh as he went out to the banks of the Nile River. Picture the scene: there was Pharaoh—the most powerful king upon earth, possessing the very power of life and death over men—standing by the Nile River surrounded by his government advisors. Then suddenly, out of nowhere, the messenger of God appears. Immediately, he began to proclaim God's will: "Let God's people go—free them to live and serve God."

God hates slavery. He hates oppression, abuse, brutality, and savagery. No person is to mistreat other people. No leader, whether in government, business, organization, or family, is to abuse a person's freedom. No leader is to abuse a person's freedom to live, work, or serve God. God's will is life, liberty, and justice for all. God has no favorites and He shows no partiality. Neither are we to show favoritism or partiality toward people: we are not to be prejudiced against people because of race, color, ability, handicap, nor for any other reason.

This is the will of God that is to be proclaimed to the world, both to the leaders and the citizens of every nation. The LORD is the Savior in every land. He is the only living and true God, and He demands that all enslaved and oppressed people be let go—that they be freed to live and to serve the LORD God of the universe.

"...proclaim liberty throughout all the land unto all the inhabitants thereof" (Le.25:10).

"And the second [is] like, [namely] this, Thou shalt love thy neighbour as thyself. There is none other commandment greater than these" (Mk.12:31).

"And he said unto them, Ye know how that it is an unlawful thing for a man that is a Jew to keep company, or come unto one of another nation; but God hath showed me that I should not call any man common or unclean" (Ac.10:28).

"For there is no difference between the Jew and the Greek: for the same Lord over all is rich unto all that call upon him" (Ro.10:12).

"Love worketh no ill to his neighbour: therefore love is the fulfilling of the law" (Ro.13:10).

"There is neither Jew nor Greek, there is neither bond nor free, there is neither male nor female: for ye are all one in Christ Jesus" (Ga.3:28).

"For all the law is fulfilled in one word, even in this; Thou shalt love thy neighbour as thyself" (Ga.5:14).

"If ye fulfil the royal law according to the scripture, Thou shalt love thy neighbour as thyself, ye do well" (Js.2:8).

[2] (8:21) **Judgment**: there was the warning and pronouncement of judgment.

a. The reason for the judgment is clearly stated: Pharaoh had rejected God. He refused to obey God, refused to free God's people. Note that this is a warning. Pharaoh is given time to repent; he has the opportunity to turn to God and to renounce his terrible sin of greed and pride that had led to the enslavement of God's people. Pharaoh was given time to show true repentance, time to free God's people.

b. The judgment was to be a repulsive plague: a plague of flies was to swarm over the land, so many billions that everything would be covered, even the very space where a person tried to stand, sit, or lie. The flies were to be so thick that they would literally...

- cover everyone
- fill the houses
- blacken the ground
- blacken the atmosphere surrounding a person

What was going to cause so many flies to swarm over Egypt? God. He no doubt caused a multiplication of flies in the breeding manure of animals and in the puddles left by the receding waters of the Nile.

Thought 1. God warns us of judgment to come. But right now His Word is only a warning; judgment has not yet fallen, not the full force of God's holy, eternal wrath. We still have time to repent, time to turn from our sinful ways and turn to God. This we must do while there is still time.

"I acknowledged my sin unto thee, and mine iniquity have I not hid. I said, I will confess my transgressions unto the LORD; and thou forgavest the iniquity of my sin....For this shall every one that is godly pray unto thee in a time when thou mayest be found" (Ps.32:5-6).

"But as for me, my prayer is unto thee, O LORD, in an acceptable time: O God, in the multitude of thy mercy hear me, in the truth of thy salvation" (Ps.69:13).

"To day if ye will hear his voice, Harden not your heart, as in the provocation, and as in the day of temptation in the wilderness: When your fathers tempted me, proved me, and saw my work. Forty years long was I grieved with this generation, and said, It is a people that do err in their heart, and they have not known my ways: Unto whom I sware in my wrath that they should not enter into my rest" (Ps.95:7-11).

"Thus saith the LORD, In an acceptable time have I heard thee, and in a day of salvation have I helped thee: and I will preserve thee" (Is.49:8).

"And now, because ye have done all these works, saith the LORD, and I spake unto you, rising up early and speaking, but ye heard not; and I called you, but ye answered not....And I will cast you out of my sight, as I have cast out all your brethren, even the whole seed of Ephraim" (Je.7:13, 15).

"But if the wicked will turn from all his sins that he hath committed, and keep all my statutes, and do that which is lawful and right, he shall surely live, he shall not die" (Eze.18:21).

"Cast away from you all your transgressions, whereby ye have transgressed; and make you a new heart and a new spirit: for why will ye die, O house of Israel?" (Eze.18:31).

"Therefore also now, saith the LORD, turn ye even to me with all your heart, and with fasting, and with weeping, and with mourning" (Joel 2:12).

"And saying, Repent ye: for the kingdom of heaven is at hand" (Mt.3:2).

"Then began he to upbraid the cities wherein most of his mighty works were done, because they repented not" (Mt.11:20).

"I tell you, Nay: but, except ye repent, ye shall all likewise perish" (Lu.13:3).

3 (8:22-23) **God, Proof of—Flies—Separation, Spiritual**: there was the purpose for the judgment. God's purpose for sending this judgment was to prove that He is the LORD, the Savior *in every land*. He is the only true and living Savior *within every land*, the only living and true God who can truly deliver people *within every land*.

The LORD was in the land of Egypt, and He is *in every land*. He is the only living and true God in every land; thus He is the only Redeemer, the only true Savior in every land. No matter where the land or place is, the LORD (Jehovah, Yahweh) is there: the Savior and Deliverer of every person and of every being throughout the universe is there.

Note how God proved this to the Egyptians. He protected His people:

⇒ God kept the flies out of Goshen, where Israel lived.
⇒ God made a distinction between His people and Pharaoh's people.

The proof was irrefutable, incontestable, undeniable. The LORD, the true and living Savior, was in Egypt. How did Pharaoh and the Egyptians know this? How do we know this? Because God's judgment fell only in the land of Egypt, only upon the Egyptians. The judgment did not fall in the land of believers, the land of Goshen. The evil enslavers were punished, and the believers of God were delivered. Flies swarmed all over the sinners, literally covering them, but not a fly touched those who followed God. The LORD proved that He is truly the Savior in every land. He is the only true and living Savior who lives everywhere, in every land. Note how this struck a death blow against the fly gods of Egypt. There was only one God who had power and could protect people from the flies: the LORD, the only true and living Savior. The fly god of Egypt (Beelzebub or Khephera) was nothing but a lifeless idol.

"Know therefore this day, and consider it in thine heart, that the LORD he is God in heaven above, and upon the earth beneath: there is none else" (De.4:39).

"Whither shall I go from thy spirit? or whither shall I flee from thy presence? If I ascend up into heaven, thou art there: if I make my bed in hell, behold, thou art there. If I take the wings of the morning, and dwell in the uttermost parts of the sea; Even there shall thy hand lead me, and thy right hand shall hold me" (Ps.139:7-10).

"The eyes of the LORD are in every place, beholding the evil and the good" (Pr.15:3).

"Thus saith the LORD, The heaven is my throne, and the earth is my footstool: where is the house that ye build unto me? and where is the place of my rest?" (Is.66:1).

"Can any hide himself in secret places that I shall not see him? saith the LORD. Do not I fill heaven and earth? saith the LORD" (Je.23:24).

"God that made the world and all things therein, seeing that he is Lord of heaven and earth, dwelleth not in temples made with hands; Neither is worshipped with men's hands, as though he needed any thing, seeing he giveth to all life, and breath, and all things; And hath made of one blood all nations of men for to dwell on all the face of the earth, and hath determined the times before appointed, and the bounds of their habitation; That they should seek the Lord, if haply they might feel after him, and find him, though he be not far from every one of us: For in him we live, and move, and have our being; as certain also of your own poets have said, For we are also his offspring. Forasmuch then as we are the offspring of God, we ought not to think that the Godhead is like unto gold, or silver, or stone, graven by art and man's device. And the times of this ignorance God winked at; but now commandeth all men every where to repent: Because he hath appointed a day, in the which he will judge the world in righteousness by that man whom he hath ordained; whereof he hath given assurance unto all men, in that he hath raised him from the dead" (Ac.17:24-31).

DEEPER STUDY # 1

(8:22) **Goshen, Land of**: this area of Egypt is where Joseph's family settled during the great famine. Goshen proved to be a blessing to Israel: it was an excellent place to raise families, farm, and set up ranches. Israel prospered in their temporary home. Note how God provided a good place for His people as He prepared them for life in the promised land. (See note—Gen.46:31-34 for more discussion.)

"And thou shalt dwell in the land of Goshen, and thou shalt be near unto me, thou, and thy children, and thy children's children, and thy flocks, and thy herds, and all that thou hast" (Ge.45:10).

"And he sent Judah before him unto Joseph, to direct his face unto Goshen; and they came into the land of Goshen. And Joseph made ready his chariot, and went up to meet Israel his father, to Goshen, and presented himself unto him; and he fell on his neck, and wept on his neck a good while" (Ge.46:28-29).

"That ye shall say, Thy servants' trade hath been about cattle from our youth even until now, both we, *and* also our fathers: that ye may dwell in the land of Goshen; for every shepherd *is* an abomination unto the Egyptians. Then Joseph came and told Pharaoh, and said, My father and my brethren, and their flocks, and their herds, and all that they have, are come out of the land of Canaan; and, behold, they *are* in the land of Goshen" (Ge.46:34-47:1).

"They said moreover unto Pharaoh, For to sojourn in the land are we come; for thy servants have no pasture for their flocks; for the famine *is* sore in the land of Canaan: now therefore, we pray thee, let thy servants dwell in the land of Goshen" (Ge.47:4).

"The land of Egypt *is* before thee; in the best of the land make thy father and brethren to dwell; in the land of Goshen let them dwell: and if thou knowest *any* men of activity among them, then make them rulers over my cattle" (Ge.47:6).

"And Israel dwelt in the land of Egypt, in the country of Goshen; and they had possessions therein, and grew, and multiplied exceedingly" (Ge.47:27).

"And all the house of Joseph, and his brethren, and his father's house: only their little ones, and their flocks, and their herds, they left in the land of Goshen" (Ge.50:8).

"And I will sever in that day the land of Goshen, in which my people dwell, that no swarms *of flies* shall be there; to the end thou mayest know that I *am* the LORD in the midst of the earth" (Ex.8:22).

"Only in the land of Goshen, where the children of Israel *were,* was there no hail" (Ex.9:26).

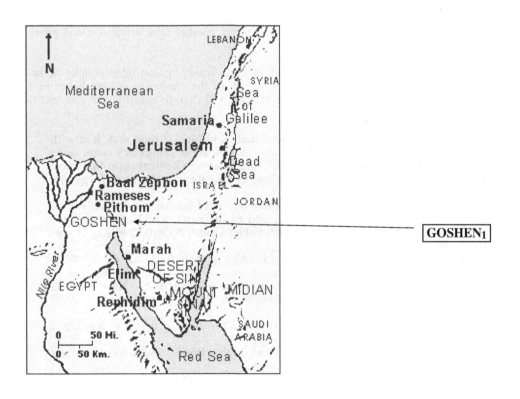

GOSHEN₁

---

1 Map from *Life Application*® *Bible*. Used by permission.

4 (8:24) **Judgment—Flies—Plagues, The Ten**: the day of judgment arrived. Dense swarms of flies filled the houses and lands. The land was literally blackened and ruined by the flies.

Thought 1. The warning of judgment was preached to Pharaoh, but he ignored it. We, too, are warned of judgment, but far too many of us are doing just what Pharaoh did: ignoring the warning. The hand of God's judgment fell upon the Egyptians: the day of judgment did come, and it is coming for us. God's hand of judgment is going to fall upon us just as it fell upon Pharaoh.

"When the Son of man shall come in his glory, and all the holy angels with him, then shall he sit upon the throne of his glory: And before him shall be gathered all nations: and he shall separate them one from another, as a shepherd divideth [his] sheep from the goats: And he shall set the sheep on his right hand, but the goats on the left....Then shall he say also unto them on the left hand, Depart from me, ye cursed, into everlasting fire, prepared for the devil and his angels" (Mt.25:31-33, 41).

"Because he hath appointed a day, in the which he will judge the world in righteousness by that man whom he hath ordained; whereof he hath given assurance unto all men, in that he hath raised him from the dead" (Ac.17:31).

"In the day when God shall judge the secrets of men by Jesus Christ according to my gospel" (Ro.2:16).

"So then every one of us shall give account of himself to God" (Ro.14:12).

"For we must all appear before the judgment seat of Christ; that every one may receive the things done in his body, according to that he hath done, whether it be good or bad" (2 Co.5:10).

"And I saw the dead, small and great, stand before God; and the books were opened: and another book was opened, which is the book of life: and the dead were judged out of those things which were written in the books, according to their works" (Re.20:12).

5 (8:25-29) **Judgment—Deliverance—Profession, False**: there was the response to the judgment: a cry for deliverance. The judgment of God once again brought Pharaoh to his knees. The outline points give a clear picture of what now happened.

⇒ Pharaoh called for Moses and offered to compromise: to let Israel sacrifice to God, but only in Egypt (v.25).
⇒ But Moses rejected the compromise, because the sacrifice of animals was offensive to the Egyptians (vv.26-27). Sacrificing animals before the Egyptians could possibly cause an uprising against the Israelites. Remember, the Egyptians detested the Israelites and shepherds (Ge.43:32; 46:34). Moreover, the Israelites had to obey God. They had to go into the wilderness three days away in order to worship God at Mt. Sinai.
⇒ Pharaoh gave in to Moses' compromise, but he insisted that Israel not try to escape from Egypt(v.28).
⇒ Pharaoh begged for prayer and deliverance from the judgment (v.28). And note: while he was begging, the flies filled the room and swarmed all around his head.
⇒ Moses promised deliverance: he assured Pharaoh of his prayers and of God's deliverance (v.29).
⇒ But note: Moses warned Pharaoh against acting deceitfully, against making another false profession and promise (v.29).

Thought 1. God's chastisement falls upon us when we sin against Him and do wrong against other people. Sometimes the chastisement is mild; sometimes it is heavy. Whatever the weight of the chastisement—no matter how much we are suffering—if we cry out to God for help, He will deliver us. God will stop the chastisement and restore the joy of life and salvation to us.

"But if from thence thou shalt seek the LORD thy God, thou shalt find him, if thou seek him with all thy heart and with all thy soul. When thou art in tribulation, and all these things are come upon thee, even in the latter days, if thou turn to the LORD thy God, and shalt be obedient unto his voice; (For the LORD thy God is a merciful God;) he will not forsake thee, neither destroy thee, nor forget the covenant of thy fathers which he sware unto them" (De.4:29-31).

"This poor man cried, and the LORD heard him, and saved him out of all his troubles" (Ps.34:6).

"Hear my cry, O God; attend unto my prayer. From the end of the earth will I cry unto thee, when my heart is overwhelmed: lead me to the rock that is higher than I. For thou hast been a shelter for me, and a strong tower from the enemy" (Ps.61:1-3).

"He shall call upon me, and I will answer him: I will be with him in trouble; I will deliver him, and honour him" (Ps.91:15).

"Then shalt thou call, and the LORD shall answer; thou shalt cry, and he shall say, Here I am. If thou take away from the midst of thee the yoke, the putting forth of the finger, and speaking vanity" (Is.58:9).

"And it shall come to pass, that before they call, I will answer; and while they are yet speaking, I will hear" (Is.65:24).

"Call unto me, and I will answer thee, and show thee great and mighty things, which thou knowest not" (Je.33:3).

"And I say unto you, Ask, and it shall be given you; seek, and ye shall find; knock, and it shall be opened unto you" (Lu.11:9).

176

6 (8:30-31) **Prayer—Deliverance, from Judgment**: there was the deliverance. Moses immediately got alone and cried out to God. He became the intercessor for Egypt. He prayed and prayed for God to remove His hand of judgment from the Egyptian people. And God heard his prayer. God delivered Egypt, removed His hand of judgment: the flies left; not a single one remained to pester the people.

Thought 1. God answers prayer. If we sincerely cry out to Him for deliverance, He hears our cry.
(1)   Hannah cried out to God and God heard her prayer.

> **"For this child I prayed; and the LORD hath given me my petition which I asked of him" (1 S.1:27).**

(2)   Samuel cried out to God and God heard his prayer.

> **"And Samuel took a sucking lamb, and offered it for a burnt offering wholly unto the LORD: and Samuel cried unto the LORD for Israel; and the LORD heard him. And as Samuel was offering up the burnt offering, the Philistines drew near to battle against Israel: but the LORD thundered with a great thunder on that day upon the Philistines, and discomfited them; and they were smitten before Israel" (1 S.7:9-10).**

(3)   Solomon cried out to God and God heard his prayer.

> **"And the LORD said unto him, I have heard thy prayer and thy supplication, that thou hast made before me: I have hallowed this house, which thou hast built, to put my name there for ever; and mine eyes and mine heart shall be there perpetually" (1 K.9:3).**

(4)   Elijah cried out to God and God heard his prayer.

> **"Hear me, O LORD, hear me, that this people may know that thou art the LORD God, and that thou hast turned their heart back again. Then the fire of the LORD fell, and consumed the burnt sacrifice, and the wood, and the stones, and the dust, and licked up the water that was in the trench" (1 K.18:37-38).**

(5)   Hezekiah cried out to God and God heard his prayer.

> **"Now therefore, O LORD our God, I beseech thee, save thou us out of his hand, that all the kingdoms of the earth may know that thou art the LORD God, even thou only. Then Isaiah the son of Amoz sent to Hezekiah, saying, Thus saith the LORD God of Israel, That which thou hast prayed to me against Sennacherib king of Assyria I have heard" (2 K.19:19-20).**

(6)   Jehoshaphat cried out to God and God heard his prayer.

> **"And it came to pass, when the captains of the chariots saw Jehoshaphat, that they said, It is the king of Israel. Therefore they compassed about him to fight: but Jehoshaphat cried out, and the LORD helped him; and God moved them to depart from him" (2 Chr.18:31).**

(7)   Ezra cried out to God and God heard his prayer.

> **"So we fasted and besought our God for this: and he was intreated of us" (Ezr.8:23).**

(8)   Zacharias cried out to God and God heard his prayer.

> **"But the angel said unto him, Fear not, Zacharias: for thy prayer is heard; and thy wife Elisabeth shall bear thee a son, and thou shalt call his name John" (Lu.1:13).**

(9)   The early church cried out to God and God heard its prayer.

> **"And when they had prayed, the place was shaken where they were assembled together; and they were all filled with the Holy Ghost, and they spake the word of God with boldness" (Ac.4:31).[2]**

7 (8:32) **Backsliding—Turning Back—Forsaking, God—Apostasy**: there was the sin of turning back. Pharaoh hardened his heart; he would not free the people. He had made a *promise* to God and he had made a *profession* to the messenger of God. Moreover, Moses had even warned him to make sure, absolutely sure, that he was sincere, that his

---

[2] *The New Thompson Chain Reference Bible*. (Indianapolis, IN: B.B. Kirkbride Bible Co., Inc., 1964), Condensed Cyclopedia of Topics and Text, Number 2818, p.109.

profession was genuine. The implication was clear: if he made a false profession, if he acted deceitfully, a far worse judgment was going to fall upon him.

Thought 1. We must be genuine in dealing with God. God cannot be deceived. If we make a false profession, God knows that our profession is false. God knows when we...
- backslide
- turn back
- fall into sin
- forsake Him
- choose the world over Him

Turning back to the world, its possessions and pleasures, is dangerous. We put our souls in peril and endanger our eternity. We must, therefore, always guard against turning back and forsaking God.

"The LORD is with you, while ye be with him; and if ye seek him, he will be found of you; but if ye forsake him, he will forsake you " (2 Chr.15:2).

"The hand of our God is upon all them for good that seek him; but his power and his wrath is against all them that forsake him" (Ezr.8:22).

"And I will utter my judgments against them touching all their wickedness, who have forsaken me, and have burned incense unto other gods, and worshipped the works of their own hands" (Je.1:16).

"For my people have committed two evils; they have forsaken me the fountain of living waters, and hewed them out cisterns, broken cisterns, that can hold no water" (Je.2:13).

"And it shall come to pass, when ye shall say, Wherefore doeth the LORD our God all these things unto us? then shalt thou answer them, Like as ye have forsaken me, and served strange gods in your land, so shall ye serve strangers in a land that is not yours" (Je.5:19).

"Thou hast forsaken me, saith the LORD, thou art gone backward: therefore will I stretch out my hand against thee, and destroy thee; I am weary with repenting" (Je.15:6).

"[The ungodly] which have forsaken the right way, and are gone astray, following the way of Balaam the son of Bosor, who loved the wages of unrighteousness....These are wells without water, clouds that are carried with a tempest; to whom the mist of darkness is reserved for ever" (2 Pe.2:15, 17).

"For if after they have escaped the pollutions of the world through the knowledge of the Lord and Saviour Jesus Christ, they are again entangled therein, and overcome, the latter end is worse with them than the beginning. For it had been better for them not to have known the way of righteousness, than, after they have known it, to turn from the holy commandment delivered unto them" (2 Pe.2:20-21).

"So I sware in my wrath, They shall not enter into my rest. Take heed, brethren, lest there be in any of you an evil heart of unbelief, in departing from the living God....And to whom sware he that they should not enter into his rest, but to them that believed not? So we see that they could not enter in because of unbelief" (He.3:11-12, 18-19).

1. The declaration of God's Word, His will a. Moses was to go to Pharaoh b. Moses was to proclaim God's Word: Let my people go—free them to serve & worship me **2. The warning of judgment** a. The cause for judgment: Refusing to obey God b. The judgment: A severe disease (murrain, anthrax) was to strike the livestock which were in the field	**CHAPTER 9** **F. The Fifth Plague—A Severe Disease Struck & Killed All Livestock in the Field: Proof That the Hand of God Controls the Animal Life of the World, 9:1-7** Then the LORD said unto Moses, Go in unto Pharaoh, and tell him, Thus saith the LORD God of the Hebrews, Let my people go, that they may serve me. 2 For if thou refuse to let them go, and wilt hold them still, 3 Behold, the hand of the LORD is upon thy cattle which is in the field, upon the horses, upon the asses, upon	the camels, upon the oxen, and upon the sheep: there shall be a very grievous murrain. 4 And the LORD shall sever between the cattle of Israel and the cattle of Egypt: and there shall nothing die of all that is the children's of Israel. 5 And the LORD appointed a set time, saying, To morrow the LORD shall do this thing in the land. 6 And the LORD did that thing on the morrow, and all the cattle of Egypt died: but of the cattle of the children of Israel died not one. 7 And Pharaoh sent, and, behold, there was not one of the cattle of the Israelites dead. And the heart of Pharaoh was hardened, and he did not let the people go.	**3. The purpose of the judgment** a. To prove that "the hand of the LORD" controls the animal life of the world b. The proof: God protected the livestock of His people 1) No animal of His people died 2) God set a definite time for the judgment: The very next day **4. The day of judgment arrived** a. All the livestock of the Egyptians died, all that were in the fields b. No livestock of Israel died **5. The response to the judgment** a. Pharaoh sent men to investigate b. Pharaoh's heart was hard: He would not free the people

DIVISION III

THE TEN PLAGUES AND EGYPT: GOD'S JUDGMENT UPON THOSE WHO REJECT HIM AND OPPRESS HIS PEOPLE, 7:8–11:10

F. The Fifth Plague—A Severe Disease Struck and Killed All Livestock in the Field: Proof That the Hand of God Controls the Animal Life of the World, 9:1-7

(9:1-7) **Introduction**: the ancient Egyptians were an idolatrous people. They denied and rejected the only living and true God. They apparently believed that the spirit of some god lived in every thing and in every area of life. Consequently, there were Egyptians who worshipped everything ranging from man himself (humanism) over to four-footed animals and creeping things. But in addition to being idolaters, the Egyptians had become a brutal and savage people. They abused and enslaved other races of people, including the very people upon earth who bore testimony to the only true and living God (Jehovah, Yahweh).

God had been patient long enough with the Egyptians. He was now demanding repentance, and when the Egyptians refused to repent, He was executing justice and chastising them. God was not wiping them out—as they themselves were guilty of doing to so many people—but He was chastening them by sending catastrophic plagues upon them and their nation.

Now, once again, God was ready to offer the Egyptians an opportunity to repent. But tragically, they would again reject God: they would still refuse to repent of their terrible evil of idolatry, of brutalizing and enslaving people. They would still refuse to free God's people, the Israelites, the only people upon earth who were still following the living and true God. This passage covers: *The Fifth Plague—A Severe Disease Struck and Killed All Livestock in the Field: Proof That the Hand of God Controls the Animal Life of the World,* 9:1-7.

1. The declaration of God's Word, His will (v.1).
2. The warning of judgment (vv.2-3).
3. The purpose of the judgment (vv.3-5).
4. The day of judgment arrived (v.6).
5. The response to the judgment (v.7).

1 (9:1) **Hebrews, The—Israel—Liberty—Freedom**: there was the declaration of God's Word, His will. Again, Moses was to go to Pharaoh and proclaim the Word of God to him. Remember: Pharaoh had cried out for deliverance from the last plague launched by God. But after God had removed the plague, Pharaoh had turned back and refused to follow through with his decision. He had refused to free God's people, refused to repent of the terrible evil of slavery, of brutalizing people—all because of cheap labor and greed. (See notes—Ex.8:2-4; 9:34-35 for more discussion.) But God is patient and not willing that any person or people should perish, not even the worst sinner or most evil person upon earth. Thus, God sent His messenger back to Pharaoh to proclaim God's Word, His will. God wanted to give Pharaoh and the Egyptians another opportunity to repent. Moses declared the great message of God against brutalizing and enslaving people.

Note that the LORD called Himself "the LORD God of the Hebrews." Remember, about 700 years earlier, practically every person upon earth had forsaken and denied God. But God, being God, could not allow His purpose for man to be defeated. Consequently, He chose one man, Abraham, and from him created a whole new race of people who were to fulfill God's purposes upon earth. The new race of people was the Hebrews, the nation Israel. The Hebrews were to be...

- God's witnesses upon earth
- God's witnesses to the only living and true God

- God's witnesses to the promised land of heaven
- God's witnesses to a great nation of people, a great body of believers down through the generations
- God's witnesses to the promised seed, the coming Savior of the world, the Lord Jesus Christ

As with any body of professing people, not all Hebrews living during the Egyptian bondage believed and followed after God. But enough did that God still called them His people and still referred to Himself as the LORD God of the Hebrews. The point is this: Pharaoh and the Egyptians were enslaving the believers of that day, the very people who followed after God. God despises slavery, despises the oppression of any people, despises the abuse of any person. But God especially despises the oppression of the very people who believe and follow Him. Thus God demands: "Let my people go—free them to live and serve me" (v.1).

"O LORD my God, in thee do I put my trust: save me from all them that persecute [oppress, enslave] me, and deliver me: Lest he tear my soul like a lion, rending it in pieces, while there is none to deliver" (Ps.7:1-2).

"My times are in thy hand: deliver me from the hand of mine enemies, and from them that persecute me. Make thy face to shine upon thy servant: save me for thy mercies' sake" (Ps.31:15-16).

"How many are the days of thy servant? when wilt thou execute judgment on them that persecute me? The proud have digged pits for me, which are not after thy law. All thy commandments are faithful: they persecute me wrongfully; help thou me. They had almost consumed me upon earth; but I forsook not thy precepts" (Ps.119:84-87).

"Princes have persecuted me without a cause: but my heart standeth in awe of thy word" (Ps.119:161).

"For the enemy hath persecuted [oppressed] my soul; he hath smitten my life down to the ground; he hath made me to dwell in darkness, as those that have been long dead. Therefore is my spirit overwhelmed within me; my heart within me is desolate" (Ps.143:3-4).

"O LORD, thou knowest: remember me, and visit me, and revenge me of my persecutors; take me not away in thy longsuffering: know that for thy sake I have suffered rebuke" (Je.15:15).

"Remember, O LORD, what is come upon us: consider, and behold our reproach. Our inheritance is turned to strangers, our houses to aliens. We are orphans and fatherless, our mothers are as widows. We have drunken our water for money; our wood is sold unto us. Our necks are under persecution: we labour, and have no rest. We have given the hand to the Egyptians, and to the Assyrians, to be satisfied with bread" (Lam.5:1-6).

2 (9:2-3) **Judgment—Animals—Livestock—Warning**: there was the warning of judgment.

a. The cause for this particular judgment was the same as the cause for the other judgments: Pharaoh refused to obey God. But note, this was only the warning of judgment to come. The judgment had not yet fallen upon Pharaoh and his people. They still had time to repent, still had time to heed God's Word. In what seems like His eternal patience, God was giving Pharaoh yet another chance.

b. But note the judgment that was to fall if Pharaoh refused to acknowledge God and do what God said: a severe disease was to strike the livestock. What was the disease? The Hebrew word is *deber,* a word used for general diseases or plagues.

⇒ The KJV translates it as *murrain,* which is a pestilence or plague that attacks domestic animals and plants.
⇒ The NIV simply translates it as "terrible plague."

Most commentators feel that the disease was some form of *anthrax. Anthrax* is an infectious disease of warm-blooded animals. It is caused by a spore-forming bacteria, and can be passed on to people if they touch anything that has been in touch with the infected animal. The flies that had infested the land may have passed the anthrax bacteria to the livestock. Anthrax causes ulcers in the body and lesions in the lungs. Consequently, this plague was to be a catastrophic plague upon Egypt. The judgment was to strike all the livestock in the fields…

- horses
- donkeys
- camels
- cattle
- sheep
- goats

This judgment obviously wrecked the Egyptian economy and greatly affected the day-to-day life of the people. The horses, donkeys, and camels were used for transportation and work; the smaller livestock were used for their skins and wool for clothing; and undoubtedly cattle and other animals were used for food. This meant that most of the industries and every family within Egypt were severely affected.

Pharaoh and his people desperately needed to heed this warning from God. There was no need—it made absolutely no sense—for them to bring God's judgment down upon their nation and upon themselves, no sense for them to go through so much suffering.

Thought 1. We must heed the warning of judgment: God's judgment is coming. Every one of us must give an account to God for the things we have done. It makes no sense for us to ignore, deny, and neglect God's warning. It makes no sense for us to bring God's judgment upon our heads, no sense for us to go through the suffering of the eternal judgment that is coming.

"Also unto thee, O LORD, belongeth mercy: for thou renderest to every man according to his work" (Ps.62:12).

"Nevertheless, if thou warn the wicked of his way to turn from it; if he do not turn from his way, he shall die in his iniquity; but thou hast delivered thy soul" (Eze.33:9).

"But I say unto you, It shall be more tolerable for Tyre and Sidon at the day of judgment, than for you" (Mt.11:22).

"Woe unto the world because of offences! for it must needs be that offences come; but woe to that man by whom the offence cometh! Wherefore if thy hand or thy foot offend thee, cut them off, and cast [them] from thee: it is better for thee to enter into life halt or maimed, rather than having two hands or two feet to be cast into everlasting fire. And if thine eye offend thee, pluck it out, and cast [it] from thee: it is better for thee to enter into life with one eye, rather than having two eyes to be cast into hell fire" (Mt.18:7-9).

"And whosoever shall not receive you, nor hear you, when ye depart thence, shake off the dust under your feet for a testimony against them. Verily I say unto you, It shall be more tolerable for Sodom and Gomorrha in the day of judgment, than for that city" (Mk.6:11).

"And if ye call on the Father, who without respect of persons judgeth according to every man's work, pass the time of your sojourning here in fear" (1 Pe.1:17).

"And, behold, I come quickly; and my reward is with me, to give every man according as his work shall be" (Re.22:12).

3 (9:3-5) **Idolatry—Judgment—Worship, False—Animals—Livestock—Plague:** there was the purpose for the judgment.

Why was God sending this particular plague upon the Egyptians? Because they worshipped the animals of the earth. They obviously believed that the spirit of some god lived in every living thing upon earth. Thus, they had taken some animals and molded their images into wood, stone, and metal. They had created idols as symbols of the gods whose spirits supposedly indwelt the animals. And they worshipped these gods, praying that they would take care of their livestock: grant good products and meat from them, make them very reproductive. Some of the animal gods were...

- the bull-gods: Apis, Mnevis, Ptah, and Bakis
- the cow-god: Hathor
- the ram-god: Khnum
- the calf-god: Ra
- the jackal-headed god: Anubis

God used the judgment of this plague to rebuke and ridicule the false worship of animals. No animal of the world and no god of animals controls the animal life of the world. There are not gods of this animal and gods of that animal. There is only one true and living God, the *LORD Himself* (Jehovah, Yahweh). And it is the hand of the LORD that controls the animals and livestock of the world.

How do we know this? What is the proof of God's control over the animals of the world? Note what He did: God protected the livestock of His people.

⇒ No animal of His people died.
⇒ God set a definite time for the judgment: the very next day.

God destroyed the livestock of the evil sinners and saved the livestock of the believers. He controlled which livestock lived and which livestock died. The hand of the LORD...

- is sovereign over the animal life of this world
- is in control of the animal life of this world

Thought 1. Idolatry is sin, a terrible evil, an evil that will condemn us to the eternal judgment of God. It is foolish, absolutely foolish, to worship the animals of the earth. Any thinking and honest person should know that anything that dies and remains dead is dead, not living. And we need a living God, not some dead god who supposedly lives in a dead animal. There is only one true and living LORD, only one LORD who controls the animal life of this world, the LORD God Himself (Jehovah, Yahweh). We absolutely must not worship the idols of this world, the idols of animals created in the imaginations of people.

"Thou shalt not make unto thee any graven image, or any likeness of any thing that is in heaven above, or that is in the earth beneath, or that is in the water under the earth" (Ex.20:4).
"Ye shall make you no idols nor graven image, neither rear you up a standing image, neither shall ye set up any image of stone in your land, to bow down unto it: for I am the LORD your God" (Le.26:1).

"I am the LORD: that is my name: and my glory will I not give to another, neither my praise to graven images" (Is.42:8).
"Little children, keep yourselves from idols" (1 Jn.5:21).

4 (9:6) **Judgment—Livestock—Animals:** the day of judgment arrived. All the livestock of the Egyptians died, all that were in the fields. But note, no livestock of the Israelites died, not even one animal.

Thought 1. God's judgment is sure, certain. The hand of God's judgment is going to fall upon us if we do not heed His warning: repent and obey Him.

"The burden of Egypt. Behold, the LORD rideth upon a swift cloud, and shall come into Egypt: and the idols of Egypt shall be moved at his presence, and the heart of Egypt shall melt in the midst of it" (Is.19:1).

"For the Son of man shall come in the glory of his Father with his angels; and then he shall reward every man according to his works" (Mt.16:27).

"And then shall appear the sign of the Son of man in heaven: and then shall all the tribes of the earth mourn, and they shall see the Son of man coming in the clouds of heaven with power and great glory" (Mt.24:30).

"Therefore be ye also ready: for in such an hour as ye think not the Son of man cometh" (Mt.24:44).

"And as it is appointed unto men once to die, but after this the judgment" (He.9:27).

"And Enoch also, the seventh from Adam, prophesied of these, saying, Behold, the Lord cometh with ten thousands of his saints, To execute judgment upon all, and to convince all that are ungodly among them of all their ungodly deeds which they have ungodly committed, and of all their hard speeches which ungodly sinners have spoken against him" (Jude 14-15).

"Behold, he cometh with clouds; and every eye shall see him, and they also which pierced him: and all kindreds of the earth shall wail because of him" (Re.1:7).

5 (9:7) **Judgment—Heart, Hard—Hard - Hardness—Rejection, Of God—Unbelief**: there was the response to the judgment.

a. Note that Pharaoh sent some officials to investigate the cattle of the Israelites, to see if they were infected and had died. He no doubt intended to replenish his own livestock and the livestock of the Egyptians by confiscating most if not all of the surviving livestock of the Israelites. Pharaoh discovered just what he had been told: God had protected the Israelites from His hand of judgment.

b. What was Pharaoh's response to the hand of God's judgment? He could easily see that the LORD had power over the animal life of the world. The animals and lives of the Egyptian people were not under the control of the animal gods he and his people worshipped. They and their livestock were under the power of the LORD God of Moses. This should have softened Pharaoh and led him to repentance. But note: Pharaoh's heart was hard: he would not let God's people go. He still would not obey God. He just would not repent of his terrible evil of idolatry and greed, the greed that drives a person to take advantage of cheap labor and to oppress people.

Thought 1. God warns us against a hard heart. Hardness of heart will cause the hand of the LORD's judgment to fall upon us.

"Harden not your heart, as in the provocation, and as in the day of temptation in the wilderness: When your fathers tempted me, proved me, and saw my work. Forty years long was I grieved with this generation, and said, It is a people that do err in their heart, and they have not known my ways: Unto whom I sware in my wrath that they should not enter into my rest" (Ps.95:8-11).

"Happy is the man that feareth alway: but he that hardeneth his heart shall fall into mischief" (Pr.28:14).

"He, that being often reproved hardeneth his neck, shall suddenly be destroyed, and that without remedy" (Pr.29:1).

"Who among you will give ear to this? who will hearken and hear for the time to come? Who gave Jacob for a spoil, and Israel to the robbers? did not the LORD, he against whom we have sinned? for they would not walk in his ways, neither were they obedient unto his law. Therefore he hath poured upon him the fury of his anger, and the strength of battle: and it hath set him on fire round about, yet he knew not; and it burned him, yet he laid it not to heart" (Is.42:23-25).

"But after thy hardness and impenitent heart treasurest up unto thyself wrath against the day of wrath and revelation of the righteous judgment of God" (Ro.2:5).

"But exhort one another daily, while it is called To day; lest any of you be hardened through the deceitfulness of sin" (He.3:13).

	G. The Sixth Plague—Festering Boils Afflicted Man & Animal: Proof that God Has Power Over Body & Health, 9:8-12	all the land of Egypt. 10 And they took ashes of the furnace, and stood before Pharaoh; and Moses sprinkled it up toward heaven; and it became a boil breaking forth with blains upon man, and upon beast.	c. God's messengers obeyed Him d. God sent a plague of festering boils upon man & animal[DSI]
1. The day of judgment arrived a. The LORD gave a charge to Moses & Aaron: Toss handfuls of ashes or soot up into the air in the sight of Pharaoh b. The result: The ash would become fine dust that would cause festering boils to break out on man & animals	8 And the LORD said unto Moses and unto Aaron, Take to you handfuls of ashes of the furnace, and let Moses sprinkle it toward the heaven in the sight of Pharaoh. 9 And it shall become small dust in all the land of Egypt, and shall be a boil breaking forth with blains upon man, and upon beast, throughout	11 And the magicians could not stand before Moses because of the boils; for the boil was upon the magicians, and upon all the Egyptians. 12 And the LORD hardened the heart of Pharaoh, and he hearkened not unto them; as the LORD had spoken unto Moses.	2. The purposes for the judgment a. To prove that God holds power over body & health b. To prove that God can stop men from standing against Him 3. The response to the judgment a. God hardened Pharaoh's heart b. Pharaoh would not listen to the messengers of God

DIVISION III

THE TEN PLAGUES AND EGYPT: GOD'S JUDGMENT UPON THOSE WHO REJECT HIM AND OPPRESS HIS PEOPLE, 7:8–11:10

G. The Sixth Plague—Festering Boils Afflicted Man and Animal: Proof that God Has Power Over Body and Health, 9:8-12

(9:8-12) **Introduction**: God alone has control over body and health, not the gods created by the imaginations of men. We can do a lot to increase the strength of our health, but in the final analysis…

- positive thinking does not control body and health
- the gods of religion and man do not control body and health
- the science and technology of man do not control body and health
- the hands of physicians and nurses do not control body and health

As stated, we can do a lot to care for our bodies and health. But there is only one Person who holds the supreme control over body and health, the LORD Himself (Jehovah, Yahweh).

The Egyptians did not believe this. They believed that the fate of body and health was controlled by the science and technology of that day and by the high priests of religion or the occult. Note how Pharaoh had both sorcerers and magicians serving in his cabinet of government. They served right along with the professional politicians, the wise men of that day. (See note—Ex.7:10-13 for more discussion.)

Both body and health on this earth and in the future world were placed into the hands of mere men and the man-made gods they followed. And, tragically, down through the ages, people have placed the destiny of their health and body into the hands of the prophets of this world, the prophets of religion, science, technology, government, sorcerers, witches, and a host of other imagined deliverers of body and health.

But this God hates: He despises idolatry, despises people dooming themselves to an eternity of hell because of some false and terrible lie. There is only one true and living God, only one LORD who has the power to control body and health: the LORD God Himself (Jehovah, Yahweh). This the LORD was going to prove to the Egyptians. This is the great lesson the Egyptians needed to learn and the same lesson we need to learn: *The Sixth Plague—Festering Boils Afflicted Man and Animal: Proof that God Has Power Over Body and Health, 9:8-12.*

1. The day of judgment arrived (vv.8-10).
2. The purposes for the judgment (v.11).
3. The response to the judgment (v.12).

1 (9:8-10) **Judgment—Disease—Plague—Boils**: the day of judgment arrived. For the second time, there was no warning of this judgment. But Pharaoh was bound to know it was coming. He was bound to be having thoughts such as these:

> *Is it possible that the LORD is not going to let Egypt alone, not until I and my people repent and do exactly what the God of Moses is demanding: turn to Him and forsake our sins, the evil of idolatry and slavery? Could the LORD of Moses continue to send judgment after judgment upon Egypt unless we free God's people?*

As stated, Pharaoh's mind was probably filled with thoughts such as these. Consequently, there was no need for God to warn the king of this judgment. He knew it was coming and he had plenty of time to repent and lead his people to repent.

a. The LORD gave a charge to Moses and Aaron: toss handfuls of ashes or soot up into the air in the presence of Pharaoh (v.8). The Hebrew word for *ashes* (piah) actually means *soot*. Note that this symbolic act was to be done in the very sight of Pharaoh himself.

b. The result would be dramatic: the soot was to symbolize fine dust blowing all over the land of Egypt. God would then cause blowing dust and festering boils to break out on man and animal (v.9).

Note that the dust was to be taken from a furnace. The Egyptians had oppressed the Israelites by forcing them to bake brick around the hot furnaces of Egypt. Now the soot of the furnace was to be made a curse to them, a curse of terrible pain and suffering.

c. God's messengers obeyed God. Moses and Aaron immediately went to a furnace, took some soot, and apparently marched straight to the king (v.10). Moses himself tossed the soot into the air.

d. And just as God had said, festering boils immediately began to break out on both the people and animals.

Thought 1. What God says will happen. There is no stopping His Word: once He has spoken, the event will take place. God declares two critical facts that should concern us.

(1) We must repent, turn away from the evil of our ways and turn to God.

"Let the wicked forsake his way, and the unrighteous man his thoughts: and let him return unto the Lord, and he will have mercy upon him; and to our God, for he will abundantly pardon" (Is.55:7).

"But if the wicked will turn from all his sins that he hath committed, and keep all my statutes, and do that which is lawful and right, he shall surely live, he shall not die" (Eze.18:21).

"I tell you, Nay: but, except ye repent, ye shall all likewise perish" (Lu.13:3).

"Repent therefore of this thy wickedness, and pray God, if perhaps the thought of thine heart may be forgiven thee" (Ac.8:22).

"And the times of this ignorance God winked at; but now commandeth all men every where to repent" (Ac.17:30).

(2) If we reject God—if we refuse to repent and obey Him—then the plague of God's judgment will fall upon us.

"I the Lord search the heart, I try the reins, even to give every man according to his ways, and according to the fruit of his doings" (Je.17:10).

"When the Son of man shall come in his glory, and all the holy angels with him, then shall he sit upon the throne of his glory: And before him shall be gathered all nations: and he shall separate them one from another, as a shepherd divideth [his] sheep from the goats: And he shall set the sheep on his right hand, but the goats on the left" (Mt.25:31-33).

"For we must all appear before the judgment seat of Christ; that every one may receive the things done in his body, according to that he hath done, whether it be good or bad" (2 Co.5:10).

"And if ye call on the Father, who without respect of persons judgeth according to every man's work, pass the time of your sojourning here in fear" (1 Pe.1:17).

"The Lord knoweth how to deliver the godly out of temptations, and to reserve the unjust unto the day of judgment to be punished" (2 Pe.2:9).

DEEPER STUDY # 1
(9:10) **Chart—Disease—Health**: because of the length of this chart, it is being placed at the end of this outline study and commentary.

---

2 (9:11) **Judgment—Health—Body, the Human—Sickness—Power, of God**: the purpose of the judgment was twofold.

a. God's purpose was to prove that the Lord and the Lord alone held power over the body and health (v.11). What was stated in the Introduction (9:8-12) bears repeating, for it is so important for the technological and scientific ages of men. Body and health can be helped and sometimes strengthened (only sometimes) by man, but...

- positive thinking does not control body and health
- religion and the priests of religion do not control body and health
- sorcery and the occult do not control body and health
- physicians and nurses do not control body and health

The Lord Himself (Jehovah, Yahweh) is sovereign over body and health. He and He alone holds the power and controls the destiny of body and health for both man and animal.

b. God's second purpose for plaguing the Egyptians with festering boils was this: to prove that the Lord can stop men from standing against Him, stop them anytime He wills. Note how v.11 begins: "the magicians [false messengers] could not stand before Moses." They had been standing against him, standing against God. But not now, and note why. Because the plague of God's judgment, the festering boils, had stricken them. The purpose of God is clear: God was clearly demonstrating that He had the power to stop the false messengers from standing against Him. He had the power to stop them anytime He willed. They claimed to be the priests of the gods who ruled over body and health. But they were deceived, blinded by their own human reasoning and the scientific technology and advancements of their day. They trusted the abilities and dreams of men and rejected the only living and true God.

Thought 1. Our bodies are subject to accident, sickness, disease, and eventually death. There are not imaginary gods controlling our health nor what happens to our bodies. We do not have to appease this god and that god and another god and so on *ad infinitum*. We do not have to satisfy all the gods of people's imaginations, hoping that we will find one god who will help us. Neither are we left hopeless when science, technology, and medicine can no longer help us.

Health is in the LORD's hands. What happens to us is in the hands of the God of salvation, the God who loves us so much that He will deliver us. A person is a fool to follow any other 'so-called' god, the helpless gods imagined by men. When the LORD (Jehovah, Yahweh) loves us like He does and longs to deliver us like He does, we are fools to continue rejecting, denying, and ignoring Him. Our bodies rest in His hands. We must, therefore, cry to Him and trust Him to take care of us and to look after our bodies. And we must trust Him to eventually transfer us into the promised land of heaven itself. In heaven, that glorious world of perfection, there is no pain, suffering, thirst, hunger, or death.

"And said, If thou wilt diligently hearken to the voice of the LORD thy God, and wilt do that which is right in his sight, and wilt give ear to his commandments, and keep all his statutes, I will put none of these diseases upon thee, which I have brought upon the Egyptians: for I am the LORD that healeth thee" (Ex.15:26).

"And the LORD will take away from thee all sickness, and will put none of the evil diseases of Egypt, which thou knowest, upon thee; but will lay them upon all them that hate thee" (De.7:15).

"I said, LORD, be merciful unto me: heal my soul; for I have sinned against thee" (Ps.41:4).

"For they [God's Words] are life unto those that find them, and health to all their flesh" (Pr.4:22).

"But he was wounded for our transgressions, he was bruised for our iniquities: the chastisement of our peace was upon him; and with his stripes we are healed" (Is.53:5).

"Return, ye backsliding children, and I will heal your backslidings. Behold, we come unto thee; for thou art the LORD our God" (Je.3:22).

"For I will restore health unto thee, and I will heal thee of thy wounds, saith the LORD" (Je.30:17).

"Come, and let us return unto the LORD: for he hath torn, and he will heal us; he hath smitten, and he will bind us up" (Ho.6:1).

"The Spirit of the Lord [is] upon me, because he hath anointed me to preach the gospel to the poor; he hath sent me to heal the brokenhearted, to preach deliverance to the captives, and recovering of sight to the blind, to set at liberty them that are bruised" (Lu.4:18).

"In the midst of the street of it [New Jerusalem , the capital of heaven], and on either side of the river, was there the tree of life, which bare twelve manner of fruits, and yielded her fruit every month: and the leaves of the tree were for the healing of the nations" (Re.22:2).

"Is any among you afflicted? let him pray. Is any merry? let him sing psalms. Is any sick among you? let him call for the elders of the church; and let them pray over him, anointing him with oil in the name of the Lord" (Js.5:13-14).

3 (9:12) **Heart, Hard—Hard - Hardened—Unbelief—Rejection, of God**: the response to the judgment was unbeliev-ably tragic. Unbelievable because God had given Pharaoh chance after chance, opportunity after opportunity. Pharaoh should have led his people to repent of the evil of their idolatry and greed. And the Egyptians were greedy, so greedy that they sought cheap labor in order to fill their pockets and increase their own comfort—even to the point of oppressing and enslaving people.

The point is this: Pharaoh was not willing to repent nor willing to lead his people to obey God. Despite all his suffer-ing, he was still unwilling to yield to God. He was still unwilling...

- to believe that God was sovereign, in control of all things
- to believe that there was only one true and living God
- to believe that there was only one LORD, only one Savior and Redeemer of men (Jehovah, Yahweh)

Pharaoh's heart was hard, very hard. He just would not listen to the messenger of God. And no amount of trouble, no matter how severe the trouble was, was going to make him believe and obey God.

Thought 1. Many of us are just as Pharaoh was: hard, stubborn, rock-like. Terrible things have happened to us, and they should have pointed us toward God and led us to cry out to Him. But far too many of us refuse to surrend-er to God. We reject, deny, and ignore God. And so many of us even *curse God*, using His holy and righteous name in vain. What terrible evil erupts from a hard heart! Evil that dooms the unrepentant soul to an everlasting hell.

"So I spake unto you; and ye would not hear, but rebelled against the commandment of the LORD, and went presumptuously up into the hill [to commit idolatry]" (De.1:43).

"Many sorrows shall be to the wicked: but he that trusteth in the LORD, mercy shall compass him about" (Ps.32:10).

"[That they] might not be as their fathers, a stubborn and rebellious generation; a generation that set not their heart aright, and whose spirit was not stedfast with God" (Ps.78:8).

"To whom he said, This is the rest wherewith ye may cause the weary to rest; and this is the re-freshing: yet they would not hear" (Is.28:12).

"For thus saith the Lord GOD, the Holy One of Israel; In returning and rest shall ye be saved; in quietness and in confidence shall be your strength: and ye would not" (Is.30:15).

"Hearken unto me, ye stouthearted, that are far from righteousness" (Is.46:12).

"Because I knew that thou art obstinate, and thy neck is an iron sinew, and thy brow brass" (Is.48:4).

"If ye will not hear, and if ye will not lay it to heart, to give glory unto my name, saith the LORD of hosts, I will even send a curse upon you, and I will curse your blessings: yea, I have cursed them already, because ye do not lay it to heart" (Mal.2:2).

"But chiefly them that walk after the flesh in the lust of uncleanness, and despise government. Presumptuous are they, selfwilled, they are not afraid to speak evil of dignities [heavenly beings]" (2 Pe.2:10).

DEEPER STUDY # 1

(9:10) **Chart—Disease—Health**: God has much to say about the human body and its health. Scripture is filled with reference after reference about this important subject. This chart is only a sample to show God's enormous interest in our body and health.

GOD'S POWER OVER THE BODY AND HEALTH

Medical Condition	Symptoms	Scripture Reference
Alcoholism	Addicted to alcohol. The alcoholic has a psychological need for alcohol, a need that continues to crave even when family, friends, and work are harmed.	"And be not drunk with wine, wherein is excess; but be filled with the Spirit" (Ep.5:18).
Atrophy	Muscles that grow weak due to disease or a lack of use. Control of the limb is hampered by extreme pain and stiffness.	"And it came to pass also on another sabbath, that he entered into the synagogue and taught: and there was a man whose right hand was withered" (Lu.6:6).
Baldness	The loss of hair on the head can be caused by... • aging • tight hairstyle • excessive hair treatments • skin diseases or infections • stress • high fever • poor eating habits (poor nutrition)	"And the man whose hair is fallen off his head, he *is* bald; *yet is* he clean. And he that hath his hair fallen off from the part of his head toward his face, he *is* forehead bald: *yet is* he clean" (Le.13:40-41).
Boil	A painful skin disease caused by bacteria. Boils are evidenced... • by swelling of parts of the skin • by red or pink bumps • by a fever and a sapping of strength	"So went Satan forth from the presence of the LORD, and smote Job with sore boils from the sole of his foot unto his crown" (Jb.2:7).
Consumption	Probably a wasting disease like dysentery. (Other medical sources point toward tuberculosis.)[1]	"I also will do this unto you; I will even appoint over you terror, consumption, and the burning ague, that shall consume the eyes, and cause sorrow of heart: and ye shall sow your seed in vain, for your enemies shall eat it" (Le.26:16).
Deafness	The partial or complete loss of hearing caused by reasons of... • heredity • injury • disease	"Then Jesus answering said unto them, Go your way, and tell John what things ye have seen and heard; how that the blind see, the lame walk, the lepers are cleansed, the deaf hear, the dead are raised, to the poor the gospel is preached" (Lu.7:22).

---

1 *Illustrated Stedman's Medical Dictionary, 24th Edition*. (Baltimore MD: Williams & Wilkins, 1982), p. 315).

GOD'S POWER OVER THE BODY AND HEALTH

Medical Condition	Symptoms	Scripture Reference
Demon possession	A demon can cause physical illness. Scripture notes occasions of... • violent behavior • muteness (unable to speak) • blindness • great suffering • convulsions • raving madness (insanity)	"And his fame went throughout all Syria: and they brought unto him all sick people that were taken with divers diseases and torments, and those which were possessed with devils, and those which were lunatic, and those that had the palsy; and he healed them" (Mt.4:24).
Dropsy	Abnormal amount of fluid that fills up tissues in the body, making breathing difficult	"And, behold, there was a certain man before him which had the dropsy" (Lu.14:2).
Dwarf	A serious retardation of growth in the length of the limbs (arms and legs) and the trunk	"Or crookbacked [hunchback], or a dwarf, or that hath a blemish in his eye, or be scurvy, or scabbed, or hath his stones broken" (Le.21:20).
Dumbness	The inability to speak either clearly or at all	"And they bring unto him one that was deaf, and had an impediment in his speech; and they beseech him to put his hand upon him" (Mk.7:32).
Dysentery	Severe attacks of diarrhea that result in a loss of fluids and minerals. Symptoms can include... • a water-like stool • intense cramping in the abdomen • low-grade fever • nausea and/or vomiting • headaches	"And after all this the LORD smote him in his bowels with an incurable disease. And it came to pass, that in process of time, after the end of two years, his bowels fell out by reason of his sickness: so he died of sore diseases. And his people made no burning for him, like the burning of his fathers" (2 Chr.21:18-19).
Epilepsy	A seizure occurs when the electrical discharges of the brain become scattered. This condition is then accompanied by a loss of consciousness with convulsions.	"Lord, have mercy on my son: for he is lunatic, and sore vexed: for ofttimes he falleth into the fire, and oft into the water" (Mt.17:15).
Fever	A higher than normal (98.6 degrees F.) body temperature	"And when Jesus was come into Peter's house, he saw his wife's mother laid, and sick of a fever. And he touched her hand, and the fever left her: and she arose, and ministered unto them" (Mt.8:14-15).
Fiery heat (Heat Stroke)	Heat stroke victims often face... • a fever of 105 degrees F. • rapid heartbeat • shortness of breath • extremely high or low blood pressure • confusion • seizures, coma, and sometimes death	"The LORD shall smite thee with a consumption, and with a fever, and with an inflammation, and with an extreme burning, and with the sword, and with blasting, and with mildew; and they shall pursue thee until thou perish" (De.28:22).
Headache	Extreme pain centered in the head. Different types of headaches cause different kinds of pain: ⇒ dull, tension headache ⇒ throbbing, vascular headache ⇒ nausea, migraine headache ⇒ sharp, neuralgia (pain that follows a specific nerve) headache	"And he said unto his father, My head, my head. And he said to a lad, Carry him to his mother" (2 K.4:19).

GOD'S POWER OVER THE BODY AND HEALTH

Medical Condition	Symptoms	Scripture Reference
Hemorrhage	Uncontrolled bleeding from internal organs, especially in the head, chest, or abdomen. Hemorrhaging is serious and life-threatening. If it is not treated, it can lead to… • shock • unconsciousness • death	"And a woman having an issue of blood twelve years, which had spent all her living upon physicians, neither could be healed of any, Came behind *him,* and touched the border of his garment: and immediately her issue of blood stanched" (Lu.8:43-44).
Impediment of speech	Unable to speak clearly, with articulation. An organic obstruction to speech. Typical symptoms would include… • clipping the beginning of a word • clipping the ending of a word • using one letter for another	"And they bring unto him one that was deaf, and had an impediment in his speech; and they beseech him to put his hand upon him" (Mk.7:32).
Indigestion	Unable to digest food properly, the following symptoms may appear: ⇒ bloated feeling in the upper abdomen ⇒ heartburn from the gastric juices from the stomach to the esophagus ⇒ nausea	"Drink no longer water, but use a little wine for thy stomach's sake and thine often infirmities" (1 Ti.5:23).
Infirmity	A broad term, but probably polio in this case. Polio is a viral infection that attacks the brain and spinal cord. Acute symptoms are… • headache and fever • stiffness in the back and neck • weakening muscles • difficulty in swallowing • paralysis • respiratory failure	"And a certain man was there, which had an infirmity thirty and eight years" (Jn.5:5).
Inflammation	Caused by an infection from a microorganism, the skin swells. Other symptoms are stinging pain, heat, and redness.	"The LORD will smite thee with the botch of Egypt, and with the emerods, and with the scab, and with the itch, whereof thou canst not be healed" (De.28:27).
Insanity	A serious defect in the brain which causes the person to act irrationally. The thought processes are no longer logical, reasonable, or rational.	"Lord, have mercy on my son: for he is lunatic, and sore vexed: for ofttimes he falleth into the fire, and oft into the water" (Mt.17:15).
Itch	A skin irritation caused by a tiny mite	"The LORD will smite thee with the botch of Egypt, and with the emerods, and with the scab, and with the itch, whereof thou canst not be healed" (De.28:27).
Leprosy	A gross destruction of the skin that had no natural cure or treatment during Bible times. Symptoms are… • a loss of feeling in a patch of skin • damage to the nervous system • potential paralysis • loss of extremities	"And it came to pass, when he was in a certain city, behold a man full of leprosy: who seeing Jesus fell on *his* face, and besought him, saying, Lord, if thou wilt, thou canst make me clean. And he put forth *his* hand, and touched him, saying, I will: be thou clean. And immediately the leprosy departed from him" (Lu.5:12-13).

GOD'S POWER OVER THE BODY AND HEALTH

Medical Condition	Symptoms	Scripture Reference
Obesity	A major weight disorder caused by... • heredity • overeating • lack of exercise • more than the average amount of fat cells A person is considered obese when 20% or more of the normal body weight is exceeded.	"And he brought the present unto Eglon king of Moab: and Eglon *was* a very fat man" (Jud.3:17).
Palsy	Paralysis occurs when there is damage to the motor function areas of the central nervous system.	"And saying, Lord, my servant lieth at home sick of the palsy, grievously tormented" (Mt.8:6).
Scurvy	A festering form of skin disease caused by a severe lack of vitamin C. Symptoms that appear are... • progressive weakness • sore gums • loose teeth • swollen and sore joints • anemia	"Blind, or broken, or maimed, or having a wen, or scurvy, or scabbed, ye shall not offer these unto the LORD, nor make an offering by fire of them upon the altar unto the LORD" (Le.22:22).
Skin diseases	A wide variety: Baldness, Boil, Caul, Inflammation, Itch, Leprosy, Scabies, Scab, Sore, Scurvy, Tetter, & Ulcer	"The LORD shall smite thee in the knees, and in the legs, with a sore botch that cannot be healed, from the sole of thy foot unto the top of thy head" (De.28:35).
Starvation	A total lack of food necessary to live. Starvation occurs when the body tears down protein tissues in order to use the amino acids to sustain energy. When the body uses up between 25% to 33% of its protein structures, death is forthcoming.	"And thou shalt eat the fruit of thine own body, the flesh of thy sons and of thy daughters, which the LORD thy God hath given thee, in the siege, and in the straitness, wherewith thine enemies shall distress thee" (De.28:53).
Tetter	Vitiligo (area of skin with no pigment). The symptoms are a slowly growing white or dark brown patches of skin.	"Then the priest shall look: and, behold, *if* the bright spots in the skin of their flesh *be* darkish white; it *is* a freckled spot *that* groweth in the skin; he *is* clean" (Le.13:39).
Tumor	An abnormal enlargement on or in some part of the body. Similar to normal tissue, a tumor has no useful purpose. Tumors are not always cancerous.	"But the hand of the LORD was heavy upon them of Ashdod, and he destroyed them, and smote them with emerods [tumors], *even* Ashdod and the coasts thereof" (1 S.5:6).
Ulcer	A break-down of the skin on or inside the body that eventually destroys the flesh underneath	"The LORD will smite thee with the botch of Egypt, and with the emerods [ulcers], and with the scab, and with the itch, whereof thou canst not be healed" (De.28:27).
Worms	Digested with either infected food or water, worms live within the body, eating what it provides.	"And immediately the angel of the Lord smote him, because he gave not God the glory: and he was eaten of worms, and gave up the ghost" (Ac.12:23).

* Note: We were greatly helped by *The Zondervan Pictorial Encyclopedia of the Bible* in devising this chart.[2]

2 *The Zondervan Pictorial Encyclopedia of the Bible,* Vol.2. Merrill C. Tenney, General Editor. (Grand Rapids, MI: Zondervan Corporation), pp.132-141.

1. The declaration of God's Word, His will

a. Moses was to rise up early, go & stand before Pharaoh

b. Moses was to proclaim God's Word

  1) Let God's people go—free them to live & serve God

  2) If Pharaoh rejected God's Word, the full force of judgment was to fall

2. The overall purposes for the judgments

a. To prove the LORD has no equal

  1) He alone is God

  2) He is sovereign & omnipotent: He could have already wiped the Egyptians off the face of the earth

b. To prove that God controls all people, nations, & rulers

  1) He raised up Pharaoh

  2) God's purpose: To demonstrate His power & to declare His name in all the earth

3. The warning of judgment

a. The cause for the judgment: Self-exaltation against God's people

b. The judgment: The worst hail storm to ever strike was to fall upon Egypt

c. The demonstration of God's mercy: Instructed Pharaoh to order his people to put their livestock & everything else in a place of shelter—lest all be destroyed

d. The people who feared God's Word obeyed

e. The people who ignored God's Word disobeyed

4. The day of judgment arrived

a. God's instruction to Moses: To stretch out his hand toward the sky so that hail would fall

b. Moses' obedience

H. The Seventh Plague— A Catastrophic Hail & Thunderstorm: Proof That the Earth Is the LORD's, 9:13-35

13 And the LORD said unto Moses, Rise up early in the morning, and stand before Pharaoh, and say unto him, Thus saith the LORD God of the Hebrews, Let my people go, that they may serve me.
14 For I will at this time send all my plagues upon thine heart, and upon thy servants, and upon thy people; that thou mayest know that there is none like me in all the earth.
15 For now I will stretch out my hand, that I may smite thee and thy people with pestilence; and thou shalt be cut off from the earth.
16 And in very deed for this cause have I raised thee up, for to show in thee my power; and that my name may be declared throughout all the earth.
17 As yet exaltest thou thyself against my people, that thou wilt not let them go?
18 Behold, to morrow about this time I will cause it to rain a very grievous hail, such as hath not been in Egypt since the foundation thereof even until now.
19 Send therefore now, and gather thy cattle, and all that thou hast in the field; for upon every man and beast which shall be found in the field, and shall not be brought home, the hail shall come down upon them, and they shall die.
20 He that feared the word of the LORD among the servants of Pharaoh made his servants and his cattle flee into the houses:
21 And he that regarded not the word of the LORD left his servants and his cattle in the field.
22 And the LORD said unto Moses, Stretch forth thine hand toward heaven, that there may be hail in all the land of Egypt, upon man, and upon beast, and upon every herb of the field, throughout the land of Egypt.
23 And Moses stretched

forth his rod toward heaven: and the LORD sent thunder and hail, and the fire ran along upon the ground; and the LORD rained hail upon the land of Egypt.
24 So there was hail, and fire mingled with the hail, very grievous, such as there was none like it in all the land of Egypt since it became a nation.
25 And the hail smote throughout all the land of Egypt all that was in the field, both man and beast; and the hail smote every herb of the field, and brake every tree of the field.
26 Only in the land of Goshen, where the children of Israel were, was there no hail.
27 And Pharaoh sent, and called for Moses and Aaron, and said unto them, I have sinned this time: the LORD is righteous, and I and my people are wicked.
28 Intreat the LORD (for it is enough) that there be no more mighty thunderings and hail; and I will let you go, and ye shall stay no longer.
29 And Moses said unto him, As soon as I am gone out of the city, I will spread abroad my hands unto the LORD; and the thunder shall cease, neither shall there be any more hail; that thou mayest know how that the earth is the LORD's.
30 But as for thee and thy servants, I know that ye will not yet fear the LORD God.
31 And the flax and the barley was smitten: for the barley was in the ear, and the flax was bolled.
32 But the wheat and the rie were not smitten: for they were not grown up.
33 And Moses went out of the city from Pharaoh, and spread abroad his hands unto the LORD: and the thunders and hail ceased, and the rain was not poured upon the earth.
34 And when Pharaoh saw that the rain and the hail and the thunders were ceased, he sinned yet more, and hardened his heart, he and his servants.
35 And the heart of Pharaoh was hardened, neither would he let the children of Israel go; as the LORD had spoken by Moses.

c. The judgment fell: God sent thunder & hail, & lightning flashed back & forth upon the ground

  1) God rained hail on the land

  2) Hail fell

  3) Lightning flashed

  4) The worst storm to ever strike the nation of Egypt fell upon the people

  5) Hail struck everything in the fields: People, animals & vegetation—all the people, all the animals, every crop, & every tree

d. The protection of the land of Goshen, where Israel lived

5. The response to the judgment: A cry for deliverance

a. Pharaoh sent for Moses: He confessed his sin, that the Lord was right & he & his people were wrong

b. Pharaoh pleaded for prayer: That the hail & thunder stop

c. Pharaoh promised to free God's people, to let Israel go

6. The purpose for the judgment & deliverance

a. To prove that the earth is the LORD's

b. To prove that the LORD is merciful

  1) Merciful despite the hard heart of man

  2) Merciful even in the midst of judgment: The plague fell upon the food supply, but God mercifully allowed some crops to escape destruction

7. The deliverance from judgment

a. Moses left Pharaoh & went out of the city

b. Moses prayed to God: Spread out his hands toward the LORD

c. The result: The thunder, hail, & rain stopped

8. The sin of turning back: Pharaoh & his officials sinned again—they hardened their hearts

a. When: After the storm was over

b. The result:

  1) Pharaoh hardened his heart & refused to free Israel

  2) Pharaoh rejected God: Refused to obey God

DIVISION III

THE TEN PLAGUES AND EGYPT: GOD'S JUDGMENT UPON THOSE WHO REJECT HIM AND OPPRESS HIS PEOPLE, 7:8–11:10

H. The Seventh Plague—A Catastrophic Hail and Thunderstorm: Proof That the Earth Is the LORD's, 9:13-35

(9:13-35) **Introduction**: Who rules over the earth? Is there one god who controls the fruitfulness of the earth, another god who controls the water of the earth, and still another god who controls the rain and sunshine and on and on? Are there many gods who control the earth and the affairs of history and men? Does it really matter who men worship just so man calls *the* being god? Is there honestly no difference between religions? No difference between the various gods worshipped by men?

Scripture declares a glorious truth: there is only one living and true God, only one LORD of the whole earth, the LORD *Jehovah-Yahweh* Himself. Scripture declares there is no other God, that all gods worshipped by men are but the creation of man's wild and depraved imaginations: idols made from man's ideas and from wood, stone, and metal. Scripture declares that man himself is not even a god; no matter how high or how powerful he becomes, man is not God, not even a god unto himself.

There is only one living and true God. There is only one God of the earth. This is the great lesson taught by this passage: *The Seventh Plague—A Catastrophic Hail and Thunderstorm: Proof That the Earth is the LORD's,* 9:13-35.

1. The declaration of God's Word, His will (vv.13-14).
2. The overall purposes for the judgment (vv.14-16).
3. The warning of judgment (vv.17-21).
4. The day of judgment arrived (vv.22-26).
5. The response to the judgment: a cry for deliverance (vv.27-28).
6. The purpose for the judgment and deliverance (vv.29-32).
7. The deliverance from judgment (v.33).
8. The sin of turning back: Pharaoh and his officials sinned again—they hardened their hearts (vv.34-35).

[1] (9:13-14) **Long-suffering, of God—Judgment—Liberty—Freedom**: there was the declaration of God's Word, His will. Six times God had told Moses to go and proclaim His Word to Pharaoh. Six times Pharaoh had refused to heed God's Word. Now, for a seventh time, God instructed Moses to go to Pharaoh. Note how long-suffering God is: God still had not given up on Pharaoh and his people. God still wanted them to turn from their terrible evil of idolatry and oppression of God's people. Therefore, God instructed Moses to rise up early, go and stand before Pharaoh. Moses was to proclaim God's Word...

- Pharaoh was to let God's people go—free them to live and serve God. But note: this time Moses was to add a second point, a terrifying point, to his message.
- Pharaoh was marked for terrible destruction. If Pharaoh rejected God's Word, the full force of God's judgments was to fall upon him and his people. Nothing would be able to prevent the utter destruction of any who refused to repent of their terrible idolatry and the oppression of God's people.

Thought 1. God's will is for people to live and serve Him in freedom. Any person, ruler, or nation who rejects God and oppresses people is doomed, doomed to suffer the judgment of God. The rejection of God—of His Word, His will—and the oppression of people marks a person for the wrath of God.

"And the LORD said unto Samuel...they have not rejected thee, but they have rejected me, that I should not reign over them" (1 S.8:7).

"Kiss the Son, lest he be angry, and ye perish from the way, when his wrath is kindled but a little. Blessed are all they that put their trust in him" (Ps.2:12).

"But my people would not hearken to my voice; and Israel would none of me. So I gave them up unto their own hearts' lust: and they walked in their own counsels. Oh that my people had hearkened unto me, and Israel had walked in my ways!" (Ps.81:11-13).

"Because I have called, and ye refused; I have stretched out my hand, and no man regarded; But ye have set at nought all my counsel, and would none of my reproof: I also will laugh at your calamity; I will mock when your fear cometh; When your fear cometh as desolation, and your destruction cometh as a whirlwind; when distress and anguish cometh upon you" (Pr.1:24-27).

"For that they hated knowledge, and did not choose the fear of the LORD: They would none of my counsel: they despised all my reproof. Therefore shall they eat of the fruit of their own way, and be filled with their own devices. For the turning away of the simple shall slay them, and the prosperity of fools shall destroy them" (Pr.1:29-32).

"He that oppresseth the poor reproacheth his Maker: but he that honoureth him hath mercy on the poor" (Pr.14:31).

"He that believeth on the Son hath everlasting life: and he that believeth not the Son shall not see life; but the wrath of God abideth on him" (Jn.3:36).

"For the wrath of God is revealed from heaven against all ungodliness and unrighteousness of men, who hold the truth in unrighteousness" (Ro.1:18).

"But unto them that are contentious, and do not obey the truth, but obey unrighteousness, indignation and wrath" (Ro.2:8).

"Let no man deceive you with vain words: for because of these things cometh the wrath of God upon the children of disobedience" (Ep.5:6).

2 (9:14-16). **Power, of God—Sovereignty, of God—God, Nature**: there were the overall purposes for the judgments.

a. The first overall purpose was to prove that the LORD has no equal (vv.14-15). Note that two facts are given to prove this point.

1) There is no one like the LORD in all the earth. He and He alone is the only living and true God. Remember, God had already proven this fact in the plagues. He had deliberately launched each of the plagues against a particular god worshipped by the Egyptians. God took each plague and tried to show that...

- there is only one God, only one true and living God
- the gods imagined and dreamed up by men are false gods: nothing but idols made of ideas, wood, stone, and metal
- man himself is not even a god: even if he is the most powerful ruler upon earth, he is nothing more than mere man, temporary and subject to the frailties of the human flesh

God had taken each of the plagues and clearly demonstrated that He has no equal, that there is no one like God in all the earth. The LORD (Jehovah, Yahweh) is the only living and true God in all the universe.

2) God alone is sovereign and omnipotent. God could have already wiped the Egyptians off the face of the earth. Again, the plagues prove this fact. God is sovereign and omnipotent, all-powerful. God has control...

- over the heavens and earth
- over the animals of the earth
- over man
- over life and death
- over the entire universe

The LORD is the only living and true God, sovereign and omnipotent. The LORD has no equal. There is no one like the LORD in all the earth.

b. The second overall purpose for the judgments was to prove that God controls the people, nations, rulers, and governments of this world (v.16). God raised up Pharaoh and set him on the throne of Egypt for a very specific purpose: to demonstrate the LORD's power and to declare His name in all the earth. (Paul used this verse to declare the sovereignty of God (Ro.9:17).

God wanted Pharaoh and the world to know His power, that He is beyond question sovereign and omnipotent over all the world. Note what Scripture says: God took Pharaoh, a man of unbelievable brutality and evil, and made an example of him before the whole world (v.16). God showed the world...

- that He is sovereign and omnipotent, the Sovereign LORD and Majesty of the universe
- that He is in charge of events, even in charge of evil rulers
- that He does chastise and judge evil rulers and sinful people
- that people in the most horrible circumstances imaginable, even people who are brutalized and enslaved, can call out to God for deliverance, and God will deliver them

God took this man Pharaoh, whose heart was so hard and evil, and declared to the world: God's power is real. God's sovereign and omnipotent power rules the world.

Note the result of God's power demonstrated in Pharaoh: God's name was to be declared throughout all the earth down through all the ages. And believers have done just this.

⇒ Jethro proclaimed the power of God over all gods.

> **"Now I know that the LORD is greater than all gods: for in the thing wherein they dealt proudly he was above them" (Ex.18:11).**

⇒ Paul the apostle declared that God's raising up of Pharaoh is proof of God's sovereignty over the universe.

> **"For the scripture saith unto Pharaoh, Even for this same purpose have I raised thee up, that I might show my power in thee, and that my name might be declared throughout all the earth" (Ro.9:17).**

⇒ Preachers and believers down through the centuries have been proclaiming the name of the LORD because of the judgments of God upon Pharaoh and his people. This study is proof of the fact.

Thought 1. The LORD has no equal. There is no one like the LORD in all the earth. He and He alone is sovereign and omnipotent within the universe. The LORD alone has power over the people, nations, rulers, and governments of the world. God alone is the Sovereign LORD and Majesty of the universe.

> **"That men may know that thou, whose name alone is JEHOVAH, art the most high over all the earth" (Ps.83:18)**
> **"Know therefore this day, and consider it in thine heart, that the LORD he is God in heaven above, and upon the earth beneath: there is none else" (De.4:39).**
> **"Both riches and honour come of thee, and thou reignest over all; and in thine hand is power and might; and in thine hand it is to make great, and to give strength unto all" (1 Chr.29:12).**
> **"He leadeth princes away spoiled, and overthroweth the mighty" (Jb.12:19).**
> **"The LORD sitteth upon the flood; yea, the LORD sitteth King for ever" (Ps.29:10).**

"For the LORD most high is terrible; he is a great King over all the earth" (Ps.47:2).

"The LORD reigneth, he is clothed with majesty; the LORD is clothed with strength, wherewith he hath girded himself: the world also is stablished, that it cannot be moved" (Ps.93:1).

"For I know that the LORD is great, and that our Lord is above all gods. Whatsoever the LORD pleased, that did he in heaven, and in earth, in the seas, and all deep places" (Ps.135:5-6).

"The king's heart is in the hand of the LORD, as the rivers of water: he turneth it whithersoever he will" (Pr.21:1).

"Thus saith the LORD, thy redeemer, and he that formed thee from the womb, I am the LORD that maketh all things; that stretcheth forth the heavens alone; that spreadeth abroad the earth by myself; That frustrateth the tokens of the liars, and maketh diviners mad; that turneth wise men backward, and maketh their knowledge foolish" (Is.44:24-25).

"Daniel answered and said, Blessed be the name of God for ever and ever: for wisdom and might are his: And he changeth the times and the seasons: he removeth kings, and setteth up kings: he giveth wisdom unto the wise, and knowledge to them that know understanding: He revealeth the deep and secret things: he knoweth what is in the darkness, and the light dwelleth with him" (Da.2:20-22).

"And all the inhabitants of the earth are reputed as nothing: and he doeth according to his will in the army of heaven, and among the inhabitants of the earth: and none can stay his hand, or say unto him, What doest thou?" (Da.4:35).

"And lead us not into temptation, but deliver us from evil: For thine is the kingdom, and the power, and the glory, for ever" (Mt.6:13).

"God that made the world and all things therein, seeing that he is Lord of heaven and earth, dwelleth not in temples made with hands" (Ac.17:24).

"Thou wilt say then unto me, Why doth he yet find fault? For who hath resisted his will? Nay but, O man, who art thou that repliest against God? Shall the thing formed say to him that formed it, Why hast thou made me thus? Hath not the potter power over the clay, of the same lump to make one vessel unto honour, and another unto dishonour?" (Ro.9:19-21).

3 (9:17-21) **Judgment—Warning**: there was the warning and proclamation of judgment.

a. The cause for the judgment was found in the hearts of Pharaoh and his people (v.17). The hearts of Pharaoh and his people were set against God's people. They exalted themselves against God's people. Pharaoh was a great king, and the Egyptian people were a great people in the eyes of the world. In comparison, God's people at their very best had been poor shepherds. And now they were slaves, a people oppressed and brutalized. Nevertheless, they were the very people who followed after the living and true God; therefore, they were very special to God. Note that God calls them "My people."

⇒ Any man who exalts himself against God's people is counted as exalting himself against God.
⇒ Any man or nation who oppresses God's people is counted as oppressing God.
⇒ Any man or nation who abuses God's people is counted as abusing God.

Consequently, the judgment of God was bound to fall upon Pharaoh and his people. God would just not allow His people to be trampled upon, insulted, and abused.

b. The judgment was to be life-threatening: the worst hail-storm ever to strike Egypt was to fall upon the nation (v.18).

c. But note the demonstration of God's mercy. God instructed Pharaoh to order his people to put their servants, livestock, and possessions in a place of shelter—lest all be destroyed. Note that every person, animal, and possession left out in the open was to be killed or destroyed. This is a strong example of God's long-suffering and mercy. Just picture the holocaust launched by Pharaoh and his people against God's people, how savage and brutal the treatment of God's people had been. No doubt thousands had been killed in the holocaust of the enslavement and brutality. Yet here is God demonstrating His mercy and long-suffering, not willing that a single Egyptian should perish. He is going to judge them, but in the very midst of the judgment, He makes a way to escape. And He forewarns them and tells them exactly how to escape. All they have to do is believe, take Him at His Word and obey. Do exactly what He says.

d. There were some people who feared God's Word and obeyed; therefore, they escaped the judgment of God (v.20). The *Expositor's Bible Commentary* says this:

There were some who "feared the word of the LORD" (v.20) and acted accordingly. This is belief as it should be, resulting in...

• action based on confidence in the Word of the LORD.

Some Egyptians must have received Moses' word as being from God Himself; for they became a part of that mixed company of Gentile believers who left Egypt with Israel (see 12:38).[1]

Matthew Henry says this:

Even among the servants of Pharaoh there were some that trembled at God's Word.[2]

e. There were, of course, people who ignored God's Word and suffered the consequences: they left their servants and animals in the fields, and they were all killed (v.21).

[1] Frank E. Gaebelein, Editor. *Expositor's Bible Commentary*, Vol.2, p.362. (The statement is set apart for emphasis.)
[2] Matthew Henry, *Matthew Henry's Commentary*. (Old Tappan, NJ: Fleming H. Revell Co.), p.308.

Thought 1. God warns us of coming judgment. And He has provided shelter for us in the Lord Jesus Christ. It is up to us to seek shelter in Christ, to cast our lives and trust upon Him. He is our shelter in the time of storm.

"I am the door: by me if any man enter in, he shall be saved, and shall go in and out, and find pasture" (Jn.10:9).

"Neither is there salvation in any other: for there is none other name under heaven given among men, whereby we must be saved" (Ac.4:12).

"But we believe that through the grace of the Lord Jesus Christ we shall be saved, even as they" (Ac.15:11).

"But God commendeth his love toward us, in that, while we were yet sinners, Christ died for us. Much more then, being now justified by his blood, we shall be saved from wrath through him" (Ro.5:8-9).

"For God hath not appointed us to wrath, but to obtain salvation by our Lord Jesus Christ" (1 Th.5:9).

"And being made perfect, he became the author of eternal salvation unto all them that obey him" (He.5:9).

4 (9:22-26) **Judgment—Hail—Storm—Protection, of God**: the day of judgment arrived.

a. God gave His instructions to Moses. Moses was to stretch his hand toward the sky, and God would send His terrifying judgment upon the land.

b. Moses obeyed God: he did exactly what God had instructed him to do (v.23).

c. The judgment of God fell: God sent thunder and hail, and lightning flashed back and forth upon the ground (vv.23-25). Note how the judgment is described:

⇒ God rained hail on the land (v.23).
⇒ Hail fell (v.24).
⇒ Lightning flashed (v.24).
⇒ The worst storm ever to strike the nation of Egypt fell upon the people (v.24).
⇒ Hail struck everything in the fields: people, animals, and vegetation (v.25). Note how devastating the destruction was. It was catastrophic. Everything out in the open was totally destroyed: all the people, all the animals, every crop, and every tree.

d. But note that God protected both His people and their land, the land of Goshen.

Thought 1. The judgment of God is going to fall upon the earth. But the person who truly believes and follows God will not face the doom of God's judgment. The LORD (Jehovah, Yahweh) is the only living and true Redeemer; He is the only Savior of man. He and He alone judges the unbeliever and saves the believer.

"He only is my rock and my salvation; he is my defense; I shall not be greatly moved" (Ps.62:2).

"I the LORD search the heart, I try the reins, even to give every man according to his ways, and according to the fruit of his doings" (Je.17:10).

"For the Son of man shall come in the glory of his Father with his angels; and then he shall reward every man according to his works" (Mt.16:27).

"When the Son of man shall come in his glory, and all the holy angels with him, then shall he sit upon the throne of his glory: And before him shall be gathered all nations: and he shall separate them one from another, as a shepherd divideth [his] sheep from the goats: And he shall set the sheep on his right hand, but the goats on the left" (Mt.25:31-33).

"The Lord knoweth how to deliver the godly out of temptations, and to reserve the unjust unto the day of judgment to be punished" (2 Pe.2:9).

"But the heavens and the earth, which are now, by the same word are kept in store, reserved unto fire against the day of judgment and perdition of ungodly men" (2 Pe.3:7).

"And Enoch also, the seventh from Adam, prophesied of these, saying, Behold, the Lord cometh with ten thousands of his saints, To execute judgment upon all, and to convince all that are ungodly among them of all their ungodly deeds which they have ungodly committed, and of all their hard speeches which ungodly sinners have spoken against him" (Jude 14-15).

"And, behold, I come quickly; and my reward is with me, to give every man according as his work shall be" (Re.22:12).

5 (9:27-28) **Judgment—Deliverance**: there was the response to the judgment: a cry for deliverance.

a. Pharaoh sent for Moses and confessed his sin: that the LORD was right and he and his people were wrong (v.27). Note that Pharaoh used the very same words that we use when we are repenting of sin: "I have sinned." Note that he also confessed that his people were sinful and that both they and he deserved the judgment of God.

b. Pharaoh pleaded for prayer: he asked Moses to pray that the hail and thunder stop (v.28).

c. Pharaoh promised to free God's people, to let Israel go (v.28). He promised to turn from his evil ways, to free the people he had enslaved and treated so savagely.

d. Moses assured Pharaoh of God's deliverance (v.29).

Thought 1. Was the confession and repentance of Pharaoh sincere? Not everyone who confesses and repents of sin is sincere. Not everyone who makes promises to God during moments of crisis is genuine. Therefore, when we confess and repent of sin, we must be sincere and *follow through*. We must do exactly what we have promised God.

"And they come unto thee [Ezekiel, the preacher] as the people cometh, and they sit before thee as my people, and they hear thy words, but they will not do them: for with their mouth they show much love, but their heart goeth after their covetousness" (Eze.33:31).
"Not every one that saith unto me, Lord, Lord, shall enter into the kingdom of heaven; but he that doeth the will of my Father which is in heaven" (Mt.7:21).
"He answered and said unto them, Well hath Esaias prophesied of you hypocrites, as it is written, This people honoureth me with [their] lips, but their heart is far from me" (Mk.7:6).
"They profess that they know God; but in works they deny him, being abominable, and disobedient, and unto every good work reprobate" (Tit.1:16).

6 (9:29-32) **Judgment—Deliverance—Mercy, of God—Long-suffering**: the purpose for the judgment and deliverance was twofold.

a. The first purpose was to prove that the whole earth is the LORD's (v.29). The earth is not under the control of the gods created by the Egyptians nor by any other people. No god created by the mind or hands of man controls the earth and what happens:

⇒ not the Egyptian water god, Iris.
⇒ not the Egyptian fire and lightning god, Siris.
⇒ not the Egyptian god of the atmosphere, Shu.

None of these could control nature nor provide protection against the devastating forces of nature. Neither can the gods worshipped by men today. Neither can man himself. No one can control nature and the devastating forces of nature, no one except the LORD Himself. The LORD and the LORD alone is sovereign over the earth. The earth is the LORD's: it is under His control alone.

"Now therefore, if ye will obey my voice indeed, and keep my covenant, then ye shall be a peculiar treasure unto me above all people: for all the earth is mine" (Ex.19:5).
"Thou, even thou, art LORD alone; thou hast made heaven, the heaven of heavens, with all their host, the earth, and all things that are therein, the seas, and all that is therein, and thou preservest them all; and the host of heaven worshippeth thee" (Ne.9:6).
"The earth is the LORD's, and the fulness thereof; the world, and they that dwell therein" (Ps.24:1).
"For every beast of the forest is mine, and the cattle upon a thousand hills" (Ps.50:10).
"The heavens are thine, the earth also is thine: as for the world and the fulness thereof, thou hast founded them" (Ps.89:11).
"The silver is mine, and the gold is mine, saith the LORD of hosts" (Hag.2:8).

b. The second purpose for this judgment and deliverance was to prove that the LORD is merciful.
1) The LORD is merciful despite the hard heart of man. Note what Moses declared: God knew that the king and his officials still did not fear the LORD (v.30). They still were not ready to repent of their terrible evil of worshipping false gods and enslaving people. But God would still have mercy and stop the judgment. He still wanted Pharaoh and his people to repent, believe, and obey God.
2) Note also that the LORD was merciful even in the midst of judgment. God's judgment of hail upon the food supply fell, but God mercifully allowed some crops to escape destruction (vv.31-32).

Thought 1. God is merciful. He is not willing that any person perish. He wants every one of us to repent, to turn from false worship and from any mistreatment of people.

"The Lord is not slack concerning his promise, as some men count slackness; but is longsuffering to us-ward, not willing that any should perish, but that all should come to repentance" (2 Pe.3:9)
"But he, being full of compassion, forgave their iniquity, and destroyed them not: yea, many a time turned he his anger away, and did not stir up all his wrath" (Ps.78:38).
"But thou, O Lord, art a God full of compassion, and gracious, longsuffering, and plenteous in mercy and truth" (Ps.86:15).
"And it shall come to pass, after that I have plucked them out I will return, and have compassion on them, and will bring them again, every man to his heritage, and every man to his land" (Je.12:15).
"It is of the LORD's mercies that we are not consumed, because his compassions fail not" (Lam.3:22).
"But though he cause grief, yet will he have compassion according to the multitude of his mercies" (Lam.3:32).
"And rend your heart, and not your garments, and turn unto the LORD your God: for he is gracious and merciful, slow to anger, and of great kindness, and repenteth him of the evil" (Joel 2:13).
"He will turn again, he will have compassion upon us; he will subdue our iniquities; and thou wilt cast all their sins into the depths of the sea" (Mi.7:19).

7 (9:33) **Deliverance—Prayer—Intercession**: there was the deliverance from judgment. Moses left Pharaoh and went out of the city. He got all alone with God, and note what he did: he spread out his hands toward the LORD. This is a picture of crying out to God. Moses was interceding for the lost people of Egypt. What was the result of his intercession? God heard his cry. God stopped the judgment, stopped the thunder, hail, and rain.

Thought 1. People are lost and dying without knowing God, without truly knowing Him. There is a great need for intercessors, for true believers to get all alone and seek the face of God for the lost. One of the crying needs of the hour is for intercessors, true intercessors.

"Thus I fell down [prayed, interceded] before the LORD forty days and forty nights, as I fell down at the first; because the LORD had said he would destroy you" (De.9:25).

"And Abraham drew near, and said, Wilt thou also destroy the righteous with the wicked? Peradventure there be fifty righteous within the city: wilt thou also destroy and not spare the place for the fifty righteous that are therein? That be far from thee to do after this manner, to slay the righteous with the wicked: and that the righteous should be as the wicked, that be far from thee: Shall not the Judge of all the earth do right? And the LORD said, If I find in Sodom fifty righteous within the city, then I will spare all the place for their sakes. And Abraham answered and said, Behold now, I have taken upon me to speak unto the Lord, which am but dust and ashes: Peradventure there shall lack five of the fifty righteous: wilt thou destroy all the city for lack of five? And he said, If I find there forty and five, I will not destroy it. And he spake unto him yet again, and said, Peradventure there shall be forty found there. And he said, I will not do it for forty's sake. And he said unto him, Oh let not the Lord be angry, and I will speak: Peradventure there shall thirty be found there. And he said, I will not do it, if I find thirty there. And he said, Behold now, I have taken upon me to speak unto the Lord: Peradventure there shall be twenty found there. And he said, I will not destroy it for twenty's sake. And he said, Oh let not the Lord be angry, and I will speak yet but this once: Peradventure ten shall be found there. And he said, I will not destroy it for ten's sake" (Ge.18:23-32).

8 (9:34-35) **Turning Back—Rejection, of God—Heart, Hard—Hard - Hardening**: there was the sin of turning back. Pharaoh and his officials sinned again: they hardened their hearts. When? After the storm was over. After God had stopped the judgment, they soon ignored the promise they had made to God. The cost of freeing over two million slaves was just too a high a price to pay. The entire economy of Egypt was already devastated by the plagues. And the loss of free slave-labor could be so catastrophic that the economy might never recover. Moreover, the slaves could help rebuild the nation, and their help to rebuild the economy was desperately needed.

Once the judgment had passed, Pharaoh and his officials apparently hoped against hope. They deceived themselves into thinking that the judgments were perhaps only natural catastrophes. Obviously, their thoughts ran something like this:

Perhaps nothing else will happen. Perhaps, just perhaps, there is no Sovereign LORD over the universe, no true and living God, only the gods created by the minds and hands of men. Maybe the catastrophes were just natural quirks of nature that sometimes happen.

The result of such self-deceptive, dishonest, and faulty thinking was twofold.
⇒ Pharaoh hardened his heart and refused to free Israel
⇒ Pharaoh rejected God: refused to obey God

Thought 1. A hard heart is a terrible thing. A hard heart causes a person to turn away from God, to forsake God. A hard heart dooms a person to the eternal judgment of God.

"The LORD is with you, while ye be with him; and if ye seek him, he will be found of you; but if ye forsake him, he will forsake you" (2 Chr.15:2).

"The hand of our God is upon all them for good that seek him; but his power and his wrath is against all them that forsake him" (Ezr.8:22).

"And I will utter my judgments against them touching all their wickedness, who have forsaken me, and have burned incense unto other gods, and worshipped the works of their own hands" (Je.1:16).

"For my people have committed two evils; they have forsaken me the fountain of living waters, and hewed them out cisterns, broken cisterns, that can hold no water" (Je.2:13).

"Thou hast forsaken me, saith the LORD, thou art gone backward: therefore will I stretch out my hand against thee, and destroy thee; I am weary with repenting" (Je.15:6).

"And it shall come to pass, when ye shall say, Wherefore doeth the LORD our God all these things unto us? then shalt thou answer them, Like as ye have forsaken me, and served strange gods in your land, so shall ye serve strangers in a land that is not yours" (Je.5:19).

"But though he had done so many miracles before them, yet they believed not on him" (Jn.12:37).

"Take heed, brethren, lest there be in any of you an evil heart of unbelief, in departing from the living God" (He.3:12).

CHAPTER 10

I. The Eighth Plague—Locusts Swarmed Over the Land: Proof That the LORD Is the Great Savior of Mankind, 10:1-20

1. **The purpose for God's judgments**
   a. That God might demonstrate one clear fact: He judges the sin & evil of hard hearts[DS1]
   b. That believers might teach the judgment of God to succeeding generations: God clearly has the power to execute judgment
   c. That believers might know this fact: God is the LORD, the Savior (Jehovah, Yahweh)

2. **The declaration of God's Word, His will**
   a. Moses & Aaron asked the key question: How long will you refuse to humble yourself before God?
   b. Moses & Aaron presented God's demand: Free God's people

3. **The warning & proclamation of judgment**
   a. The opportunity to repent & obey God
   b. The judgment: Locusts would swarm over Egypt
      1) Would cover the earth
      2) Would devour what little vegetation was not destroyed by the hail storm

      3) Would fill all Egyptian houses: Even the houses of Egypt's officials
      4) Would be the most severe locust plague in Egyptian history

4. **The attempt to compromise with God**
   a. The king's advisors suggested he compromise: Let the people go & worship their God
      1) Because Moses was a snare
      2) Because Egypt was ruined
   b. The king offered a compromise: He would free the people to go, but he wanted

And the LORD said unto Moses, Go in unto Pharaoh: for I have hardened his heart, and the heart of his servants, that I might show these my signs before him:
2 And that thou mayest tell in the ears of thy son, and of thy son's son, what things I have wrought in Egypt, and my signs which I have done among them; that ye may know how that I am the LORD.
3 And Moses and Aaron came in unto Pharaoh, and said unto him, Thus saith the LORD God of the Hebrews, How long wilt thou refuse to humble thyself before me? let my people go, that they may serve me.
4 Else, if thou refuse to let my people go, behold, to morrow will I bring the locusts into thy coast:
5 And they shall cover the face of the earth, that one cannot be able to see the earth: and they shall eat the residue of that which is escaped, which remaineth unto you from the hail, and shall eat every tree which groweth for you out of the field:
6 And they shall fill thy houses, and the houses of all thy servants, and the houses of all the Egyptians; which neither thy fathers, nor thy fathers' fathers have seen, since the day that they were upon the earth unto this day. And he turned himself, and went out from Pharaoh.
7 And Pharaoh's servants said unto him, How long shall this man be a snare unto us? let the men go, that they may serve the LORD their God: knowest thou not yet that Egypt is destroyed?
8 And Moses and Aaron were brought again unto Pharaoh: and he said unto

them, Go, serve the LORD your God: but who are they that shall go?
9 And Moses said, We will go with our young and with our old, with our sons and with our daughters, with our flocks and with our herds will we go; for we must hold a feast unto the LORD.
10 And he said unto them, Let the LORD be so with you, as I will let you go, and your little ones: look to it; for evil is before you.
11 Not so: go now ye that are men, and serve the LORD; for that ye did desire. And they were driven out from Pharaoh's presence.
12 And the LORD said unto Moses, Stretch out thine hand over the land of Egypt for the locusts, that they may come up upon the land of Egypt, and eat every herb of the land, even all that the hail hath left.
13 And Moses stretched forth his rod over the land of Egypt, and the LORD brought an east wind upon the land all that day, and all that night; and when it was morning, the east wind brought the locusts.
14 And the locusts went up over all the land of Egypt, and rested in all the coasts of Egypt: very grievous were they; before them there were no such locusts as they, neither after them shall be such.
15 For they covered the face of the whole earth, so that the land was darkened; and they did eat every herb of the land, and all the fruit of the trees which the hail had left: and there remained not any green thing in the trees, or in the herbs of the field, through all the land of Egypt.
16 Then Pharaoh called for Moses and Aaron in haste; and he said, I have sinned against the LORD your God, and against you.
17 Now therefore forgive, I pray thee, my sin only this once, and intreat the LORD your God, that he may take away from me this death only.

to know who would be going

   1) Moses' reply: Everyone—all the people—& all the livestock

   2) The king's reaction & threat: "Never! May God help you if I ever let you take the women & children with you. You are bent on evil (escape)"
   3) The king's compromise: Only the men could go
   4) The messengers of God were escorted (angrily) out of the king's presence

5. **The day of judgment arrived**
   a. God charged His servant: Stretch out your hand over Egypt & the locusts will swarm over the land & devour everything left from the hail storm

   b. God's servant obeyed: He stretched out his rod over the land
   c. God's judgment fell
      1) The signs of judgment appeared: An east wind blew all day & night—still giving time to repent
      2) The next morning the locusts came
         • Invaded all Egypt
         • Settled in every area
         • Unbelievably great numbers
         • Worst plague ever
         • Covered the entire ground
         • So numerous, darkness covered all Egypt
         • Devoured & destroyed all vegetation & food supply
         • Nothing green remained, nothing on the trees & nothing on the plants

6. **The response to the judgment: A cry for deliverance**
   a. Pharaoh confessed his sin

   b. Pharaoh asked for forgiveness
   c. Pharaoh asked for prayer: That God would remove the deadly plague

7. The deliverance from judgment			
a. God's messenger interceded, prayed	18 And he went out from Pharaoh, and intreated the LORD.	sea; there remained not one locust in all the coasts of Egypt.	Sea of Reeds (Red Sea)
b. God heard His messenger & stopped the judgment: Changed the east wind to a west wind that carried the locusts into the	19 And the LORD turned a mighty strong west wind, which took away the locusts, and cast them into the Red	20 But the LORD hardened Pharaoh's heart, so that he would not let the children of Israel go.	8. The sin of turning back a. God hardened Pharaoh's heart b. Pharaoh would not free God's people

DIVISION III

THE TEN PLAGUES AND EGYPT: GOD'S JUDGMENT UPON THOSE WHO REJECT HIM AND OPPRESS HIS PEOPLE, 7:8–11:10

I. The Eighth Plague—Locusts Swarmed Over the Land: Proof That the LORD Is the Great Savior of Mankind, 10:1-20

(10:1-20) **Introduction—God, Nature of**: God is the LORD, the great Savior of believers. Man is guilty of all forms of sin and evil, and God is going to judge all people of all generations for their sins and evil. This is pictured in the ten plagues of God's judgment that fell upon Egypt. Pharaoh and his people were guilty of the worst kinds of sins and evil, the evils of...

- injustice
- idolatry
- slavery
- brutality
- savagery
- murder
- greed

- worldliness
- immorality
- skepticism
- agnosticism
- rebellion against God
- rejection of God
- hardness of heart

Pharaoh and his people were worthy of judgment, so God was executing His justice upon them. God was rectifying all the wrongs they had committed against Him and against so many people on earth, in particular the people of God. But note the crucial point: God is not only just, God is merciful. The LORD God is the great God of salvation and redemption. The LORD saves and delivers us. This is the great lesson of this passage: God judges us, yes, but God also redeems us. He saves and delivers us. This is: *The Eighth Plague—Locusts Swarmed Over the Land: Proof That the LORD Is the Great Savior of Mankind,* 10:1-20.

1. The purpose for God's judgments (v.1-2).
2. The declaration of God's Word, His will (v.3).
3. The warning and proclamation of judgment (v.4-6).
4. The attempt to compromise with God (v.7-11).
5. The day of judgment arrived (v.12-15).
6. The response to the judgment: a cry for deliverance (v.16-17).
7. The deliverance from judgment (v.18-19).
8. The sin of turning back (v.20).

1 (10:1-2) **Judgment—Heart, Hard—Teach - Teaching**: there was the purpose for God's judgments. Why was God chastising and judging Egypt? Launching plague after plague upon the people? God Himself tells us in these two verses.

a. God wanted to demonstrate His judgment, that He clearly judges the sin and evil of hard hearts (v.1. See DEEPER STUDY # 1—Ex.10:1 for more discussion). Man needed to know this fact, to have the fact forever written upon his mind. God judges sin and evil. The ancient Egyptians were terrible sinners:

⇒ a savage and ruthless people who brutalized and enslaved others.
⇒ a brutal, merciless people who abused and killed others at will.
⇒ a prideful, self-sufficient people who rejected and denied the only living and true God.
⇒ a skeptical, idolatrous people who worshipped everything from man himself to birds, four-footed beasts, and creeping things.
⇒ a prejudicial, bigoted people who oppressed God's people, the very people who taught the truth of God and gave the hope of living forever to man.
⇒ a worldly, carnal people who were given over to greed, bright lights, pleasures, and the lusts of the flesh.

God had no choice: He had to chastise and judge the king and his people. He had to correct them. But note: God had a larger purpose than just judging the Egyptians for their evil and worldliness. God was going to demonstrate His judgment to the entire world, that He clearly judges sin and evil.

Thought 1. People may deny the fact, but denial does not stop the truth. God is going to judge the world, the sin and evil of people. This fact was clearly demonstrated in God's judgment upon the Egyptians. This was one of God's purposes for sending the ten plagues upon Egypt.

"The fool hath said in his heart, There is no God. They are corrupt, they have done abominable works, there is none that doeth good. The LORD looked down from heaven upon the children of men, to see if there were any that did understand, and seek God. They are all gone aside, they are all together become filthy: there is none that doeth good, no, not one. Have all the workers of iniquity no knowledge? who eat up my people as they eat bread, and call not upon the LORD" (Ps.14:1-4).

"And I will utter my judgments against them touching all their wickedness, who have forsaken me, and have burned incense unto other gods, and worshipped the works of their own hands" (Je.1:16).

"He that believeth on the Son hath everlasting life: and he that believeth not the Son shall not see life; but the wrath of God abideth on him" (Jn.3:36).

"For the wrath of God is revealed from heaven against all ungodliness and unrighteousness of men, who hold the truth in unrighteousness" (Ro.1:18).

"But unto them that are contentious, and do not obey the truth, but obey unrighteousness, indignation and wrath" (Ro.2:8).

"But fornication, and all uncleanness, or covetousness, let it not be once named among you, as becometh saints; neither filthiness, nor foolish talking, nor jesting, which are not convenient: but rather giving of thanks. For this ye know, that no whoremonger, nor unclean person, nor covetous man, who is an idolater, hath any inheritance in the kingdom of Christ and of God. Let no man deceive you with vain words: for because of these things cometh the wrath of God upon the children of disobedience" (Ep.5:3-6).

"Take heed, brethren, lest there be in any of you an evil heart of unbelief, in departing from the living God" (He.3:12).

b. God wanted believers to teach the judgment of God as well: He wanted them to teach the judgment of God to succeeding generations, that God is going to judge the world. He clearly has the power to execute judgment (v.2).

The judgment of God must be taught as well as the mercy of God. Our own children, as well as the unbelievers of the world, must be taught the judgment of God. God is just, perfectly just, and He wills that every one of us be treated justly...

• that every injustice we have suffered be made right
• that every injustice we have committed against others be made right
• that every injustice we have committed against God be made right

Therefore, God must execute justice; He must judge the world in *righteousness*. Therefore, God wants all believers to teach the truth of His judgment to their children, as well as to the unbelievers of the world. This was one of the very reasons God sent His plagues, His judgment, upon Egypt. The ten plagues stand as a picture before the world, a picture declaring that God judges sin and evil, a picture that the terrible day of God's judgment is coming. The day is coming when God is going to judge the world in righteousness, and the ten plagues show us this fact. The day of judgment—the day when every person must give an account to God—is coming.

Thought 1. God does not want our children to suffer the coming judgment upon sin and evil. God wants our children to escape the judgment. Therefore, it is our duty to teach the judgment of God: our duty to tell them about God's terrible plagues of judgment cast upon the evil and sin of the Egyptians.

"Only take heed to thyself, and keep thy soul diligently, lest thou forget the things which thine eyes have seen, and lest they depart from thy heart all the days of thy life: but teach them thy sons, and thy sons' sons" (De.4:9).

"And thou shalt teach them diligently unto thy children, and shalt talk of them when thou sittest in thine house, and when thou walkest by the way, and when thou liest down, and when thou risest up" (De.6:7).

"And that their children, which have not known any thing, may hear, and learn to fear the LORD your God" (De.31:13).

"Train up a child in the way he should go: and when he is old, he will not depart from it" (Pr.22:6).

"Whom shall he teach knowledge? and whom shall he make to understand doctrine? them that are weaned from the milk, and drawn from the breasts" (Is.28:9).

"So when they had dined, Jesus saith to Simon Peter, Simon, [son] of Jonas, lovest thou me more than these? He saith unto him, Yea, Lord; thou knowest that I love thee. He saith unto him, Feed my lambs" (Jn.21:15).

c. God also wanted believers to learn another fact from His judgment upon Egypt: that God is the LORD, the great Savior and Redeemer (Jehovah, Yahweh). God had delivered His people from the terrible judgments that were falling upon Egypt (Ex.8:22-23; 9:4), and He was going to deliver His people from Egyptian slavery, deliver them to the promised land. God is the LORD, the great Savior, Redeemer, and Deliverer of the world. Remember, the name LORD means just this: God is the God of salvation, redemption, and deliverance—the God who establishes the covenant of redemption and salvation with man; the God who reveals Himself as the LORD, the great Redeemer of mankind.

Thought 1. Salvation is found in the LORD and in the LORD alone. No one else, not a single person nor any manmade god...
• can save us from the bondages of this world that lead to death
• can lead us to promised land of heaven and give us eternal life

Only the LORD Himself can do this. Only He can save us. This was one of the reasons God launched His judgments upon Egypt, so that we might know that God is the LORD, the great Savior of mankind. The LORD is our great Savior, Redeemer, and Deliverer.

"The LORD is my light and my salvation; whom shall I fear? the LORD is the strength of my life; of whom shall I be afraid?" (Ps.27:1).

"But the salvation of the righteous is of the LORD: he is their strength in the time of trouble" (Ps.37:39).

"Behold, God is my salvation; I will trust, and not be afraid: for the LORD JEHOVAH is my strength and my song; he also is become my salvation" (Is.12:2).

"And it shall be said in that day, Lo, this is our God; we have waited for him, and he will save us: this is the LORD; we have waited for him, we will be glad and rejoice in his salvation" (Is.25:9).

"The LORD thy God in the midst of thee is mighty; he will save, he will rejoice over thee with joy; he will rest in his love, he will joy over thee with singing" (Zep.3:17).

"For unto you is born this day in the city of David a Saviour, which is Christ the Lord" (Lu.2:11).

"For the Son of man is come to seek and to save that which was lost" (Lu.19:10).

"For God sent not his Son into the world to condemn the world; but that the world through him might be saved" (Jn.3:17).

"Neither is there salvation in any other: for there is none other name under heaven given among men, whereby we must be saved" (Ac.4:12).

"Him hath God exalted with his right hand to be a Prince and a Saviour, for to give repentance to Israel, and forgiveness of sins" (Ac.5:31).

"This is a faithful saying, and worthy of all acceptation, that Christ Jesus came into the world to save sinners; of whom I am chief" (1 Ti.1:15).

"Wherefore he is able also to save them to the uttermost that come unto God by him, seeing he ever liveth to make intercession for them" (He.7:25).

DEEPER STUDY # 1

(10:1) Judgment, Judicial—Hard - Hardness—Hearts, Hardened: Scripture says that God hardened Pharaoh's heart and the hearts of his servants. What does this mean? It does not mean...

- that God doomed Pharaoh to hell
- that God interfered with Pharaoh's soul
- that God destroyed Pharaoh's will, his ability to choose God
- that God kept Pharaoh from living a righteous life

Pharaoh's heart was hard because he had made it hard through the years, made it hard by the decisions he had made. Time and again he had made decision after decision to do wrong, and as he did, the law of human nature, the very law of conditioning, set in. The more Pharaoh chose wrong, the easier it was to choose wrong. And he chose to do more and more wrong. Thus his heart became encrusted and rock-like. He found it easier and easier to reject God and give in to the lusts of the human flesh. Thus it can be said that God made Pharaoh's heart hard; that is, the law established by God from the very first of creation—the law of human nature, the law of conditioning—made Pharaoh's heart hard.

Pharaoh made his own heart hard by choosing to do wrong time and again. He conditioned himself, his own flesh and mind, to do more and more wrong and to reject God time and again. His conscience and inner knowledge of righteousness had just become hardened, more and more encrusted and rock-like.

Thus Scripture declares that God hardened Pharaoh's heart. But remember: God hardened Pharaoh's heart because his heart deserved to be hardened. Pharaoh had...

- chosen to worship false gods and idols all his life
- chosen to live an ungodly and unrighteous life
- treated others unjustly and unfairly
- brutalized and enslaved people
- rejected the pleas of God time and again
- rejected the plagues and warnings of God
- rejected God's messenger (Moses) who proclaimed the message of God (See DEEPER STUDY # 1—Ex.4:21 for more discussion.)

---

2 (10:3) **Freedom—Liberty—Pride**: there was the declaration of God's Word, His will. Moses and Aaron went to the palace of Pharaoh.

a. They asked the key question: How long will you refuse to humble yourself before God? Remember, Pharaoh had professed his sin and promised to obey God; he had promised to repent of his hardness against God and to free God's people (Ex.9:27). But once the former judgment had passed, he soon forgot his confession and promises: he turned away from God, more hardened than ever. He became stubborn, stiff-necked, obstinate, and unyielding to God.

b. They presented God's demand: free God's people (see note—Ex.9:1 for discussion).

Thought 1. Why does man refuse to humble himself before God? Because God demands our life, all we are and have, the actual sacrifice of everything. Why? In order to get the Word of God, the gospel of salvation, out to the world. The heart of Pharaoh is a tragic picture of man's heart: full of...

- pride
- self-sufficiency
- a hunger for money
- a hunger for power

- self-centeredness
- selfishness
- greed
- carnality
- idolatry
- false worship

The very thought that our hearts are full of such things is repulsive to some people. No matter what Scripture says about sin and judgment, we stick our heads up against the truth: we become stubborn, stiff-necked, obstinate, and unyielding to God. God wants to know something from our hard hearts: How long will we refuse to humble ourselves before Him?

"The wicked in his pride doth persecute the poor: let them be taken in the devices that they have imagined" (Ps.10:2).

"Therefore pride compasseth them about as a chain; violence covereth them as a garment" (Ps.73:6).

"Thou hast rebuked the proud that are cursed, which do err from thy commandments" (Ps.119:21).

"These six things doth the LORD hate: yea, seven are an abomination unto him: A proud look, a lying tongue, and hands that shed innocent blood, An heart that deviseth wicked imaginations, feet that be swift in running to mischief, A false witness that speaketh lies, and he that soweth discord among brethren" (Pr.6:16-19).

"When pride cometh, then cometh shame: but with the lowly is wisdom" (Pr.11:2).

"Pride goeth before destruction, and an haughty spirit before a fall" (Pr.16:18).

"He loveth transgression that loveth strife: and he that exalteth his gate seeketh destruction" (Pr.17:19).

"An high look, and a proud heart, and the plowing of the wicked, is sin" (Pr.21:4).

"For thou hast said in thine heart, I will ascend into heaven, I will exalt my throne above the stars of God: I will sit also upon the mount of the congregation, in the sides of the north: I will ascend above the heights of the clouds; I will be like the most High. Yet thou shalt be brought down to hell, to the sides of the pit" (Is.14:13-15).

"Though thou exalt thyself as the eagle, and though thou set thy nest among the stars, thence will I bring thee down, saith the LORD" (Obad.4).

"Love not the world, neither the things that are in the world. If any man love the world, the love of the Father is not in him. For all that is in the world, the lust of the flesh, and the lust of the eyes, and the pride of life, is not of the Father, but is of the world" (1 Jn.2:15-16).

3 (10:4-6) **Warning—Judgment—Opportunity—Chance, Second**: there was the warning and proclamation of judgment.

a. God gave Pharaoh and his people an opportunity to repent and obey Him (v.4). Note that this is a warning of coming judgment. The judgment was not to fall until the next day. Pharaoh had time to think and repent, plenty of time (see Ex.9:5).

b. God described the devastating judgment that was to fall upon Egypt (v.4-6). The judgment was going to be catastrophic, devastating: locusts would swarm all over Egypt.

⇒ The locusts would cover the whole face of the earth (v.5).
⇒ The locusts would devour what little vegetation was not destroyed by the hail storm (v.5).
⇒ The locusts would fill all Egyptian houses, even the houses of Egyptian officials (v.6).
⇒ The locusts would bring the most severe locust plague in all Egyptian history (v.6).

Thought 1. The plague of locusts has always struck terror in people, so much so that it has become a terrifying symbol of God's judgment. God warns us that judgment, terrible judgment, is coming. The statistics are absolute and accurate: there is not even one percent error in these statistics: everyone of us will die. Not one of us will escape death. After death, the judgment. This is exactly what Scripture says.

"And as it is appointed unto men once to die, but after this the judgment" (He.9:27).

"Though hand join in hand, the wicked shall not be unpunished: but the seed of the righteous shall be delivered" (Pr.11:21).

"Therefore thus saith the LORD, Behold, I will bring evil upon them, which they shall not be able to escape; and though they shall cry unto me, I will not hearken unto them" (Je.11:11).

"For when they shall say, Peace and safety; then sudden destruction cometh upon them, as travail upon a woman with child; and they shall not escape" (1 Th.5:3).

"How shall we escape, if we neglect so great salvation; which at the first began to be spoken by the Lord, and was confirmed unto us by them that heard him" (He.2:3).

4 (10:7-11) **Compromise—Half-Hearted**: there was an attempt to compromise with God. What then happened is interesting and full of drama.

a. The king's advisors suggested he compromise, that he let the Israelites go and worship their God (v.7). Up until now, the advisors had been silent, but the situation was now desperate. They gave two reasons for their counsel to compromise:

⇒ because Moses was a dangerous snare. They blamed Moses for the terrible judgments that were falling upon Egypt. They suggested that Moses was setting a snare, a dangerous trap to destroy them.
⇒ because Egypt was almost ruined. The advisors were obviously becoming impatient with Pharaoh's obstinacy and blindness to the destruction of the nation.

b. The king sent for Moses and Aaron and offered a compromise. He would free the people to go and worship the LORD, but he wanted to know who would be going (v.8).
⇒ Moses replied that everyone (all the people) and all the livestock would be going (v.9).
⇒ Upon hearing this, the king reacted and threatened the messengers of God: "Never! May God help you if I ever let you take the women and children with you. You are bent, planning an evil [escape]."
⇒ After threatening them, the king offered a compromise: only the men could go (v.11).
⇒ The messengers of God were then escorted angrily out of the king's presence (v.11).

Thought 1. God does not compromise with sin and evil. Pharaoh was willing to grant God's people the right to worship, but not to live in freedom and liberty. He was willing to go half way with God, but not all the way. However, God does not accept a half-hearted commitment. God does not compromise. God demands total obedience: that we do all He says, that we believe and follow Him with all our hearts.

"And thou shalt love the LORD thy God with all thine heart, and with all thy soul, and with all thy might" (De.6:5).
"Blessed are they that keep his testimonies, and that seek him with the whole heart" (Ps.119:2).
"Trust in the LORD with all thine heart; and lean not unto thine own understanding" (Pr.3:5).
"My son, give me thine heart, and let thine eyes observe my ways" (Pr.23:26).
"And ye shall seek me, and find me, when ye shall search for me with all your heart" (Je.29:13).
"Therefore also now, saith the LORD, turn ye even to me with all your heart, and with fasting, and with weeping, and with mourning" (Joel 2:12).
"I beseech you therefore, brethren, by the mercies of God, that ye present your bodies a living sacrifice, holy, acceptable unto God, which is your reasonable service. And be not conformed to this world: but be ye transformed by the renewing of your mind, that ye may prove what is that good, and acceptable, and perfect, will of God" (Ro.12:1-2).

5 (10:12-15) **Judgment—Locusts—Plagues, The Ten**: the day of judgment arrived.

a. God charged His servant: stretch out your hand over Egypt and the locusts will swarm over the land and devour everything left from the hail storm (v.12).
b. God's servant obeyed: he stretched out his rod over the land (v.13).
c. Immediately, God's judgment fell (v.13-15). Note exactly what happened: the mercy of God is clearly seen once again.
1) The signs of judgment appeared, but the judgment did not actually fall, not yet. An east wind blew all day and night: the Egyptians still had time to repent. God was still extending His mercy to the very people who had committed so many terrible atrocities against His people for so long. But this was to be the last night they had to repent. If they refused to repent of their evil atrocities and turn to God, the judgment was to fall the very next morning. Note what happened.
2) The next morning the locusts came. They...
• invaded all Egypt (v.14)
• settled in every area (v.14)
• were unbelievably numerous (v.14)
• brought the worst plague ever (v.14)
• covered the entire ground (v.15)
• were so numerous that darkness covered all Egypt (v.15)
• devoured and destroyed all vegetation and food supply (v.15)
• left nothing green, absolutely nothing on the trees and nothing on the plants (v.15)

Thought 1. The day of judgment will arrive; it is coming.
⇒ Rejecting God will not stop God's judgment.
⇒ Denying God will not stop God's judgment.
⇒ Ignoring God will not stop God's judgment.
⇒ Skepticism will not stop God's judgment.
⇒ Atheism will not stop God's judgment.
⇒ Thinking that God's judgment is not coming will not stop God's judgment.
⇒ Believing that there is no such thing as God's judgment will not stop God's judgment.

Denying and refusing to believe something will not stop it from happening, not if it is true. The LORD *is*—He does *exist*; He is the true and living God—and He is a rewarder to those who diligently seek after Him.

"But without faith it is impossible to please him: for he that cometh to God must believe that he is, and that he is a rewarder of them that diligently seek him" (He.11:6).

But if we refuse to believe God, rejecting Him and His warning, then God's eternal judgment is going to fall upon us. We cannot escape His judgment.

> "For the wrath of God is revealed from heaven against all ungodliness and unrighteousness of men, who hold the truth in unrighteousness....And even as they did not like to retain God in their knowledge, God gave them over to a reprobate mind, to do those things which are not convenient; Being filled with all unrighteousness, fornication, wickedness, covetousness, maliciousness; full of envy, murder, debate, deceit, malignity; whisperers, Backbiters, haters of God, despiteful, proud, boasters, inventors of evil things, disobedient to parents, Without understanding, covenantbreakers, without natural affection, implacable, unmerciful: Who knowing the judgment of God, that they which commit such things are worthy of death, not only do the same, but have pleasure in them that do them" (Ro.1:18, 28-32).

> "Now the works of the flesh are manifest, which are these; Adultery, fornication, uncleanness, lasciviousness, Idolatry, witchcraft, hatred, variance, emulations, wrath, strife, seditions, heresies, Envyings, murders, drunkenness, revellings, and such like: of the which I tell you before, as I have also told you in time past, that they which do such things shall not inherit the kingdom of God" (Ga.5:19-21).

> "But the heavens and the earth, which are now, by the same word are kept in store, reserved unto fire against the day of judgment and perdition of ungodly men" (2 Pe.3:7).

> "And Enoch also, the seventh from Adam, prophesied of these, saying, Behold, the Lord cometh with ten thousands of his saints, To execute judgment upon all, and to convince all that are ungodly among them of all their ungodly deeds which they have ungodly committed, and of all their hard speeches which ungodly sinners have spoken against him" (Jude 14-15).

> "And I saw a great white throne, and him that sat on it, from whose face the earth and the heaven fled away; and there was found no place for them. And I saw the dead, small and great, stand before God; and the books were opened: and another book was opened, which is the book of life: and the dead were judged out of those things which were written in the books, according to their works. And the sea gave up the dead which were in it; and death and hell delivered up the dead which were in them: and they were judged every man according to their works. And death and hell were cast into the lake of fire. This is the second death. And whosoever was not found written in the book of life was cast into the lake of fire" (Re.20:11-15).

> "But the fearful, and unbelieving, and the abominable, and murderers, and whoremongers, and sorcerers, and idolaters, and all liars, shall have their part in the lake which burneth with fire and brimstone: which is the second death" (Re.21:8).

6 (10:16-17) **Profession, False—Intercession—Forgiveness**: there was the response to the judgment: a confession of sin. In desperation, Pharaoh called for Moses and Aaron to come and to come quickly. Note exactly what he did: he made what seemed to be a genuine confession. He confessed that he had sinned against the LORD and against His messenger, Moses.

a. Pharaoh asked for forgiveness. Note how he worded it: this one more time. He was saying, "This is it. I will accept God and His Word, obey Him and follow through with my promise" (v.17).

b. Pharaoh then asked for prayer, that God remove the deadly plague (v.17).

Thought 1. A sincere profession made to God is not enough. Sincerity of heart will not get us to heaven. For example, we can be taking a trip to New York, Tokyo, or any other place and be as sincere as we can be about reaching our destination. But if we are on the wrong road, we will miss the city. Our sincerity and traveling along toward a certain destination does not help us unless we are on the right road. We have to be sure—absolutely sure—that we have taken the right road to reach our destination. The only way to God is through His Son, Jesus Christ.

> "For God so loved the world, that he gave his only begotten Son, that whosoever believeth in him should not perish, but have everlasting life" (Jn.3:16).

> "Then Simon Peter answered him, Lord, to whom shall we go? thou hast the words of eternal life" (Jn.6:68).

> "I said therefore unto you, that ye shall die in your sins: for if ye believe not that I am [he], ye shall die in your sins" (Jn.8:24).

> "Jesus saith unto him, I am the way, the truth, and the life: no man cometh unto the Father, but by me" (Jn.14:6).

> "Neither is there salvation in any other: for there is none other name under heaven given among men, whereby we must be saved" (Ac.4:12).

> "For other foundation can no man lay than that is laid, which is Jesus Christ" (1 Co.3:11).

> "For there is one God, and one mediator between God and men, the man Christ Jesus; Who gave himself a ransom for all, to be testified in due time" (1 Ti.2:5-6).

7 (10:18-19) **Deliverance—Judgment**: there was the deliverance from the judgment. Moses left the palace and presence of Pharaoh and got alone with God. He prayed and prayed to the LORD, the great Deliverer and Savior. The LORD and the LORD alone could stop the judgment of locusts. And note, the LORD did. He changed the east wind to a west wind that carried the locusts into the Sea of Reeds. (The Hebrew here is *Yam Suph* which means Sea of Reeds. See DEEPER STUDY # 1—Ex.14:16-18 for more discussion.)

Note the sovereignty of God, His power over the wind. One fact is clearly seen throughout the ten plagues: God is sovereign. He rules over the whole universe, over all nature and events.

Thought 1. The LORD is our Redeemer. He and He alone can deliver us from the chastisement and judgment that are due us. And He will, if we will pray and ask Him.

"But if from thence thou shalt seek the LORD thy God, thou shalt find him, if thou seek him with all thy heart and with all thy soul. When thou art in tribulation, and all these things are come upon thee, even in the latter days, if thou turn to the LORD thy God, and shalt be obedient unto his voice; (For the LORD thy God is a merciful God;) he will not forsake thee, neither destroy thee, nor forget the covenant of thy fathers which he sware unto them" (De.4:29-31).

"This poor man cried, and the LORD heard him, and saved him out of all his troubles" (Ps.34:6).

"From the end of the earth will I cry unto thee, when my heart is overwhelmed: lead me to the rock that is higher than I" (Ps.61:2).

"He shall call upon me, and I will answer him: I will be with him in trouble; I will deliver him, and honour him" (Ps.91:15).

"Then shalt thou call, and the LORD shall answer; thou shalt cry, and he shall say, Here I am. If thou take away from the midst of thee the yoke, the putting forth of the finger, and speaking vanity" (Is.58:9).

"And it shall come to pass, that before they call, I will answer; and while they are yet speaking, I will hear" (Is.65:24).

"And I say unto you, Ask, and it shall be given you; seek, and ye shall find; knock, and it shall be opened unto you" (Lu.11:9).

8 (10:20) **Turning Back—Heart, Hard—Hard - Hardened—Apostasy—Rejection**: there was the sin of turning back. This was a terrible, terrible tragedy. Pharaoh once again hardened his heart, and God once again had to act upon his heart. God hardened Pharaoh's heart; that is, God let his heart run the course of human nature. God let the law of human nature, *the law of conditioning*, take its effect. God allowed Pharaoh's rejection to harden his own heart more and more. The result: his heart became hardened, more rock-hard than ever, and he would not repent of his idolatry and oppression of people. He would not obey God and free God's people.

Thought 1. Turning back from God is a dangerous thing. Turning back and not fulfilling one's promise to follow God will doom one to the terrible judgment that is coming.

"And they remembered that God was their rock, and the high God their redeemer. Nevertheless they did flatter him with their mouth, and they lied unto him with their tongues" (Ps.78:35-36).

"Hear ye this, O house of Jacob, which are called by the name of Israel, and are come forth out of the waters of Judah, which swear by the name of the LORD, and make mention of the God of Israel, but not in truth, nor in righteousness" (Is.48:1).

"Not every one that saith unto me, Lord, Lord, shall enter into the kingdom of heaven; but he that doeth the will of my Father which is in heaven. Many will say to me in that day, Lord, Lord, have we not prophesied in thy name? and in thy name have cast out devils? and in thy name done many wonderful works? And then will I profess unto them, I never knew you: depart from me, ye that work iniquity" (Mt.7:21-23).

"He answered and said unto them, Well hath Esaias prophesied of you hypocrites, as it is written, This people honoureth me with [their] lips, but their heart is far from me" (Mk.7:6).

"They profess that they know God; but in works they deny him, being abominable, and disobedient, and unto every good work reprobate" (Tit.1:16).

J. The Ninth Plague—Darkness Covered the Land: Proof That God Has Power Over the Light & Darkness of the Earth, 10:21-29

1. **The day of judgment arrived**
   a. God charged His servant: Stretch out your hand toward the sky & thick darkness will spread over Egypt, a darkness so thick it can be felt
   b. God's servant obeyed
   c. The judgment: A thick darkness fell, a darkness that lasted three days
      1) So thick, could not see
      2) So thick, afraid to arise
2. **The purpose of the judgment: To prove that God has power over light & darkness**
3. **The attempt to compromise with God**

21 And the LORD said unto Moses, Stretch out thine hand toward heaven, that there may be darkness over the land of Egypt, even darkness which may be felt.
22 And Moses stretched forth his hand toward heaven; and there was a thick darkness in all the land of Egypt three days:
23 They saw not one another, neither rose any from his place for three days: but all the children of Israel had light in their dwellings.
24 And Pharaoh called unto Moses, and said, Go ye, serve the LORD; only let your flocks and your herds be stayed: let your little ones also go with you.
25 And Moses said, Thou must give us also sacrifices and burnt offerings, that we may sacrifice unto the LORD our God.
26 Our cattle also shall go with us; there shall not an hoof be left behind; for thereof must we take to serve the LORD our God; and we know not with what we must serve the LORD, until we come thither.
27 But the LORD hardened Pharaoh's heart, and he would not let them go.
28 And Pharaoh said unto him, Get thee from me, take heed to thyself, see my face no more; for in that day thou seest my face thou shalt die.
29 And Moses said, Thou hast spoken well, I will see thy face again no more.

a. Pharaoh offered to free everyone but the animals to go & worship the LORD
b. Moses rejected the compromise
   1) The animals would be needed to make sacrifices to God
   2) Just what animals would not be known until they reached their destination
   3) Thus, Israel had to take all the animals

4. **The insanity of a hard heart: God hardened Pharaoh's heart**
   a. Pharaoh refused to free Israel
   b. Pharaoh reacted in wrath
      1) Told Moses to get out of his sight
      2) Threatened to kill Moses if he ever saw him again
   c. God's final rejection: His servant would never appear before Pharaoh again

DIVISION III

THE TEN PLAGUES AND EGYPT: GOD'S JUDGMENT UPON THOSE WHO REJECT HIM AND OPPRESS HIS PEOPLE, 7:8–11:10

J. The Ninth Plague—Darkness Covered the Land: Proof That God Has Power Over the Light and Darkness of the Earth, 10:21-29

(10:21-29) **Introduction—Egypt**: the hand of God's judgment was falling upon the unrighteousness and ungodliness of the Egyptians (see Ro.1:18-32). Through the ages the Egyptians had become…
- a cesspool of immorality: adultery, fornication, and homosexuality
- a ruthless and savage power that brutalized and enslaved whole nations of people
- an industrial center based upon greed and cheap labor
- a depraved society obsessed with the bright lights and the fleshly, carnal pleasures of this world
- an indulgent and uncommitted people, a people whose will to advance as a society had become weak and lazy

On and on the list could go. The Egyptians had long ago forsaken God and set out to build their own society and nation apart from God. In fact, they had dreamed up their own gods. They were worshipping everything ranging from the idealistic worship of man himself (humanism) over to the worship of idols, idols formed from wood, stone, and metal. Millions, including Pharaoh himself, had even turned to sorcery and the occult.

Moreover the Egyptians had become a brutal and savage people: they oppressed and enslaved millions of people, even the very people who were still following after the living and true God.

God had been patient with the Egyptians for centuries, just as Scripture teaches that He is patient with all peoples of the world. God is not willing that any person or nation of people perish, but that all come to repentance (2 Pe.3:9). But the day came when it was time for justice to be executed, when the evil of the Egyptians had to be judged. But even then as we have seen, God was merciful and patient. Before He launched His plagues of judgment upon Egypt, He called them to repentance. He warned them of the coming judgment, and then He gave them a whole day and night to repent before He launched His judgment. This was true in all but two cases, and even then Pharaoh expected the hand of God's judgment (see note—Ex.8:16-18; 9:8-10). He knew that God was not going to leave Egypt alone, not until he and his people repented of their evil ways, in particular the evil of idolatry and of enslaving and brutalizing people.

The point is this: God had already called the Egyptians to repentance on *eight* different occasions. But Pharaoh had rejected God's plea each time. They had chosen to live in spiritual darkness, a darkness that had blinded them almost beyond seeing the truth. God's patience had just about reached the end: the king and his people had almost hardened their hearts beyond any chance of ever repenting. God knew this, but He still longed for the Egyptians to never perish, to know Him and to live righteous and pure lives. Thus God set out to give the Egyptians another chance, a ninth opportunity to repent.

Note the enormous patience and mercy of God. Not only had He been patient and merciful with the Egyptians for centuries, but here He was showing patience and mercy even in the midst of judging the Egyptians. This is: *The Ninth Plague—Darkness Covered the Land: Proof That God Has Power Over the Light & Darkness of the Earth,* 10:21-29.

1. The day of judgment arrived (vv.21-23).
2. The proof of God's power: He protected His people (v.23).
3. The attempt to compromise with God (vv.24-26).
4. The insanity of a hard heart: God hardened Pharaoh's heart (vv.27-29).

1 (10:21-23) **Judgment—Darkness**: the day of judgment arrived. Note again, no warning of this judgment was given. However, Pharaoh had to know that it was coming. The God who could cast so many plagues upon Egypt was not going to give up until Pharaoh obeyed God. These were bound to be the thoughts of Pharaoh. It was just a matter of whether Pharaoh could outlast the God of Moses, a matter of whether he was going to repent and do what God was demanding: repent of the evil of idolatry, of the terrible sin of oppressing and brutalizing people. Pharaoh was set against God: he was going to withstand God as long as he could, forever if possible. God knew that Pharaoh was expecting another judgment: it was just a matter of when. Therefore, God launched this judgment without warning.
 a. God gave a charge to his servant, Moses: stretch out your hand toward the sky, and thick darkness will spread over Egypt, a darkness so thick it can be felt (v.21). Imagine a pitch black darkness for three days and three nights. This is the judgment being described, a darkness that can literally be felt...
 • a frightening, fearsome darkness
 • an eerie, creeping darkness
 • a ghostly, scary darkness
 • a strange, weird darkness
 • a mysterious, supernatural darkness

 b. God's servant obeyed. Moses stretched his hand toward heaven (v.22).
 c. The judgment: a thick darkness fell upon Egypt, a darkness that lasted three days. Imagine living in pitch black darkness for three days. Scripture says that the people were literally imprisoned by the *chain of darkness*. The darkness was...
 • so thick the people could not see one another
 • so thick the people were even afraid to arise

The people were confined to their houses; terror seized them; few of them had the courage to arise out of bed, and the few who did stumbled about so much they most likely returned to bed. Matthew Henry says this:

> No doubt [the darkness]...terrified them. The cloud of locusts, which had darkened the land (v.15), was nothing [compared] to this. The tradition of the Jews is [this]: in this darkness they were terrified by the [unusual sight]...of evil spirits, or ...by dreadful sounds and murmurs which they made, or [which is not less frightful] by the horrors of their own consciences; and this is the plague which...Ps.78:49 [may refer to].
> "He cast upon them the fierceness of His anger, wrath, and indignation, and trouble, by sending evil angels among them..."
> ...to those to whom the devil has been a deceiver He will, at length, be a terror.[1]

Thought 1. Man has chosen to live in spiritual darkness, a darkness so thick that few people ever see the truth. This is willful darkness, a deliberate decision by man to live in spiritual darkness; consequently, the judgment of God is coming. And when God launches His judgment, there will be no escape, not for any of us. Even as the Egyptians were held by the chain of darkness, we shall be held by the chain of God's hand to face the execution of justice. We shall be judged for what we have done upon this earth, every one of us.

"Also unto thee, O Lord, belongeth mercy: for thou renderest to every man according to his work" (Ps.62:12).
"I the LORD search the heart, I try the reins, even to give every man according to his ways, and according to the fruit of his doings" (Je.17:10).
"For the Son of man shall come in the glory of his Father with his angels; and then he shall reward every man according to his works" (Mt.16:27).
"When the Son of man shall come in his glory, and all the holy angels with him, then shall he sit upon the throne of his glory: And before him shall be gathered all nations: and he shall separate them one from another, as a shepherd divideth [his] sheep from the goats: And he shall set the sheep on his right hand, but the goats on the left" (Mt.25:31-33).
"For we must all appear before the judgment seat of Christ; that every one may receive the things done in his body, according to that he hath done, whether it be good or bad" (2 Co.5:10).
"And if ye call on the Father, who without respect of persons judgeth according to every man's work, pass the time of your sojourning here in fear" (1 Pe.1:17).
"And I saw the dead, small and great, stand before God; and the books were opened: and another book was opened, which is the book of life: and the dead were judged out of those things which were written in the books, according to their works" (Re.20:12).
"And, behold, I come quickly; and my reward is with me, to give every man according as his work shall be" (Re.22:12).

[1] Matthew Henry. *Matthew Henry's Commentary*, p.313.

206

2 (10:23) **Plagues, Purpose—Power, of God—Protection, of God's People—Israel**: there was the purpose and proof of God's power: He protected His people. Note that God's people had light in their houses. This demonstrated a great fact: there is only one God who has power over light and darkness, the LORD Himself. The LORD cast darkness upon those who rejected Him, and He gave light to those who followed Him.

The Egyptians worshipped a sun-god named *Ra*. He was one of their chief deities; therefore, when God cast darkness upon Egypt, He proved...

- that there is only one living and true God who controls light and darkness, the LORD Himself
- that the LORD (Jehovah, Yahweh) is the God of Salvation and Redemption, that He truly delivers His people from judgment

Pharaoh could not have missed the point. The people of God had been protected by the LORD, whereas *Ra* had done absolutely nothing to protect the Egyptians. The God of Moses had the power both to judge and to deliver. It was His power that was supreme, far, far superior to the sun-god *Ra*. Note: once again, God had proven His power. God had demonstrated the most wonderful truths to Egypt:

⇒ that He is the only living and true God.
⇒ that He is omnipotent, possessing the power to control both light and darkness.
⇒ that He has the power to both judge and deliver people.
⇒ that all other gods are helpless and hopeless before the LORD God.
⇒ that all other gods are, in fact, just figments of man's imagination.

Thought 1. God alone has power over light and darkness. But more than this, God has power over all things, over both heaven and earth and all that is therein. God is sovereign over all, and He is omnipotent, all-powerful.

"**Know therefore this day, and consider it in thine heart, that the LORD he is God in heaven above, and upon the earth beneath: there is none else**" (De.4:39).
"**Both riches and honour come of thee, and thou reignest over all; and in thine hand is power and might; and in thine hand it is to make great, and to give strength unto all**" (1 Chr.29:12).
"**The LORD sitteth upon the flood; yea, the LORD sitteth King for ever**" (Ps.29:10).
"**For the LORD most high is terrible; he is a great King over all the earth**" (Ps.47:2).
"**That men may know that thou, whose name alone is JEHOVAH, art the most high over all the earth**" (Ps.83:18).
"**The LORD reigneth, he is clothed with majesty; the LORD is clothed with strength, wherewith he hath girded himself: the world also is stablished, that it cannot be moved**" (Ps.93:1).
"**Whatsoever the LORD pleased, that did he in heaven, and in earth, in the seas, and all deep places**" (Ps.135:6).
"**Daniel answered and said, Blessed be the name of God for ever and ever: for wisdom and might are his: And he changeth the times and the seasons: he removeth kings, and setteth up kings: he giveth wisdom unto the wise, and knowledge to them that know understanding: He revealeth the deep and secret things: he knoweth what is in the darkness, and the light dwelleth with him**" (Da.2:20-22).
"**And all the inhabitants of the earth are reputed as nothing: and he doeth according to his will in the army of heaven, and among the inhabitants of the earth: and none can stay his hand, or say unto him, What doest thou?**" (Da.4:35).
"**God that made the world and all things therein, seeing that he is Lord of heaven and earth, dwelleth not in temples made with hands**" (Ac.17:24).
"**Thou wilt say then unto me, Why doth he yet find fault? For who hath resisted his will? Nay but, O man, who art thou that repliest against God? Shall the thing formed say to him that formed it, Why hast thou made me thus? Hath not the potter power over the clay, of the same lump to make one vessel unto honour, and another unto dishonour?**" (Ro.9:19-21).

3 (10:24-26) **Compromise—Negotiate**: there was the attempt to compromise with God. At some point, Pharaoh realized that the darkness had completely stopped the nation of Egypt dead in its tracks. The halls of government, the economy, the military, and all other areas of life had ceased to function. The whole nation, everything and everyone, was enveloped in darkness. Nothing, absolutely nothing, could be carried on—no business, no work, no construction, no buying and selling, not even the securing of food. Even the basic essentials and necessities of human life could not be handled. Blanketed in pitch black darkness, life and survival could not last, not for long. Pharaoh had no choice: he sent for Moses. Stumbling through the darkness, the officials eventually reached Moses and brought him to Pharaoh.

a. Pharaoh offered to free all of God's people to go and worship the LORD. But note: he was not willing for them to take the animals (v.24). He would keep the animals as hostages to guarantee that the Israelites would return to Egypt.
b. Moses rejected the compromise:
⇒ The animals would be needed to make sacrifices to God (v.25).
⇒ Just what animals would be needed would not be known until they reached their destination (v.26).
⇒ Thus, Israel had to take all the animals.

Thought 1. God cannot compromise with man. To lower His standards would make God less than perfect, less than God. God could never agree for man to abuse, brutalize, and enslave other people—not for greed, not for money, not so one race of people can live off the servitude of another race. God's will is for man to live in peace and reconciliation, to live together as neighbors, neighbors who practice brotherly love. For this reason, God could never compromise with men over the issue of sin and evil.

"**God is not a man, that he should lie; neither the son of man, that he should repent: hath he said, and shall he not do it? or hath he spoken, and shall he not make it good? Behold, I have received commandment to bless: and he hath blessed; and I cannot reverse it**" (Nu.23:19-20).

"**And also the Strength of Israel will not lie nor repent: for he is not a man, that he should repent**" (1 S.15:29).

"**The counsel of the LORD standeth for ever, the thoughts of his heart to all generations**" (Ps.33:11).

"**For ever, O LORD, thy word is settled in heaven. Thy faithfulness is unto all generations: thou hast established the earth, and it abideth. They continue this day according to thine ordinances: for all are thy servants**" (Ps.119:89-91).

"**I know that, whatsoever God doeth, it shall be for ever: nothing can be put to it, nor any thing taken from it: and God doeth it, that men should fear before him**" (Ec.3:14).

"**For I am the LORD, I change not; therefore ye sons of Jacob are not consumed**" (Mal.3:6).

"**For the gifts and calling of God are without repentance**" (Ro.11:29).

"**Wherein God, willing more abundantly to show unto the heirs of promise the immutability of his counsel, confirmed it by an oath: That by two immutable things, in which it was impossible for God to lie, we might have a strong consolation, who have fled for refuge to lay hold upon the hope set before us**" (He.6:17-18).

"**Every good gift and every perfect gift is from above, and cometh down from the Father of lights, with whom is no variableness, neither shadow of turning**" (Js.1:17).

---

4 (10:27-29) **Heart, Hard—Hard - Hardened—Rejection, of God**: there was the insanity of a hard heart: God hardened Pharaoh's heart.

a. Pharaoh refused to free Israel: he just was not going to let them go (v.27).
b. Pharaoh reacted in wrath (v.28). Pharaoh was upset, provoked, angered to no end. He became enraged:
 ⇒ He told Moses to get out of his sight.
 ⇒ He threatened to kill Moses if he ever saw him again.

c. This led to God's final rejection: his servant broke the conference off. He would never again see the face of Pharaoh (v.29).

Thought 1. People can do some unreasonable things, very unreasonable, some things that approach insanity. But nothing is any more insane than...
• a hard heart
• rejection of God
• denying God
• wrath against God's message

"**And the LORD said unto Samuel, Hearken unto the voice of the people in all that they say unto thee: for they have not rejected thee, but they have rejected me, that I should not reign over them**" (1 S.8:7).

"**But my people would not hearken to my voice; and Israel would none of me. So I gave them up unto their own hearts' lust: and they walked in their own counsels. Oh that my people had hearkened unto me, and Israel had walked in my ways!**" (Ps.81:11-13).

"**Because I have called, and ye refused; I have stretched out my hand, and no man regarded; But ye have set at nought all my counsel, and would none of my reproof: I also will laugh at your calamity; I will mock when your fear cometh; When your fear cometh as desolation, and your destruction cometh as a whirlwind; when distress and anguish cometh upon you. Then shall they call upon me, but I will not answer; they shall seek me early, but they shall not find me**" (Pr.1:24-28).

"**He therefore that despiseth, despiseth not man, but God, who hath also given unto us his holy Spirit**" (1 Th.4:7-8).

CHAPTER 11

K. The Tenth Plague—Death of the Firstborn Announced: Proof That God is the God of True Believers, 11:1-10

1. The charge of God given to God's servant
 a. Announce one more plague, a plague that would cause Pharaoh to free the people

 b. Instruct God's people to ask the Egyptians for silver & gold (wages due for decades of slave-labor)

  1) The Egyptians gave because God stirred them to favor His people
  2) The Egyptians gave because they held Moses in such high esteem

2. The warning & proclamation of judgment
 a. God Himself will execute the judgment, right about midnight
 b. The judgment:
  1) All the firstborn among men & animals will die

And the Lord said unto Moses, Yet will I bring one plague more upon Pharaoh, and upon Egypt; afterwards he will let you go hence: when he shall let you go, he shall surely thrust you out hence altogether.

2 Speak now in the ears of the people, and let every man borrow of his neighbour, and every woman of her neighbour, jewels of silver, and jewels of gold.

3 And the Lord gave the people favour in the sight of the Egyptians. Moreover the man Moses was very great in the land of Egypt, in the sight of Pharaoh's servants, and in the sight of the people.

4 And Moses said, Thus saith the Lord, About midnight will I go out into the midst of Egypt:

5 And all the firstborn in the land of Egypt shall die, from the firstborn of Pharaoh that sitteth upon his throne, even unto the firstborn of the maidservant that is behind the mill; and all the firstborn of beasts.

6 And there shall be a great cry throughout all the land of Egypt, such as there was none like it, nor shall be like it any more.

7 But against any of the children of Israel shall not a dog move his tongue, against man or beast: that ye may know how that the Lord doth put a difference between the Egyptians and Israel.

8 And all these thy servants shall come down unto me, and bow down themselves unto me, saying, Get thee out, and all the people that follow thee: and after that I will go out. And he went out from Pharaoh in a great anger.

9 And the Lord said unto Moses, Pharaoh shall not hearken unto you; that my wonders may be multiplied in the land of Egypt.

10 And Moses and Aaron did all these wonders before Pharaoh: and the Lord hardened Pharaoh's heart, so that he would not let the children of Israel go out of his land.

  2) All Egypt will cry out in anguish—cry louder than ever before or ever again

3. The purpose of the judgment
 a. To prove that God is the God of true believers: He protected His people
 b. To stir Egypt (the world) to know one simple fact: There is a difference between unbelievers & believers
 c. To force Egypt to free God's people

4. The conclusion: Facts to keep in mind about the plagues
 a. Why judgment fell: Because Pharaoh would not listen
 b. God's purpose: To make His power known
 c. God's servants were faithful
 d. God's judgment was just: Pharaoh's heart was hard & evil
  1) He rejected God's warning & mercy time and again
  2) He enslaved God's people

DIVISION III

THE TEN PLAGUES AND EGYPT: GOD'S JUDGMENT UPON THOSE WHO REJECT HIM AND OPPRESS HIS PEOPLE, 7:8–11:10

K. The Tenth Plague—Death of the Firstborn Announced: Proof That God is the God of True Believers, 11:1-10

(11:1-10) **Introduction—Greed—Discrimination**: keep one picture in mind when studying the plagues of God's judgment upon ancient Egypt. Pharaoh and his officials were facing two real, live crises.

The first major crisis was the economic crisis created by the plagues, in particular the crisis caused by…
- the livestock disease (Ex.9:7)
- the hail storm (Ex.9:13-35)
- the locusts (Ex.10:1-20)

There was little livestock left in the nation and little if any crops or vegetation left. Egypt and its economy was catastrophically devastated. The government no doubt confiscated much of Israel's livestock and traded for food from neighboring countries as well as lived off what food had been stored for emergencies. But still there were bound to be shortages of everything basic to the survival of the nation and its economy. In addition, we can imagine the fear of a threat from some nearby enemy who was just waiting for Egypt to become weak.

The second major crisis was the demand that the enslaved Israelites be set free. Israel numbered more than two million people by this time (Ex.12:37). Remember: children within every society have been forced to work up until recent history. The number of working Israelites would, therefore, number over a million workers, most likely over two million. The situation boiled down to a political and economic decision:
⇒ If the government leaders freed the Israelites, how would Egypt rebuild its economy? One fact was sure: they could rebuild the economy much quicker with the help of one million working slaves than they could without the one million workers—if the plagues stopped. Consequently, in the counsel of the officials, they were no doubt making the decision not to free the slaves…
- hoping against hope
- seeking compromises (which Pharaoh did)
- trusting that eventually the plagues would stop

This gives some idea of the crises the king and his government officials were facing. Cabinet meetings must have continued day by day long into the nights during the crises of the plagues.

But note this fact: people, no matter who they are, are more important than the economy and the welfare of one race or one nation. We are all created by the Lord God Himself; therefore, as members of the human race, we are all brothers and sisters before Him. We are to have what Scripture calls *brotherly love* for one another. We are to love one another as neighbors. It was this that Egypt so miserably failed to do, and nothing on earth was going to stir the most powerful nation upon earth to treat other people as equal neighbors and brothers before the Lord. Why? Because they rejected the only living and true God and were worshipping the false gods and religions created by the imaginations of men. Thus the truth of God and of His holy will was foreign to them, the truth...

- of being created equally with other races of people
- of being neighbors
- of co-existing equally
- of brotherly love

The truth of the living God was just foreign to the ancient Egyptians. Consequently, what happens so often to people who do not really know the Lord happened to them: they thought themselves to be a superior race of people. They considered themselves to be more powerful, more intellectual, and a superior breed of people. In their minds, the Egyptians were genetically a superior race of people. They were certainly wealthier and more powerful. Consequently, they enslaved and brutalized people. Ferociously, the slave-drivers forced the slaves to do the menial and degrading jobs—the demeaning, base, inhuman, beastly work that had to be done. Sometimes slaves, not animals, were even used to push the millstone around, grinding the grain. This work, as well as all slave-labor, is inhumane and brutish to man. Moreover, it curses God's Word and denies God, that there is a Creator who has created us all equally, created us all to be His people.

Therefore, God's patience ended. Every nation and person upon earth must always remember this one fact: there is an end to God's patience. There is a time when God is forced to step in, chastise and judge people. We can harden our hearts, become so rock-like and stiff-necked against God, that we go beyond the point of ever repenting. We can reach a point when we will never repent. When does a person reach that point? Only God knows. No one can ever know the heart of another person, not well enough to know if that person could ever repent of his sins. As stated, only God can know the spiritual hardness of the human heart.

God knew the hearts of the Egyptians, both the heart of Pharaoh and the hearts of his people. God knew that Pharaoh and his people had reached the point of never repenting, that they never would repent. Remember, the ancient Egyptians were guilty of terrible, horrible evil.

⇒ They were guilty of atrocity heaped upon atrocity, of brutalizing and enslaving people.
⇒ They were guilty of oppressing and brutalizing the very people who were attempting to serve and live for God upon this earth.
⇒ They were guilty of rejecting God and worshipping the false idols and religions created by the imaginations of men.

God had seen and been hurt enough. His heart had been cut to the core because of the sinful and evil ways of the Egyptians. Pharaoh and his people were not going to repent of their idolatry and evil enslavement of people. They were not going to free God's people, not of their own free will. God had no choice; He had to force the Egyptians to free Israel. Thus He laid the plans to launch one final plague of judgment. This one final plague would cause the king of Egypt and his officials to beg God's people to leave Egypt. This is the discussion of this important passage of Scripture: *The Tenth Plague—Death of the Firstborn Announced: Proof That God is the God of True Believers,* 11:1-10.

1. The charge of God given to God's servant (vv.1-3).
2. The warning and proclamation of judgment (vv.4-6).
3. The purpose of the judgment (vv.7-8).
4. The conclusion: facts to keep in mind about the plagues (vv.9-10).

---

1 (11:1-3) **Justice—Retribution**: there was the charge given to God's servant.

a. Moses was to announce one more plague, a plague that would cause Pharaoh to free the people (v.1). The Hebrew word used here for plague (nega) means far more than a grievous and sorrowful event. The word means *a stroke, a blow*.[1] Thus, the tenth plague was to bring far more than just grief upon the Egyptians. The plague would be launched by the stroke and blow of God's own hand, the stroke and blow of His *almighty power*. The stroke of God's *mighty hand* would cause Pharaoh to free God's people. In fact, the blow of God's hand would cause such havoc that Pharaoh would literally *drive* the Israelites out of Egypt.

b. Note what God now charged Moses to do: instruct God's people to ask the Egyptians for silver and gold. The Egyptians owed enormous wages to Israel for decades of forced slave labor. In addition, the Egyptians had probably confiscated and stolen most of the valuables and possessions of the Israelites when they enslaved them. The Egyptians owed the people of God so much, they could never have repaid them. But God wanted justice executed: He wanted Israel paid a great sum for the past injustices done them. What caused the Egyptians to freely give the Israelites their silver and gold?

1) The Egyptians gave because God stirred them to favor His people (v.3).
⇒ God obviously aroused fear within the Egyptians. The God of the Hebrews had sent plague after plague upon Egypt, and all the while the Israelites had been protected. No doubt the Egyptians feared the Israelites, feared them because of their power with God.

---

[1] F.B. Huey, *Exodus*, p.50.

⇒ God apparently aroused guilt within the Egyptians. They had mistreated and oppressed the people of God, abused and brutalized them, cheated and stolen from them. The Egyptians were obviously making restitution either to ease their own consciences or else to please the God of the Hebrews.

2) The Egyptians gave because they held Moses in such high esteem (v.3). Just imagine how highly the people regarded Moses, this man through whom the finger of God worked so mightily.
⇒ The magicians were unable to stand before him (Ex.8:18-19).
⇒ The government officials knew of his power and some even believed his message (Ex.9:20; 10:7).

Thought 1. Two lessons can be clearly seen in God's charge to Moses.
(1) There is a day when justice has to be executed, a day when the door to mercy and salvation is closed. That day had arrived for Pharaoh and his people. The day is coming when the door of mercy and salvation will also be closed to us.

"Therefore thus saith the Lord, Behold, I will bring evil upon them, which they shall not be able to escape; and though they shall cry unto me, I will not hearken unto them" (Je.11:11).
"Though they dig into hell, thence shall mine hand take them; though they climb up to heaven, thence will I bring them down" (Am.9:2).
"For when they shall say, Peace and safety; then sudden destruction cometh upon them, as travail upon a woman with child; and they shall not escape" (1 Th.5:3).
"How shall we escape, if we neglect so great salvation; which at the first began to be spoken by the Lord, and was confirmed unto us by them that heard him" (He.2:3).
"Behold, I stand at the door, and knock: if any man hear my voice, and open the door, I will come in to him, and will sup with him, and he with me" (Re.3:20).

(2) The day is coming when God will execute justice to believers, a day when believers will be paid and rewarded for their service here upon earth.

"His lord said unto him, Well done, good and faithful servant; thou hast been faithful over a few things, I will make thee ruler over many things: enter thou into the joy of thy lord" (Mt.25:23).
"Blessed [are] those servants, whom the lord when he cometh shall find watching: verily I say unto you, that he shall gird himself, and make them to sit down to meat, and will come forth and serve them" (Lu.12:37).
"In my Father's house are many mansions: if [it were] not [so], I would have told you. I go to prepare a place for you. And if I go and prepare a place for you, I will come again, and receive you unto myself; that where I am, [there] ye may be also" (Jn.14:2-3).
"But glory, honour, and peace [shall be given], to every man that worketh good, to the Jew first, and also to the Gentile" (Ro.2:10).
"For I reckon that the sufferings of this present time are not worthy to be compared with the glory which shall be revealed in us" (Ro.8:18).
"For our light affliction, which is but for a moment, worketh for us a far more exceeding and eternal weight of glory" (2 Co.4:17).
"Knowing that whatsoever good thing any man doeth, the same shall he receive of the Lord, whether he be bond or free" (Ep.6:8).
"For our conversation [conduct] is in heaven; from whence also we look for the Saviour, the Lord Jesus Christ: Who shall change our vile body, that it may be fashioned like unto his glorious body, according to the working whereby he is able even to subdue all things unto himself" (Ph.3:20-21).
"When Christ, who is our life, shall appear, then shall ye also appear with him in glory" (Col.3:4).
"And when the chief Shepherd shall appear, ye shall receive a crown of glory that fadeth not away" (1 Pe.5:4).
"Beloved, now are we the sons of God, and it doth not yet appear what we shall be: but we know that, when he shall appear, we shall be like him; for we shall see him as he is" (1 Jn.3:2).
"And I heard a voice from heaven saying unto me, Write, Blessed are the dead which die in the Lord from henceforth: Yea, saith the Spirit, that they may rest from their labours; and their works do follow them" (Re.14:13).
"And God shall wipe away all tears from their eyes; and there shall be no more death, neither sorrow, nor crying, neither shall there be any more pain: for the former things are passed away" (Re.21:4).

2 (11:4-6) **Judgment—Death—Warning**: there was the warning and proclamation of judgment. This warning actually took place during the ninth plague when Pharaoh had Moses brought to him (Ex.10:24-29). God had obviously given Moses these instructions before he was taken to Pharaoh for their last confrontation. This means that God had prepared Moses for the abrupt end of their meeting, sharing that Pharaoh was going to react in wrath and threaten the very life of Moses. The point to keep in mind is this: what Moses now told Pharaoh actually took place in their meeting during the ninth plague. Note the warning given to Pharaoh.

a. God Himself would execute the judgment about midnight (v.4). The Hebrew is emphatic and dramatic: "I, I [the Lord] will go out" [ani yose], that is, *march* throughout Egypt. And note when: right after midnight.

b. The judgment was to bring a night of horror and terror (v.5-6). All the firstborn among men and animals were to die: all during that one night; all somewhere between midnight and daybreak. The judgment was to fall upon the firstborn son of Pharaoh as well as the firstborn son of the slave girl, and even upon the firstborn of animals. No person was too high or powerful and none too low or weak to escape the plague of God's final judgment.

All Egyptians would cry out in anguish, cry louder than ever before or ever again (v.6).

There is some historical evidence apart from the Bible that verifies the death of the firstborn among the Egyptians. *The Expositor's Bible Commentary* says the following:

> A possible historical reminiscence of this event has been uncovered by Mordechai Gilula (:The Smiting of the Firstborn; An Egyptian Myth?" Tel Aviv, 4 [1977]: 94-95).
> ⇒ In the Pre-Mosaic Pyramid Texts (par.339 a-b), there is a reference to "that day of slaying the firstborn" spelled smsw in Egyptian.
> ⇒ Likewise, the Pre-Mosaic Coffin Texts (VI:178) refer to "that night of slaying the firstborn," while another coffin text has both "that night...that day of slaying the firstborn" (II:163 b-c).
> ⇒ In the Coffin Texts the Egyptian word for "firstborn" is wr or wrw, meaning "great" or "eldest." Interestingly the firstborn in the Coffin Texts are gods, while the Pyramid Texts do not say.[2]

Thought 1. God warns us: judgment is coming and there will be no escape.

> "Nevertheless, if thou warn the wicked of his way to turn from it; if he do not turn from his way, he shall die in his iniquity; but thou hast delivered thy soul" (Eze.33:9).
>
> "For the wrath of God is revealed from heaven against all ungodliness and unrighteousness of men, who hold the truth in unrighteousness; Because that which may be known of God is manifest in them; for God hath showed it unto them. For the invisible things of him from the creation of the world are clearly seen, being understood by the things that are made, even his eternal power and Godhead; so that they are without excuse....And even as they did not like to retain God in their knowledge, God gave them over to a reprobate mind, to do those things which are not convenient; Being filled with all unrighteousness, fornication, wickedness, covetousness, maliciousness; full of envy, murder, debate, deceit, malignity; whisperers, Backbiters, haters of God, despiteful, proud, boasters, inventors of evil things, disobedient to parents, Without understanding, covenantbreakers, without natural affection, implacable, unmerciful: Who knowing the judgment of God, that they which commit such things are worthy of death, not only do the same, but have pleasure in them that do them" (Ro.1:18-20, 28-32).
>
> "Know ye not that the unrighteous shall not inherit the kingdom of God? Be not deceived: neither fornicators, nor idolaters, nor adulterers, nor effeminate, nor abusers of themselves with mankind, Nor thieves, nor covetous, nor drunkards, nor revilers, nor extortioners, shall inherit the kingdom of God" (1 Co.6:9-10).
>
> "Let him that is taught in the word communicate unto him that teacheth in all good things. Be not deceived; God is not mocked: for whatsoever a man soweth, that shall he also reap. For he that soweth to his flesh shall of the flesh reap corruption; but he that soweth to the Spirit shall of the Spirit reap life everlasting" (Ga.6:6-8).
>
> "For this ye know, that no whoremonger, nor unclean person, nor covetous man, who is an idolater, hath any inheritance in the kingdom of Christ and of God. Let no man deceive you with vain words: for because of these things cometh the wrath of God upon the children of disobedience" (Ep.5:5-6).

3 (11:7-8) **Protection, of God's People—Believers, Distinctiveness of**: there was the purpose for the judgment. Three purposes are given for this particular plague.

a. Purpose 1: to prove that God is the God of true believers: He protected His people (v.7). God's protection was to be so strong that a dog would not even bark, much less growl, at a believer during the night of the judgment. God's people were to experience the peace and tranquillity of God Himself during the judgment.

b. Purpose 2: to stir Egypt (the world) to know one simple fact: there is a difference between unbelievers and believers (v.7). God Himself had made a distinction between Egypt and Israel, between unbelievers and believers. Unbelievers do not follow God. They turn away from God, reject, deny, and even curse Him. Unbelievers just have nothing to do with God. Therefore, God cannot take care of them, neither upon this earth nor in the day of judgment. They have to stand alone and face the judgment of God alone.

But this is not true with believers. Believers follow God and cast themselves upon the mercy of God, trusting Him to take care of them. And because they cast themselves upon Him, He is able to take care of them.

c. Purpose 3: to force Egypt to free God's people. God's people were going to be freed. God was going to make sure they were set free. This judgment was to cause the rulers of Egypt to bow before Moses and beg that he and God's people leave Egypt.

2 Frank E. Gaebelein, Editor. *The Expositor's Bible Commentary*, Vol.2, pp.369-370.

Note that Moses left Pharaoh in a spirit of "hot anger" (v.8, NIV). Why?

The stupidity and waste of all those lives just because of stubborn sinfulness made Moses exceedingly angry. To be in the presence of evil and not be angry is a dreadful spiritual and moral malady.[3]

Thought 1. There is a difference between Egypt and Israel, between the unbelievers and believers of this world.
⇒ The difference is God's presence and care, God's protection and safety, God's promise of heaven and eternity.
⇒ The difference is also the believers' struggle to live a righteous and godly life, to serve and witness for God, and to have compassion for the needy and lost of this world.

> **"I am a companion of all them that fear thee, and of them that keep thy precepts" (Ps.119:63).**
> **"He that walketh with wise men shall be wise: but a companion of fools shall be destroyed" (Pr.13:20).**
> **"For I say unto you, That except your righteousness shall exceed [the righteousness] of the scribes and Pharisees, ye shall in no case enter into the kingdom of heaven" (Mt.5:20).**
> **"Awake to righteousness, and sin not; for some have not the knowledge of God: I speak this to your shame" (1 Co.15:34).**
> **"Wherefore come out from among them, and be ye separate, saith the Lord, and touch not the unclean thing; and I will receive you, And will be a Father unto you, and ye shall be my sons and daughters, saith the Lord Almighty" (2 Co.6:17-18).**
> **"Being filled with the fruits of righteousness, which are by Jesus Christ, unto the glory and praise of God" (Ph.1:11).**
> **"Teaching us that, denying ungodliness and worldly lusts, we should live soberly, righteously, and godly, in this present world; Looking for that blessed hope, and the glorious appearing of the great God and our Saviour Jesus Christ" (Tit.2:12-13).**
> **"But the day of the Lord will come as a thief in the night; in the which the heavens shall pass away with a great noise, and the elements shall melt with fervent heat, the earth also and the works that are therein shall be burned up. Seeing then that all these things shall be dissolved, what manner of persons ought ye to be in all holy conversation [conduct] and godliness, Looking for and hasting unto the coming of the day of God, wherein the heavens being on fire shall be dissolved, and the elements shall melt with fervent heat? Nevertheless we, according to his promise, look for new heavens and a new earth, wherein dwelleth righteousness. Wherefore, beloved, seeing that ye look for such things, be diligent that ye may be found of him in peace, without spot, and blameless" (2 Pe.3:10-14).**

4 (11:9-10) **Plagues, The Ten—Judgment**: this is the conclusion to the ten plagues; there are several facts to keep in mind about the plagues.
a. Fact 1: Why did God's judgment fall upon Egypt? Why was it necessary for Pharaoh and the Egyptians to suffer the judgment of God? Because Pharaoh and the Egyptians would not listen to God's call to repentance (v.9). Always remember, the Egyptians were guilty of terrible evil: they had rejected God centuries before and turned to the worship of false gods and religions. And just as tragic, they had committed atrocity after atrocity against many of the peoples of the known world of that day. They enslaved people and brutalized them under the heavy weight of savage slave-drivers.

Thought 1. Many a person hears the Word of God just as Pharaoh did, and still they do not listen. They refuse to listen. The result: they reject God, deny Him, and even curse Him.

> **"And the Lord said unto Samuel, Hearken unto the voice of the people in all that they say unto thee: for they have not rejected thee, but they have rejected me, that I should not reign over them" (1 S.8:7).**
> **"But they mocked the messengers of God, and despised his words, and misused his prophets, until the wrath of the Lord arose against his people, till there was no remedy" (2 Chr.36:16).**
> **"But my people would not hearken to my voice; and Israel would none of me. So I gave them up unto their own hearts' lust: and they walked in their own counsels. Oh that my people had hearkened unto me, and Israel had walked in my ways!" (Ps.81:11-13).**
> **"I have called, and ye refused; I have stretched out my hand, and no man regarded" (Pr.1:24).**
> **"To whom shall I speak, and give warning, that they may hear? behold, their ear is uncircumcised [closed, shut], and they cannot hearken: behold, the word of the Lord is unto them a reproach; they have no delight in it" (Je.6:10).**
> **"Yea, they made their hearts as an adamant stone, lest they should hear the law, and the words which the Lord of hosts hath sent in his spirit by the former prophets: therefore came a great wrath from the Lord of hosts" (Zec.7:12).**
> **"He that rejecteth me, and receiveth not my words, hath one that judgeth him: the word that I have spoken, the same shall judge him in the last day" (Jn.12:48).**

---

3 Frank E. Gaebelein, Editor. *The Expositor's Bible Commentary*, Vol.2, p.370.

b. Fact 2: God's purpose for the plagues of judgment was to make His power known (v.9). As just pointed out, the Egyptians were a sinful and evil people: they worshipped false idols and religions, and they brutalized and enslaved people. Yet God did not want a single Egyptian to perish, but all to come to repentance. This was the reason He worked the miracles of the plagues: to prove...

- that all the gods and religions worshipped by the Egyptians were false
- that there was only one living and true God, the LORD Himself (Jehovah, Yahweh)
- that the LORD was the only God of salvation, redemption, and deliverance

> "Behold, God is my salvation; I will trust, and not be afraid: for the Lord JEHOVAH is my strength and my song; he also is become my salvation" (Is.12:2).
> "The Lord is my light and my salvation; whom shall I fear? the Lord is the strength of my life; of whom shall I be afraid?" (Ps.27:1).
> "But the salvation of the righteous is of the Lord: he is their strength in the time of trouble" (Ps.37:39).
> "And it shall be said in that day, Lo, this is our God; we have waited for him, and he will save us: this is the Lord; we have waited for him, we will be glad and rejoice in his salvation" (Is.25:9).
> "The Lord thy God in the midst of thee is mighty; he will save, he will rejoice over thee with joy; he will rest in his love, he will joy over thee with singing" (Zep.3:17).
> "For God sent not his Son into the world to condemn the world; but that the world through him might be saved" (Jn.3:17).
> "Neither is there salvation in any other: for there is none other name under heaven given among men, whereby we must be saved" (Ac.4:12).
> "Him hath God exalted with his right hand to be a Prince and a Saviour, for to give repentance to Israel, and forgiveness of sins" (Ac.5:31).
> "Wherefore he is able also to save them to the uttermost that come unto God by him, seeing he ever liveth to make intercession for them" (He.7:25).

c. Fact 3: God's servants were faithful (v.10). Moses and Aaron did exactly what God instructed them to do. They proclaimed the message of God to Pharaoh, and they worked the miracles God gave them the power to perform. They preached God's Word and called the Egyptians to repentance, to repent of the terrible evil of idolatry and of enslaving people.

> "And Moses verily was faithful in all his house, as a servant, for a testimony of those things which were to be spoken after" (He.3:5).
> "Whereupon, O king Agrippa, I [Paul] was not disobedient unto the heavenly vision" (Ac.26:19).
> "Moreover it is required in stewards, that a man be found faithful" (1 Co.4:2).
> "Blessed are they that do his commandments, that they may have right to the tree of life, and may enter in through the gates into the city" (Re.22:14).
> "Now therefore, if ye will obey my voice indeed, and keep my covenant, then ye shall be a peculiar treasure unto me above all people: for all the earth is mine" (Ex.19:5).
> "As the Lord commanded Moses his servant, so did Moses command Joshua, and so did Joshua; he left nothing undone of all that the Lord commanded Moses" (Jos.11:15).
> "For he [Hezekiah] clave to the Lord, and departed not from following him, but kept his commandments, which the Lord commanded Moses" (2 K.18:6).

d. Fact 4: God's judgment was just. Pharaoh's heart was hard and evil (v.10). As the leader of Egypt, he took the lead in rejecting God, in rejecting God's warning and mercy time and again. He took the lead in worshipping the false religions and gods created by the imaginations of men. Moreover, he took the lead in enslaving and brutalizing people, even the very people upon earth who were attempting to follow God in his day and time.

Thought 1. God has the power to judge and the power to save man. Both powers will be demonstrated before every person who has ever lived.
(1) God is going to judge the world.

> "When the Son of man shall come in his glory, and all the holy angels with him, then shall he sit upon the throne of his glory: And before him shall be gathered all nations: and he shall separate them one from another, as a shepherd divideth [his] sheep from the goats: And he shall set the sheep on his right hand, but the goats on the left" (Mt.25:31-33).
> "And as it is appointed unto men once to die, but after this the judgment" (He.9:27).
> "But the heavens and the earth, which are now, by the same word are kept in store, reserved unto fire against the day of judgment and perdition of ungodly men" (2 Pe.3:7).
> "And Enoch also, the seventh from Adam, prophesied of these, saying, Behold, the Lord cometh with ten thousands of his saints, To execute judgment upon all, and to convince all that are ungodly among them of all their ungodly deeds which they have ungodly committed, and of all their hard speeches which ungodly sinners have spoken against him" (Jude 14-15).
> "And I saw the dead, small and great, stand before God; and the books were opened: and another book was opened, which is the book of life: and the dead were judged out of those things which were written in the books, according to their works" (Re.20:12).

(2) God will save all who call upon Him.

"For God so loved the world, that he gave his only begotten Son, that whosoever believeth in him should not perish, but have everlasting life" (Jn.3:16).

"And it shall come to pass, that whosoever shall call on the name of the Lord shall be saved" (Ac.2:21).

"For the wages of sin is death; but the gift of God is eternal life through Jesus Christ our Lord" (Ro.6:23).

"That if thou shalt confess with thy mouth the Lord Jesus, and shalt believe in thine heart that God hath raised him from the dead, thou shalt be saved. For with the heart man believeth unto righteousness; and with the mouth confession is made unto salvation" (Ro.10:9-10).

"For whosoever shall call upon the name of the Lord shall be saved" (Ro.10:13).

"For by grace are ye saved through faith; and that not of yourselves: it is the gift of God" (Ep.2:8).

"[God] who will have all men to be saved, and to come unto the knowledge of the truth" (1 Ti.2:4).

DIVISION IV

THE PASSOVER AND THE TENTH PLAGUE: DELIVERANCE FROM GOD'S JUDGMENT— LIBERATED, SET FREE, 12:1–13:16

(12:1–13:16) **DIVISION OVERVIEW—Israel—Deliverance**: this division of Exodus covers the great deliverance of Israel from Egyptian slavery, and how the Israelites were to celebrate their deliverance. Very simply stated, the Passover is the celebration of...

- Israel's First Great Emancipation
- Israel First Day of Independence[1]

Imagine, if you will, a dark night like any other Egyptian night. But this one particular night was strangely different. An ominous, apprehensive sense filled the air as Israel waited to see if their careful preparation of the Passover lamb would enable them to survive the night.

Cries of unmeasured grief pierced the night as Egyptian mothers and fathers held the lifeless bodies of their firstborn children. For the Israelites, Passover was a night where *obedience to God* was the literal difference between life and death. Clutching their own firstborn children, every Hebrew mother and father breathed a grateful prayer to God, a prayer of relief. The death angel took note of the blood of the lamb on their doors and passed over them. This sacred institution, the Passover, would become one of Israel's defining moments in history—freedom from their Egyptian masters. It would be a night that every child in every generation would hear about again and again: the story of how God delivered His people from judgment through the blood of the Passover lamb. Note these important items before we begin our study:

1. The greatest event in the history of ancient Israel was the event Scripture now covers: the deliverance of Israel from Egyptian slavery. How was God going to deliver His people?

⇒ First, by blood, the blood of the Passover lamb. God was going to send the tenth and final plague of His judgment upon Egypt, the plague of death, the death of the firstborn. But there was an escape: the blood of the lamb. If a person would sacrifice a lamb and smear its blood on the door posts of the house, God would pass over the house and not judge nor strike down the firstborn. The death of the lamb became a substitute for the believer. The person who believed God, who believed that the blood of the sacrificial lamb would save him, would escape the plague of death.

⇒ Second, by power, the power of God to deliver His people through the Red Sea and to destroy the Egyptian army.

Note that the deliverance of Israel is a picture (symbol, type) of how God delivers a person from the sins and enslavements of this world (Egypt) and from the coming plague of death that is to fall upon us all. God delivers us by the blood of His Son, the Lord Jesus Christ, the Lamb of God who takes away the sin of the world. God also delivers us by His power, the power of His Spirit to guide and give us victory over all the temptations and trials of this life.

2. Scripture itself tells us exactly what the Passover is, exactly what the Passover means. God told Moses to declare this wonderful truth: that God would *pass over* and not cast His judgment upon any person who believed in the blood of the lamb, any person who believed enough to place himself behind the blood of the lamb.

> **"For I will pass through the land of Egypt this night, and will smite all the firstborn in the land of Egypt, both man and beast; and against all the gods of Egypt I will execute judgment: I am the LORD. And the blood shall be to you for a token upon the houses where ye are: and when I see the blood, I will pass over you, and the plague shall not be upon you to destroy you, when I smite the land of Egypt" (Ex.12:12-13).**

> **"For the LORD will pass through to smite the Egyptians; and when he seeth the blood upon the lintel, and on the two side posts, the LORD will pass over the door, and will not suffer the destroyer to come in unto your houses to smite you" (Ex.12:23).**

> **"That ye shall say, It is the sacrifice of the LORD's passover, who passed over the houses of the children of Israel in Egypt, when he smote the Egyptians, and delivered our houses. And the people bowed the head and worshipped" (Ex.12:27).**

---

[1] F.B. Huey, *Exodus*, p.55.

3. The Passover meant to Israel just what the cross means to the Christian believer: deliverance from slavery—freedom and liberty—wrought by God's mighty power.

⇒ The blood of the Passover lamb caused God's judgment of death to *pass over* the Israelite believer. The blood of the Passover lamb led to a new and glorious life of liberty and freedom for the Israelite believer.

⇒ The blood of Christ, the Lamb of God Himself, delivers the genuine believer of any race from death. The blood of Christ frees the genuine believer from sin, death, and hell. The blood of our Lord gives us a new life of freedom and liberty that goes on eternally.

4. There is a very close tie between the Passover and the crucifixion of Christ. All Scripture declares this close tie.
a. Isaiah prophesied that the Lamb of God was to be slaughtered for the people.

"Surely he hath borne our griefs, and carried our sorrows: yet we did esteem him stricken, smitten of God, and afflicted. But he was wounded for our transgressions, he was bruised for our iniquities: the chastisement of our peace was upon him; and with his stripes we are healed. All we like sheep have gone astray; we have turned every one to his own way; and the LORD hath laid on him the iniquity of us all. He was oppressed, and he was afflicted, yet he opened not his mouth: he is brought as a lamb to the slaughter, and as a sheep before her shearers is dumb, so he openeth not his mouth" (Is.53:4-7).

b. Jesus Christ was *celebrating the Passover* with His disciples when He made the phenomenal revelation: He Himself was the Passover Lamb to be slain for the sins of the world.

"For this is my blood of the new testament, which is shed for many for the remission of sins" (Mt.26:28).

c. John the Baptist proclaimed that Jesus Christ was the Lamb of God who took away the sins of the world.

"The next day John seeth Jesus coming unto him, and saith, Behold the Lamb of God, which taketh away the sin of the world" (Jn.1:29).
"And looking upon Jesus as he walked, he saith, Behold the Lamb of God!" (Jn.1:36).

d. Paul the Apostle declared that Jesus Christ was *our Passover* who was sacrificed for us. Therefore, we must purge the evil out of our lives and live righteous lives, lives of sincerity and truth.

"Purge out therefore the old leaven, that ye may be a new lump, as ye are unleavened. For even Christ our passover is sacrificed for us: Therefore let us keep the feast, not with old leaven, neither with the leaven of malice and wickedness; but with the unleavened bread of sincerity and truth" (1 Co.5:7-8).

e. Peter declared that Jesus Christ was the Lamb whose blood cleanses us from sin.

"Forasmuch as ye know that ye were not redeemed with corruptible things, as silver and gold, from your vain conversation [conduct, behavior] received by tradition from your fathers; But with the precious blood of Christ, as of a lamb without blemish and without spot" (1 Pe.1:18-19).

f. The Book of Hebrews declares that Jesus Christ is the sacrifice that bears our sins and secures eternal redemption for us.

"Neither by the blood of goats and calves, but by his own blood he entered in once into the holy place, having obtained eternal redemption for us" (He.9:12).
"So Christ was once offered to bear the sins of many; and unto them that look for him shall he appear the second time without sin unto salvation" (He.9:28).

g. The great book of *Revelation* declares time and again that Jesus Christ is the Lamb of God.

"And when he had taken the book, the four beasts and four and twenty elders fell down before the Lamb, having every one of them harps, and golden vials full of odours, which are the prayers of saints. And they sung a new song, saying, Thou art worthy to take the book, and to open the seals thereof: for thou wast slain, and hast redeemed us to God by thy blood out of every kindred, and tongue, and people, and nation; And hast made us unto our God kings and priests: and we shall reign on the earth" (Re.5:8-10).
"And they sing the song of Moses the servant of God, and the song of the Lamb, saying, Great and marvellous are thy works, Lord God Almighty; just and true are thy ways, thou King of saints" (Re.15:3. See Re.7:9; 12:11; 13:8; 14:1; 15:3; 17:14; 19:9; 21:22.)

5. The Passover is a story of both judgment and deliverance. Judgment is never a pretty sight, but God never winks at sin nor turns His head, ignoring injustice. After holding His wrath for years, Egypt had gone too far. Pharaoh and his people had rejected God and had cruelly mistreated masses of people upon earth, including the very people who believed and bore witness to the only living and true God. Therefore, God had no choice but to execute justice upon the evil

Egyptians and to save all those who truly believed and followed Him. God will spare no energy when His love is scorned and His people are abused.

> "And the Lord shall deliver me from every evil work, and will preserve me unto his heavenly kingdom: to whom be glory for ever and ever" (2 Ti.4:18).
> "The Lord knoweth how to deliver the godly out of temptations, and to reserve the unjust unto the day of judgment to be punished" (2 Pe.2:9).
> "For the LORD loveth judgment, and forsaketh not his saints; they are preserved for ever: but the seed of the wicked shall be cut off" (Ps.37:28).
> "But I am poor and needy; yet the Lord thinketh upon me: thou art my help and my deliverer; make no tarrying, O my God" (Ps.40:17).
> "No weapon that is formed against thee shall prosper; and every tongue that shall rise against thee in judgment thou shalt condemn. This is the heritage of the servants of the LORD, and their righteousness is of me, saith the LORD" (Is.54:17).
> "I the LORD search the heart, I try the reins, even to give every man according to his ways, and according to the fruit of his doings" (Je.17:10).

6. The Passover was instituted to celebrate Israel's deliverance from Egyptian slavery. The celebration of the Passover celebrated the great emancipation of Israel. It was Israel's great Independence Day.[2]

7. The Passover is closely tied to the Feast of Unleavened Bread. The blood of the lamb had saved the Israelites who had believed and obeyed God. But God intended to do more than just deliver His people from the slavery of Egypt (the world). Therefore, as they prepared the Passover meal, God instructed the Israelites to put all leaven (yeast) and all leavened bread out of their house. They were to eat only unleavened bread and take only unleavened bread with them as they walked out of Egypt (the world) and marched toward the promised land of God (heaven). Why did God give this unusual instruction to the Israelites?

- Because their salvation and deliverance were to be immediate: they had to leave Egypt (the world) and its enslavement quickly, immediately
- Because leaven symbolizes evil throughout Scripture

Simply stated, God wanted the Feast of Unleavened Bread to remind His people of His miraculous deliverance, of the time when they had to rush out of Egypt away from the evils of Egypt and its enslavements. God wanted to remind His people that they had been given a new life, a life that was marching toward the promised land of God. Spiritually, this symbolizes the utter necessity for the Christian believer to *rush away* from the world with all its leaven (evil) and to walk in *newness of life* as we march to the promised land of God.

> "Know ye not, that so many of us as were baptized into Jesus Christ were baptized into his death? Therefore we are buried with him by baptism into death: that like as Christ was raised up from the dead by the glory of the Father, even so we also should walk in newness of life" (Ro.6:3-4).
> "Therefore if any man be in Christ, he is a new creature; old things are passed away; behold, all things are become new" (2 Co.5:17).
> "As ye have therefore received Christ Jesus the Lord, so walk ye in him" (Col.2:6).
> "He that saith he abideth in him ought himself also so to walk, even as he walked" (1 Jn.2:6).

8. The Passover actually included three major celebrations. By tying these three events together, God stressed this important truth: It was God and God alone who delivered Israel from Egyptian slavery. As they began their march to the promised land, each one of the celebrations focused the hearts of God's people on God's great deliverance:

⇒ The Passover itself *focused* upon God's great redemption, His salvation and deliverance of the believer who hid behind the blood of the sacrificial lamb.

⇒ The Feast of Unleavened Bread *focused* upon the necessity of fleeing—quickly fleeing—the slavery of Egypt (the world), of immediately marching to the promised land.

⇒ The dedication of the firstborn *focused* upon the utter necessity of dedicating the firstborn to God. God was the Savior of the firstborn; therefore, the firstborn belonged to Him and was to be dedicated to Him. And note: by giving the firstborn to God, the parents would set the precedent of giving all their children to God, of teaching them that God is the great Savior and Deliverer of us all.

9. The Passover is one of the clearest and most descriptive types in all the Old Testament. The types are discussed as the various subjects are covered by Scripture.

10. The Passover is a wonderful highlight in the Book of Exodus. The subjects covered in the two chapters stress the importance of the Passover in the life of ancient Israel and in the life of the believer.

---

[2] F.B. Huey, *Exodus*, p.55.

THE PASSOVER AND THE TENTH PLAGUE: DELIVERANCE FROM GOD'S JUDGMENT— LIBERATED, SET FREE, 12:1–13:16

A. The Passover: The First Basic Essential for Redemption—an Unblemished Lamb, 12:1-13

B. The Feast of Unleavened Bread: The Second Basic Essential for Redemption—Putting All Leaven, All Evil, Out of One's Life, 12:14-20

C. The Tenth Plague, the Death of the Firstborn and the Passover: Deliverance from God's Judgment—Liberated, Set Free, 12:21-51

D. The Dedication of the Firstborn: Remembering God's Great Deliverance, 13:1-16

CHAPTER 12

IV. THE PASSOVER & THE TENTH PLAGUE: DELIVERANCE FROM GOD'S JUDGMENT— LIBERATED, SET FREE, 12:1–13:16

A. The Passover: The First Basic Essential for Redemption—An Unblemished Lamb, 12:1-13

1. The significance of the Passover feast: The calendar was changed—Passover month was to begin Israel's year[DS1]

2. The persons to observe the feast
  a. The whole congregation of Israel
  b. Each family, each household was to secure one lamb: On the 10th day
  c. Small households were to share their lamb with neighbors

3. The lamb's qualifications
  a. To be one year old
  b. To be without blemish
  c. To be either a sheep or a goat

4. The lamb's sacrifice
  a. To slaughter at a specific, set time: At evening on the 14th day of the month

And the LORD spake unto Moses and Aaron in the land of Egypt, saying,
2 This month shall be unto you the beginning of months: it shall be the first month of the year to you.
3 Speak ye unto all the congregation of Israel, saying, In the tenth day of this month they shall take to them every man a lamb, according to the house of their fathers, a lamb for an house:
4 And if the household be too little for the lamb, let him and his neighbour next unto his house take it according to the number of the souls; every man according to his eating shall make your count for the lamb.
5 Your lamb shall be without blemish, a male of the first year: ye shall take it out from the sheep, or from the goats:
6 And ye shall keep it up until the fourteenth day of the same month: and the whole assembly of the congregation of Israel shall kill it in the evening.
7 And they shall take of the blood, and strike it on the two side posts and on the upper door post of the houses, wherein they shall eat it.
8 And they shall eat the flesh in that night, roast with fire, and unleavened bread; and with bitter herbs they shall eat it.
9 Eat not of it raw, nor sodden at all with water, but roast with fire; his head with his legs, and with the purtenance thereof.
10 And ye shall let nothing of it remain until the morning; and that which remaineth of it until the morning ye shall burn with fire.
11 And thus shall ye eat it; with your loins girded, your shoes on your feet, and your staff in your hand; and ye shall eat it in haste: it is the LORD's passover.
12 For I will pass through the land of Egypt this night, and will smite all the firstborn in the land of Egypt, both man and beast; and against all the gods of Egypt I will execute judgment: I am the LORD.
13 And the blood shall be to you for a token upon the houses where ye are: and when I see the blood, I will pass over you, and the plague shall not be upon you to destroy you, when I smite the land of Egypt.

  b. To smear some blood on the sides & tops of the door frames
  c. To roast & eat the meat; to also eat some unleavened bread & bitter herbs
  d. To roast the whole animal over a fire—its head, legs, & inner parts: Not to eat the lamb raw nor cooked in water
  e. To let nothing remain until morning: To burn whatever was left
  f. To eat in haste & to be dressed, ready to quickly walk out

5. The lamb's purpose: To be a substitute in death for believers
  a. The purpose concerned judgment: God was to execute judgment upon Egypt (the world)—including man, animals, & all the false gods
  b. The purpose concerned belief in God: The blood was a sign that a person *believed* God— the blood caused God to pass over & not condemn the believer

DIVISION IV

THE PASSOVER AND THE TENTH PLAGUE: DELIVERANCE FROM GOD'S JUDGMENT—LIBERATED, SET FREE, 12:1–13:16

A. The Passover: The First Basic Essential for Redemption—An Unblemished Lamb, 12:1-13

(12:1-13) **Introduction**: the Passover deals with the judgment of God and the deliverance of God.
  ⇒ The Passover deals with the judgment of God upon the unbelievers of this world, upon the evil oppressors and the ungodly and unrighteous of this world.
  ⇒ The Passover deals with the deliverance of God, His deliverance of all who believe in and diligently follow Him.

The importance of the Passover can never be over-stressed. It was without question the most significant day in Israel's history. Grasp the magnitude of what God was doing in the Passover:
  ⇒ God had a plan to save and deliver His people, all of them.
  ⇒ God had a plan to judge the evil and brutal Egyptians while protecting His people, every one of them.
  ⇒ God had a plan to show every future believer the importance of the blood of the Passover Lamb.
  ⇒ God had a plan for the forgiveness of sin, every sin that Jesus Christ would willingly take upon Himself.

The subject of this great passage is: *The Passover: The First Basic Essential for Redemption—An Unblemished Lamb,* 12:1-13.
1. The significance of the Passover feast: the calendar was changed—Passover month was to begin Israel's year (vv.1-2).
2. The persons to observe the feast (vv.3-4).
3. The lamb's qualifications (v.5).
4. The lamb's sacrifice (vv.6-11).
5. The lamb's purpose: to be a substitute in death for believers (vv.12-13).

1 (12:1-2) **Lamb—Belief—Sacrifice—Passover**: the Passover was the most significant event in Israel's history, so significant that God used the Passover to change the very calendar of Israel. Passover was an event that was different from all other events in Israel's history: it marked the very night when God delivered His people...

- from the slavery of the Egyptians (the world)
- from the plague of death

The Exodus from Egypt marked a whole new way of life for God's people. Thus God wanted their new way of life marked with a significant event, an event that would always stir them to remember the Passover, the great night of His deliverance. How could God do this? By giving them a new calendar. Their new year was to begin during the very month of the Passover. From then on, the first month of Israel's year was to be the month called *Abib,* which corresponds to today's March–April. In Palestine, these were the months that began Spring. The word Abib means "young head of grain" which pictures the new "life-giving nature of springtime."[1]

Note: Israel switched calendars after the Babylonian exile (586 B.C.). They switched to the Babylonian calendar which observed the new year in the Spring, the month of *Nisan* (Est.3:7; Ne.2:1).

Thought 1. Passover marked a *new beginning*. The old year was suddenly broken off, a new year was begun. This is true of conversion: the person's old life is suddenly broken off; a new life in Christ is begun. A person who believes in Jesus Christ, in His sacrificial death for them...

- passes from death to life
- passes from the judgment of God to the acceptance of God

The person's conversion becomes the greatest day of his life. He turns away from his *old life* and begins to live a *new life*, walking toward the *promised land* of God.

"A new heart also will I give you, and a new spirit will I put within you: and I will take away the stony heart out of your flesh, and I will give you an heart of flesh" (Eze.36:26).
"And said, Verily I say unto you, Except ye be converted, and become as little children, ye shall not enter into the kingdom of heaven" (Mt.18:3).
"Jesus answered and said unto him, Verily, verily, I say unto thee, Except a man be born again, he cannot see the kingdom of God" (Jn.3:3).
"Repent ye therefore, and be converted, that your sins may be blotted out, when the times of refreshing shall come from the presence of the Lord" (Ac.3:19).
"Therefore if any man be in Christ, he is a new creature: old things are passed away; behold, all things are become new" (2 Co.5:17).
"For in Christ Jesus neither circumcision availeth any thing, nor uncircumcision, but a new creature" (Ga.6:15).
"That ye put off concerning the former conversation the old man, which is corrupt according to the deceitful lusts; And be renewed in the spirit of your mind; And that ye put on the new man, which after God is created in righteousness and true holiness" (Ep.4:22-24).
"Ye have put off the old man with his deeds; And have put on the new man, which is renewed in knowledge after the image of him that created him" (Col.3:9-10).

Thought 2. The beginning of a new life for the Israelites was marked by a new calendar. Likewise the life of Christ is marked by a new calendar. The climax of His life was His resurrection from death. When He arose, He arose to a *new life,* a life that was to live eternally in the glory of heaven. Such an event astounds the world, so much so that the world measures its seasons and history from the date of His birth.

DEEPER STUDY # 1
(12:1-2) **Calendar, Hebrew—Symbol—Type**: because of the length of this Deeper Study, it is being placed at the end of this commentary to keep from breaking the flow of a person's study. (Please see DEEPER STUDY #1 at the conclusion of this commentary study.)

---

2 (12:3-4) **Passover—Feasts—Family**: Who was to observe the Passover feast?

a. The whole congregation of Israel. Note that Israel was called a *congregation* (edah). This is the first time this term is used in Scripture. The term is used over one hundred times to refer to the people of God who gathered together either to worship the LORD or to hear the Word of the LORD.

Note this fact as well: there is also another Hebrew word for *congregation* (qahal). This word is often used in Deuteronomy and in the Prophetic books and is said to mean the same as the New Testament Greek word for *assembly* or *church* (ekklesia).[2] Obviously, when God looked upon Israel, He saw the persons who truly believed Him, the true believers scattered all over the nation, and He called them His *congregation* of people.

b. Each family, each household was to celebrate the feast of Passover. Each household was to secure one lamb on the tenth day of the month. Note that the Passover was *family-centered*. J. Vernon McGee says this:

---

[1] Ronald F. Youngblood. *Exodus,* p. 58-59.
[2] Frank E. Gaebelein, Editor. *The Expositor's Bible Commentary*, Vol.2, p.372.

When Israel entered Egypt, it was as a family. When they made their exit from Egypt, it was as a nation. The interesting point is that God puts the emphasis on the family here because the family comprises the building blocks out of which the nation was made....An old cliché says, "No nation is stronger than the families of that nation."

The Israelites have become a nation and God is going to deliver them, but He will do it by families and by the individuals in the family. There was to be a lamb in every house.[3]

c. Small households were to share their lamb with neighbors (v.4). J. Vernon McGee has another excellent explanation of this particular point:

This verse does not say anything about the lamb being too little for the household. This would not happen; the lamb is sufficient. It is possible, however, that the household might be too little for the lamb. God is interested in each individual member of the family. Each family was to have a lamb, but what if a man and his wife were childless or had married children who lived apart from them? This couple is then supposed to join with a neighbor who is in the same position and divide the lamb. Each individual in each family is to receive a part of the lamb. The celebration of the Feast of the Passover is to be a personal, private matter. It is redemption for the nation, yes, but it centers in the family. It must be received and accepted by each individual member in the family. The Passover is a family affair.

God is presenting the modus operandi by which He is going to save individuals. No one is saved because he is the member of a nation or a family....each member of [a] family made a transaction with the Lamb; each had to partake of the Lamb....Every member had to exhibit his faith in this way.

...Each one [had] to participate and partake of [the lamb] in order to come in under the protection and the redemption of the blood that is out on the doorpost of the house.[4]

Thought 1. The importance of the family focusing upon the *Lamb of God* cannot be overstressed. Parents must take the lead in drawing their children around the Lamb of God, Christ Himself. This has been God's instruction from the very beginning of human history.

"Only take heed to thyself, and keep thy soul diligently, lest thou forget the things which thine eyes have seen, and lest they depart from thy heart all the days of thy life: but teach them thy sons, and thy sons' sons" (De.4:9).

"And these words, which I command thee this day, shall be in thine heart: And thou shalt teach them diligently unto thy children, and shalt talk of them when thou sittest in thine house, and when thou walkest by the way, and when thou liest down, and when thou risest up" (De.6:6-7).

"Gather the people together, men, and women, and children, and thy stranger that is within thy gates, that they may hear, and that they may learn, and fear the LORD your God, and observe to do all the words of this law: And that their children, which have not known any thing, may hear, and learn to fear the LORD your God, as long as ye live in the land whither ye go over Jordan to possess it" (De.31:12-13).

"There was not a word of all that Moses commanded, which Joshua read not before all the congregation of Israel, with the women, and the little ones, and the strangers that were conversant among them" (Jos.8:35).

"And Jehoash did that which was right in the sight of the LORD all his days wherein Jehoiada the priest instructed him" (2 K.12:2).

"Come, ye children, hearken unto me: I will teach you the fear of the LORD" (Ps.34:11).

"My son, forget not my law; but let thine heart keep my commandments" (Pr.3:1).

"Train up a child in the way he should go: and when he is old, he will not depart from it" (Pr.22:6).

"Whom shall he teach knowledge? and whom shall he make to understand doctrine? them that are weaned from the milk, and drawn from the breasts" (Is.28:9).

"So when they had dined, Jesus saith to Simon Peter, Simon, [son] of Jonas, lovest thou me more than these? He saith unto him, Yea, Lord; thou knowest that I love thee. He saith unto him, Feed my lambs [little ones]" (Jn.21:15).

"When I call to remembrance the unfeigned faith that is in thee [Timothy], which dwelt first in thy grandmother Lois, and thy mother Eunice; and I am persuaded that in thee also" (2 Ti.1:5).

"And that from a child thou [Timothy] hast known the holy scriptures, which are able to make thee wise unto salvation through faith which is in Christ Jesus" (2 Ti.3:15).

[3] (12:5) **Lamb—Passover**: What were the qualifications for the Passover lamb? God laid down very specific qualifications for the lamb that was to be chosen as the Passover lamb (v.5). The lamb...
- was to be one year old, that is, in its prime
- was to be without blemish or defect, that is, perfect
- was to be either a sheep or a goat

---

3 J. Vernon McGee. *Thru the Bible,* Vol.1. (Nashville, TN: Thomas Nelson Publishers, 1981), p.236.
4 ibid., p.236-237.

The lamb had to be as stated: one year old, in its prime, and *without any blemish or defect whatsoever*. This was the law laid down by God throughout Scripture. The point being made was this: God is perfect, perfect in holiness and righteousness. Therefore, whatever is given to God must be perfect in order to be acceptable to Him.

> **"And whosoever offereth a sacrifice of peace offerings unto the LORD to accomplish his vow, or a freewill offering in beeves or sheep, it shall be perfect to be accepted; there shall be no blemish therein" (Le.22:21).**

But note the problem with the gifts of sacrifice offered by the Israelites. The same problem exists with the gifts and sacrifices we offer to God.

> **"Gifts and sacrifices...[these] could not make him that did the service perfect, as pertaining to the conscience" (He.9:9).**

Any honest and thinking person knows that we can never be perfect, not absolutely perfect. How then can we ever be acceptable to God? By faith in the *Perfect Lamb of God*, the Son of God Himself, the Lord Jesus Christ. God accepts and counts our faith in His Son as *perfection*. We are not perfect and never will be, but if we believe—truly believe—in the perfect Lamb of God, the Lord Jesus Christ, God counts our belief as perfection. He justifies us, counts us as though we are sinless. This is the wonderful mercy of God.

⇒ The believers of old believed the promise of God, that the blood of the unblemished lamb would save them. Therefore, God accepted the believers' faith in His promise and counted the believers as acceptable to Him.
⇒ The believer today believes the promise of God's Son, that His blood cleanses us from all sin and makes us acceptable to God. Therefore, God accepts our belief in Christ and counts us perfect and acceptable in Christ, the Lamb of God who takes away the sins of the world.

Thought 1. The Passover lamb was a type of the Lord Jesus Christ.
(1) The Passover sacrifice was to a be a lamb or a young goat. The lamb was a picture of the Lord Jesus Christ, the Lamb of God Himself. Note this: Jesus Christ was not only the promised seed and Savior who was promised to Abraham and his descendants, not only the promised seed and Savior who was to come and save the world—Jesus Christ was the Lamb of God Himself, the Lamb of God who was to be slain for the sins of the world. Jesus Christ was the Lamb of God symbolized in the Passover lamb. This is exactly what Scripture proclaims.

> **"The next day John seeth Jesus coming unto him, and saith, Behold the Lamb of God, which taketh away the sin of the world" (Jn.1:29).**
> **"And looking upon Jesus as he walked, he saith, Behold the Lamb of God!" (Jn.1:36).**
> **"In whom we have redemption through his blood, the forgiveness of sins, according to the riches of his grace" (Ep.1:7).**
> **"Forasmuch as ye know that ye were not redeemed with corruptible things, as silver and gold, from your vain conversation received by tradition from your fathers; But with the precious blood of Christ, as of a lamb without blemish and without spot" (1 Pe.1:18-19).**
> **"After this I beheld, and, lo, a great multitude, which no man could number, of all nations, and kindreds, and people, and tongues, stood before the throne, and before the Lamb, clothed with white robes, and palms in their hands" (Re.7:9).**
> **"And they overcame him [Satan] by the blood of the Lamb, and by the word of their testimony; and they loved not their lives unto the death" (Re.12:11).**
> **"And all that dwell upon the earth shall worship him, whose names are not written in the book of life of the Lamb slain from the foundation of the world" (Re.13:8).**
> **"And I looked, and, lo, a Lamb stood on the mount Sion, and with him an hundred forty and four thousand, having his Father's name written in their foreheads" (Re.14:1).**
> **"And they sing the song of Moses the servant of God, and the song of the Lamb, saying, Great and marvellous are thy works, Lord God Almighty; just and true are thy ways, thou King of saints" (Re.15:3).**
> **"And he saith unto me, Write, Blessed are they which are called unto the marriage supper of the Lamb. And he saith unto me, These are the true sayings of God" (Re.19:9).**
> **"And I saw no temple therein: for the Lord God Almighty and the Lamb are the temple of it" (Re.21:22).**

(2) The Passover lamb was to be one year old, in its prime. Jesus Christ offered Himself up while in the strength and vigor of life, not as a child, nor as an elderly person.
(3) The Passover lamb was to be without blemish or defect. Jesus Christ was without blemish or defect. He knew no sin whatsoever; He was the *perfect* Son of God.

> **"And he made his grave with the wicked, and with the rich in his death; because he had done no violence, neither was any deceit in his mouth" (Is.53:9).**
> **"Which of you convinceth me of sin? And if I say the truth, why do ye not believe me?" (Jn.8:46).**

"For he hath made him to be sin for us, who knew no sin; that we might be made the righteousness of God in him" (2 Co.5:21).

"For we have not an high priest which cannot be touched with the feeling of our infirmities; but was in all points tempted like as we are, yet without sin" (He.4:15).

"For such an high priest became us, who is holy, harmless, undefiled, separate from sinners, and made higher than the heavens" (He.7:26).

"How much more shall the blood of Christ, who through the eternal Spirit offered himself without spot to God, purge your conscience from dead works to serve the living God?" (He.9:14).

"But with the precious blood of Christ, as of a lamb without blemish and without spot" (1 Pe.1:19).

"Who did no sin, neither was guile found in his mouth" (1 Pe.2:22).

"And ye know that he was manifested to take away our sins; and in him is no sin" (1 Jn.3:5).

4 (12:6-11) **Lamb—Passover—Sacrifices—Sacrificial System**: the instructions governing the lamb's sacrifice were also very specific (v.6).

a. The lamb had to be slaughtered and it had to be slaughtered at a very specific time: at evening on the fourteenth day of the month (v.6).

Thought 1. Note two clear symbols.
(1) Symbol 1: the lamb had to die, to be slaughtered. This symbolizes that Jesus Christ had to die: it was necessary that He die. Why?
(a) Because the penalty for sin is death; the penalty for our rebellion and insurrection against God is death.

"For all have sinned, and come short of the glory of God" (Ro.3:23).

"For the wages of sin is death; but the gift of God is eternal life through Jesus Christ our Lord" (Ro.6:23).

"For to be carnally minded is death" (Ro.8:6).

"Then when lust hath conceived, it bringeth forth sin: and sin, when it is finished, bringeth forth death" (Js.1:15).

"But the fearful, and unbelieving, and the abominable, and murderers, and whoremongers, and sorcerers, and idolaters, and all liars, shall have their part in the lake which burneth with fire and brimstone: which is the second death" (Re.21:8).

"He, that being often reproved hardeneth his neck, shall suddenly be destroyed, and that without remedy" (Pr.29:1).

"The soul that sinneth, it shall die" (Eze.18:4).

(b) Because there can be only one way to escape the penalty of sin and death. Someone—a perfect and sinless person who is acceptable to God—has to step forward and do two things for us:
⇒ Take the penalty of our sin upon Himself
⇒ Pay the penalty for our sin

"But he was wounded for our transgressions, he was bruised for our iniquities: the chastisement of our peace was upon him; and with his stripes we are healed" (Is.53:5).

"He was oppressed, and he was afflicted, yet he opened not his mouth: he is brought as a lamb to the slaughter, and as a sheep before her shearers is dumb, so he openeth not his mouth" (Is.53:7).

"Christ hath redeemed us from the curse of the law, being made a curse for us: for it is written, Cursed is every one that hangeth on a tree" (Ga.3:13).

"But we see Jesus, who was made a little lower than the angels for the suffering of death, crowned with glory and honour; that he by the grace of God should taste death for every man" (He.2:9).

"So Christ was once offered to bear the sins of many; and unto them that look for him shall he appear the second time without sin unto salvation" (He.9:28).

(c) Because God the Father predestined the death of His Son, predestined that the way of salvation and redemption would be by the blood of the cross.

"Ye men of Israel, hear these words; Jesus of Nazareth, a man approved of God among you by miracles and wonders and signs, which God did by him in the midst of you, as ye yourselves also know: Him, being delivered by the determinate counsel and foreknowledge of God, ye have taken, and by wicked hands have crucified and slain" (Ac.2:22-23).

"But when the fulness of the time was come, God sent forth his Son, made of a woman, made under the law, To redeem them that were under the law, that we might receive the adoption of sons" (Ga.4:4-5).

"But we see Jesus, who was made a little lower than the angels for the suffering of death, crowned with glory and honour; that he by the grace of God should taste death for every man" (He.2:9).

"And almost all things are by the law purged with blood; and without shedding of blood is no remission" (He.9:22).

(2) Symbol 2: the lamb had to be slaughtered at a very specific time. This symbolized that Jesus Christ had to come to earth and die at a particular time, that His death and the time of His death were set by God. God sent His Son to earth in the fulness of time.

"And saying, The time is fulfilled, and the kingdom of God is at hand: repent ye, and believe the gospel" (Mk.1:15).

"Him, being delivered by the determinate counsel and foreknowledge of God, ye have taken, and by wicked hands have crucified and slain" (Ac.2:23).

"But when the fulness of the time was come, God sent forth his Son, made of a woman, made under the law, To redeem them that were under the law, that we might receive the adoption of sons" (Ga.4:4-5).

"For there is one God, and one mediator between God and men, the man Christ Jesus; Who gave himself a ransom for all, to be testified in due time" (1 Ti.2:5-6).

"Now once in the end of the world hath he appeared to put away sin by the sacrifice of himself. And as it is appointed unto men once to die, but after this the judgment: So Christ was once offered to bear the sins of many; and unto them that look for him shall he appear the second time without sin unto salvation" (He.9:26-28).

b. The blood of the lamb was to be smeared on the sides and tops of the door frames (v.7). If a person believed God—believed that God would save the person behind the blood—the person would smear the blood on the door frame. If the person did not believe God, he would not smear the blood. The person's faith in God—in His Word, in the blood—saved him. This is exactly what Scripture says:

"Through faith he kept the passover, and the sprinkling of blood, lest he that destroyed the firstborn should touch them" (He.11:28).

Scripture declares the glorious truth of *substitutionary death*: the sacrifice and its blood symbolizes the substitution of one life for another. The lamb and its blood were offered as a substitute for the believer.

"For the life of the flesh is in the blood: and I have given it to you upon the altar to make an atonement for your souls: for it is the blood that maketh an atonement for the soul" (Le.17:11).

Thought 1. This symbolized the covering of the blood of Christ. We must make sure that we ourselves are covered and that our homes, our entire families, are covered by the blood of our Lord. Jesus Christ died for us. He is our *Substitute* in death: He died *for* us; He sacrificed His life *for* us.

"For this is my blood of the new testament, which is shed for many for the remission of sins" (Mt.26:28).

"Much more then, being now justified by his blood, we shall be saved from wrath through him" (Ro.5:9).

"Purge out therefore the old leaven, that ye may be a new lump, as ye are unleavened. For even Christ our passover is sacrificed for us" (1 Co.5:7).

"Who gave himself for our sins, that he might deliver us from this present evil world, according to the will of God and our Father" (Ga.1:4).

"In whom we have redemption through his blood, the forgiveness of sins, according to the riches of his grace" (Ep.1:7).

"For ye are dead, and your life is hid with Christ in God [hid in the death of Christ]" (Col.3:3).

"Who gave himself for us, that he might redeem us from all iniquity, and purify unto himself a peculiar people, zealous of good works" (Tit.2:14).

"And almost all things are by the law purged with blood; and without shedding of blood is no remission" (He.9:22).

"So Christ was once offered to bear the sins of many; and unto them that look for him shall he appear the second time without sin unto salvation" (He.9:28).

"Forasmuch as ye know that ye were not redeemed with corruptible things, as silver and gold, from your vain conversation [behavior] received by tradition from your fathers; But with the precious blood of Christ, as of a lamb without blemish and without spot" (1 Pe.1:18-19).

"Who his own self bare our sins in his own body on the tree, that we, being dead to sins, should live unto righteousness: by whose stripes ye were healed" (1 Pe.2:24).

"For Christ also hath once suffered for sins, the just for the unjust, that he might bring us to God, being put to death in the flesh, but quickened by the Spirit" (1 Pe.3:18).

"The blood of Jesus Christ his Son cleanseth us from all sin" (1 Jn.1:7).

Thought 2. The blood smeared on the door frame was a public profession. Neighbors, friends, and family—all clearly saw that a person believed God and believed in God's Word, His promises, and His coming judgment. This is a strong challenge to us: that we bear witness to Christ, that we proclaim openly and unashamedly that we believe in God's promises and in His coming judgment.

"I will mention the lovingkindnesses of the LORD, and the praises of the LORD, according to all that the LORD hath bestowed on us" (Is.63:7).

"Go ye therefore, and teach all nations, baptizing them in the name of the Father, and of the Son, and of the Holy Ghost: Teaching them to observe all things whatsoever I have commanded you: and, lo, I am with you alway, [even] unto the end of the world" (Mt.28:19-20).

"And he said unto them, Go ye into all the world, and preach the gospel to every creature" (Mk.16:15).

"But ye shall receive power, after that the Holy Ghost is come upon you: and ye shall be witnesses unto me both in Jerusalem, and in all Judaea, and in Samaria, and unto the uttermost part of the earth" (Ac.1:8).

"For we cannot but speak the things which we have seen and heard" (Ac.4:20).

"Go, stand and speak in the temple to the people all the words of this life" (Ac.5:20).

"These things speak, and exhort, and rebuke with all authority. Let no man despise thee" (Tit.2:15).

"But sanctify the Lord God in your hearts: and be ready always to give an answer to every man that asketh you a reason of the hope that is in you with meekness and fear" (1 Pe.3:15).

c. The believers were to roast and eat the meat. They were also to eat some unleavened bread and bitter herbs (v.8). Again, note that the Passover was family-centered: the family was to eat the Passover together, to worship and celebrate the feast *together*.

Thought 1. This particular point symbolizes three things.
(1) The eating of the Passover lamb symbolizes that we are definitely to *eat* (partake, assimilate) the merits of Christ's death, that we are to partake of the death of Christ.
(2) The unleavened bread symbolizes *righteousness*: we must *eat*, partake of, the righteousness of the Lord Jesus Christ.

"This is the bread which cometh down from heaven, that a man may eat thereof, and not die. I am the living bread which came down from heaven: if any man eat of this bread, he shall live for ever: and the bread that I will give is my flesh, which I will give for the life of the world. The Jews therefore strove among themselves, saying, How can this man give us his flesh to eat? Then Jesus said unto them, Verily, verily, I say unto you, Except ye eat the flesh of the Son of man, and drink his blood, ye have no life in you. Whoso eateth my flesh, and drinketh my blood, hath eternal life; and I will raise him up at the last day. For my flesh is meat indeed, and my blood is drink indeed. He that eateth my flesh, and drinketh my blood, dwelleth in me, and I in him. As the living Father hath sent me, and I live by the Father: so he that eateth me, even he shall live by me. This is that bread which came down from heaven: not as your fathers did eat manna, and are dead: he that eateth of this bread shall live for ever" (Jn.6:50-58).

(3) The bitter herbs symbolized the bitter days of Israel's slavery (see Ex.1:14). This is a picture of our enslavement to sin. The horrible days of our enslavement to sin are never to be forgotten. Our hearts are to be constantly broken over sin.

"Jesus answered them, Verily, verily, I say unto you, Whosoever committeth sin is the servant of sin" (Jn.8:34).

"Know ye not, that to whom ye yield yourselves servants to obey, his servants ye are to whom ye obey; whether of sin unto death, or of obedience unto righteousness? But God be thanked, that ye were the servants of sin, but ye have obeyed from the heart that form of doctrine which was delivered you. Being then made free from sin, ye became the servants of righteousness" (Ro.6:16-18).

"For the wages of sin is death; but the gift of God is eternal life through Jesus Christ our Lord" (Ro.6:23).

Thought 2. What a lesson for the church: to be family-centered! But how many churches are really family-centered? How many programs and activities of the church place the family together? How much of the church is organized and planned to separate and divide the family? How much focuses upon the *togetherness* of the family? Are there churches who contribute to the division of the family?

d. The believer was to roast the whole animal over a fire: its head, legs, and inner parts. The animal was not to be eaten raw nor cooked in water (v.9). Note that the lamb was prepared in a very specific way, with very specific instructions. No other way was acceptable.

Thought 1. This symbolizes that the death of Christ was specifically spelled out. Thus, we must accept Christ exactly as He was prepared and offered by God. There is no other way to be saved, no other way whatsoever. Some people may consider the blood of Christ repulsive, disgusting, or offensive. They may even reject the death of Christ as the way by which man becomes acceptable to God. Nevertheless, God is very specific: there is no other way to God, no way except by the blood of Jesus Christ.

"For this is my blood of the new testament, which is shed for many for the remission of sins" (Mt.26:28).

226

"I said therefore unto you, that ye shall die in your sins: for if ye believe not that I am [he], ye shall die in your sins" (Jn.8:24).

"I am the good shepherd: the good shepherd giveth his life for the sheep" (Jn.10:11).

"Much more then, being now justified by his blood, we shall be saved from wrath through him" (Ro.5:9).

"Neither is there salvation in any other: for there is none other name under heaven given among men, whereby we must be saved" (Ac.4:12).

"Take heed therefore unto yourselves, and to all the flock, over the which the Holy Ghost hath made you overseers, to feed the church of God, which he hath purchased with his own blood" (Ac.20:28).

"Much more then, being now justified by his blood, we shall be saved from wrath through him" (Ro.5:9).

"In whom we have redemption through his blood, the forgiveness of sins, according to the riches of his grace" (Ep.1:7).

"How much more shall the blood of Christ, who through the eternal Spirit offered himself without spot to God, purge your conscience from dead works to serve the living God?" (He.9:14).

"And almost all things are by the law purged with blood; and without shedding of blood is no remission" (He.9:22).

"But if we walk in the light, as he is in the light, we have fellowship one with another, and the blood of Jesus Christ his Son cleanseth us from all sin" (1 Jn.1:7).

"Yet it pleased the LORD to bruise him; he hath put him to grief: when thou shalt make his soul an offering for sin, he shall see his seed, he shall prolong his days, and the pleasure of the LORD shall prosper in his hand" (Is.53:10).

e. The believer was to let no food remain until morning. He was to burn whatever was left (v.10).

Thought 1. This symbolizes that all of Christ is to be *eaten* (assimilated, taken in, digested). Nothing of Christ is to be left out: not His cross, not His demand for self-denial, not His righteousness. We are to digest all of Christ into our lives, all of His righteousness and teachings. We are to follow Christ in everything.

"Therefore we are buried with him by baptism into death: that like as Christ was raised up from the dead by the glory of the Father, even so we also should walk in newness of life" (Ro.6:4).

"Purge out therefore the old leaven, that ye may be a new lump, as ye are unleavened. For even Christ our passover is sacrificed for us: Therefore let us keep the feast, not with old leaven, neither with the leaven of malice and wickedness; but with the unleavened bread of sincerity and truth" (1 Co.5:7-8).

"As ye have therefore received Christ Jesus the Lord, so walk ye in him" (Col.2:6).

"Wherefore he is able also to save them to the uttermost that come unto God by him, seeing he ever liveth to make intercession for them" (He.7:25).

"But if we walk in the light, as he is in the light, we have fellowship one with another, and the blood of Jesus Christ his Son cleanseth us from all sin" (1 Jn.1:7).

"He that saith he abideth in him ought himself also so to walk, even as he walked" (1 Jn.2:6).

f. The believer was to eat in haste and to be dressed, ready to quickly walk out and march toward the promised land (v.11). The believer was to waste no time in separating from Egypt and beginning his new life of freedom.

Thought 1. This symbolizes that we are to *eat*, partake of, Christ quickly. We are to lay hold of the death of Christ immediately. The hour is urgent: now is the day of salvation. We are to immediately accept Christ, rush away from the world and begin our *new life*, our *new life* marching to the promised land of heaven. We are to live as though Christ might return today.

"And saying, Repent ye: for the kingdom of heaven is at hand" (Mt.3:2).

"Therefore be ye also ready: for in such an hour as ye think not the Son of man cometh" (Mt.24:44).

"Watch therefore, for ye know neither the day nor the hour wherein the Son of man cometh" (Mt.25:13).

"Watch ye therefore: for ye know not when the master of the house cometh, at even, or at midnight, or at the cockcrowing, or in the morning" (Mk.13:35).

"Behold, now is the accepted time; behold, now is the day of salvation" (2 Co.6:2).

"And the times of this ignorance God winked at; but now commandeth all men every where to repent" (Ac.17:30).

"Behold, I come as a thief. Blessed is he that watcheth, and keepeth his garments, lest he walk naked, and they see his shame" (Re.16:15).

"And, behold, I come quickly; and my reward is with me, to give every man according as his work shall be" (Re.22:12).

"See, I have set before thee this day life and good, and death and evil" (De.30:15).

"I call heaven and earth to record this day against you, that I have set before you life and death, blessing and cursing: therefore choose life, that both thou and thy seed may live" (De.30:19).

"And Elijah came unto all the people, and said, How long halt ye between two opinions? if the LORD be God, follow him: but if Baal, then follow him. And the people answered him not a word" (1 K.18:21).

"Choose you this day whom ye will serve; whether the gods which your fathers served that were on the other side of the flood, or the gods of the Amorites, in whose land ye dwell: but as for me and my house, we will serve the LORD" (Jos.24:15).

5 (12:12-13) **Lamb—Sacrifices—Sacrificial System—Passover**: What was God's purpose for the Passover lamb? In substituting the lamb's death for the firstborn of Israel? Just this: God was symbolizing that there had to be a substitute in death for the believers. The purpose for the Passover lamb concerned two things (vv.12-13).

a. The first purpose concerned *judgment*. God was to execute judgment upon Egypt (the world), including both man and animal, and also upon all the false gods of Egypt (v.12). Remember the Egyptians were an idolatrous people who had rejected God ages before. They wanted to live like they wanted and do their own thing. Therefore, they wanted nothing to do with the righteousness demanded by God. They turned to the worship of false gods, the false gods of man's imaginations. The result was terrible: they created gods in their own image, gods that allowed them to live like they wanted: selfish, immoral, greedy, covetous, unrighteous lives. The Egyptians became what we all become when we reject the only true God of righteousness, the LORD God Himself (Jehovah, Yahweh): they became an evil people. They were a people who trampled other people under foot, enslaving them and brutalizing them. They had even enslaved and launched a holocaust against the very people who believed in the only true and living God, the ancient Israelites. The Egyptians had reached the point of no return, the point of never repenting. Therefore, God was about to execute judgment upon Egypt, a judgment that would fall upon all Egypt, including all the people, animals, and the false gods worshipped by the people.

> "For the Egyptians buried all their firstborn, which the LORD had smitten among them: upon their gods also the LORD executed judgments" (Nu.33:4).

Note: by judging the firstborn of *animals*, God was striking at the very gods of the Egyptians. Remember, they had imagined and created gods that were closely linked to various animals of the earth. Thus God was striking a death blow to the so-called gods by striking dead the firstborn of all animals. The gods of the Egyptians were powerless to stop the judgment of God. The judgment demonstrated that the fancied gods of Egypt were false gods, that the people were actually following a false, worthless, and empty worship (see note, pt.6—Ex.7:8-11:10). Thus the Passover concerned judgment. How could a person escape the judgment of God? How could a person stir God to *pass over* him and his family? By faith. Note the next point.

b. The second purpose of the Passover Lamb concerned faith, belief in God: the blood of the Passover lamb smeared upon the door posts was a sign that a person believed God. The blood caused God to *pass over* and not condemn the believer (v.13).

Simply stated: if a person believed God—really believed—he would smear the blood on the door posts of his house. If he did not believe God, he would not smear the blood. As in all situations, some persons believed God and some did not. Some escaped the judgment of God and some did not. Scripture even tells us that some of the Egyptians and perhaps other nationalities believed God and joined the Israelites (Ex.12:38).

Thought 1. Several lessons can be learned from this point.
(1) The person who does not trust Jesus Christ shall face the judgment of God.

> "And this is the condemnation, that light is come into the world, and men loved darkness rather than light, because their deeds were evil" (Jn.3:19).
> "I said therefore unto you, that ye shall die in your sins: for if ye believe not that I am [he], ye shall die in your sins" (Jn.8:24).
> "Because he hath appointed a day, in the which he will judge the world in righteousness by that man whom he hath ordained [Jesus Christ]; whereof he hath given assurance unto all men, in that he hath raised him from the dead" (Ac.17:31).
> "In the day when God shall judge the secrets of men by Jesus Christ according to my gospel" (Ro.2:16).

(2) The people's faith in the blood saved them. Our faith in the blood of Jesus Christ saves us. Note that the Israelites were not saved because they had godly parents nor because they were living good, honest, and moral lives. Neither are we. We are all saved by the blood of the Lamb, saved because we believe that the blood of the Lamb covers our sin.

> "Take heed therefore unto yourselves, and to all the flock, over the which the Holy Ghost hath made you overseers, to feed the church of God, which he hath purchased with his own blood" (Ac.20:28).
> "But God commendeth his love toward us, in that, while we were yet sinners, Christ died for us. Much more then, being now justified by his blood, we shall be saved from wrath through him" (Ro.5:8-9).
> "How much more shall the blood of Christ, who through the eternal Spirit offered himself without spot to God, purge your conscience from dead works to serve the living God?" (He.9:14).
> "Through faith he [Moses] kept the passover, and the sprinkling of blood, lest he that destroyed the firstborn should touch them" (He.11:28).
> "Unto him that loved us, and washed us from our sins in his own blood" (Re.1:5).

(3) The blood of the sacrificed lamb symbolized the substitution of one life for another. The blood of Jesus Christ symbolizes our death, if we truly trust His blood to cover us. We are redeemed when we trust the blood of Jesus Christ.

> **"Purge out therefore the old leaven, that ye may be a new lump, as ye are unleavened. For even Christ our passover is sacrificed for us" (1 Co.5:7).**
>
> **"Neither by the blood of goats and calves, but by his own blood he entered in once into the holy place, having obtained eternal redemption for us. For if the blood of bulls and of goats, and the ashes of an heifer sprinkling the unclean, sanctifieth to the purifying of the flesh: How much more shall the blood of Christ, who through the eternal Spirit offered himself without spot to God, purge your conscience from dead works to serve the living God?" (He.9:12-14).**
>
> **"And almost all things are by the law purged with blood; and without shedding of blood is no remission" (He.9:22).**
>
> **"Forasmuch as ye know that ye were not redeemed with corruptible things, as silver and gold, from your vain conversation received by tradition from your fathers; But with the precious blood of Christ, as of a lamb without blemish and without spot" (1 Pe.1:18-19).**
>
> **"And they sung a new song, saying, Thou art worthy to take the book, and to open the seals thereof: for thou wast slain, and hast redeemed us to God by thy blood out of every kindred, and tongue, and people, and nation; And hast made us unto our God kings and priests: and we shall reign on the earth" (Re.5:9-10).**

(4) The Lamb of God alone takes away the sins of the world.

> **"In whom we have redemption through his blood, the forgiveness of sins, according to the riches of his grace" (Ep.1:7).**
>
> **"But if we walk in the light, as he is in the light, we have fellowship one with another, and the blood of Jesus Christ his Son cleanseth us from all sin" (1 Jn.1:7).**
>
> **"The next day John seeth Jesus coming unto him, and saith, Behold the Lamb of God, which taketh away the sin of the world" (Jn.1:29).**
>
> **"Again the next day after John stood, and two of his disciples; And looking upon Jesus as he walked, he saith, Behold the Lamb of God!" (Jn.1:35-36).**
>
> **"He was oppressed, and he was afflicted, yet he opened not his mouth: he is brought as a lamb to the slaughter, and as a sheep before her shearers is dumb, so he openeth not his mouth" (Is.53:7).**

Thought 2. J. Vernon McGee has an excellent application on this point:

> *God said that when he saw the blood, he would pass over that home. The blood was not some mystic or superstitious sign. A great principle runs all the way through the Word of God that without shedding of blood, there is no remission of sins. In other words, God cannot arbitrarily or big-heartedly shut His eyes to sin and do nothing about it, any more than can a judge today when the guilty are brought before him. The judge should apply the law to the guilty, and the penalty should be paid. Part of our problem in America today is the laxity in law enforcement. But God's law is inexorable in the universe— "The soul that sinneth, it shall die." The death sentence is upon all of us. But God is gracious, and an innocent life may be substituted for the guilty. Up until Christ came, it was a lamb. Then Jesus was "...the Lamb of God, which taketh away the sin of the world" (Jn.1:29). If we receive Christ, we are saved from the judgment that we deserve as sinners.* [5]

---

5 J. Vernon McGee. *Thru the Bible,* Vol.1, p.239.

DEEPER STUDY # 1
(12:1-2) **Calendar, Hebrew:**

SIGNIFICANT EVENTS IN THE HEBREW CALENDAR

Sacred Month	Secular Month	Hebrew Name	Modern Name	Feast or Event	Farm Seasons **	Bible Ref.	Old Testament Meaning	New Testament Meaning
1	7	Abib; Nisan	March–April	Passover	Harvesting barley and flax; Later Spring rains	Ex.12:2; 13:4; 23:15; 34:18; De.16:1; Ne.2:1; Est..3:7	Redemption from Egypt's bondage	Christ's Crucifixion
				Unleaven-ed Bread;			Purging of all leaven (a symbol of sin)	Justification/ Sanctification
				Firstfruits		Le.23:10-12		Resurrection of Christ
2	8	Ziv or Zif Iyyar +	April–May	Second or "Little Passover"	Barley harvest; Dry season begins	1K.6:1, 37	33rd day of the Omer (Sabbath), a minor holiday	
3	9	Sivan	May-June	Pentecost (Weeks)	Wheat harvest	Est.8:9	A Giving of Thanks for the First Harvest	The Coming of the Holy Spirit and The Birth of the Church
4	10	Tammuz +	June-July	Fast to remember the breach in Jerusalem's wall	Tending the vines (grapes, olives, figs, pomegranates, etc.)	Je.52:5-6		
5	11	Ab +	July-August	Fast for the destruction of the Temple (by Babylon-OT & Rome-NT) (Mt.24:1-3)	Ripening of the vines			
6	12	Elul	August-September		Harvesting of the vines	Ne.6:15		

There were two other significant events in the Hebrew calendar: *The Sabbatical Year* and *The Year of Jubilee*. *The Sabbatical Year* was celebrated every seven years. During the seventh year the land was given rest from agricultural use and debts were forgiven (see Ex.23:10-11; Le.25:1-7; De.15:1 for more information). *The Year of Jubilee* was celebrated at the end of every forty-ninth year on the Day of Atonement. On this special day, the trumpet would sound out the message of freedom to all the inhabitants of the land who had been held in bondage. In addition, all property was to be returned to the original owners who had been forced to give it up because of poverty. This meant that all prices in the economy throughout the forty-nine years were to be fairly adjusted according to the closeness to The Year of Jubilee (see Le.25:8-17).

230

Sacred Month	Secular Month	Hebrew Name	Modern Name	Feast or Event	Farm Seasons **	Bible Ref.	Old Testament Meaning	New Testament Meaning
7	1 (Beginning of the civil year)	Ethanim Tishri +	September-October	Trumpets	Plowing of the fields: Early autumn rains	1K.8:2; Joel 2:23	A Somber Assembly in Preparation for the Day of Atonement	The Rapture of the Church & The Bodily Return of Christ
				Atonement (Yom Kippur)			A National Day of Repentance (yearly)	Forgiveness of Sins
				Tabernacles (Booths)			A Celebration for the Harvest	The Kingdom of God on Earth
				Branches or Palms				
8	2	Bul Marcheshvan +	October-November		Planting of the crops: Wheat & barley esp.	1K.6:38		
9	3	Kislev or Chislev or Chisleu	November-December	Hanukkah Feast of Dedication	Winter begins	Ne.1:1; Zec.7:1 (Extra-Biblical Source: 2 Macc.1:9)		
10	4	Tebeth	December-January	Fast remembering Nebuchadnezzar's siege of Jerusalem		Est.2:16 2 K.25:1		
11	5	Shebat or Sebat	January-February	Jewish Arbor Day	Blossoming of trees	Zec.1:7		
12	6	Adar *	February-March	Fast of Esther	Blooming of almond trees; Harvesting of citrus fruit	Ezr.6:15; Est.3:7,13 8:12;9:1, 15,17,19, 21,26-28		
				Purim			Israel was delivered from their enemies: a time to share with each other & with the poor	

* Note: An additional month (Second Adar or Adar Sheni or Veadar) was added to the Hebrew calendar about every three years. This was how the lunar calendar corresponded to the solar year.

+ Hebrew names of the month that are not in the Bible are marked with a plus sign (+). These are known as "Post-exilic" names, from the period of history known as "The Babylonian Exile."

**The idea for listing the Farm Seasons was stirred by the *NIV Study Bible*, Grand Rapids, MI: Zondervan Bible Publishers, 1985, pp.102-103.

TYPES, SYMBOLS, AND PICTURES
(Exodus 12:1-13)

Historical Term	Type or Picture (Scriptural Basis for Each)	Life Application for Today's Believer	Biblical Application
The Passover Feast (Ex.12:1-13; 12:21-27)	*Salvation: Deliverance from God's judgment. God's judgment passes over all who hide behind the blood of the Passover Lamb.* **"And it shall come to pass, when your children shall say unto you, What mean ye by this service? That ye shall say, It *is* the sacrifice of the LORD's passover, who passed over the houses of the children of Israel in Egypt, when he smote the Egyptians, and delivered our houses"** (Ex.12:26-27).	God's judgment passes over all who hide behind the blood of Jesus Christ, the Lamb of God. The Son of God Himself, the Lord Jesus Christ, has delivered the believer from eternal judgment.	*"Through faith he [Moses] kept the passover, and the sprinkling of blood, lest he that destroyed the firstborn should touch them"* (He.11:28). *"The next day John seeth Jesus coming unto him, and saith, Behold the Lamb of God, which taketh away the sin of the world"* (Jn.1:29). *"Purge out therefore the old leaven, that ye may be a new lump, as ye are unleavened. For even Christ our passover is sacrificed for us"* (1 Co.5:7). *"He that believeth on the Son hath everlasting life: and he that believeth not the Son shall not see life; but the wrath of God abideth on him"* (Jn.3:36). *"But God commendeth his love toward us, in that, while we were yet sinners, Christ died for us. Much more then, being now justified by his blood, we shall be saved from wrath through him"* (Ro.5:8-9).
The Passover Lamb *"without blemish [defect or imperfection]"* (Ex.12:5)	*Purity and perfection* **"Your lamb shall be without blemish [defect], a male of the first year: ye shall take *it* out from the sheep, or from the goats"** (Ex.12:5).	Jesus Christ is the Passover Lamb who lived a pure, sinless, and perfect life.	*"For he hath made him to be sin for us, who knew no sin; that we might be made the righteousness of God in him"* (2 Co.5:21). *"The next day John seeth Jesus coming unto him, and saith, Behold the Lamb of God, which taketh away the sin of the world"* (Jn.1:29). *"And being made perfect, he became the author of eternal salvation unto all them that obey him"* (He.5:9). *(see He.4:15; 7:26; 9:14; 1 Pe.1:18-19; 2:22)*
The Slaughter of the Lamb (Ex.12:7, 13; 12:21-23)	*Substitutionary atonement: The lamb had to die for the believer: its blood had to be smeared on the doorposts to save the believer.* **"And they shall take of the blood, and strike *it* on the two side posts and on the upper door post of the houses, wherein they shall eat it....And the blood shall be to you for a token upon the houses where ye are: and when I see the**	Jesus Christ, the Lamb of God, died for man. He gave His life for man. The life, the very death and blood, of Jesus Christ was offered upon the cross as a substitute for the believer. Scripture declares this glorious truth, the truth of the *substitutionary death* of Jesus Christ.	*"But he was wounded for our transgressions, he was bruised for our iniquities: the chastisement of our peace was upon him; and with his stripes we are healed....He was oppressed, and he was afflicted, yet he opened not his mouth: he is brought as a lamb to the slaughter, and as a sheep before her shearers is dumb, so he openeth not his mouth"* (Is.53:5, 7).

TYPES, SYMBOLS, AND PICTURES
(Exodus 12:1-13)

Historical Term	Type or Picture (Scriptural Basis for Each)	Life Application for Today's Believer	Biblical Application
The Slaughter of the Lamb (continued) (Ex.12:7, 13; 12:21-23)	**blood, I will pass over you, and the plague shall not be upon you to destroy you, when I smite the land of Egypt" (Ex.12:7, 13).**		*"But God commendeth his love toward us, in that, while we were yet sinners, Christ died for us" (Ro.5:8).* *"For Christ also hath once suffered for sins, the just for the unjust, that he might bring us to God, being put to death in the flesh, but quickened by the Spirit" (1 Pe.3:18).* *"Who his own self bare our sins in his own body on the tree, that we, being dead to sins, should live unto righteousness: by whose stripes ye were healed" (1 Pe.2:24).* (see Ro.3:25; 1 Co.5:7; Ga.3:13; He.2:9; 10:4; 13:11-12; 1 Jn.2:2)
The Blood from the Lamb (Ex.12:7, 13; 12:21-23)	*The forgiveness of sin: The blood of the lamb smeared on the doorposts...* • hid the believer with all his weaknesses & sins behind the blood • made the believer acceptable to God **"And they shall take of the blood, and strike** *it* **on the two side posts and on the upper door post of the houses, wherein they shall eat it....And the blood shall be to you for a token upon the houses where ye are: and when I see the blood, I will pass over you, and the plague shall not be upon you to destroy you, when I smite the land of Egypt" (Ex.12:7, 13; see Ex.12:21-23).**	The shed blood of Jesus Christ... • provides forgiveness of sin • makes the believer acceptable to God • delivers the believer from the wrath of God, the judgment to come	*"The next day John seeth Jesus coming unto him, and saith, Behold the Lamb of God, which taketh away the sin of the world" (Jn.1:29).* *"In whom we have redemption through his blood, the forgiveness of sins, according to the riches of his grace" (Ep.1:7).* *"For this is my blood of the new testament, which is shed for many for the remission of sins" (Mt.26:28).* *"And ye know that he was manifested to take away our sins; and in him is no sin" (1 Jn.3:5).* *"Unto him that loved us, and washed us from our sins in his own blood" (Re.1:5).* (see Jn.3:16; Jn.3:17-18; Ac.5:31; Ro.5:9; Ga.1:4; Ga.3:13; He.9:22; 9:26-28; 1 Pe.3:18; Re.1:5; Is.53:5)
The Bitter Herbs (Ex.12:8)	*The bitter days of Israel's slavery [to sin]* **"And they shall eat the flesh in that night, roast with fire, and unleavened bread;** *and* **with bitter herbs they shall eat it" (Ex.12:8).**	Slavery is sin, the height of evil. To suffer the cruel bondage of slavery is to suffer the most brutal evil imaginable. There is no joy—only bitterness—in being a slave to such an evil. This is a clear picture of man's slavery to sin. Sin is a cruel master: it enslaves people to such bondages as... • the lust of the flesh • the lust of the eyes • the pride of life	*"Jesus answered them, Verily, verily, I say unto you, Whosoever committeth sin is the servant of sin" (Jn.8:34).* *"For I know that in me (that is, in my flesh,) dwelleth no good thing: for to will is present with me; but how to perform that which is good I find not. For the good that I would I do not: but the evil which I would not, that I do. Now if I do that I would not, it is no more I that do it, but sin*

233

TYPES, SYMBOLS, AND PICTURES
(Exodus 12:1-13)

Historical Term	Type or Picture (Scriptural Basis for Each)	Life Application for Today's Believer	Biblical Application
The Bitter Herbs (continued) (Ex.12:8)		But there is glorious news. Jesus Christ has broken the power of sin. Jesus Christ can take a person & set him free from the lethal bondage of sin.	*that dwelleth in me" (Ro.7:18-20).* "Who gave himself for our sins, that he might deliver us from this present evil world, according to the will of God and our Father" (Ga.1:4). "Stand fast therefore in the liberty wherewith Christ hath made us free, and be not entangled again with the yoke of bondage" (Ga.5:1). "For ye have not received the spirit of bondage again to fear; but ye have received the Spirit of adoption, whereby we cry, Abba, Father" (Ro.8:15).* (see Ro.7:14-25; 8:1-2)
The Roasting and Eating of the Passover Lamb (Ex.12:9-11)	*Identifying with the lamb's death* "Eat not of it raw, nor sodden at all with water, but roast *with* fire; his head with his legs, and with the purtenance thereof. And ye shall let nothing of it remain until the morning; and that which remaineth of it until the morning ye shall burn with fire. And thus shall ye eat it; *with* your loins girded, your shoes on your feet, and your staff in your hand; and ye shall eat it in haste: it *is* the LORD's passover" (Ex.12:9-11).	The believer cannot partake in Christ's death from afar—it is a personal decision... • to partake of Christ by believing in Christ • to partake of Christ by living a life that dies to self and lives for Christ	"For God so loved the world, that he gave his only begotten Son, that whosoever believeth in him should not perish, but have everlasting life" (Jn.3:16). "Moreover, brethren, I declare unto you the gospel which I preached unto you, which also ye have received, and wherein ye stand; By which also ye are saved, if ye keep in memory what I preached unto you, unless ye have believed in vain. For I delivered unto you first of all that which I also received, how that Christ died for our sins according to the scriptures" (1 Co.15:1-3). "And he said to [them] all, If any [man] will come after me, let him deny himself, and take up his cross daily, and follow me" (Lu.9:23). "And that he died for all, that they which live should not henceforth live unto themselves, but unto him which died for them, and rose again" (2 Co.5:15). (see Jn.5:25; Ro.10:9-10; Ga.2:20; Tit.2:14)

	B. The Feast of Unleavened Bread: The Second Basic Essential for Redemption—Putting All Leaven, All Evil, Out of One's Life, 12:14-20	that which every man must eat, that only may be done of you.
		17 And ye shall observe the feast of unleavened bread; for in this selfsame day have I brought your armies out of the land of Egypt: therefore shall ye observe this day in your generations by an ordinance for ever.
1. The significance of the feast: To be celebrated annually, forever—as a permanent ordinance	14 And this day shall be unto you for a memorial; and ye shall keep it a feast to the LORD throughout your generations; ye shall keep it a feast by an ordinance for ever.	
	15 Seven days shall ye eat unleavened bread; even the first day ye shall put away leaven out of your houses: for whosoever eateth leavened bread from the first day until the seventh day, that soul shall be cut off from Israel.	18 In the first month, on the fourteenth day of the month at even, ye shall eat unleavened bread, until the one and twentieth day of the month at even.
2. The instructions governing the feast		19 Seven days shall there be no leaven found in your houses: for whosoever eateth that which is leavened, even that soul shall be cut off from the congregation of Israel, whether he be a stranger, or born in the land.
a. To eat seven days		
b. To put all leaven (symbolizing evil) out of one's house, out of one's presence		
c. The importance: To cut off anyone who disobeys	16 And in the first day there shall be an holy convocation, and in the seventh day there shall be an holy convocation to you; no manner of work shall be done in them, save	20 Ye shall eat nothing leavened; in all your habitations shall ye eat unleavened bread.
d. To observe two special holy days of worship:		
• The first day, which was the celebration of the Passover		
• The seventh day, which ended the feast of unleavened bread		

• No work was to be done during these two days, only cooking & eating	
3. The purpose of the feast	
a. To be the celebration of God's great deliverance	
b. To be the great celebration of eating only unleavened bread, symbolizing...	
• the quick flight to a new life marching to the promised land	
• the putting of leaven (evil) out of one's house	
4. The critical importance of the feast	
a. A person was to be cut off, excommunicated or executed, from the congregation if he ate leavened bread (evil), no matter who he was	
b. A person had to eat unleavened bread (symbolizing righteousness), no matter where he lived	

DIVISION IV

THE PASSOVER AND THE TENTH PLAGUE: DELIVERANCE FROM GOD'S JUDGMENT—LIBERATED, SET FREE, 12:1–13:16

B.   The Feast of Unleavened Bread: The Second Basic Essential for Redemption—Putting All Leaven, All Evil, Out of One's Life, 12:14-20

(12:14-20) **Introduction**: once a person has been saved, a matter of critical importance arises:
⇒ He must immediately flee the evil of his past life.
⇒ He must immediately rush to live a life of righteousness as he marches to the promised land of heaven.

This was the picture, the symbol, God wanted seen in the Feast of Unleavened Bread. Picture the scene: there was an Israelite family standing around their table in the wee hours of the morning. They had been slaves all their lives: mistreated, abused, and brutalized. But there they were…
*   fully dressed
*   sandals on their feet
*   staffs in their hands
*   ready to go

Thank God, they were to be free at last. When the orders came to march, they were to be ready, ready right then and there. Very little time had been given to prepare. They were even to take unleavened bread, bread without yeast. There was no time to let the leaven or yeast do its work, no time to let it permeate the bread.

This was the picture being painted by the unleavened bread. Note that leaven is mentioned eight times in this passage. Leaven or yeast causes dough to ferment. Because of the fermentation effect, leaven was used to picture corruption and evil in the world, to show how sin permeates and spreads throughout the world and in the hearts of men. Throughout Scripture, leaven symbolizes evil. This means that unleavened bread symbolizes *righteousness*: we are to eat the bread of righteousness.
⇒ Historically, the Feast of Unleavened Bread was to remind God's people of the time when they had to rush out of Egypt, away from the evils of Egypt (the world) and of enslavement.
⇒ Spiritually, the feast symbolizes the utter necessity for the Christian believer to rush away from the world with all its evil (leaven) and to rush toward the promised land of heaven.

The Feast of Unleavened Bread was to remind God's people of the time when they had to rush to their *new life* in the promised land of Canaan. They had to rush forth into freedom with only unleavened bread. Spiritually, this symbolizes the utter necessity for the Christian believer to rush forth with the unleavened bread of righteousness. The Christian believer is to march forth toward the promised land, digesting only unleavened bread, only the bread of life, the bread of righteousness.

This is the interesting subject of this passage: *The Feast of Unleavened Bread: The Second Basic Essential for Redemption—Putting All Leaven, All Evil, Out of One's Life*, 12:14-20.

1. The significance of the feast: to be celebrated annually, forever—as a permanent ordinance (v.14).
2. The instructions governing the feast (v.15-16).
3. The purpose of the feast (v.17-19).
4. The critical importance of the feast (v.19-20).

1 (12:14) **Feasts—Unleavened Bread—Righteousness—Passover**: there was the significance of the Feast of Unleavened Bread. Its significance was found in three facts.

a. The feast was instituted by God Himself. God instructed Moses and Aaron to establish the feast. The feast was so important that God Himself felt compelled to establish its celebration. Note that the feast was to be celebrated every year, and it was to be a lasting ordinance of Israel.

b. The Feast of Unleavened Bread was a part of the Passover, but it was also considered a separate and distinct feast. They were both celebrated at the same time, and they were a part of one another. Nevertheless, they were two distinct feasts, symbolizing two different truths. The Passover was celebrated on the first day of the Feast of Unleavened Bread. *The Expositor's Bible Commentary* makes the following points.

    1) Both names are used to refer to the same feast:
      ⇒ Both feasts are called the Passover (Ex.34:25; Eze.45:21).
      ⇒ Both feasts are also called the Feast of Unleavened Bread (De.16:16; 2 Chr.30:13, 21; Ezr.6:22).
    2) Both feasts are also treated separately (Le.23:5-6; Nu.28:16-17; 2 Chr.35:1, 17; Ezr.6:19-22; Eze.45:21).
    3) The New Testament also uses each name to refer to the same feasts:
      ⇒ The Passover (pascha, Jn.2:13, 23; 6:4; 11:55).
      ⇒ The unleavened bread (azymos, Mt.26:17; Lu.22:1, 7).[1]

c. Leaven symbolizes evil and unleaven symbolizes righteousness. As stated above, this feast was to remind the Israelites of God's great deliverance, just how quickly God had delivered them. The people had been forced to rush out of Egypt, to quickly rush from the evil of slavery. They had to begin their march to freedom so quickly that they had time to prepare only unleavened bread. The leaven was to forever symbolize the evil of Egyptian slavery. And the unleavened bread was to forever symbolize the utter necessity of rushing to their *new life* in the promised land, a *new life* of righteousness under God's leadership and rule.

Thought 1. The person who is truly saved by Jesus Christ is born again: he has a new life. As the believer marches to the promised land of heaven, he is to live for Christ:

(1) He is to live a righteous, godly life.

> "Know ye not, that so many of us as were baptized into Jesus Christ were baptized into his death? Therefore we are buried with him by baptism into death: that like as Christ was raised up from the dead by the glory of the Father, even so we also should walk in newness of life" (Ro.6:3-4).
>
> "Knowing this, that our old man is crucified with him, that the body of sin might be destroyed, that henceforth we should not serve sin" (Ro.6:6).
>
> "Let not sin therefore reign in your mortal body, that ye should obey it in the lusts thereof. Neither yield ye your members as instruments of unrighteousness unto sin: but yield yourselves unto God, as those that are alive from the dead, and your members as instruments of righteousness unto God" (Ro.6:12-13).
>
> "I beseech you therefore, brethren, by the mercies of God, that ye present your bodies a living sacrifice, holy, acceptable unto God, which is your reasonable service. And be not conformed to this world: but be ye transformed by the renewing of your mind, that ye may prove what is that good, and acceptable, and perfect, will of God" (Ro.12:1-2).
>
> "Therefore if any man be in Christ, he is a new creature: old things are passed away; behold, all things are become new" (2 Co.5:17).
>
> "And that ye put on the new man, which after God is created in righteousness and true holiness" (Ep.4:24).
>
> "Teaching us that, denying ungodliness and worldly lusts, we should live soberly, righteously, and godly, in this present world; Looking for that blessed hope, and the glorious appearing of the great God and our Saviour Jesus Christ" (Tit.2:12-13).
>
> "But the day of the LORD will come as a thief in the night; in the which the heavens shall pass away with a great noise, and the elements shall melt with fervent heat, the earth also and the works that are therein shall be burned up. Seeing then that all these things shall be dissolved, what manner of persons ought ye to be in all holy conversation and godliness, Looking for and hasting unto the coming of the day of God, wherein the heavens being on fire shall be dissolved, and the elements shall melt with fervent heat? Nevertheless we, according to his promise, look for new heavens and a new earth, wherein dwelleth righteousness. Wherefore, beloved, seeing that ye look

---

[1] Frank E. Gaebelein. *The Expositor's Bible Commentary*, Vol.2, p.374.

for such things, be diligent that ye may be found of him in peace, without spot, and blameless" (2 Pe.3:10-14).

"Love not the world, neither the things that are in the world. If any man love the world, the love of the Father is not in him. For all that is in the world, the lust of the flesh, and the lust of the eyes, and the pride of life, is not of the Father, but is of the world" (1 Jn.2:15-16).

(2) He is to live a life studying the pure, unleavened Word of God.

"Search the scriptures; for in them ye think ye have eternal life: and they are they which testify of me" (Jn.5:39).

"These were more noble than those in Thessalonica, in that they received the word with all readiness of mind, and searched the scriptures daily, whether those things were so" (Ac.17:11).

"And now, brethren, I commend you to God, and to the word of his grace, which is able to build you up, and to give you an inheritance among all them which are sanctified" (Ac.20:32).

"For whatsoever things were written aforetime were written for our learning, that we through patience and comfort of the scriptures might have hope" (Ro.15:4).

"Study to show thyself approved unto God, a workman that needeth not to be ashamed, rightly dividing the word of truth" (2 Ti.2:15).

"All scripture is given by inspiration of God, and is profitable for doctrine, for reproof, for correction, for instruction in righteousness" (2 Ti.3:16).

"As newborn babes, desire the sincere milk of the word, that ye may grow thereby: If so be ye have tasted that the LORD is gracious" (1 Pe.2:2-3).

"Wherewithal shall a young man cleanse his way? by taking heed thereto according to thy word....Thy word have I hid in mine heart, that I might not sin against thee" (Ps.119:9, 11).

"Seek ye out of the book of the LORD, and read: no one of these shall fail" (Is.34:16).

[2] (12:15-16) **Feast—Unleavened Bread—Evil—Righteousness**: there were the instructions of God governing the Feast of Unleavened Bread.

a. The feast was to be celebrated for seven days (v.15). Unleavened bread and only unleavened bread was to be eaten during the seven days. This shows how significant this feast was to God. He wanted His people to spend an entire week, seven full days...

- focusing upon their desperate flight from the evils of Egypt (a symbol of the world)
- focusing upon their excited flight to freedom and to the promised land (a symbol of heaven)

b. A person was to put all leaven (evil) out of his house, out of his presence (v.15).

Thought 1. Leaven symbolizes evil in the Scripture. We must put all evil out of our lives and out of our homes.

"If iniquity be in thine hand, put it far away, and let not wickedness dwell in thy tabernacles" (Jb.11:14).

"Then Jesus said unto them, Take heed and beware of the leaven of the Pharisees and of the Sadducees" (Mt.16:6).

"A little [evil] leaven leaveneth the whole lump" (Ga.5:9).

"That ye put off concerning the former conversation [behavior] the old man, which is corrupt according to the deceitful lusts" (Ep.4:22).

"Lie not one to another, seeing that ye have put off the old man with his deeds" (Col.3:9).

"Wherefore seeing we also are compassed about with so great a cloud of witnesses, let us lay aside every weight, and the sin which doth so easily beset us, and let us run with patience the race that is set before us" (He.12:1).

"Dearly beloved, I beseech you as strangers and pilgrims, abstain from fleshly lusts, which war against the soul" (1 Pe.2:11).

c. The importance of the feast is seen in the punishment to be imposed upon the disobedient. Any person who disobeyed, who ate leaven, was to be cut off (v.15). What does cut off mean? Some commentators say that a person was to be banished and excommunicated from the community of believers. Other commentators say that a person was to be executed (see Ex.31:14; Le.20:2-3).

Thought 1. This pictures the awesome importance of repentance, of turning to Christ and putting evil out of our lives. If we do not, then we are to be cut off from God. We shall face the terrifying judgment of hell, of existing eternally without God.

"He that pursueth evil pursueth it to his own death" (Pr.11:19).

"The soul that sinneth, it shall die" (Eze.18:4).

"When the Son of man shall come in his glory, and all the holy angels with him, then shall he sit upon the throne of his glory: And before him shall be gathered all nations: and he shall separate them one from another, as a shepherd divideth [his] sheep from the goats: And he shall set the sheep on his right hand, but the goats on the left....Then shall he say also unto them on the left hand, Depart from me, ye cursed, into everlasting fire, prepared for the devil and his angels" (Mt.25:31-33, 41).

"For the wages of sin is death; but the gift of God is eternal life through Jesus Christ our Lord" (Ro.6:23).

"And to you who are troubled rest with us, when the Lord Jesus shall be revealed from heaven with his mighty angels, In flaming fire taking vengeance on them that know not God, and that obey not the gospel of our Lord Jesus Christ" (2 Th.1:7-8).

"And Enoch also, the seventh from Adam, prophesied of these, saying, Behold, the Lord cometh with ten thousands of his saints, To execute judgment upon all, and to convince all that are ungodly among them of all their ungodly deeds which they have ungodly committed, and of all their hard speeches which ungodly sinners have spoken against him" (Jude 14-15).

 d. God's people were to observe two special holy days of worship (v.16):
  ⇒ The *first day*, which was the celebration of the Passover. The Passover actually began the Feast of Unleavened Bread, which was to last seven days.
  ⇒ The *seventh day*, which ended the Feast of Unleavened Bread.

Note a significant fact: no work was to be done during the two special days of worship, only cooking and eating. The only activity allowed was that of preparing food to eat.

Thought 1. This stresses the importance of celebrating religious ordinances and holidays. God emphasized them. He gave strict instructions to Israel: they were to celebrate two holy days within seven days of each other. How much more should we remember holy days, the days that celebrate the Lord's great work of salvation?
(1) We should celebrate the birth of our Lord.

  "Now when Jesus was born in Bethlehem of Judaea in the days of Herod the king, behold, there came wise men from the east to Jerusalem, Saying, Where is he that is born King of the Jews? for we have seen his star in the east, and are come to worship him" (Mt.2:1-2).
  "And there were in the same country shepherds abiding in the field, keeping watch over their flock by night. And, lo, the angel of the Lord came upon them, and the glory of the Lord shone round about them: and they were sore afraid. And the angel said unto them, Fear not: for, behold, I bring you good tidings of great joy, which shall be to all people. For unto you is born this day in the city of David a Saviour, which is Christ the Lord. And this shall be a sign unto you; Ye shall find the babe wrapped in swaddling clothes, lying in a manger. And suddenly there was with the angel a multitude of the heavenly host praising God, and saying, Glory to God in the highest, and on earth peace, good will toward men" (Lu.2:8-14).

(2) We should celebrate the death and resurrection of our Lord.

  "Know ye not, that so many of us as were baptized into Jesus Christ were baptized into his death? Therefore we are buried with him by baptism into death: that like as Christ was raised up from the dead by the glory of the Father, even so we also should walk in newness of life. For if we have been planted together in the likeness of his death, we shall be also in the likeness of his resurrection" (Ro.6:3-5).

(3) We should celebrate the conversion and baptism of new believers.

  "Go ye therefore, and teach all nations, baptizing them in the name of the Father, and of the Son, and of the Holy Ghost: Teaching them to observe all things whatsoever I have commanded you: and, lo, I am with you alway, [even] unto the end of the world" (Mt.28:19-20).
  "Then Peter said unto them, Repent, and be baptized every one of you in the name of Jesus Christ for the remission of sins, and ye shall receive the gift of the Holy Ghost" (Ac.2:38).

(4) We should celebrate the death of our Lord in the Lord's Supper.

  "And he took bread, and gave thanks, and brake [it], and gave unto them, saying, This is my body which is given for you: this do in remembrance of me. Likewise also the cup after supper, saying, This cup [is] the new testament in my blood, which is shed for you" (Lu.22:19-20).
  "For I [Paul] have received of the Lord that which also I delivered unto you, That the Lord Jesus the same night in which he was betrayed took bread: And when he had given thanks, he brake it, and said, Take, eat: this is my body, which is broken for you: this do in remembrance of me. After the same manner also he took the cup, when he had supped, saying, This cup is the new testament in my blood: this do ye, as oft as ye drink it, in remembrance of me" (1 Co.11:23-25).

3 (12:17-19) **Unleavened Bread—Feast—Leaven—Evil**: there were two purposes for celebrating the feast.
 a. The feast celebrated God's great deliverance out of Egypt (v.17).

238

Thought 1. Egypt represented the world and its evil of enslavement. The believer has been saved and delivered from being enslaved to the world and its evil. Man looks at the world and becomes enslaved by the world's ways, the way of...

- bright lights
- pleasures
- possessions
- power
- position

- recognition
- honor
- fame
- greed
- wealth

- comfort
- ease
- drink
- food (gluttony)

The world has a seed of corruption lying at its core, a seed of corruption that causes deterioration, wasting away, and eventually death. But note: man is not only enslaved by the ways of the world, he is enslaved by the seed of corruption that leads him to age and die, that carries him into the grave. (See notes—2 Pe.1:4. Also see notes—Mt.6:19; 8:17; 1 Co.15:50 for more discussion.)

But this is the glorious message of God's power to deliver people: God can deliver us even as He delivered the Israelites out of Egypt and its evil. Through Christ, we can be delivered from the enslavement and evil of this world.

"For the Son of man is come to seek and to save that which was lost [hopeless and helpless]" (Lu.19:10).

"The next day John seeth Jesus coming unto him, and saith, Behold the Lamb of God, which taketh away the sin of the world" (Jn.1:29).

"For God so loved the world, that he gave his only begotten Son, that whosoever believeth in him should not perish, but have everlasting life. For God sent not his Son into the world to condemn the world; but that the world through him might be saved" (Jn.3:16-17).

"Who gave himself for our sins, that he might deliver us from this present evil world, according to the will of God and our Father" (Ga.1:4).

"Who his own self bare our sins in his own body on the tree, that we, being dead to sins, should live unto righteousness: by whose stripes ye were healed" (1 Pe.2:24).

"And he is the propitiation [sacrifice, covering] for our sins: and not for ours only, but also for the sins of the whole world" (1 Jn.2:2).

b. The feast was the great celebration of eating only unleavened bread. The eating of unleavened bread celebrated two great events (vv.18-19).
1) The quick flight to a *new life*, a *new life* that had escaped Egypt (the world) and was marching to the promised land of God (v.18). Remember the picture painted in the Introduction (Ex.12:14-20). The Israelites had little time to prepare before the judgment of God fell upon Egypt (the world). They were to get ready immediately, get ready to flee Egypt and begin their march to the promised land. The time was short, very short, so short they had to take only unleavened bread. There was not time to let leaven (yeast) ferment the bread.

Thought 1. The unleavened bread symbolized the utter necessity for the believer to get ready now, to immediately flee the evil of the world and begin the march to the promised land of heaven. There is little time before the judgment of God falls upon the world.

"Therefore be ye also ready: for in such an hour as ye think not the Son of man cometh" (Mt.24:44).

"And while they went to buy, the bridegroom came; and they that were ready went in with him to the marriage: and the door was shut" (Mt.25:10).

"Watch therefore, for ye know neither the day nor the hour wherein the Son of man cometh" (Mt.25:13).

"Watch ye therefore: for ye know not when the master of the house cometh, at even, or at midnight, or at the cockcrowing, or in the morning" (Mk.13:35).

"So that servant came, and showed his Lord these things. Then the master of the house being angry said to his servant, go out quickly into the streets and lanes of the city, and bring in hither the poor, and the maimed, and the halt, and the blind" (Lu.14:21).

"Behold, now is the accepted time; behold, now is the day of salvation" (2 Co.6:2).

"For when they shall say, Peace and safety; then sudden destruction cometh upon them, as travail upon a woman with child; and they shall not escape" (1 Th.5:3).

"How shall we escape, if we neglect so great salvation; which at the first began to be spoken by the Lord, and was confirmed unto us by them that heard him" (He.2:3).

2) The unleavened bread celebrated the putting of leaven—all leaven—out of one's house (v.19). Remember, leaven symbolizes evil and unleaven symbolizes righteousness.

Thought 1. A person is to act quickly and put evil—all evil—out of his life.
(1) He is to be clean, free from all sin: cleansed by the blood of Christ.

"Wash you, make you clean; put away the evil of your doings from before mine eyes; cease to do evil" (Is.1:16).

"Wash thine heart from wickedness, that thou mayest be saved. How long shall thy vain thoughts lodge within thee?" (Je.4:14).

"Then Jesus said unto them, Take heed and beware of the leaven of the Pharisees and of the Sadducees....Then understood they how that he bade them not beware of the leaven of bread, but of the doctrine of the Pharisees and of the Sadducees" (Mt.16:6, 12).

"And now why tarriest thou? arise, and be baptized, and wash away thy sins, calling on the name of the LORD" (Ac.22:16).

"But God commendeth his love toward us, in that, while we were yet sinners, Christ died for us. Much more then, being now justified by his blood, we shall be saved from wrath through him" (Ro.5:8-9).

"Your glorying is not good. Know ye not that a little leaven leaveneth the whole lump? Purge out therefore the old leaven, that ye may be a new lump, as ye are unleavened. For even Christ our passover is sacrificed for us: Therefore let us keep the feast, not with old leaven, neither with the leaven of malice and wickedness; but with the unleavened bread of sincerity and truth" (1 Co.5:6-8).

"Having therefore these promises, dearly beloved, let us cleanse ourselves from all filthiness of the flesh and spirit, perfecting holiness in the fear of God" (2 Co.7:1).

"Ye did run well; who did hinder you that ye should not obey the truth? This persuasion cometh not of him that calleth you. A little leaven leaveneth the whole lump" (Ga.5:7-9).

"If a man therefore purge himself from these, he shall be a vessel unto honour, sanctified, and meet for the master's use, and prepared unto every good work" (2 Ti.2:21).

"Draw nigh to God, and he will draw nigh to you. Cleanse your hands, ye sinners; and purify your hearts, ye double minded" (Js.4:8).

"The blood of Jesus Christ his Son cleanseth us from all sin" (1 Jn.1:7).

"Unto him that loved us, and washed us from our sins in his own blood" (Re.1:5).

(2) A person who has put evil out of his life—who has been cleansed by the blood of Christ—must begin immediately to eat the unleavened bread of righteousness, the *Bread of Life* itself. He must begin to walk in *newness of life*.

"Sow to yourselves in righteousness, reap in mercy; break up your fallow ground: for it is time to seek the LORD, till he come and rain righteousness upon you" (Ho.10:12).

"Therefore we are buried with him by baptism into death: that like as Christ was raised up from the dead by the glory of the Father, even so we also should walk in newness of life" (Ro.6:4).

"Then Jesus said unto them, Verily, verily, I say unto you, Moses gave you not that bread from heaven; but my Father giveth you the true bread from heaven. For the bread of God is he which cometh down from heaven, and giveth life unto the world. Then said they unto him, Lord, evermore give us this bread. And Jesus said unto them, I am the bread of life: he that cometh to me shall never hunger; and he that believeth on me shall never thirst." (Jn.6:32-35).

"I am that bread of life. Your fathers did eat manna in the wilderness, and are dead. This is the bread which cometh down from heaven, that a man may eat thereof, and not die. I am the living bread which came down from heaven: if any man eat of this bread, he shall live for ever: and the bread that I will give is my flesh, which I will give for the life of the world" (Jn.6:48-51).

"This is that bread which came down from heaven: not as your fathers did eat manna, and are dead: he that eateth of this bread shall live for ever" (Jn.6:58).

"Awake to righteousness, and sin not; for some have not the knowledge of God: I speak this to your shame" (1 Co.15:34).

"Stand therefore, having your loins girt about with truth, and having on the breastplate of righteousness" (Ep.6:14).

"But thou, O man of God, flee these things; and follow after righteousness, godliness, faith, love, patience, meekness. Fight the good fight of faith, lay hold on eternal life, whereunto thou art also called, and hast professed a good profession before many witnesses" (1 Ti.6:11-12).

"For the grace of God that bringeth salvation hath appeared to all men, Teaching us that, denying ungodliness and worldly lusts, we should live soberly, righteously, and godly, in this present world" (Tit.2:11-12).

4 (12:19-20) **Feast—Unleavened Bread—Judgment—Righteousness—Believer, Life of**: there was the critical importance of observing the feast. The importance was shown in one very specific instruction given by God.

A person, no matter who he was, was to be cut off, executed, or excommunicated from the congregation if he ate leavened bread (evil) (v.19). Keep in mind that commentators differ as to the meaning of "cut off," some feeling that it means to be banished or excommunicated; others feeling that it means execution (see Ex.31:14; Le.20:2-3).

Note that the penalty was to apply to strangers or aliens among Israel. There were a large number of Egyptians and other nationalities who had apparently turned to the LORD during the plagues of judgment, and they were marching with the Israelites toward the promised land (Ex.12:38). The native-born refers to Israelites, the true descendants of Abraham.

The point is this: the Feast of Unleavened Bread was so important that a person had no choice. He had to eat only unleavened bread; if he ate leavened bread, he was cut off. He was either banished from the fellowship or executed.

Thought 1. We must not eat leaven, must not have any part with evil. We must never...
- partake of evil
- assimilate evil
- digest evil
- take evil into our lives

"Depart from evil, and do good; seek peace, and pursue it" (Ps.34:14).

"Ye that love the LORD, hate evil: he preserveth the souls of his saints; he delivereth them out of the hand of the wicked" (Ps.97:10).

"Turn not to the right hand nor to the left: remove thy foot from evil" (Pr.4:27).

"A wise man feareth, and departeth from evil: but the fool rageth, and is confident" (Pr.14:16).

"And oppress not the widow, nor the fatherless, the stranger, nor the poor; and let none of you imagine evil against his brother in your heart" (Zec.7:10).

"Let love be without dissimulation [hypocrisy]. Abhor that which is evil; cleave to that which is good" (Ro.12:9).

"Now these things were our examples, to the intent we should not lust after evil things, as they also lusted" (1 Co.10:6).

"Abstain from all appearance of evil" (1 Th.5:22).

"Let him eschew [turn from] evil, and do good; let him seek peace, and ensue it" (1 Pe.3:11).

TYPES, SYMBOLS, AND PICTURES
(Exodus 12:14-20)

Historical Term	Type or Picture (Scriptural Basis for Each)	Life Application for Today's Believer	Biblical Application
Leaven (Ex.12:14-20)	*Evil* "Seven days shall ye eat unleavened bread; even the first day ye shall put away leaven [evil] out of your houses: for whosoever eateth leavened bread from the first day until the seventh day, that soul shall be cut off from Israel" (Ex.12:15; see Ex.12:19-20; Ex.12:39).	The believer must take personal responsibility for purging the evil out of his life... • by getting rid of all sin (Col.3:8-9) • by getting rid of the sin that so easily entangles him (He.12:1) • by abstaining even from the appearance of evil (1 Th.5:22) • by constantly searching his heart for unconfessed sin (Ps.139; 23-24) • by never making peace with sin, by making it a despised habit, a hated foe, a defeated enemy	*"Then Jesus said unto them, Take heed and beware of the leaven [evil] of the Pharisees and of the Sadducees" (Mt.16:6).* *"Your glorying is not good. Know ye not that a little leaven leaveneth the whole lump? Purge out therefore the old leaven, that ye may be a new lump, as ye are unleavened. For even Christ our passover is sacrificed for us: Therefore let us keep the feast, not with old leaven, neither with the leaven of malice and wickedness; but with the unleavened bread of sincerity and truth" (1 Co.5:6-8).* *"Abstain from all appearance of evil" (1 Th.5:22).* *"Now these things were our examples, to the intent we should not lust after evil things, as they also lusted" (1 Co.10:6).* *(see Ro.12:9; Ga.5:9; Col. 3:8-10; He.12:1; 1 Pe.3:11; 1 Jn.1:9; Ps.51:1-13; 139:23-24)*
Unleavened Bread (Ex.12:14-20)	In fleeing Egypt, the Israelite did not have time to allow the leaven (yeast) to ferment in the bread. He had to take unleavened bread. (1)This is a picture of urgency, haste, readiness: the believer must be immediately ready to leave Egypt (the world) & quickly begin the march to the promised land. (2)This is a picture of the	There is the urgent need for a person... • to rush away from the world, to be immediately converted and to quickly begin his march to the promised land of heaven • to leave his *old life* behind and to begin his *new life of righteousness*	*"Behold, now is the accepted time; behold, now is the day of salvation" (2 Co.6:2).* *"Christ was raised up from the dead by the glory of the Father, even so we also should walk in newness of life" (Ro.6:4).* *"Therefore if any man be in Christ, he is a new creature: old things are passed away; behold, all things are become new" (2 Co.5:17).*

TYPES, SYMBOLS, AND PICTURES
(Exodus 12:14-20)

Historical Term	Type or Picture (Scriptural Basis for Each)	Life Application for Today's Believer	Biblical Application
	believer's *new life of righteousness:* the believer must leave his *old life* in Egypt and begin his march to the promised land. "And ye shall observe *the feast of* unleavened bread; for in this selfsame day have I brought your armies out of the land of Egypt: therefore shall ye observe this day in your generations by an ordinance for ever" (Ex.12:17).		*"But now ye also put off all these; anger, wrath, malice, blasphemy, filthy communication out of your mouth. Lie not one to another, seeing that ye have put off the old man with his deeds; And have put on the new man, which is renewed in knowledge after the image of him that created him"* (Col.3:8-10). *(see 2 Co.6:17-18; Mt. 24:44; 25:13; He.2:3; Ep.4:24; Col.3:8-10)*

1. The warning to escape the coming judgment: Declared by Moses to the elders of Israel

a. Select & sacrifice the Passover lamb, family by family
1) Take hyssop & smear the blood on your door frame
2) Do not go out at night—stay inside all night: Under the protection of the blood

b. Accept, believe the message of judgment & deliverance
1) The LORD will judge, strike down the Egyptians (the world)
2) The LORD will pass over, not destroy the believers protected by the blood

c. Observe the ceremony as a lasting ordinance: Even in the promised land

d. Proclaim the meaning of the Passover to children
1) Explain the Passover sacrifice (lamb)
2) Explain how the LORD judged the Egyptians but passed over—protected & did not destroy—the Israelites who believed

e. The two absolute essentials
1) The people bowed and worshipped God
2) The people obeyed God

2. The judgment of God struck Egypt (a type of the world)

a. The judgment: Death of the firstborn
b. The judgment was universal
1) Struck all families from the palace to the dungeon
2) Struck all livestock

3. The judgment achieved its purpose

a. Purpose 1: Pharaoh & his

C. The Tenth Plague, The Death of the Firstborn & the Passover: Deliverance from God's Judgment—Liberated, Set Free, 12:21-51

21 Then Moses called for all the elders of Israel, and said unto them, Draw out and take you a lamb according to your families, and kill the passover.
22 And ye shall take a bunch of hyssop, and dip it in the blood that is in the bason, and strike the lintel and the two side posts with the blood that is in the bason; and none of you shall go out at the door of his house until the morning.
23 For the LORD will pass through to smite the Egyptians; and when he seeth the blood upon the lintel, and on the two side posts, the LORD will pass over the door, and will not suffer the destroyer to come in unto your houses to smite you.
24 And ye shall observe this thing for an ordinance to thee and to thy sons for ever.
25 And it shall come to pass, when ye be come to the land which the LORD will give you, according as he hath promised, that ye shall keep this service.
26 And it shall come to pass, when your children shall say unto you, What mean ye by this service?
27 That ye shall say, It is the sacrifice of the LORD's passover, who passed over the houses of the children of Israel in Egypt, when he smote the Egyptians, and delivered our houses. And the people bowed the head and worshipped.
28 And the children of Israel went away, and did as the LORD had commanded Moses and Aaron, so did they.
29 And it came to pass, that at midnight the LORD smote all the firstborn in the land of Egypt, from the firstborn of Pharaoh that sat on his throne unto the firstborn of the captive that was in the dungeon; and all the firstborn of cattle.
30 And Pharaoh rose up in the night, he, and all his servants, and all the Egyptians;

and there was a great cry in Egypt; for there was not a house where there was not one dead.
31 And he called for Moses and Aaron by night, and said, Rise up, and get you forth from among my people, both ye and the children of Israel; and go, serve the LORD, as ye have said.
32 Also take your flocks and your herds, as ye have said, and be gone; and bless me also.
33 And the Egyptians were urgent upon the people, that they might send them out of the land in haste; for they said, We be all dead men.
34 And the people took their dough before it was leavened, their kneading troughs being bound up in their clothes upon their shoulders.
35 And the children of Israel did according to the word of Moses; and they borrowed of the Egyptians jewels of silver, and jewels of gold, and raiment:
36 And the LORD gave the people favour in the sight of the Egyptians, so that they lent unto them such things as they required. And they spoiled the Egyptians.
37 And the children of Israel journeyed from Rameses to Succoth, about six hundred thousand on foot that were men, beside children.
38 And a mixed multitude went up also with them; and flocks, and herds, even very much cattle.
39 And they baked unleavened cakes of the dough which they brought forth out of Egypt, for it was not leavened; because they were thrust out of Egypt, and could not tarry, neither had they prepared for themselves any victual.
40 Now the sojourning of the children of Israel, who dwelt in Egypt, was four hundred and thirty years.
41 And it came to pass at the end of the four hundred and thirty years, even the selfsame day it came to pass, that all the hosts of the LORD went out from the land of Egypt.
42 It is a night to be much observed unto the LORD for

people cried out in anguish & wept over their dead: Justice was executed upon their terrible evil

b. Purpose 2: Pharaoh called for Moses & Aaron & freed God's people; the hardhearted & proud—those who had rejected God—were humbled
1) Freed everyone including their herds
2) Asked for a blessing from the LORD

c. Purpose 3: Pharaoh & his people urged God's people to leave immediately; they feared God's judgment would kill them all

4. The judgment was escaped by Israel (God's people, believers): The great exodus—free at last

a. Obeyed God's instructions
b. Took only unleavened bread
c. Asked the Egyptians for gifts: Symbolized restitution, paying back what had been stolen & what was due for their enslavement & decades of unpaid labor

d. Started their freedom march
1) A multitude of Israelites began the march, 600,000 men alone (over 2 million total)
2) A large mixed multitude of Egyptians, other slaves, & animals journeyed with them
3) They also baked & took unleavened bread (symbolically left all leaven—evil—behind in Egypt [the world])

e. Rushed, left & separated themselves from Egypt immediately: No time to even prepare food

f. Cut off all attachments & heritage of 430 years[DS1]

g. The wonderful fact: God gloriously delivered His people from Egypt (symbolically, the world)

5. The judgment & the Passover deliverance was always to be

observed by those who be-lieve—strictly observed	bringing them out from the land of Egypt: this is that night of the LORD to be observed of all the children of Israel in their generations.	Israel shall keep it.	the whole congregation
a. Separation was an absolute essential when observing 1) Was not to be eaten by a foreigner	43 And the LORD said unto Moses and Aaron, This is the ordinance of the passover: There shall no stranger eat thereof:	48 And when a stranger shall sojourn with thee, and will keep the passover to the LORD, let all his males be circumcised, and then let him come near and keep it; and he shall be as one that is born in the land: for no uncircumcised person shall eat thereof.	6) Could be eaten by other nationalities (proselytes) if circumcised
2) Could be eaten by a circumcised slave	44 But every man's servant that is bought for money, when thou hast circumcised him, then shall he eat thereof.		7) Was not to be eaten by uncircumcised males
3) Was not to be eaten by a temporary or a hired worker 4) Could be eaten only within the house of faith: No meat was to be taken outside of the house & no bone of the lamb was to be broken 5) Was to be celebrated by	45 A foreigner and an hired servant shall not eat thereof. 46 In one house shall it be eaten; thou shalt not carry forth ought of the flesh abroad out of the house; neither shall ye break a bone thereof. 47 All the congregation of	49 One law shall be to him that is homeborn, and unto the stranger that sojourneth among you. 50 Thus did all the children of Israel; as the LORD commanded Moses and Aaron, so did they. 51 And it came to pass the selfsame day, that the LORD did bring the children of Israel out of the land of Egypt by their armies.	8) The same law was to apply to both the native-born & to the foreigner b. Obedience was an absolute essential: All Israel obeyed c. The wonderful result repeated: The LORD gloriously delivered the Israelites

DIVISION IV

THE PASSOVER AND THE TENTH PLAGUE: DELIVERANCE FROM GOD'S JUDGMENT—LIBERATED, SET FREE, 12:1–13:16

C. The Tenth Plague, The Death of the Firstborn and the Passover: Deliverance from God's Judgment—Liberated, Set Free, 12:21-51

(12:21-51) **Introduction**: "Free! Free at last! Thank God Almighty, I'm free at last." These words, shouted out by Martin Luther King in the 20th century, must have resounded within the hearts of all the Israelites as they marched out of Egypt. For centuries the Israelites had been enslaved and brutalized by the Egyptians; now they were being set free...

- set free to pursue life, liberty, and justice for all
- set free to worship and serve God with all their hearts
- set free to begin the great march toward the promised land of Canaan

Ancient Egypt was guilty of the most horrendous evils imaginable, and they had flaunted their evil before the very face of God Himself. They were...

- guilty of idolatry—worshipping the false gods created by man's imaginations.
- guilty of rejecting God—committing rebellion and insurrection against Him, and even denying and cursing Him.
- guilty of gross immorality, of becoming a cesspool of unnatural and inhuman affection—all running wild in a blazing flame of lust: adultery, fornication, licentiousness, homosexuality.
- guilty of greed and covetousness—of filling their pockets and seeking wealth through the cheap labor and enslavement of others.
- guilty of indulging the flesh, of living a life of license, ease, comfort—guilty of building a society based upon slave-labor.
- guilty of brutalizing and enslaving people—enslaving the very people who believed and followed the only living and true God.

Despite the great achievements of ancient Egypt, the evils of the Egyptian people were horrible. They rejected the only living and true God and committed atrocity after atrocity against other races of people. They savagely brutalized and enslaved people.

As we have seen, God had seen enough evil and wickedness within Egyptian society. The day for executing justice against the ancient Egyptians had come. God had launched nine judgments against the evil and brutal Egyptians. Throughout the entire period of plagues, the king was to lead his people to repent, but he refused. Now he and his people had gone too far, beyond the point of repentance. God knew they would never repent, never turn to Him, and never free the people of God. Consequently, God was now ready to launch the tenth plague of judgment, a judgment that would drive the Egyptians to free God's people. This was the great day of Israel's *deliverance from slavery*, the launch of their *freedom march* to the promised land of God. This is: *The Tenth Plague, The Death of the Firstborn and the Passover: Deliverance from God's Judgment—Liberated, Set Free,* 12:21-51.

1. The warning to escape the coming judgment: declared by Moses to the elders of Israel (vv.21-28).
2. The judgment struck Egypt (a type of the world) (v.29).
3. The judgment achieved its purpose (vv.30-33).
4. The judgment was escaped by Israel (God's people, believers): the great exodus—free at last (vv.34-41).
5. The judgment and the Passover deliverance was always to be observed by those who believed—strictly observed (vv.42-51).

1 (12:21-28) **Passover, The—Lamb—Judgment—Animals, Sacrifice of—Faith**: there was the warning to escape the coming judgment. The hand of God's judgment was ready to fall: the tenth plague was to occur immediately. Thus Moses called all the elders together and gave them the instructions concerning the Passover. He spelled out exactly what God had told him. The elders were to take the instructions of God to the people they represented. God's people had to be saved: the hand of God's judgment was to pass over all those who truly believed Him. Note five facts.

a. The people were to select and sacrifice the Passover lamb, family by family (vv.21-22). Two new instructions governing the Passover are given here. (See outline and notes—Ex.12:1-13 for the instructions given earlier.)

1) A branch of hyssop was to be used to smear the blood on the door frame of a house (v.22). *Hyssop* (ezob) was apparently a small, bushy plant with leaves that easily absorbed liquid. It was the plant used to lift the moisture of vinegar up to Jesus' lips when He hung on the cross. The plant is referred to twelve different times in Scripture:
⇒ ten times in the Old Testament (Le.14:4, 6, 49, 51, 52; Nu.19:6, 18; Ex.12:22; 1 K.4:33; Ps.51:7).
⇒ two times in the New Testament (Jn.19:29; He.9:19-20).

2) The second new instruction regarding the Passover concerned safety and security. No person was to go out of the house at night. Everyone was to stay inside all night, stay inside under the protection of the blood (v.22). Believers were not to leave the house until morning, not to leave the safety of the blood until they were called to march out of Egypt to the promised land. Why? What was wrong with walking outdoors during the night? Two things.
⇒ First, the person who walked out into the world of Egypt would have removed himself from the safety of the blood. If God had allowed a person to roam about out in the streets of the world, the very meaning of the lamb's blood would have been lost. God's very purpose was to teach the people that their salvation lay in the safety of the lamb's blood.
⇒ Second, if a person was out roaming about and busily engaged in some worldly affair or pleasure, he would miss the call to leave Egypt. He would miss the call to go home to the promised land.

Thought 1. The application is clear.
(1) We must hide ourselves behind the blood of Christ. Protection from the hand of God's judgment is not found in the world. It is found in the blood of Christ.

> **"Come, my people, enter thou into thy chambers, and shut thy doors about thee: hide thyself as it were for a little moment, until the indignation be overpast. For, behold, the LORD cometh out of his place to punish the inhabitants of the earth for their iniquity: the earth also shall disclose her blood, and shall no more cover her slain" (Is.26:20-21).**
> **"In whom we have redemption through his blood, even the forgiveness of sins" (Col.1:14).**
> **"Who his own self bare our sins in his own body on the tree, that we, being dead to sins, should live unto righteousness: by whose stripes ye were healed" (1 Pe.2:24).**
> **"For Christ also hath once suffered for sins, the just for the unjust, that he might bring us to God, being put to death in the flesh, but quickened by the Spirit" (1 Pe.3:18).**
> **"But if we walk in the light, as he is in the light, we have fellowship one with another, and the blood of Jesus Christ his Son cleanseth us from all sin" (1 Jn.1:7).**

(2) We must stay behind the blood of Christ. We must not roam back out into the world of sin and ungodly pleasure. We must separate ourselves from the world and refuse to live a life of worldliness. We must live for God and be ready when He calls us home to the promised land of heaven.

> **"And take heed to yourselves, lest at any time your hearts be overcharged with surfeiting, and drunkenness, and cares of this life, and [so] that day come upon you unawares. For as a snare shall it come on all them that dwell on the face of the whole earth. Watch ye therefore, and pray always, that ye may be accounted worthy to escape all these things that shall come to pass, and to stand before the Son of man" (Lu.21:34-36).**
> **"Be ye not unequally yoked together with unbelievers: for what fellowship hath righteousness with unrighteousness? and what communion hath light with darkness?" (2 Co.6:14).**
> **"Wherefore come out from among them, and be ye separate, saith the Lord, and touch not the unclean thing; and I will receive you, And will be a Father unto you, and ye shall be my sons and daughters, saith the Lord Almighty" (2 Co.6:17-18).**
> **"For this ye know, that no whoremonger, nor unclean person, nor covetous man, who is an idolater, hath any inheritance in the kingdom of Christ and of God. Let no man deceive you with vain words: for because of these things cometh the wrath of God upon the children of disobedience" (Ep.5:5-6).**
> **"Love not the world, neither the things that are in the world. If any man love the world, the love of the Father is not in him. For all that is in the world, the lust of the flesh, and the lust of the eyes, and the pride of life, is not of the Father, but is of the world" (1 Jn.2:15-16).**

b. The people were to accept, to believe the message of judgment and deliverance (v.23).
1) God was going to judge, strike down the ancient Egyptians (v.23). Every person was going to suffer the hand of God's judgment. The firstborn son of every family was condemned to die—all because of the evil of the ancient Egyptians throughout all the centuries of their history. Moreover, the ancient Egyptians enslaved, brutalized, savagely abused, and murdered God's people, the very people who wanted to serve the only living and true God.
2) God would *pass over*, not destroy, the believers protected by the blood (v.23).

Note this: the only way to be saved and delivered from God's judgment was by the blood of the sacrificed lamb. The sacrificed lamb died *in place* of the firstborn who took shelter behind the blood. Thus the sacrificed lamb...

• was the *substitute* for the believer
• was the *way of redemption and deliverance* for the believer

There was no other way a person could be saved—redeemed and delivered—no other way except by the blood of the sacrificed lamb. If a person believed the message from God, he would believe the Word of God and hide behind the blood. If a person did not believe the message from God, he would not hide behind the blood.

God's promise was clear: He would *pass over* and not destroy the believers protected by the blood of the lamb. Exactly what happened to the believers and unbelievers will be seen in the next point (see note—Ex.12:29).

Thought 1. Remember two facts, two clear teachings of Scripture:
(1) The Passover lamb was only a type of *the Lamb of God* who was to come and save the world. Jesus Christ is the Lamb of God who takes away the sin of the world. Jesus Christ is *the Lamb* chosen and provided by God Himself, not by man. God Himself has acted in perfection and provided the perfect Passover Lamb, the only Lamb whose blood can truly cleanse us from sin and deliver us from the hand of God's judgment.
(2) In the terrifying day of judgment, God is not going to ask...
   • what church we belonged to
   • how moral and just we have been
   • how many good works we have done
   • how often we attended church

God is going to ask one thing and one thing only: Have we trusted the blood of Jesus Christ to cleanse us from sin? Are we coming to Him—approaching God—through the blood of the Lamb of God, the Lord Jesus Christ? He is our Passover Lamb; He was sacrificed "once for all" for us.

"Christ our passover is sacrificed for us" (1 Co.5:7).
"Who needeth not daily, as those high priests, to offer up sacrifice, first for his own sins, and then for the people's: for this he did once, when he offered up himself" (He.7:27).
"The next day John seeth Jesus coming unto him, and saith, Behold the Lamb of God, which taketh away the sin of the world" (Jn.1:29).
"For this is my blood of the new testament, which is shed for many for the remission of sins" (Mt.26:28).
"Much more then, being now justified by his blood, we shall be saved from wrath through him" (Ro.5:9).
"In whom we have redemption through his blood, the forgiveness of sins, according to the riches of his grace" (Ep.1:7).
"Neither by the blood of goats and calves, but by his own blood he entered in once into the holy place, having obtained eternal redemption for us. For if the blood of bulls and of goats, and the ashes of an heifer sprinkling the unclean, sanctifieth to the purifying of the flesh: How much more shall the blood of Christ, who through the eternal Spirit offered himself without spot to God, purge your conscience from dead works to serve the living God?" (He.9:12-14).
"Forasmuch as ye know that ye were not redeemed with corruptible things, as silver and gold, from your vain conversation received by tradition from your fathers; But with the precious blood of Christ, as of a lamb without blemish and without spot" (1 Pe.1:18-19).
"And from Jesus Christ, who is the faithful witness, and the first begotten of the dead, and the prince of the kings of the earth. Unto him that loved us, and washed us from our sins in his own blood" (Re.1:5).

c. The Passover was to be observed as a lasting ordinance. God's people were to observe the Passover even when they reached and entered the promised land (vv.24-25).
d. God's people were to proclaim the meaning of the Passover to their children (vv.26-27).
   ⇒ They were to explain the Passover sacrifice of the lamb (v.27).
   ⇒ They were to explain how the LORD judged the Egyptians but *passed over*—protected and did not destroy—the Israelites who believed God's Word (v.27).

Thought 1. Children are to be taught the story of the Passover lamb, how Jesus Christ is *the Lamb of God* who takes away the sin of the world. They are to be taught the meaning of the cross, the meaning of the blood of the Lord Jesus Christ.

"Only take heed to thyself, and keep thy soul diligently, lest thou forget the things which thine eyes have seen, and lest they depart from thy heart all the days of thy life: but teach them thy sons, and thy sons' sons" (De.4:9).
"And these words, which I command thee this day, shall be in thine heart: And thou shalt teach them diligently unto thy children, and shalt talk of them when thou sittest in thine house, and when thou walkest by the way, and when thou liest down, and when thou risest up" (De.6:6-7).
"And he did that which was right in the sight of the LORD, according to all that his father Amaziah did" (2 Chr.26:4).

"Train up a child in the way he should go: and when he is old, he will not depart from it" (Pr.22:6).

"So when they had dined, Jesus saith to Simon Peter, Simon, [son] of Jonas, lovest thou me more than these? He saith unto him, Yea, Lord; thou knowest that I love thee. He saith unto him, Feed my lambs" (Jn.21:15).

"When I [Paul] call to remembrance the unfeigned faith that is in thee [Timothy], which dwelt first in thy grandmother Lois, and thy mother Eunice; and I am persuaded that in thee also" (2 Ti.1:5).

e. There were two absolute essentials which the people did (vv.27-28).
1) The people bowed their heads and worshipped God (v.27). They heard the message of God and they accepted God's Word. They acknowledged God: bowed their heads in reverence and worshipped Him. They were thankful, ever so thankful, that God had made a way...
   • for them to be saved
   • for them to escape the coming judgment of God
   • for them to be delivered from the enslavement of Egypt

2) The people obeyed God. They did exactly what God commanded (v.28).

Thought 1. God tells us how to be saved from the coming judgment: we must seek safety behind the blood of His Son, Jesus Christ. We must believe God: accept His Word and acknowledge Him.
⇒ We must reverence Him, bow our heads and worship Him.
⇒ We must obey Him and hide behind the blood of His Son, the Lord Jesus Christ.

"For when we were yet without strength, in due time Christ died for the ungodly" (Ro.5:6).

"But God commendeth his love toward us, in that, while we were yet sinners, Christ died for us" (Ro.5:8).

"Purge out therefore the old leaven, that ye may be a new lump, as ye are unleavened. For even Christ our passover is sacrificed for us" (1 Co.5:7).

"For I delivered unto you first of all that which I also received, how that Christ died for our sins according to the scriptures" (1 Co.15:3).

"Who gave himself for our sins, that he might deliver us from this present evil world, according to the will of God and our Father" (Ga.1:4).

"Who his own self bare our sins in his own body on the tree, that we, being dead to sins, should live unto righteousness: by whose stripes ye were healed" (1 Pe.2:24).

"For Christ also hath once suffered for sins, the just for the unjust, that he might bring us to God, being put to death in the flesh, but quickened by the Spirit" (1 Pe.3:18).

2 (12:29) **Judgment—Egypt—Firstborn—Plagues, The Ten**: the judgment of God struck Egypt. God had warned the Egyptians, but they had rejected His warning. They had refused to repent of their terrible evil: they had gone so far in their rebellion against God that they were beyond repenting.
⇒ They had continued to reject God and His warning, to deny that a sovereign, omnipotent God existed.
⇒ They had continued to commit atrocity after atrocity against people, in particular God's people.
⇒ They had continued in their obstinate unbelief, worshipping idols and refusing to free God's people.

God had no choice: judgment had to fall. And fall it did. At midnight, horror and terror struck all Egypt: all the firstborn of Egypt were struck down. The firstborn of every family from the palace to the dungeon became sick and died. The judgment of God fell equally upon all, upon the wealthy and the powerful as well as the poor and the weak. Even the firstborn of animals died. Why? Why did God strike dead the firstborn of animals? For one strong reason: by judging the firstborn of animals, God was striking at the very gods of the Egyptians. Remember, they had imagined and created gods that were closely linked to various animals of the earth. Thus God was striking a death blow to the so-called gods by striking dead the firstborn of all animals.

Note: it was the LORD Himself who executed justice upon the Egyptians. Remember: in addition to their idolatry and rejection of God and their evil enslavement of people, the Egyptians had launched a holocaust against all the Hebrew male babies, killing them all at birth (Ex.1:15-22). Now God was executing equal justice upon them: their firstborn sons were dying by the thousands.

Thought 1. In Scripture, Egypt is a type of the world; therefore, what happened to Egypt stands as a critical warning to us. The day of judgment is coming, a worldwide, universal day of judgment. Every soul who refuses to hide behind the blood of God's Lamb will face the terrifying judgment of the LORD Himself. This is the clear declaration of God's Word.

"And before him shall be gathered all nations: and he shall separate them one from another, as a shepherd divideth [his] sheep from the goats: And he shall set the sheep on his right hand, but the goats on the left....Then shall he say also unto them on the left hand, Depart from me, ye cursed, into everlasting fire, prepared for the devil and his angels" (Mt.25:32-33, 41).

"Because he hath appointed a day, in the which he will judge the world in righteousness by that man whom he hath ordained; whereof he hath given assurance unto all men, in that he hath raised him from the dead" (Ac.17:31).

""In the day when God shall judge the secrets of men by Jesus Christ according to my gospel (Ro.2:16).

"So then every one of us shall give account of himself to God" (Ro.14:12).

"For we must all appear before the judgment seat of Christ; that every one may receive the things done in his body, according to that he hath done, whether it be good or bad" (2 Co.5:10).

"And I saw a great white throne, and him that sat on it, from whose face the earth and the heaven fled away; and there was found no place for them. And I saw the dead, small and great, stand before God; and the books were opened: and another book was opened, which is the book of life: and the dead were judged out of those things which were written in the books, according to their works. And the sea gave up the dead which were in it; and death and hell delivered up the dead which were in them: and they were judged every man according to their works. And death and hell were cast into the lake of fire. This is the second death. And whosoever was not found written in the book of life was cast into the lake of fire" (Re.20:11-15).

3 (12:30-33) **Judgment—Justice**: the judgment achieved its purpose.

a. Purpose One: Pharaoh and his people cried out in anguish and wept over their dead. Justice was executed upon their terrible evil. No one could help the Egyptians; no one could comfort them. No one could deliver them from the hand of God's judgment. It was too late. God's judgment had fallen. Justice had been executed. There was nothing left except the...

- suffering
- pain
- hurt
- grief

The unbelievers had rejected God too long. They had gone beyond the point of repentance, beyond the point of ever turning away from their evil. And God was forced to act in justice and judgment.

b. Purpose Two: during that very night, Pharaoh called for Moses and Aaron and freed God's people (vv.31-32). The hard-hearted and proud—those who had rejected God—were humbled.

⇒ Pharaoh freed all God's people, including their herds and flocks (v.32).

⇒ Pharaoh begged Moses to seek the LORD for a blessing upon himself and Egypt (v.32).

Remember, Pharaoh (the authority of the government which he represented) was considered to be a god. The king and the state were worshipped by the people: their first loyalty and allegiance were committed to the king and the state. Yet here the king was powerless to protect himself and his nation from the hand of God's judgment. The most powerful man and people upon earth were powerless against the only living and true God, against the day God had set to execute justice upon the evil unbelievers of Egypt.

c. Purpose Three: Pharaoh and his people urged God's people to leave immediately. They feared that God might immediately execute justice upon them all, that He might kill them all.

Thought 1. Maxie Dunnam has an excellent statement concerning the judgment of God that is worthy of being quoted in its entirety.

> *There can be no covering up or diminishing the reality of divine judgment. The fact is set forth on page after page of Bible history. God judged Adam and Eve, expelling them from the garden and pronouncing curses on their future earthly life. God judged the corrupt world of Noah's day, sending a flood to destroy humankind. God judged Sodom and Gomorrah, engulfing them in a volcanic catastrophe (Ge.19:24). And God judged Pharaoh and the Egyptians just as He had foretold He would (Ge.15:14), unleashing against them the terrors of the ten plagues.*
>
> *There are "big judgments" about which we all know. Apart from these, the pages of the Bible are literally filled with judgment. Those who don't study the Bible seriously nonchalantly suggest that when you leave the Old Testament and come to the New, the theme of divine judgment fades almost to nothing. That isn't so. Even a cursory reading of the New Testament reveals God's action as judge. In fact, the entire New Testament is overshadowed by the certainty of a coming day of universal judgment which was set forth by Jesus Himself. It's not easy to forget that picture, the powerful imagery of it—the sheep separated from the goats, the righteous on the right hand of God and the unrighteous on the left, the righteous invited into the presence of the Lord, the unrighteous condemned to eternal punishment where there is "weeping and gnashing of teeth" (Matt.8:12).*
>
> *The picture in the New Testament is that the world's Savior, Jesus Christ, is also the world's judge. Listen to Jesus Himself:*
>
> > *"For the Father judges no one, but has committed all judgment to the Son, that all should honor the Son just as they honor the Father. He who does not honor the Son does not honor the Father who sent Him.'*
> >
> > *"Most assuredly, I say to you, he who hears My word and believes in Him who sent Me has everlasting life, and shall not come into judgment, but has passed from death into life. Most assuredly, I say to you, the hour is coming, and now is, when the dead will hear the voice of the Son of God; and those who hear will live. For as the Father has life in Himself, so He has granted the Son to have life in Himself, and has given Him authority to execute judgment also, because He is the Son of Man. Do*

not marvel at this; for the hour is coming in which all who are in the graves will hear His voice and come forth—those who have done good, to the resurrection of life, and those who have done evil, to the resurrection of condemnation" (John 5:22-29).

"There is no way to cover up or diminish the reality of divine judgment."[1]

"And then shall appear the sign of the Son of man in heaven: and then shall all the tribes of the earth mourn, and they shall see the Son of man coming in the clouds of heaven with power and great glory" (Mt.24:30).

"And whosoever shall not receive you, nor hear you, when ye depart thence, shake off the dust under your feet for a testimony against them. Verily I say unto you, It shall be more tolerable for Sodom and Gomorrha in the day of judgment, than for that city" (Mk.6:11).

"Whosoever therefore shall be ashamed of me and of my words in this adulterous and sinful generation; of him also shall the Son of man be ashamed, when he cometh in the glory of his Father with the holy angels" (Mk.8:38).

"And this is the condemnation, that light is come into the world, and men loved darkness rather than light, because their deeds were evil" (Jn.3:19).

"But we are sure that the judgment of God is according to truth against them which commit such things" (Ro.2:2).

"And to you who are troubled rest with us, when the Lord Jesus shall be revealed from heaven with his mighty angels, In flaming fire taking vengeance on them that know not God, and that obey not the gospel of our Lord Jesus Christ: Who shall be punished with everlasting destruction from the presence of the Lord, and from the glory of his power" (2 Th.1:7-9).

"Behold, he cometh with clouds; and every eye shall see him, and they also which pierced him: and all kindreds of the earth shall wail because of him" (Re.1:7).

4 (12:34-41) **Judgment—Security—Protection—Israel**: the judgment was escaped by Israel, the people of God, the believers of that day. The great exodus now took place. God's people were free, free at last. The Scripture and the outline points describe the scene as well as it can be pictured.

a. God's people obeyed His instructions exactly as He had commanded (v.34).

b. God's people took only unleavened bread, carrying it on their shoulders with the kneading troughs wrapped in clothing.

c. As instructed, God's people requested silver, gold, and clothing from the Egyptians (v.35). The Egyptians had no doubt stolen all the valuables of the Israelites when they had enslaved them. Moreover, as slaves, the Israelites were paid little if any wages for their labor throughout the decades of the enslavement. The Egyptians owed the Israelites more back wages than they could ever conceivably pay. Note that the LORD Himself worked upon the hearts of the Egyptians and stirred them to favor His people with gifts that probably amounted to great wealth.

d. God's people started their great *freedom march* (vv.37-39).

⇒ Over six-hundred thousand men alone, age twenty and above, left Egypt and marched toward the promised land (Nu.1:3). This means that with women and children included there were over two million, perhaps three or four million Israelites who began the great march.

⇒ Moreover, a mixed multitude left with the Israelites. The mixed multitude obviously included some who were a mixed breed, resulting from the intermarriage of Israelites with Egyptians. There were also some Egyptians and other slaves and some animals that journeyed with God's people (vv.38-39). The mixed multitude would later cause serious problems for God's people. The book of Numbers will show us that they were the ringleaders of the agitators and trouble-makers among God's true people.

⇒ Note, they also baked and took unleavened bread. They did not take time to allow the yeast to leaven the bread. (Remember: leaven symbolizes evil in the Scripture. The symbolic picture is this: as God's people marched forth to the promised land, they were leaving all leaven—all evil—behind in Egypt [the world].) They were leaving their *old life* and beginning a *new life*, marching forth to the promised land of God.

e. God's people rushed, left and separated themselves from Egypt immediately. There was not even time to prepare food (v.39).

f. God's people cut off all attachments to Egypt (symbolically, the world). They cut all attachments to the place that had held them under its power and dominion for four-hundred and thirty years (v.40).

g. There was the most wonderful fact: God gloriously delivered His people from Egypt (symbolically, the world) (v.41).

Thought 1. People are to be free, free to seek the promised land of God. Freedom and liberty for all people is God's will. No government and no person is to keep us from following God, nor from seeking the promised land of God. We are to be free to worship and serve the LORD God Himself.

"The Spirit of the LORD GOD is upon me; because the LORD hath anointed me to preach good tidings unto the meek; he hath sent me to bind up the brokenhearted, to proclaim liberty to the captives, and the opening of the prison to them that are bound" (Is.61:1).

---

[1] Maxie Dunnam. *Mastering the Old Testament, Exodus,* p.137-138.

"For there is no difference between the Jew and the Greek: for the same Lord over all is rich unto all that call upon him" (Ro.10:12).

"There is neither Jew nor Greek, there is neither bond nor free, there is neither male nor female: for ye are all one in Christ Jesus" (Ga.3:28).

"For, brethren, ye have been called unto liberty; only use not liberty for an occasion to the flesh [for license, indulgence, lawlessness], but by love serve one another" (Ga.5:13).

"As free, and not using your liberty for a cloke of maliciousness [against others], but as the servants of God" (1 Pe.2:16).

Thought 2. God will deliver us from the enslavements of this world. No matter what the enslavements are and no matter how strong their grip, God has the power to break the grip—the power to save and deliver us.

"Knowing this, that our old man is crucified with him, that the body of sin might be destroyed, that henceforth we should not serve sin. For he that is dead is freed from sin" (Ro.6:6-7).

"Who gave himself for our sins, that he might deliver us from this present evil world, according to the will of God and our Father" (Ga.1:4).

"Now unto him that is able to do exceeding abundantly above all that we ask or think, according to the power that worketh in us" (Ep.3:20).

"And the Lord shall deliver me from every evil work, and will preserve me unto his heavenly kingdom: to whom be glory for ever and ever" (2 Ti.4:18).

"Forasmuch then as the children are partakers of flesh and blood, he also himself likewise took part of the same; that through death he might destroy him that had the power of death, that is, the devil; And deliver them who through fear of death were all their lifetime subject to bondage" (He.2:14-15).

"Wherefore he is able also to save them to the uttermost that come unto God by him, seeing he ever liveth to make intercession for them" (He.7:25).

"The Lord knoweth how to deliver the godly out of temptations, and to reserve the unjust unto the day of judgment to be punished" (2 Pe.2:9).

"And he said, The LORD is my rock, and my fortress, and my deliverer" (2 S.22:2).

"But I am poor and needy; yet the LORD thinketh upon me: thou art my help and my deliverer; make no tarrying, O my God" (Ps.40:17).

"Surely he shall deliver thee from the snare of the fowler, and from the noisome pestilence" (Ps.91:3).

"Fear thou not; for I am with thee: be not dismayed; for I am thy God: I will strengthen thee; yea, I will help thee; yea, I will uphold thee with the right hand of my righteousness" (Is.41:10).

DEEPER STUDY # 1

(12:40-41) **Generation—History**: Israel was in Egypt for four-hundred and thirty years. Just think: four-hundred and thirty long years. Allow the magnitude of all those years to sink in and remember, most of the years were spent in slavery. Then let your imagination explore what can transpire in four-hundred and thirty years:

⇒ If a generation is forty years, then almost eleven generations of Israelites lived in Egypt.
⇒ Four-hundred and thirty times crops were planted.
⇒ Four-hundred and thirty times crops were harvested.
⇒ Millions of Israelites were born.
⇒ Millions of Israelites died.
⇒ Four-hundred and thirty years were spent constructing buildings, roads, pyramids, and other projects.
⇒ Four-hundred and thirty years of political leadership changed.
⇒ Four-hundred and thirty years were spent waiting to become free, free to live in the promised land of Canaan.

And throughout all the four-hundred and thirty years, God remembered His people and the promises that He had made to them. God remembered His promise to give the promised land (heaven) and the promised seed (the Savior) to believers, to all those who genuinely believed and followed Him. Note what it was that made God remember His covenant:

1. God remembered His covenant because He loved and cared for His people: God saw the suffering and pain of their slavery.

"And God heard their groaning, and God remembered his covenant with Abraham, with Isaac, and with Jacob" (Ex.2:24).

"And I have also established my covenant with them, to give them the land of Canaan, the land of their pilgrimage, wherein they were strangers. And I have also heard the groaning of the children of Israel, whom the Egyptians keep in bondage; and I have remembered my covenant" (Ex.6:4-5).

2. God remembered His covenant because He is faithful. He keeps His Word.

"Know therefore that the LORD thy God, he is God, the faithful God, which keepeth covenant and mercy with them that love him and keep his commandments to a thousand generations" (De.7:9).

"My covenant will I not break, nor alter the thing that is gone out of my lips" (Ps.89:34).

"He hath remembered his covenant for ever, the word which he commanded to a thousand generations. Which covenant he made with Abraham, and his oath unto Isaac; And confirmed the same unto Jacob for a law, and to Israel for an everlasting covenant" (Ps.105:8-10).

> "For all the promises of God in him are yea, and in him Amen, unto the glory of God by us" (2 Co.1:20).

3. God remembered His covenant because he wants all people to be saved.

> "And I will establish my covenant between me and thee and thy seed after thee in their generations for an everlasting covenant, to be a God unto thee, and to thy seed after thee" (Ge.17:7).
> "That at that time ye were without Christ, being aliens from the commonwealth of Israel, and strangers from the covenants of promise, having no hope, and without God in the world" (Ep.2:12).
> "But now hath he obtained a more excellent ministry, by how much also he is the mediator of a better covenant, which was established upon better promises. For if that first covenant had been fault-less, then should no place have been sought for the second. For finding fault with them, he saith, Be-hold, the days come, saith the Lord, when I will make a new covenant with the house of Israel and with the house of Judah: Not according to the covenant that I made with their fathers in the day when I took them by the hand to lead them out of the land of Egypt; because they continued not in my cove-nant, and I regarded them not, saith the Lord. For this is the covenant that I will make with the house of Israel after those days, saith the Lord; I will put my laws into their mind, and write them in their hearts: and I will be to them a God, and they shall be to me a people" (He.8:6-10).
> "The Lord is not slack concerning his promise, as some men count slackness; but is longsuffering to us-ward, not willing that any should perish, but that all should come to repentance" (2 Pe.3:9).

5 (12:42-51) **Judgment—Passover**: the judgment and the Passover deliverance were always to be remembered and cel-ebrated. Remember, the Passover celebrated God's great deliverance of the Israelite believer. The Passover was to be strictly observed by those who believed. Again, God established the Passover as a lasting ordinance for His people. Note three significant facts.

a. Separation was an absolute essential in the observance of the Passover (vv.43-49). Only the person who identified with the people of God could take part in the Passover.

⇒ The Passover was not to be eaten by foreigners (v.43).
⇒ The Passover could be eaten by slaves only if they had been circumcised (v.44).
⇒ The Passover could not be eaten by a temporary resident nor by a hired worker (v.45).
⇒ The Passover was to be eaten only within the house of faith. No meat was to be taken outside the house, and no bone of the lamb was to be broken (v.46). Note: this was a prophecy concerning the bones of Christ: no bone of Christ was to be broken (Jn.19:36).
⇒ The Passover was to be celebrated by the whole congregation (v.47).
⇒ The Passover was to be eaten by other nationalities or proselytes only if they were circumcised (v.48).
⇒ The Passover was not to be eaten by any uncircumcised male (v.48[b]).
⇒ The same laws governing the Passover were to apply to both the native-born and to the foreigner (v.49)

b. Obedience was an absolute essential (v.50). Note that all Israel obeyed God, did exactly what God had commanded through His messengers, Moses and Aaron.

c. Note that the wonderful result is repeated: the LORD gloriously delivered His people out of Egyptian slavery (v.51). The Israelites who believed and obeyed God were saved by the mighty hand of God, and they began their great march to-ward the promised land.

Thought 1. If we have placed ourselves behind the blood of Christ, God has gloriously saved us. No matter who we are, no matter how terrible a sinner we have been, God saves us if we trust the blood of Christ. But note: once we are saved and delivered from the enslavements of this world, two things become absolutely essential.

(1) Separation from the world is absolutely essential.

> "Depart from me, ye evildoers: for I will keep the commandments of my God" (Ps.119:115).
> "Depart ye, depart ye, go ye out from thence, touch no unclean thing; go ye out of the midst of her; be ye clean, that bear the vessels of the LORD" (Is.52:11).
> "And be not conformed to this world: but be ye transformed by the renewing of your mind, that ye may prove what is that good, and acceptable, and perfect, will of God" (Ro.12:2).
> "Wherefore come out from among them, and be ye separate, saith the Lord, and touch not the unclean thing; and I will receive you, And will be a Father unto you, and ye shall be my sons and daughters, saith the Lord Almighty" (2 Co.6:17-18).
> "And have no fellowship with the unfruitful works of darkness, but rather reprove them" (Ep.5:11).
> "Love not the world, neither the things that are in the world. If any man love the world, the love of the Father is not in him. For all that is in the world, the lust of the flesh, and the lust of the eyes, and the pride of life, is not of the Father, but is of the world" (1 Jn.2:15-16).

(2) Obedience becomes absolutely essential.

> "Now therefore, if ye will obey my voice indeed, and keep my covenant, then ye shall be a peculiar treasure unto me above all people: for all the earth is mine" (Ex.19:5).
> "O that there were such an heart in them, that they would fear me, and keep all my commandments always, that it might be well with them, and with their children for ever!" (De.5:29).
> "This book of the law shall not depart out of thy mouth; but thou shalt meditate therein day and night, that thou mayest observe to do according to all that is written therein: for then thou shalt make thy way prosperous, and then thou shalt have good success" (Jos.1:8).
> "Not every one that saith unto me, Lord, Lord, shall enter into the kingdom of heaven; but he that doeth the will of my Father which is in heaven" (Mt.7:21).
> "Therefore whosoever heareth these sayings of mine, and doeth them, I will liken him unto a wise man, which built his house upon a rock: And the rain descended, and the floods came, and the winds blew, and beat upon that house; and it fell not: for it was founded upon a rock. And every one that heareth these sayings of mine, and doeth them not, shall be likened unto a foolish man, which built his house upon the sand: And the rain descended, and the floods came, and the winds blew, and beat upon that house; and it fell: and great was the fall of it" (Mt.7:24-27).
> "He that hath my commandments, and keepeth them, he it is that loveth me: and he that loveth me shall be loved of my Father, and I will love him, and will manifest myself to him" (Jn.14:21).
> "Jesus answered and said unto him, If a man love me, he will keep my words: and my Father will love him, and we will come unto him, and make our abode with him" (Jn.14:23).
> "If ye keep my commandments, ye shall abide in my love; even as I have kept my Father's commandments, and abide in his love" (Jn.15:10).
> "Ye are my friends, if ye do whatsoever I command you" (Jn.15:14).
> "Blessed are they that do his commandments, that they may have right to the tree of life, and may enter in through the gates into the city" (Re.22:14).

Thought 2. Note two significant facts about the strict regulations governing the Passover.

(1) Separation—ritual purity—was an absolute essential to partake of *the Passover* (See point 1 above). The same is true with the Lord's Supper. Spiritual purity—repentance and asking God to forgive one's sins—is an absolute essential before partaking of the Lord's Supper.

> "But let a man examine himself, and so let him eat of that bread, and drink of that cup" (1 Co.11:28).
> "And when a stranger shall sojourn with thee, and will keep the passover to the LORD, let all his males be circumcised, and then let him come near and keep it; and he shall be as one that is born in the land: for no uncircumcised person shall eat thereof" (Ex.12:48).

(2) No bone on the Passover lamb could be broken (v.46). This was a picture of what was to happen to Christ. No bone of Christ, the Lamb of God, was broken.

This is a picture of *unity*. The parts of the lamb were not to be divided: the lamb was to remain a *unified body*. The family members were not to be divided: the family was to remain *together*, hid behind the blood of the lamb as *one body*, as one *unified* family.

Jesus Christ died without a single bone being broken. Not a part was dismembered. All parts of His body remained unified. Jesus Christ is the Head of one body (the church), a body...

- that has many members
- that has different gifts
- that has been called to serve the Lamb of God in unity, without division

> "The Jews therefore, because it was the preparation, that the bodies should not remain upon the cross on the sabbath day, (for that sabbath day was an high day,) besought Pilate that their legs might be broken, and that they might be taken away. Then came the soldiers, and brake the legs of the first, and of the other which was crucified with him. But when they came to Jesus, and saw that he was dead already, they brake not his legs....For these things were done, that the scripture should be fulfilled, A bone of him shall not be broken" (Jn.19:31-33, 36).

TYPES, SYMBOLS, AND PICTURES
(Exodus 12:21-51)

Historical Term	Type or Picture (Scriptural Basis for Each)	Life Application for Today's Believer	Biblical Application
No Broken Bones on the Lamb (Ex.12:46)	*A picture of unity: The parts of the lamb were not to be divided: the lamb was to remain a unified body. The family members were not to be divided: the family was to be hid behind the blood of the lamb as one body, as one unified family.* **"In one house shall it be eaten; thou shalt not carry forth ought of the flesh abroad out of the house; neither shall ye break a bone thereof"** (Ex.12:46).	Jesus Christ died without a single bone being broken. Not a part was dismembered. All parts of His body remained unified. Jesus Christ is the Head of one body (the church), a body… • that has many members • that has different gifts • that has been called to serve the Lamb of God in unity, without division	*"For these things were done, that the scripture should be fulfilled, A bone of him shall not be broken"* (Jn.19:36). *"Now ye are the body of Christ, and members in particular. And God hath set some in the church, first apostles, secondarily prophets, thirdly teachers, after that miracles, then gifts of healings, helps, governments, diversities of tongues"* (1 Co.12:27-28). *"But now hath God set the members every one of them in the body, as it hath pleased him….That there should be no schism in the body; but that the members should have the same care one for another"* (1 Co.12:18, 25). *"I in them, and thou in me, that they may be made perfect in one; and that the world may know that thou hast sent me, and hast loved them, as thou hast loved me"* (Jn.17:23). *(see Ro.12:4-5; 1 Co.12:12-13; Ep.1:23; 4:11-12; Col.1:24; Ac.2:1; 1:14; 2:42-47)*

CHAPTER 13

D. The Dedication of the Firstborn: Remembering God's Great Deliverance, 13:1-16

1. **Dedicate (sanctify, set apart) the firstborn child & animal to God**
   a. Is the commandment of God (v.1)
   b. Is to include both man & animal
2. **Follow these instructions in the dedication of the firstborn**
   a. Remember God's deliverance out of Egypt & slavery: Symbolizing deliverance from the world & from slavery to sin
   b. Eat no leavened bread: Symbolizing that you are to allow no evil in your lives
   c. Remember the very day & month of God's deliverance
   d. Always keep this great dedication of deliverance once a year—even after God's deliverance into the promised land (symbolizing heaven): Even after reaching a state of abundance & plenty, of spiritual victory, peace, & rest
   e. Eat unleavened bread for 7 days: Symbolizing that you are to take in only righteousness
   f. Worship on the 7th day
   g. Let no leavened bread nor leaven (yeast) be seen with you nor in your homes: Symbolizing that no evil was to be seen in your life or home
   h. Share your testimony of deliverance with your son
   i. Make the dedication a sign
      1) A reminder that your

And the LORD spake unto Moses, saying,
2 Sanctify unto me all the firstborn, whatsoever openeth the womb among the children of Israel, both of man and of beast: it is mine.
3 And Moses said unto the people, Remember this day, in which ye came out from Egypt, out of the house of bondage; for by strength of hand the LORD brought you out from this place: there shall no leavened bread be eaten.
4 This day came ye out in the month Abib.
5 And it shall be when the LORD shall bring thee into the land of the Canaanites, and the Hittites, and the Amorites, and the Hivites, and the Jebusites, which he sware unto thy fathers to give thee, a land flowing with milk and honey, that thou shalt keep this service in this month.
6 Seven days thou shalt eat unleavened bread, and in the seventh day shall be a feast to the LORD.
7 Unleavened bread shall be eaten seven days; and there shall no leavened bread be seen with thee, neither shall there be leaven seen with thee in all thy quarters.
8 And thou shalt show thy son in that day, saying, This is done because of that which the LORD did unto me when I came forth out of Egypt.
9 And it shall be for a sign unto thee upon thine hand,

and for a memorial between thine eyes, that the LORD's law may be in thy mouth: for with a strong hand hath the LORD brought thee out of Egypt.
10 Thou shalt therefore keep this ordinance in his season from year to year.
11 And it shall be when the LORD shall bring thee into the land of the Canaanites, as he sware unto thee and to thy fathers, and shall give it thee,
12 That thou shalt set apart unto the LORD all that openeth the matrix, and every firstling that cometh of a beast which thou hast; the males shall be the LORD's.
13 And every firstling of an ass thou shalt redeem with a lamb; and if thou wilt not redeem it, then thou shalt break his neck: and all the firstborn of man among thy children shalt thou redeem.
14 And it shall be when thy son asketh thee in time to come, saying, What is this? that thou shalt say unto him, By strength of hand the LORD brought us out from Egypt, from the house of bondage:
15 And it came to pass, when Pharaoh would hardly let us go, that the LORD slew all the firstborn in the land of Egypt, both the firstborn of man, and the firstborn of beast: therefore I sacrifice to the LORD all that openeth the matrix, being males; but all the firstborn of my children I redeem.
16 And it shall be for a token upon thine hand, and for frontlets between thine eyes: for by strength of hand the LORD brought us forth out of Egypt.

hands, eyes, & mouth are to keep God's law
   2) The reason: Because God delivered you

j. Keep the dedication at the appointed time year by year

3. **Honor God when He delivers you into Canaan: Symbolizing the promised land of salvation, freedom, victory, peace, & rest**
   a. By giving the firstborn to the LORD: Both animal & man

   b. By redeeming the firstborn of donkeys & of man: That is, by buying them back for a price[DS1]
      1) The price for a donkey: A lamb
      2) The price for a son: Five shekels (Nu.18:16)
   c. By sharing the great dedication with your children
      1) Sharing God's great deliverance

      2) Sharing God's judgment upon Egypt

      3) Sharing that your child belongs to the LORD, his life, hands, & eyes: Because the LORD delivered His people

DIVISION IV

THE PASSOVER AND THE TENTH PLAGUE: DELIVERANCE FROM GOD'S JUDGMENT—LIBERATED, SET FREE, 12:1–13:16

D. The Dedication of the Firstborn: Remembering God's Great Deliverance, 13:1-16

(13:1-16) **Introduction**: within the family, one thing is of critical importance to God: children. God wants children to be saved, to know that God is the God of salvation, of redemption, and deliverance.

This is what the dedication of the firstborn was all about: remembering and teaching the children of God's people that He had delivered His people out of Egypt, out of the land of slavery. Down through the generations, God wanted every child of His people to know this one great fact: He is the God of salvation, redemption, and deliverance.

How could God best do this? How could He best make sure that His people never forgot...

- that He is the God of salvation and redemption?
- that they must teach this great truth to their children?

By establishing a day of dedication, a day when His people would dedicate their firstborn sons to Him. This God did in founding the great day called, "The Dedication of the Firstborn." But God did more than this: He tied the day to the Passover and the Feast of Unleavened Bread. Remember:

⇒ The Passover was the great day when God's judgment had fallen upon the firstborn of Egypt, but had *passed over* all who had placed themselves behind the blood of the sacrificial lamb. The Passover was the greatest day in the life of Israel, the day when God delivered His people from Egyptian slavery (a symbol of the world and of man's enslavement to the evils of the world). (See outline and notes—Ex.12:21-51 for more discussion.)

⇒ The Feast of Unleavened Bread was a seven day celebration of the Passover. The eating of the Passover lamb was celebrated on the first day of the feast. Unleavened bread reminded the Israelites of the urgency of fleeing the evil of slavery, that they must immediately begin the march to the promised land.

⇒ The Dedication of the Firstborn was to remind the Israelites...

• that God had delivered Israel from Egyptian slavery, that God had actually adopted Israel as His firstborn son (Ex.4:22).

• that every family was to teach their children of God's great redemption. By dedicating the firstborn to God, the parents would set the precedent, the pattern of dedicating all their children to God.

The point to see is this: the Passover, the Feast of Unleavened Bread, and the Dedication of the Firstborn were all tied together. All three celebrations focused upon the greatest day in the life of Israel, the day of God's great deliverance from Egyptian slavery. It was the day when the people of God began their great march to the promised land. But each celebration focused upon one separate feature of God's great deliverance; each was to remind the believer of one special truth of God's great deliverance:

⇒ The Passover *focused* upon God's great redemption, His salvation and deliverance of the believer who hid behind the blood of the sacrificial lamb.

⇒ The Feast of Unleavened Bread *focused* upon the necessity of fleeing the slavery of Egypt (the world), of immediately marching to the promised land.

⇒ The Dedication of the Firstborn *focused* upon the utter necessity of dedicating the firstborn to God. And note: by giving the firstborn to God, the parents would set the precedent of giving all their children to God, of teaching them that God is the great Savior and Deliverer of men.

This is the important subject of this passage: *The Dedication of the Firstborn: Remembering God's Great Deliverance,* 13:1-16.

1. Dedicate (sanctify, set apart) the firstborn to God (vv.1-2).
2. Follow these instructions in the dedication of the firstborn (vv.3-10).
3. Honor God when He delivers you into Canaan: symbolizing the promised land of salvation, victory, peace, and rest (vv.11-16).

1 (13:1-2) **Child—Firstborn—Dedication—Sanctification**: dedicate—sanctify, set apart—the firstborn to God.

a. This was the commandment of God (v.1). The *Dedication of the Firstborn* was not a dedication service established by man, not a celebration that man felt was needed, that he founded. The dedication of the firstborn was so important that God Himself founded and established the celebration. It was a celebration, a day that was to be kept because God Himself commanded it to be kept.

b. Note this fact as well: the firstborn of both man and animal were to be dedicated to God. God's redemption is so important that He wanted it never forgotten, so important that He wanted the firstborn animal dedicated to Him as well as the firstborn son. The point was this: everything that a person had *came from God*—everything. Everything was either given by God or else redeemed, saved and delivered by God. He and He alone was the true and living LORD, the Creator and Redeemer of mankind. He had proven this fact in the great Passover and deliverance of His people. This was never to be forgotten. It was a fact that was to be kept before the minds of God's people. How? By setting up a permanent dedication service. Every time a firstborn child or animal was born, the firstborn was to be dedicated to God.

c. Note the clear-cut declaration of God: "The firstborn...it is mine" (KJV); "The first offspring...belongs to me" (NIV).

Thought 1. The application to us is twofold:

(1) We are to remember the day of God's redemption, the day of our salvation. We are to remember the day God saved and delivered us from Egypt, from the world and its enslavement to sin and evil. How are we to remember the great day of deliverance? By dedicating our firstborn child to God. We are to take our firstborn child and give the child to God. We are to set the child apart to God, and by so doing set the precedent of giving all our children to God.

"Only take heed to thyself, and keep thy soul diligently, lest thou forget the things which thine eyes have seen, and lest they depart from thy heart all the days of thy life: but teach them thy sons, and thy sons' sons" (De.4:9).

"And all Judah stood before the LORD, with their little ones, their wives, and their children" (2 Chr.20:13).

"Also that day they offered great sacrifices, and rejoiced: for God had made them rejoice with great joy: the wives also and the children rejoiced: so that the joy of Jerusalem was heard even afar off" (Ne.12:43).

"Come, ye children, hearken unto me: I will teach you the fear of the LORD" (Ps.34:11).

"Lo, children are an heritage of the LORD: and the fruit of the womb is his reward" (Ps.127:3).

"Remember now thy Creator in the days of thy youth, while the evil days come not, nor the years draw nigh, when thou shalt say, I have no pleasure in them" (Ec.12:1).

(2) We are to give the first of everything to God, not only our children, but the first of all our possessions.

"And blessed be the most high God, which hath delivered thine enemies into thy hand. And he gave him tithes of all" (Ge.14:20).

"And this stone, which I have set for a pillar, shall be God's house: and of all that thou shalt give me I will surely give the tenth unto thee" (Ge.28:22).

"Ye shall offer at your own will a male without blemish, of the beeves, of the sheep, or of the goats. But whatsoever hath a blemish, that shall ye not offer: for it shall not be acceptable for you. And whosoever offereth a sacrifice of peace offerings unto the LORD to accomplish his vow, or a freewill offering in beeves or sheep, it shall be perfect to be accepted; there shall be no blemish therein. Blind, or broken, or maimed, or having a wen, or scurvy, or scabbed, ye shall not offer these unto the LORD, nor make an offering by fire of them upon the altar unto the LORD. Either a bullock or a lamb that hath any thing superfluous or lacking in his parts, that mayest thou offer for a freewill offering; but for a vow it shall not be accepted. Ye shall not offer unto the LORD that which is bruised, or crushed, or broken, or cut; neither shall ye make any offering thereof in your land. Neither from a stranger's hand shall ye offer the bread of your God of any of these; because their corruption is in them, and blemishes be in them: they shall not be accepted for you" (Le.22:19-25).

"And all the tithe of the land, whether of the seed of the land, or of the fruit of the tree, is the LORD's: it is holy unto the LORD" (Le.27:30).

"Because all the firstborn are mine; for on the day that I smote all the firstborn in the land of Egypt I hallowed unto me all the firstborn in Israel, both man and beast: mine shall they be: I am the LORD" (Nu.3:13).

"That thou shalt take of the first of all the fruit of the earth, which thou shalt bring of thy land that the LORD thy God giveth thee, and shalt put it in a basket, and shalt go unto the place which the LORD thy God shall choose to place his name there. And thou shalt go unto the priest that shall be in those days, and say unto him, I profess this day unto the LORD thy God, that I am come unto the country which the LORD sware unto our fathers for to give us. And the priest shall take the basket out of thine hand, and set it down before the altar of the LORD thy God" (De.26:2-4).

"And as soon as the commandment came abroad, the children of Israel brought in abundance the firstfruits of corn, wine, and oil, and honey, and of all the increase of the field; and the tithe of all things brought they in abundantly" (2 Chr.31:5).

"Honour the LORD with thy substance, and with the firstfruits of all thine increase: So shall thy barns be filled with plenty, and thy presses shall burst out with new wine" (Pr.3:9-10).

"A son honoureth his father, and a servant his master: if then I be a father, where is mine honour? and if I be a master, where is my fear? saith the LORD of hosts unto you, O priests, that despise my name. And ye say, Wherein have we despised thy name? Ye offer polluted bread upon mine altar; and ye say, Wherein have we polluted thee? In that ye say, The table of the LORD is contemptible. And if ye offer the blind for sacrifice, is it not evil? and if ye offer the lame and sick, is it not evil? offer it now unto thy governor; will he be pleased with thee, or accept thy person? saith the LORD of hosts" (Mal.1:6-8).

"Bring ye all the tithes into the storehouse, that there may be meat in mine house, and prove me now herewith, saith the LORD of hosts, if I will not open you the windows of heaven, and pour you out a blessing, that there shall not be room enough to receive it" (Mal.3:10).

"But seek ye first the kingdom of God, and his righteousness; and all these things shall be added unto you" (Mt.6:33).

2 (13:3-10) **Firstborn—Dedication—Children**: follow these instructions in the dedication of the firstborn.

a. Remember God's deliverance out of slavery and Egypt (v.3). Remember that Egypt symbolizes the world. Therefore, this symbolizes our deliverance from the world and from being enslaved to the sin of the world.

b. Eat no leavened bread (v.3). Remember that leaven symbolizes evil within the world. Therefore this symbolizes that we are to allow no evil within our lives. We are not to eat, digest, nor partake of any evil whatsoever.

c. Remember the very day and month of God's great deliverance (v.4). No believer should ever forget the great day of God's deliverance, of his conversion. We should always remember the day that God redeemed and saved us.

d. Always keep this great dedication of deliverance once a year—even after God's deliverance into the promised land (v.5). Remember, the promised land symbolizes both heaven and a state of spiritual victory, peace, and rest (see DEEPER STUDY # 1—Ex.2:24; also see note—Ge.12:1). The point for us is clear: no matter how spiritually mature we become—no matter what state and experience of peace and rest we achieve in Christ—we should never forget our conversion experience. We should always remember the great day God delivered us from sin, the day He started us out on the great march toward the promised land of heaven.

e. Eat unleavened bread for seven days (v.6). Remember that unleavened bread symbolizes righteousness. As we march to the promised land of heaven, it symbolizes the urgency of immediately beginning to live a righteous life. We must eat, digest, and partake only of righteousness; and we must be quick to do it.

f. Worship on the seventh day (v.6). The picture for us is descriptive: as we walk about remembering the great deliverance of God, putting all evil out of our lives, and partaking only of righteousness, we are to set apart one day of every week for God, one day that is to be totally given over to worship and rest. (See outline and notes—Ge.2:1-3; Ex.20:8-11 for more discussion.)

g. Obey a critical point—let no leavened bread nor leaven (yeast) be seen with you nor in your homes (v.7). Note how strict the prohibition concerning leaven was and how often God stressed it throughout these chapters dealing with the Passover.

⇒ A person was not to eat any leaven, none whatsoever.

⇒ A person was not even to look upon leaven: no leaven whatsoever was to be seen.

⇒ A person was not even to allow leaven in his house during the seven days of the Feast of Unleavened Bread. The Jews became so conscientious about this that they took candles and searched the crevices and cracks of their homes and under and behind their furniture trying to make absolutely sure that there was no leaven in the house.

Thought 1. What a lesson for us in searching out the leaven of evil in our hearts and lives! We must search ever so diligently and make sure—absolutely sure—that there is no evil in our lives. When the light of God's Word and Spirit discovers sin within us, we must confess it and cast it out. We must get all sin out of our lives and homes. We must not even look upon anything that causes sin.

"Then Jesus said unto them, Take heed and beware of the leaven of the Pharisees and of the Sadducees....Then understood they how that he bade them not beware of the leaven of bread, but of the [false] doctrine of the Pharisees and of the Sadducees" (Mt.16:6, 12).

"Purge out therefore the old leaven, that ye may be a new lump, as ye are unleavened. For even Christ our passover is sacrificed for us: Therefore let us keep the feast, not with old leaven, neither with the leaven of malice and wickedness; but with the unleavened bread of sincerity and truth" (1 Co.5:7-8).

"A little leaven [evil] leaveneth the whole lump" (Ga.5:9).

"That ye put off concerning the former conversation the old man, which is corrupt according to the deceitful lusts" (Ep.4:22).

"Wherefore seeing we also are compassed about with so great a cloud of witnesses, let us lay aside every weight, and the sin which doth so easily beset us, and let us run with patience the race that is set before us" (He.12:1).

"Dearly beloved, I beseech you as strangers and pilgrims, abstain from fleshly lusts, which war against the soul" (1 Pe.2:11).

"If iniquity be in thine hand, put it far away, and let not wickedness dwell in thy tabernacles" (Jb.11:14).

"Let the wicked forsake his way, and the unrighteous man his thoughts: and let him return unto the LORD, and he will have mercy upon him; and to our God, for he will abundantly pardon" (Is.55:7).

h. Share your testimony of deliverance with your son (v.8). We must tell our children what the LORD has done for us in His great deliverance from the world and its evil.

i. Make the dedication a sign—a visible and strong testimony—of what God has done for you (v.9). Note that a person's whole body—his hands, eyes, and mouth—was to be totally given over to keep God's law. God had done a marvelous thing for the believer among the Israelites: He had delivered them with His mighty hand. Therefore, they were to commit their total being to God. F.B. Huey says this:

Other peoples often had a mark branded or tattooed on the hand or another part of the body with the name or symbol of the deity they worshipped and whose protection they enjoined to ward off evil spirits. Sometimes they wore a sacred badge or jeweled ornament on the forehead as a symbol of devotion to their god. For the Israelites the Passover with its Feast of Unleavened Bread, not tattoos or other external symbols, would serve as their identification with their deity.[1]

The Expositor's Bible Commentary says this:

The Jewish practice of writing Exodus 13:1-16 out on two of the four strips of parchment (along with Deut.6:4-9 and 11;13-21 on the other two) and placing them in two cubical leather boxes (tepillin; cf. "phylacteries," Matt.23:5) that were strapped on to the forehead and left arm seems to have originated in the Babylonian captivity. These were worn especially at daily morning prayers. This, was however, to exchange the intended inner reality for an external ritualism. The word was to activate their lips, hearts, and hands, not to be trapped in a box.[2]

Thought 1. The believer's whole body—his hands, eyes, and mouth—are to be totally given over to God. The believer...

• is to use his hands only for righteousness, never unrighteousness

• is to keep his eyes only on the moral and righteous, never the immoral and unrighteous

---

[1] F.B. Huey, Jr. *Exodus*, p.61.

[2] Frank E. Gaebelein, Editor. *The Expositor's Bible Commentary*, Vol.2, pp.382-383.

- is to use his mouth only for righteousness and truth, never unrighteousness and untruth

"Ye have heard that it was said by them of old time, Thou shalt not commit adultery: But I say unto you, That whosoever looketh on a woman to lust after her hath committed adultery with her already in his heart. And if thy right eye offend thee, pluck it out, and cast [it] from thee: for it is profitable for thee that one of thy members should perish, and not [that] thy whole body should be cast into hell. And if thy right hand offend thee, cut it off, and cast [it] from thee: for it is profitable for thee that one of thy members should perish, and not [that] thy whole body should be cast into hell" (Mt.5:27-30).

"Let all bitterness, and wrath, and anger, and clamour, and evil speaking, be put away from you, with all malice" (Ep.4:31).

"And the tongue is a fire, a world of iniquity: so is the tongue among our members, that it defileth the whole body, and setteth on fire the course of nature; and it is set on fire of hell" (Js.3:6).

"Wherefore laying aside all malice, and all guile, and hypocrisies, and envies, and all evil speakings" (1 Pe.2:1).

"For he that will love life, and see good days, let him refrain his tongue from evil, and his lips that they speak no guile" (1 Pe.3:10).

"Keep thy tongue from evil, and thy lips from speaking guile" (Ps.34:13).

"Let thine eyes look right on, and let thine eyelids look straight before thee" (Pr.4:25).

"He that keepeth his mouth keepeth his life: but he that openeth wide his lips shall have destruction" (Pr.13:3).

"He that walketh righteously, and speaketh uprightly; he that despiseth the gain of oppressions, that shaketh his hands from holding of bribes, that stoppeth his ears from hearing of blood, and shutteth his eyes from seeing evil; He shall dwell on high: his place of defence shall be the munitions of rocks: bread shall be given him; his waters shall be sure" (Is.33:15-16).

j. Keep the dedication at the appointed time year by year (v.10). The Dedication of the Firstborn, of the believer's children to God, was to be faithfully celebrated.

Thought 1. Three very important lessons are seen in the instructions governing the Dedication of the Firstborn.
(1) We must dedicate our firstborn child to God. By giving our firstborn child to God, we will set the precedent and pattern of dedicating all our children to the LORD.
(2) We must take the leaven of evil and put it out of our lives and homes. And we must be strict about the matter, ever so diligent in searching out any evil and casting it out (repenting).
(3) We must eat only unleavened bread, that is eat and digest only righteousness, only the life of Christ: only the purity, goodness, and righteousness of His being.

"Blessed [are] they which do hunger and thirst after righteousness: for they shall be filled" (Mt.5:6).

"Purge out therefore the old leaven, that ye may be a new lump, as ye are unleavened. For even Christ our passover is sacrificed for us: Therefore let us keep the feast, not with old leaven, neither with the leaven of malice and wickedness; but with the unleavened bread of sincerity and truth" (1 Co.5:7-8).

"Stand therefore, having your loins girt about with truth, and having on the breastplate of righteousness" (Ep.6:14).

"Being filled with the fruits of righteousness, which are by Jesus Christ, unto the glory and praise of God" (Ph.1:11).

"As ye have therefore received Christ Jesus the Lord, so walk ye in him: Rooted and built up in him, and stablished in the faith, as ye have been taught, abounding therein with thanksgiving" (Col.2:6-7).

"But thou, O man of God, flee these things; and follow after righteousness, godliness, faith, love, patience, meekness. Fight the good fight of faith, lay hold on eternal life, whereunto thou art also called, and hast professed a good profession before many witnesses" (1 Ti.6:11-12).

"Study to show thyself approved unto God, a workman that needeth not to be ashamed, rightly dividing the word of truth" (2 Ti.2:15).

"Teaching us that, denying ungodliness and worldly lusts, we should live soberly, righteously, and godly, in this present world; Looking for that blessed hope, and the glorious appearing of the great God and our Saviour Jesus Christ" (Tit.2:12-13).

"Wherefore laying aside all malice, and all guile, and hypocrisies, and envies, and all evil speakings, As newborn babes, desire the sincere milk of the word, that ye may grow thereby: If so be ye have tasted that the Lord is gracious" (1 Pe.2:1-3).

3 (13:11-16) **Dedication—Firstborn—Children**: honor God when He delivers you into Canaan. Remember, Canaan symbolizes the promised land of heaven and of salvation, victory, peace, and rest. (See DEEPER STUDY # 1—Ex.2:24 for more discussion.) The Israelites were to honor God by doing three very important things.

a. The firstborn was to be dedicated to God (v.12). The firstborn was to be offered up to God as a sacrifice. Why? To remind the Israelites that God was the source of their lives...
- the only living and true God
- the Redeemer, their only Savior and Deliverer, the One who had delivered them from the slavery of Egypt and given them the promised land

b. There were to be two exceptions to the sacrificing and slaying of the firstborn, that of donkeys and of man (v.12).
⇒ Donkeys were to be redeemed with a lamb. A lamb was to be sacrificed instead of a donkey. This was either because a donkey was considered an unclean animal or because it was useful for work (see Ex.34:20; Nu.18:15). Whatever the reason, a lamb was to be substituted for a donkey. Note this fact as well: God meant that the Dedication of the Firstborn was to be observed by everyone. If a person began to slip back from observing the offering of the firstborn to God, then the legal authorities were to take the donkey and break its neck. The donkey was the LORD's not the man's; therefore no man was to refuse to redeem his donkey.
⇒ The firstborn son of a family was redeemed with five shekels (Ex.13:13; 34:20). This passage does not give the amount; the five shekels is spelled out later (Nu.18:16).

F.B. Huey makes an important point that needs to be noted by all generations of men:

The firstborn male of animals was to be sacrificed to the Lord, but the firstborn son was to be redeemed (Exod. 13:13; 34:20). This provision is an important reminder that human sacrifice was never sanctioned by God (Deut.18:10; Lev.18:21; 20:2-5), though the Israelites themselves gave their children as sacrifice, as did their pagan neighbors (cf. 2 Kings 3:27; 16:3; 17:31; 21:6; 2 Chron.33:6; Ezek.16:20, 21). The prophets constantly spoke out against this abhorrent practice (cf. Isa.57:4, 5; Jer.7:30-34; 19:4-9; 44:6-10; Ezek.16:20).[3]

c. Parents were to share the great dedication with their children (vv.14-16).
1) Parents were to share that the LORD Himself—His mighty hand—had delivered them from Egypt, from the land of slavery.
2) Parents were to share God's judgment upon Egypt (v.15). It was the LORD Himself who had struck down all the firstborn of Egypt, both men and animals.
3) Parents were to share that their children belonged to the LORD—the children's life, hands, and eyes—all belonged to the LORD (v.16). The parents and the children all belonged to the LORD because the LORD had delivered His people by His mighty hand out of Egypt.

Thought 1. The lesson for us is clearly illustrated. We are to teach our children three great lessons.
(1) God alone is the Great Deliverer; they must be redeemed by God's mighty hand through His Son, the Lord Jesus Christ.

"For all have sinned, and come short of the glory of God; Being justified freely by his grace through the redemption that is in Christ Jesus" (Ro.3:23-24).
"Christ hath redeemed us from the curse of the law, being made a curse for us: for it is written, Cursed is every one that hangeth on a tree" (Ga.3:13).
"Who hath delivered us from the power of darkness, and hath translated us into the kingdom of his dear Son: In whom we have redemption through his blood, even the forgiveness of sins" (Col.1:13-14).
"Who gave himself for us, that he might redeem us from all iniquity, and purify unto himself a peculiar people, zealous of good works" (Tit.2:14).
"Neither by the blood of goats and calves, but by his own blood he entered in once into the holy place, having obtained eternal redemption for us" (He.9:12).
"Forasmuch as ye know that ye were not redeemed with corruptible things, as silver and gold, from your vain conversation received by tradition from your fathers; But with the precious blood of Christ, as of a lamb without blemish and without spot" (1 Pe.1:18-19).

(2) God's judgment fell upon Egypt, and it is going to fall upon all unbelievers.

"When the Son of man shall come in his glory, and all the holy angels with him, then shall he sit upon the throne of his glory: And before him shall be gathered all nations: and he shall separate them one from another, as a shepherd divideth [his] sheep from the goats: And he shall set the sheep on his right hand, but the goats on the left....Then shall he say also unto them on the left hand, Depart from me, ye cursed, into everlasting fire, prepared for the devil and his angels" (Mt.25:31-33, 41).
"Because he hath appointed a day, in the which he will judge the world in righteousness by that man whom he hath ordained; whereof he hath given assurance unto all men, in that he hath raised him from the dead" (Ac.17:31).
"In the day when God shall judge the secrets of men by Jesus Christ according to my gospel" (Ro.2:16).
"And as it is appointed unto men once to die, but after this the judgment" (He.9:27).
"The Lord knoweth how to deliver the godly out of temptations, and to reserve the unjust unto the day of judgment to be punished" (2 Pe.2:9).
"And Enoch also, the seventh from Adam, prophesied of these, saying, Behold, the Lord cometh with ten thousands of his saints, To execute judgment upon all, and to convince all that are ungodly among them of all their ungodly deeds which they have ungodly committed, and of all their hard speeches which ungodly sinners have spoken against him" (Jude 14-15).
"And I saw a great white throne, and him that sat on it, from whose face the earth and the heaven fled away; and there was found no place for them. And I saw the dead, small and great, stand

---

[3] F.B. Huey, Jr. *Exodus*, p.62.

before God; and the books were opened: and another book was opened, which is the book of life: and the dead were judged out of those things which were written in the books, according to their works. And the sea gave up the dead which were in it; and death and hell delivered up the dead which were in them: and they were judged every man according to their works. And death and hell were cast into the lake of fire. This is the second death. And whosoever was not found written in the book of life was cast into the lake of fire" (Re.20:11-15).

(3) Our child belongs to God; we dedicated him or her to the LORD when they were born.

> "And he lifted up his eyes, and saw the women and the children; and said, Who are those with thee? And he said, The children which God hath graciously given thy servant" (Ge.33:5).
> "And Joseph said unto his father, They are my sons, whom God hath given me in this place. And he said, Bring them, I pray thee, unto me, and I will bless them" (Ge.48:9).
> "And I took your father Abraham from the other side of the flood, and led him throughout all the land of Canaan, and multiplied his seed, and gave him Isaac" (Jos.24:3).
> "He maketh the barren woman to keep house, and to be a joyful mother of children. Praise ye the LORD" (Ps.113:9).
> "Lo, children are an heritage of the LORD: and the fruit of the womb is his reward" (Ps.127:3).
> "Behold, I and the children whom the LORD hath given me are for signs and for wonders in Israel from the LORD of hosts, which dwelleth in mount Zion" (Is.8:18).

Thought 2. A question that has often concerned some people is perhaps answered here: What happens to small children who die and were too young to know right from wrong? J. Vernon McGee has this to say:

> The children of Israel were to put the blood of the lamb outside on the door. Upon seeing the blood, the death angel would pass over the house. I believe there is a picture given here that will answer a question that is asked many times: What will happen to the little children of believers at the time of the Rapture? If small children are in the house when the Lord comes for His own, will He take the Mom and Dad and leave the little ones behind? This chapter shows us that God will not leave the young ones behind.
> Inside the home the family is eating the lamb, and by faith they are partaking of Christ. The young children do not know what is taking place. Will they be left behind in Egypt when Israel goes out from the land? If a little one has not yet reached the age of accountability, will he be slain? Oh no, friend, the blood covers everyone in the family. God will not leave small children behind at the time of the Rapture any more than He left them behind when the Israelites were redeemed and left the land of Egypt.[4]

DEEPER STUDY # 1

(13:13) **Redeem—Redemption—Ransom**: in its most basic meaning, the word *redeem* (Hebrew, padah) means to buy back for a price, to ransom, to liberate. F.B. Huey says this:

> The word found in 13:13 for "redeem" (Hebrew, padah) always is used of persons and living beings in the Old Testament; it is a term from commercial law and emphasizes payment (the New Testament equivalent is agorazo, from a word meaning "to buy at the market place," Gal.3:13; Rev.5:9). In its secular usage redemption was the recovery by payment of something for its original owner that had been alienated from him. Sometimes instead of redeeming a son Israelite parents devoted their son to the Lord for service as priests, as in the case of Samuel (1 S.1:11, 22)."[5]

Two facts are important to note: God is the Sovereign LORD and Majesty of the universe. God, therefore, has the sovereign right to redeem (liberate) people.

1. Note how the word *redeem* (padah) is used in relation to individuals.
   ⇒ The Psalmist cried out for God to redeem him.

   > "But as for me, I will walk in mine integrity: redeem me, and be merciful unto me" (Ps.26:11).
   > "Arise for our help, and redeem us for thy mercies' sake" (Ps.44:26).

   ⇒ God redeemed the soul of the Psalmist.

   > "My lips shall greatly rejoice when I sing unto thee; and my soul, which thou hast redeemed" (Ps.71:23).

   ⇒ God redeemed David's soul from distress.

   > "And the king sware, and said, As the LORD liveth, that hath redeemed my soul out of all distress" (1 K.1:29).

---

4 J. Vernon McGee. *Thru the Bible*, Vol.1, p.237.
5 F.B. Huey, Jr. *Exodus*, p.62.

2. Note how the word *redeem* (padah) is used in relation to Israel.

⇒ The Psalmist cried out for God to redeem Israel.

"Redeem Israel, O God, out of all his troubles" (Ps.25:22).

⇒ The Psalmist declared that God shall redeem Israel from sin.

"And he shall redeem Israel from all his iniquities" (Ps.130:8).

⇒ God redeemed Israel to be His people and to glorify Himself through them.

"And what one nation in the earth is like thy people, even like Israel, whom God went to redeem for a people to himself, and to make him a name, and to do for you great things and terrible, for thy land, before thy people, which thou redeemedst to thee from Egypt, from the nations and their gods?" (2 S.7:23).

⇒ God charged Israel with transgression and with lying despite the fact that He had redeemed them.

"Woe unto them! for they have fled from me: destruction unto them! because they have transgressed against me: though I have redeemed them, yet they have spoken lies against me" (Ho.7:13).

TYPES, SYMBOLS, AND PICTURES
(Exodus 13:1-16)

Historical Term	Type or Picture (Scriptural Basis for Each)	Life Application for Today's Believer	Biblical Application
The Dedication of the Firstborn (Ex.13:2)	*Sanctification: Setting apart a life for God* **"Sanctify unto me all the firstborn, whatsoever openeth the womb among the children of Israel, *both* of man and of beast: it *is* mine" (Ex.13:2).**	God demands that we be sanctified (holy) completely and totally set apart to God. We must be constantly reminded... • that Jesus Christ is our sanctification (1 Co.1:30) • that Jesus Christ sanctifies us through His blood (He.13:12) • that we are chosen by God through the sanctifying work of the Holy Spirit (1 Pe.1:2) • that Jesus Christ gave Him-self for the church, that He might sanctify it (Ep.5:26) • that we are sanctified through the truth, through God's Word (Jn.17:17) • that we are to be sanctified [holy] vessels, fit for God to use (2 Ti.2:21) • that God's will is for us to live sanctified, pure, and holy lives (Lu. 1:74; 2 Co. 7:10; 1 Th.4:3)	*"But of him are ye in Christ Jesus, who of God is made unto us wisdom, and righteousness, and sanctification, and redemption" (1 Co.1:30).* *"Wherefore Jesus also, that he might sanctify the people with his own blood, suffered without the gate" (He.13:12).* *"Sanctify them through thy truth: thy word is truth" (Jn.17:17).* *"If a man therefore purge himself from these, he shall be a vessel unto honour, sanctified, and meet for the master's use, and prepared unto every good work" (2 Ti.2:21).* *"For this is the will of God, even your sanctification, that ye should abstain from fornication" (1 Th. 4:3).* *(see Pr.3:9-10; Mt.6:33; 1 Pe.1:2; Ep.5:26)*

DIVISION V

THE RED SEA AND THE WILDERNESS WANDERINGS: THE BELIEVER'S TRIALS AS HE JOURNEYS TO THE PROMISED LAND, 13:17–18:27

(13:17–18:27) **DIVISION OVERVIEW—Wilderness Wanderings—Israel—World, Described**: after centuries of shattered dreams, Israel was finally free. God had delivered Israel from Egypt and its enslavement, and now, the people were marching to the promised land. But lying between Egypt and the promised land of Canaan was a *vast wilderness*, a desert, a dreadful and fearful desert, a wilderness that was...

- dry
- parched
- waterless
- barren
- uncultivated
- unfruitful
- desolate
- empty
- uninhabited

The desert wilderness was a dangerous land with its wild, ferocious animals and venomous snakes and scorpions. Nevertheless, the Israelites had to march through the wilderness if they were to reach the promised land. The most direct route would have taken them several weeks at most to reach their destination. But, surprisingly, God did not lead Israel straight to the promised land. God kept Israel in the wilderness for *forty years—forty long years* (Nu.14:33; De.29:5). God led Israel to *wander* all throughout the desert wilderness, to meander and roam here and there and then back again. For *forty long years* God kept Israel in the wilderness wandering about. In fact, this period of Israel's history is known as *The Wilderness Wanderings*. Imagine! A journey that would take just a few short weeks took forty years, forty long, weary years (Nu.32:13).

Now, why did God keep the Israelites in the desert wilderness for *forty long years* before He led them into the promised land. Why did God lead His people in a meandering route before entering the promised land? There are several passages of Scripture that tell us, that clearly show why God led Israel through the *wilderness wanderings*.

A. THE PURPOSES FOR THE WILDERNESS WANDERINGS STATED BY THE OLD TESTAMENT

1. God led the Israelites through the *wilderness wanderings* to humble them: this God did by revealing the sinful nature of the human heart.

"And thou shalt remember all the way which the LORD thy God led thee these forty years in the wilderness, to humble thee" (De.8:2).

The wilderness wanderings reveal the true heart of man, the true nature of the human heart. The wilderness wanderings show that the human heart is...

- A heart that is hard and filled with unbelief.

   "(Harden not your hearts, as in the provocation, in the day of temptation in the wilderness: When your fathers tempted me, proved me, and saw my works forty years. Wherefore I was grieved with that generation, and said, They do alway err in their heart; and they have not known my ways. So I sware in my wrath, They shall not enter into my rest.) Take heed, brethren, lest there be in any of you an evil heart of unbelief, in departing from the living God. But exhort one another daily, while it is called To day; lest any of you be hardened through the deceitfulness of sin" (He.3:8-13).
   "But with whom was he grieved forty years? was it not with them that had sinned, whose carcases fell in the wilderness? And to whom sware he that they should not enter into his rest, but to them that believed not? So we see that they could not enter in because of unbelief" (He.3:17-19).
   "Let us labour therefore to enter into that rest, lest any man fall after the same example of unbelief" (He.4:11).

- A heart that disobeys God, willfully and knowingly disobeys Him.

   "And it came to pass, that there went out some of the people on the seventh day for to gather [manna], and they found none. And the LORD said unto Moses, How long refuse ye to keep my commandments and my laws [to keep the Sabbath holy]?" (Ex.16:27-28).

- A heart that murmurs, grumbles, and complains.

> "And the people murmured against Moses, saying, What shall we drink?" (Ex.15:24).
> "And the whole congregation of the children of Israel murmured against Moses and Aaron in the wilderness" (Ex.16:2).

- A heart that is always finding fault in others and blaming others.

> "Wherefore the people did chide with Moses, and said, Give us water that we may drink. And Moses said unto them, Why chide ye with me? wherefore do ye tempt the LORD?" (Ex.17:2).

- A heart that contends and argues with others.

> "When they have a matter, they come unto me; and I judge between one and another, and I do make them know the statutes of God, and his laws" (Ex.18:16).

2. God led the Israelites through the *wilderness wanderings* to test them, to see if they would obey God or not. The *wilderness wanderings* show us how disobedient we really are, how much we must pray and stay on our faces before God...
- that we must draw near and fellowship with Him, live and walk in His presence
- that we must learn to trust and depend upon Him

> "And thou shalt remember all the way which the LORD thy God led thee these forty years in the wilderness, to humble thee, and to prove thee, to know what was in thine heart, whether thou wouldest keep his commandments, or no" (De.8:2).
> "He found him in a desert land, and in the waste howling wilderness; he led him about, he instructed him, he kept him as the apple of his eye" (De.32:10).
> "Trust in the LORD with all thine heart; and lean not unto thine own understanding. In all thy ways acknowledge him, and he shall direct thy paths" (Pr.3:5-6).
> "Ye are my witnesses, saith the LORD, and my servant whom I have chosen: that ye may know and believe me, and understand that I am he: before me there was no God formed, neither shall there be after me" (Is.43:10).
> "Seek ye the LORD while he may be found, call ye upon him while he is near" (Is.55:6).

3. God led the Israelites through the *wilderness wanderings* to reveal that life is a *pilgrimage of faith*, that people needed to learn to trust God more and more. People need God—His love, grace, and strength—to reach the promised land. The believer could never reach the promised land by himself—through his own strength and efforts, no matter how strong or courageous. The believer could never overcome the lurking dangers nor find his way out of the vast unmarked terrain of the wilderness and reach the promised land, not all alone, not without God's help. To march through the desert wilderness the believer must learn that he needs God, and that his need is desperate. The believer needs...
- God's mercy and grace
- God's presence and love
- God's provision and supply
- God's power and deliverance

> "And thou shalt remember all the way which the LORD thy God led thee these forty years in the wilderness....And he humbled thee, and suffered thee to hunger, and fed thee with manna, which thou knewest not, neither did thy fathers know....Thy raiment waxed not old upon thee, neither did thy foot swell, these forty years" (De.8:2, 3, 4).
> "He found him in a desert land, and in the waste howling wilderness; he led him about, he instructed him, he kept him as the apple of his eye" (De.32:10).
> "Cease ye from man, whose breath is in his nostrils: for wherein is he to be accounted of?" (Is.2:22).
> "Thus saith the LORD; Cursed be the man that trusteth in man, and maketh flesh his arm, and whose heart departeth from the LORD" (Je.17:5).
> "But seek ye first the kingdom of God, and his righteousness; and all these things shall be added unto you" (Mt.6:33).
> "For by grace are ye saved through faith; and that not of yourselves: it is the gift of God: Not of works, lest any man should boast" (Ep.2:8-9).

4. God led the Israelites through the *wilderness wanderings* to reveal that man does not live by bread alone, but by every word that proceeds out of the mouth of God. The *wilderness wanderings* show us...
- that man is not satisfied nor fulfilled with physical things alone; spiritual things are also needed, especially the Word of God
- that man cannot walk through life trusting the words of men to carry him through the wilderness of life. He has to walk trusting the Word of God to conquer the wilderness and to reach the promised land

> "And thou shalt remember all the way which the LORD thy God led thee these forty years in the wilderness....And he humbled thee, and suffered thee to hunger, and fed thee with manna, which thou

knewest not, neither did thy fathers know; that he might make thee know that man doth not live by bread only, but by every word that proceedeth out of the mouth of the LORD doth man live" (De.8:2, 3).

"And now, brethren, I commend you to God, and to the word of his grace, which is able to build you up, and to give you an inheritance among all them which are sanctified" (Ac.20:32).

"All scripture is given by inspiration of God, and is profitable for doctrine, for reproof, for correction, for instruction in righteousness" (2 Ti.3:16).

5. God led the Israelites through the *wilderness wanderings* to teach them to fear God, to fear His chastening hand so much that they would obey Him. As Israel walked through the wilderness, they saw God chastening and correcting the persons who did their own thing and disobeyed God. Throughout life we often witness the chastening hand of God. By this, we learn to fear God. We learn that He loves us and because He loves us, He will correct us. The point is this: God will chasten us if we disobey Him. Hence, His chastening hand stirs us to fear and obey Him.

"And thou shalt remember all the way which the LORD thy God led thee these forty years in the wilderness....Thou shalt also consider in thine heart, that, as a man chasteneth his son, so the LORD thy God chasteneth thee. Therefore thou shalt keep the commandments of the LORD thy God, to walk in his ways, and to fear him" (De.8:2, 5-6).

"Blessed is the man whom thou chastenest, O LORD, and teachest him out of thy law" (Ps.94:12).

"My son, despise not the chastening of the LORD; neither be weary of his correction: For whom the LORD loveth he correcteth; even as a father the son in whom he delighteth" (Pr.3:11-12).

"Every branch in me that beareth not fruit he taketh away: and every [branch] that beareth fruit, he purgeth it, that it may bring forth more fruit" (Jn.15:2).

"And ye have forgotten the exhortation which speaketh unto you as unto children, My son, despise not thou the chastening of the Lord, nor faint when thou art rebuked of him: For whom the Lord loveth he chasteneth, and scourgeth every son whom he receiveth. If ye endure chastening, God dealeth with you as with sons; for what son is he whom the father chasteneth not?" (He.12:5-7).

6. God led the Israelites through the *wilderness wanderings* to teach them to praise the LORD, to bless Him for His abundant provision and supply and for the glorious promise of the promised land.

"And thou shalt remember all the way which the LORD thy God led thee these forty years in the wilderness....For the LORD thy God bringeth thee into a good land, a land of brooks of water, of fountains and depths that spring out of valleys and hills; A land of wheat, and barley, and vines, and fig trees, and pomegranates; a land of oil olive, and honey; A land wherein thou shalt eat bread without scarceness, thou shalt not lack any thing in it; a land whose stones are iron, and out of whose hills thou mayest dig brass. When thou hast eaten and art full, then thou shalt bless the LORD thy God for the good land which he hath given thee" (De.8:2, 7-10).

"But as it is written, Eye hath not seen, nor ear heard, neither have entered into the heart of man, the things which God hath prepared for them that love him" (1 Co.2:9).

"But the day of the Lord will come as a thief in the night; in the which the heavens shall pass away with a great noise, and the elements shall melt with fervent heat, the earth also and the works that are therein shall be burned up. Seeing then that all these things shall be dissolved, what manner of persons ought ye to be in all holy conversation and godliness, Looking for and hasting unto the coming of the day of God, wherein the heavens being on fire shall be dissolved, and the elements shall melt with fervent heat? Nevertheless we, according to his promise, look for new heavens and a new earth, wherein dwelleth righteousness" (2 Pe.3:10-13).

"And I saw a new heaven and a new earth: for the first heaven and the first earth were passed away; and there was no more sea. And I John saw the holy city, new Jerusalem, coming down from God out of heaven, prepared as a bride adorned for her husband. And I heard a great voice out of heaven saying, Behold, the tabernacle of God is with men, and he will dwell with them, and they shall be his people, and God himself shall be with them, and be their God. And God shall wipe away all tears from their eyes; and there shall be no more death, neither sorrow, nor crying, neither shall there be any more pain: for the former things are passed away" (Re.21:1-4).

"And he showed me a pure river of water of life, clear as crystal, proceeding out of the throne of God and of the Lamb. In the midst of the street of it, and on either side of the river, was there the tree of life, which bare twelve manner of fruits, and yielded her fruit every month [an abundance of harvest and food]: and the leaves of the tree were for the healing of the nations. And there shall be no more curse: but the throne of God and of the Lamb shall be in it; and his servants shall serve him: And they shall see his face; and his name shall be in their foreheads. And there shall be no night there; and they need no candle, neither light of the sun; for the Lord God giveth them light: and they shall reign for ever and ever" (Re.22:1-5).

7. God led the Israelites through the *wilderness wanderings* because of their sin. The *wilderness wanderings* were the judgment of God upon the people because of their unbelief and sins.

"And the LORD spake unto Moses and unto Aaron, saying, How long shall I bear with this evil congregation, which murmur against me? I have heard the murmurings of the children of Israel, which they murmur against me. Say unto them, As truly as I live, saith the LORD, as ye have spoken in mine ears, so will I do to you: Your carcases shall fall in this wilderness; and all that were numbered of you, according to your whole number, from twenty years old and upward, which have murmured against me, Doubtless ye shall not come into the land, concerning which I sware to make you dwell therein, save Caleb the son of Jephunneh, and Joshua the son of Nun. But your little ones, which ye said should be a prey, them will I bring in, and they shall know the land which ye have despised. But as for you, your carcases, they shall fall in this wilderness. And your children shall wander in the wilderness forty years, and bear your whoredoms, until your carcases be wasted in the wilderness. After the number of the days in which ye searched the land, even forty days, each day for a year, shall ye bear your iniquities, even forty years, and ye shall know my breach of promise. I the LORD have said, I will surely do it unto all this evil congregation, that are gathered together against me: in this wilderness they shall be consumed, and there they shall die" (Nu.14:26-35).

"And the LORD'S anger was kindled against Israel, and he made them wander in the wilderness forty years, until all the generation, that had done evil in the sight of the LORD, was consumed" (Nu.32:13).

"Harden not your hearts, as in the provocation, in the day of temptation in the wilderness: When your fathers tempted me, proved me, and saw my works forty years. Wherefore I was grieved with that generation, and said, They do alway err in their heart; and they have not known my ways. So I sware in my wrath, They shall not enter into my rest.) Take heed, brethren, lest there be in any of you an evil heart of unbelief, in departing from the living God" (He.3:8-12).

"While it is said, To day if ye will hear his voice, harden not your hearts, as in the provocation. For some, when they had heard, did provoke: howbeit not all that came out of Egypt by Moses. But with whom was he grieved forty years? was it not with them that had sinned, whose carcases fell in the wilderness? And to whom sware he that they should not enter into his rest, but to them that believed not? So we see that they could not enter in because of unbelief" (He.3:15-19).

B. THE PURPOSES FOR THE WILDERNESS WANDERINGS STATED BY THE NEW TESTAMENT

1. The wilderness wanderings were appointed by God to be an example for us, a warning to keep us from setting our hearts on evil things as the Israelites did.

"Moreover, brethren, I would not that ye should be ignorant, how that all our fathers were under the cloud, and all passed through the sea; And were all baptized unto Moses in the cloud and in the sea; And did all eat the same spiritual meat; And did all drink the same spiritual drink: for they drank of that spiritual Rock that followed them: and that Rock was Christ. But with many of them God was not well pleased: for they were overthrown in the wilderness. Now these things were our examples, to the intent we should not lust after evil things, as they also lusted. Neither be ye idolaters, as were some of them; as it is written, The people sat down to eat and drink, and rose up to play. Neither let us commit fornication, as some of them committed, and fell in one day three and twenty thousand. Neither let us tempt Christ, as some of them also tempted, and were destroyed of serpents. Neither murmur ye, as some of them also murmured, and were destroyed of the destroyer. Now all these things happened unto them for examples: and they are written for our admonition, upon whom the ends of the world are come. Wherefore let him that thinketh he standeth take heed lest he fall" (1 Co.10:1-12; see outlines and notes—1 Co.10:1-13 for more discussion).

2. The wilderness wanderings were appointed by God to be written down in Scripture, recorded to teach us how to walk through the wilderness of this world, through all the trials, problems, and sufferings of life. We are to walk in hope, the hope of Christ and of the promised land...
   * walk enduring all the trials of life
   * walk gaining comfort and encouragement from the Scriptures (from the lessons learned from the experiences of Israel)

"For whatsoever things were written aforetime were written for our learning, that we through patience and comfort of the scriptures might have hope" (Ro.15:4).

Israel's journey—the *wilderness wanderings*—was neither easy nor appreciated. It took a supreme act of God's power to pry open Pharaoh's grip on the Israelites, but it took the simple act of unbelief for Israel to squander their newfound freedom. The *promised land* was theirs to reach and enjoy, but the journey exposed the hardness and unbelief of their hearts. Their hardness and unbelief brought the judgment of God down upon them, and they were never allowed to enter the promised land of God (Nu.14:30; see Nu.26:65; 32:11; 32:13; De.1:35-36; Jos.5:6; Ps.95:10-11; Eze.20:15-16; He.3:18-19; 4:6).
   ⇒ Their hearts should have been filled with gratitude for God's great goodness. Instead the trials of the *wilderness wanderings* reflected what was really lying within each person's heart, a spirit of unbelief.
   ⇒ Their hearts should have marched in victory, marched with a spirit of assurance, knowing that God would guide and take care of them. Instead they wandered about filled with a spirit of murmuring, grumbling, and complaining.
   ⇒ Their hearts should have been filled with a spirit of fear, reverence, and worship because of God's great power demonstrated in the terrifying plagues cast upon Egypt. Instead they were filled with a spirit of idolatry and sexual immorality (Ex.32:1-6; 1 Co.10:1-12).

Indeed, Israel's experience was a tragic experience. But it will be an even greater tragedy if we do not learn from Israel's failure in the *wilderness wanderings*. As we walk through the wilderness of this world, we must do as Scripture says above: learn from Israel's story. This is the fascinating study of this division of Scripture: THE RED SEA AND THE WILDERNESS WANDERINGS: THE BELIEVER'S TRIALS AS HE JOURNEYS TO THE PROMISED LAND, 13:17-18:27.

DIVISION V

THE RED SEA AND THE WILDERNESS WANDERINGS: THE BELIEVER'S TRIALS AS HE JOURNEYS TO THE PROMISED LAND, 13:17–18:27

A. Beginning the Wilderness Journey: God's Guidance by Day and by Night, 13:17-22

B. The First Crisis of Israel in the Wilderness: Crossing the Red Sea: God's Great Deliverance, 14:1-31

C. Moses' Great Song of Praise: Praising God for His Great Deliverance, 15:1-21

D. The Second Crisis of Israel in the Wilderness—Bitter Water at Marah: Bitter Experiences Made Sweet and Pure, 15:22-27

E. The Third Crisis of Israel in the Wilderness—Hunger: The Two Great Sins of Israel, That of Grumbling and Disobedience (Unbelief), 16:1-36

F. The Fourth Crisis of Israel in the Wilderness—Thirst: God's Provision of Water, 17:1-7

G. The Fifth Crisis of Israel in the Wilderness—Warfare: Victory Through Prevailing Prayer, 17:8-16

H. The Sixth Crisis of Israel in the Wilderness—Marital Separation and Overwork: Helping Others, 18:1-27

	V. THE RED SEA & THE WILDERNESS WANDERINGS: THE BELIEVER'S TRIALS AS HE JOURNEYS TO THE PROMISED LAND, 13:17–18:27	wilderness of the Red sea: and the children of Israel went up harnessed out of the land of Egypt.	c. God led His people in an orderly fashion: Marching in military rank & file
		19 And Moses took the bones of Joseph with him: for he had straitly sworn the children of Israel, saying, God will surely visit you; and ye shall carry up my bones away hence with you.	**2. God led His people to focus upon great faith: They honored the great faith of Joseph, his faith in the promised land—demonstrated in his wish to be buried there**
	A. Beginning the Wilderness Journey: God's Guidance by Day & by Night, 13:17-22	20 And they took their journey from Succoth, and encamped in Etham, in the edge of the wilderness.	**3. God led His people by His very own presence—every step of the way**
1. God led His people away from trouble	17 And it came to pass, when Pharaoh had let the people go, that God led them not through the way of the land of the Philistines, although that was near; for God said, Lest peradventure the people repent when they see war, and they return to Egypt:	21 And the LORD went before them by day in a pillar of a cloud, to lead them the way; and by night in a pillar of fire, to give them light; to go by day and night:	a. Led from Succoth to Etham[DS1,2]
a. God knew two significant facts			b. Used the pillar of cloud & fire
1) The shortest route went through the land of enemies, the Philistines			1) The pillar of cloud by day
2) His people were not strong enough to fight			2) The pillar of fire by night
b. God led His people toward the Red Sea	18 But God led the people about, through the way of the	22 He took not away the pillar of the cloud by day, nor the pillar of fire by night, from before the people.	c. Led His people faithfully: Neither pillar ever left its place in guiding the people

DIVISION V

THE RED SEA AND THE WILDERNESS WANDERINGS: THE BELIEVER'S TRIALS AS HE JOURNEYS TO THE PROMISED LAND, 13:17–18:27

A. Beginning the Wilderness Journey: God's Guidance by Day and by Night, 13:17-22

(13:17-22) **Introduction**: God leads His dear people. God leads us day by day and night by night. Throughout life we face problems and difficulties, trials and temptations that are ever so...

• rough	• stressful	• back-breaking
• hard	• discouraging	• crumbling
• trying	• disappointing	• unchangeable
• pressuring	• defeating	• hopeless

There just seems to be no way out, no solution, no way to conquer, triumph, or overcome. But this is not true: it is a defeating lie. God cares for us and God will lead us out of the problem. God will give us the way and the strength to overcome and conquer no matter what the difficulty may be. God will guide us by day and by night—every day and every night—if we will only follow Him. This is the great lesson to be learned from the very beginning of Israel's wilderness wanderings. This is: *Beginning the Wilderness Journey: God's Guidance by Day and by Night,* 13:17-22.

1. God led His people away from trouble (vv.17-18).
2. God led His people to focus upon great faith: they honored the great faith of Joseph in the promised land—demonstrated in his wish to be buried there (v.19).
3. God led His people by His very own presence—every step of the way (vv.20-22).

1 (13:17-18) **Guidance—Problems—Difficulties**: God led His people away from trouble. He was their Scout, their Pioneer, their Guide, their Leader.
a. God knew two significant facts.
1) The shortest route to the promised land went up along the coast of the Mediterranean Sea right through the land of the Philistines. The Philistines were to become aggressive, bitter enemies of God's people. God knew that the Philistines would feel threatened by two or three million people marching through their land, that they would attack His people.
2) God's people were just not strong enough to fight. Moreover, they had few if any weapons with which to fight. They had been reared as slaves, not warriors. They had no military training whatsoever. They had the spirit of slaves—broken, slavish spirits—not the spirit of soldiers. God knew exactly what His people needed:
⇒ They needed to be forever freed of fearing the Egyptians; therefore, God was planning to destroy the Egyptian army in the Red Sea
⇒ They needed to be hardened and toughened by living in the wilderness for several decades before facing the enemies who would stand against their entering the promised land
⇒ They needed to be humbled and proven, to see exactly what was in their hearts, whether or not they would keep God's commandments

"And thou shalt remember all the way which the LORD thy God led thee these forty years in the wilderness, to humble thee, and to prove thee, to know what was in thine heart, whether thou wouldest keep his commandments, or no" (De.8:2).

⇒ They needed to worship and serve God at Mt. Sinai, the mountain of God.

"And he said, Certainly I will be with thee; and this shall be a token [sign] unto thee, that I have sent thee: When thou hast brought forth the people out of Egypt, ye shall serve God upon this mountain" (Ex.3:12).

⇒ They needed to be given the laws of God and molded into a strong nation of people before entering the promised land (Ex.20:1f).
⇒ They needed to travel all about throughout the wilderness—hundreds of miles—in order to learn to trust God before they could inherit the promised land, to trust God as their...
  • Savior   • Provider
  • Guide   • Protector
  • Source   • Hope

"He found him [Israel] in a desert land, and in the waste howling wilderness; he led him about, he instructed him, he kept him as the apple of his eye" (De.32:10).
"And he led them [Israel] forth by the right way, that they might go to a city of habitation" (Ps.107:7).
"These all died in faith, not having received the promises, but having seen them afar off, and were persuaded of them, and embraced them, and confessed that they were strangers and pilgrims on the earth. For they that say such things declare plainly that they seek a country. And truly, if they had been mindful of that country from whence they came out, they might have had opportunity to have returned. But now they desire a better country, that is, an heavenly: wherefore God is not ashamed to be called their God: for he hath prepared for them a city" (He.11:13-16).

b. God led His people toward the Red Sea. What we commonly call the Red Sea is better translated the Sea of Reeds (yam-suph). The Sea of Reeds or *yam-suph* was most likely what we know as the Red Sea. But this is disputable. Many Bible-believing commentators feel that the Red Sea is too far south to fit the description in Exodus 14:2. Whatever our own personal conclusion, the Red Sea of that day would not include the extension of the sea, not include the Gulf of Suez that has been constructed by man. (See DEEPER STUDY # 4—Ex.14:16-18 for more discussion.)

c. God led His people in an orderly fashion. That is, they marched in some form of military rank and file (v.18). The Israelites knew that the Egyptians could change their minds and begin to pursue them at any moment. If they had marched forth like a mob in a disorderly fashion, they would have no sense of strength, no sense that they could protect themselves despite their enormous numbers. Order and organization always encourages people, especially when there is the possibility of trouble. Thus God encouraged the people by having Moses organize them into divisions, divisions of some military rank and file. Like a mighty army, they marched forth toward the promised land. The sight of two plus million people marching in military file must have been an awesome sight, a sight that stirred and excited the hearts of God's people beyond expression. The electrifying sense of confidence, strength, and power must have surged through their bodies, just because of the shear fact that they formed such an enormous army of people.

Thought 1. God knows how to lead us away from trouble. He knows our weaknesses, both psychologically and physically. He knows exactly how much we can bear. God will always lead us...
  • to the right people
  • to the right place
  • to do the right thing
  • to know what to do

God will always lead and guide us. Our task is simply to seek and follow Him.

"Lead me, O LORD, in thy righteousness because of mine enemies; make thy way straight before my face" (Ps.5:8).
"Teach me thy way, O LORD, and lead me in a plain path, because of mine enemies" (Ps.27:11).
"For this God is our God for ever and ever: he will be our guide even unto death" (Ps.48:14).
"Give us help from trouble: for vain is the help of man. Through God we shall do valiantly: for he it is that shall tread down our enemies" (Ps.60:11-12).
"Thou leddest thy people like a flock by the hand of Moses and Aaron" (Ps.77:20).
"If I take the wings of the morning, and dwell in the uttermost parts of the sea; Even there shall thy hand lead me, and thy right hand shall hold me" (Ps.139:9-10).
"And thine ears shall hear a word behind thee, saying, This is the way, walk ye in it, when ye turn to the right hand, and when ye turn to the left" (Is.30:21).
"Fear thou not; for I am with thee: be not dismayed; for I am thy God: I will strengthen thee; yea, I will help thee; yea, I will uphold thee with the right hand of my righteousness" (Is.41:10).
"Howbeit when he, the Spirit of truth, is come, he will guide you into all truth: for he shall not speak of himself; but whatsoever he shall hear, [that] shall he speak: and he will show you things to come" (Jn.16:13).

"There hath no temptation taken you but such as is common to man: but God is faithful, who will not suffer you to be tempted above that ye are able; but will with the temptation also make a way to escape, that ye may be able to bear it" (1 Co.10:13).

Thought 2. The world is like a wilderness, a wilderness through which we must struggle in order to survive. The church has been placed in the world to show us how to survive in the wilderness. As we journey through the wilderness of this world, we must stand together, stand in one spirit, stand in unity. A strong show of unity will protect us and keep our enemies at bay, enemies like:
⇒ Satan

"And I say also unto thee, That thou art Peter, and upon this rock I will build my church; and the gates of hell shall not prevail against it" (Mt.16:18).
"Submit yourselves therefore to God. Resist the devil, and he will flee from you" (Js.4:7).
"Be sober, be vigilant; because your adversary the devil, as a roaring lion, walketh about, seeking whom he may devour: Whom resist stedfast in the faith, knowing that the same afflictions are accomplished in your brethren that are in the world" (1 Pe.5:8-9).

⇒ fear

"For God hath not given us the spirit of fear; but of power, and of love, and of a sound mind" (2 Ti.1:7).

⇒ condemnation

"There is therefore now no condemnation to them which are in Christ Jesus, who walk not after the flesh, but after the Spirit" (Ro.8:1).

⇒ the world

"For whatsoever is born of God overcometh the world: and this is the victory that overcometh the world, even our faith" (1 Jn.5:4).

2 (13:19) **Faith—Guidance—Joseph—Promised Land**: God led His people to focus upon great faith. This is seen in the honor they paid to the great faith of Joseph, his great faith in the promised land. Note that some person in Israel had kept the bones of Joseph for over 400 years. God's people now fulfilled the wish of Joseph to be buried in the promised land: they took his bones with them as they began their great march to the promised land of God.

The point to note is this: Joseph believed God. He believed the great promises of God, the promises that God had given to Abraham and Isaac and to Jacob who was Joseph's father. What were the promises that Joseph believed? They are found in what we call the Abrahamic Covenant.
⇒ There was the promise of the promised seed, including both the seed of a great nation of people and the seed of the Savior, the Lord Jesus Christ. (See DEEPER STUDY # 2—Ex.1:6-7; outline and notes—Ge.12:2-3; Ge.12:3.)
⇒ There was the promise of the promised land, including both the land of Canaan and the eternal land of heaven. (See DEEPER STUDY # 1—Ex.2:24; outline and notes—Ge.12:1.)

Now note this fact: Israel believed the promises of God, the promises of the Abrahamic Covenant. How do we know this? Note what they did: they carried the bones of Joseph with them as they began their march to the promised land. Why did they carry his bones? Because they believed God. They believed—hoped, expected—that God was going to lead them to the promised land and then give the land to them. They believed in the hope of the promised land: in the peace, rest, security, and provision that they would find there. Within their hearts, God's people knew that God was going to lead them to the promised land. Therefore, they set out to fulfill the wish and hope of Joseph, to take his bones to the *promised land of God*.

Thought 1. Today, we know that the promise of the promised seed is true: the Lord Jesus Christ, the Savior of the world, has already come to save us. Moreover, there has been a great nation of people born of Abraham's seed, the nation of Israel and a great body of believers from both Israel and all the other nations of the earth.

We can rest assured of this one fact: the promise of the promised land is also true. God is leading and will continue to lead all believers to the promised land of heaven.

"But the day of the Lord will come as a thief in the night; in the which the heavens shall pass away with a great noise, and the elements shall melt with fervent heat, the earth also and the works that are therein shall be burned up. Seeing then that all these things shall be dissolved, what manner of persons ought ye to be in all holy conversation and godliness. Looking for and hasting unto the coming of the day of God, wherein the heavens being on fire shall be dissolved, and the elements shall melt with fervent heat? Nevertheless we, according to his promise, look for new heavens and a new earth, wherein dwelleth righteousness" (2 Pe.3:10-13).
"And I saw a new heaven and a new earth: for the first heaven and the first earth were passed away; and there was no more sea. And I John saw the holy city, new Jerusalem [the capital of the new universe], coming down from God out of heaven, prepared as a bride adorned for her husband. And I

269

heard a great voice out of heaven saying, Behold, the tabernacle of God is with men, and he will dwell with them, and they shall be his people, and God himself shall be with them, and be their God. And God shall wipe away all tears from their eyes; and there shall be no more death, neither sorrow, nor crying, neither shall there be any more pain: for the former things are passed away" (Re.21:1-4).

"Of old hast thou laid the foundation of the earth: and the heavens are the work of thy hands. They shall perish, but thou shalt endure: yea, all of them shall wax old like a garment; as a vesture shalt thou change them, and they shall be changed: but thou art the same, and thy years shall have no end" (Ps.102:25-27).

"And all the host of heaven shall be dissolved, and the heavens shall be rolled together as a scroll: and all their host shall fall down, as the leaf falleth off from the vine, and as a falling fig from the fig tree" (Is.34:4).

"Lift up your eyes to the heavens, and look upon the earth beneath: for the heavens shall vanish away like smoke, and the earth shall wax old like a garment, and they that dwell therein shall die in like manner: but my salvation shall be for ever, and my righteousness shall not be abolished" (Is.51:6).

"For, behold, I create new heavens and a new earth: and the former shall not be remembered, nor come into mind" (Is.65:17).

"For as the new heavens and the new earth, which I will make, shall remain before me, saith the LORD, so shall your seed and your name remain" (Is.66:22).

"By faith Abraham, when he was called to go out into a place which he should after receive for an inheritance, obeyed; and he went out, not knowing whither he went. By faith he sojourned in the land of promise, as in a strange country, dwelling in tabernacles with Isaac and Jacob, the heirs with him of the same promise: for he looked for a city which hath foundations, whose builder and maker is God....These all died in faith, not having received the promises, but having seen them afar off, and were persuaded of them, and embraced them, and confessed that they were strangers and pilgrims on the earth. For they that say such things declare plainly that they seek a country. And truly, if they had been mindful of that country from whence they came out, they might have had opportunity to have returned. But now they desire a better country, that is, an heavenly: wherefore God is not ashamed to be called their God: for he hath prepared for them a city" (He.11:8-10, 13-16).

"But ye are come unto mount Sion, and unto the city of the living God, the heavenly Jerusalem, and to an innumerable company of angels" (He.12:22).

"For here have we no continuing city [a perfect heavenly city], but we seek one to come" (He.13:14).

"And I John saw the holy city, new Jerusalem, coming down from God out of heaven, prepared as a bride adorned for her husband. And I heard a great voice out of heaven, saying, Behold, the tabernacle of God is with men, and he will dwell with them, and they shall be his people, and God himself shall be with them, and be their God. And God shall wipe away all tears from their eyes; and there shall be no more death, neither sorrow, nor crying, neither shall there be any more pain: for the former things are passed away" (Re.21:2-4).

"And he carried me away in the spirit to a great and high mountain, and showed me that great city, the holy Jerusalem, descending out of heaven from God" (Re.21:10).

3 (13:20-22) **Guidance—Pillar of Cloud and Fire—Cloud—Faithfulness, of God**: God led His people by His very own presence, every step of the way.

a. God led His people to move from Succoth to Etham, to camp over on the very edge of the desert (v.20). (See DEEPER STUDY #1,2—Ex.13:20.) This was another detour leading south, away from the promised land. Why? Because of the Egyptian fortifications on the edge of the Desert of Shur.

These forts protected Egypt from invaders, and they obviously posed a threat to the Israelites. The Israelites appeared to be sitting ducks for Pharaoh's vengeance. They seemed to be surrounded...
• by a hostile and onrushing Egyptian army
• by an uncrossable Red Sea
• by an unknown and dangerous wilderness

But God had a plan, a plan for a glorious escape when all hope seemed to be lost. The *great escape* being planned by God was beginning to unfold.

"I waited patiently for the LORD; and he inclined unto me, and heard my cry. He brought me up also out of an horrible pit, out of the miry clay, and set my feet upon a rock, and established my goings" (Ps.40:1-2).

"God is our refuge and strength, a very present help in trouble" (Ps.46:1).

"Be still, and know that I am God: I will be exalted among the heathen, I will be exalted in the earth" (Ps.46:10).

"Come and see the works of God: he is terrible in his doing toward the children of men. He turned the sea into dry land: they went through the flood on foot: there did we rejoice in him" (Ps.66:5-6).

"Surely he shall deliver thee from the snare of the fowler, and from the noisome pestilence" (Ps.91:3).

"I wait for the LORD, my soul doth wait, and in his word do I hope. My soul waiteth for the Lord more than they that watch for the morning: I say, more than they that watch for the morning. Let

Israel hope in the LORD: for with the LORD there is mercy, and with him is plenteous redemption" (Ps.130:5-7).

"And he said, The LORD is my rock, and my fortress, and my deliverer" (2 S.22:2).

"Be not afraid of their faces: for I am with thee to deliver thee, saith the LORD" (Je.1:8).

"He delivereth and rescueth, and he worketh signs and wonders in heaven and in earth, who hath delivered Daniel from the power of the lions" (Da.6:27).

b. Note how God led His people. He used a pillar of cloud to guide them by day, a cloud that became a cloud of fire at night. The cloud is actually called "the pillar of cloud by day and the pillar of fire by night" (vv.21-22). What was this pillar of cloud and pillar of fire?

The Expositor's Bible Commentary says this:

This single "pillar" (14:24), which was a cloud by day and a fire by night, whose width at the base was sufficiently large to provide cover for Israel from the intense heat (Ps.105:39), was a visible symbol of the presence of Yahweh in their midst.
   - *The pillar of the cloud and fire was but another name for "the angel of God"...Exodus 14:19 equates the two as does 23:20-23.*
   - *God's Name was "in" this angel who went before them to bring them into Canaan (23:20-23).*
   - *He was the "angel of his presence" (Isa.63:8-9).*
   - *Malachi 3:1 calls this angel the "messenger of the covenant," who is equated with the Lord, the owner of the temple.*

Obviously, then the Christ of the NT is the shekinah glory or Yahweh of the OT. Through this cloudy pillar the Lord would speak to Moses (33:9-11) and to the people (Ps.99:6-7). Such easy movement from the pillar of cloud and fire to the angel and back to the Lord himself has already been met in the same interchange between the burning bush, the angel, and the Lord in chapter 3.[1]

The Compact Bible Dictionary says this:

God guided Israel out of Egypt and through the wilderness by a pillar of cloud by day. This became a pillar of fire by night that they might travel by night in escaping from the Egyptian army (Exod.13:21-22). When the Egyptians overtook the Israelites, the angel of the Lord removed this cloudy, fiery pillar from before them and placed it behind them as an effective camouflage (Exod.14:19, 20, 24).
   ⇒ *The pillar of cloud stood over the tent of meeting outside the camp, whenever the Lord met Moses there (Exod.33:7-11).*
   ⇒ *The Lord came down for judgment in the cloud (Nu.12).*

No natural phenomenon and fire fits the Biblical description: the cloud and fire were divine manifestations, in a form sufficiently well-defined to be called a pillar."[2]

It is probably best to picture the cloud as being just what Scripture says, a cloud. It would seem that the LORD caused a cloud to form above the children of Israel, a cloud that remained during their forty year wilderness wanderings.
   ⇒ The cloud protected the people from the heat of the sun when needed (Ex.13:21-22).
   ⇒ The cloud became a cloud of fire by night providing light for the people when needed (Ex.13:21).
   ⇒ There was only one pillar, not two, one "pillar of fire and cloud" (Ex.14:24).
   ⇒ The cloud could not be driven away by the wind (Ne.9:19; Ps.78:14).
   ⇒ The LORD Himself was in the cloud. The cloud was the visible symbol of God's presence among His people (Ex.13:21; 14:24).
   ⇒ The LORD often spoke to the people from the cloud (Nu.12:5-6; De.31:15-16; Ps.99:6-7).
   ⇒ Israel often remembered the cloud (Ps.78:14; 105:39).

Note one other fact: the pillar of cloud and fire was a symbol, a picture of baptism. The New Testament says that the Israelites were baptized into Moses in the cloud. How? By placing themselves under the guidance and command of the cloud. The cloud was given by God to show Moses where to lead the Israelites. Therefore, when they followed the cloud, they were placing themselves under the guidance and command of Moses. They were identifying themselves—proclaiming themselves—to be followers of God and of His appointed leader, Moses.

"Moreover, brethren, I would not that ye should be ignorant, how that all our fathers were under the cloud, and all passed through the sea; And were all baptized unto Moses in the cloud and in the sea" (1 Co.10:1-2).

c. God led His people faithfully: neither the pillar of cloud by day nor the pillar of fire by night ever left its place in guiding the people of God (v.22). Remember the wilderness or desert was a wasted, barren, desolate, hot, and dry place. There were no roads, no signs, and no guides to lead God's people over the desert. Most likely, none of the people had

---

[1] Frank E. Gaebelein, Editor. *The Expositor's Bible Commentary*, Vol.2, p.385. (The quote has been outlined by us for clarity.)
[2] Alton T. Bryant, Editor. *The Compact Bible Dictionary* (Grand Rapids, MI: Zondervan Publishing House, 1967), p.461. (The quote has been outlined by us for clarity.)

ever been across the desert. They were on their own, left totally to themselves but for one Person: God Himself. How faithful was God? His presence never left them, not for a moment. The pillar of cloud and of fire never left its place, never. God led His dear people every step of their journey as they marched to the promised land.

Thought 1. We who have believed—truly believed in Christ—are marching to the promised land of heaven. As we march, we can rest assured of this one great fact: God leads us by His very own presence, and He will never leave us. No matter what problems arise and no matter how severe the circumstances may be, God will guide us every step of the way. He will never forsake us.

"And, behold, I am with thee, and will keep thee in all places whither thou goest, and will bring thee again into this land; for I will not leave thee, until I have done that which I have spoken to thee of" (Ge.28:15).

"And he said, My presence shall go with thee, and I will give thee rest" (Ex.33:14).

"Thou shalt guide me with thy counsel, and afterward receive me to glory" (Ps.73:24).

"When thou passest through the waters, I will be with thee; and through the rivers, they shall not overflow thee: when thou walkest through the fire, thou shalt not be burned; neither shall the flame kindle upon thee" (Is.43:2).

"Lo, I am with you alway, [even] unto the end of the world" (Mt.28:20).

DEEPER STUDY # 1

(13:20) **Succoth—Cities**: this was an Egyptian city. Note these facts:
- ⇒ Succoth was Israel's first stop when they left Egypt (see Ex.12:37; 13:20; and Nu.33:5-6).
- ⇒ The Hebrew meaning for Succoth is *booths*.
- ⇒ Succoth is likely the site of the modern day Egyptian City Tel el-Maskhutah, a border city in the eastern section of the biblical land of Goshen, west of the bitter lakes.[3]
- ⇒ The same name was also given to a city in Canaan during the time of Jacob (see Ge.33:17).

DEEPER STUDY # 2

(13:20) **Etham—Cities**: this was an Egyptian city that probably served as a fort to protect the border of Egypt. Note:
- ⇒ This is the location where Israel camped after leaving the city of Succoth.
- ⇒ Etham was located on the edge of the wilderness of Shur.
- ⇒ The probable Hebrew meaning of the word Etham is *fort*.

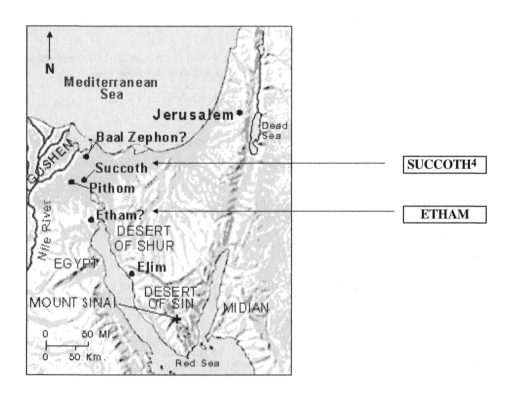

---

[3] *Zondervan Pictorial Encyclopedia of the Bible*, Vol.5:529.
[4] Map from *Life Application® Bible*. Used by permission.

TYPES, SYMBOLS, AND PICTURES
(Exodus 13:17-22)

Historical Term	Type or Picture (Scriptural Basis for Each)	Life Application for Today's Believer	Biblical Application
The Wilderness Wanderings (Journey) (Ex.13:17-18:27)	*The pilgrimage (journey, wanderings) of the believer...* • *as he turns away from Egypt (the world) & leaves behind his old life.* • *as he turns to begin his new life by marching to the promised land.* • *as he marches through the wilderness [trials] of this world & conquers all that the wilderness throws against him.* **"But God led the people about, through the way of the wilderness of the Red sea: and the children of Israel went up harnessed [marching in military rank] out of the land of Egypt" (Ex.13:18).** (see Nu.14:33; De.8:2-3, 5-6; 32:10)	Once a person has been saved—turned to God from the world (Egypt), turned away from his old life—he begins his *new life* (in Christ). He immediately begins to march to the promised land of heaven. His new life is the *pilgrimage* of the Christian believer: a march through the *wilderness* of this world, through all that the wilderness throws up against him... • trials • temptations • problems • difficulties • obstacles • accidents • sufferings • death	*"Now all these things happened unto them for ensamples: and they are written for our admonition, upon whom the ends of the world are come" (1 Co. 10:11).* *"And, behold, I am with thee, and will keep thee in all places whither thou goest, and will bring thee again into this land; for I will not leave thee, until I have done that which I have spoken to thee of" (Ge.28:15).* *"When thou passest through the waters, I will be with thee; and through the rivers, they shall not overflow thee: when thou walkest through the fire, thou shalt not be burned; neither shall the flame kindle upon thee" (Is.43:2).* *"There hath no temptation taken you but such as is common to man: but God is faithful, who will not suffer you to be tempted above that ye are able; but will with the temptation also make a way to escape, that ye may be able to bear it" (1 Co.10:13).* *(see Mt. 4:1-11; Lu. 4:1-13; 2 S.22:2; Je.1:8; He.2:14-15)*
The Pillar of Cloud and Fire (Ex.13:21)	*A picture of God's awesome presence and guidance. This cloud was...* • *a source of light* • *a source for direction* • *a source of protection* • *a picture of baptism* **"And the LORD went before them by day in a pillar of a cloud, to lead them the way; and by night in a pillar of fire, to give them light; to go by day and night: He took not away the pillar of the cloud by day, nor the pillar of fire by night, from before the people" (Ex. 13:21-22; see Ex.14:19-20).**	God has promised His presence, guidance, & protection as we journey through the wilderness of this world, journey to the promised land of heaven. God's presence and guidance... • will guide us with His counsel (Ps.73:24) • will show us the exact way to go (Is.42:16) • will protect & deliver us (Ps.34:7; see Ps. 91:4) • will be with us through all—no matter what (Ge.28:15; Ex. 33:14) • will lead us to the green pastures & still waters (Ps.23:2)	*"Thou wilt show me the path of life: in thy presence is fulness of joy; at thy right hand there are pleasures for evermore" (Ps.16:11).* *"Thy word is a lamp unto my feet, and a light unto my path" (Ps.119:105).* *"I will instruct thee and teach thee in the way which thou shalt go: I will guide thee with mine eye" (Ps.32:8).* *"He maketh me to lie down in green pastures: he leadeth me beside the still waters" (Ps.23:2).* *"For this God is our God for ever and ever: he will be our guide even unto death" (Ps.48:14).* *"Thou shalt guide me with thy counsel, and afterward receive me to glory" (Ps.73:24).*

273

CHAPTER 14

B. The First Crisis of Israel in the Wilderness—Crossing the Red Sea: God's Great Deliverance, 14:1-31

1. Scene 1: God's plan & purpose
a. God's instructions to Moses
  1) To turn back
  2) To camp by the sea, opposite Baal-zephon near Pi-hahiroth, between Migdol & the sea[DS1,2,3]

b. God's purpose
  1) To make Pharaoh think Israel was trapped between the sea & the desert
  2) To gain glory through Pharaoh & his army: By executing justice upon them
  3) To prove the truth to the Egyptians once more, that God is the LORD

2. Scene 2: Pharaoh's change of mind & pursuit of God's people (a symbol of an evil leader, of the world)
a. Pharaoh & his officials changed their minds about freeing God's people

b. Pharaoh mobilized his massive army

  1) Six hundred of his best chariots
  2) All the other chariots

  3) All his horsemen & troops
c. Pharaoh pursued the Israelites & overtook them

3. Scene 3: The fear & cry of God's people
a. They saw the Egyptian army & were stricken with terror:

b. Some cried out to the LORD

c. Others complained & mur-

And the LORD spake unto Moses, saying,

2 Speak unto the children of Israel, that they turn and encamp before Pi-hahiroth, between Migdol and the sea, over against Baal-zephon: before it shall ye encamp by the sea.

3 For Pharaoh will say of the children of Israel, They are entangled in the land, the wilderness hath shut them in.

4 And I will harden Pharaoh's heart, that he shall follow after them; and I will be honoured upon Pharaoh, and upon all his host; that the Egyptians may know that I am the LORD. And they did so.

5 And it was told the king of Egypt that the people fled: and the heart of Pharaoh and of his servants was turned against the people, and they said, Why have we done this, that we have let Israel go from serving us?

6 And he made ready his chariot, and took his people with him:

7 And he took six hundred chosen chariots, and all the chariots of Egypt, and captains over every one of them.

8 And the LORD hardened the heart of Pharaoh king of Egypt, and he pursued after the children of Israel: and the children of Israel went out with an high hand.

9 But the Egyptians pursued after them, all the horses and chariots of Pharaoh, and his horsemen, and his army, and overtook them encamping by the sea, beside Pi-hahiroth, before Baal-zephon.

10 And when Pharaoh drew nigh, the children of Israel lifted up their eyes, and, behold, the Egyptians marched after them; and they were sore afraid: and the children of Israel cried out unto the LORD.

11 And they said unto Moses, Because there were no graves in Egypt, hast thou taken us away to die in the wilderness? wherefore hast thou dealt thus with us, to carry us forth out of Egypt?

12 Is not this the word that we did tell thee in Egypt, saying, Let us alone, that we may serve the Egyptians? For it had been better for us to serve the Egyptians, than that we should die in the wilderness.

13 And Moses said unto the people, Fear ye not, stand still, and see the salvation of the LORD, which he will show to you to day: for the Egyptians whom ye have seen to day, ye shall see them again no more for ever.

14 The LORD shall fight for you, and ye shall hold your peace.

15 And the LORD said unto Moses, Wherefore criest thou unto me? speak unto the children of Israel, that they go forward:

16 But lift thou up thy rod, and stretch out thine hand over the sea, and divide it: and the children of Israel shall go on dry ground through the midst of the sea.

17 And I, behold, I will harden the hearts of the Egyptians, and they shall follow them: and I will get me honour upon Pharaoh, and upon all his host, upon his chariots, and upon his horsemen.

18 And the Egyptians shall know that I am the LORD, when I have gotten me honour upon Pharaoh, upon his chariots, and upon his horsemen.

19 And the angel of God, which went before the camp of Israel, removed and went behind them; and the pillar of the cloud went from before their face, and stood behind them:

20 And it came between the camp of the Egyptians and the camp of Israel; and it was a cloud and darkness to them, but it gave light by night to these: so that the one came not near the other all the night.

mured against God's leader
  1) Complained that they were going to die in the wilderness

  2) Complained that they would have been better to remain slaves than to die in the desert

4. Scene 4: The great message of victory & deliverance
a. Fear not
b. Stand still—stand firm—& watch the salvation of the LORD
  1) The Egyptians will be destroyed
  2) The LORD Himself will fight for you
  3) Stand still: Watch
c. Stop crying out to God: Arise—go forward, move on

5. Scene 5: God's great purpose in dividing the Red Sea[DS4]

a. That His people might be delivered from their enemy

b. That God might gain glory through Pharaoh & his army: By executing justice upon them
  1) Proved His sovereignty, power, & control: "I will"
  2) Proved His execution of justice & judgment, His execution of righteousness
c. That the Egyptians might know that God is the LORD, the God of deliverance & salvation

6. Scene 6: The great deliverance
a. Delivered by the angel of God: Moved from the front of His people to the rear (moved from leading to protecting)
b. Delivered by the pillar of cloud: Shifted also
  1) Was placed between the Egyptians & God's people
  2) Was a wall of darkness to the Egyptians, but a wall of light to God's people

c. Delivered by God's Almighty power 1) God made a way to escape • Made a strong east wind that blew the sea back all night • Dried the ground 2) God delivered His people • They walked through the sea on dry ground • The waters formed a wall on the right & left d. Delivered by God's presence & control 1) The Egyptians pursued Israel into the sea 2) God looked down upon the Egyptians • Caused them to become confused: The pillar of cloud & fire disturbed & troubled them • Caused the chariots to ram each other & knocked off their wheels • Struck fear in their hearts, crying out for a retreat e. Delivered by God's execution of justice & judgment	21 And Moses stretched out his hand over the sea; and the LORD caused the sea to go back by a strong east wind all that night, and made the sea dry land, and the waters were divided. 22 And the children of Israel went into the midst of the sea upon the dry ground: and the waters were a wall unto them on their right hand, and on their left. 23 And the Egyptians pursued, and went in after them to the midst of the sea, even all Pharaoh's horses, his chariots, and his horsemen. 24 And it came to pass, that in the morning watch the LORD looked unto the host of the Egyptians through the pillar of fire and of the cloud, and troubled the host of the Egyptians, 25 And took off their chariot wheels, that they drave them heavily: so that the Egyptians said, Let us flee from the face of Israel; for the LORD fighteth for them against the Egyptians. 26 And the LORD said unto Moses, Stretch out thine hand	over the sea, that the waters may come again upon the Egyptians, upon their chariots, and upon their horsemen. 27 And Moses stretched forth his hand over the sea, and the sea returned to his strength when the morning appeared; and the Egyptians fled against it; and the LORD overthrew the Egyptians in the midst of the sea. 28 And the waters returned, and covered the chariots, and the horsemen, and all the host of Pharaoh that came into the sea after them; there remained not so much as one of them. 29 But the children of Israel walked upon dry land in the midst of the sea; and the waters were a wall unto them on their right hand, and on their left. 30 Thus the LORD saved Israel that day out of the hand of the Egyptians; and Israel saw the Egyptians dead upon the sea shore. 31 And Israel saw that great work which the LORD did upon the Egyptians: and the people feared the LORD, and believed the LORD, and his servant Moses.	1) God instructed Moses to stretch his hand over the sea: The waters would flow back over the Egyptians (the enemies) 2) Moses obeyed God 3) God executed justice upon the Egyptians (the enemy) • The LORD caused the sea to flow back • The Egyptians were swept into the sea • The water covered the chariots & horsemen, the entire army: Not one survived **7. Scene 7: The LORD's salvation of His people** a. Fact 1: Israel walked through the sea on dry ground b. Fact 2: God saved Israel from the Egyptians (the enemy) c. Fact 3: Israel saw the dead, their evil enslavers, lying upon the shore d. Fact 4: God's purpose was accomplished 1) God's people saw His power 2) God's people feared Him 3) God's people believed in Him & in His messenger

DIVISION V

THE RED SEA AND THE WILDERNESS WANDERINGS: THE BELIEVER'S TRIALS AS HE JOURNEYS TO THE PROMISED LAND, 13:17–18:27

B.   The First Crisis of Israel in the Wilderness—Crossing the Red Sea: God's Great Deliverance, 14:1-31

(14:1-31) **Introduction:** life is often cruel, very cruel. Hopes that have risen to great heights sink in disappointment. Everywhere, every day, thousands of people are facing…

- disease
- deformity
- accident
- suffering
- death
- loss of job
- shortage of money
- bankruptcy
- broken relationships

"Where is God when we really need Him?" becomes the cry of the human heart. This was the very situation confronting Israel. The Israelites had been freed from the cruel hand of Pharaoh, but for what reason? To perish like hunted animals? There they stood trapped by the Red Sea and the surrounding Egyptian army. Up against insurmountable odds, Israel had to face:

⇒ a man whose hardened heart made him crazy with hate, hatred for them.
⇒ 600 chosen chariots plus all the other chariots and horses of Egypt.
⇒ the most powerful army on the face of the earth.

But note: the problem was not Pharaoh and his great military power. The problem was not the Red Sea. The problem was closer to home. The problem was the hearts of the Israelites, the secret thoughts of the heart that wondered…

- "God, why are you allowing this to happen?"
- "Why me? This is not fair.."
- "If only we had stayed in Egypt, life would be so much simpler."

We can only imagine the scene as Pharaoh rushed to capture the Israelites:

⇒ Mothers were clutching children, trying to make their final memories of freedom as least painful as possible.
⇒ Perhaps some were contemplating throwing themselves into the Red Sea, allowing the waters to become their final resting place.
⇒ Others were determined to go down fighting.

Scripture states that the people bitterly accused Moses and God of being cruel. This stinging yet false charge cut to the core. Any other man would have thrown up his hands and waved the white flag of surrender to Pharaoh, but not Moses. Instead, Moses pointed the people to the LORD. He knew that God was in complete control of the situation. God was preparing to do something great, something so marvelous, so extraordinary that it would be recorded as one of the greatest acts in history. God was going to make them eyewitnesses of His great power, a power that can deliver us from any trial, any circumstance:

⇒ sickness   ⇒ divorce
⇒ injury   ⇒ broken relationships
⇒ loss of job   ⇒ bankruptcy
⇒ poverty

This is the message of this great Scripture: *The First Crisis of Israel in the Wilderness—Crossing the Red Sea: God's Great Deliverance,* 14:1-31.
1. Scene 1: God's plan and purpose (vv.1-4).
2. Scene 2: Pharaoh's change of mind and pursuit of God's people (a symbol of an evil leader, of the world) (vv.5-9).
3. Scene 3: the fear and cry of God's people (vv.10-12).
4. Scene 4: the great message of victory and deliverance (vv.13-15).
5. Scene 5: God's great purpose in dividing the Red Sea (vv.16-18).
6. Scene 6: the great deliverance (vv.19-28).
7. Scene 7: the LORD'S salvation of his people (vv.29-31).

1 (14:1-4) **Israel—Egypt—Baal-zephon—Justice, of God—Glory, of God—God, Proof of**: the first scene is that of God's plan and purpose.
a. God gave a strange, surprising instruction to Moses. He told Moses to change directions, to turn back and pitch camp by the Red Sea...
  • opposite Baal-zephon and near Pi-hiharoth
  • between Migdol and the sea

Strange, surprising instructions! Israel had already reached the edge of the desert, and the people were ready to begin their march to Horeb or Mt. Sinai where they were to worship God. Then they were to march on toward the promised land of Canaan. But here God was instructing them to turn back and camp at the edge of the sea. Why? Why would God want Israel to backtrack and camp by the sea?
b. God had three major purposes for leading Israel by the sea (vv.3-4).
  1) God wanted Pharaoh to think that Israel was trapped between the sea and the desert (v.3). Very simply, Pharaoh would hear that Israel was camped by the sea, and he would immediately know that he could trap them there. They would be in a defenseless, helpless position. He could recapture them and bring them back to Egypt as slaves. The loss of free labor and wealth suffered by freeing the two million plus slaves was bound to be a terrible blow to the economy of Egypt. Pharaoh and his people had no doubt been facing crisis after crisis since the Israelites had fled the country.
      Thus when Pharaoh's spies brought word to him that the Israelites were camped by the sea, he and his officials knew they could easily recapture the slaves. They knew they could regain their free labor and the enormous wealth the Israelites had taken with them as they fled Egypt (see note—Ex.12:34-41).
  2) God was to gain glory through Pharaoh and his army, gain glory over the evil empire of ancient Egypt and gain glory over all the false gods of the Egyptians. God was going to execute justice upon Pharaoh and his military: they were to be destroyed because of their hard hearts, because of the terrible evil of idolatry, because of enslaving and brutalizing other people, especially the people of God.
  3) God wanted the Egyptians to know that He is the LORD, the only true Savior and Deliverer of man, the only living and true God (v.4). The gods of Egypt were false. God wanted the Egyptians to know that they were worshipping and following false gods. No man-made god would be able to deliver Pharaoh and his army, no god of man's imagination was going to be able to stop the LORD from judging the Egyptians. The Egyptians were to know beyond any question that there is only one living and true God, the LORD Himself (Jehovah, Yahweh).
      Thus, by executing judgment upon Pharaoh and his army, God was giving the surviving Egyptians an opportunity to repent, to turn away from their evil and idolatrous ways and to turn to the LORD Himself. Even in judgment, God was showing mercy upon the Egyptian people.

Thought 1. There is only one living and true God, only one true *Savior* and *Deliverer* of mankind, the LORD Himself. Scripture declares this truth over and over.

> **"For God so loved the world, that he gave his only begotten Son, that whosoever believeth in him should not perish, but have everlasting life" (Jn.3:16).**
> **"Then Simon Peter answered him, Lord, to whom shall we go? thou hast the words of eternal life" (Jn.6:68).**
> **"I said therefore unto you, that ye shall die in your sins: for if ye believe not that I am [he], ye shall die in your sins" (Jn.8:24).**

"Neither is there salvation in any other: for there is none other name under heaven given among men, whereby we must be saved" (Ac.4:12).

DEEPER STUDY # 1
(14:2) **Pi-hiharoth—Cities or Areas**: located by the Red Sea, this was the setting for one of Israel's greatest moments, the moment when God miraculously defeated Pharaoh's mighty army at the Red Sea. There are three dominant views of Pi-hahiroth's exact location.
⇒ The first view places Pi-hahiroth near the Mediterranean Sea on Lake Sirbonis.
⇒ The second view has the location just north of the modern Suez.
⇒ The third and most likely view places Pi-hahiroth near the modern Tell Defneh (the ancient Egyptian Tahpanhes).

DEEPER STUDY # 2
(14:2) **Migdol—Cities or Areas**: the name of an area in western Egypt. The Hebrew word means *fort* or *watchtower*.
⇒ It was between Migdol and the Red Sea that Israel camped while they waited for an apparent destructive blow from Pharaoh or a saving act from God (Ex.14:2).
⇒ The geographical location of Migdol was just west of the Red Sea (Ex.14:2).
⇒ Migdol was Israel's final encampment in Egypt (Ex.14:2, see Nu.33:7).
⇒ During the time of the prophet Jeremiah, many of the rebellious Israelites fled to Migdol and practiced idolatry (see Je.44:1-14; 46:14).[1]

DEEPER STUDY # 3
(14:2) **Baal-zephon—Cities or Areas**: the name means *Baal of the North*. Note these striking facts about this place:
⇒ Baal-zephon was named for an Egyptian deity. It was the perfect place for God's people to observe Pharaoh's on-rushing army.
⇒ Baal-zephon became a visual aid for Israel to see God's glory—the glory of Almighty God versus those who worshipped the false gods of Egypt (Ex.14:2; 14:9; Nu.33:7).

"To whom will ye liken me, and make *me* equal, and compare me, that we may be like? They lavish gold out of the bag, and weigh silver in the balance, *and* hire a goldsmith; and he maketh it a god: they fall down, yea, they worship. They bear him upon the shoulder, they carry him, and set him in his place, and he standeth; from his place shall he not remove: yea, *one* shall cry unto him, yet can he not answer, nor save him out of his trouble. Remember this, and show yourselves men: bring it again to mind, O ye transgressors. Remember the former things of old: for I *am* God, and *there is* none else; *I am* God, and *there is* none like me" (Is.46:5-9).

---

2 (14:5-9) **Pharaoh—Egypt, Military of; Economy of**: the second scene was dramatic: Pharaoh's change of mind and pursuit of God's people. Note the fast moving drama of Scripture that is described ever so rapidly.

a. Pharaoh and his officials changed their minds about freeing God's people (v.15). Remember the economy of Egypt had been catastrophically devastated by the plagues. God had launched the plagues to execute justice upon Pharaoh and his people. The Egyptians needed to rebuild their nation. Every industry had obviously been affected: farming, construction, mining, metal, food, and the service industries.

But Pharaoh and his officials not only had to deal with a devastated economy, they had to deal with the loss of most of their labor force and with the loss of economic wealth. Remember, there were over six-hundred thousand Israelite men alone, and most of them would have large families. Just imagine the impact of losing more than two million slave-laborers, all cheap and free laborers.

Moreover, there was gold, silver, and other gifts given by the Egyptians to each Israelite family—just to get rid of them lest the plagues of God continue to fall upon Egypt (see note—Ex.12:34-41). The combined wealth would have amounted to millions of dollars. Just a small amount of gold and silver and other valuables—worth say a hundred dollars—given to each family would have amounted to sixty million dollars. Whatever the wealth given, it was enormous.

The reality of the lost wealth and the loss of free labor was bound to severely impact the rebuilding of Egypt's economy. The Egyptians could rebuild the nation much quicker if they could recapture the Israelites, enslave them, and confiscate their enormous wealth. Pharaoh and his officials had no doubt been discussing this fact in their cabinet meetings as they met to handle the devastated economy of the nation. Thus when they heard that the Israelites slaves were camped between the sea and the desert, it is easy to imagine...
• the rage and indignation of Pharaoh and his officials
• the thoughts of revenge that were stirred within their minds
• the proud heart that thrust itself against God and His people
• the roar of the lion [Satan] that was set to devour God's people

What was God's reaction against their plan to launch a savage, brutal attack? God hardened their hearts. That is, He gave them up to the passion of their hard hearts. He allowed their hearts to become harder and harder in their evil passions. Note what happened.

---

[1] *The Compact Bible Dictionary,* Edited by T. Alton Bryant, p.361.

b. Pharaoh mobilized his massive army (vv.6-9). This is seen in the fact...
- that Pharaoh mobilized six hundred of his best chariots as well as many of the other chariots of Egypt. By "best chariots" is meant 600 of the most advanced war machines of that day.
- that Pharaoh placed officers over all the chariots. A certain number of chariots must have been assigned to a large number of foot soldiers.

Just imagine! Six-hundred of the latest chariots to be built for warfare and hundreds of other chariots mobilized for battle. The number of foot soldiers no doubt numbered in the tens of thousands.

But this was not all. Pharaoh mobilized his horsemen and the troops that supported them. As stated, the army was of enormous size. A major military campaign was being planned and launched against God's people, a campaign to capture and enslave and bring them back to Egypt.

c. And then the armed march began. Pharaoh pursued the Israelites and overtook them where they were camping by the sea (v.9).

Thought 1. The world and its rulers, governments, and people are fickle. They move from policy to policy, turning back and changing from what they often promised. This is especially true in dealing with God's people. For awhile, the world may grant peace to God's people, allowing them the freedom of speech and worship. But the world can change overnight and turn away from the right of worship and free speech. The world can attempt to deny believers the right to teach and bear testimony for the only living and true God. Thus, believers must always be prepared for the turning away of the world, for the persecution of the world.

"Behold, I send you forth as sheep in the midst of wolves: be ye therefore wise as serpents, and harmless as doves. But beware of men: for they will deliver you up to the councils, and they will scourge you in their synagogues; And ye shall be brought before governors and kings for my sake, for a testimony against them and the Gentiles." (Mt.10:16-18; see Lu.21:12).

"Then shall they deliver you up to be afflicted, and shall kill you: and ye shall be hated of all nations for my name's sake" (Mt.24:9).

"If the world hate you, ye know that it hated me before [it hated] you. If ye were of the world, the world would love his own: but because ye are not of the world, but I have chosen you out of the world, therefore the world hateth you. Remember the word that I said unto you, The servant is not greater than his lord. If they have persecuted me, they will also persecute you; if they have kept my saying, they will keep yours also. But all these things will they do unto you for my name's sake, because they know not him that sent me" (Jn.15:18-21).

"They shall put you out of the synagogues: yea, the time cometh, that whosoever killeth you will think that he doeth God service. And these things will they do unto you, because they have not known the Father, nor me" (Jn.16:2-3).

"For unto you it is given in the behalf of Christ, not only to believe on him, but also to suffer for his sake" (Ph.1:29).

"Yea, and all that will live godly in Christ Jesus shall suffer persecution" (2 Ti.3:12).

3 (14:10-12) **Fear—Faithlessness—Complaining—Blaming Others**: the third scene was that of fright and terror. It was the fear and cry of God's people. When God's people saw the world's most powerful army marching over the horizon toward them, they were as any unarmed people would be: stricken with fear (v.10).
⇒ Some cried out to God for help (v.10).
⇒ Others cried out against God's leader, complained and turned against him. They accused Moses of bringing them into the wilderness to be slaughtered by the Egyptians army. The accusers reminded Moses that they had asked him in Egypt to leave them alone. Slavery was far better than death in the desert (vv.11-12)!

The people of God felt hopeless and helpless. There they were a defenseless people, including women and children, about to be attacked by the mightiest army on earth. They saw no way of deliverance and were gripped with a deep, intense despair. They blamed and condemned God's leader. They forgot God's mighty arm of salvation and deliverance.

Thought 1. The point to see is the fright of God's people and their lack of faith. Fear—terrible fear—would be natural in such a situation. Crying out to God would be a natural, normal reaction. But not complaining nor turning against God's leader. This revealed a shallow, weak faith. The people were not trusting God to deliver them. Their memories were short lived. Just think about what God had done for them.
⇒ God had just demonstrated His mighty power in launching the ten plagues of judgment upon Egypt. And all the Israelites had witnessed God's mighty power.
⇒ God had just delivered the Israelites from enslavement in Egypt.
⇒ God had been guiding them step by step since they had been set free.
⇒ In addition, God had promised to take them into the promised land of Canaan.

The moment called for faith, strong faith in God's promise, and in His mighty arm that had been proven time and time again. But faith was lacking. They felt there was no deliverance available, no possible way they could be saved from so great an enemy. But God's Word is clear: we are not to fear. No matter how severe the circumstance, no matter how terrible the problem, no matter how hopeless and helpless the situation may seem—the believer is never to be overtaken by fear and faithlessness.

"And he did not many mighty works there because of their unbelief" (Mt.13:58).

"And immediately Jesus stretched forth [his] hand, and caught him, and said unto him, O thou of little faith, wherefore didst thou doubt?" (Mt.14:31).

"Then Jesus answered and said, O faithless and perverse generation, how long shall I be with you? how long shall I suffer you? bring him hither to me" (Mt.17:17).

"And he said unto them, Why are ye so fearful? how is it that ye have no faith?" (Mk.4:40).

"Art thou the Christ? tell us. And he said unto them, If I tell you, ye will not believe" (Lu.22:67).

"Then he said unto them, O fools, and slow of heart to believe all that the prophets have spoken" (Lu.24:25).

"But though he had done so many miracles before them, yet they believed not on him" (Jn.12:37).

Thought 2. Fear is one of the worst nightmares people can face as they journey through the wilderness of the world. Fear causes people to...

- worry incessantly about money
- fight among themselves
- be overly concerned with appearance
- isolate themselves
- make rash, hurried decisions
- spew out false accusations
- grasp after friendships
- strike out at people
- become physically sick
- ignore God
- withdraw into a shell
- steal, lie, cheat, abuse, fight, kill

What is a person to do when fear strikes? There is only one antidote, only one true remedy: the Lord Jesus Christ. Jesus Christ can bring peace and calm to our lives. He can deliver us from fear. This is the clear declaration of Scripture.

"But the very hairs of your head are all numbered. Fear ye not therefore, ye are of more value than many sparrows" (Mt.10:30-31).

"Peace I leave with you, my peace I give unto you: not as the world giveth, give I unto you. Let not your heart be troubled, neither let it be afraid" (Jn.14:27).

"These things I have spoken unto you, that in me ye might have peace. In the world ye shall have tribulation: but be of good cheer; I have overcome the world" (Jn.16:33).

"Be careful for nothing [do not be anxious nor fear]; but in every thing by prayer and supplication with thanksgiving let your requests be made known unto God. And the peace of God, which passeth all understanding, shall keep your hearts and minds through Christ Jesus" (Ph.4:6-7).

"For God hath not given us the spirit of fear; but of power, and of love, and of a sound mind" (2 Ti.1:7).

"Yea, though I walk through the valley of the shadow of death, I will fear no evil: for thou art with me; thy rod and thy staff they comfort me" (Ps.23:4).

"The Lord will give strength unto his people; the Lord will bless his people with peace" (Ps.29:11).

"Fear thou not; for I am with thee: be not dismayed; for I am thy God: I will strengthen thee; yea, I will help thee; yea, I will uphold thee with the right hand of my righteousness" (Is.41:10).

"Fear not: for I have redeemed thee, I have called thee by thy name; thou art mine" (Is.43:1).

"When thou passest through the waters, I will be with thee; and through the rivers, they shall not overflow thee: when thou walkest through the fire, thou shalt not be burned; neither shall the flame kindle upon thee" (Is.43:2).

"Who shall separate us from the love of Christ? *shall* tribulation, or distress, or persecution, or famine, or nakedness, or peril, or sword?...Nay, in all these things we are more than conquerors through him that loved us. For I am persuaded, that neither death, nor life, nor angels, nor principalities, nor powers, nor things present, nor things to come, Nor height, nor depth, nor any other creature, shall be able to separate us from the love of God, which is in Christ Jesus our Lord" (Ro.8:35, 37-39).

"For he is our peace, who hath made both one, and hath broken down the middle wall of partition *between us*" (Ep.2:14).

4 (14:13-15) **Victory—Salvation—Deliverance—Perseverance—Stedfastness—Fear—Fearlessness—Still, Be—Firm, Stand—Courage:** the fourth scene is one of the greatest challenges issued to man. It is the great message of victory and deliverance. Note that God's servant did not react nor strike out against the complainers and his accusers. With great composure of mind, Moses shouted out three challenges to the people of God.

a. Fear not (v.13). Picture the scene. There were God's people confronted by a raging sea in front of them and a raging army behind them. Thousands and thousands of soldiers, horsemen, and chariots were marching toward them, and there was no place to flee. They were hemmed in. How could they not fear? A terrifying fear would be a normal reaction in facing such an impossible situation. But there was God's messenger shouting out: "Fear not!"

Thought 1. No matter the problem that confronts us, God's message is always, "Fear not." The problem may be...

- bankruptcy
- unemployment
- financial difficulties
- a severed relationship
- a family problem
- conflict
- disease
- accident
- death of a loved one
- temptation
- sin

On and on the list could go. But we must never despair. God's first message to us is always, "Fear not."

"And he answered, Fear not: for they that be with us are more than they that be with them" (2 K.6:16).
"I will not be afraid of ten thousands of people, that have set themselves against me round about" (Ps.3:6).
"Though an host should encamp against me, my heart shall not fear: though war should rise against me, in this will I be confident" (Ps.27:3).
"Thou shalt not be afraid for the terror by night; nor for the arrow that flieth by day" (Ps.91:5).
"The LORD is on my side; I will not fear: what can man do unto me?" (Ps.118:6).
"When thou liest down, thou shalt not be afraid: yea, thou shalt lie down, and thy sleep shall be sweet" (Pr.3:24).
"Fear thou not; for I am with thee: be not dismayed; for I am thy God: I will strengthen thee; yea, I will help thee; yea, I will uphold thee with the right hand of my righteousness" (Is.41:10).
"Fear not: for I have redeemed thee, I have called thee by thy name; thou art mine. When thou passest through the waters, I will be with thee; and through the rivers, they shall not overflow thee: when thou walkest through the fire, thou shalt not be burned; neither shall the flame kindle upon thee" (Is.43:1-2).
"But the very hairs of your head are all numbered. Fear ye not therefore, ye are of more value than many sparrows" (Mt.10:30-31).
"Forasmuch then as the children are partakers of flesh and blood, he also himself likewise took part of the same; that through death he might destroy him that had the power of death, that is, the devil; And deliver them who through fear of death were all their lifetime subject to bondage" (He.2:14-15).
"And when I saw him, I fell at his feet as dead. And he laid his right hand upon me, saying unto me, Fear not; I am the first and the last: I am he that liveth, and was dead; and, behold, I am alive for evermore, Amen; and have the keys of hell and of death" (Re.1:17-18).

b. The second challenge to God's people was a most difficult thing to do: stand still—stand firm—and watch the salvation of the LORD (vv.13-14). Imagine! Standing there were God's people with the mightiest army in the world marching down upon them. What would their natural reaction be? To flee, to get away, to run wherever they could. But there was God's leader shouting out, "Be still—stand firm—watch the salvation of the LORD." And then Moses declared the wonderful truth of God's promise:
⇒ The enemy, the Egyptians, will be destroyed.
⇒ The LORD Himself will fight for you.
⇒ Just stand still, stand firm: watch.

Thought 1. When a severe problem confronts us, a problem that seems to have no solution, what is the natural tendency of our hearts? Often to flee, to get away, to run wherever we can.
But this is not God's way. God's way is to stand still, stand firm: watch the salvation of the LORD. God wants to deliver us. We must, therefore, stand firm, not give up, cave in, nor flee away. We must be steadfast: stand still, wait upon God's mighty arm to save and deliver us.

"Hearken unto this, O Job: stand still, and consider the wondrous works of God" (Jb.37:14).
"Be still, and know that I am God: I will be exalted among the heathen, I will be exalted in the earth" (Ps.46:10).
"Behold, God is my salvation; I will trust, and not be afraid: for the LORD JEHOVAH is my strength and my song; he also is become my salvation" (Is.12:2).
"For the Egyptians shall help in vain, and to no purpose: therefore have I cried concerning this, Their strength is to sit still" (Is.30:7).
"For God hath not given us the spirit of fear; but of power, and of love, and of a sound mind" (2 Ti.1:7).

c. The third challenge in facing problems is a surprising challenge. Stop crying out to God and complaining: arise, go forward, move on (v.15). Moses had just proclaimed a stirring challenge to the people: "Do not fear, stand still; believe God; watch the salvation of the LORD." But as soon as Moses completed his challenge, he walked over to his tent and became gripped with fear himself. He obviously become despondent and hopeless, gripped by a terrifying sense of helplessness. But note what happened: God met His dear servant's need. God told Moses in no uncertain terms: "Why are you crying out to me? Stop crying! Get up! Arise! Tell the people to go forward!" And Moses did.

Thought 1. In facing any problem there is a time for prayer and for crying out to God, a time for studying and analyzing the problem and planning what one can do. But there is also...
• a time to stop crying out and praying
• a time to quit blaming others for the problem
• a time to stop analyzing and planning
• a time to arise, go forward, and move on—trusting God to roll the walls of the problem back

(1) God demands that we arise and go forth: that we be diligent, stedfast, and unmovable in life.

"He that endureth to the end shall be saved" (Mt.10:22).
"Moreover it is required in stewards, that a man be found faithful [diligent]" (1 Co.4:2).

"Therefore, my beloved brethren, be ye stedfast, unmoveable, always abounding in the work of the Lord, forasmuch as ye know that your labour is not in vain in the Lord" (1 Co.15:58).

"And let us not be weary in well doing: for in due season we shall reap, if we faint not" (Ga.6:9).

"Moses my servant is dead; now therefore arise, go over this Jordan, thou, and all this people, unto the land which I do give to them, even to the children of Israel" (Jos.1:2).

"The righteous also shall hold on his way, and he that hath clean hands shall be stronger and stronger" (Jb.17:9).

"They go from strength to strength, every one of them in Zion appeareth before God" (Ps.84:7).

(2) God demands zeal in life.

"Say not ye, There are yet four months, and [then] cometh harvest? behold, I say unto you, Lift up your eyes, and look on the fields; for they are white already to harvest" (Jn.4:35).

"So we laboured in the work: and half of them held the spears from the rising of the morning till the stars appeared" (Ne.4:21).

"For Zion's sake will I not hold my peace, and for Jerusalem's sake I will not rest, until the righteousness thereof go forth as brightness, and the salvation thereof as a lamp that burneth" (Is.62:1).

"And he said unto them, How is it that ye sought me? wist [knew] ye not that I must be about my Father's business?" (Lu.2:49).

"Return to thine own house, and show how great things God hath done unto thee. And he went his way, and published throughout the whole city how great things Jesus had done unto him" (Lu.8:39).

"Jesus saith unto them, My meat is to do the will of him that sent me, and to finish his work" (Jn.4:34).

"I must work the works of him that sent me, while it is day: the night cometh, when no man can work" (Jn.9:4).

"How God anointed Jesus of Nazareth with the Holy Ghost and with power: who went about doing good, and healing all that were oppressed of the devil; for God was with him" (Ac.10:38).

"This man was instructed in the way of the Lord; and being fervent in the spirit, he spake and taught diligently the things of the Lord, knowing only the baptism of John" (Ac.18:25).

5 (14:16-18) **Red Sea—Israel, Deliverance of—Pharaoh—Egypt—God, Glory of**: the fifth scene covers God's purpose for dividing the Red Sea. God had a threefold purpose for performing this remarkable miracle.

a. God divided the Red Sea so that His people might be delivered from their enemies (v.16). God instructed Moses to lift up his rod and stretch out his hand over the sea. The result would be a phenomenal miracle: the waters would divide so that God's people could march through the sea on dry ground (v.16).

Remember who the people were standing there on the seashore, the people about to be attacked and enslaved by the most powerful army in the world. They were *God's people*...

• the people chosen by Him to be His witnesses upon earth, witnessing that He is the only living and true God, the only Savior and Redeemer of mankind.
• the people who had been given the great promises of God, the promise of the promised land and the promise of the promised seed, the coming Savior of the world, the Lord Jesus Christ.

God had promised to deliver His people from the bondage of slavery and to lead them to the promised land of Canaan (a symbol of heaven). And God's promise to His people is never broken. He will move heaven and earth to keep His promise from ever being broken. If God had left the Israelites alone to fend for themselves on the seashore, they would have been defeated and enslaved.

This is the first reason God divided the Red Sea: to keep His promise to Israel, to deliver His people from certain death and enslavement.

b. God divided the Red Sea so that He might gain glory through Pharaoh and his army, gain glory by executing justice and judgment upon them (v.17). How did God gain glory through this event?

1) God proved His sovereignty. Note the "I wills":
⇒ "I will harden."
⇒ "I will be honored."

God is the sovereign LORD and majesty of the universe; therefore, He can do as He wills. He told Moses that He Himself was in charge of this event, not man. Pharaoh was not in charge, neither were Moses and the Israelites. God was in charge; He was in total control of all that was to happen. Thus the very demonstration of God's sovereignty, of His control of the event, was to bring great glory to God.

2) God proved His justice and judgment, that He executes righteousness. The Egyptians were tyrants who brutalized and enslaved people. Moreover, they were an idolatrous people who rejected and denied the LORD (*Jehovah, Yahweh*), the only true and living God, the only true Savior and Redeemer of mankind. God had given the Egyptians opportunity after opportunity to repent of their evil and turn to Him. But they had rejected and become so hard-hearted that they were obstinate. They had reached the point where they would never repent. Consequently, the day of judgment had arrived. It was time for God to execute justice upon Pharaoh and his army. By miraculously destroying the greatest army on earth, God was to gain glory. God was to demonstrate that He is God Almighty, the Sovereign LORD and Majesty who executes justice upon the evil and idolatrous people of this earth.

281

c. God divided the Red Sea so that the Egyptians might know that God is the LORD, the only God of deliverance and salvation (v.18). God told Moses that He was going to…
- divide the Red Sea
- open a way for Israel to walk on dry ground through the sea
- arouse the Egyptian army to pursue Israel through the sea
- destroy the Egyptian army

Once God had so miraculously done all this, the Egyptians who survived were bound to know one great fact: the LORD (*Jehovah, Yahweh*) was the true and living God. No god of the Egyptians possessed such power. No god imagined and made by man could perform such feats. And note: no Egyptian god was able to…
- forewarn the Egyptians of the coming destruction
- save the Egyptians from being destroyed

The Sovereign God, the God who had power to deliver and save people and to destroy His enemies, was the God proclaimed by Israel: the LORD Himself (*Jehovah, Yahweh*).

> **"Know therefore this day, and consider it in thine heart, that the LORD he is God in heaven above, and upon the earth beneath: there is none else" (De.4:39).**
> **"Thou, even thou, art LORD alone; thou hast made heaven, the heaven of heavens, with all their host, the earth, and all things that are therein, the seas, and all that is therein, and thou preservest them all; and the host of heaven worshippeth thee" (Ne.9:6).**
> **"The earth is the LORD's, and the fulness thereof; the world, and they that dwell therein" (Ps.24:1).**
> **"The heavens are thine, the earth also is thine: as for the world and the fulness thereof, thou hast founded them" (Ps.89:11).**
> **"Thus saith the LORD, The heaven is my throne, and the earth is my footstool: where is the house that ye build unto me? and where is the place of my rest?" (Is.66:1).**
> **"God that made the world and all things therein, seeing that he is Lord of heaven and earth, dwelleth not in temples made with hands; Neither is worshipped with men's hands, as though he needed any thing, seeing he giveth to all life, and breath, and all things; And hath made of one blood all nations of men for to dwell on all the face of the earth, and hath determined the times before appointed, and the bounds of their habitation; That they should seek the Lord, if haply they might feel after him, and find him, though he be not far from every one of us: For in him we live, and move, and have our being; as certain also of your own poets have said, For we are also his offspring. Forasmuch then as we are the offspring of God, we ought not to think that the Godhead is like unto gold, or silver, or stone, graven by art and man's device. And the times of this ignorance God winked at; but now commandeth all men every where to repent: Because he hath appointed a day, in the which he will judge the world in righteousness by that man whom he hath ordained; whereof he hath given assurance unto all men, in that he hath raised him from the dead" (Ac.17:24-31).**

DEEPER STUDY # 4

(14:16-18) **Sea, The Red—Red Sea**: this sea is one of the most heralded bodies of water in the history of the Israelites.
- ⇒ The Red Sea became the gateway to freedom for Israel.
- ⇒ The Red Sea was miraculously used by God as an instrument of judgment upon Pharaoh's army: they were drowned in the sea as they pursued the Israelites, hoping to capture and enslave them again (Ex.14:23-28; Ps.136:15; He.11:29).
- ⇒ The Red Sea is known as *Yam Suph*, which means "Sea of Reeds" in Hebrew.[2]
- ⇒ The exact crossing site of the Israelites is unknown, although different commentators speculate on possible sites:
  - The northern end of the Gulf of Suez.[3]
  - The southern end of Lake Menzaleh, about 20 miles east of the city of Rameses.[4]
  - The water of the Bitter Lakes, "which may have been an extension of the Gulf of Suez in that day."[5]
  - John I. Durham states: "*The major difficulty in plotting the route of the Exodus lies not in the lack of information supplied in Exodus, but in our ignorance of the identification and correct location of the places in Exodus.*"[6]

Durham's point is well stated. The issue is not to split theological hairs, but to study what God has clearly said in His Word. What God has said about the Red Sea and its impact upon Israel is well documented in Scripture.

---

2 *NIV Study Bible*, p. 107.

3 ibid., p. 106.

4 ibid., p. 107.

5 Leon Wood, *A Survey of Israel's History*. (Grand Rapids, MI: Zondervan Publishing House, 1982), p. 130.

6 John I. Durham. *Word Biblical Commentary, Exodus*. (Waco, TX: Word, Inc. 1987), p. 185.

1. The Red Sea played an important part in the Ten Plagues:

> "And the LORD turned a mighty strong west wind, which took away the locusts, and cast them into the Red sea; there remained not one locust in all the coasts of Egypt" (Ex.10:19).

2. The Red Sea proved to be Israel's doorway to escape from Egypt:

> "But God led the people about, *through* the way of the wilderness of the Red sea: and the children of Israel went up harnessed out of the land of Egypt" (Ex.13:18).
> "Pharaoh's chariots and his host hath he cast into the sea: his chosen captains also are drowned in the Red sea" (Ex.15:4).

3. The Red Sea would be a marker that would *define the limits* of the promised land.

> "And I will set thy bounds from the Red sea even unto the sea of the Philistines, and from the desert unto the river: for I will deliver the inhabitants of the land into your hand; and thou shalt drive them out before thee" (Ex.23:31).

4. The Red Sea would be a constant reminder to future generations of God's deliverance of Israel.

> "And what he did unto the army of Egypt, unto their horses, and to their chariots; how he made the water of the Red sea to overflow them as they pursued after you, and *how* the LORD hath destroyed them unto this day" (De.11:4).
> "For we have heard how the LORD dried up the water of the Red sea for you, when ye came out of Egypt; and what ye did unto the two kings of the Amorites, that *were* on the other side Jordan, Sihon and Og, whom ye utterly destroyed" (Jos.2:10).
> "For the LORD your God dried up the waters of Jordan from before you, until ye were passed over, as the LORD your God did to the Red sea, which he dried up from before us, until we were gone over" (Jos.4:23).
> "And I brought your fathers out of Egypt: and ye came unto the sea; and the Egyptians pursued after your fathers with chariots and horsemen unto the Red sea" (Jos.24:6).
> "And didst see the affliction of our fathers in Egypt, and heardest their cry by the Red sea" (Ne.9:9).
> "Our fathers understood not thy wonders in Egypt; they remembered not the multitude of thy mercies; but provoked *him* at the sea, *even* at the Red sea" (Ps.106:7).
> "He rebuked the Red sea also, and it was dried up: so he led them through the depths, as through the wilderness" (Ps.106:9).
> "To him which divided the Red sea into parts: for his mercy *endureth* for ever" (Ps.136:13).
> "But overthrew Pharaoh and his host in the Red sea: for his mercy *endureth* for ever" (Ps.136:15).
> "He brought them out, after that he had showed wonders and signs in the land of Egypt, and in the Red sea, and in the wilderness forty years" (Ac.7:36).
> "By faith they passed through the Red sea as by dry *land:* which the Egyptians assaying [trying] to do were drowned" (He.11:29).

---

6 (14:19-28) **Red Sea—Deliverance, of God—Salvation—Pillar of Cloud and Fire—Israel—Egypt, Army of**: the sixth scene was the mighty deliverance of God. What now happened was a dramatic display of God's omnipotence, of His Almighty power.

a. The angel of God moved from the front of His people to the rear (v.19). He moved to stand between Israel and the Egyptians. He moved to protect God's people from the attack of the Egyptians.

> **Thought 1**. Throughout Scripture, the angels of God are seen taking an active role in the defense of the believer. God's holy messengers are on alert, watching out for all of us who truly believe and follow Christ. (See note—Ge.28:12-15; He.1:4-14 for more discussion.)

> "For he shall give his angels charge over thee, to keep thee in all thy ways" (Ps.91:11).
> "Who maketh his angels spirits; his ministers a flaming fire" (Ps.104:4).
> "Then the devil leaveth him, and, behold, angels came and ministered unto him" (Mt.4:11).
> "Thinkest thou that I cannot now pray to my Father, and he shall presently give me more than twelve legions of angels?" (Mt.26:53).
> "And he was there in the wilderness forty days, tempted of Satan; and was with the wild beasts; and the angels ministered unto him" (Mk.1:13).
> "For it is written, He shall give his angels charge over thee, to keep thee" (Lu.4:10).
> "And of the angels he saith, Who maketh his angels spirits, and his ministers a flame of fire" (He.1:7).
> "And all the angels stood round about the throne, and about the elders and the four beasts, and fell before the throne on their faces, and worshipped God" (Re.7:11).

b. The pillar of cloud moved to the rear of the Israelites as well, moved and hung between God's people and the Egyptians (vv.19-20). And note what happened: the pillar of cloud...
- was placed between the Egyptians and God's people (v.20)
- was a wall of darkness to the Egyptians but a wall of light to God's people (v.20)

This meant that the Egyptians lost sight of the Israelites. They were unable to pursue the people of God. There was a pitch black darkness between them. The cloud apparently lowered itself to cover the earth with a heavy, thick fog. The soupy fog blacked out all light from the moon and stars: there was obviously pitch black darkness, a total inability to see but a few feet in front of oneself.

c. God's Almighty power was demonstrated through his servant Moses. Moses stretched out his hand over the sea and God's power acted.
  1) God made a way to escape (v.21):
    ⇒ He made a strong east wind that blew the sea back all night. The waters stood upright, piled up, and congealed.
    ⇒ He dried the ground of the sea bed.

    Note the word *divided* (yibbakeu or baqa). It is the word used for splitting rocks and wood or for splitting asunder the earth with a violent earthquake.[7] The LORD actually split asunder the sea and made a valley, a passageway through the sea. The passageway or valley must have been at least a half mile wide for two to three million people to pass through in one night. And this they did, for they had crossed to the other side by the morning watch, somewhere between 2-6 a.m. (see v.24).

  2) God delivered His people (v.22). They walked through the sea on dry ground, and the raging waters formed a wall to the right and left of the people as they marched through. No doubt the leaders, Moses and Aaron, stepped out first and led the way, encouraging the people of God to follow. Picture the scene: there were teeming thousands of Israelites—about two to three million people—backed up all along the seashore, all standing in orderly, military file-like divisions.

    Every eye was fastened upon the unbelievable, the two surging, massive walls of water that had divided and made a half-mile passage through the sea. The emotions—all kinds of emotions: wonder, marvel, apprehension—were all rushing through the hearts and minds of the onlookers.

    Then, all of a sudden, the sound of the trumpet—the signal to march forth—was sounded. And every eye that could see the two servants of God, Moses and Aaron, watched as they began to walk side by side down into the bed of the sea. There were towering walls of water hanging and raging for hundreds of feet above their heads. The first division of people standing next to the two leaders slowly followed, and then the second followed the first, and the third the second, each gaining the courage from those who marched safely ahead of them. For hours the divisions of God's people marched through the sea until finally the last division arrived safely on the opposite shore. All night they had marched, all night they had witnessed...
- the miraculous power of God
- the mighty deliverance of God

    They had experienced a true miracle. God had rolled back the mighty waters of the Red Sea—God had temporarily intervened and changed the laws of nature in order to deliver His people from their enemies.

    The great expositor George Bush descriptively pictures the scene:

> *Countless eyes fastened on Moses and Aaron...these venerated leaders advanced together into the untrodden path, and at once the yielding waters divide, and contrary to all the laws of fluids stand erect on either hand like walls of solid ice! The bed of the sea appears between them, and lost in the amazement on this highway of the Lord's ransomed they pass through dry-shod and reach in safety the opposite shore!*[8]

Thought 1. How did God divide the Red Sea and make a passageway that was at least one-half mile wide? And how did God dry the bed of the Sea so that two to three million people could walk upon the dry ground without getting bogged down—all within one night? By His omnipotent power. God is God, the LORD God of redemption—of deliverance and salvation. The LORD can redeem, deliver, and save whom He will. He so chose to deliver Israel, to save them from the oppressive Egyptians.

"The waters saw thee, O God, the waters saw thee; they were afraid: the depths also were troubled. The clouds poured out water: the skies sent out a sound: thine arrows also went abroad. The voice of thy thunder was in the heaven: the lightnings lightened the world: the earth trembled and shook. Thy way is in the sea, and thy path in the great waters, and thy footsteps are not known. Thou leddest thy people like a flock by the hand of Moses and Aaron" (Ps.77:16-20).

"He turned the sea into dry land: they went through the flood on foot: there did we rejoice in him" (Ps.66:6).

"He divided the sea, and caused them to pass through; and he made the waters to stand as an heap" (Ps.78:13).

"Art thou not it [the arm of the Lord] which hath dried the sea, the waters of the great deep; that hath made the depths of the sea a way for the ransomed to pass over?" (Is.51:10).

---

[7] George Bush. *Exodus*, p.178.
[8] ibid., p.178.

"Then he remembered the days of old, Moses, and his people, saying, Where is he that brought them up out of the sea with the shepherd of his flock? where is he that put his holy Spirit within him? That led them by the right hand of Moses with his glorious arm, dividing the water before them, to make himself an everlasting name? That led them through the deep, as an horse in the wilderness, that they should not stumble?" (Is.63:11-13).

d. God's presence and control delivered His people (vv.23-27).
   1) The Egyptians pursued Israel into the sea (v.23). What would cause Pharaoh to order his troops to pursue Israel through the sea?
   ⇒ Perhaps blind rage? Hardness of heart? Bitter hatred and revenge?
   ⇒ All of the above were perhaps involved. In picturing the scene, the pillar of cloud (heavy fog) had probably lifted, dissipating just enough to arouse Pharaoh to begin his mad pursuit. In addition, the Egyptians could no doubt hear the noise of the fleeing Israelites. Pharaoh could tell they were fleeing, and he was not about to let them escape. The idea that God had rolled the waters of the Red Sea back and made a pathway through the bed of the sea would never have crossed Pharaoh's mind. He obviously thought that the Israelites were marching along the seashore or else weaving themselves somehow back inland. In picturing the situation, we must always keep in mind the following fact: it is doubtful that Pharaoh and his army were able to see well enough through the fog to know that they were pursuing Israel into the dried bed of the sea between two awesome, terrifying walls of water, towering perhaps a hundred or more feet into the air. They, of course, could hear the noise of the storm and of the storm-tossed, raging, violent waves. But God apparently kept the heavy, dense fog hanging all around the Egyptian army so that they could not know that they were marching into a potential trap.
   2) God looked down upon the Egyptians (vv.24-25). The phrase "looked down" (shaqaph) is always tied to God looking down in mercy or in wrath.[9] In this event, God looked down in wrath and judgment upon the Egyptians:
   ⇒ He caused them to become confused: the pillar of cloud and fire disturbed and troubled them.
   ⇒ He caused the chariots to ram each other, knocking off some of their wheels.
   ⇒ He struck fear in their hearts and they cried out for a retreat.

Again, George Bush paints a descriptive picture of this event:

> *"Let us flee," was the cry that resounded in every direction, through the broken and trembling ranks, but, alas, it was now too late. All attempts at flight were vain. The day of [God's] forbearance was passed. The measure of their iniquity was full. The tyrant and his people had hardened themselves in rebellion against God till his patience was exhausted, and the day of vengeance was come. They are first frightened into despair, and then plunged into destruction.[10]*

e. God delivered His people by executing justice and judgment upon the Egyptians (vv.26-28). Note what happened:
   1) God instructed Moses to stretch his hand over the sea: the waters were to flow back over the Egyptians (v.26).
   2) Moses obeyed God (v.27).
   3) God executed justice upon the Egyptians (v.27).
   ⇒ The LORD caused the sea to flow back (v.27).
   ⇒ The Egyptians were swept into the sea (v.27).
   ⇒ The water covered the chariots and horsemen, the entire army: not one survived (v.28).

The Psalmist tells us that God caused a severe storm to break loose upon the Egyptians. *The Expositor's Bible Commentary* says this:

> *The pillar of fire must have suddenly lit up the sky with such a flash in the darkness that the chariots careened against one another.*
> *Meanwhile there also was unleashed such a spectacular display of thunder, lightning, rain, and earthquake that the boldest and most arrogant of Egypt's charioteers were struck with terror. So we would understand from Psalm 77:16-20.[11]*

"The waters saw thee, O God, the waters saw thee; they were afraid: the depths also were troubled. The clouds poured out water: the skies sent out a sound: thine arrows also went abroad. The voice of thy thunder was in the heaven: the lightnings lightened the world: the earth trembled and shook. Thy way is in the sea, and thy path in the great waters, and thy footsteps are not known. Thou leddest thy people like a flock by the hand of Moses and Aaron" (Ps.77:16-20).

"Nevertheless he saved them for his name's sake, that he might make his mighty power to be known. He rebuked the Red sea also, and it was dried up: so he led them through the depths, as through the wilderness. And he saved them from the hand of him that hated them, and redeemed them from the hand of the enemy. And the waters covered their enemies: there was not one of them left" (Ps.106:8-11).

---

9 George Bush. *Exodus*, p.181.
10 ibid., p.181.
11 Frank E. Gaebelein, Editor. *The Expositor's Bible Commentary*, Vol.2, p.390.

Thought 1. The point to see is this glorious fact: God always delivers His people. No matter what the problem or difficulty is, God will deliver us. God will even move heaven and earth—override the very laws of nature if need be—to deliver us. This is His promise: He will deliver us.

"And he said, The LORD is my rock, and my fortress, and my deliverer" (2 S.22:2).
"Surely he shall deliver thee from the snare of the fowler, and from the noisome pestilence" (Ps.91:3).
"For thou hast delivered my soul from death, mine eyes from tears, and my feet from falling" (Ps.116:8; see 116:1-9).
"And even to your old age I am he; and even to hoar [gray] hairs will I carry you: I have made, and I will bear; even I will carry, and will deliver you" (Is.46:4).
"Be not afraid of their faces: for I am with thee to deliver thee, saith the LORD" (Je.1:8).
"There hath no temptation taken you but such as is common to man: but God is faithful, who will not suffer you to be tempted above that ye are able; but will with the temptation also make a way to escape, that ye may be able to bear it" (1 Co.10:13).
"And the Lord shall deliver me from every evil work, and will preserve me unto his heavenly kingdom: to whom be glory for ever and ever" (2 Ti.4:18).
"Forasmuch then as the children are partakers of flesh and blood, he also himself likewise took part of the same; that through death he might destroy him that had the power of death, that is, the devil; And deliver them who through fear of death were all their lifetime subject to bondage" (He.2:14-15).
"The Lord knoweth how to deliver the godly out of temptations, and to reserve the unjust unto the day of judgment to be punished" (2 Pe.2:9).

7 (14:29-31) **Deliverance—Salvation—Israel—Egypt**: the seventh scene was the LORD's salvation of His people. Four astounding facts are reemphasized in these three verses.
a. Fact 1: Israel walked through the sea on dry ground (v.29).
b. Fact 2: God saved Israel from the ancient Egyptians (v.30).
c. Fact 3: Israel saw the dead, their evil enslavers lying upon the seashore (v.30).
d. Fact 4: God's purpose was accomplished (v.31).
⇒ God's people saw His power.
⇒ God's people feared Him.
⇒ God's people believed in Him and in His messenger. The people now placed their trust in God and in the leadership of Moses. They were now ready—fully ready—to follow God and His servant to the promised land.

Thought 1. The one thing God wants above all else is trust. God wants us to believe Him, to trust Him.

"Trust in the LORD, and do good; so shalt thou dwell in the land, and verily thou shalt be fed....Commit thy way unto the LORD; trust also in him; and he shall bring it to pass" (Ps.37:3, 5).
"Trust in the LORD with all thine heart; and lean not unto thine own understanding" (Pr.3:5).
"Thou wilt keep him in perfect peace, whose mind is stayed on thee: because he trusteth in thee. Trust ye in the LORD for ever: for in the LORD JEHOVAH is everlasting strength" (Is.26:3-4).
"Ye are my witnesses, saith the LORD, and my servant whom I have chosen: that ye may know and believe me, and understand that I am he: before me there was no God formed, neither shall there be after me" (Is.43:10).
"Who is among you that feareth the LORD, that obeyeth the voice of his servant, that walketh in darkness, and hath no light? let him trust in the name of the LORD, and stay upon his God" (Is.50:10).

TYPES, SYMBOLS, AND PICTURES
(Exodus 14:1-31)

Historical Term	Type or Picture (Scriptural Basis for Each)	Life Application for Today's Believer	Biblical Application
The Red Sea (Ex.14:13-31)	*A picture of deliverance through the greatest trials and obstacles* "And Moses said unto the people, Fear ye not, stand still, and see the salvation of the Lord, which he will show to you to day: for the Egyptians whom ye have seen to day, ye shall see them again no more for ever" (Ex.14:13). "And Moses stretched out his hand over the sea;	God promises to deliver us through all the trials and temptations of life, no matter how... • difficult • terrorizing • frightening • fearful • impossible	*"But I am poor and needy; yet the Lord thinketh upon me: thou art my help and my deliverer; make no tarrying, O my God" (Ps.40:17).* *"Fear thou not; for I am with thee: be not dismayed; for I am thy God: I will strengthen thee; yea, I will help thee; yea, I will uphold thee with the right hand of my righteousness" (Is.41:10).*

TYPES, SYMBOLS, AND PICTURES
(Exodus 14:1-31)

Historical Term	Type or Picture (Scriptural Basis for Each)	Life Application for Today's Believer	Biblical Application
The Red Sea (continued) (Ex.14:13-31)	and the LORD caused the sea to go back by a strong east wind all that night, and made the sea dry land, and the waters were divided. And the children of Israel went into the midst of the sea upon the dry ground: and the waters were a wall unto them on their right hand, and on their left" (Ex.14:21-22). "And Moses stretched forth his hand over the sea...And the waters returned, and covered the chariots, and the horsemen, and all the host of Pharaoh that came into the sea after them; there remained not so much as one of them" (Ex.14:26-28).		*"And the Lord shall deliver me from every evil work, and will preserve me unto his heavenly kingdom: to whom be glory for ever and ever" (2 Ti.4:18).* *"Who delivered us from so great a death, and doth deliver: in whom we trust that he will yet deliver us" (2 Co.1:10).* *(see Jn.16:13; 1 Co.10:13; He.2:14-15; 13:5-6; 2 Pe.2:9; Is.30:21; Ps.48:14; 73:24; Ge.28:15; Ex.33:14; De.20:1; Ps.91:3; Is.46:4; Je.1:8;)*
Pharaoh's Defeat (Ex.14:13-31)	*A picture of God's complete and total victory over enemies* "And the waters returned, and covered the chariots, and the horsemen, *and* all the host of Pharaoh that came into the sea after them; there remained not so much as one of them" (Ex.14:28).	Jesus Christ—through His death and resurrection—has conquered all the evil forces of the physical world and of the spiritual world. He now rules... • over the principalities and powers and rulers of this dark world • over the wicked forces of the spiritual world (Satan and his wicked angels) (Remember: Pharaoh symbolizes Satan.)	*"Now is the judgment of this world: now shall the prince of this world be cast out" (Jn.12:31).* *"[The power of God] which he wrought in Christ, when he raised him from the dead, and set him at his own right hand in the heavenly places, Far above all principality, and power, and might, and dominion, and every name that is named, not only in this world, but also in that which is to come: And hath put all things under his feet, and gave him to be the head over all things to the church" (Ep.1:20-22).* *"And having spoiled principalities and powers [upon the cross], he made a show of them openly, triumphing over them in it" (Col.2:15).* *(see Ps.7:11; 2:8-9; Jn.16:11; Col.1:16-17; He.2:14-15; 2 Pe.2:4, 6, 9; Re.20:10; 21:8)*

1. A song of God's praise
a. Because the LORD had gloriously triumphed : He had hurled the armed horsemen into the sea

b. Because the LORD is worthy of praise & renewed commitment
1) My strength & my song
2) My salvation
3) My God
4) My father's God

2. A song of God's great deliverance
a. Delivered by His name: The LORD, a warrior
1) Hurled Pharaoh's chariots & army into the sea
2) Drowned the best of Pharaoh's officers in the Red Sea
3) Covered and sank them in the depths like a stone
b. Delivered by His right hand of power
1) Was majestic in power
2) Destroyed the enemy
c. Delivered by the greatness of His majesty
1) Overthrew those who opposed Him
2) Sent forth His wrath & consumed the enemy
d. Delivered by His mighty control over the waters: Symbolized in the blast of His nostrils
1) He piled up the waters
2) He stood the waters upright
3) He congealed the waters
e. Delivered by His glorious triumph over the bitter hatred of the enemy, over their boasting & pride
1) The enemies' boastings: "I" and "my" (6 times)
2) God destroyed them: Covered them with the sea & they sank like lead in the mighty waters
f. Delivered by the glory of His person: No god is like Him

CHAPTER 15

C. Moses' Great Song of Praise: Praising God for His Great Deliverance, 15:1-21

Then sang Moses and the children of Israel this song unto the LORD, and spake, saying, I will sing unto the LORD, for he hath triumphed gloriously: the horse and his rider hath he thrown into the sea.
2 The LORD is my strength and song, and he is become my salvation: he is my God, and I will prepare him an habitation; my father's God, and I will exalt him.
3 The LORD is a man of war: the LORD is his name.
4 Pharaoh's chariots and his host hath he cast into the sea: his chosen captains also are drowned in the Red sea.
5 The depths have covered them: they sank into the bottom as a stone.
6 Thy right hand, O LORD, is become glorious in power: thy right hand, O LORD, hath dashed in pieces the enemy.
7 And in the greatness of thine excellency thou hast overthrown them that rose up against thee: thou sentest forth thy wrath, which consumed them as stubble.
8 And with the blast of thy nostrils the waters were gathered together, the floods stood upright as an heap, and the depths were congealed in the heart of the sea.
9 The enemy said, I will pursue, I will overtake, I will divide the spoil; my lust shall be satisfied upon them; I will draw my sword, my hand shall destroy them.
10 Thou didst blow with thy wind, the sea covered them: they sank as lead in the mighty waters.
11 Who is like unto thee, O LORD, among the gods? who

Is like thee, glorious in holiness, fearful in praises, doing wonders?
12 Thou stretchedst out thy right hand, the earth swallowed them.
13 Thou in thy mercy hast led forth the people which thou hast redeemed: thou hast guided them in thy strength unto thy holy habitation.
14 The people shall hear, and be afraid: sorrow shall take hold on the inhabitants of Palestina.
15 Then the dukes of Edom shall be amazed; the mighty men of Moab, trembling shall take hold upon them; all the inhabitants of Canaan shall melt away.
16 Fear and dread shall fall upon them; by the greatness of thine arm they shall be as still as a stone; till thy people pass over, O LORD, till the people pass over, which thou hast purchased.
17 Thou shalt bring them in, and plant them in the mountain of thine inheritance, in the place, O LORD, which thou hast made for thee to dwell in, in the Sanctuary, O Lord, which thy hands have established.
18 The LORD shall reign for ever and ever.
19 For the horse of Pharaoh went in with his chariots and with his horsemen into the sea, and the LORD brought again the waters of the sea upon them; but the children of Israel went on dry land in the midst of the sea.
20 And Miriam the prophetess, the sister of Aaron, took a timbrel in her hand; and all the women went out after her with timbrels and with dances.
21 And Miriam answered them, Sing ye to the LORD, for he hath triumphed gloriously; the horse and his rider hath he thrown into the sea.

---

1) Majestic in holiness
2) Awesome in glory
3) Working wonders (NIV)
4) Caused the earth to swallow the enemy

3. A song of God's glorious purpose: To lead the redeemed to God's holy dwelling (the promised land)
a. The source of God's purpose: His mercy, His love
b. The impact of God's leadership & guidance
1) Nations will hear & tremble
2) Enemies will be in anguish
3) Leaders will be terrified & tremble
4) Enemies who stand against the march of God's people to God's dwelling (the promised land) will melt away
5) People will be gripped with fear & dread, as still as stone: Until God's redeemed people reach God's dwelling (the promised land)

c. The promise of God to His people: The LORD will bring them in & plant them on the mountain of His inheritance
1) The very place made for God's dwelling
2) The very sanctuary established by God's hands
3) The very place where the LORD will reign forever

4. A song of special praise & dance: Sung by the women of God's people
a. When: After God's glorious deliverance
1) After the destruction of the Egyptian army
2) After the Israelites walked through the Red Sea
b. Miriam the prophetess led the dance & praise[DS1]

c. The song:
1) The LORD has triumphed gloriously
2) He has thrown the armed horsemen into the sea

DIVISION V

THE RED SEA AND THE WILDERNESS WANDERINGS: THE BELIEVER'S TRIALS AS HE JOURNEYS TO THE PROMISED LAND, 13:17–18:27

C. **Moses' Great Song of Praise: Praising God for His Great Deliverance, 15:1-21**

(15:1-21) **Introduction**: God delivers His people through the trials of life. When we experience His deliverance—the power of His hand upon our lives—our hearts are always filled with joy and rejoicing. Praise floods our hearts. And usually, the greater the deliverance, the greater the praise lifted up to God.

This is what happened to the Israelites. God's great deliverance at the Red Sea was the most wonderful deliverance Israel was ever to experience as a nation. God knew this; therefore, in His infinite wisdom, He stirred Moses to record the praise of his heart forever in Holy Scripture. The song is usually divided into five sections or stanzas.

⇒ Verses 1-5
⇒ Verses 6-8
⇒ Verses 9-10
⇒ Verses 11-12
⇒ Verses 13-18

However, this division seems to focus present-day thought and divisions upon the song. It seems far more natural to look at the song as a whole with Moses declaring how God Himself delivered His people, gloriously delivered them.

Note that Moses' sister Miriam also led the women in singing praises to God (vv.19-21). Both songs are obviously two of the oldest songs ever recorded in written form.

This is the subject of the present passage, this is: *Moses' Great Song of Praise: Praising God for His Great Deliverance,* 15:1-21.

1. A song of God's praise (vv.1-2).
2. A song of God's great deliverance (vv.3-12).
3. A song of God's glorious purpose: to lead the redeemed to God's holy dwelling (the promised land) (vv.13-18).
4. A song of special praise and dance: sung by the women of God's people (vv.19-21).

---

1 (15:1-2) **Song—Worship—Praise—Thanksgiving—God, Names - Titles—Moses—Deliverance**: the song in this passage is a song of God's praise. It is sung to the LORD. The LORD is the focus of the praise. He is addressed thirteen times in this passage, in just twenty-one verses.

• The song sung by Moses addresses God ten times as LORD (Jehovah, Yahweh) (vv.1, 2, 3, 6, 11, 16, 17, 18)
• The song of Moses also addresses God as Adonay one time (v.17)
• The brief song sung by Miriam (vv.19-21) addresses the LORD two times (vv.19, 21)

Moses and the Israelites were flooded with the joy of the moment, and their hearts were just overflowing with a spirit of rejoicing and praise to God. Two reasons are given for Israel breaking out in song.

a. The LORD had gloriously triumphed on behalf of His people: He had hurled the armed horsemen of their enemies into the sea. The LORD had gloriously delivered them from being recaptured and enslaved again by the Egyptians. Moreover, the LORD had miraculously drowned the Egyptian army in the Red Sea. He had made absolutely sure that the ancient Egyptians would never again enslave His people. This was the greatest day of redemption in the history of Israel. God had redeemed them, saved and delivered them from their enemies.

b. The LORD was, therefore, worthy of praise and renewed commitment (v.2). Note how personal the LORD was to the Israelite believer during these moments. His *relationship to the LORD* was very personal. His heart just broke forth praising God for the personal relationship God had made possible and wrought.

1) The LORD is "my strength" (v.2). No matter what trial confronts the believer, God strengthens the believer to face the trial of...
• problems
• temptations
• sufferings
• evil persecution

The believer is weak within himself, but the LORD is always present with him. The LORD is his strength. This the Israelites, God's people, were declaring.

2) The LORD is "my song" (v.2). The believer faces the same trials and sorrows upon earth as unbelievers do. Both believers and unbelievers suffer upon earth; often believers suffer more because of the persecution and hatred of the world. Nevertheless, God comforts the believer and gives him the peace and security of His Holy Spirit. The believer knows that the world and its afflictions can take his life, but not his soul. He knows that he is going to serve God forever in the new heavens and earth. Therefore, the believer is to...
• joy in trials
• rejoice through sufferings
• sing in the face of sorrow

The believer is weak within himself, but the LORD is always present with him. It is the presence of the LORD that always puts the song within the believer's heart. Moses and the true believers among Israel knew this glorious truth; therefore, they led all the people in declaring the glorious truth: "The LORD is my song."

3) The LORD is "my salvation" (v.2). The enemies of the world—including evil men, sin, death, and hell—are always attacking and threatening the believer. But God is the believer's Savior: He will deliver and save the believer from all that opposes him.

4) The LORD is "my God" (v.2). He is the true and living God. God had just proven this once again by miraculously delivering His people through the Red Sea and destroying their enemies. The miracle had just taken

place. It was time for God's people to reaffirm their faith and declare that God is "my God." It was time for them to praise and make a renewed commitment to Him. Each Israelite had reason to stand up and shout...
- "The LORD, He is my God."
- "I will prepare my heart for His *indwelling presence*."

5) The LORD is "my father's God." Their fathers had taught them to believe God and His great promises to His people. Their fathers were strong in faith and God had blessed them ever so richly. Therefore, the Israelites declared that they were committing themselves to follow the God of their fathers. He was worthy to be followed. This He had just proven by delivering them so miraculously through the Red Sea.

2 (15:3-12) **Deliverance—God, Power—Song**: the song was a song of God's great deliverance. Six facts are declared about God's great deliverance.
a. God delivered His people by His name: He is the LORD, and the LORD is a warrior (vv.3-5). The very name LORD (Jehovah, Yahweh) means that God is our Redeemer, Deliverer, Savior. The LORD...
- fights for us
- stands against our enemies for us
- conquers all opposition for us
- triumphs and gains the victory over all the forces of evil for us

This the LORD did for Israel:
⇒ He hurled Pharaoh's chariots and army into the sea (v.4).
⇒ He drowned the best of Pharaoh's officers in the Red Sea (v.4).
⇒ He covered and sank them in the depths like a stone (v.5).

Note the emphasis upon the water where Israel crossed:
⇒ The army was cast into the sea.
⇒ The army was drowned in the Red Sea.
⇒ The army was covered by the depths.
⇒ The army sank to the bottom like a stone.

The point: the place where Israel crossed the sea was not a shallow place, not only ankle or knee deep. It was a large body of water, a body so large that it drowned the Egyptian army when God released the two walls of water to flow back together again. A miracle? Yes! A phenomenal, miraculous work of God—all to save His people just as He had promised He would.

Thought 1. The very name LORD is the picture of a warrior who delivers, saves, and redeems us from the enemies of this world (see Ex.14:14). The LORD is the warrior who saved Israel from being slaughtered and enslaved by the Egyptian army. Similarly, the LORD is the warrior who will save us from our enemies.

"**The LORD shall fight for you, and ye shall hold your peace**" (Ex.14:14).
"**With him is an arm of flesh; but with us is the LORD our God to help us, and to fight our battles**" (2 Chr.32:8).
"**Lift up your head, O ye gates; and be ye lift up, ye everlasting doors; and the King of glory shall come in. Who is this King of glory? The LORD strong and mighty, the LORD mighty in battle**" (Ps.24:7-8).
"**Jesus [our Lord] answered and said, This voice came not because of me, but for your sakes. Now is the judgment of this world: now shall the prince of this world be cast out**" (Jn.12:30-31).
"**These things I have spoken unto you, that in me ye might have peace. In the world ye shall have tribulation: but be of good cheer; I have overcome the world**" (Jn.16:33).
"**Then cometh the end, when he shall have delivered up the kingdom to God, even the Father; when he shall have put down all rule and all authority and power**" (1 Co.15:24).
"**And then shall that Wicked be revealed, whom the Lord shall consume with the spirit of his mouth, and shall destroy with the brightness of his coming**" (2 Th.2:8).
"**Forasmuch then as the children are partakers of flesh and blood, he [the Lord Jesus Christ] also himself likewise took part of the same; that through death he might destroy him that had the power of death, that is, the devil; And deliver them who through fear of death were all their lifetime subject to bondage**" (He.2:14-15).
"**He that committeth sin is of the devil; for the devil sinneth from the beginning. For this purpose the Son of God was manifested, that he might destroy the works of the devil**" (1 Jn.3:8).
"**And I saw, and behold a white horse: and he that sat on him had a bow; and a crown was given unto him: and he went forth conquering, and to conquer**" (Re.6:2).
"**These shall make war with the Lamb, and the Lamb shall overcome them: for he is Lord of lords, and King of kings: and they that are with him are called, and chosen, and faithful**" (Re.17:14).

b. God delivered His people by His right hand of power (v.6). The *right hand* is a symbol of power. In reference to God, it refers to His omnipotent power. God is omnipotent: all power belongs to Him. He can do anything, and nothing is too hard for Him. God's right hand can roll back and make a passage-way through the waters of any sea—if He so wills. God can reverse any law of nature as He wills. The Israelites had just witnessed this astounding miracle of God. Their song declared the glorious fact:

⇒ The right hand of the LORD was majestic in power.
⇒ The right hand of the LORD destroyed and dashed the Egyptian army into pieces.

Thought 1. God is omnipotent. He has the power to deliver and save us from any force, no matter how evil, terrible, or terrifying. He even has the power to save and deliver us from death, the power to plant the seed of eternal life in us.

"Both riches and honour come of thee, and thou reignest over all; and in thine hand is power and might; and in thine hand it is to make great, and to give strength unto all" (1 Chr.29:12).

"I know that thou canst do every thing, and that no thought can be withholden from thee" (Jb.42:2).

"But our God is in the heavens: he hath done whatsoever he hath pleased" (Ps.115:3).

"Yea, before the day was I am he; and there is none that can deliver out of my hand: I will work, and who shall let [hinder, stop] it?" (Is.43:13).

"But Jesus beheld [them], and said unto them, With men this is impossible; but with God all things are possible" (Mt.19:26).

"For with God nothing shall be impossible" (Lu.1:37).

"Now unto him that is able to do exceeding abundantly above all that we ask or think, according to the power that worketh in us" (Ep.3:20).

"For our conversation [citizenship] is in heaven; from whence also we look for the Saviour, the Lord Jesus Christ: Who shall change our vile body, that it may be fashioned like unto his glorious body, according to the working whereby he is able even to subdue all things unto himself" (Ph.3:20-21).

"And the Lord shall deliver me from every evil work, and will preserve me unto his heavenly kingdom: to whom be glory for ever and ever" (2 Ti.4:18).

c. God delivered His people by the greatness of His majesty (v.7). Note that Pharaoh and his army are said to have risen up against God, not Israel. God counts believers as His own, as His very own people, as His very own family. Therefore, to rise up against believers is the same as rising up against their Father, against God Himself.
⇒ God overthrew those who opposed Him. The word *overthrew* (haras) is the picture of destroying a building. The enemies of God set out to destroy the building of God, His people, His Old Testament body of believers. Therefore, God destroyed the building of their army.[1]
⇒ God sent forth His wrath and consumed them as stubble. He consumed them as though their building was nothing but stubble.

The majesty of God is so glorious—so brilliant and bright—that it can consume the mightiest army upon earth, consume it as though it is nothing more than mere stubble.

"Thine, O LORD, is the greatness, and the power, and the glory, and the victory, and the majesty: for all that is in the heaven and in the earth is thine; thine is the kingdom, O LORD, and thou art exalted as head above all" (1 Chr.29:11).

"With God is terrible majesty. Touching the Almighty, we cannot find him out: he is excellent in power, and in judgment, and in plenty of justice" (Jb.37:22-23).

"The voice of the LORD is powerful; the voice of the LORD is full of majesty" (Ps.29:4).

"The LORD reigneth, he is clothed with majesty; the LORD is clothed with strength, wherewith he hath girded himself: the world also is stablished, that it cannot be moved" (Ps.93:1).

"For all the gods of the nations are idols: but the LORD made the heavens. Honour and majesty are before him: strength and beauty are in his sanctuary" (Ps.96:5-6).

"Enter into the rock, and hide thee in the dust, for fear of the LORD, and for the glory of his majesty. The lofty looks of man shall be humbled, and the haughtiness of men shall be bowed down, and the LORD alone shall be exalted in that day. For the day of the LORD of hosts shall be upon every one that is proud and lofty, and upon every one that is lifted up; and he shall be brought low" (Is.2:10-12).

"For thus saith the high and lofty One that inhabiteth eternity, whose name is Holy; I dwell in the high and holy place, with him also that is of a contrite and humble spirit, to revive the spirit of the humble, and to revive the heart of the contrite ones" (Is.57:15).

"Now unto him that is able to keep you from falling, and to present you faultless before the presence of his glory with exceeding joy, To the only wise God our Saviour, be glory and majesty, dominion and power, both now and ever" (Jude 24-25).

d. God delivered His people by His mighty control over the waters (v.8). Note that the "blast of God's nostrils" is said to have caused the strong east wind that divided the Red Sea (14:21). This is simply descriptive language, a poetic way to declare God's control over the waters. The fact is unquestionable, obvious: the blast of God's nostrils, the blast of God's control...
• piled up the waters
• stood the stormy, surging waters upright
• congealed the deep waters

---

[1] Frank E. Gaebelein, Editor. *The Expositor's Bible Commentary*, Vol.2, p.394.

e. God delivered His people by His glorious triumph over the bitter hatred of the enemy, over their pride and boastings (vv.9-10). The spirit of the Egyptians is exposed in these two verses. They had been gripped with a spirit of bitter hatred against the Israelite slaves. To the Egyptian mind, the Israelites were the scum of the earth, descendants of detestable shepherds, a people worthy only to be enslaved. Moreover, the Israelites were the cause for the ten plagues being launched against Egypt, the cause for the destruction of Egypt and its economy. The Egyptians had always loathed the Israelites, but after the terrible destruction of their nation by the God of the Israelites, their loathing grew to hatred—bitter hatred. Thus, the Egyptians had vowed to utterly destroy God's people.

1) Note the sixfold vow and boastings of the Egyptian army. It is as though they are so bent on pursuing and destroying God's people that they can hardly catch their breath. The picture is that of a heaving chest and a breathless voice boasting…
- "I will pursue."
- "I will overtake."
- "I will divide the spoils."
- "I will gorge myself on them" (NIV).
- "I will draw my sword."
- "My hand shall destroy them" (v.9).

2) But God had promised to deliver His people, and this He did. He fulfilled His promise. God caused the wind to blow and note what happened:
⇒ The sea covered the Egyptian army and they sank like lead in the mighty waters (v.10).

Thought 1. The world hates believers. Believers live righteous and pure lives; they teach love and compassion, un-selfishness and giving, giving even to the point of sacrifice. The world despises this way of life. The worldly of the world want to…
- do their own thing
- live their own way
- get and possess all they can
- be comfortable and indulge their desires

Thus the life of believers and the life of the worldly are at odds. The result is tragic: the worldly ridicule and persecute believers. But God has promised a glorious triumph over the worldly of this earth. He has promised to deliver us from this world. And God will fulfill His promise; this is the strong declaration of Scripture.

"He shall deliver thee in six troubles: yea, in seven there shall no evil touch thee" (Jb.5:19).
"Surely he shall deliver thee from the snare of the fowler, and from the noisome pestilence" (Ps.91:3).
"There hath no temptation taken you but such as is common to man: but God is faithful, who will not suffer you to be tempted above that ye are able; but will with the temptation also make a way to escape, that ye may be able to bear it" (1 Co.10:13).
"And the Lord shall deliver me from every evil work, and will preserve me unto his heavenly kingdom: to whom be glory for ever and ever" (2 Ti.4:18).
"The Lord knoweth how to deliver the godly out of temptations, and to reserve the unjust unto the day of judgment to be punished" (2 Pe.2:9).

f. God delivered His people by His matchless person: no god is like Him (vv.1-12). No person, no being—real or imagined—can compare with God. This the LORD had just proven.
⇒ Egypt was renowned for its gods, but they were nothing but man-made gods. They were mere idols who were helpless in protecting the Egyptians from the execution of God's holy justice.
⇒ The leaders, kings, and princes of this world are often treated as gods, but they are mere men. They are only frail, limited, and mortal, totally incapable of standing before or against the LORD.

The song of Moses graphically declares the truth: "Who is like you, O LORD, among the gods? Who is like you…"
- majestic in holiness
- awesome in glory
- working wonders

What wonder? The LORD stretched out His right hand, and the earth swallowed the enemy of His people. No man-made god could keep God from executing justice upon the oppressors and evil persecutors of His people.

"He is the Rock, his work is perfect: for all his ways are judgment: a God of truth and without in-iquity, just and right is he" (De.32:4).
"For the LORD loveth judgment, and forsaketh not his saints; they are preserved for ever: but the seed of the wicked shall be cut off" (Ps.37:28).
"Of the increase of his government and peace there shall be no end, upon the throne of David, and upon his kingdom, to order it, and to establish it with judgment and with justice from henceforth even for ever. The zeal of the LORD of hosts will perform this" (Is.9:7).
"In those days, and at that time, will I cause the Branch of righteousness to grow up unto David; and he shall execute judgment and righteousness in the land" (Je.33:15).

"And I will set my glory among the heathen, and all the heathen shall see my judgment that I have executed, and my hand that I have laid upon them" (Eze.39:21).

"Art thou not from everlasting, O LORD my God, mine Holy One? we shall not die. O LORD, thou hast ordained them for judgment; and, O mighty God, thou hast established them for correction" (Hab.1:12).

"But we are sure that the judgment of God is according to truth against them which commit such things. And thinkest thou this, O man, that judgest them which do such things, and doest the same, that thou shalt escape the judgment of God?" (Ro.2:2-3).

"The Lord knoweth how to deliver the godly out of temptations, and to reserve the unjust unto the day of judgment to be punished" (2 Pe.2:9).

3 (15:13-18) **Song—Purpose, of God—Land, The Promised—Guidance, of God**: the song is a song of God's glorious purpose: to lead the redeemed to His holy dwelling, that is, to *the promised land*. This passage is definitely referring to *the promised land*. Note that enemies would stand in the way as Israel marched to claim their promised inheritance, but God would cause the hearts of the enemy to melt. God was going to bring His people to their inheritance, to the promised land, to the very sanctuary where the presence of the LORD dwelt (a symbol of heaven). (See DEEPER STUDY # 1—Ex.2:24; note—Ge.12:1 for more discussion.)

Note a significant fact: these verses point to the future. They declare the assurance of God's people in the great promise of God. What promise?

⇒ That God was going to lead His people to the promised land; that God was going to make absolutely sure that His people received their promised inheritance, the inheritance of the promised land (see 1 S.26:19; Ps.79:1).

The Scripture and outline points cover the message proclaimed by the song. God's glorious purpose is to lead His redeemed people to His holy dwelling, to the promised land (symbolically, the promised land of heaven where His holy presence dwells eternally).

a. The source of God's great purpose is His mercy, His love (v.13). God had demonstrated His mercy and love by redeeming His people. He had saved them from the bondage of slavery by delivering them from their enemies through the Red Sea.

The point is clear: in looking to the future, God's people could trust the mercy and love of God. God's mercy and love would continue to lead His people until they reached the promised land.

Thought 1. It is God's mercy and love that redeems us, that saves and delivers us throughout life. We can rest assured: God's mercy and love will lead us to the promised land, the promised inheritance of living with God eternally.

"For God so loved the world, that he gave his only begotten Son, that whosoever believeth in him should not perish, but have everlasting life" (Jn.3:16).

"But God, who is rich in mercy, for his great love wherewith he loved us, Even when we were dead in sins, hath quickened us together with Christ, (by grace ye are saved;) And hath raised us up together, and made us sit together in heavenly places in Christ Jesus: That in the ages to come he might show the exceeding riches of his grace in his kindness toward us through Christ Jesus" (Ep.2:4-7).

"Not by works of righteousness which we have done, but according to his mercy he saved us, by the washing of regeneration, and renewing of the Holy Ghost; Which he shed on us abundantly through Jesus Christ our Saviour; That being justified by his grace, we should be made heirs according to the hope of eternal life" (Tit.3:5-7).

"Blessed be the God and Father of our Lord Jesus Christ, which according to his abundant mercy hath begotten us again unto a lively hope by the resurrection of Jesus Christ from the dead, To an inheritance incorruptible, and undefiled, and that fadeth not away, reserved in heaven for you" (1 Pe.1:3-4).

b. The impact of God's leadership and guidance was clearly seen: it was a clear demonstration of God's awesome power (vv.14-16). God's hand would rest powerfully upon His people. Note the impact upon Israel's enemies. Fear would grip them. Note the five different descriptions of the fear.

⇒ Nations would hear and tremble.
⇒ Enemies would be in anguish.
⇒ Leaders would be terrified and tremble.
⇒ Enemies would melt away, the enemies who stood against the march of God's people to God's dwelling (the promised land).
⇒ People would be gripped with fear and dread, as still as stone, until God's redeemed people reached God's dwelling (the promised land).

Thought 1. No enemy will ever be able to stop God from leading us to the promised land of heaven. God protects and guides us day by day, and He will protect and guide us until He is ready to take us home to heaven.

"For the eyes of the LORD run to and fro throughout the whole earth, to show himself strong in the behalf of them whose heart is perfect toward him. Herein thou hast done foolishly: therefore from henceforth thou shalt have wars" (2 Chr.16:9).

"The LORD is my shepherd; I shall not want. He maketh me to lie down in green pastures: he leadeth me beside the still waters. He restoreth my soul: he leadeth me in the paths of righteousness for his name's sake. Yea, though I walk through the valley of the shadow of death, I will fear no evil: for thou art with me; thy rod and thy staff they comfort me. Thou preparest a table before me in the presence of mine enemies: thou anointest my head with oil; my cup runneth over. Surely goodness and mercy shall follow me all the days of my life: and I will dwell in the house of the LORD [heaven] for ever" (Ps.23:1-6).

"The angel of the LORD encampeth round about them that fear him, and delivereth them" (Ps.34:7).

"For this God is our God for ever and ever: he will be our guide even unto death" (Ps.48:14).

"Thou shalt guide me with thy counsel, and afterward receive me to glory" (Ps.73:24).

"In my Father's house are many mansions: if [it were] not [so], I would have told you. I go to prepare a place for you. And if I go and prepare a place for you, I will come again, and receive you unto myself; that where I am, [there] ye may be also" (Jn.14:2-3).

"For our conversation [citizenship] is in heaven; from whence also we look for the Saviour, the Lord Jesus Christ: Who shall change our vile body, that it may be fashioned like unto his glorious body, according to the working whereby he is able even to subdue all things unto himself" (Ph.3:20-21).

4 (15:19-21) **Miriam—Song—Praise**: the song stirred a special praise and dance by the women of God's people. These three verses cover what is called "The Song of Miriam." Remember, Miriam was the sister of Moses, the older sister who had so lovingly looked after him when he was a tiny baby. (See outline and notes—Ex.3:1-10 for more discussion.)

a. When did Miriam sing this song? Right after God's glorious deliverance (v.19). Scripture says...
- right after God destroyed the Egyptian army in the sea
- right after the Israelites walked on dry land through the sea

b. Miriam led all the Israelite women in dancing and praising the LORD (v.20). Note that Miriam is called a prophetess. (See DEEPER STUDY # 1—Ex.15:20 for discussion.)

c. The song of Miriam was sung to the LORD (v.21). The song focused upon two great facts:
1) The King James Version declares this:
   ⇒ The LORD has *triumphed gloriously*.
   ⇒ The LORD has thrown the horse and rider into the sea.

2) The New American Standard declares this:
   ⇒ The LORD is *highly exalted*.
   ⇒ The LORD has hurled the horse and rider into the sea.

Thought 1. God delivers His people. He always has and He always will deliver us from evil, even from the final evil, that of death and hell.

"And he said, The LORD is my rock, and my fortress, and my deliverer" (2 S.22:2).

"And even to your old age I am he; and even to hoar [gray] hairs will I carry you: I have made, and I will bear; even I will carry, and will deliver you" (Is.46:4).

"Be not afraid of their faces: for I am with thee to deliver thee, saith the LORD" (Je.1:8).

"There hath no temptation taken you but such as is common to man: but God is faithful, who will not suffer you to be tempted above that ye are able; but will with the temptation also make a way to escape, that ye may be able to bear it" (1 Co.10:13).

"And the Lord shall deliver me from every evil work, and will preserve me unto his heavenly kingdom: to whom be glory for ever and ever" (2 Ti.4:18).

"Forasmuch then as the children are partakers of flesh and blood, he also himself likewise took part of the same; that through death he might destroy him that had the power of death, that is, the devil; And deliver them who through fear of death were all their lifetime subject to bondage" (He.2:14-15).

"The Lord knoweth how to deliver the godly out of temptations, and to reserve the unjust unto the day of judgment to be punished" (2 Pe.2:9).

DEEPER STUDY # 1
(15:20) **Prophetess**: the calling of the prophetess is the same calling as a prophet. The prophetess was a woman called by God to be God's spokeswoman. She was called, appointed, and anointed by God...
- to declare God's Word
- to be the messenger of God
- to be endued with the very power and authority of God

Scripture mentions several other women who were called by God to receive the prophetic gift to speak for Him, to be His prophetesses:
⇒ Deborah (Jud.4:4)
⇒ Isaiah's wife (Is.8:3)
⇒ Huldah (2 K.22:14)
⇒ Noadiah (Ne.6:14)
⇒ Anna (Lu.2:36)
⇒ Philip's daughters (Ac.21:9)

	D. The Second Crisis of Israel in the Wilderness—Bitter Water at Marah: Bitter Experiences Made Sweet & Pure, 15:22-27	him a tree, which when he had cast into the waters, the waters were made sweet: there he made for them a statute and an ordinance, and there he proved them,	He showed Moses a piece of wood that purified, sweetened, the water
1. The first crisis: Thirst			**4. The purpose of God: To test His people**
a. Moses led the people from the Red Sea into the wilderness of Shur:*DS1* Went three days & found *no water*	22 So Moses brought Israel from the Red sea, and they went out into the wilderness of Shur; and they went three days in the wilderness, and found no water.	26 And said, If thou wilt diligently hearken to the voice of the LORD thy God, and wilt do that which is right in his sight, and wilt give ear to his commandments, and keep all his statutes, I will	**5. The result of the crisis: The LORD made a great covenant & promise**
			a. The covenant: Conditional
			1) If diligently listen
			2) If do what is right
			3) If obey commandments
b. Moses led them to Marah:*DS2* Found water, but it was *bitter*	23 And when they came to Marah, they could not drink of the waters of Marah, for they were bitter: therefore the name of it was called Marah.	put none of these diseases upon thee, which I have brought upon the Egyptians: for I am the LORD that healeth thee.	b. The Lord's promise
			1) He would not have to chastise them with the diseases brought upon the Egyptians
2. The first terrible sin of Israel: Complaining, grumbling, murmuring	24 And the people murmured against Moses, saying, What shall we drink?	27 And they came to Elim, where were twelve wells of water, and threescore and ten palm trees: and they en-	2) He would always provide for them: "I am the LORD who heals you"*DS3*
3. The cry of God's servant to the LORD & the LORD's provision:	25 And he cried unto the LORD; and the LORD showed	camped there by the waters.	**6. The abundant provision of God: Led them to Elim which had twelve springs & seventy palm trees*DS4***

DIVISION V

THE RED SEA AND THE WILDERNESS WANDERINGS: THE BELIEVER'S TRIALS AS HE JOURNEYS TO THE PROMISED LAND, 13:17–18:27

D. The Second Crisis of Israel in the Wilderness, Bitter Water at Marah: Bitter Experiences Made Sweet and Pure, 15:22-27

(15:22-27) **Introduction**: complaining, grumbling, and murmuring are terrible sins. Think of the hurt and pain we feel when people grumble against us, especially when the complaint threatens our…

- lives
- friendships
- reputations
- characters
- work
- relationships
- attachments
- positions
- employment
- promotions
- investments

Complaining, grumbling, and murmuring hurt and cause pain. But more than this, complaining and grumbling show a great distrust in God:

⇒ It shows that we do not believe God is in control and that He is going to work things out.
⇒ It shows that we are distrusting God's power, questioning His goodness to take care of the situation.

This is the subject of this important passage of Scripture. It covers the first terrible sin of the Israelites, that of complaining. They grumbled and murmured against their leader, God's dear servant Moses. This is: *The Second Crisis of Israel in the Wilderness, Bitter Water at Marah: Bitter Experiences Made Sweet and Pure*, 15:22-27.

1. The first crisis: thirst (vv.22-23).
2. The first terrible sin of Israel: complaining, grumbling, murmuring (v.24).
3. The cry of God's servant to the Lord and the Lord's provision for His people: He showed Moses a piece of wood that purified, sweetened, the water (v.25).
4. The purpose of God: to test His people (25).
5. The result of the crisis: the Lord made a great law and promise (vv.25-26).
6. The abundant provision of God: led them to Elim which had twelve springs and seventy palm trees (v.27).

1 (15:22-23) **Israel—Wilderness Wanderings—Thirst—Trials**: the first crisis faced by Israel in the *wilderness wanderings* was that of thirst.
a. Moses led the Israelites from the Red Sea, beginning their march to Mt. Sinai. To reach Sinai they had to cross the desert of Shur (see DEEPER STUDY # 1—Ex.15:22 for more discussion). It was the desert that created the problem: they traveled and found *no water*. Imagine two to three million people marching across a desert for three days and finding *no water*. The water supply of some families had run low, and apparently the supply of others had run out. Being out in the desert with no water was as severe a crisis as could be faced. It was a matter of life and death—survival was at stake, the survival of several million people including children. What could be done?

b. Moses led them to a place where there was supposed to be water, to *Marah*. But shockingly, the water had become polluted: the water was *bitter,* unfit to drink (see Deeper Study # 2, *Marah*—Ex.15:23). From the reaction of the people, it was apparently so bitter that they were afraid to drink it, feeling it was unsafe.

Thought 1. Remember these facts.
⇒ The Israelites had just been *delivered by God* from Egyptian slavery. Their deliverance is a picture of the believer's redemption, of his deliverance from the enslavement of the world to sin and death.
⇒ The Israelites had just begun their wilderness journey, their journey to the promised land of Canaan. This is a picture of the believer beginning his Christian life and walk, his journey throughout life to the promised land of heaven.
⇒ Thus, the crisis of the bitter waters of Marah is a picture of the bitter trials that confront the believer as he walks throughout life, marching to the promised land of heaven.

Now, just think of the bitter trials that confront us throughout life, such bitter trials as...
* no water
* no food
* no home
* accidents
* divorce
* suffering
* deformity
* death
* loss of job
* financial loss
* severe temptation
* failed plans
* frustrations
* disappointments
* sorrows
* despondency

Bitter trials are the normal experience of human life. They confront us all, and they perplex and puzzle us. Believers often ask, "Why has God let this happen to me?" Trials and temptations are common to all people. When they strike us, the question is: How are we going to react? Are we going to trust God to help and strengthen us, or grumble and complain and perhaps curse God?

"Why art thou cast down, O my soul?" (Ps.42:5).
"There hath no temptation taken you but such as is common to man: but God is faithful, who will not suffer you to be tempted above that ye are able; but will with the temptation also make a way to escape, that ye may be able to bear it" (1 Co.10:13).
"For verily, when we were with you, we told you before that we should suffer tribulation; even as it came to pass, and ye know" (1 Th.3:4).
"Beloved, think it not strange concerning the fiery trial which is to try you, as though some strange thing happened unto you: But rejoice, inasmuch as ye are partakers of Christ's sufferings; that, when his glory shall be revealed, ye may be glad also with exceeding joy" (1 Pe.4:12-13).

Thought 2. After traveling for three days in the hot, dry desert, the Israelites must have burst forth with joy at finding water. But what a terrible disappointment! Bitter, undrinkable water!
The bitter, undrinkable water is a picture of the bitter waters of the world, the bitter trials and experiences of this world. The person who drinks from the waters of this earth is doomed to disappointment. The waters of this earth will prove to be bitter:
⇒ alcohol
⇒ drugs
⇒ sex
⇒ wealth
⇒ pleasure
⇒ fame
⇒ recognition
⇒ power
⇒ position
⇒ beauty
⇒ possessions

The waters of the earth never satisfy the thirst of the human heart. Only Jesus Christ can satisfy the thirst of the heart. He is the living water.

"Jesus answered and said unto her, Whosoever drinketh of this water shall thirst again: But whosoever drinketh of the water that I shall give him shall never thirst; but the water that I shall give him shall be in him a well of water springing up into everlasting life" (Jn.4:13-14).
"In the last day, that great [day] of the feast, Jesus stood and cried, saying, If any man thirst, let him come unto me, and drink. He that believeth on me, as the scripture hath said, out of his belly shall flow rivers of living water" (Jn.7:37-38).
"Blessed [are] they which do hunger and thirst after righteousness: for they shall be filled" (Mt.5:6).
"They shall hunger no more, neither thirst any more; neither shall the sun light on them, nor any heat" (Re.7:16).
"And the Spirit and the bride say, Come. And let him that heareth say, Come. And let him that is athirst come. And whosoever will, let him take the water of life freely" (Re.22:17).
"Ho, every one that thirsteth, come ye to the waters, and he that hath no money; come ye, buy, and eat; yea, come, buy wine and milk without money and without price" (Is.55:1).

DEEPER STUDY # 1
(15:22) **Shur, Desert of**: this desert stretched from the northeast section of Egypt over to the northwestern part of the Sinai Desert. It reached down southward to the mountains of Sinai. Shur is also called "the desert of Etham" (Nu.33:8). Apparently "Shur" was the Hebrew word for the desert and "Etham" the Egyptian word.[1]

[1] Frank E. Gaebelein, Editor. *The Expositor's Bible Commentary*, Vol.2, p.398.

⇒ The word "Shur" means *wall*, referring to a *fortress wall*.
⇒ The Desert of Shur is a significant part of the Old Testament lands where the patriarchs traveled and lived.
  • There were Sarah and Abraham.

> **"And the angel of the LORD found her [Hagar] by a fountain of water in the wilderness, by the fountain in the way to Shur" (Ge.16:7).**
> **"And Abraham [and his family] journeyed from thence toward the south country, and dwelled between Kadesh and Shur, and sojourned in Gerar" (Ge.20:1).**

  • There were the descendents of Ishmael.

> **"And they dwelt from Havilah unto Shur, that is before Egypt, as thou goest toward Assyria: and he died in the presence of all his brethren" (Ge.25:18).**

  • There were Moses and the Israelites.

> **"So Moses brought Israel from the Red sea, and they went out into the wilderness of Shur; and they went three days in the wilderness, and found no water" (Ex.15:22).**

  • There was King Saul who fought the Amalekites.

> **"And Saul smote the Amalekites from Havilah until thou comest to Shur, that is over against Egypt" (1 S.15:7).**

  • There were David and his men who fought the Geshurites, the Gezrites, and the Amalekites whose roots were in Shur.

> **"And David and his men went up, and invaded the Geshurites, and the Gezrites, and the Amalekites: for those nations were of old the inhabitants of the land, as thou goest to Shur, even unto the land of Egypt" (1 S.27:8).**

DEEPER STUDY # 2
(15:23) **Marah**: the word means *bitter*. The water was obviously polluted by some mineral that made it impure and unfit for drinking.
⇒ Marah was probably the area known today as *Ain Hawarah*. This lies several miles inland from the sea, about forty-seven miles southeast of Suez and only about seven miles from the Red Sea.[2]
⇒ Marah was about a three day journey into the wilderness of Etham. The Israelites camped at Marah and demonstrated a spirit of terrible unbelief, a spirit of complaining and grumbling against the Lord and His appointed leader, Moses (Ex.15:23; Nu.33:8).

---

[2] (15:24) **Complaining—Grumbling—Murmuring—Sin—Israel**: this is the first terrible sin of Israel, that of complaining, grumbling, and murmuring. This was to be a sin constantly committed when the Israelites faced a crisis. Keep in mind what the Israelites had just experienced three days earlier: the great deliverance of God through the Red Sea. Moreover, throughout the previous year or two, they had witnessed the awesome power of God through the ten plagues of judgment cast upon the Egyptians. But here they were, three days later—just three days after their great Red Sea deliverance—complaining and grumbling against God's servant. They should have remembered God...
  • remembered His great power and love
  • remembered His great care and provision

They should have trusted God to provide water. They should have bowed in prayer, calling upon God to show their leader, Moses, where water was. Imagine what a glorious picture of trust and victory that would have been: two to three million people—men, women, and children—all bowing together in military file on the desert sands, all praying and calling out to God for help through the crisis.

But this was not to be. They were immature believers: unspiritual, unstable, and carnal (fleshly). Their carnal hearts of unbelief took over, and the Israelites complained, grumbled, and murmured against God's leader. This was the first terrible sin of Israel, and it was to be a sin committed time and again by them. In fact, every time they faced a crisis, they were to complain and murmur. Note these examples:

⇒ They complained and grumbled because they had no food.

> **"And the whole congregation of the children of Israel murmured against Moses and Aaron in the wilderness" (Ex.16:2).**

---

2 *Zondervan Pictorial Encyclopedia of the Bible*, Vol.4:70.

⇒ They complained and grumbled because they had no water.

"**And the people thirsted there for water; and the people murmured against Moses, and said, Wherefore is this that thou hast brought us up out of Egypt, to kill us and our children and our cattle with thirst?" (Ex.17:3).**

⇒ They complained and grumbled because of the trials they were facing throughout their wilderness wanderings: they wished to return to Egypt.

"**And all the children of Israel murmured against Moses and against Aaron: and the whole congregation said unto them, Would God that we had died in the land of Egypt! or would God we had died in this wilderness! And wherefore hath the LORD brought us unto this land, to fall by the sword, that our wives and our children should be a prey? were it not better for us to return into Egypt? And they said one to another, Let us make a captain, and let us return into Egypt" (Nu.14:2-4).**

⇒ They complained and grumbled because they became tired of their leaders, tired of Moses' and Aaron's leadership.

"**For which cause both thou and all thy company are gathered together against the LORD: and what is Aaron, that ye murmur against him?" (Nu.16:11).**

⇒ They complained and grumbled because of God's judgment, because God executed justice upon the Israelites who sinned.

"**But on the morrow all the congregation of the children of Israel murmured against Moses and against Aaron, saying, Ye have killed the people of the LORD" (Nu.16:41).**

As stated in the Introduction, complaining and grumbling are signs of distrust, of terrible unbelief in God. When we complain and grumble, we reveal a heart of unbelief and distrust. We reveal that we do not believe God's power and goodness. We do not believe that God is in control, that He will work the situation out. A heart that trusts God will always pray, asking God to help. The trusting heart never complains nor grumbles against people and situations, especially not against fellow believers and certainly not against the dear servants of God. Note these facts about complaining and grumbling.

a. Complaining and grumbling are not against the servant of God but against the Lord Himself.

"**And Moses said, This shall be, when the LORD shall give you in the evening flesh to eat, and in the morning bread to the full; for that the LORD heareth your murmurings which ye murmur against him: and what are we? your murmurings are not against us, but against the LORD" (Ex.16:8).**

b. Complaining and grumbling are often due to a person not believing God's Word nor listening to His voice.

"**Yea, they despised the pleasant land, they believed not his word: But murmured in their tents, and hearkened not unto the voice of the LORD" (Ps.106:24-25).**

c. Complaining and grumbling are often due to the foolishness and sin of man himself.

"**The foolishness of man perverteth his way: and his heart fretteth against the LORD" (Pr.19:3).**
"**Wherefore doth a living man complain, a man for the punishment of his sins?" (Lam.3:39).**

d. Complaining and grumbling are to have no part in the believer's life.

"**Do all things without murmurings and disputings" (Ph.2:14).**

e. Complaining and grumbling shall be severely judged by God.

"**Neither murmur ye, as some of them also murmured, and were destroyed of the destroyer" (1 Co.10:10).**
"**Behold, the Lord cometh with ten thousands of his saints, To execute judgment upon all, and to convince all that are ungodly among them of all their ungodly deeds which they have ungodly committed, and of all their hard speeches which ungodly sinners have spoken against him. These are murmurers, complainers, walking after their own lusts; and their mouth speaketh great swelling words, having men's persons in admiration because of advantage" (Jude 14-16).**

Thought 1. People thirst for contentment, for an elusive peace of mind. To find contentment and peace, they thirst and thirst after all kinds of things. And the world offers all kinds of things to people, claiming that they will satisfy the thirst of the human heart. But the waters, the things offered by the world, are bitter; they leave a bitter taste in our mouths and do not quench our thirst. Despite this, every day, all over the world, men drink from the bitter wells of the earth, the bitter waters of...

- pleasure
- fame
- illicit sex
- a shallow form of religion
- material possessions
- position

- power
- money
- property
- bright lights and stardom
- self-gratification
- idolatry

Blinded by a craving that never satisfies, men drink their fill of these waters. They drink and drink, but in the end a bitter taste in the mouth is the only thing that lingers.

What is the answer to the bitter waters of experience as the believer journeys in the wilderness of the world? The answer comes from Jesus Christ Himself. Only He has the power to sweeten the bitter waters of life. How does Christ create this great antidote for a world sickened by drinking polluted waters? Jesus Christ has poured His life into this world and flooded the world with Living waters, waters that satisfy the thirst of the human heart, that give life to man. The Scriptures declare that He is the only alternative to drinking the bitter waters of this earth!

"Jesus answered and said unto her, If thou knewest the gift of God, and who it is that saith to thee, Give me to drink; thou wouldest have asked of him, and he would have given thee living water" (Jn.4:10).

"And he showed me a pure river of water of life, clear as crystal, proceeding out of the throne of God and of the Lamb. In the midst of the street of it, and on either side of the river, *was there* the tree of life, which bare twelve *manner* of fruits, *and* yielded her fruit every month: and the leaves of the tree *were* for the healing of the nations" (Re.22:1-2).

"And the Spirit and the bride say, Come. And let him that heareth say, Come. And let him that is athirst come. And whosoever will, let him take the water of life freely" (Re.22:17).

"The LORD is my shepherd; I shall not want. He maketh me to lie down in green pastures: he leadeth me beside the still waters. He restoreth my soul: he leadeth me in the paths of righteousness for his name's sake" (Ps.23:1-3).

"They shall be abundantly satisfied with the fatness of thy house; and thou shalt make them drink of the river of thy pleasures" (Ps.36:8).

"Behold, God is my salvation; I will trust, and not be afraid: for the LORD JEHOVAH is my strength and my song; he also is become my salvation. Therefore with joy shall ye draw water out of the wells of salvation" (Is.12:2-3).

"They shall not hunger nor thirst; neither shall the heat nor sun smite them: for he that hath mercy on them shall lead them, even by the springs of water shall he guide them" (Is.49:10).

"Ho, every one that thirsteth, come ye to the waters, and he that hath no money; come ye, buy, and eat; yea, come, buy wine and milk without money and without price" (Is.55:1).

Thought 2. Man is thirsty, thirsty for satisfaction and fulfillment, completion and purpose, meaning and significance, acceptance and recognition, joy and happiness, love and friendship.

The world offers water to man, water that claims to quench man's thirst. And when man looks at the world, he sees the appealing water, water that *looks like* it will quench his thirst. But when he drinks the water, it is bitter. The waters of the world fill men with...

- bitter fulfillment and satisfaction
- bitter completion and purpose
- bitter meaning and significance

- bitter acceptance and recognition
- bitter joy and happiness
- bitter love and friendship

The waters of the world—all of them without exception—leave man with bitter achievement and success, bitter gratification and pleasure. Only one person can sweeten the waters of life for man: the Lord Jesus Christ Himself, the living water. The water that Jesus Christ gives can actually sweeten the experiences of life. This is exactly what Scripture says.

"Blessed [are] they which do hunger and thirst after righteousness: for they shall be filled" (Mt.5:6).

"But whosoever drinketh of the water that I shall give him shall never thirst; but the water that I shall give him shall be in him a well of water springing up into everlasting life" (Jn.4:14).

"In the last day, that great [day] of the feast, Jesus stood and cried, saying, If any man thirst, let him come unto me, and drink. He that believeth on me, as the scripture hath said, out of his belly shall flow rivers of living water" (Jn.7:37-38).

"For the Lamb which is in the midst of the throne shall feed them, and shall lead them unto living fountains of waters: and God shall wipe away all tears from their eyes" (Re.7:17).

---

3 (15:25) **Prayer—Crying, To God—Intercession**: What did God's servant do? Moses did exactly what he should have done: he got alone with God and cried out in prayer. And note what the Lord did: He met the need of His dear servant and of His people. Despite the people's carnality and sin, despite their unbelief and grumbling, God met their need. God showed Moses a tree that would purify and make the water clean and sweet for drinking. Moses took some wood from the tree and threw it into the water, making the water become clear and pure.

Thought 1. The Lord met the need of the Israelites. He provided clear, pure water for them. Note two lessons.
(1) God delivered the Israelites from the severe crisis that had threatened their lives. But note why: because the servant of God got alone and cried out to God. The servant of God prayed and interceded: in desperation he pleaded for God to help deliver the people out of their life-threatening crisis. What a lesson for government leaders and for ministers.

> "But if from thence thou shalt seek the LORD thy God, thou shalt find him, if thou seek him with all thy heart and with all thy soul" (De.4:29).
> "This poor man cried, and the LORD heard him, and saved him out of all his troubles" (Ps.34:6).
> "From the end of the earth will I cry unto thee, when my heart is overwhelmed: lead me to the rock that is higher than I" (Ps.61:2).
> "He shall call upon me, and I will answer him: I will be with him in trouble; I will deliver him, and honour him" (Ps.91:15).
> "Then shalt thou call, and the LORD shall answer; thou shalt cry, and he shall say, Here I am. If thou take away from the midst of thee the yoke, the putting forth of the finger, and speaking vanity" (Is.58:9).
> "And it shall come to pass, that before they call, I will answer; and while they are yet speaking, I will hear" (Is.65:24).
> "And I say unto you, Ask, and it shall be given you; seek, and ye shall find; knock, and it shall be opened unto you" (Lu.11:9).
> "Elias was a man subject to like passions as we are, and he prayed earnestly that it might not rain: and it rained not on the earth by the space of three years and six months" (Js.5:17).

(2) God will take the bitter experiences of our lives and sweeten them. He will purify and clean up the bitter experiences of life. Just imagine all the trouble, problems, difficulties, trials, and temptations of life—God will take the bitterness out of them all. He will enable us to bear them all. God will strengthen us to conquer and walk through them all—victoriously and triumphantly.

> "Blessed is the man that endureth temptation: for when he is tried, he shall receive the crown of life, which the Lord hath promised to them that love him" (Js.1:12).
> "And we know that all things work together for good to them that love God, to them who are the called according to his purpose" (Ro.8:28).
> "There hath no temptation taken you but such as is common to man: but God is faithful, who will not suffer you to be tempted above that ye are able; but will with the temptation also make a way to escape, that ye may be able to bear it" (1 Co.10:13).
> "For our light affliction, which is but for a moment, worketh for us a far more exceeding and eternal weight of glory" (2 Co.4:17).
> "And he said unto me, My grace is sufficient for thee: for my strength is made perfect in weakness. Most gladly therefore will I rather glory in my infirmities, that the power of Christ may rest upon me" (2 Co.12:9).
> "Beloved, think it not strange concerning the fiery trial which is to try you, as though some strange thing happened unto you: But rejoice, inasmuch as ye are partakers of Christ's sufferings; that, when his glory shall be revealed, ye may be glad also with exceeding joy" (1 Pe.4:12-13).
> "And God shall wipe away all tears from their eyes; and there shall be no more death, neither sorrow, nor crying, neither shall there be any more pain: for the former things are passed away" (Re.21:4).
> "Many are the afflictions of the righteous: but the LORD delivereth him out of them all" (Ps.34:19).
> "The LORD will strengthen him upon the bed of languishing: thou wilt make all his bed in his sickness" (Ps.41:3).
> "When thou passest through the waters, I will be with thee; and through the rivers, they shall not overflow thee: when thou walkest through the fire, thou shalt not be burned; neither shall the flame kindle upon thee" (Is.43:2).

Thought 2. J. Vernon McGee has an interesting comment on this point (we have set the Scripture off in outline form for simplicity):

> *What was it that made the bitter water of Marah sweet? We are told that a tree cast into the water made it sweet.*
> ⇒ *Deuteronomy 21:23 says, "he that is hanged is accursed of God...."*
> ⇒ *Galatians 3:13...says, "Cursed is every one that hangeth on a tree."*
>
> *Jesus Christ died on a tree, and it is that cross that makes the experiences of life sweet. He tasted death for every man, and took the sting out of death. "O death where is thy sting? O grave, where is thy victory?" says 1 Corinthians 15:55. It is the cross of Christ that makes sweet the Marah experiences of life.*[3]

---

[3] J. Vernon McGee. *Thru the Bible*, Vol.1, p.251.

4 (15:25) **Test - Testing**: this is a very significant point. This point shows us why the Israelites were unable to find water out in the desert. God was behind the entire experience, behind the crisis. God had purposed that the Israelites would be unable to find water. Why? To *test* them. What does this mean, that God *tested* Israel? That God *tests* people?

⇒ God *tests* people in order to humble them and to reveal what is in their hearts.

> "And thou shalt remember all the way which the LORD thy God led thee these forty years in the wilderness, to humble thee, and to prove thee, to know what was in thine heart, whether thou wouldest keep his commandments, or no" (De.8:2).
> "Who fed thee in the wilderness with manna, which thy fathers knew not, that he might humble thee, and that he might prove thee, to do thee good at thy latter end" (De.8:16).
> "Thou has proved mine heart; thou hast visited me in the night; thou has tried me, and shalt find nothing; I am purposed that my mouth shall not transgress" (Ps.17:3).
> "And it came to pass after these things, that God did tempt Abraham, and said unto him, Abraham: and he said, Behold, here I am. And he said, Take now thy son, thine only son Isaac, whom thou lovest, and get thee into the land of Moriah; and offer him there for a burnt offering upon one of the mountains which I will tell thee of" (Ge.22:1-2).

⇒ God *tests* people in order to strengthen them and to keep them from sinning.

> "And Moses said unto the people, Fear not: for God is come to prove you, and that his fear may be before your faces, that ye sin not" (Ex.20:20).

⇒ God *tests* people in order to see if they will obey Him.

> "Then said the LORD unto Moses, Behold, I will rain bread from heaven for you; and the people shall go out and gather a certain rate every day, that I may prove them, whether they will walk in my law, or not" (Ex.16:4).

⇒ God *tests* people in order to refine them and to stir them to live righteous lives.

> "And I will bring the third part through the fire, and will refine them as silver is refined, and will try them as gold is tried: they shall call on my name, and I will hear them: I will say, It is my people: and they shall say, The LORD is my God" (Zec.13:9).
> "And he shall sit as a refiner and purifier of silver: and he shall purify the sons of Levi, and purge them as gold and silver, that they may offer unto the LORD an offering in righteousness" (Mal.3:3).

⇒ God *tests* people in order to judge and reward them.

> "Every man's work shall be made manifest: for the day shall declare it, because it shall be revealed by fire; and the fire shall try every man's work of what sort it is" (1 Co.3:13).

⇒ God *tests* people to see if they genuinely trust Him.

> "When Jesus then lifted up [his] eyes, and saw a great company come unto him, he saith unto Philip, Whence shall we buy bread, that these may eat? And this he said to prove him: for he himself knew what he would do" (Jn.6:5-6).

⇒ God *tests* people so that they will learn more and more patience and endurance.

> "My brethren, count it all joy when ye fall into divers temptations; Knowing this, that the trying of your faith worketh patience" (Js.1:2-3).
> "And not only so, but we glory in tribulations also: knowing that tribulation worketh patience; And patience, experience; and experience, hope: And hope maketh not ashamed; because the love of God is shed abroad in our hearts by the Holy Ghost which is given unto us" (Ro.5:3-5).

5 (15:25-26) **Covenant—Promise—Chastisement—Obedience**: the LORD now made a covenant, a great promise to His people. Simply stated, God told His people in one word what He expected: obedience. If they obeyed Him, He *would not chastise them*. But if they disobeyed Him, He would have to chastise them. In fact, He would have to chastise them by afflicting them with the very diseases of the Egyptians. Why the diseases of the Egyptians? No doubt because of the Scriptural principle of judgment. God had delivered the Israelites by inflicting judgment upon the Egyptians because of their unbelief and distrust of God. Therefore, if the Israelites sinned by disbelieving and distrusting God, they would suffer the same penalty as did the Egyptians. The great expositor Matthew Henry says this:

> Let not the Israelites think, because **God** had...highly honoured them...that...he would connive at their sins and let them do as they would. No, God is no respecter of persons; a rebellious Israelite [would] fare no better than a rebellious Egyptian.[4]

The Scriptural principle of judgment is just this:

---

4 Matthew Henry. *Matthew Henry's Commentary*, Vol.1, p.339.

⇒ Whatever we sow, we shall reap, and whatever we measure out to others shall be measured out to us.

> **"Be not deceived; God is not mocked: for whatsoever a man soweth, that shall he also reap. For he that soweth to his flesh shall of the flesh reap corruption; but he that soweth to the Spirit shall of the Spirit reap life everlasting" (Ga.6:7-8).**
> **"For with what judgment ye judge, ye shall be judged: and with what measure ye mete, it shall be measured to you again" (Mt.7:2).**

The Scripture clearly spells out the covenant and the great promise God was making to the Israelites. Note, what we are calling a covenant was a statute, a decree, a law being laid down by God. Remember, a law or decree is set: it is permanent. If the law is obeyed, then the promise is certain. The promise will be fulfilled.

a. There was the covenant: the people were to obey the Lord...
  • to diligently listen to Him
  • to do what is right
  • to hear and keep His commandments (see Je.7:22-23)

b. There was the LORD's promise. If His people obeyed Him...
  • He would not have to chastise them with the diseases brought upon the Egyptians (see De.28:60)
  • He would always be able to provide for them; that is, He would be able to heal them (See DEEPER STUDY # 3— Ex.15:26.)

Thought 1. God does chastise us, all of us who truly believe in Him. He chastises us because He loves us. True chastisement is always for a child's good, and a loving father always chastises and disciplines his child when his child goes astray. Thus it is with God. God chastises us to correct, to keep us...
  • from going deeper and deeper into sin
  • from being enslaved more and more by sin
  • from damaging our bodies
  • from bringing guilt and pain into our lives
  • from destroying ourselves
  • from stumbling or crashing headlong into some accident
  • from killing ourselves
  • from dooming ourselves to an eternity of separation from God

> **"Thou shalt also consider in thine heart, that, as a man chasteneth his son, so the LORD thy God chasteneth thee" (De.8:5).**
> **"Blessed is the man whom thou chastenest, O LORD, and teachest him out of thy law" (Ps.94:12).**
> **"My son, despise not the chastening of the LORD; neither be weary of his correction: For whom the LORD loveth he correcteth; even as a father the son in whom he delighteth" (Pr.3:11-12).**
> **"Every branch in me that beareth not fruit he taketh away: and every [branch] that beareth fruit, he purgeth it, that it may bring forth more fruit" (Jn.15:2).**
> **"And ye have forgotten the exhortation which speaketh unto you as unto children, My son, despise not thou the chastening of the Lord, nor faint when thou art rebuked of him: For whom the Lord loveth he chasteneth, and scourgeth every son whom he receiveth. If ye endure chastening, God dealeth with you as with sons; for what son is he whom the father chasteneth not?" (He.12:5-7).**
> **"As many as I love, I rebuke and chasten: be zealous therefore, and repent" (Re.3:19).**

DEEPER STUDY # 3

(15:26) **God, Names - Titles**: the Hebrew *Yahweh Rophe* means "the LORD who heals." The LORD had just made the bitter water of Marah pure, clear, and sweet—fit to drink. The LORD had *healed* the water. God is declaring that He is the Healer, the LORD who heals people, who heals both their bodies and spirits. He will take care of His people, look after them as they journey through the *wilderness wanderings* of life, through all the trials and problems of life.

> **"So Abraham prayed unto God: and God healed Abimelech, and his wife, and his maidservants; and they bare children" (Ge.20:17).**
> **"And they said, If ye send away the ark of the God of Israel, send it not empty; but in any wise return him a trespass offering: then ye shall be healed, and it shall be known to you why his hand is not removed from you" (1 S.6:3).**
> **"If my people, which are called by my name, shall humble themselves, and pray, and seek my face, and turn from their wicked ways; then will I hear from heaven, and will forgive their sin, and will heal their land" (2 Chr.7:14).**
> **"And the LORD hearkened to Hezekiah, and healed the people" (2 Chr.30:20).**
> **"Blessed is he that considereth the poor: the LORD will deliver him in time of trouble" (Ps.41:4).**
> **"Who forgiveth all thine iniquities; who healeth all thy diseases" (Ps.103:3).**
> **"He healeth the broken in heart, and bindeth up their wounds" (Ps.147:3).**
> **"But he was wounded for our transgressions, he was bruised for our iniquities: the chastisement of our peace was upon him; and with his stripes we are healed" (Is.53:5).**
> **"Return, ye backsliding children, and I will heal your backslidings. Behold, we come unto thee; for thou art the LORD our God" (Je.3:22).**

"They have healed also the hurt of the daughter of my people slightly, saying, Peace, peace; when there is no peace" (Je.6:14).

"For I will restore health unto thee, and I will heal thee of thy wounds, saith the LORD; because they called thee an Outcast, saying, This is Zion, whom no man seeketh after" (Je.30:17).

"Come, and let us return unto the LORD: for he hath torn, and he will heal us; he hath smitten, and he will bind us up" (Ho.6:1).

6 (15:27) **Elim—God, Provision**: the LORD's great goodness is vividly seen in what then happened. God abundantly provided for His people. He led them to Elim, an oasis in the barren desert. Elim was a flourishing area: there were twelve springs and seventy palm trees there. (See DEEPER STUDY #4, *Elim*—Ex.15:27.) The point to see is God's abundant provision for His dear people. Although it is not mentioned, the people had obviously repented of their terrible sin of complaining, grumbling, and murmuring; and God had forgiven them, pouring out the abundance of His blessing upon them. His provision was just overflowing upon His dear people.

Thought 1. God meets our needs, abundantly meets them.
(1) God fills us with joy and satisfaction: He leads us to draw water out of the wells of salvation.

"Therefore with joy shall ye draw water out of the wells of salvation" (Is.12:3).

"Thou wilt show me the path of life: in thy presence is fulness of joy; at thy right hand there are pleasures for evermore" (Ps.16:11).

"And the ransomed of the LORD shall return, and come to Zion with songs and everlasting joy upon their heads: they shall obtain joy and gladness, and sorrow and sighing shall flee away" (Is.35:10).

"These things have I spoken unto you, that my joy might remain in you, and [that] your joy might be full" (Jn.15:11).

"Hitherto have ye asked nothing in my name: ask, and ye shall receive, that your joy may be full" (Jn.16:24).

"For the kingdom of God is not meat and drink; but righteousness, and peace, and joy in the Holy Ghost" (Ro.14:17).

(2) God always makes us lie down in green pastures and leads us beside the still waters, even when facing the terrible trials of this life. God's provision is always sufficient to take care of us, no matter what confronts us.

"And ye shall serve the LORD your God, and he shall bless thy bread, and thy water; and I will take sickness away from the midst of thee" (Ex.23:25).

"And the LORD thy God will make thee plenteous in every work of thine hand, in the fruit of thy body, and in the fruit of thy cattle, and in the fruit of thy land, for good: for the LORD will again rejoice over thee for good, as he rejoiced over thy fathers" (De.30:9).

"They shall be abundantly satisfied with the fatness of thy house; and thou shalt make them drink of the river of thy pleasures" (Ps.36:8).

"Blessed be the Lord, who daily loadeth us with benefits, even the God of our salvation" (Ps.68:19).

"Then shall he give the rain of thy seed, that thou shalt sow the ground withal; and bread of the increase of the earth, and it shall be fat and plenteous: in that day shall thy cattle feed in large pastures" (Is.30:23).

"Bring ye all the tithes into the storehouse, that there may be meat in mine house, and prove me now herewith, saith the LORD of hosts, if I will not open you the windows of heaven, and pour you out a blessing, that there shall not be room enough to receive it" (Mal.3:10).

"But seek ye first the kingdom of God, and his righteousness; and all these things shall be added unto you" (Mt.6:33).

"I am come that they might have life, and that they might have [it] more abundantly" (Jn.10:10).

"And God is able to make all grace abound toward you; that ye, always having all sufficiency in all things, may abound to every good work" (2 Co.9:8).

"Now unto him that is able to do exceeding abundantly above all that we ask or think, according to the power that worketh in us" (Ep.3:20).

"But my God shall supply all your need according to his riches in glory by Christ Jesus" (Ph.4:19).

DEEPER STUDY # 4
(15:27) **Elim**: the location of Elim was in the fruitful, well-watered valley that is known today as Wadi Gharandel.
⇒ Elim lies between the desert of Shur and the desert of Sin.
⇒ The region is said to have a rainy season that sends torrents of water flowing down the valley.[5]
⇒ The area was always lush and green: it had twelve different springs of water that would have flowed out and formed pools and creeks.

5 Frank E. Gaebelein, Editor. *The Expositor's Bible Commentary*, Vol.2, p.399.

⇒ There were seventy palm trees, and no doubt because of its fruitful soil, many other different kinds of fruit trees.

⇒ Israel arrived at Elim on the fifteenth day of the second month after leaving Egypt.

"And they took their journey from Elim, and all the congregation of the children of Israel came unto the wilderness of Sin, which is between Elim and Sinai, on the fifteenth day of the second month after their departing out of the land of Egypt" (Ex.16:1).

TYPES, SYMBOLS, AND PICTURES
(Exodus 15:22-27)

Historical Term	Type or Picture (Scriptural Basis for Each)	Life Application for Today's Believer	Biblical Application
The Bitter Waters at Marah (Ex.15:22-26)	*Bitter trials of life* **"And when they came to Marah, they could not drink of the waters of Marah, for they were bitter: therefore the name of it was called Marah. And the people murmured against Moses, saying, What shall we drink? And he cried unto the LORD; and the LORD showed him a tree, which when he had cast into the waters, the waters were made sweet: there he made for them a statute and an ordinance, and there he proved them"** (Ex.15:23-25).	God will take the bitter experiences of our lives and sweeten them. He will purify and clean up the bitter experiences of life. Just imagine all the trouble, problems, difficulties, trials, and temptations of life... • God will take the bitterness out of them all • God will enable us to bear them all • God will strengthen us to conquer and walk through them all—victoriously and triumphantly	*"Many are the afflictions of the righteous: but the LORD delivereth him out of them all"* (Ps.34:19). *"The LORD will strengthen him upon the bed of languishing: thou wilt make all his bed in his sickness"* (Ps.41:3). *"Surely he shall deliver thee from the snare of the fowler, and from the noisome pestilence"* (Ps.91:3). *"Fear thou not; for I am with thee: be not dismayed; for I am thy God: I will strengthen thee; yea, I will help thee; yea, I will uphold thee with the right hand of my righteousness"* (Is.41:10). *"And we know that all things work together for good to them that love God, to them who are the called according to his purpose"* (Ro.8:28).

CHAPTER 16

E. The Second Crisis of Israel in the Wilderness—Hunger: The Two Great Sins of Israel, That of Grumbling & Disobedience (Unbelief), 16:1-36

1. The crisis of hunger: The first great sin committed again, that of complaining & grumbling (unbelief)
a. The people left Elim & marched to the desert of Sin:^{DS1} On the 15th day of the second month, exactly one month after leaving Egypt
b. The people grumbled against God's servants

1) The reason: Hunger—had run out of food supplies
2) The terrible depth of their sinful grumbling
• Would rather have died in Egypt in one of God's plagues than in the desert
• Doubted God's goodness & care (unbelief)

2. God promised to meet the needs of His grumbling people
a. God would provide bread from heaven
b. God would, however, test their faith
1) By charging them to gather bread every day for that day:
2) By commanding that they gather twice as much bread on the sixth day

c. God would prove Himself
1) In the evening the LORD would use His provision to prove that it was He who saved them

2) In the morning the LORD would use His provision to prove His glory
3) The reason: Because the people grumbled & complained against Him
d. God gave a warning: Grumbling is not against God's servants, but against God Himself

And they took their journey from Elim, and all the congregation of the children of Israel came unto the wilderness of Sin, which is between Elim and Sinai, on the fifteenth day of the second month after their departing out of the land of Egypt.
2 And the whole congregation of the children of Israel murmured against Moses and Aaron in the wilderness:
3 And the children of Israel said unto them, Would to God we had died by the hand of the LORD in the land of Egypt, when we sat by the flesh pots, and when we did eat bread to the full; for ye have brought us forth into this wilderness, to kill this whole assembly with hunger.
4 Then said the LORD unto Moses, Behold, I will rain bread from heaven for you; and the people shall go out and gather a certain rate every day, that I may prove them, whether they will walk in my law, or no.
5 And it shall come to pass, that on the sixth day they shall prepare that which they bring in; and it shall be twice as much as they gather daily.
6 And Moses and Aaron said unto all the children of Israel, At even, then ye shall know that the LORD hath brought you out from the land of Egypt:
7 And in the morning, then ye shall see the glory of the LORD; for that he heareth your murmurings against the LORD: and what are we, that ye murmur against us?
8 And Moses said, This shall be, when the LORD shall give you in the evening flesh to eat, and in the morning bread to the full; for that the LORD heareth your murmurings which ye murmur against him: and what are we? your murmurings are not

against us, but against the LORD.
9 And Moses spake unto Aaron, Say unto all the congregation of the children of Israel, Come near before the LORD: for he hath heard your murmurings.
10 And it came to pass, as Aaron spake unto the whole congregation of the children of Israel, that they looked toward the wilderness, and, behold, the glory of the LORD appeared in the cloud.
11 And the LORD spake unto Moses, saying,
12 I have heard the murmurings of the children of Israel: speak unto them, saying, At even ye shall eat flesh, and in the morning ye shall be filled with bread; and ye shall know that I am the LORD your God.
13 And it came to pass, that at even the quails came up, and covered the camp: and in the morning the dew lay round about the host.
14 And when the dew that lay was gone up, behold, upon the face of the wilderness there lay a small round thing, as small as the hoar frost on the ground.
15 And when the children of Israel saw it, they said one to another, It is manna: for they wist not what it was. And Moses said unto them, This is the bread which the LORD hath given you to eat.
16 This is the thing which the LORD hath commanded, Gather of it every man according to his eating, an omer for every man, according to the number of your persons; take ye every man for them which are in his tents.
17 And the children of Israel did so, and gathered, some more, some less.
18 And when they did mete it with an omer, he that gathered much had nothing over, and he that gathered little had no lack; they gathered every man according to his eating.
19 And Moses said, Let no man leave of it till the morning.
20 Notwithstanding they hearkened not unto Moses; but some of them left of it until the morning, and it bred worms, and stank: and Moses

e. God laid down the prerequisite for receiving the bread of God: The people had to come, to draw near God

1) The people obeyed: They looked to the cloud (symbolized God's presence)
2) The results: The glory of the LORD shone in the cloud^{DS2}

f. God restressed the facts
1) He had heard the people's grumblings
2) He would meet their needs
3) His purpose: That they might know that He is the LORD their God
g. God fulfilled His promise
1) God gave the meat He had promised: The quail came & covered the camp that very evening
2) God gave the bread—the manna from heaven—He had promised
• The next morning after the dew had melted, the ground was covered with thin flakes that looked like frost
• The Israelites called it manna, meaning "what is it": It was the bread promised by God

3. The people failed the test: They disobeyed God
a. God's first commandment was obeyed: To gather only what was needed for each person within a tent, an omer (two quarts or one tenth of a bushel)
1) The people obeyed: Each gathered exactly what was needed
2) The people strictly obeyed: They actually measured the amount—no one had too much nor too little

b. God's second commandment was disobeyed: Not to keep any manna overnight
1) Some people disobeyed: Kept it until morning
2) The manna was full of maggots & smelled
3) Moses was angered

305

4) God's mercy was demonstrated: He still gave manna
  • The people gathered every morning
  • The sun melted all leftovers

c. God's third commandment was disobeyed: To gather twice as much bread on the 6th day

1) The people's experience: They gathered twice as much bread on the 6th day & the rulers gave a report to Moses

2) The people were supposed to cook what was needed for the Sabbath on the 6th day: Because the Sabbath was a day of rest, a holy day to the LORD:

3) Some of the people obeyed, & the manna did not stink nor have maggots

4) The third commandment was reemphasized & restressed
  • The Sabbath day was to be a day given to the LORD
  • Six days' food was to be gathered, but no food was to be gathered on the Sabbath day

5) Some of the people disobeyed God: Went out on the Sabbath to gather manna & found none

6) God rebuked the people & gave a strong charge to them: Must keep in mind

was wroth with them.
21 And they gathered it every morning, every man according to his eating: and when the sun waxed hot, it melted.
22 And it came to pass, that on the sixth day they gathered twice as much bread, two omers for one man: and all the rulers of the congregation came and told Moses.
23 And he said unto them, This is that which the LORD hath said, To morrow is the rest of the holy sabbath unto the LORD: bake that which ye will bake to day, and seethe that ye will seethe; and that which remaineth over lay up for you to be kept until the morning.
24 And they laid it up till the morning, as Moses bade: and it did not stink, neither was there any worm therein.
25 And Moses said, Eat that to day; for to day is a sabbath unto the LORD: to day ye shall not find it in the field.
26 Six days ye shall gather it; but on the seventh day, which is the sabbath, in it there shall be none.
27 And it came to pass, that there went out some of the people on the seventh day for to gather, and they found none.
28 And the LORD said unto Moses, How long refuse ye to keep my commandments

and my laws?
29 See, for that the LORD hath given you the sabbath, therefore he giveth you on the sixth day the bread of two days; abide ye every man in his place, let no man go out of his place on the seventh day.
30 So the people rested on the seventh day.
31 And the house of Israel called the name thereof Manna: and it was like coriander seed, white; and the taste of it was like wafers made with honey.
32 And Moses said, This is the thing which the LORD commandeth, Fill an omer of it to be kept for your generations; that they may see the bread wherewith I have fed you in the wilderness, when I brought you forth from the land of Egypt.
33 And Moses said unto Aaron, Take a pot, and put an omer full of manna therein, and lay it up before the LORD, to be kept for your generations.
34 As the LORD commanded Moses, so Aaron laid it up before the Testimony, to be kept.
35 And the children of Israel did eat manna forty years, until they came to a land inhabited; they did eat manna, until they came unto the borders of the land of Canaan.
36 Now an omer is the tenth part of an ephah.

that the LORD Himself has established the Sabbath
  • He gave six days to gather bread
  • He demanded that everyone rest & worship on the Sabbath

  • The people obeyed

4. The manna (bread) memorialized: Commanded by God
a. The manna described[DS3]
  1) Was white like coriander seed
  2) Tasted like honey wafers
b. The commandment of God: To keep an omer (two quarts) of manna as a testimony to future generations—declaring how God fed Israel in the wilderness

  1) Moses instructed Aaron to do as God had commanded

  2) Aaron obeyed: Kept a jar of manna until the Ark of Testimony was built

c. God's provision of manna lasted for forty years: Until His people reached the promised land

d. God's daily provision was abundant: one omer per person (two quarts)

DIVISION V

THE RED SEA AND THE WILDERNESS WANDERINGS: THE BELIEVER'S TRIALS AS HE JOURNEYS TO THE PROMISED LAND, 13:17–18:27

E.   The Third Crisis of Israel in the Wilderness—Hunger: The Two Great Sins of Israel, That of Grumbling and Disobedience (Unbelief), 16:1-36

(16:1-36) **Introduction**: one of the most basic needs of man is the need for food. Without food, a person starves to death. Consequently, when a person's food supply is threatened...
  • he complains—grumbles and murmurs against the weather, some crop disease, or God
  • he blames the circumstances, the government, the economy, the grocery store, the farmer, his employer—just whoever or whatever is causing the shortage of food

A person's trust in God and others is soon lost when his food supply is threatened. Trust in God far too often crumbles when hunger or any other serious trial confronts a person. This was the very situation facing the Israelites...
  • that of hunger
  • that of complaining, grumbling, and murmuring
  • that of failing to trust God to meet their need

But these things should never be. We should never complain nor fail to trust God, not because of hunger nor because of any other serious circumstance that might confront us. God loves and cares for us. And God has promised to take care of our needs in every circumstance, even in life-threatening circumstances. God's promise is clear:

"But seek ye first the kingdom of God, and his righteousness; and all these things shall be added unto you" (Mt.6:33).

This is the great lesson of this passage: *The Third Crisis of Israel in the Wilderness—Hunger: The Two Great Sins of Israel, That of Grumbling and Disobedience (Unbelief)*, 16:1-36.

1. The crisis of hunger: the first great sin committed again, that of complaining and grumbling (unbelief) (vv.1-3).
2. The promise of God: to meet the needs of His grumbling people (vv.4-15).
3. The test of the people: they failed the test—disobeyed God (vv.16-30).
4. The manna (bread) memorialized: commanded by God (vv.31-36).

1 (16:1-3) **Hunger—Complaining—Grumbling—Murmuring—Moses—Aaron—Israel—Sin**: there was the crisis of hunger, and the first great sin of Israel was committed again, that of complaining and grumbling.

a. The people left Elim and marched to the desert of Sin (see DEEPER STUDY # 1—Ex.16:1 for more discussion). Note that God's people marched to the desert of Sin exactly one month after leaving Egypt. How quickly God's people forget the deliverance, care, goodness, and blessings of God! Just one month earlier, God had miraculously delivered His people out of Egyptian slavery. Yet, here they were committing a terrible sin. Note what the sin was.

b. The people complained—grumbled and murmured—against God's servants Moses and Aaron. Why? Because they were hungry: they had used up all their food supply. Before they left Egypt, they had apparently been instructed to take along one month's supply of food, and now they had no food left. A crisis existed and the situation looked hopeless. Where in the desert could two to three million people possibly find enough food to keep them alive? Such an enormous food source just did not exist, not out in the wilderness of the desert. The people knew this, and they obviously began to talk about the problem among themselves. The talk soon became a complaint, and the people began to grumble and murmur against their leaders, Moses and Aaron.

This God's people should not have done. Instead of grumbling and complaining, God's people should have gone to their leaders, presented the problem, and suggested that they all—both leaders and people—seek God together. The people should have trusted God, trusted His goodness and power to deliver them. But this they did not do. They showed unbelief in God...

- distrusted His concern and care
- distrusted His goodness
- distrusted His power
- distrusted His provision

And note the terrible depth of their distrust and unbelief, the scorching heat of their sinful grumbling: they would rather have died in Egypt in one of God's plagues than to die of starvation out in the desert. At least in Egypt they had meat and bread. The Hebrew has the idea of *pots of meat*—all they could eat.

What audacity! What an affront against God! What rashness, arrogance, gall, rudeness, and defiance. What a terrible thing to say in the face of God! And after He had done so much for them.

⇒ Remember God's wonderful deliverance from Egyptian slavery.
⇒ Remember God's astounding power demonstrated at the Red Sea.
⇒ Remember God's glorious provision of water to take care of their thirst

All this had all taken place within the last thirty days. Time and again over a period of thirty days, God had gloriously delivered and provided for His dear people. But murmurers have short memories. And here they were wallowing around in the pit of sinful grumbling, showing that their hearts were full of...

- selfishness
- unbelief
- distrust
- carnal, fleshly thoughts

Thought 1. Our memories of the "good old days," of the past, are often magnified and exaggerated. This was certainly true of the Israelites, and it is true of us. In looking back to their days in Egypt, the Israelites could not have had enough to eat. Meat and plenty of food are never a part of the everyday diet of slaves nor of the poor of any society. The Israelites had short memories and warped perspectives. They had forgotten their days of affliction as slaves to the world of Egypt.

This shows the great crisis the Israelites were facing. They were facing starvation. A spirit of hopelessness gripped them. They knew there was no place out in the desert where enough food could be found to feed them, not two to three million people. Nevertheless, when a crisis arises for the believer—the genuine believer—he is to call upon God, not grumble and complain. In facing problems, we are to trust God—believe that God cares, that He loves us, that He will help us through the problem—no matter how severe the problem may be.

"The LORD is my strength and my shield; my heart trusted in him, and I am helped: therefore my heart greatly rejoiceth; and with my song will I praise him" (Ps.28:7).

"Oh how great is thy goodness, which thou hast laid up for them that fear thee; which thou hast wrought for them that trust in thee before the sons of men!" (Ps.31:19).

"The LORD redeemeth the soul of his servants: and none of them that trust in him shall be desolate" (Ps.34:22).

"Trust in the LORD, and do good; so shalt thou dwell in the land, and verily thou shalt be fed" (Ps.37:3).

"Commit thy way unto the LORD; trust also in him; and he shall bring it to pass" (Ps.37:5).

"But I am poor and needy; yet the Lord thinketh upon me: thou art my help and my deliverer; make no tarrying, O my God" (Ps.40:17).

"Thou wilt keep him in perfect peace, whose mind is stayed on thee: because he trusteth in thee" (Is.26:3).

"Trust ye in the LORD for ever: for in the LORD JEHOVAH is everlasting strength" (Is.26:4).

"Fear thou not; for I am with thee: be not dismayed; for I am thy God: I will strengthen thee; yea, I will help thee; yea, I will uphold thee with the right hand of my righteousness" (Is.41:10).

"Let your conversation [behavior, conduct] be without covetousness; and be content with such things as ye have: for he hath said, I will never leave thee, nor forsake thee. So that we may boldly say, The Lord is my helper, and I will not fear what man shall do unto me" (He.13:5-6).

Thought 2. J. Vernon McGee has an excellent application of this point.

The children of Israel...despised God's heavenly food and complained about eating it. They grew tired of eating manna. They longed for the fleshpots of Egypt. They wanted to go back to that from which they had been delivered.

That is the story, I am afraid, of some people who have been converted, and have been delivered out of "Egypt" [the world, the old life]. Every now and then they take a side trip back to get the leeks, the onions, and the garlic. There are Christians today who need to make a complete break with the old life. Friend, you can't go on living like the world, living on the things of Egypt, and be serviceable to God and have the peace of God in your heart. There must be a break with Egypt. We must live on the true Manna that comes from heaven, even the Lord Jesus Christ.[1]

DEEPER STUDY # 1

(16:1) **Desert of Sin**: this was a place, the actual name of a desert in the days of Moses. The word "sin" must not be confused with the theological word *sin*. The "Desert of Sin" was probably taken from the word *Sinai* or the bush *Seneh*. The desert was probably named the "Desert of Sin" because of its terrain, most likely referring to a rocky area with thornbushes scattered across the landscape. The desert was most likely located in the southwestern Sinai, close to the area of modern *Debbet er-Ramleh*.

---

2 (16:4-15) **Complaining—Grumbling—Murmuring—Manna—Supply—Provision—Blessing—Testing**: there was God's promise to meet the needs of His grumbling people.

a. God promised to provide *bread from heaven* for His people (v.4). The only conceivable way two to three million people could be fed out in the wilderness of a desert—fed for over forty years—would be by a miracle from God. This was exactly what God was promising: to feed His people Himself, to feed them in such a way that His existence, love, and care could never be questioned nor doubted. (See DEEPER STUDY # 3—Ex.16:31 for more discussion.)

b. God would, however, test the faith of His people (v.4). God was going to test their faith in two ways:
⇒ By charging His people to gather bread every day for that particular day. They were to gather *only one day's supply*, no more and no less. By laying down this restriction, God tested their trust in Him. They had to trust God *day by day* for food.
⇒ By commanding that they gather twice as much food on the sixth day (v.5). This commandment would test the obedience of the people. Would they gather twice as much as commanded and rest on the seventh day, or would they go out and work to gather their food on the seventh day? Just what the people did will be seen later (note 3—Ex.16:16-30).

c. God would prove Himself (vv.6-7). God's servants went before God's people and declared His wonderful promise:
⇒ In the evening, the LORD would use His provision to prove that it was He who saved them and brought them out of the land of Egyptian slavery (v.6).
⇒ In the morning, the LORD would use His provision to prove His glory (v.7).
⇒ Why was the LORD going to do this? Because the LORD was going to prove Himself—that He was truly the LORD—because the people had grumbled and complained against Him (v.7).

d. Now note: God gave a warning. Grumbling is not against God's servants but against God Himself (v.8). This is true in two ways.
1) God, not His servant, is the person who leads His people. God, not the servants of God, had delivered the Israelites from their enslavement in Egypt (the world) and led them to begin their march to the promised land. God in His sovereign leadership had led the Israelites to be where they were, not Moses and Aaron. Therefore, their complaint, although spoken against Moses and Aaron, was really directed against God and His leadership.

---

[1] J. Vernon McGee. *Thru the Bible*, Vol.1, p.254-255.

2) Complaining and grumbling show distrust in God, that a person does not believe God cares and will work things out for good. Therefore, when we complain and grumble, we are saying to God that we do not trust Him, do not trust that He loves us and will deliver us. Our complaining and grumbling is not against God's servant, not really. It is against God.

> "Harden not your heart, as in the provocation, and as in the day of temptation in the wilderness: When your fathers tempted me, proved me, and saw my work. Forty years long was I grieved with this generation, and said, It is a people that do err in their heart, and they have not known my ways: Unto whom I sware in my wrath that they should not enter into my rest" (Ps.95:8-11).
>
> "The foolishness of man perverteth his way: and his heart fretteth against the LORD" (Pr.19:3).
>
> "Happy is the man that feareth alway: but he that hardeneth his heart shall fall into mischief" (Pr.28:14).
>
> "He, that being often reproved hardeneth his neck, shall suddenly be destroyed, and that without remedy" (Pr.29:1).
>
> "Who art thou that judgest another man's servant? to his own master he standeth or falleth. Yea, he shall be holden up: for God is able to make him stand" (Ro.14:4).
>
> "Neither murmur ye, as some of them also murmured, and were destroyed of the destroyer. Now all these things happened unto them for ensamples: and they are written for our admonition, upon whom the ends of the world are come. Wherefore let him that thinketh he standeth take heed lest he fall" (1 Co.10:10-12).
>
> "Wherefore, my beloved, as ye have always obeyed, not as in my presence only, but now much more in my absence, work out your own salvation with fear and trembling. For it is God which worketh in you both to will and to do of his good pleasure. Do all things without murmurings and disputings [arguing]" (Ph.2:12-14).
>
> "(Harden not your hearts, as in the provocation, in the day of temptation in the wilderness: When your fathers tempted me, proved me, and saw my works forty years. Wherefore I was grieved with that generation, and said, They do alway err in their heart; and they have not known my ways. So I sware in my wrath, They shall not enter into my rest.) Take heed, brethren, lest there be in any of you an evil heart of unbelief, in departing from the living God. But exhort one another daily, while it is called To day; lest any of you be hardened through the deceitfulness of sin" (He.3:8-13).
>
> "Let us labour therefore to enter into that rest, lest any man fall after the same example of unbelief [Israel's unbelief]" (He.4:11).

e. God laid down the prerequisite for receiving the bread of God: the people had to come, to draw near God (vv.9-10). When believers sin against God by complaining and grumbling, they must come before the LORD and draw near Him. The idea is that of confession and repentance: the people were to draw near God, come before Him and confess and repent of their complaining and grumbling.

Note that the people obeyed: they looked to the cloud which symbolized God's very presence (v.10). What they witnessed was a phenomenal sight: the glory of the LORD shone in the cloud (v.10. See DEEPER STUDY # 2—Ex.16:10 for more discussion.)

Thought 1. How often God would grant a clear, intense sense of His glory and presence—if we would only draw near Him. If we would only spend long sessions of meditation and prayer in His presence. How much power would be present in our lives and ministries if we often got alone with God for long periods of time.

> "Let us draw near with a true heart in full assurance of faith, having our hearts sprinkled from an evil conscience, and our bodies washed with pure water" (He.10:22).
>
> "Draw nigh to God, and he will draw nigh to you. Cleanse your hands, ye sinners; and purify your hearts, ye double minded" (Js.4:8).

f. God restressed the facts (vv.11-12). Note that He restated the facts to Moses: He had heard the people's grumblings and He would meet their needs. But He was doing it for a very specific purpose: that they might learn the truth, learn more and more that He is the LORD their God. God wanted the truth driven more and more into their hearts and lives, that He and He alone is the only living and true God. He and He alone was to be their God, the LORD of their lives.

g. God fulfilled His promise (vv.13-15).

1) God gave the meat He had promised. The quail came and covered the camp that very evening (v.13). Imagine enough quail to feed two to three million people every day of the week for forty years. Moreover, imagine the quail always landing right where the Israelites were camped. The provision of the quail was beyond all question a spectacular miracle of God.

2) God gave the bread He had promised—the manna from heaven (vv.13-15).

⇒ The next morning after the dew had melted, the ground was covered with thin flakes that looked like frost (v.14).

⇒ The Israelites had never seen the thin flakes before. Thus they called it manna, which means "What is it?" (v.15). Moses informed the people that it was the bread from heaven that had been promised by God. (See DEEPER STUDY # 3—Ex.16:31 for more discussion.)

Thought 1. Man is hungry, hungry for all kinds of things. But lying at the very base of his hunger is the craving for...

- purpose and fulfillment
- acceptance and recognition
- love and friendship
- joy and pleasure

The world offers food to satisfy and fulfill man's hunger. And when a man looks at the world, he sees an appealing offer to feed him, to feed him with...

- drugs
- alcohol
- sex (illicit sex)
- pleasure
- bright lights
- success

- stimulation
- excitement
- position
- honor
- fame
- beauty

- popularity
- riches
- property
- power
- control

But tragically, these things never satisfy; they never fill the deepest recesses of man's heart. The world leaves man empty, leaves him with a sense of empty gratification and pleasure and with unfilled achievement and success.

There is only one way man's hunger can be satisfied: he must eat, partake of the bread from heaven: the Lord Jesus Christ. Only Jesus Christ can satisfy the hunger of man's heart. Only Jesus Christ can give life to man. Jesus Christ is the Bread of Life. He is the bread given by God to satisfy the hunger of man's soul.

> **"Then Jesus said unto them, Verily, verily, I say unto you, Moses gave you not that bread from heaven; but my Father giveth you the true bread from heaven. For the bread of God is he which cometh down from heaven, and giveth life unto the world" (Jn.6:32-33).**

> **"And Jesus said unto them, I am the bread of life: he that cometh to me shall never hunger; and he that believeth on me shall never thirst" (Jn.6:35).**

> **"I am that bread of life. Your fathers did eat manna in the wilderness, and are dead. This is the bread which cometh down from heaven, that a man may eat thereof, and not die. I am the living bread which came down from heaven: if any man eat of this bread, he shall live for ever: and the bread that I will give is my flesh, which I will give for the life of the world" (Jn.6:48-51).**

> **"This is that bread which came down from heaven: not as your fathers did eat manna, and are dead: he that eateth of this bread shall live for ever" (Jn.6:58).**

> **"Wherefore do ye spend money for that which is not bread? and your labour for that which satisfieth not? hearken diligently unto me, and eat ye that which is good, and let your soul delight itself in fatness" (Is.55:2).**

DEEPER STUDY # 2

(16:10) **God, Glory of—Glory, of God—Shekinah Glory**: the glory of the LORD appeared in the cloud. This was the Shekinah Glory, the cloud that symbolized God's presence. It was the very cloud that had guided Israel out of Egypt and that was to rest upon the tabernacle (Ex.40:34-38). The Shekinah Glory was also to rest above the mercy seat in the most holy place of the tabernacle. Scripture describes the glory of the LORD as follows:

1. The glory of the LORD is like a consuming fire.

> **"And the sight of the glory of the LORD was like devouring fire on the top of the mount in the eyes of the children of Israel" (Ex.24:17).**

2. The glory of the LORD is like a pillar of fire that radiates light.

> **"And the LORD went before them by day in a pillar of a cloud, to lead them the way; and by night in a pillar of fire, to give them light; to go by day and night: He took not away the pillar of the cloud by day, nor the pillar of fire by night, from before the people" (Ex.13:21-22).**

3. The glory of the LORD is like a fiery furnace.

> **"For ye are not come unto the mount that might be touched, and that burned with fire, nor unto blackness, and darkness, and tempest....For our God is a consuming fire" (He.12:18, 29).**

4. The glory of the LORD is like a light that radiates splendor, a light that is so full of splendor that Peter called it "the excellent glory."

> **"For he received from God the Father honour and glory, when there came such a voice to him from the excellent glory, This is my beloved Son, in whom I am well pleased" (2 Pe.1:17).**

5. The glory of the LORD is a light so glorious and brilliant that there is no need for a sun.

"Having the glory of God: and her light was like unto a stone most precious, even like a jasper stone, clear as crystal....And the city had no need of the sun, neither of the moon, to shine in it: for the glory of God did lighten it, and the Lamb is the light thereof" (Re.21:11, 23).

6. The glory of the LORD is a light so brilliant that no man can approach it.

"Who only hath immortality, dwelling in the light which no man can approach unto; whom no man hath seen, nor can see: to whom be honour and power everlasting" (1 Ti.6:16).

3 (16:16-30) **Disobedience—Test - Testing—Manna—Hoarding**: the people failed the test of God. They disobeyed God. God gave the people three different commands concerning the manna. Note the response to each command.
  a. God's first command was obeyed (vv.16-18). He instructed the people to gather only the amount of manna that was needed for each person within a tent, an omer (two quarts) for each person. Note:
  ⇒ The people obeyed. Each person gathered exactly what was needed (v.17).
  ⇒ The people strictly obeyed: they actually measured the amount gathered. No person kept more nor had less than what he should (v.18).

  b. God's second command was disobeyed (vv.19-21). The servant of God (Moses) declared God's command: the manna was not to be kept overnight. Why? The reason is obvious: this was the test of God.
  ⇒ This was one of the ways God was going to expose the human heart, that it is selfish and carnal.
  ⇒ This was the way God was going to teach His people that they must trust Him day by day, trust Him for the provisions of life.

Picture what God's people were being asked to do: to go to bed at night without a morsel of food in the house, to trust God totally for their daily bread.

But keep this fact in mind: they were expecting to march straight to the promised land of Canaan, expecting to be in the desert for only a brief period of time. They had no idea whatsoever that they would be wandering about in the wilderness for *forty long years*, no idea that they were being asked to trust God for their daily bread for so long a period, for forty years.

But note: this was exactly what God's people are supposed to do: trust Him day by day, trust Him every day of their lives.
  1) What did the Israelites do? Some of them disobeyed God and kept a portion of manna overnight. They were not quite sure that God had actually provided the manna, that there would be manna available the next morning. They just did not trust the promise of God, did not believe God would continue to meet their needs. They acted selfishly, coveting and hoarding the manna.
  2) Note what happened: the manna was full of maggots and stunk—was unfit to eat—when the disbelievers arose the next morning.
  3) The servant of God, Moses, was justifiably angered with the people (v.20).
  4) But God demonstrated His mercy: He continued to provide for the people, continued to give the manna—the bread from heaven—to them (v.21). And note: the people gathered the manna every morning, day by day; and when the sun came up, the manna melted.

Thought 1. Two very important lessons can be learned from the disobedience of the Israelites, from their unbelief, their distrust of God.
(1) We must learn to trust God for the provisions of life, day by day, every day of our lives. Trusting God does not mean trusting Him now and then, here and there, for a while as we wish. God demands that we trust Him always, every moment of every day.

"The LORD redeemeth the soul of his servants: and none of them that trust in him shall be desolate" (Ps.34:22).
"Trust in the LORD, and do good; so shalt thou dwell in the land, and verily thou shalt be fed" (Ps.37:3).
"Commit thy way unto the LORD; trust also in him; and he shall bring it to pass" (Ps.37:5).
"They that trust in the LORD shall be as mount Zion, which cannot be removed, but abideth for ever" (Ps.125:1).
"The fear of man bringeth a snare: but whoso putteth his trust in the LORD shall be safe" (Pr.29:25).
"Thou wilt keep him in perfect peace, whose mind is stayed on thee: because he trusteth in thee. Trust ye in the LORD for ever: for in the LORD JEHOVAH is everlasting strength" (Is.26:3-4).
"But seek ye first the kingdom of God, and his righteousness; and all these things shall be added unto you" (Mt.6:33).
"Jesus said unto him, If thou canst believe, all things [are] possible to him that believeth" (Mk.9:23).
"But without faith it is impossible to please him: for he that cometh to God must believe that he is, and that he is a rewarder of them that diligently seek him" (He.11:6).
"For whatsoever is born of God overcometh the world: and this is the victory that overcometh the world, even our faith" (1 Jn.5:4).

(2) We must arise early every day and gather the manna of God, the Bread from heaven. To stay physically healthy, we have to eat every day. The same is true spiritually. To stay spiritually healthy, we must seek the spiritual nourishment to strengthen and carry us through the day. That is, we must arise early enough every day to spend time with the Lord Jesus Christ...

- in worship and devotions
- in feasting and partaking of Him
- in nourishing ourselves spiritually, nourishing ourselves enough to last us all day

Once the sun rises, the manna is melted. The activities of the world begin when the sun rises; the hope of having time to gather the manna of spiritual nourishment is slim. The suggestion of God's Word is strong: we should arise early—before the activities of the day crowd in upon us—to gather the manna of spiritual nourishment.

⇒ Jacob arose early in the morning to worship and pray.

> **"And Jacob rose up early in the morning, and took the stone that he had put for his pillows, and set it up for a pillar, and poured oil upon the top of it" (Ge.28:18).**

⇒ Samuel's parents arose early in the morning to worship and pray.

> **"And they rose up in the morning early, and worshipped before the LORD, and returned, and came to their house to Ramah: and Elkanah knew Hannah his wife; and the LORD remembered her" (1 S.1:19).**

⇒ Hezekiah arose early in the morning to worship and pray.

> **"Then Hezekiah the king rose early, and gathered the rulers of the city, and went up to the house of the LORD" (2 Chr.29:20).**

⇒ Job arose early in the morning to worship and pray.

> **"And it was so, when the days of their feasting were gone about, that Job sent and sanctified them, and rose up early in the morning, and offered burnt offerings according to the number of them all: for Job said, It may be that my sons have sinned, and cursed God in their hearts. Thus did Job continually" (Jb.1:5).**

⇒ David arose early in the morning to worship and pray.

> **"Awake up, my glory; awake, psaltery and harp: I myself will awake early" (Ps.57:8).**

⇒ The Psalmist arose early in the morning to worship and pray.

> **"I prevented [preceded] the dawning of the morning, and cried: I hoped in thy word" (Ps.119:147).**

⇒ Jesus Christ arose early in the morning to worship and pray.

> **"And in the morning, rising up a great while before day, he went out, and departed into a solitary place, and there prayed" (Mk.1:35).**

⇒ Scripture had predicted that Jesus Christ would be awakened morning by morning to listen to God His Father.

> **"The Lord GOD hath given me the tongue of the learned, that I should know how to speak a word in season to him that is weary: he wakeneth morning by morning, he wakeneth mine ear to hear as the learned" (Is.50:4).**

Thought 2. There is a strong lesson here about storing up and hoarding the manna. We must never hide nor hoard "the bread from heaven," Jesus Christ. Jesus Christ is the only spiritual food that can satisfy the human heart. We must therefore share the bread of life, Jesus Christ, with the world.

> **"But ye shall receive power, after that the Holy Ghost is come upon you: and ye shall be witnesses unto me both in Jerusalem, and in all Judaea, and in Samaria, and unto the uttermost part of the earth" (Ac.1:8).**
> **"For we cannot but speak the things which we have seen and heard" (Ac.4:20).**
> **"Go, stand and speak in the temple to the people all the words of this life" (Ac.5:20).**
> **"Be not thou therefore ashamed of the testimony of our Lord, nor of me his prisoner: but be thou partaker of the afflictions of the gospel according to the power of God" (2 Ti.1:8).**
> **"These things speak, and exhort, and rebuke with all authority. Let no man despise thee" (Tit.2:15).**

"But sanctify the Lord God in your hearts: and be ready always to give an answer to every man that asketh you a reason of the hope that is in you with meekness and fear" (1 Pe.3:15).

c. God's third command was also disobeyed (vv.22-27). God commanded the people to gather twice as much bread on the sixth day, two omers (four quarts) for each person. Note what happened.
   1) The people gathered twice as much bread on the sixth day and the rulers gave the good report to Moses (v.22).
   2) The people were supposed to cook what was needed for the Sabbath on the sixth day (v.23). Why? Because the Sabbath was a day of rest, a holy day to the LORD.
   3) Did the people obey God? Some did. And the manna did not stink nor get maggots in it (v.24).
   4) Now, note what the messenger of God did. He restressed, reemphasized the third command (vv.25-26). The point is clear: the Sabbath day was to be a day given to the LORD (v.25).
   ⇒ Six days were to be used for gathering food, but no food was to be gathered on the Sabbath day (v.26).

   God had His messenger stress the command time and again. There could be no misunderstanding: the people knew exactly what they were to do.
   5) Again, did the people obey God? Some did not: they disobeyed God (v.27). Despite the clear, unquestionable command of God, some of the people deliberately chose to act on their own, to do their own thing. They rebelled against God's command and disobeyed Him. They went out on the Sabbath day to gather manna. But note: they found none.
   6) What was God's response? He rebuked the people and gave a strong charge to them (vv.28-30).
   ⇒ He rebuked them with a question: How long would they disobey him and His laws (v.28)?
   ⇒ He gave them a strong charge: they must keep in mind that the LORD Himself established the Sabbath. The facts were clear:
      • The LORD had given six days to gather bread, to work (v.29)
      • The LORD demanded that everyone rest and worship on the Sabbath day (v.29)
      Note: the people obeyed (v.30).

Thought 1. Two clear lessons are seen in this experience of Israel.
(1) We must obey God. God means what he says, and He expects us to obey Him. We must never disobey Him, not deliberately, not in rebellion.

   "Now therefore, if ye will obey my voice indeed, and keep my covenant, then ye shall be a peculiar treasure unto me above all people: for all the earth is mine" (Ex.19:5).
   "O that there were such an heart in them, that they would fear me, and keep all my commandments always, that it might be well with them, and with their children for ever!" (De.5:29).
   "This day the LORD thy God hath commanded thee to do these statutes and judgments: thou shalt therefore keep and do them with all thine heart, and with all thy soul" (De.26:16).
   "This book of the law shall not depart out of thy mouth; but thou shalt meditate therein day and night, that thou mayest observe to do according to all that is written therein: for then thou shalt make thy way prosperous, and then thou shalt have good success" (Jos.1:8).
   "And Samuel said, Hath the LORD as great delight in burnt offerings and sacrifices, as in obeying the voice of the LORD? Behold, to obey is better than sacrifice, and to hearken than the fat of rams" (1 S.15:22).
   "And if thou wilt walk in my ways, to keep my statutes and my commandments, as thy father David did walk, then I will lengthen thy days" (1 K.3:14).
   "Not every one that saith unto me, Lord, Lord, shall enter into the kingdom of heaven; but he that doeth the will of my Father which is in heaven" (Mt.7:21).
   "Therefore whosoever heareth these sayings of mine, and doeth them, I will liken him unto a wise man, which built his house upon a rock" (Mt.7:24).
   "Jesus answered and said unto him, If a man love me, he will keep my words: and my Father will love him, and we will come unto him, and make our abode with him" (Jn.14:23).
   "If ye keep my commandments, ye shall abide in my love; even as I have kept my Father's commandments, and abide in his love....Ye are my friends, if ye do whatsoever I command you" (Jn.15:10, 14).
   "Blessed are they that do his commandments, that they may have right to the tree of life, and may enter in through the gates into the city" (Re.22:14).

(2) We must keep the LORD'S Day every week (v.23). The LORD'S Day is...
   • a day of rest
   • a holy day to the LORD (v.23)

   We must, therefore, guard the LORD'S Day. We must not *gather*, that is, work on His day. We must set aside one day a week for rest and holy worship just as He commands.
   (a) We are to keep the LORD'S Day.

   "Remember the sabbath day, to keep it holy" (Ex.20:8).
   "Six days thou shalt work, but on the seventh day thou shalt rest: in earing time and in harvest thou shalt rest" (Ex.34:21).

"Blessed is the man that doeth this, and the son of man that layeth hold on it; that keepeth the sabbath from polluting it, and keepeth his hand from doing any evil" (Is.56:2).

"If thou turn away thy foot from the sabbath, from doing thy pleasure on my holy day; and call the sabbath a delight, the holy of the LORD, honourable; and shalt honour him, not doing thine own ways, nor finding thine own pleasure, nor speaking thine own words: Then shalt thou delight thyself in the LORD; and I will cause thee to ride upon the high places of the earth, and feed thee with the heritage of Jacob thy father: for the mouth of the LORD hath spoken it" (Is.58:13-14).

(b) We are to do good on the Lord's Day.

"How much then is a man better than a sheep? Wherefore it is lawful to do well on the sabbath days" (Mt.12:12).

"And when the sabbath day was come, he began to teach in the synagogue: and many hearing him were astonished, saying, From whence hath this man these things? and what wisdom is this which is given unto him, that even such mighty works are wrought by his hands?" (Mk.6:2).

"If a man on the sabbath day receive circumcision, that the law of Moses should not be broken; are ye angry at me, because I have made a man every whit whole on the sabbath day?" (Jn.7:23).

"And it was the sabbath day when Jesus made the clay, and opened his eyes" (Jn.9:14).

"And on the sabbath we went out of the city by a river side, where prayer was wont to be made; and we sat down, and spake unto the women which resorted thither" (Ac.16:13).

"And Paul, as his manner was, went in unto them, and three sabbath days reasoned with them out of the scriptures" (Ac.17:2).

(c) The early disciples worshipped God on the Lord's Day.

"And upon the first day of the week, when the disciples came together to break bread, Paul preached unto them, ready to depart on the morrow; and continued his speech until midnight" (Ac.20:7).

"Upon the first day of the week let every one of you lay by him in store, as God hath prospered him, that there be no gatherings when I come" (1 Co.16:2).

"I was in the Spirit on the Lord's day, and heard behind me a great voice, as of a trumpet, Saying, I am Alpha and Omega, the first and the last: and, What thou seest, write in a book, and send it unto the seven churches which are in Asia; unto Ephesus, and unto Smyrna, and unto Pergamos, and unto Thyatira, and unto Sardis, and unto Philadelphia, and unto Laodicea" (Re.1:10-11).

4 (16:31-36) **Manna—Memorial**: there was the command that the manna—the bread from heaven—be memorialized.

a. Note the description of the manna (v.31). (See DEEPER STUDY # 3—Ex.16:31 for more discussion.)

b. God commanded that an omer (two quarts) of the manna be kept as a memorial for future generations (vv.32-34). God wanted a testimony for future generations: a testimony that declared how He had fed His people after He delivered them out of Egypt.

Note that Moses instructed Aaron to do as God had commanded (v.33), and that Aaron obeyed. He kept a jar of manna until the Ark of Testimony was built (v.34). Note: three items were to be kept in the Ark of the Testimony or what we usually call the Ark of the Covenant (which was to be built in the form of a chest) (see He.9:4).

⇒ The manna which was kept in a gold pot.
⇒ Aaron's rod which budded (Nu.17:10).
⇒ The two tablets containing the ten commandments.

c. God's provision of manna lasted for forty years, a phenomenal miracle. God provided manna for His people until they reached the fertile, fruitful soil of the promised land (v.35).

d. And note: God's daily provision was abundant. One omer (two quarts) was provided for each person.

Thought 1. The faithfulness of God should be memorialized in the heart of every believer. God is faithful to us. If we obey Him, truly follow Him, He fulfills His promises to us. He looks after us and takes care of us.

"Know therefore that the LORD thy God, he is God, the faithful God, which keepeth covenant and mercy with them that love him and keep his commandments to a thousand generations" (De.7:9).

"Blessed be the LORD, that hath given rest unto his people Israel, according to all that he promised: there hath not failed one word of all his good promise, which he promised by the hand of Moses his servant" (1 K.8:56).

"Thy mercy, O LORD, is in the heavens; and thy faithfulness reacheth unto the clouds" (Ps.36:5).

"I will sing of the mercies of the LORD for ever: with my mouth will I make known thy faithfulness to all generations" (Ps.89:1).

"God is faithful, by whom ye were called unto the fellowship of his Son Jesus Christ our Lord" (1 Co.1:9).

"But the Lord is faithful, who shall stablish you, and keep you from evil" (2 Th.3:3).

"If we believe not, yet he abideth faithful: he cannot deny himself" (2 Ti.2:13).

"Wherefore in all things it behoved him to be made like unto his brethren, that he might be a merciful and faithful high priest in things pertaining to God, to make reconciliation for the sins of the people" (He.2:17).

"Let us hold fast the profession of our faith without wavering; (for he is faithful that promised)" (He.10:23).

"Wherefore let them that suffer according to the will of God commit the keeping of their souls to him in well doing, as unto a faithful Creator" (1 Pe.4:19).

DEEPER STUDY # 3

(16:31) **Bread, From Heaven—Jesus Christ, Bread of God—Manna**: God promised to feed the Israelites with bread from heaven. The Israelites called this bread *manna*. Manna looked like resin or a coriander seed. The coriander seed is a small white grain that is used for seasoning. *Manna* tasted like honey wafers (Ex.16:31) or like wafers made with olive oil (Nu.11:8). The manna could be ground with a handmill or crushed in some form of mortar and cooked or baked in pots (Nu.8:7-8). Note three significant pictures—three important lessons—that can be drawn from the manna.

1. The manna was the bread given by God to save Israel from physical death (starvation). Jesus Christ is the Bread of God given to save man from spiritual death. This means the manna was a type of the *Bread of Heaven,* a picture of the Lord Jesus Christ Himself. Note what Jesus Christ claimed for Himself:

a. Jesus Christ claimed that He is the true bread from heaven.

> "Then Jesus said unto them, Verily, verily, I say unto you, Moses gave you not that bread from heaven; but my Father giveth you the true bread from heaven" (Jn.6:32).

b. Jesus Christ claimed that He is the bread of God who came down from heaven.

> "For the bread of God is he which cometh down from heaven, and giveth life unto the world" (Jn.6:33).

c. Jesus Christ claimed that He is the bread of life.

> "And Jesus said unto them, I am the bread of life: he that cometh to me shall never hunger; and he that believeth on me shall never thirst" (Jn.6:35).
> "I am that bread of life" (Jn.6:48).

d. Jesus Christ claimed that He is the living bread which came down from heaven.

> "I am the living bread which came down from heaven: if any man eat of this bread, he shall live for ever: and the bread that I will give is my flesh, which I will give for the life of the world.... This is that bread which came down from heaven: not as your fathers did eat manna, and are dead: he that eateth of this bread shall live for ever" (Jn.6:51, 58).

e. Jesus Christ claimed that whoever ate, that is, partook, of Him as the bread of life would live forever.

> "This is that bread which came down from heaven: not as your fathers did eat manna, and are dead: he that eateth of this bread shall live for ever" (Jn.6:58).

f. Jesus Christ claimed that whoever came to Him would never hunger nor ever thirst.

> "And Jesus said unto them, I am the bread of life: he that cometh to me shall never hunger; and he that believeth on me shall never thirst" (Jn.6:35).

2. The manna was sent by God, but the people had to gather it. Jesus Christ was sent by God, but we have to receive Him.

> "But as many as received him, to them gave he power to become the sons of God, even to them that believe on his name" (Jn.1:12).
> "For God so loved the world, that he gave his only begotten Son, that whosoever believeth in him should not perish, but have everlasting life" (Jn.3:16).
> "Behold, I stand at the door, and knock: if any man hear my voice, and open the door, I will come in to him, and will sup with him, and he with me" (Re.3:20).

3. The manna was the daily bread for the redeemed, the bread upon which they were to feast. And note, they had to arise early to gather the manna or else the sun melted the manna. The picture is clear: believers must arise early every day to gather the manna of God, the Bread from heaven. We must arise early to receive our spiritual nourishment through prayer and the study of God's Holy Word. And we must remember: when the sun rises, the manna melts. The activities of the day begin to press in upon us when the sun rises. The point: we must arise early to feed upon the Bread of Life, the Lord Jesus Christ. We must seek Him in prayer and in the study of His Word, seek Him early every day. (See note, Thought 1, pt.2—Ex.16:16-30 for discussion.)

"But if from thence thou shalt seek the LORD thy God, thou shalt find him, if thou seek him with all thy heart and with all thy soul" (De.4:29).

"And it shall be with him, and he shall read therein all the days of his life: that he may learn to fear the LORD his God, to keep all the words of this law and these statutes, to do them" (De.17:19).

"But his delight is in the law of the LORD; and in his law doth he meditate day and night" (Ps.1:2).

"When I remember thee upon my bed, and meditate on thee in the night watches" (Ps.63:6).

"My meditation of him shall be sweet: I will be glad in the LORD" (Ps.104:34).

"And I will delight myself in thy commandments, which I have loved" (Ps.119:47).

"My hands also will I lift up unto thy commandments, which I have loved; and I will meditate in thy statutes" (Ps.119:48).

"The law of thy mouth is better unto me than thousands of gold and silver" (Ps.119:72).

"I remember the days of old; I meditate on all thy works; I muse on the work of thy hands" (Ps.143:5).

"Seek ye the LORD while he may be found, call ye upon him while he is near" (Is.55:6).

"Thy words were found, and I did eat them; and thy word was unto me the joy and rejoicing of mine heart: for I am called by thy name, O LORD God of hosts" (Je.15:16).

"These were more noble than those in Thessalonica, in that they received the word with all readiness of mind, and searched the scriptures daily, whether those things were so" (Ac.17:11).

"And now, brethren, I commend you to God, and to the word of his grace, which is able to build you up, and to give you an inheritance among all them which are sanctified" (Ac.20:32).

"For whatsoever things were written aforetime were written for our learning, that we through patience and comfort of the scriptures might have hope" (Ro.15:4).

"Study to show thyself approved unto God, a workman that needeth not to be ashamed, rightly dividing the word of truth" (2 Ti.2:15).

"As newborn babes, desire the sincere milk of the word, that ye may grow thereby: If so be ye have tasted that the Lord is gracious" (1 Pe.2:2-3).

TYPES, SYMBOLS, AND PICTURES
(Exodus 16:1-36)

Historical Term	Type or Picture (Scriptural Basis for Each)	Life Application for Today's Believer	Biblical Application
Manna (Ex.16:1-36)	*God's provision: The Bread from heaven* "Then said the LORD unto Moses, Behold, I will rain bread from heaven for you; and the people shall go out and gather a certain rate every day, that I may prove them, whether they will walk in my law, or no" (Ex.16:4).	The Lord Jesus Christ is the Bread from Heaven—the Bread of Life—a life that sustains the believer both now and forever.	"Then Jesus said unto them, Verily, verily, I say unto you, Moses gave you not that bread from heaven; but my Father giveth you the true bread from heaven" (Jn.6:32-33). "And Jesus said unto them, I am the bread of life: he that cometh to me shall never hunger; and he that believeth on me shall never thirst" (Jn.6:35). "I am that bread of life. Your fathers did eat manna in the wilderness, and are dead. This is the bread which cometh down from heaven, that a man may eat thereof, and not die. I am the living bread which came down from heaven: if any man eat of this bread, he shall live for ever: and the bread that I will give is my flesh, which I will give for the life of the world" (Jn.6:48-51; see Jn.6:58).

| 1. The crisis: Thirst—the Israelites had no water to drink
a. Left the desert of Sin & were led from place to place by God
b. Camped at Rephidim[DS1]
c. The crisis: No water

2. The terrible sin of Israel
a. They looked to Moses not to God: Argued, grumbled
b. They tested God: Questioned His goodness & care—demanded that He prove Himself, provide for them
c. They accused Moses of being an impostor: Misleading them, leading them to their death | **CHAPTER 17**

F. The Fourth Crisis of Israel in the Wilderness—Thirst: God's Provision of Water, 17:1-7

And all the congregation of the children of Israel journeyed from the wilderness of Sin, after their journeys, according to the commandment of the LORD, and pitched in Rephidim: and there was no water for the people to drink. 2 Wherefore the people did chide with Moses, and said, Give us water that we may drink. And Moses said unto them, Why chide ye with me? wherefore do ye tempt the LORD? 3 And the people thirsted there for water; and the people murmured against Moses, and said, Wherefore is this that thou hast brought us up out of Egypt, to kill us and | our children and our cattle with thirst? 4 And Moses cried unto the LORD, saying, What shall I do unto this people? they be almost ready to stone me. 5 And the LORD said unto Moses, Go on before the people, and take with thee of the elders of Israel; and thy rod, wherewith thou smotest the river, take in thine hand, and go. 6 Behold, I will stand before thee there upon the rock in Horeb; and thou shalt smite the rock, and there shall come water out of it, that the people may drink. And Moses did so in the sight of the elders of Israel. 7 And he called the name of the place Massah, and Meribah, because of the chiding of the children of Israel, and because they tempted the LORD, saying, Is the LORD among us, or not? | 3. The cry of God's servant: He cried out to the LORD
a. He cried out for direction
b. The people threatened his life

4. The provision of God
a. God told His messenger to walk ahead of the people: To take some of the elders & his staff with him

b. God promised to stand before His servant by the rock in Horeb[DS2]
c. God instructed His servant to strike the rock & promised that water would flow out of it
d. God's servant obeyed

5. The place memorialized
a. Named Massah: Test, testing
b. Named Meribah: Arguing, quarreling, strife, contention |

DIVISION V

THE RED SEA AND THE WILDERNESS WANDERINGS: THE BELIEVER'S TRIALS AS HE JOURNEYS TO THE PROMISED LAND, 13:17–18:27

F. The Fourth Crisis of Israel in the Wilderness—Thirst: God's Provision of Water, 17:1-7

(17:1-7) **Introduction**: the craving for water, the need to moisten parched lips, is one of the strongest drives that a man has. As long as a man's thirst is quenched, he can go on about his normal life. However, if water is withheld for a long period of time, the body begins to dehydrate. If water is not provided soon after dehydration, the man will become sick and eventually die.

Now note: physical thirst is a picture of spiritual thirst. Men who sense spiritual thirst will do anything to satisfy their thirst. Spiritual thirst is a normal thing, but it becomes abnormal when man tries to satisfy his thirst with the things of the world…

- immoral sex
- fleshly pleasures
- selfish power
- self-centered fame
- possessions
- property
- recognition
- position
- worldly friends
- pornography
- overeating

The thirst of the human heart can be met by God and by God alone. This is the much needed lesson of this passage: *The Fourth Crisis of Israel in the Wilderness—Thirst: God's Provision of Water*, 17:1-7.
1. The crisis: thirst—the Israelites had no water to drink (v.1).
2. The terrible sin of Israel (vv.2-3).
3. The cry of God's servant: he cried out to the LORD (v.4).
4. The provision of God (vv.5-6).
5. The place memorialized (v.7).

1 (17:1) **Trial—Thirst—Water—Crisis—Israel**: there was the crisis of thirst, of coming to a place and finding no water to drink. Israel had left the desert of Sin and marched to Rephidim where they were expecting to find water. But when they arrived, they discovered to their horror that the creeks were dry. There was no water.

The people had been wandering about in the desert for days, perhaps weeks; and remember, there were two to three million of them. They were tired, weary, and thirsty—totally exhausted. Nerves were on edge. Water supplies had no doubt been running low for days, and each family had been rationing their water supply. When they reached Rephidim, they obviously had run completely out of water. Then they heard the most frightening words imaginable: "No water. The creeks are dry."

A crisis existed, the most severe crisis that a people could face out in the dry, barren desert: no water. It was a matter of life and death, of survival. What were they to do? What could they do?

Now, note a significant fact: it was the LORD Himself who had led them to camp at Rephidim, who had led them by the pillar of cloud, by His very own presence. Why? Why would the LORD lead them to a place where there was *no water?* The answer lies in the name of *the LORD.* The LORD (Jehovah, Yahweh) means the God of revelation and deliverance.

⇒ The LORD was obviously planning to reveal Himself at Rephidim, to reveal that He is the God of salvation and deliverance, the God who saves and delivers His people through all the trials of life.

⇒ The LORD was obviously planning to test His people at Rephidim, to test and strengthen their faith: to teach them to trust Him more and more, to trust Him to take care of them and their needs more and more.

⇒ The LORD was obviously planning to glorify Himself at Rephidim, to glorify Himself by proving that He is truly God, the God who saves and delivers His people through all the trials and problems of life.

Thought 1. What causes so many trials and problems in life? Often, we do. We are often the cause of problems and trials, of bringing affliction into our own lives. We act foolishly and abuse our bodies, break the law, mistreat others, act irresponsibly, misbehave, fail to take care of things, and on and on the list could go. We often cause many of the problems and trials that confront us.

But note: sometimes trials arise in our lives that are beyond our control, trials that we did absolutely nothing to cause. These are often caused by God. God sometimes puts us in situations that really try us, that cause serious problems for us. Why?

(1) God uses trials to test, prove, and strengthen us. God uses trials to arouse us...
  • to cry out to Him for help
  • to trust Him more and more
  • to become stronger and stronger in enduring and in standing up for Him
  • to be a strong testimony and witness for Him that He does truly exist and can deliver and save those who trust Him
  • to draw closer and closer to Him in prayer, trust, fellowship, and communion

"And thou shalt remember all the way which the LORD thy God led thee these forty years in the wilderness, to humble thee, and to prove thee, to know what was in thine heart, whether thou wouldest keep his commandments, or no" (De.8:2).

"But he knoweth the way that I take: when he hath tried me, I shall come forth as gold" (Jb.23:10).

"For thou, O God, hast proved us: thou hast tried us, as silver is tried" (Ps.66:10).

"When Jesus then lifted up [his] eyes, and saw a great company come unto him, he saith unto Philip, Whence shall we buy bread, that these may eat?" (Jn.6:5).

"And not only so, but we glory in tribulations also: knowing that tribulation worketh patience; And patience, experience; and experience, hope: And hope maketh not ashamed; because the love of God is shed abroad in our hearts by the Holy Ghost which is given unto us" (Ro.5:3-5).

"For our light affliction, which is but for a moment, worketh for us a far more exceeding and eternal weight of glory" (2 Co.4:17).

"My brethren, count it all joy when ye fall into divers temptations; Knowing this, that the trying of your faith worketh patience. But let patience have her perfect work, that ye may be perfect and entire, wanting nothing" (Js.1:2-4).

(2) God uses trials to glorify and praise Himself. When the LORD delivers and saves us through a trial, we glorify and praise God for delivering us.

"When thou hast eaten and art full, then thou shalt bless the Lord thy God for the good land which he hath given thee" (De.8:10).

"And let them sacrifice the sacrifices of thanksgiving, and declare his works with rejoicing" (Ps.107:22).

"Giving thanks unto the Father, which hath made us meet [fit, qualified] to be partakers of the inheritance of the saints in light" (Col.1:12).

"Wherein ye greatly rejoice, though now for a season, if need be, ye are in heaviness through manifold temptations: That the trial of your faith, being much more precious than of gold that perisheth, though it be tried with fire, might be found unto praise and honour and glory at the appearing of Jesus Christ" (1 Pe.1:6-7).

(3) God uses trials to reveal that He is the God of salvation and deliverance, the God who saves and delivers His people through all the trials of life. Thereby people know that God is the LORD...
  • that *He does exist*
  • that He is *the only living and true God*

"Thus saith the LORD, In this thou shalt know that I am the LORD: behold, I will smite with the rod that is in mine hand upon the waters which are in the river, and they shall be turned to blood" (Ex.7:17).

"And Moses said unto Pharaoh, Glory over me: when shall I intreat for thee, and for thy servants, and for thy people, to destroy the frogs from thee and thy houses, that they may remain in the river only? And he said, To morrow. And he said, Be it according to thy word: that thou mayest know that there is none like unto the LORD our God" (Ex.8:9-10).

"And I will sever in that day the land of Goshen, in which my people dwell, that no swarms of flies shall be there; to the end thou mayest know that I am the LORD in the midst of the earth. And I will put a division between my people and thy people: to morrow shall this sign be" (Ex.8:22-23).

"And Moses said unto him, As soon as I am gone out of the city, I will spread abroad my hands unto the LORD; and the thunder shall cease, neither shall there be any more hail; that thou mayest know how that the earth is the LORD's" (Ex.9:29).

"Ye are my witnesses, saith the LORD, and my servant whom I have chosen: that ye may know and believe me, and understand that I am he: before me there was no God formed, neither shall there be after me. I, even I, am the LORD; and beside me there is no saviour. I have declared, and have saved, and I have showed, when there was no strange god among you: therefore ye are my witnesses, saith the LORD, that I am God. Yea, before the day was I am he; and there is none that can deliver out of my hand: I will work, and who shall let it?" (Is.43:10-13).

"And I [Paul] said, Who art thou, Lord? And he said, I am Jesus whom thou persecutest. But rise, and stand upon thy feet: for I have appeared unto thee for this purpose, to make thee a minister and a witness both of these things which thou hast seen, and of those things in the which I will appear unto thee; Delivering thee from the people, and from the Gentiles, unto whom now I send thee, To open their eyes, and to turn them from darkness to light, and from the power of Satan unto God, that they may receive forgiveness of sins, and inheritance among them which are sanctified by faith that is in me" (Ac.26:15-18).

DEEPER STUDY # 1

(17:1) **Rephidim—Massah—Meribah—The Wilderness Journey**: the meaning of the word *Rephidim* is *refreshments*. Scripture states that it was hardly a refreshment for the people of God. For them Rephidim became…

⇒ a place of unbelief (Ex.17:1-3).

"And all the congregation of the children of Israel journeyed from the wilderness of Sin, after their journeys, according to the commandment of the LORD, and pitched in Rephidim: and *there was* no water for the people to drink. Wherefore the people did chide with Moses, and said, Give us water that we may drink. And Moses said unto them, Why chide ye with me? wherefore do ye tempt the LORD? And the people thirsted there for water; and the people murmured against Moses, and said, Wherefore *is* this *that* thou hast brought us up out of Egypt, to kill us and our children and our cattle with thirst?" (Ex.17:1-3).

⇒ a place of unfaithfulness to God (Ex.17:7).

"And he called the name of the place Massah, and Meribah, because of the chiding of the children of Israel, and because they tempted the LORD, saying, Is the LORD among us, or not?" (Ex.17:7).

⇒ a place of battle with Amalek (Ex.17:8-16).

"Then came Amalek, and fought with Israel in Rephidim" (Ex.17:8).

⇒ a place where Moses struck the rock to secure water (Ex.17:1-7; 19:2).

"Behold, I will stand before thee there upon the rock in Horeb; and thou shalt smite the rock, and there shall come water out of it, that the people may drink. And Moses did so in the sight of the elders of Israel" (Ex.17:6).

⇒ a place where God delivered His people (Ps.81:7).

"Thou calledst in trouble, and I delivered thee; I answered thee in the secret place of thunder: I proved thee at the waters of Meribah" (Ps.81:7).

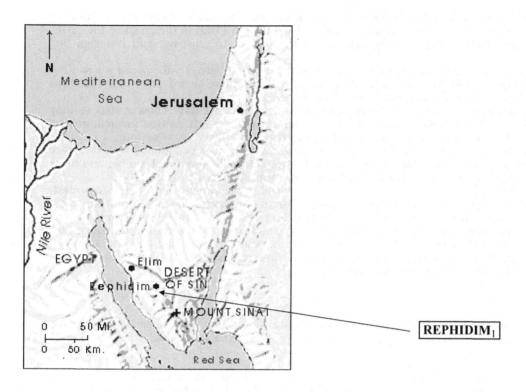

REPHIDIM[1]

2 (17:2-3) **Israel—Grumbling—Complaining—Murmuring**: there was the terrible sin of Israel. What did Israel do? Did they pass the test of God? Did they trust God, trust His goodness: believe that He loved them and cared for them? Note what they did.

a. The Israelites looked to a man not to God; they had their eyes and hopes placed upon an earthly leader not upon the LORD. Note what happened: they argued and grumbled against their earthly leader, Moses (v.2). They demanded of Moses, "Give us water." They treated him as though he were a magician, as though he could work miracles and meet their needs.

The point is this: the people's eyes were on Moses and not on God. They focused upon Moses as a wonder worker, as a worker of miracles. A man was the object of their attention and loyalty not God.

> **Thought 1**. Our trust must always be in God not in man. In the terrifying and difficult trials of life, man can be of little help. Man can help us very little if at all when facing...
> - terminal illness
> - very old age
> - a terrible accident
> - the death of a loved one
> - an awful tragedy
> - bankruptcy
> - natural disasters
> - life-threatening situations
> - a supervisor's hatred or anger

Our hope is in God not in earthly leaders. Therefore, we must learn to look to God not to men for help.

> "Oh how great is thy goodness, which thou hast laid up for them that fear thee; which thou hast wrought for them that trust in thee before the sons of men!" (Ps.31:19).
> "The LORD redeemeth the soul of his servants: and none of them that trust in him shall be desolate" (Ps.34:22).
> "Trust in the LORD, and do good; so shalt thou dwell in the land, and verily thou shalt be fed" (Ps.37:3).
> "Commit thy way unto the LORD; trust also in him; and he shall bring it to pass" (Ps.37:5).
> "It is better to trust in the LORD than to put confidence in man" (Ps.118:8).
> "It is better to trust in the LORD than to put confidence in princes" (Ps.118:9).
> "Trust in the LORD with all thine heart; and lean not unto thine own understanding" (Pr.3:5).
> "Cease ye from man, whose breath is in his nostrils: for wherein is he to be accounted of?" (Is.2:22).
> "Trust ye in the LORD for ever: for in the LORD JEHOVAH is everlasting strength" (Is.26:4).
> "Woe to the rebellious children, saith the LORD, that take counsel, but not of me; and that cover with a covering, but not of my spirit, that they may add sin to sin: That walk to go down into Egypt, and have not asked at my mouth; to strengthen themselves in the strength of Pharaoh, and to trust in the shadow of Egypt!" (Is.30:1-2).

---

1 Map from *Life Application*® *Bible.* Used by permission.

"Woe to them that go down to Egypt for help; and stay on horses, and trust in chariots, because they are many; and in horsemen, because they are very strong; but they look not unto the Holy One of Israel, neither seek the LORD!" (Is.31:1).

"Now the Egyptians are men, and not God; and their horses flesh, and not spirit. When the LORD shall stretch out his hand, both he that helpeth shall fall, and he that is holpen shall fall down, and they all shall fail together" (Is.31:3).

"Who is among you that feareth the LORD, that obeyeth the voice of his servant, that walketh in darkness, and hath no light? let him trust in the name of the LORD, and stay upon his God" (Is.50:10).

"Thus saith the LORD; Cursed be the man that trusteth in man, and maketh flesh his arm, and whose heart departeth from the LORD" (Je.17:5).

"When Ephraim saw his sickness, and Judah saw his wound, then went Ephraim to the Assyrian, and sent to king Jareb: yet could he not heal you, nor cure you of your wound" (Ho.5:13).

"And I will say to my soul, Soul, thou hast much goods laid up for many years; take thine ease, eat, drink, [and] be merry. But God said unto him, [Thou] fool, this night thy soul shall be required of thee: then whose shall those things be, which thou hast provided?" (Lu.12:19-20).

b. The Israelites tested God: they were questioning God's goodness and demanding that He prove Himself, demanding that He take care of them right then and there (v.2).

How could the people question God's goodness when He had done so much for them? How could they doubt His existence and His care? Why were they complaining and grumbling and arguing with God's servant? The answer is obvious:

⇒ Because they were not a people of prayer. Instead of complaining and grumbling against God and Moses, they should have gone to Moses and suggested that they all seek God in prayer, seek Him to meet their need. Just imagine what a great sight that would have been: two to three million people on their knees together—out in the middle of the desert—crying out to God to provide water for them. What a different picture we would have in Scripture of Israel if they had only done what they should have: joined Moses in prayer, seeking God to meet their need. But this was not to be.

c. The Israelites accused Moses of being an impostor: of misleading them and leading them to their death (v.3). Note how serious the situation became: the people were ready to stone Moses (see v.4). They became violent, filled with uncontrolled anger, malice, and rage.

⇒ They forgot all about God's wonderful provisions in the past: how God had already provided water for them.
⇒ They forgot all about how gloriously God had used His servant in the past: how Moses had freed them from Egyptian slavery and led them through the Red Sea.

Death—death from thirst and dehydration—was staring them in the face, and they were terrified. They had grown so little in God and knew so little about God that they immediately turned against God's servant Moses.

Thought 1. Again, why? How could the Israelites so quickly forget God's blessings? So quickly forget how God had magnificently delivered His people?
(1) Because of their hearts and minds. Their hearts and minds were...
- carnal
- fleshly
- self-centered

"Because the carnal mind is enmity against God: for it is not subject to the law of God, neither indeed can be" (Ro.8:7).
"This I say therefore, and testify in the Lord, that ye henceforth walk not as other Gentiles walk, in the vanity of their mind" (Ep.4:17).
"Unto the pure all things are pure: but unto them that are defiled and unbelieving is nothing pure; but even their mind and conscience is defiled" (Tit.1:15).

(2) Because of unbelief and distrust. They had not grown in prayer nor in trust of the Lord. Day by day out in the wilderness wanderings they had kept their minds upon carnal things, the things of this earth instead of upon God. They had obviously thought little about God, little about His glorious person and power, little about His wonderful salvation and deliverance.
Thus, they had learned little about God...
- little about trusting and believing Him
- little about worshipping and honoring Him
- little about witnessing and bearing testimony for Him

"I said therefore unto you, that ye shall die in your sins: for if ye believe not that I am [he], ye shall die in your sins" (Jn.8:24).
"(Harden not your hearts, as in the provocation, in the day of temptation in the wilderness: When your fathers tempted me, proved me, and saw my works forty years. Wherefore I was grieved with that generation, and said, They do alway err in their heart; and they have not known my ways. So I sware in my wrath, They shall not enter into my rest.) Take heed, brethren, lest there be in any of you an evil heart of unbelief, in departing from the living God" (He.3:8-12).

"Let us labour therefore to enter into that rest, lest any man fall after the same example of unbelief" (He.4:11).

"I will therefore put you in remembrance, though ye once knew this, how that the Lord, having saved the people out of the land of Egypt, afterward destroyed them that believed not" (Jude 5).

3 (17:4) **Prayer—Intercession**: the servant of God cried out to God for help. The people were upset and impatient with Moses, to the point of violence: they were ready to stone Moses. He was experiencing what Paul was later to experience: "the more abundantly I love you, the less I be loved" (2 Co.12:15). Moses did the only thing he could: he got alone with God and cried out to God for help. Note that Moses was very upset with the Israelites: he called them "this people" ("these people" NIV) instead of "my people." The sin and personal attacks of the people against Moses had put a great distance, an alienation, between them. The prophets of God often felt this distance and alienation when the people rebelled against God and attacked them (Is.6:9; Hag.1:2).

Thought 1. Our only hope in desperate situations is to cry out in prayer to God. When nothing else can help, prayer can. God hears and answers prayer.

"Ask, and it shall be given you; seek, and ye shall find; knock, and it shall be opened unto you" (Mt.7:7).

"But if from thence thou shalt seek the LORD thy God, thou shalt find him, if thou seek him with all thy heart and with all thy soul" (De.4:29).

"This poor man cried, and the LORD heard him, and saved him out of all his troubles" (Ps.34:6).

"From the end of the earth will I cry unto thee, when my heart is overwhelmed: lead me to the rock that is higher than I" (Ps.61:2).

"Seek the LORD, and his strength: seek his face evermore" (Ps.105:4).

"And ye shall seek me, and find me, when ye shall search for me with all your heart" (Je.29:13).

4 (17:5-6) **Need - Necessities—Provision—Supply—Rock, The—Israel—Water**: there was the provision of God. God heard the cry of His dear servant, heard his desperate plea for help.

a. God told His servant to walk ahead of the people: to take with him some of the elders of Israel and his rod or staff (v.5). Why take the elders with him? To be eye-witnesses of the miracle. Why take the rod? Not to strike some plague or chastisement upon them but to call forth the power of God. God wanted to meet the need of the unbelieving and distrusting backsliders. Note the patience, forbearance, and longsuffering of God. Note His willingness to work a long time with us, longing for us to repent and trust Him—just as we should always do.

"For my name's sake will I defer mine anger, and for my praise will I refrain for thee, that I cut thee not off" (Is.48:9).

"It is of the LORD'S mercies that we are not consumed, because his compassions fail not" (Lam.3:22).

"And rend your heart, and not your garments, and turn unto the LORD your God: for he is gracious and merciful, slow to anger, and of great kindness, and repenteth him of the evil" (Joel 2:13).

"Or despisest thou the riches of his goodness and forbearance and longsuffering; not knowing that the goodness of God leadeth thee to repentance?" (Ro.2:4).

"But to Israel he saith, All day long I have stretched forth my hands unto a disobedient and gainsaying people" (Ro.10:21).

"The Lord is not slack concerning his promise, as some men count slackness; but is longsuffering to us-ward, not willing that any should perish, but that all should come to repentance" (2 Pe.3:9).

b. Now note what God promised to do for His backslidden people: He promised to stand before His servant by the *rock in Horeb* (v.6).

c. God instructed His dear servant to strike the rock, and He promised that water would flow out of it (v.6). (See DEEPER STUDY # 2—Ex.17:6 for more discussion.)

d. God's servant obeyed (v.6). Moses took his staff and struck the rock in sight of all the elders standing there. The result: water flowed out of the rock, flowed like rivers that branched out into streams.

Note another fact as well: the LORD Himself is said to have been standing there causing water to gush forth out of the rock. How was this possible? By God, by His omnipotent power. The LORD was standing there by the rock and when Moses struck it, the LORD caused a river and springs of water to flow out of the rock or out of the ground from under the rock. This is exactly what is declared in other Scriptures.

"Moreover, brethren, I would not that ye should be ignorant, how that all our fathers were under the cloud, and all passed through the sea; And were all baptized unto Moses in the cloud and in the sea; and did all eat the same spiritual meat; And did all drink the same spiritual drink: for they drank of that spiritual Rock that followed them: and that Rock was Christ" (1 Co.10:1-4).

"He clave the rocks in the wilderness, and gave them drink as out of the great depths. He brought streams also out of the rock, and caused waters to run down like rivers" (Ps.78:15-16).

"Which turned the rock into a standing water, the flint into a fountain of waters" (Ps.114:8).

Thought 1. The wilderness will leave a person dry, parched, and empty of any moisture. This is a picture of man being spiritually dry, parched, and empty. Spiritually...

- man has a dry spirit; God seems far, far away.
- man has a dry soul; a personal relationship with Christ and personal devotions are lacking.
- man has dry friendships; surface relationships are the norm.
- man has dry hearing, the words of God are only faintly heard.
- man has a dry family life, little communication and little fulfillment and love.

- man has a dry heart; tenderness dried up long ago.
- man has a dry love life; self-centeredness quenches any chance of sharing together sacrificially.
- man has a dry mind; worldly distractions rule every thought.
- man has a dry career; work has become a loathsome chore.
- man has a dry vision for the future; little hope exists for a full and satisfied life.

Empty people have a desperate need to quench their thirst. But note, there is glorious news: there is water to quench man's dry, parched thirst. There is a living water, a water that gives life to man. That water is Jesus Christ Himself. Jesus Christ is the water of life. He can quench the dry, parched thirst of man. This is the strong declaration of Scripture.

"Jesus answered and said unto her, If thou knewest the gift of God, and who it is that saith to thee, Give me to drink; thou wouldest have asked of him, and he would have given thee living water. The woman saith unto him, Sir, thou hast nothing to draw with, and the well is deep: from whence then hast thou that living water?...Jesus answered and said unto her, Whosoever drinketh of this water shall thirst again: But whosoever drinketh of the water that I shall give him shall never thirst; but the water that I shall give him shall be in him a well of water springing up into everlasting life" (Jn.4:10-11, 13-14).

"In the last day, that great [day] of the feast, Jesus stood and cried, saying, If any man thirst, let him come unto me, and drink. He that believeth on me, as the scripture hath said, out of his belly shall flow rivers of living water" (Jn.7:37-38).

"Blessed [are] they which do hunger and thirst after righteousness: for they shall be filled" (Mt.5:6).

"They shall be abundantly satisfied with the fatness of thy house; and thou shalt make them drink of the river of thy pleasures" (Ps.36:8).

"Therefore with joy shall ye draw water out of the wells of salvation" (Is.12:3).

"For I will pour water upon him that is thirsty, and floods upon the dry ground: I will pour my spirit upon thy seed, and my blessing upon thine offspring" (Is.44:3).

"Ho, every one that thirsteth, come ye to the waters, and he that hath no money; come ye, buy, and eat; yea, come, buy wine and milk without money and without price" (Is.55:1).

"And the Spirit and the bride say, Come. And let him that heareth say, Come. And let him that is athirst come. And whosoever will, let him take the water of life freely" (Re.22:17).

Thought 2. Jesus Christ declared that He is the water of life, the water that saves and gives life to man. Jesus Christ is the only water that can meet the thirst of man's soul, that can satisfy man.

"Jesus answered and said unto her, If thou knewest the gift of God, and who it is that saith to thee, Give me to drink; thou wouldest have asked of him, and he would have given thee living water" (Jn.4:10).

"Jesus answered and said unto her, Whosoever drinketh of this water shall thirst again: But whosoever drinketh of the water that I shall give him shall never thirst; but the water that I shall give him shall be in him a well of water springing up into everlasting life" (Jn.4:13-14).

"In the last day, that great [day] of the feast, Jesus stood and cried, saying, If any man thirst, let him come unto me, and drink" (Jn.7:37).

"He that believeth on me, as the scripture hath said, out of his belly shall flow rivers of living water. (But this spake he of the Spirit, which they that believe on him should receive: for the Holy Ghost was not yet given; because that Jesus was not yet glorified)" (Jn.7:38-39).

"For the Lamb which is in the midst of the throne shall feed them, and shall lead them unto living fountains of waters: and God shall wipe away all tears from their eyes" (Re.7:17).

"And he said unto me, It is done. I am Alpha and Omega, the beginning and the end. I will give unto him that is athirst of the fountain of the water of life freely" (Re.21:6).

"And the Spirit and the bride say, Come. And let him that heareth say, Come. And let him that is athirst come. And whosoever will, let him take the water of life freely" (Re.22:17).

"Ho, every one that thirsteth, come ye to the waters, and he that hath no money; come ye, buy, and eat; yea, come, buy wine and milk without money and without price. Wherefore do ye spend money for that which is not bread? and your labour for that which satisfieth not? hearken diligently unto me, and eat ye that which is good, and let your soul delight itself in fatness" (Is.55:1-2).

Thought 3. There is a great lesson here: we must learn to trust God, believe Him, depend upon Him to take care of our needs. God will meet our needs, even the most severe and difficult needs. God will do whatever is necessary to meet our needs: He will even give waters in the wilderness and rivers in the desert to take care of us (Is.43:20). Our task is to trust God, to depend upon Him.

"But seek ye first the kingdom of God, and his righteousness; and all these things shall be added unto you" (Mt.6:33).

"He that believeth on the Son hath everlasting life: and he that believeth not the Son shall not see life; but the wrath of God abideth on him" (Jn.3:36).

"I am the vine, ye [are] the branches: He that abideth in me, and I in him, the same bringeth forth much fruit: for without me ye can do nothing" (Jn.15:5).

"Not that we are sufficient of ourselves to think any thing as of ourselves; but our sufficiency is of God" (2 Co.3:5).

"And ye shall serve the LORD your God, and he shall bless thy bread, and thy water; and I will take sickness away from the midst of thee" (Ex.23:25).

"Oh how great is thy goodness, which thou hast laid up for them that fear thee; which thou hast wrought for them that trust in thee before the sons of men!" (Ps.31:19).

"Many sorrows shall be to the wicked: but he that trusteth in the LORD, mercy shall compass him about" (Ps.32:10).

"The LORD redeemeth the soul of his servants: and none of them that trust in him shall be desolate" (Ps.34:22).

"Trust in the LORD, and do good; so shalt thou dwell in the land, and verily thou shalt be fed" (Ps.37:3).

"Commit thy way unto the LORD; trust also in him; and he shall bring it to pass" (Ps.37:5).

"The fear of man bringeth a snare: but whoso putteth his trust in the LORD shall be safe" (Pr.29:25).

"Thou wilt keep him in perfect peace, whose mind is stayed on thee: because he trusteth in thee. Trust ye in the LORD for ever: for in the LORD JEHOVAH is everlasting strength" (Is.26:3-4).

"Bring ye all the tithes into the storehouse, that there may be meat in mine house, and prove me now herewith, saith the LORD of hosts, if I will not open you the windows of heaven, and pour you out a blessing, that there shall not be room enough to receive it" (Mal.3:10).

5   (17:7) **Rephidim—Massah—Meribah—Memorial**: the place of Rephidim was memorialized. Moses wanted succeeding generations to always remember what had happened at Rephidim; therefore, he gave two names to the place.

⇒   Massah, which means test, testing. This, of course, referred to the people's testing—doubting and questioning—of God.

⇒   Meribah, which means argument, contention, and strife. This referred to the people's complaining and grumbling spirit against God and His servant Moses.

Thought 1. Two important lessons must be learned from this point. We all (every believer) leave a legacy upon earth. We absolutely must not leave the legacy that the Israelites left.

(1)   The legacy of testing God: of unbelief and distrust, of doubting and questioning God, questioning His existence and His goodness.

"Well; because of unbelief they [Israel] were broken off, and thou standest by faith. Be not highminded, but fear: For if God spared not the natural branches, take heed lest he also spare not thee" (Ro.11:20-21).

"And said unto him, Art thou he that should come, or do we look for another?" (Mt.11:3).

"And he did not many mighty works there because of their unbelief" (Mt.13:58).

"Then came the disciples to Jesus apart, and said, Why could not we cast him out? And Jesus said unto them, Because of your unbelief: for verily I say unto you, If ye have faith as a grain of mustard seed, ye shall say unto this mountain, Remove hence to yonder place; and it shall remove; and nothing shall be impossible unto you" (Mt.17:19-20).

"And he said unto them, Why are ye so fearful? how is it that ye have no faith?" (Mk.4:40).

"Afterward he appeared unto the eleven as they sat at meat, and upbraided them with their unbelief and hardness of heart, because they believed not them which had seen him after he was risen" (Mk.16:14).

"And their words seemed to them as idle tales, and they believed them not" (Lu.24:11).

"Then he said unto them, O fools, and slow of heart to believe all that the prophets have spoken" (Lu.24:25).

"But though he had done so many miracles before them, yet they believed not on him" (Jn.12:37).

"The other disciples therefore said unto him, We have seen the Lord. But he said unto them, Except I shall see in his hands the print of the nails, and put my finger into the print of the nails, and thrust my hand into his side, I will not believe" (Jn.20:25).

"Take heed, brethren, lest there be in any of you an evil heart of unbelief, in departing from the living God" (He.3:12).

"Let us labour therefore to enter into that rest, lest any man fall after the same example of unbelief" (He.4:11).

"And he said unto him, If now I have found grace in thy sight, then show me a sign that thou talkest with me" (Jud.6:17).

"Who hath believed our report? and to whom is the arm of the LORD revealed?" (Is.53:1).

(2) The legacy of complaining, grumbling, and murmuring.

> "The foolishness of man perverteth his way: and his heart fretteth against the LORD" (Pr.19:3).
> "Jesus therefore answered and said unto them, Murmur not among yourselves" (Jn.6:43).
> "Neither murmur ye, as some of them also murmured, and were destroyed of the destroyer" (1 Co.10:10).
> "Do all things without murmurings and disputings" (Ph.2:14).

DEEPER STUDY # 2

(17:6) **Rock of Horeb, The**: Scripture teaches that the *rock* is a symbol of the Lord Jesus Christ. As the title of the song says, Jesus Christ is the "Rock of Ages." Time and again throughout Scripture, the rock pictures the LORD. (See outline and notes—1 Pe.2:4-8 for an in-depth study of "Christ, the Living Rock.")

1. The Israelites are said to have drunk of the spiritual rock, the Rock of Christ.

> "And did all drink the same spiritual drink: for they drank of that spiritual Rock that followed them: and that Rock was Christ" (1 Co.10:4).

What does it mean to say that Christ was the spiritual Rock that followed the Israelites? It means that He was the foundation, the support, the security, the solid footing of their lives. He was there to support them, to make them safe and secure and to provide for them, to provide whatever they needed.

2. Moses *struck the rock* and water flowed out of the rock, water that saved and brought life to the Israelites. Jesus Christ was "smitten, stricken, and afflicted" and became the fountain of living water for us all.

> "Surely he hath borne our griefs, and carried our sorrows: yet we did esteem him stricken, smitten of God, and afflicted. But he was wounded for our transgressions, he was bruised for our iniquities: the chastisement of our peace was upon him; and with his stripes we are healed" (Is.53:4-5).
> "Jesus answered and said unto her, Whosoever drinketh of this water shall thirst again: But whosoever drinketh of the water that I shall give him shall never thirst; but the water that I shall give him shall be in him a well of water springing up into everlasting life" (Jn.4:13-14).
> "In the last day, that great [day] of the feast, Jesus stood and cried, saying, If any man thirst, let him come unto me, and drink. He that believeth on me, as the scripture hath said, out of his belly shall flow rivers of living water" (Jn.7:37-38).

3. The Psalmist cried out for the Rock to help him in his distress.

> "From the end of the earth will I cry unto thee, when my heart is overwhelmed: lead me to the rock that is higher than I" (Ps.61:2).

4. Israel remembered that God was their rock.

> "And they remembered that God was their rock, and the high God their redeemer" (Ps.78:35).

5. Jesus Christ is the rock, the chief cornerstone, that determines the fate of all people.

> "Wherefore also it is contained in the scripture, Behold, I lay in Sion a chief corner stone, elect, precious: and he that believeth on him shall not be confounded. Unto you therefore which believe he is precious: but unto them which be disobedient, the stone which the builders disallowed, the same is made the head of the corner, And a stone of stumbling, and a rock of offence, even to them which stumble at the word, being disobedient: whereunto also they were appointed" (1 Pe.2:6-8).

6. Jesus Christ is the only foundation upon which people can build and base their lives.

> "For other foundation can no man lay than that is laid, which is Jesus Christ" (1 Co.3:11).

TYPES, SYMBOLS, AND PICTURES
(Exodus 17:1-7)

Historical Term	Type or Picture (Scriptural Basis for Each)	Life Application for Today's Believer	Biblical Application
The Rock at Rephidim (Ex.17:6)	*God's Provision of water* "Behold, I will stand before thee there upon the rock in Horeb; and thou shalt smite the rock, and	Jesus Christ is our Rock, the rock of our salvation... • who provides the water that saves and gives us life	*"And did all drink the same spiritual drink: for they drank of that spiritual Rock that followed them: and that Rock was Christ" (1 Co.10:4; see Is.53:4-5).*

TYPES, SYMBOLS, AND PICTURES
(Exodus 17:1-7)

Historical Term	Type or Picture (Scriptural Basis for Each)	Life Application for Today's Believer	Biblical Application
The Rock at Rephidim (continued) (Ex.17:6)	there shall come water out of it, that the people may drink. And Moses did so in the sight of the elders of Israel" (Ex.17:6). "Therefore with joy shall ye draw water out of the wells of salvation" (Is.12:3).	• who supports us during the storms of life • who is the chief cornerstone that determines the fate of us all • who is the only foundation upon which we can build and base our lives	*"Jesus answered and said unto her, Whosoever drinketh of this water shall thirst again: But whosoever drinketh of the water that I shall give him shall never thirst; but the water that I shall give him shall be in him a well of water springing up into everlasting life" (Jn.4:13-14).* *"Wherefore also it is contained in the scripture, Behold, I lay in Sion a chief corner stone, elect, precious: and he that believeth on him shall not be confounded. Unto you therefore which believe he is precious: but unto them which be disobedient, the stone which the builders disallowed, the same is made the head of the corner, And a stone of stumbling, and a rock of offence, even to them which stumble at the word, being disobedient: whereunto also they were appointed" (1 Pe.2:6-8; see 1 Co.3:11).*
Meribah (Ex. 17:7)	*Argument, contention, and strife: Complaining against God and His servants* "And the people thirsted there for water; and the people murmured against Moses, and said, Wherefore is this that thou hast brought us up out of Egypt, to kill us and our children and our cattle with thirst?...And he called the name of the place Massah, and Meribah, because of the chiding of the children of Israel, and because they tempted the LORD, saying, Is the LORD among us, or not?" (Ex.17:3, 7).	Carnal (fleshly) believers complain, murmur, & grumble. They complain against God and His servants. They are like a spiritual cancer that spreads and infects the whole body of believers.	*"Neither murmur ye, as some of them also murmured, and were destroyed of the destroyer" (1 Co.10:10).* *"Do all things without murmurings and disputings" (Ph.2:14).* *"Jesus therefore answered and said unto them, Murmur not among yourselves" (Jn.6:43).* *"If any man among you seem to be religious, and bridleth not his tongue, but deceiveth his own heart, this man's religion is vain" (Js.1:26).* *(see Ex.16:8; Ps.52:2; 106:24-25; 120:2; Js. 3:5-8; 1 Pe.3:10; Jude 14-16)*
Massah (Ex.17:7)	*The name "Massah" means testing: Doubting and questioning God* "And he called the name of the place Massah, and Meribah, because of the chiding of the children of Israel, and because they tempted the LORD, saying, Is the LORD among us, or not?" (Ex.17:7).	God is not to be doubted nor questioned. How can the creature question the LORD God... • who is the great Creator and Sustainer of the universe • who is the Sovereign Lord and Majesty of all • who is the Giver of every good and perfect gift, the Father of Light, who never changes	*"Take heed, brethren, lest there be in any of you an evil heart of unbelief, in departing from the living God" (He.3:12).* *"Because of unbelief they [Israel] were broken off, and thou standest by faith. Be not highminded, but fear: For if God spared not the natural branches, take heed lest he also spare not thee" (Ro.11:20-21).*

EXODUS 17:1-7

TYPES, SYMBOLS, AND PICTURES
(Exodus 17:1-7)

Historical Term	Type or Picture (Scriptural Basis for Each)	Life Application for Today's Believer	Biblical Application
Massah (continued) (Ex.17:7)		• who is the only living and true God	*"Then he said unto them, O fools, and slow of heart to believe all that the prophets have spoken"* (Lu.24:25). *"Art thou the Christ? tell us. And he said unto them, If I tell you, ye will not believe"* (Lu.22:67). *"But though he had done so many miracles before them, yet they believed not on him"* (Jn.12:37). *"And he did not many mighty works there because of their unbelief"* (Mt.13:58). *(see Ro.4:20; 2 Th.3:3; 1 Ti. 1:13; 2 Ti.2:13; He. 3:19; He.10:23)*

	G. The Fifth Crisis of Israel in the Wilderness—Warfare: Victory Through Prevailing Prayer, 17:8-16		
1. The crisis	8 Then came Amalek, and fought with Israel in Rephidim.	heavy; and they took a stone, and put it under him, and he sat thereon; and Aaron and Hur stayed up his hands, the one on the one side, and the other on the other side; and his hands were steady until the going down of the sun.	support in order to prevail in prayer
a. The Amakelites attacked Israel[DS1]			e. Needed others who could support & hold up God's servant: Aaron & Hur[DS2]
b. Moses appointed a commander to mobilize an army: Joshua	9 And Moses said unto Joshua, Choose us out men, and go out, fight with Amalek: to morrow I will stand on the top of the hill with the rod of God in mine hand.		
c. Moses promised to seek God, to prevail in prayer			
		13 And Joshua discomfited Amalek and his people with the edge of the sword.	**3. The results of prevailing prayer**
2. The prevailing prayer	10 So Joshua did as Moses had said to him, and fought with Amalek: and Moses, Aaron, and Hur went up to the top of the hill.	14 And the LORD said unto Moses, Write this for a memorial in a book, and rehearse it in the ears of Joshua: for I will utterly put out the remembrance of Amalek from under heaven.	a. The enemy was defeated
a. Was made while the battle was being waged			b. The victory was to be written down & remembered forever
b. Was made on a hill in sight of all: To show that victory was through the LORD alone			
c. Was of critical importance	11 And it came to pass, when Moses held up his hand, that Israel prevailed: and when he let down his hand, Amalek prevailed.		c. Judgment was pronounced upon the enemy: To be completely blotted out
1) Prevailing prayer led to advance		15 And Moses built an altar, and called the name of it Jehovah-nissi:	d. God's name was established forever: Jehovah-Nissi, the LORD is my banner[DS3]
2) Weak prayer led to retreat		16 For he said, Because the LORD hath sworn that the LORD will have war with Amalek from generation to generation.	
d. Needed a stone for rest &	12 But Moses' hands were		

DIVISION V

THE RED SEA AND THE WILDERNESS WANDERINGS: THE BELIEVER'S TRIALS AS HE JOURNEYS TO THE PROMISED LAND, 13:17–18:27

G.   The Fifth Crisis of Israel in the Wilderness—Warfare: Victory Through Prevailing Prayer, Ex.17:8-16

(17:8-16) **Introduction**: crisis—what do we do when some crisis stares us in the face? No crisis is more threatening and frightening than war—a war that is launched right at one's back door. This is what now happened to Israel, but the focus is not upon the war. The focus is upon the thing that brought about the victory: prevailing prayer—the intercession, the crying out to God. Victory against the enemies of life comes from the LORD and from the LORD alone. When the enemies of life attack us, our duty is to go before the LORD and cry out to Him for victory. This is the lesson, the great focus of this passage: *The Fifth Crisis of Israel in the Wilderness—Warfare: Victory Through Prevailing Prayer,* 17:8-16.

1. The crisis (vv.8-9).
2. The prevailing prayer (vv.10-12).
3. The results of prevailing prayer (vv.13-16).

1 (17:8-9) **Amalekites—Crisis—Israel**: there was the crisis of war.

a.   The Amalekites attacked Israel while they were camped at Rephidim. (See DEEPER STUDY # 1, *Amalekites*—Ex.17:8 for more discussion.) Why would the Amalekites attack Israel? No doubt, because they felt threatened. They were a desert people who lived just south of the promised land of Canaan. They had obviously heard about Israel being freed from Egypt and of their march to Canaan, somewhere between two to three million of them. To reach Canaan, this large mass of Israelites would have to march either through or close by the land of the Amalekites. The leaders of the Amalekites had no idea what Israel's intentions would be, to pass by their land in peace or to attack and ransack them. Consequently, the Amalekites launched a surprise attack against Israel. The attack was sudden, totally unexpected. Four facts need to be pointed out about the attack of the Amalekites.

1) The attack was most cruel and savage. It was launched first against the handicapped and the helpless: the stragglers—the sick, aged, and weary—who lagged behind the main body of travelers. Scripture says the Amalekites slaughtered them all (De.25:17-19).

2) The attack was a surprise attack launched against a mass of civilians, not against an army, totally unprovoked and uncalled for. The leaders of the Amalekites should have sent emissaries out to investigate Israel's intentions and to seek peace. The launching of an army to begin killing, maiming, raping, and enslaving people was reprehensible.

3) The Amalekites were set on annihilation of the Israelites, totally exterminating and erasing them from the face of the earth. They were driven by prejudice and bitter hatred against the Israelites, the same bitter prejudice held by many nations against the Jews down through the generations.

"They have said, Come, and let us cut them off from being a nation; that the name of Israel may be no more in remembrance....Gebal, and Ammon, and Amalek; the Philistines with the inhabitants of Tyre" (Ps.83:4, 7).

4) The Amalekites should have known that God had promised the land of Canaan to Israel. They should have known just as people today know that the Jews look upon the land of Palestine (Canaan) as the *promised land* given to them by God. But the Amalekites should have been aware of the fact far more than we are today. Why?
⇒ Because the Amalekites were the descendants of Esau, the twin brother of Jacob. And God had given the promise of the *promised land* to Jacob and his descendants. Esau knew all about the promise. And note: Amalek was the grandson of Esau. His father, Eliphaz, was the oldest son of Esau. Esau would certainly have shared the great promises of God with both his son Eliphaz and his grandson Amalek (see Ge.36:15).

The point is this: the Amalekites were distant cousins of the Israelites. They most likely knew and certainly should have known about Israel's being promised the promised land of Canaan. They should have sent emissaries and investigated Israel's intentions, not launched a savage and brutal attack against them. *The Expositor's Bible Commentary* says this:

> There is every possibility that [the Amalekites] had known about the promise of the land of Canaan that had been given to Esau's twin brother, Jacob; therefore, they should not have felt any threat to their interests in the Negev had this promise been remembered and taken seriously. After all, the promise was to be a means of blessing Amalek along with all the other nations (Ge.12:3) if only they, like Abraham, would have believed. Instead they "came" (wayyabo) and attacked Israel at Rephidim—some distance south of the north-central district of the Sinai where they lived.[1]

b. Moses appointed a commander to mobilize an army to defend Israel, the young man Joshua (v.9). Apparently, Moses had already charged Joshua with mobilizing an army for Israel. This is suggested by the quickness with which Joshua and the armed men were able to mobilize and stop the attack of the Amalekites. Remember, the attack was a surprise attack against those who lagged behind: the handicapped, sick, weary, and aged.

Where did Israel's armed forces get their weapons? Most likely from the Egyptians. When they were freed by the Egyptians, they requested wages—back pay—for their slave labor. One of the requests would have been for weapons for protection and hunting purposes out in the wilderness of the desert, weapons such as swords and bows and arrows. This would have been a natural and understandable request. There is also a possibility that they were able to recover some weapons from the Egyptians when the army was drowned in the Red Sea. In addition, they would have been making what weapons they could as they marched along from place to place in their wilderness wanderings, weapons such as long spears, slingshots, bows and arrows, and shields.

c. Note that Moses promised to seek God, to intercede for Joshua and the soldiers (v.9). Joshua was to fight; Moses was to pray. Moses promised to go to the top of the highest hill surrounding the battle field, to lift up the rod of God, appealing and calling out to God in prayer. The rod of God was looked upon as the *Banner* of Israel. Consequently, when they saw the *rod of God*—their banner—lifted high, they knew that God's servant was crying out to God. They were encouraged and motivated to fight beyond their strength. They knew that God would give them the victory over their enemy. The point is this: Moses promised the warriors of Israel that he would be their intercessor, their prayer-warrior.

Thought 1. We are often attacked by the enemies of this life, enemies such as...
- disease
- injury
- prejudice
- hatred
- temptation
- lust
- greed
- arrogance
- loneliness
- emptiness
- death

When enemies attack us, our only hope is the LORD, going before Him and crying out for help. Prevailing prayer—intercession, seeking the face of God—are our only hope.

"Seek the LORD and his strength, seek his face continually" (1 Chr.16:11).

"Ask, and it shall be given you; seek, and ye shall find; knock, and it shall be opened unto you" (Mt.7:7).

"Praying always with all prayer and supplication in the Spirit, and watching thereunto with all perseverance and supplication for all saints" (Ep.6:18).

"Pray without ceasing" (1 Th.5:17).

"And ye shall seek me, and find me, when ye shall search for me with all your heart" (Je.29:13).

DEEPER STUDY # 1
(17:8) **Amalekites**: the Amalekites were the bitter, life-long enemies of Israel. They were the first nation to physically attack God's people on their journey from Egypt to the Promised Land. A nomadic tribe, their influence stretched from the Sinai to Canaan. From their first attack on Israel at Rephidim (Ex.17:1), the Amalekites' hatred for Israel was demonstrated with disdain for God, a foolish lack of fear of Him. Significant historical events in Israel's relationship with the Amalekites were:
⇒ The Amalekites cowardly attack on the weak members of the exodus (De.25:17-18).
⇒ God's non-negotiable instructions to exterminate the Amalekites (De.25:19).

[1] Frank E. Gaebelein, Editor. *The Expositor's Bible Commentary*, Vol.2, p.408.

⇒ An embarrassing defeat to the Amalekites because of Israel's rebellion toward God (Nu.14:39-45).
⇒ An unholy alliance of the Amalekites, the king of Moab, and the Ammonites defeated God's people and captured the city of palms (most likely Jericho—De.34:3) (Jud.3:12-14).
⇒ Gideon's great victory over the combined forces of the Amalekites and Midianites (Jud.7:19-23).
⇒ King Saul's moral failure to obey the LORD's instructions to kill the Amalekites' king (Agag). This cost Saul his place as the king of Israel (1 S.15:1-23).
⇒ King David's conquests of Amalek (2 S.8:12; 1 Chr.18:11).

2 (17:10-12) Prayer, Prevailing—Prayer, Weak—Intercession—Stone, The: there was the prevailing prayer.

a. Note that Moses prayed while Joshua and the army fought: *prevailing prayer* was made while the battle was being waged (v.10).

Thought 1. The time for prevailing prayer is when the enemy attacks. Spiritually, the attack may be the fierceness of some...

- temptation
- evil thought
- lustful notion
- immoral suggestion

- urge to steal
- compulsion to lie
- act of selfishness
- temptation to cheat

Physically, the attack may be the threat of ridicule, mockery, abuse, persecution, bodily harm—even the threat of death. Whatever the attack by the enemy, the believer's hope lies in God. As soon as the attack is launched, as soon as the believer becomes aware of the attack, the believer must immediately turn to God and pray. And he must prevail in prayer.

"Seek the LORD and his strength, seek his face continually" (1 Chr.16:11).
"Ask, and it shall be given you; seek, and ye shall find; knock, and it shall be opened unto you" (Mt.7:7).
"Watch and pray, that ye enter not into temptation: the spirit indeed [is] willing, but the flesh [is] weak" (Mt.26:41).
"And he spake a parable unto them to this end, that men ought always to pray, and not to faint" (Lu.18:1).
"Hitherto have ye asked nothing in my name: ask, and ye shall receive, that your joy may be full" (Jn.16:24).
"Praying always with all prayer and supplication in the Spirit, and watching thereunto with all perseverance and supplication for all saints" (Ep.6:18).
"Pray without ceasing" (1 Th.5:17).

b. Moses did exactly what he promised he would do: he went up to the top of the highest hill. He went to the very top so everyone could see him as he sought God. Why?
c. Because of the critical importance of prevailing prayer (v.11). Note what happened.
  1) When Moses held up his hand and the rod of God, Israel advanced (v.11).
  2) When Moses' hand tired and he lowered his arm and the rod, Israel had to retreat under the onslaught of the enemy (v.11).

Why did this happen? Because God needed to teach His people a striking lesson. They were just beginning their journey to the *promised land*, and they needed to learn the basic truth of life: victory is through the LORD and through the LORD alone. In the future, no matter who the enemy was, the only hope for victory was the LORD. No one else could carry them victoriously to the *promised land*, no one except the LORD.
This was the reason God wanted Moses on top of the hill in sight of all, so they could witness the power of...

- prevailing prayer
- intercession
- crying out to God

- seeking God
- appealing to God
- trusting God

God's people, both the soldiers and the civilians, could easily see what happened when Moses was strong enough to keep the rod raised: the army of God began advancing against the enemy, began winning the battle. But they also witnessed what happened when Moses became tired and lowered the rod of God: they began losing the battle and were forced to retreat.

Thought 1. The lesson was clear: when the enemy attacks, God's people must go before God: they must...
- prevail in prayer
- become intercessors
- cry out to God
- seek God
- continuously appeal to God
- trust God

"And Jehoshaphat bowed his head with his face to the ground: and all Judah and the inhabitants of Jerusalem fell before the LORD, worshipping the LORD" (2 Chr.20:18).

"And it came to pass in those days, that he went out into a mountain to pray, and continued all night in prayer to God" (Lu.6:12).

"And he said, Let me go, for the day breaketh. And he said, I will not let thee go, except thou bless me" (Ge.32:26).

"This poor man cried, and the LORD heard him, and saved him out of all his troubles" (Ps.34:6).

"From the end of the earth will I cry unto thee, when my heart is overwhelmed: lead me to the rock that is higher than I" (Ps.61:2).

d. Note that Moses, the prayer warrior, needed a stone to sit upon for rest and support (v.12). The stone supported him, held him up, and gave him rest so that he could endure and continue to prevail in prayer.

Thought 1. Remember the stone is a symbol, a picture of the Lord Jesus Christ. (See DEEPER STUDY # 2—Ex.17:6.) As the rock of our lives, He is our...

• support
• rest
• security
• foundation

"But the LORD is my defence; and my God is the rock of my refuge" (Ps.94:22).

"He is the Rock, his work is perfect: for all his ways are judgment: a God of truth and without iniquity, just and right is he" (De.32:4).

"The stone which the builders refused is become the head stone of the corner" (Ps.118:22).

"Jesus saith unto them, Did ye never read in the scriptures, The stone which the builders rejected, the same is become the head of the corner: this is the Lord's doing, and it is marvellous in our eyes?" (Mt.21:42).

"And are built upon the foundation of the apostles and prophets, Jesus Christ himself being the chief corner stone" (Ep.2:20).

"Wherefore also it is contained in the scripture, Behold, I lay in Sion a chief corner stone, elect, precious: and he that believeth on him shall not be confounded" (1 Pe.2:6).

Thought 2. All believers have faced times in their wilderness wanderings when exhaustion and sheer fatigue hit with great force. There have been times...

• when deadlines came and went, and the harder we worked the more we fell behind
• when children demanded too much time or got into too much trouble
• when our schedules were out of control
• when finances ran low and there was simply not enough to make ends meet
• when times of personal devotion to God were pushed aside—until a more convenient time
• when a loved one forsook us or died and we were left with unbearable pain
• when life was only endured and not enjoyed
• when enemies attacked and we saw no way to escape
• when spouses just did not understand, creating tension and frustration for us
• when fellowship with the body of Christ was the last thing on our minds
• when an accident or disease hit with full force
• when everything seemed hopeless, as though all were lost

God knows that we need His support day-by-day, moment-by-moment. This is where Jesus Christ comes in. He is the Rock of our salvation. He undergirds us as we walk through the wilderness of this world. When we reach the end of our resources, He will undergird our lives. He is a rock, a support that never collapses, a source that has no limits or boundaries, a Savior who never grows weary of saving us from ourselves.

"The eternal God is thy refuge, and underneath are the everlasting arms: and he shall thrust out the enemy from before thee; and shall say, Destroy them" (De.33:27).

"The LORD is my rock, and my fortress, and my deliverer; my God, my strength, in whom I will trust; my buckler, and the horn of my salvation, and my high tower" (Ps.18:2).

"For who is God save the LORD? or who is a rock save our God? It is God that girdeth me with strength, and maketh my way perfect" (Ps.18:31-32).

"Thou hast also given me the shield of thy salvation: and thy right hand hath holden me up, and thy gentleness hath made me great" (Ps.18:35).

"The LORD liveth; and blessed be my rock; and let the God of my salvation be exalted" (Ps.18:46).

"For in the time of trouble he shall hide me in his pavilion: in the secret of his tabernacle shall he hide me; he shall set me up upon a rock" (Ps.27:5).

"Unto thee will I cry, O LORD my rock; be not silent to me: lest, if thou be silent to me, I become like them that go down into the pit" (Ps.28:1).

"Bow down thine ear to me; deliver me speedily: be thou my strong rock, for an house of defence to save me. For thou art my rock and my fortress; therefore for thy name's sake lead me, and guide me" (Ps.31:2-3).

"He brought me up also out of an horrible pit, out of the miry clay, and set my feet upon a rock, and established my goings" (Ps.40:2).

"Fear thou not; for I am with thee: be not dismayed; for I am thy God: I will strengthen thee; yea, I will help thee; yea, I will uphold thee with the right hand of my righteousness" (Is.41:10).

"And even to your old age I am he; and even to hoar [gray] hairs will I carry you: I have made, and I will bear; even I will carry, and will deliver you" (Is.46:4).

"For whosoever shall call upon the name of the Lord shall be saved" (Ro.10:13).

"Casting all your care upon him; for he careth for you" (1 Pe.5:7).

e. Note that the prayer warrior, Moses, also needed others who could help him in his intercession and appeal to God. Two other men had gone up the hill to see the LORD with Moses: Aaron and Hur. (See DEEPER STUDY # 2, *Hur*—Ex.17:12 for more discussion.)

When Moses became too tired to hold up the rod of God, the two men held up his arms for him. Note that they stayed right with Moses all day, until sunset. Keep in mind that all three of these men were servants of God. Standing there on the hill, holding up the rod of God with the battle for their very survival being waged in the valley below, these men were doing what any servant of God would be doing:

⇒ praying and crying out to God
⇒ struggling and interceding with God
⇒ begging and appealing to God

The point to see is this: one prayer warrior is often not enough. Support in prayer is needed. Others are needed when the enemy attacks and threatens God's people.

Thought 1. Every believer needs to prevail in prayer. There are times when we, our loved ones, friends, church, and believers worldwide need special prayer—special periods of intercession—of crying out to God. Therefore, we must be ready to pray and pray—ready to spend long periods of time in prayer—ready to prevail in prayer, appealing to God to give us the victory over the fierce enemies who attack us.

"And it came to pass in those days, that he went out into a mountain to pray, and continued all night in prayer to God" (Lu.6:12).

"And he said, Let me go, for the day breaketh. And he said, I will not let thee go, except thou bless me" (Ge.32:26).

"Praying always with all prayer and supplication in the Spirit, and watching thereunto with all perseverance and supplication for all saints" (Ep.6:18).

"Pray without ceasing" (1 Th.5:17).

"And ye shall seek me, and find me, when ye shall search for me with all your heart" (Je.29:13).

DEEPER STUDY # 2

(17:12) **Hur**: More than one man in the Old Testament bears the name of Hur. The most familiar is the Hur mentioned here who was the son of Caleb and Ephrath and the grandfather of Bezalel the artist (1 Chr.2:19-20).

⇒ Hur served with Moses.
⇒ Hur may have been Moses' brother-in-law, the husband of Moses' sister Miriam.[2]
⇒ Hur, along with Aaron, supported Moses as they prayed for victory during the battle (Ex.17:10-13).
⇒ Hur helped in ruling the tribes while Moses was on Mount Sinai (Ex.24:14).
⇒ Hur had a part in building the Tabernacle (Ex.31:2; 1 Chr.2:19).
⇒ A man named Hur was a Midianite king who died with Balaam (Nu.31:1-8; Jos.13:21).
⇒ A man named Hur was an officer in Solomon's charge who worked in Ephraim. This Hur's responsibility was to provide food for Solomon's palace.[3]
⇒ Hur's son was a co-ruler with Nehemiah. He helped rebuild the wall around Jerusalem (Ne.3:9).

(See Ex.17:10, 12; 24:14; 31:1-2; 35:30; 38:22; Nu.31:8; Jos.13:21; 1 K.4:8; 1 Chr.2:19-20, 50; 4:1, 4; 2 Chr.1:5; Ne.3:9).

---

3 (17:13-16) **Victory—Triumph—Amalekites—God, Names of**: there were the results of prevailing prayer.

a. The enemy was defeated (v.13). God gave His people victory over their enemy. The Amalekites were crushed.

Thought 1. The Amalekites are a picture of fierce, violent enemies, enemies whom the believer has to face as he walks through the wilderness of this world. Such enemies as...

• evil rulers	• pornography	• loss of job
• oppressive people	• lust	• lack of purpose
• drugs	• greed	• lack of money
• alcohol	• pride	• fear
• gluttony	• loneliness	• hopelessness
• immorality	• boredom	• helplessness

---

2 Flavius Josephus. *Antiquities of the Jews.* "Complete Works," III, 2, 4
3 *Zondervan Pictorial Encyclopedia of the Bible*, Vol.3:227.

Such enemies are extremely dangerous. But there is hope, glorious hope. All enemies, no matter how strong or terrible, can be defeated. We can overcome and conquer. We can gain the victory over all—no matter what confronts us. How? By God! By God's power. By calling upon the Lord for help. If we call—pray, prevail in prayer—God will hear and deliver us from the Amalekites of our day. God will give us victory over all enemies, no matter who or what they are, and no matter how ferocious their attack. Victory only comes when God's power, the power of prayer, is used to overcome the Amalekites of this day and age.

"**Ask, and it shall be given you; seek, and ye shall find; knock, and it shall be opened unto you**" (Mt.7:7).

"**And he spake a parable unto them to this end, that men ought always to pray, and not to faint**" (Lu.18:1).

"**But there shall not an hair of your head perish**" (Lu.21:18).

"**These things I have spoken unto you, that in me ye might have peace. In the world ye shall have tribulation: but be of good cheer; I have overcome the world**" (Jn.16:33).

"**Who delivered us from so great a death, and doth deliver: in whom we trust that he will yet deliver us**" (2 Co.1:10).

"**And the Lord shall deliver me from every evil work, and will preserve me unto his heavenly kingdom: to whom be glory for ever and ever**" (2 Ti.4:18).

"**Forasmuch then as the children are partakers of flesh and blood, he also himself likewise took part of the same; that through death he might destroy him that had the power of death, that is, the devil; And deliver them who through fear of death were all their lifetime subject to bondage**" (He.2:14-15).

"**The Lord knoweth how to deliver the godly out of temptations, and to reserve the unjust unto the day of judgment to be punished**" (2 Pe.2:9).

"**The Lord shall fight for you, and ye shall hold your peace**" (Ex.14:14).

"**When thou goest out to battle against thine enemies, and seest horses, and chariots, and a people more than thou, be not afraid of them: for the Lord thy God is with thee, which brought thee up out of the land of Egypt**" (De.20:1).

"**And he said, The Lord is my rock, and my fortress, and my deliverer; The God of my rock; in him will I trust: he is my shield, and the horn of my salvation, my high tower, and my refuge, my saviour; thou savest me from violence** (2 S.22:2-3).

"**Seek the Lord and his strength, seek his face continually**" (1 Chr.16:11).

"**The angel of the Lord encampeth round about them that fear him, and delivereth them**" (Ps.34:7).

"**But I am poor and needy; yet the Lord thinketh upon me: thou art my help and my deliverer; make no tarrying, O my God**" (Ps.40:17).

"**Surely he shall deliver thee from the snare of the fowler, and from the noisome pestilence**" (Ps.91:3).

"**Fear thou not; for I am with thee: be not dismayed; for I am thy God: I will strengthen thee; yea, I will help thee; yea, I will uphold thee with the right hand of my righteousness**" (Is.41:10).

"**When thou passest through the waters, I will be with thee; and through the rivers, they shall not overflow thee: when thou walkest through the fire, thou shalt not be burned; neither shall the flame kindle upon thee**" (Is.43:2).

"**Be not afraid of their faces: for I am with thee to deliver thee, saith the Lord**" (Je.1:8).

b. The victory was to be written down and remembered forever (v.14). God told Moses to write an account of the attack and victory so that Joshua and succeeding generations would always remember the event. But note: What specifically did God want His people to remember? That victory is through the Lord and through the Lord alone. When enemies attack God's people, their hope is the Lord. God's people are to go before the Lord and pray, prevail in prayer until the Lord gives the victory.

"**Then sang Moses and the children of Israel this song unto the Lord, and spake, saying, I will sing unto the Lord, for he hath triumphed gloriously: the horse and his rider hath he thrown into the sea**" (Ex.15:1).

"**O my God, I trust in thee: let me not be ashamed, let not mine enemies triumph over me**" (Ps.25:2).

"**For thou, Lord, hast made me glad through thy work: I will triumph in the works of thy hands**" (Ps.92:4).

"***And* having spoiled principalities and powers, he [Jesus Christ] made a show of them openly, triumphing over them in it**" (Col.2:15).

c. Judgment was pronounced upon the enemy: the enemy of God's people was to be completely blotted out (v.14). The Amalekites as a nation of people were to be utterly destroyed. The evil and cruelty of the Amalekites were terrible (see note—Ex.17:8-9 and DEEPER STUDY # 1—Ex.17:8 for discussion). Consequently, they were to face the judgment of God. They had set out to erase God's people from the face of the earth, but in the end, God brought the judgment of extinction to them. Their final extinction as a nation apparently took place under Saul and David (1 S.15:1-35; 2 S.1:1-8:12).

d. God's name was established forever: Moses built an altar there at Rephidim and called it *Jehovah-Nissi*, which means "the Lord is my Banner" (vv.15-16. See DEEPER STUDY # 3—Ex.17:15.) Note that Moses honored God, not Joshua. He did not have Joshua parading before the people in a triumphant march; he had an altar built to God.

333

Thought 1. There are many enemies throughout life who seek to destroy us, terrible enemies: such enemies as…

- disease
- accident
- temptation
- alcohol
- lust

- immorality
- abuse
- irresponsibility
- bankruptcy
- greed

- gluttony
- loneliness
- violence
- threats
- war

On and on the list could go, but there is hope. Deliverance is possible. Victory over all enemies can be had. Victory is through the Lord. But note: victory is through the Lord and through Him alone.

"Now thanks *be* unto God, which always causeth us to triumph in Christ, and maketh manifest the savour of his knowledge by us in every place" (2 Co.2:14).
"But thanks *be* to God, which giveth us the victory through our Lord Jesus Christ" (1 Co.15:57).
"For whatsoever is born of God overcometh the world: and this is the victory that overcometh the world, *even* our faith" (1 Jn.5:4).

DEEPER STUDY # 3

(17:15) **God, Names - Titles**: Jehovah Nissi means "the LORD is my Banner." Moses had lifted up the rod of God as the banner of Israel, as the emblem, the symbol of Israel. Remember, the rod was the symbol of God's power. Moses had cried out, praying for God to give victory over the enemy that had attacked God's people. The rod of God had been lifted up as the identifying *banner* and *symbol* that God's power was present with Israel. The LORD (Jehovah, Yahweh) was present and gave the victory. It was God's presence, salvation, and deliverance—His power—that had triumphed. Therefore, Moses declared that the Banner of Israel, the Banner of God's people, was the LORD Himself.

TYPES, SYMBOLS, AND PICTURES
(Exodus 17:8-16)

Historical Term	Type or Picture (Scriptural Basis for Each)	Life Application for Today's Believer	Biblical Application
The Stone that Moses Sat Upon (Ex.17:12)	*A picture of support and salvation* **"But Moses' hands were heavy; and they took a stone, and put *it* under him, and he sat thereon; and Aaron and Hur stayed up his hands, the one on the one side, and the other on the other side; and his hands were steady until the going down of the sun"** (Ex.17:12). **I waited patiently for the LORD; and he inclined unto me, and heard my cry. He brought me up also out of an horrible pit, out of the miry clay, and set my feet upon a rock, *and* established my goings"** (Ps.40:1-2).	Jesus Christ is the Rock of our lives, the Rock that undergirds us as we walk through the wilderness of this world. Jesus Christ is the Rock of… • our salvation • our support • our security • our foundation	*"He only is my rock and my salvation; he is my defence; I shall not be greatly moved"* (Ps.62:2). *"The stone which the builders refused is become the head stone [Jesus Christ] of the corner"* (Ps.118:22). *"And [you] are built upon the foundation of the apostles and prophets, Jesus Christ himself being the chief corner stone"* (Ep.2:20). *"For who is God save the LORD? or who is a rock save our God? It is God that girdeth me with strength, and maketh my way perfect"* (Ps.18:31-32). *"But the LORD is my defence; and my God is the rock of my refuge"* (Ps.94:22). (see 1 S.2:2; 2 S. 22:47; De.32:4; Ps.28:1; 62:2; 1 Pe.2:6-9)

TYPES, SYMBOLS, AND PICTURES
(Exodus 17:8-16)

Historical Term	Type or Picture (Scriptural Basis for Each)	Life Application for Today's Believer	Biblical Application
Jehovah Nissi: The LORD is my Banner (Ex.17:15-16)	*God's Name is the Banner of the believer. His name is the Emblem, the Symbol, the Identifying Sign of the believer.* **"And Moses built an altar, and called the name of it Jehovah-nissi [the LORD is my banner]: For he said, Because the LORD hath sworn** *that* **the LORD** *will have* **war with Amalek from generation to generation"** (Ex.17:15-16). **"Some** *trust* **in chariots, and some in horses: but we will remember the name of the LORD our God"** (Ps.20:7).	The Name of the Lord Jesus Christ is the Banner. His name is the emblem, the symbol, the identifying sign—of the believer. The name of the Lord is what the believer carries with him as he journeys through the wilderness of this world. The name of the Lord is his banner (his power), his witness, as he marches to the promised land of heaven.	*"Wherefore God also hath highly exalted him, and given him a name which is above every name: That at the name of Jesus every knee should bow, of things in heaven, and things in earth, and things under the earth; And that every tongue should confess that Jesus Christ is Lord, to the glory of God the Father"* (Ph.2:9-11). *"But these are written, that ye might believe that Jesus is the Christ, the Son of God; and that believing ye might have life through his name"* (Jn.20:31). *"Because he hath set his love upon me, therefore will I deliver him: I will set him on high because he hath known my name"* (Ps.91:14). *"Our help is in the name of the LORD, who made heaven and earth"* (Ps.124:8). *"The name of the LORD is a strong tower: the righteous runneth into it, and is safe"* (Pr.18:10). *(see Ne.9:5-6; Ps.113:1-5)*

CHAPTER 18

H. The Sixth Crisis of Israel in the Wilderness— Marital Separation & Overwork: Helping Others, 18:1-27

1. Help one: Jethro sought to reunite Moses with his family

a. Jethro, Moses' father-in-law, heard the news of all that God had done for Moses & Israel

b. Moses had sent his wife back home: Probably because of her bitter rebellion against God (see 4:24-26)

c. Moses had demonstrated great faith in naming his sons
  1) Gershom means "an alien there," a stranger, sojourner
  2) Eliezer means "my God is my helper"

d. Jethro made a decision to bring Moses' family to him in the desert: When they were camped near the mount of God (Mt. Sinai)
  1) Jethro's courtesy: Had sent a messenger to tell Moses he was coming with Moses' wife & sons
  2) Moses' kindness & reception & apparent forgiveness of his wife: Went out to meet his family & showed great humility, greeting & asking about the welfare of each one
  3) Moses' great testimony & witness for God: Shared all that the Lord had done to Pharaoh & the Egyptians & all the hardships suffered in the wilderness journey

2. Help two: Jethro publicly acknowledged God's blessing upon his son-in-law & upon Israel

a. Jethro praised God for His goodness toward Israel

b. Jethro blessed the LORD for His great deliverance of Israel from the Egyptians

c. Jethro bore a great testimony for the LORD: That He is greater than all gods

d. Jethro provided the burnt

When Jethro, the priest of Midian, Moses' father in law, heard of all that God had done for Moses, and for Israel his people, and that the LORD had brought Israel out of Egypt;

2 Then Jethro, Moses' father in law, took Zipporah, Moses' wife, after he had sent her back,

3 And her two sons; of which the name of the one was Gershom; for he said, I have been an alien in a strange land:

4 And the name of the other was Eliezer; for the God of my father, said he, was mine help, and delivered me from the sword of Pharaoh:

5 And Jethro, Moses' father in law, came with his sons and his wife unto Moses into the wilderness, where he encamped at the mount of God:

6 And he said unto Moses, I thy father in law Jethro am come unto thee, and thy wife, and her two sons with her.

7 And Moses went out to meet his father in law, and did obeisance, and kissed him; and they asked each other of their welfare; and they came into the tent.

8 And Moses told his father in law all that the LORD had done unto Pharaoh and to the Egyptians for Israel's sake, and all the travail that had come upon them by the way, and how the LORD delivered them.

9 And Jethro rejoiced for all the goodness which the LORD had done to Israel, whom he had delivered out of the hand of the Egyptians.

10 And Jethro said, Blessed be the LORD, who hath delivered you out of the hand of the Egyptians, and out of the hand of Pharaoh, who hath delivered the people from under the hand of the Egyptians.

11 Now I know that the LORD is greater than all gods: for in the thing wherein they dealt proudly he was above them.

12 And Jethro, Moses' father

in law, took a burnt offering and sacrifices for God: and Aaron came, and all the elders of Israel, to eat bread with Moses' father in law before God.

13 And it came to pass on the morrow, that Moses sat to judge the people: and the people stood by Moses from the morning unto the evening.

14 And when Moses' father in law saw all that he did to the people, he said, What is this thing that thou doest to the people? why sittest thou thyself alone, and all the people stand by thee from morning unto even?

15 And Moses said unto his father in law, Because the people come unto me to inquire of God:

16 When they have a matter, they come unto me; and I judge between one and another, and I do make them know the statutes of God, and his laws.

17 And Moses' father in law said unto him, The thing that thou doest is not good.

18 Thou wilt surely wear away, both thou, and this people that is with thee: for this thing is too heavy for thee; thou art not able to perform it thyself alone.

19 Hearken now unto my voice, I will give thee counsel, and God shall be with thee: Be thou for the people to Godward, that thou mayest bring the causes unto God:

20 And thou shalt teach them ordinances and laws, and shalt show them the way wherein they must walk, and the work that they must do.

21 Moreover thou shalt provide out of all the people able men, such as fear God, men of truth, hating covetousness; and place such over them, to be rulers of thousands, and rulers of hundreds, rulers of fifties, and rulers of tens:

22 And let them judge the people at all seasons: and it shall be, that every great matter they shall bring unto thee, but every small matter they shall judge: so shall it be

offering & other sacrifices for a worship & fellowship service: Held with Moses, Aaron, & the elders

3. Help three: Jethro saw that Moses was overworked & offered a wise solution

a. The leadership of Moses: He sat as the only judge & the people had to wait all day to see him

b. Jethro questioned the wisdom of Moses' organizational structure
  1) Jethro's question: Why did Moses alone sit as judge?
  2) Moses' answer: The people demanded his personal attention—they wanted him to interpret God's will & laws in settling disputes

c. The fact: A serious problem of leadership had developed, that of being worn out & overworked
  1) The people & Moses were both being worn out
  2) The work was too heavy for one person to handle

d. Jethro offered a wise solution to the leadership crisis
  1) Moses should be the representative before God & the primary teacher of the people
    • To teach the commandments & laws of God
    • To teach them how to live
    • To teach them their duty before God & man
  2) Moses should select capable & godly men to serve as officials
    a) Men who are incorruptible: Who hate dishonesty & greed
    b) Men who can oversee thousands, hundreds, fifties, & tens
  3) Moses should handle major & difficult cases; the judges should handle simple cases of disputes

4) Moses should organize only as God commanded 5) The results: A lighter load, less pressure, & national peace e. The wisdom of leadership: Moses listened to his father-in-law 1) He appointed capable men to serve as judges	easier for thyself, and they shall bear the burden with thee. 23 If thou shalt do this thing, and God command thee so, then thou shalt be able to endure, and all this people shall also go to their place in peace. 24 So Moses hearkened to the voice of his father in law, and did all that he had said. 25 And Moses chose able men out of all Israel, and made	them heads over the people, rulers of thousands, rulers of hundreds, rulers of fifties, and rulers of tens. 26 And they judged the people at all seasons: the hard causes they brought unto Moses, but every small matter they judged themselves. 27 And Moses let his father in law depart; and he went his way into his own land.	2) He handled the difficult cases himself f. Moses said farewell to his father-in-law: Jethro returned home

DIVISION V

THE RED SEA AND THE WILDERNESS WANDERINGS: THE BELIEVER'S TRIALS AS HE JOURNEYS TO THE PROMISED LAND, 13:17–18:27

H. The Sixth Crisis of Israel in the Wilderness—Marital Separation and Overwork: Helping Others, 18:1-27

(18:1-27) **Introduction**: overwork is a serious problem for some people. Who? Think about...
- working mothers
- single mothers who work and rear children
- men and women who have to work long hours and maybe two jobs just to make it financially
- executives, managers, and professionals who bear so much heavy responsibility
- secretaries and office workers who have so many details to look after and perform

On and on the list could go, but the picture is seen: overwork is a problem for many people throughout society. Many of our acquaintances, friends, neighbors, and even perhaps ourselves are overworked. And there seems to be no end to the problem for many of us. Overwork is such a problem that it often causes marriages and health to deteriorate, to the point that both break down. Overwork was a problem, a real crisis that confronted Moses. This is the subject of the present passage: *The Sixth Crisis of Israel in the Wilderness—Marital Separation and Overwork: Helping Others, 18:1-27.*
1. Help one: Jethro sought to reunite Moses with his family (vv.1-8).
2. Help two: Jethro publicly acknowledged God's blessing upon his son-in-law and upon Israel (vv.9-12).
3. Help three: Jethro saw that Moses was overworked and offered a wise solution (vv.13-27).

1 (18:1-8) **Jethro—Family, Division of—Father-In-Laws—Moses**: there was the first help of Jethro: he sought to reunite Moses with his family.

a. Jethro, Moses' father-in-law, heard the news of all that God had done for Moses and Israel (v.1). How? Travelers and salesmen, statesmen and businessmen—all would have spread the news all over the world. The known world of that day would have heard about Israel's great deliverance from Egyptian slavery. And the leader of Israel was Moses, Jethro's son-in-law. Hearing the news would obviously excite Jethro, for God was greatly using his son-in-law. Jethro was as any of us would be, excited—very excited—that his son-in-law was the leader of a great nation of people. (See outline and note—Ex.2:15-22 for more discussion on Jethro.)

b. Now, note this significant fact: sometime in the past, Moses had sent his wife and children back home, back to Jethro (v.2). When? And for what purpose? Scripture does not say, not definitely. Commentators suggest several major reasons:
⇒ That Moses had sent his family back for safety reasons, sent them back sometime before the beginning of his confrontations with Pharaoh and the beginning of the ten plagues.
⇒ That Moses had just recently sent his wife back home to bring Jethro to him for a visit.

A third possibility seems to more closely fit the story of Scripture. Remember the last time Scripture mentions Moses' wife Zipporah: she was in bitter rebellion against God. She had objected to the circumcision of their son so bitterly that Moses had given in to her and refused to obey God's commandment, the commandment to circumcise his son. The result: God chastised and disciplined Moses. In fact, he became so sick that he almost died. Why? Why would God chastise Moses so severely? Especially since God had just called him into the ministry? Because Moses could not be the leader of God's people if he was not going to obey and follow God. And circumcision was the first and basic sign that a person believed God and followed God.

Lying there upon his death bed, Moses somehow conveyed this to Zipporah, and she agreed to the circumcision in order to remove God's hand of chastisement upon her husband. But she agreed only outwardly, only verbally, not from the heart. She was so angry and vengeful about the situation that she took the foreskin of her son and threw it at the feet of Moses who was—keep in mind—lying in bed critically ill, on the verge of death. As she threw the bloody foreskin at Moses' feet, she shouted out: "You are a bloody husband to me" (Ex.4:24-26).

The point is this: Zipporah was in rebellion against God, bitter rebellion, and in terrible conflict with Moses and his belief in God. What did Moses do about the family crisis after God restored his health? Most commentators feel that Moses sent his wife back home, back to Jethro, after her explosion of bitter rebellion. As stated, this seems to more closely fit

Scripture. Moses probably felt that his wife's bitter rebellion against God and himself would have threatened the very mission of God; therefore, he sent her back home to her parents.

Thought 1. Family strife can hinder and hamper a person's call to serve God, especially when the strife involves a bitter rebellion against one's spouse and God. Scripture declares that families are not to live in strife, argument, bitterness, division, and rebellion, not against one another and not against God. The teaching of Scripture is clear:

"Wives, submit yourselves unto your own husbands, as unto the Lord" (Ep.5:22).

"And, ye fathers, provoke not your children to wrath: but bring them up in the nurture and admonition of the Lord" (Ep.6:4).

"Lie not one to another, seeing that ye have put off the old man with his deeds" (Col.3:9).

"Likewise, ye husbands, dwell with them according to knowledge, giving honour unto the wife, as unto the weaker vessel, and as being heirs together of the grace of life; that your prayers be not hindered" (1 Pe.3:7).

c. Note that Moses had demonstrated great faith in naming his sons (vv.3-4).
1) Moses named his oldest son "Gershom," which means "a stranger, alien, sojourner, or expulsion" (v.3). Why did Moses name his son Gershom? Because Moses was a stranger in a strange land. He was an alien, a sojourner in a land that was not his. Where was Moses' land? Why was Moses not claiming Midian as his home? Had he not settled there? Married there, and now was having children there? Moses was to live in Midian for forty years. What did Moses mean when he said that he was only a stranger in a strange land (Midian)? He would not be referring to Egypt, for he was not an Egyptian, and Egypt had enslaved his family and people.

There could be only one land to which Moses was referring: the *promised land*, the land of Canaan, which was a symbol and picture of the promised land of heaven. Moses' heart was upon the promised land of God. And he was declaring his faith in the promised land, both the promised land of Canaan and the promised land of heaven. (See DEEPER STUDY # 1—Ex.2:24; note 2—Ge.12:1 for more discussion.) The New Testament declares that the great leaders of the Bible believed in the promised land of heaven as well as the promised land of Canaan. They believed in a *heavenly country* and a *heavenly city*. Their real home was not this earth, not a worldly country or city. Their real home was a heavenly home—a heavenly country and city that are eternal—that Abraham and all believers are to inherit. Note how clearly Scripture declares this fact:

"By faith Abraham, when he was called to go out into a place which he should after receive for an inheritance, obeyed; and he went out, not knowing whither he went. By faith he sojourned in the land of promise, as in a strange country, dwelling in tabernacles with Isaac and Jacob, the heirs with him of the same promise: for he looked for a city which hath foundations, whose builder and maker is God" (He.11:8-10).

"These all died in faith, not having received the promises, but having seen them afar off, and were persuaded of them, and embraced them, and confessed that they were strangers and pilgrims on the earth. For they that say such things declare plainly that they seek a country. And truly, if they had been mindful of that country from whence they came out, they might have had opportunity to have returned. But now they desire a better country, that is, an heavenly: wherefore God is not ashamed to be called their God: for he hath prepared for them a city" (He.11:13-16. Note v.15: it clearly states that Abraham's mind was on the heavenly and eternal country. If it had not been, he would have returned to his former home. He would never have wandered about, suffering the hardships he bore. We might add, neither would have Moses.)

"But ye are come unto mount Sion, and unto the city of the living God, the heavenly Jerusalem, and to an innumerable company of angels" (He.12:22).

"For here have we no continuing city [a perfect, heavenly city], but we seek one to come" (He.13:14).

"For the promise, that he should be the heir of the world, was not to Abraham, or to his seed, through the law, but through the righteousness of faith" (Ro.4:13).

2) Moses named his younger son Eliezer which means "my God is my helper." Note why: because of God. He believed that God was the One who had delivered him from being captured and executed by Pharaoh. Therefore, he honored God by naming his son Eliezer, "my God is my helper." (See outline and notes—Ex.2:11-25 for more discussion.)

The point to see is this: Moses never lost his faith in God, not even when he was a hunted criminal by the government of Egypt, not even when he was a young man rearing his family.

"But the LORD your God ye shall fear; and he shall deliver you out of the hand of all your enemies" (2 K.17:39).

"He shall deliver thee in six troubles: yea, in seven there shall no evil touch thee" (Jb.5:19).

"Thou *art* my hiding place; thou shalt preserve me from trouble; thou shalt compass me about with songs of deliverance" (Ps.32:7).

"Surely he shall deliver thee from the snare of the fowler, and from the noisome pestilence" (Ps.91:3).

"And *even* to *your* old age I *am* he; and *even* to hoar [gray] hairs will I carry *you*: I have made, and I will bear; even I will carry, and will deliver *you*" (Is.46:4).

"Be not afraid of their faces: for I am with thee to deliver thee, saith the LORD" (Je.1:8).

"Who delivered us from so great a death, and doth deliver: in whom we trust that he will yet deliver us" (2 Co.1:10).

"And the Lord shall deliver me from every evil work, and will preserve me unto his heavenly kingdom: to whom be glory for ever and ever" (2 Ti.4:18).

d. There was Jethro's decision to bring Moses' family to him (v.5). At some point, Jethro decided to make the journey to visit Moses and to take Moses' wife and sons back to him. The situation was apparently somewhat sensitive, for note what Jethro did.
   1) Note that Jethro showed great courtesy. He sent a messenger to tell Moses that he was coming to visit and that he was bringing Moses' wife and sons with him. This was either the custom of the day or else he felt the situation between Zipporah and Moses might still be extremely sensitive. He, therefore, wanted to notify Moses ahead of time that Zipporah and the children were also coming.
   2) Note Moses' kindness and reception of his family (v.7). He went out to greet his family and showed great humility. He received them: he greeted and asked about the welfare of each.
   3) After the greetings, they no doubt went to Moses' own personal tent where he shared the great testimony of God's mighty deliverance from Egypt and through the wilderness wanderings (v.8).

Thought 1. Courtesy, kindness, receptivity, forgiveness, and sharing together—this is to always be the spirit of the believer when receiving estranged members of his family. Note: this is even to be the spirit of believers who may have been at severe odds with family members. Reconciliation and forgiveness are God's will for divided family members. God wants families reconciled and living together in forgiveness and love.

    "And forgive us our debts, as we forgive our debtors" (Mt.6:12).
    "For if ye forgive men their trespasses, your heavenly Father will also forgive you" (Mt.6:14).
    "Then came Peter to him, and said, Lord, how oft shall my brother sin against me, and I forgive him? till seven times?" (Mt.18:21).
    "And when ye stand praying, forgive, if ye have ought against any: that your Father also which is in heaven may forgive you your trespasses. But if ye do not forgive, neither will your Father which is in heaven forgive your trespasses" (Mk.11:25-26).
    "And if he trespass against thee seven times in a day, and seven times in a day turn again to thee, saying, I repent; thou shalt forgive him" (Lu.17:4).
    "And be ye kind one to another, tenderhearted, forgiving one another, even as God for Christ's sake hath forgiven you" (Ep.4:32).
    "Forbearing one another, and forgiving one another, if any man have a quarrel against any: even as Christ forgave you, so also do ye" (Col.3:13).
    "Likewise, ye husbands, dwell with them according to knowledge, giving honour unto the wife, as unto the weaker vessel, and as being heirs together of the grace of life; that your prayers be not hindered" (1 Pe.3:7).

2 (18:9-12) **Jethro—Son-in-Law—Worship:** there was the second help of Jethro: he publicly acknowledged God's blessing upon his son-in-law.
a. Jethro praised God for His goodness to Israel: he rejoiced in God's great deliverance of Israel from Egyptian slavery (v.9).
b. Jethro actually broke forth in praise to the LORD for His great deliverance (v.10). He instinctively blurted out: "Blessed be the LORD." Note that he called God the LORD (Jehovah, Yahweh), the God of deliverance, salvation, and redemption—the God who reveals Himself and makes a covenant with man. This indicates that Jethro was a true believer, a person who sincerely trusted the LORD and His great promises.
c. Jethro also bore a great testimony for God. He declared that the LORD was greater than all other gods (v.11). He was placing the LORD above all other gods worshipped by the Egyptians and others. He was declaring that there was only one sovereign LORD and Majesty of the universe, only one Deliverer and Savior, the LORD Himself. (See the confession of Naaman, 2 Ki.5:15.)
d. Jethro provided the burnt offering and altar sacrifices for a worship and fellowship service. Note that this was held with Moses and all the elders of Israel (v.12). Jethro was making a public acknowledgment of God's wonderful blessings upon his son-in-law and upon Israel.

Thought 1. How many family members are pleased with one another? So pleased that they acknowledge God's blessings upon the other members? How critical it is that we straighten out our lives, that we...
- repent and live righteous lives
- forgive and reconcile with estranged family members
- pray and seek God to bless our family members
- humbly and unselfishly acknowledge the blessings of God upon other family members
- be kind to our family members

    "By this shall all [men] know that ye are my disciples, if ye have love one to another" (Jn.13:35).
    "This is my commandment, That ye love one another, as I have loved you" (Jn.15:12).
    "Let love be without dissimulation [without hypocrisy]. Abhor that which is evil; cleave to that which is good" (Ro.12:9).

"Be kindly affectioned one to another with brotherly love; in honour preferring one another" (Ro.12:10).

"Let us therefore follow after the things which make for peace, and things wherewith one may edify another" (Ro.14:19).

"And be ye kind one to another, tenderhearted, forgiving one another, even as God for Christ's sake hath forgiven you" (Ep.4:32).

"Put on therefore, as the elect of God, holy and beloved, bowels of mercies, kindness, humbleness of mind, meekness, longsuffering" (Col.3:12).

"Wherefore comfort yourselves together, and edify one another, even as also ye do" (1 Th.5:11).

3 (18:13-27) **Work—Labor—Overwork—Crisis—Leadership—Organization—Government—Democracy**: there was the third help of Jethro: he saw that Moses was overworked and offered a wise solution. What then happened is interesting. It shows that Jethro was a man of real wisdom and that he and Moses had developed a close relationship during the forty years Moses had worked for him in Midian. (See outline and notes—Ex.2:15-22; 4:18-19 for more discussion.)

a. The next morning, no doubt very early, Moses arose and went to the tent of his headquarters. There he sat all day judging the people. He was *the only judge* for Israel, the only judge for two to three million people (v.13). The result was awful: there was a staggering backlog of cases. Many of the people were having to stand from early morning to late evening, waiting to have their cases tried before Moses.

b. Jethro questioned the wisdom of Moses' organizational structure (vv.14-15).
⇒ He asked Moses why he alone sat as judge (v.14).
⇒ Moses simply replied that the people demanded his personal attention: they wanted him to interpret God's will and laws in settling disputes (v.15).

c. Jethro responded by immediately stating an obvious fact: a serious problem of leadership had developed, that of *overwork* (vv.17-18).
⇒ Moses and the people were being worn out.
⇒ The work was too heavy for one person to handle.

d. Jethro then offered a wise solution to the leadership crisis (vv.19-23). But note, Jethro first of all appealed to God to be with Moses (v.19). What was Jethro's counsel to solve the leadership crisis?
1) First, Moses should be the representative before God and the primary teacher of the people (vv.19-20). He should...
• teach the decrees and laws of God (Note: there was a written book of God's laws existing during Moses' day)
• show the people how to live
• show the people their duty before God and man

2) Second, Moses should select capable and godly men to serve as officials (v.21). Note the qualifications of the judges to be chosen:
⇒ Men who were capable, that is, had a natural ability to judge differences between people.
⇒ Men who feared God.
⇒ Men of truth, that is, men who were trustworthy.
⇒ Men who hated dishonesty and greed.

3) Third, Moses himself should handle the major and difficult cases; the judges should handle the simple cases of disputes (v.22).
4) Fourth, Moses should organize only as God commanded (v.23).

Note the humility of Jethro. He knew that his idea should not be followed unless God approved it. This he told Moses. The result: if God allowed Moses to structure the courts of Israel like this, then it would mean a lighter load, less pressure, and national peace (v.23).

e. Note the wisdom of Moses' leadership: he listened to his father-in-law (vv.24-27). Another passage tells us that Moses actually established a democracy at this point: he presented the idea to the people and had them elect the persons to serve as their judges (v.25. See De.1:9-13.) The judges handled every issue among the people except the most difficult cases. The difficult cases were brought to Moses (v.26).

f. Jethro then returned home (v.27).

Thought 1. Overwork is a serious problem for some of God's people. Some of us have to go day and night, and we still have as much waiting on us as we just finished. What is the answer? Part of the answer is...
• restructuring the organization—just as Moses did
• structuring the workload into smaller units—just as Moses did
• delegating more and more work to others—just as Moses did
• securing more and more laborers—just as Moses did
• asking the people to help find able, godly laborers—just as Moses did
• seeking God for His solution to the problem—just as Moses did (v.23. See De.1:9-13)
• asking God for strength day by day—just as Moses surely did

"And I will give you pastors according to mine heart, which shall feed you with knowledge and understanding" (Je.3:15).

"Then saith he unto his disciples, The harvest truly [is] plenteous, but the labourers [are] few; Pray ye therefore the Lord of the harvest, that he will send forth labourers into his harvest" (Mt.9:37-38).

"Say not ye, There are yet four months, and [then] cometh harvest? behold, I say unto you, Lift up your eyes, and look on the fields; for they are white already to harvest. And he that reapeth receiveth wages, and gathereth fruit unto life eternal: that both he that soweth and he that reapeth may rejoice together" (Jn.4:35-36).

"So when they had dined, Jesus saith to Simon Peter, Simon, [son] of Jonas, lovest thou me more than these? He saith unto him, Yea, Lord; thou knowest that I love thee. He saith unto him, Feed my lambs. He saith to him again the second time, Simon, [son] of Jonas, lovest thou me? He saith unto him, Yea, Lord; thou knowest that I love thee. He saith unto him, Feed my sheep. He saith unto him the third time, Simon, [son] of Jonas, lovest thou me? Peter was grieved because he said unto him the third time, Lovest thou me? And he said unto him, Lord, thou knowest all things; thou knowest that I love thee. Jesus saith unto him, Feed my sheep" (Jn.21:15-17).

"Let the elders that rule well be counted worthy of double honour, especially they who labour in the word and doctrine" (1 Ti.5:17).

"And the things that thou hast heard of me among many witnesses, the same commit thou to faithful men, who shall be able to teach others also" (2 Ti.2:2).

"Feed the flock of God which is among you, taking the oversight thereof, not by constraint, but willingly; not for filthy lucre, but of a ready mind" (1 Pe.5:2).

TYPES, SYMBOLS, AND PICTURES
(Exodus 18:1-27)

Historical Term	Type or Picture (Scriptural Basis for Each)	Life Application for Today's Believer	Biblical Application
Eliezer, Moses' Youngest Son (Ex.18:4)	*God is my helper* "And the name of the other *was* Eliezer; for the God of my father, *said he, was* mine help, and delivered me from the sword of Pharaoh" (Ex.18:4).	God is our helper. He helps us when we are... • weak • needy • poor • helpless • distressed • fearful • criticized • condemned • attacked • lonely • empty • lost • overlooked • ignored	*"But I am poor and needy; yet the Lord thinketh upon me: thou art my help and my deliverer; make no tarrying, O my God"* (Ps.40:17). *"Fear thou not; for I am with thee: be not dismayed; for I am thy God: I will strengthen thee; yea, I will help thee; yea, I will uphold thee with the right hand of my righteousness"* (Is.41:10). *"So that we may boldly say, The Lord is my helper, and I will not fear what man shall do unto me"* (He.13:6).

OUTLINE AND SUBJECT INDEX

REMEMBER: When you look up a subject and turn to the Scripture reference, you have not just the Scripture but also an outline and a discussion (commentary) of the Scripture and subject.

This is one of the GREAT FEATURES of *The Preacher's Outline & Sermon Bible*®. Once you have all the volumes, you will have not only what all other Bible indexes give you, that is, a list of all the subjects and their Scripture references, but in addition you will have...

- an outline of every Scripture and subject in the Bible
- a discussion (commentary) on every Scripture and subject
- every subject supported by other Scripture, already written out or cross referenced

DISCOVER THE UNIQUE VALUE for yourself. Quickly glance below to the first subject of the Index. It is:

AARON
Call of. 4:13-17; 4:27-31; 5:13-27, esp. 13; 7:1-7
Family of.
Had a believing, courageous mother. 2:2
Parents were Amram & Jochebed. 6:20
Sister was Miriam. 15:20
Sons were Nadab, Abihu, Eleazer, & Ithamar. 6:23
Wife was Elisheba. 6:23
Younger brother was Moses. 2:2

Turn to the first reference. Glance at the Scripture and the outline, then read the commentary. You will immediately see the TREMENDOUS BENEFIT of the INDEX of *The Preacher's Outline & Sermon Bible*®.

OUTLINE & SUBJECT INDEX

AARON
Call of. 4:13-17; 4:27-31; 5:13-27, esp. 13; 7:1-7
Family of.
Had a believing, courageous mother. 2:2
Parents were Amram & Jochebed. 6:20
Sister was Miriam. 15:20
Sons were Nadab, Abihu, Eleazer, & Ithamar. 6:23
Wife was Elisheba. 6:23
Younger brother was Moses. 2:2
Genealogy of. Chart of. 6:13-27
Life of. Was 83 years old when called to serve God. 6:28-7:7
Ministry of.
To bear testimony & perform miracles before Pharaoh. 7:8-10; 7:17-21
Was a prophet, a spokesman for Moses. 7:1-2
Was chosen by God to help Moses deliver the Israelites from slavery. 4:13-17; 4:27-31; 6:13-27

ABASE - ABASED (See **HUMILIATION; SHAME**)
Caused by.
Hard heart. 7:22-25; 8:15; 8:19; 8:32; 9:7; 9:12; 9:34-35; 10:20; 10:27-29; 11:10
Self-glory & self-exaltation. 8:25-29; 9:7; 9:12; 10:16-17

ABIASAPH
Distant descendent of Levi. Son of Korah. 6:13-27, esp.24; 6:13-27 (Chart)

ABIB
Significance of.
First month of the Hebrew calendar. 12:1-2

Month of the Exodus, the great deliverance of Israel, & of the Passover. 12:1-2

ABIHU
Son of Aaron. 6:13-27, esp. 23; Ex.6:13-27 (Chart)

ABILITY - ABILITIES
Duty. To delegate responsibility to others. 18:13-27

ABORTION
Life of the unborn of little value to society throughout history. 1:22

ABUNDANCE - ABUNDANT (See **BLESSINGS; FRUITFUL; FULNESS, SPIRITUAL; HUNGER, SPIRITUAL; SATISFACTION, SPIRITUAL**)
Source. God. Provides food & water—an **a.** for our needs. 15:27; 16:1-36; 16:31-35; 16:31; 17:1-7

ABUSE - ABUSED (See **OPPRESSION; PERSECUTION**)

ACCEPTANCE - ACCEPTABLE
How one becomes **a.**
By acknowledging God's holiness. 3:4-6
By humility. 3:4-6
By learning from God's chastisement. 4:24-26
By obedience. 12:12-13
By surrendering to God's call. 4:18-31
By the blood of the lamb. 12:1-13; 12:21-28

ACCESS (See **APPROACH - APPROACHABLE**)
How man draws near God.
By humility, acknowledging God's holiness. 3:4-6
By the blood of the Lamb. 12:1-13; 12:21-28

ACCOUNTABLE - ACCOUNTABILITY
Duty of **a.**
To accept God's call, not make excuses. 3:11-4:17
To obey God, to keep His commandments. 15:25-26
Who is held **a.**
God's servant. 4:24-26; 4:13-17
Nations & leaders. 7:8-13; 7:14-25; 8:1-15; 8:16-19; 8:20-32; 9:1-7; 9:8-12; 9:13-35; 10:1-20; 10:21-29; 11:1-10; 15:25-26
Why people are held **a.**
Because of disobedience. 4:24-26; 15:26-27
Because of God's call. 4:13-17; 4:18-31
Because of hard hearts. (See **HEARTS, HARD**)
Because of sin, evil, idolatry, & oppression of people. 7:8-13; 7:14-25; 8:1-15; 8:16-19; 8:20-32; 9:1-7; 9:8-12; 9:13-35; 10:1-20; 10:21-29; 11:1-10

ACCUSATIONS, FALSE (See **CRITICISM; JUDGING OTHERS; SLAN-DER**)
Against Moses.
Complained, grumbled, murmured against him. 5:20-23; 14:10-12; 15:24; 16:1-3; 17:2-3
Were about to stone Moses. 17:4
Results. Pain, hurt. 5:20-23; 14:10-12, see 15; 15:22-27; 17:1-7, esp. 4

**ACKNOWLEDGE - ACKNOWLEDG-
MENT**
Who was **a**.
God.
After He gave victory over Israel's
enemies. 15:1-21; 17:13-16;
18:9-12
After He provided manna, bread
from heaven. 16:31-35
After He provided water to Israel.
17:7
After He delivered Israel through
the Red Sea. Glorious **a**. & description of God. 15:1-21
Moses. By Jethro, Moses' father-in-
law. After he heard of God's great
deliverance of Israel. 18:1-8

ADMINISTER - ADMINISTRATION
Example of.
Jethro. Advised Moses on how to organize Israel's judges. 18:13-27
Moses. Organized Israel into military
divisions to march out of Egyptian
slavery. 13:17-18; 14:19-28
Organization - Structure. Of Israel's
judges. 18:13-27

ADOPTED - ADOPTION
Moses. By Pharaoh's daughter. 2:9-10
Who is **a**. Israel.
Believers of Israel. 4:20-23, esp.22;
6:6-9
Fact. First time God called Israel His
son, His firstborn. 4:20-23, esp.22

ADULTERY (See **FORNICATION;
IMMORALITY; LUST; SEX**)

ADVERSITY (See **TRIALS - TRIBULA-
TIONS**)

AFFECTION
Example of.
Moses & Aaron for one another.
4:27-31
Moses & his father-in-law Jethro.
18:1-8

AFFLICTIONS (See **SUFFERING; TRI-
ALS**)

AGNOSTIC (See **ATHEIST; DENIAL;
HUMANISM; REJECTION; UNBE-
LIEF**)
Who was **a**. List of men who were **a**.
7:17

AGONY (See **MISERY - MISERABLE**)
Caused by.
Hunger. Israel in the wilderness wan-
derings. 16:1-3
Judgment of God. 8:7-8; 12:30-33
Slavery. Israel in bondage to Egypt.
1:8-22; 5:1-23; 6:6-9, esp. 9
Thirst. Israel in the wilderness wander-
ings. 15:22-27; 17:1-7

AGREE - AGREEMENT (See **BRO-
THERHOOD; UNITY**)

AGRICULTURE
Seasons for planting & harvesting. Hebrew Calendar. 12:1-2

ALARM - ALARMED
Caused by. Plague of death sent by God
upon the firstborn of Egypt. 12:29;
12:30-33

ALIENATED - ALIENATION
Caused by. Rebellion against God's
commandments. 4:24-26
Example of. Moses separated from his
wife. 4:24-26; 18:1-8

ALIENS (See **STRANGERS - PIL-
GRIMS**)

ALLEGIANCE (See **COMMITMENT;
DEDICATION**)

ALTAR
Built by. Moses. In honor of the LORD's
victory in Israel's first war. 17:13-16

AMALEKITES
Discussed. 17:8

AMBASSADOR (See **MESSENGER;
MINISTER; SERVANT, OF GOD**)
Example of. Aaron was chosen to be
God's **a**., God's spokesman before Pha-
raoh. 4:13-17; 4:27-31

AMBITION - AMBITIOUS (See **ASPI-
RATION**)

AMINADIB
Aaron's father-in-law. 6:13-27, esp. 23

AMORITES
Land of. Promised to Israel. 3:7-8; 3:8

AMRAM
Grandson of Jacob. Son of Levi. 6:13-27
(Chart)

ANGEL OF THE LORD (See **LORD,
ANGEL OF THE**)

ANGER (See **HOSTILITY; VIOLENCE;
WRATH**)
Caused by.
A hard heart. 10:27-29
A leader not obeying God. Moses be-
came **a**. with Pharaoh. 11:7-8
A reaction against the chastising hand
of God. 10:27-29
A rejection & rebellion against God's
commandments. 4:24-26
An injustice seen. Moses saw a man
being beaten. 2:11-12
Of God. Caused by. (See **JUDGMENT;
WRATH OF GOD**)
A man rejecting God's call (Moses).
4:13-17

ANGUISH (See **AGONY; ANXIETY**)

ANIMALS (See **LIVESTOCK**)
Of Egypt. Diseases of. Was one of the
plagues of Egypt. 9:1-7

ANTAGONISM
Example of.
Pharaoh enslaved Israel, increasing
abuse more & more. 1:11-22; 5:1-23
Pharaoh had all male babies killed to
control Israel's population. 1:15-22

ANTHRAX
A disease of animals. 9:2-3
Was one of the judgments, plagues upon
Egypt. 9:2-3

ANXIETY - ANXIOUS (See **IMPA-
TIENCE; PRESSURE; RESTLESS-
NESS; STRESS; TENSION; UNEASI-
NESS**)
Caused by.
Being falsely accused & criticized.
5:20-23; 14:10-12, see 15; 15:25;
16:1-3; 17:4
Divided family; unsupportive spouse.
4:24-26; 18:1-8
Facing impossible trials, problems, &
obstacles. 5:20-23; 14:10-12, see 15;
15:25; 16:1-3; 17:4
Murder. 2:13-14
Overwork. 18:13-27
Unbelief, not trusting God's care &
provision. 5:20-23; 14:10-12, see
15; 15:25; 16:1-3; 17:4

APOSTASY (See **BACKSLIDING;
DENIAL; FALLING AWAY - FALL,
SPIRITUAL**)

APPEARANCE - APPEARANCES
Of God.
To Israel. In the pillar of cloud in the
wilderness. 16:4-15, esp. 10
To Moses. In the burning bush. 3:1-3;
3:13-22, esp. 16

APPOINT - APPOINTED (See **CALL,
OF GOD**)
Who is **a**.
Aaron. His call by God. 4:13-17;
6:28-7:5; 7:6-7
Moses. His call by God. 3:1-10; 6:28-
7:5; 7:6-7

APPOINTED TIME (See **FULNESS OF
TIME**)

APPROACH - APPROACHABLE (See
AVAILABLE)
How one must **a**. God. Acknowledging
His holiness: respect & reverence.
3:4-6
How one should **a**. others. With respect
& courtesy. 18:1-8, esp. 5-7

AREA (See **CITIES - AREAS**)

ARGUE - ARGUMENTS (See **CON-
FLICT; CRITICISM; DIVISION**)
Example of. Israel against Moses. 14:10-
12; 15:24; 16:1-3; 17:2-3
Source - Caused by. **A**. against serving
God.
A fussing, arguing, unsupportive wife.
4:13-17
Five **a**. 3:11-4:17
Grumbling, murmuring, complaining.
14:10-12; 15:24; 16:1-3; 17:2-3
Shortage of water & food. 14:10-12;
15:24; 16:1-3; 17:2-3
Unbelief, distrust in God. 14:10-12;
15:24; 16:1-3; 17:2-3

ARK OF THE COVENANT
Contained. The manna, Aaron's rod, &
the Ten Commandments tablets.
16:31-35

ARK, THE
Meaning. 2:3

ARMY (See **MILITARY**)

ATHEIST - ATHEISM (See **AGNOSTIC; DENIAL; HUMANISM; REJECTION; UNBELIEF**)
Who was **a**.
List of men who were **a**. 7:17
Rulers who exalted themselves (man) above God. 5:2-14, esp. 2
Rulers who exalted themselves to be gods. 7:17; 8:1-15

ARROGANCE (See **BOASTING; HAUGHTINESS; PRIDE; SELF-SUFFICIENCY**)
Boasting that one does not know God. 5:22-24, esp. 2

ASH - ASHES
Fact. Used to symbolize one of God's plagues upon Egypt. 9:8-10

ASPIRE - ASPIRATION
Example. Moses **a**. to help Israel in their slavery. 2:11-25

ASSIR
Descendent of Levi. 6:13-27 (Chart)

ASSIST - ASSISTANCE (See **HELP - HELPING**)

ASSISTANT
Call of. Aaron to serve as **a**. to Moses. 4:13-17; 6:28-7:7

ASSURANCE (See **CONFIDENCE; SECURITY**)
Needed in - Is Given in.
Accepting God's call. 4:10-12
Proclaiming God's Word & in leading people. 5:20-23; 6:1-7:7

ASTROLOGY (See **MAGICIANS; SORCERY**)

ATONEMENT
Typed - Symbolized - Pictured. By the Passover Lamb. 12:5; 12:6-11; 12:12-13; 12:21-28; Intro. VII, pt.17

AUTHORITY (See **POWER**)

AVAILABLE - AVAILABILITY (See **APPROACHABLE**)
Duty. To be disciplined, scheduled in making oneself **a**. 18:13-27

AVARICE (See **COVETOUSNESS; GREED**)

AVENGE - AVENGING (See **REVENGE**)

AWE (See **FEAR; REVERENCE**)

BAAL-ZEPHON
Discussed. 14:2

BABES - BABIES
Abuse of. Attempt to kill all Israelite male **b**. 1:8-22, esp. 22

Birth of. Moses. Picture of a godly courageous mother. 2:1-10

BACKBITERS - BACKBITING (See **COMPLAINING GRUMBLING; MURMURING**)

BACKSLIDING (See **COMPROMISE; DOUBLE-MINDED; FALLING AWAY; FICKLENESS; HALF-HEARTED; TURNING BACK**)
Caused by.
Trials. Severe trials. Of Israel in the wilderness. 12:10-12; 15:22-27; 16:1-36; 17:1-7
Unbelief. Of Israel in the wilderness. 12:10-12; 15:22-27; 16:1-36; 17:1-7
Results.
Complaining, grumbling, murmuring. 5:20-23; 15:25; 17:4
Rejecting leaders. 5:20-23; 15:25; 17:4

BAPTISM - BAPTIZED
Of Israel. Were **b**. into Moses by the pillar of cloud. 13:20-22

BARRIERS (See **BIGOTRY; DISCRIMINATION; DIVISION; PREJUDICE**)

BATH - BATHING
Example of. Pharaoh's daughter when she found Moses. 2:5-8

BEGUILE (See **DECEIVE - DECEPTION**)

BEHAVE - BEHAVIOR (See **BELIEVER**, Duty)

BELIEVE - BELIEVING - BELIEFS (See **FAITH; OBEDIENCE; TRUST**)
Duty.
To **b**. God day by day, trust Him every day. 16:16-30
To **b**. in the blood of the lamb, the Lamb of God. 12:1-13:16; 12:1-13; 12:21-28
To **b**. that God will give us victory over all our enemies. 17:8-16
To **b**. that God will provide for us. 15:22-27; 16:1-3; 16:4-15; 16:16-30
To **b**., to diligently listen to God. 15:25-26
Result. Health & the healing touch of God. 15:25-26

BELIEVER - BELIEVERS (See **PILGRIM; SOJOURNER**)
Distinctiveness of. Is a difference between believers & unbelievers. 11:7-8
Duty. To seek deeper experiences with the LORD. 3:1-3
Fact. **B**. were the promised seed promised to Abraham. 1:6-7
Life & walk. (See **WILDERNESS WANDERINGS**)
To obey God while walking through the wilderness of this world. 15:26-27
To pray & trust God to meet one's needs, not complain & grumble. 5:20-23; 14:10-12; 15:25; 17:4; 17:8-16

Title - Name - Identity.
Israel of God. Intro. VII, pt.1
Pilgrim. 13:17-18:27, Intro. VII, pt.25
Redeemed, the. 15:13-18

BENEVOLENCE (See **GIVING; MINISTERING; STEWARDSHIP**)

BEREAVEMENT (See **GRIEF; SORROW**)
Example of. Egyptian agonizing **b**. over death of firstborn. 12:30-33

BETRAYAL - BETRAYED (See **APOSTASY; BACKSLIDING; DENIAL**)

BIBLE (See **WORD OF GOD**)
Fact. Exodus is a book that exposes the truth, the sins of God's people. Intro. V, Special Features
Purpose of. To teach us how to walk through the wilderness (trials) of this world. 13:17-18:27 (pt.B)

BIGOTRY (See **BARRIERS; DISCRIMINATION; PARTIALITY; PREJUDICE**)

BIRDS
B. used by God. Doves. Used to feed the Israelites in the wilderness. 16:4-15, esp. 12-13

BIRTH, NEW (See **BORN AGAIN; NEW CREATION; NEW LIFE**)

BITTER - BITTERNESS (See **COMPLAINING; GRUMBLING; MURMURING**)

BLAME - BLAMING OTHERS
Caused by.
Not trusting God nor waiting for God's timing. 5:20-23; see 6:1-7:7
Not trusting God, unbelief. 14:10-12; 15:22-27; 16:1-36; 17:1-7
Example of. Israel **b**. Moses at the Red Sea when faced with a serious problem. 14:10-12

BLAMELESS - BLAMELESSNESS (See **CLEANLINESS; FORGIVENESS; PURITY; SPOTLESS**)

BLESS - BLESSINGS (See **ABUNDANCE; FULNESS, SPIRITUAL; HUNGER, SPIRITUAL; SATISFACTION, SPIRITUAL**)
What the **b**. are.
Bread. 16:1-36
Call of God. 3:1-10
Deliverance through the greatest of trials: the Red Sea. 14:1-31
Food. 16:1-36
His presence, guidance by day & by night. 13:17-22
Necessities of life. 15:22-27; 16:1-36; 17:1-7
Victory over enemies—all trials. 17:8-16
Water. 15:22-27; 17:1-7

BLOOD (See **JESUS CHRIST**, Blood of)

345

BOASTING - BOASTERS (See **GLORY-
ING IN MAN; HAUGHTINESS;
PRIDE; SELF-SUFFICIENCY**)
What men **b**.
    That they do not know the LORD. 5:2-
    14; esp. 2
    That they (men) are their own gods.
    5:2-14, esp. 2; 8:1-15
Who **b**. World leaders. Pharaoh. 5:2-14,
    esp. 2

BODY, HUMAN
Care of. By God. Is under God's control.
    9:8-12
Fact. Not controlled by man, not in the
    final analysis. 9:11

BOILS
Fact. Was one of the plagues against
    Egypt. 9:12

BOLD - BOLDNESS
Example of.
    Moses & Aaron. Went before Pharaoh
    & declared God's Word. 5:1
    Moses. In declaring God's message of
    victory & deliverance. 14:13-15

BONDAGE (See **SLAVERY – ENSLAVE-
MENT; YOKE**)
What enslaves - Things that hold men
in **b**.
    Evil rulers. Pharaoh held Israel in **b**.
    1:8-22
    Greed, covetousness, money, econom-
    ic stability. 8:2-4; 11:1-10

BONDAGE, SPIRITUAL (See **SIN**)
Symbolized - Typed - Pictured.
    By Egypt. 1:11-14; 3:7-8; 12:1-13:16
    (pt. 1, 7); 12:6-11 (pt.6); 12:14-20;
    12:29; 12:34-43; 13:1-16; 13:17-
    18:27; 13:19; Intro.VII, pt.2
    By Pharaoh. 1:11-14; 3:7-8; Intro.VII,
    pt.3

BONE - BONES
Fact. Joseph's **b**. were taken back to the
    promised land by Moses. 13:19
Prophecies concerning **b**. Passover
    lamb's **b**. Not to be broken. Prophecy of
    Christ. 12:42-51, esp. 46; Intro.VII,
    pt.23

BORN AGAIN (See **BIRTH, NEW; NEW
CREATION; NEW LIFE; REDEMP-
TION; SALVATION**)

BRAG - BRAGGING (See **ARROGANCE;
BOASTING; GLORYING IN MAN;
PRIDE**)

BREAD
How to secure. By trusting the LORD's
    provision. 16:1-36
Type - Symbol - Picture of.
    Jesus Christ. 16:31; 17:5-6; Intro.VII,
    pt.31
    Spiritual nourishment. 16:16-30;
    16:31; Intro.VII, pt.30

BREAD OF LIFE
Christ is the Bread of Life. 16:1-36;
    16:31; Intro.VII, pt.30
Duty. To eat, partake of the Bread of
    Life. 16:31; Intro.VII, pt.30

Symbolized - Typed - Pictured. By the
    manna, the bread given to Israel by
    God. 16:31; Intro.VII, pt.30

BREAD, UNLEAVENED
Feast of. Was closely tied to the Passov-
    er. 12:1-13:16 (pt.7) ; Intro.VII, pt.22
Type - Symbol - Picture.
    Of righteousness. 14:20; Intro.VII,
    pt.22
    Of the believer's new life: the urgency
    to march to the promised land. 12:1-
    13:16 (pt.7); 14:20; Intro.VII, pt.22

BREAKING THE LAW (See **LAW,
BREAKING THE**)

BRICK - BRICKS
Fact. Israel was forced to make **b**. as
    slaves in Egypt. 1:11-14

BROKEN-HEARTED (See **CONTRI-
TION; GRIEF; SORROW; SORROW,
GODLY**)
Caused by.
    Rejection. By one's own people. Mo-
    ses an example. 5:20-23; 15:25; 17:4
    The burdens & sufferings of people.
    2:11; 5:20-23
    The sins, complaining, & unbelief of
    people. 5:20-23; 14:13-15, esp. 15;
    15:25; 17:4

BROTHERHOOD (See **FELLOWSHIP;
NEIGHBOR; ONENESS; UNITY**)
Basis of.
    God's plan: care for one's family.
    Jethro reunited Moses & his wife.
    18:1-8
    God's call. 4:13-17; 4:27-31
Destruction of **b**. Caused by.
    Complaining, grumbling, murmuring.
    15:24; 17:2-3
    Secret sin. Exposure of. 2:13-15
Essential - Importance of **b**.
    In prayer. 17:10-12
    In warfare. 17:8-16
Example of.
    Jethro, Moses father-in-law. Were re-
    united after some time of separation.
    18:1-8
    Moses & Aaron. Were reunited after
    40 years' separation. 4:27-32

BRUISED, THE (See **BROKEN-
HEARTED**)
    Needs met - Healing of. By God. Called
    Moses, even after he was **b**., rejected by
    his people. 2:11-25; 3:1-10

BUILD - BUILDING (See **CONSTRUC-
TION**)

BULRUSH REED, THE
Fact. Moses was hidden in the **b**. by his
    mother. 2:3-4

BURDEN - BURDENED (See **BROKEN-
HEARTED; COMPASSION**)
For whom. The enslaved, oppressed, suf-
    fering. Moses **b**. for his people. 2:11;
    5:20-22; 15:25; 17:4

BUSH, THE BURNING
Where God met Moses. 3:1-3

BUSINESS (See **ORGANIZATION; RE-
SPONSIBILITY**)
Error - Danger.
    Lack of organization. 18:13-27
    Not delegating responsibility.
    18:13-27
    Overwork. 18:13-27

BUSYBODY - BUSYBODIES (See
**COMPLAINING; GRUMBLING;
MURMURING**)

BUSYNESS
Caused by.
    Lack of organization. 18:13-27
    Not delegating responsibility.
    18:13-27

CALAMITIES (See **CATASTROPHE;
DISASTERS; JUDGMENT; PLAGUES**)
Caused by.
    Chastisement. (See **CHASTISE-
MENT**)
    Judgment. Upon those who reject God
    & brutally oppress people. 7:8-11:10
    Sin, evil, rejection & cursing of God.
    7:8-11:10

CALENDAR
Hebrew. Chart of. 12:1-2

CALL - CALLED (See **CHOSEN**)
Discussed.
    The call itself. Described. 3:4-6
    The kind of person **c**. 3:1-3
Of whom.
    Aaron. 4:13-17; 4:27-31; 5:1-13, esp.
    13; 17:1-7
    Chart. A survey (list & study) of dif-
    ferent people **c**. 3:9-10
    Moses.
        A study of God's call to serve.
        3:1-10
        First **c**. 3:1-10
        Second **c**. 6:28-7:7
Purpose. Why God calls a person to serve
    Him. 3:7-8
Rejected - Refused. (See **EXCUSES**)
    By Moses. Five excuses. 3:11–4:17
Surrender to. Moses. 4:18-31

CALLOUS (See **HARD - HARDNESS;
INSENSITIVE**)

CANAAN (See **LAND, THE PROM-
ISED**)
Description. Land flowing with milk
    & honey. 3:7-8
Fact. Was promised to the Israelites
    by God. 2:23-25; 2:24; 3:7-8;
    15:13-18
Name of. Palestine. 15:13-18,
    esp. 14
Type - Symbol - Picture. Of heaven.
    2:23-25; 2:24; 3:7-8; 15:13-18

CANAANITES
Discussed. 3:8

**CAPTIVE - CAPTIVITY - CAPTI-
VATED** (See **BONDAGE; ENSLAVE-
MENT; SLAVERY**)
Duty toward. To be compassionate. (See
COMPASSION)
Prophecies concerning.
Israel being c. in Egypt. Fulfilled.
1:11-14; see Gen.15:7-21, esp. 13-
14; 50:24-26
Israel being delivered from Egypt. Ful-
filled. 12:34-41, esp. 40-41; see
Ge.15:7-21; 50:24-26

CARE - CARING (See **COMPASSION;
MINISTERING; SERVICE**)
Example of.
Midwives. Saving the Hebrew babies
from Pharaoh. 1:15-21
Moses' mother for his as a baby.
2:1-10
Moses. Looking upon his enslaved
people & feeling compassion. 2:11
Pharaoh's daughter. 2:5-8

CARMI
Grandson of Jacob. Son of Reuben. 6:13-
27 (Chart)

CARNAL - CARNALITY (See **LUST**)
Caused by. Unbelief, distrust. 5:20-23;
5:22-27; 14:10-12; 15:22-27; 16:1-36;
17:1-7
Results.
Can bring terrible change to our lives.
Example. Moses. 2:11-12
Craves after the flesh pots of the
world. 16:1-3; 17:2-3
Craves after the security of the world
instead of God. 14:10-12
Grumbling, complaining, murmuring.
14:10-12; 15:24; 16:1-3; 17:2-3
Immorality. Wanting men & women,
sex. 1:1-5; 3:8
Murder. Example. Moses. 2:11-12
Ruined testimony. Example. Moses.
2:13-15

**CATASTROPHE - CATASTROPHIC
EVENTS** (See **CALAMITIES; DISAS-
TERS**)
Caused by.
Chastisement. (See **CHASTISE-
MENT**)
God. As judgment. 7:8-11:10
Sin, evil, rejection & cursing of God.
7:8-11:10

CENSOR - CENSORING (See **JUDGING
OTHERS**)
Example of. The Israelites c. Moses. Accused him of misleading them. 5:20-
23; 14:10-12; 15:24; 16:1-3; 17:2-3

CEREMONY - CEREMONIAL LAW
(See **RITUAL**)
Dedication of the Firstborn. (See
FIRSTBORN)
Feast of Unleavened Bread. (See **UN-
LEAVENED BREAD, FEAST OF**)
Passover Feast, The. (See **PASSOVER**)

CHANCE, SECOND (See **SECOND
CHANCE**)

CHARACTER
Example of highest c. Moses. 3:1-3
Of believers. (See **BELIEVERS**, Duty)
Of unbelievers. (See **UNBELIEVERS**,
Nature)

CHARGE - CHARGED (See **EXHORT -
EXHORTATION**)

CHARIOT
Fact. Egypt used 600 of the most modern
c. & hundreds more against Israel. 14:5-9

CHART
Listed.
Calendar, Hebrew. 12:1-2
Diseases in the Bible. 9:10
The God of history. 7:5
Genealogy.
Of Aaron. 6:13-27
Of Jacob. 1:1-5; 6:13-27
Of Moses. 6:13-27
Types, Symbols, Pictures. Intro. VII,
Types Chart

CHASTEN - CHASTISEMENT (See
DISCIPLINE, GODLY)
Example of.
Moses. Because he failed to obey God.
4:24-26
Israel. Because of disobedience.
16:16-30, esp. 19-20, 27-30
How a person is c.
Afflicted with disease, illness. 15:25-26
Rebuked, corrected. 16:16-30, esp.
19-20, 27-30
Why a believer is c. Disobedience.
15:25-26; 16:16-30, esp. 19-20, 27-30
Why God c. Because He loves us.
15:25-26

CHEER - CHEERFULNESS (See **JOY;
REJOICING**)

CHIDE - CHIDING (See **ACCUSA-
TIONS, FALSE; REBUKE; RE-
PROVE; SCOLD**)

**CHILD - CHILDREN - CHILDLIKE-
NESS** (See **FAMILY; PARENTS**)
Abuse of. Slaughtered by Pharaoh.
1:15-21
Duty toward.
To do all one can to save if abused.
1:15-21; 2:1-10
To see c. as gifts from God. 2:2
To teach that God is the God of salva-
tion & deliverance. 13:1-16
To teach the judgment of God to c.
10:1-2
To teach the Passover, that Jesus Chr-
ist is the Lamb of God. 12:21-28
To teach three great lessons. 13:11-16

CHOSEN (See **CALL - CALLED**)
Who the c. are.
Aaron. 4:13-17; 6:13-7:7; 15:13-18
Israel. 1:1-7; 1:6-7; 2:23-25; 2:24
Moses. 3:1-10; 3:11-4:17; 6:13-7:7

CHRISTIAN - CHRISTIANS (See **BE-
LIEVERS**)

CHRONOLOGY
Of the main characters & events in Exodus. Intro. VIII, Timeline

CHURCH (See **WORSHIP**)
Need - Needs.
To be unified, living together in one
spirit, as one body. 12:42-51,
esp. 46
To see the holiness & glory of God.
3:1-10
Problems within. (See **CARNAL**)
Worship. (See **WORSHIP**)

CIRCUMCISION
Discussed.
Three critical facts about c. 4:24-26
What c. was. Why God gave c.
4:24-26
Importance of.
Essential before taking part in the
Passover. 12:42-51
Failure to be c. Caused chastisement
by God. 4:24-26

CIRCUMSTANCES (See **TRIALS**)

**CITIES - AREAS - GEOGRAPHICAL
LOCATIONS - NATIONS - PLACES**
(See **DESERT; MOUNTAINS; RIV-
ERS; SEAS**)
Amorites, Land of. 3:8
Baal-zephon. 14:2
Canaanites, Land of. 3:8
Desert of Shur. 15:22
Desert of Sin. 16:2
Egypt. 1:8; Intro. VI
Elim. 15:27
Etham. 13:20
Hittites, Land of. 3:8
Hivites, Land of. 3:8
Israel. 1:1-7
Jebusites, Land of. 3:8
Marah. 15:23
Midian, Land of. 2:15-22
Migdol. 14:2
Mount Horeb. 3:1
Nile. 7:14-25; 7:17-19; 7:20-22
Perizzites, Land of. 3:8
Pi Hahiroth. 14:2
Pithom. 1:11
Rameses. 1:11
Red Sea. 14:16-18
Rephidim. 17:2
Succoth. 13:20

CITIZENSHIP (See **GOVERNMENT**)

CIVIL AUTHORITIES (See **GOVERN-
MENT; RULERS**)
Duty. To structure government for effi-
ciency. 18:13-22
Sins of.
Broken promises. 8:7-8; 8:25-29;
9:27-28; 10:16-17; 10:24-26
Double-minded. Pharaoh agreed to
free the enslaved Israelites, then
changed time & again. 8:7-8; 8:25-
29; 9:27-28;10:16-17; 10:24-26

CIVILIZATION (See **CITIZENSHIP;
SOCIETY; WORLD**)

CLAMOR - CLAMORING (See **COM-
PLAINING; GRUMBLING; MUR-
MURING**)

CLEAN - CLEANLINESS - CLEANSED
(See BLAMELESS; FORGIVENESS; PURITY; SPOTLESS)

How to be cleansed.
By Jesus Christ. 3:7-8
By the blood of the Passover lamb, Christ Himself. 12:1-13:16 (pt.4); 12:1-13; 12:21-28

CLOSE-MINDEDNESS (See HARDNESS OF HEART; STUBBORN)

CLOUD
Used by God. To lead & guide the Israelites in the wilderness wanderings. 13:20-22

CLOUD, PILLAR OF CLOUD & FIRE
Discussed. 13:20-22
Purpose of.
To defend Israel. 14:19-28, esp. 19-20
To guide Israel. 13:20-22
To manifest, show forth, God's glory. 16:4-15, esp. 9-10

COMFORT - COMFORTED (See SECURITY)
Source. God's great provision.
In giving us the hope of the promised land. 2:24; 3:7-8
In meeting our needs. 15:27

COMMANDMENT
Duty.
To keep the Sabbath c. 16:16-30, esp. 25-29
To obey God's c. 15:26-27
Subject of c.
All c. 15:26-27
Sabbath. 16:16-30, esp. 25-29
Warning.
Against disobeying the c.: will result in chastisement. 15:26-27
Against failing to keep the c. 16:16-30, esp. 28-29

COMMISSION (See WITNESSING)
Given to.
Israel. To be missionary force to the world. 1:1-22 (pt.2)
Moses. 3:1-10

COMMIT - COMMITMENT (See DEDICATION; SURRENDER)
Call to c. To the mission of God. Moses called. 3:1-10; 6:28-7:7

COMMUNE - COMMUNION (See DEDICATION; DEVOTION; MEDITATION; PRAYER)
How one can c. with God.
By crying out in prayer. 5:21-23; 6:1-5
By intercessory prayer. 17:8-16
By reverencing & humbling oneself before God. 3:1-10

COMMUNITY (See CONGREGATION)

COMPASSION (See BROKEN-HEARTED; BURDEN)
Of God.
For the crushed, broken, desperate. 6:1-5, esp. 5
Stirred by the sufferings of His people. 2:23-25; 3:7-8; 3:9-10; 6:1-5, esp. 5; 6:6-9

Results.
Can change our lives. 2:11
Meets the needs of the world. 2:11

COMPLACENT - COMPLACENCY
(See DULLNESS, SPIRITUAL; SLEEP, SPIRITUAL; SLOTHFUL)
In accepting oppression & persecution. 5:20-23; 14:10-12; 16:1-3; 17:2-3
Results. Fighting against God's call. Moses made up five excuses. 3:11-4:17

COMPLAIN - COMPLAINING (See GRUMBLING; MURMURING; JUDGING OTHERS; SLANDER; TROUBLE-MAKER)
Caused by.
Being upset with one's leader. 5:20-23; 17:2-3
Carnality. 14:10-12; 15:24; 16:1-3; 17:2-3
Questioning God's care & provision. 14:10-12; 15:24; 16:1-3; 17:2-3
Unbelief. 14:10-12; 15:24; 16:1-3; 17:2-3
Characteristic - Trait. Of carnal, distrustful persons. 14:10-12; 15:24; 16:1-3; 17:2-3
Discussed. 15:24
Fact. Is not against God's servants, but against God Himself. 16:4-15
Of Israel.
At Egypt. Against Moses. Because of Pharaoh's reaction against him: more intense oppression. 5:20-23
At Marah. Over bitter water. 15:22-27; 15:24
At Rephidim. Because of no water. 17:1-7
At the Red Sea. Faced with an impossible situation. 14:10-12
At the wilderness of Sin. Because of no food. 16:1-3
One of two great sins of Israel. 16:1-36; 16:1-3
Results. Causes pain, hurt. 14:10-12, see 15; 15:22-27; 15:25; 17:4

COMPROMISE (See BACKSLIDING; FICKLENESS; HALF-HEARTED; INCONSISTENCY; INSTABILITY)
Caused by.
False religion & worship. 3:8
Greed, love of money. 10:7-11; 10:24-26
Worldliness: lusting after sex, pleasure, & possessions. 3:8
Example of. Pharaoh. Attempted to c. with God. 10:7-11; 10:24-26
Fact. God does not c. with sin & evil. 10:7-11; 10:24-26
Illustration of. Israel c. with worldliness of Canaanites. 3:8

CONCEIT - CONCEITED (See PRIDE)

CONCERN - CONCERNED (See CARE - CARING; COMPASSION; MINISTERING)

CONDEMN - CONDEMNATION (See JUDGMENT)

CONFESS - CONFESSION (See DECISION; PROFESSION, SPIRITUAL or RELIGIOUS)

CONFESSION, FALSE (See DECEIT; DENY - DENIAL; HYPOCRISY; LYING; PROFESSION, FALSE; REJECTION; UNBELIEF)
Example of. Pharaoh. 8:15; 8:32
Fact. Sincerity is not enough. 10:16-17

CONFIDENCE (See ASSURANCE; SECURITY; SELF-CONFIDENCE)

CONFLICT (See DIVISION - DISSENSION; STRIFE)
Caused by.
Carnality. 2:11-12; 2:13-15; 14:10-12; 15:24; 16:1-3; 17:2-3
Feeling threatened. 17:8
Greed, love of money. 8:2-4; 11:1-10, esp. 7-8
Unbelief, distrust in God's care & provision. 5:20-23; 14:10-12; 15:24; 16:1-3; 17:2-3
How to overcome.
By faith & confidence in God. 14:13-15; 16:4-15
By prayer. 5:20-23; 15:25; 17:4

CONFORM - CONFORMED - CONFORMITY (See COMPROMISE; WORLDLINESS)

CONGREGATION (See COMMUNITY)
Name - Title - Identity. Israel. 12:3-4, esp. 3; 12:19-20; 12:42-51, esp. 47

CONQUER - CONQUEST (See OVERCOMERS; TRIUMPH; VICTORY)

CONSECRATION (See CEREMONY; COMMISSION; COMMITMENT; DEDICATION; DEVOTION)

CONSISTENT - CONSISTENCY (See COMMITMENT; DEDICATION)

CONSOLATION (See COMFORT)

CONSTANCY (See ENDURANCE; PERSEVERANCE; STEDFASTNESS)

CONSTRUCTION
Example of. The Israelites. As slaves c. cities, pyramids, & roads for Egypt. 1:11-14

CONTEMPT (See DESPISE; PREJUDICE)
Example of. Egyptians detested the Israelites. 8:25-29

CONTENT - CONTENTMENT (See JOY)
Source of. God's promise of the promised land of heaven. 2:24

CONTENTION - CONTENTIOUS (See ARGUMENT; STRIFE)

CONTINUE - CONTINUING (See ENDURANCE; PERSEVERANCE)

CONTRARY (See STRIFE; STUBBORN)

CONTRITE - CONTRITION (See BROKEN-HEARTED; HUMILITY; REPENTANCE; SORROW, GODLY)

CONTROVERSY (See **ARGUMENT; CRITICISM; DIVISION; JUDGING OTHERS; STRIFE**)

CONVERSATION (See **TONGUE**)

CONVERSION - CONVERTED
Symbolized - Typed - Pictured. By the Feast of Unleavened Bread. 12:1-13:16 (pt.7); 12:14-20; 12:34-41, esp. 39; Intro. VII, pt.22

CONVICTION
Example. Pharaoh. Sensed he had sinned against the LORD. 9:27-28; 10:16-17

COOPERATION (See **BROTHER-HOOD; UNITY**)
Essential - Necessary.
In prayer. 17:10-12
In warfare. 17:8-16

CORIANDER SEED
Fact. Was compared to the manna (bread) that fed the Israelites daily. 16:31-36, esp. 31

COUNTERFEIT (See **HYPOCRISY; PROFESSION, FALSE**)

COURAGE - COURAGEOUS (See **BOLDNESS**)
Duty.
Not to fear impossible problems & trials, but to stand firm & be **c**. 14:13-15
To be **c**. & declare God's will & Word to nations & rulers. 5:1; 7:10; 10:3
Failure in. Arguing against God's call. 3:11-4:17
To stand before impossible odds—problems, difficulties, trials—to stand **c**. 14:13-15

COURT, JUDICIAL
Organization of - Structure of. **C**. of Israel. 18:13-27

COVENANT
Discussed. Abrahamic **c**. 1:6-7; 2:23-25; 2:24
Listed. Of obedience. Demanded by God. 15:25-26
Why God remembers His **c**. Three reasons. 12:40-41

COVET - COVETOUSNESS (See **GREED**)

COWARDICE (See **FEAR**)

CRAFTINESS (See **DECEPTION**)

CREATION
Source of **c**. God. Created & controls the most minute elements. 8:16-19

CRISIS - CRISES (See **TRIALS – TRIB-ULATIONS**)

CRITICISM - CRITICIZER - CRITI-CIZING (See **ARGUMENTS; COM-PLAINING; CONFLICT; DIVISION; GRUMBLING; JUDGING OTHERS; MURMURING; SLANDER**)
Caused by.
Being upset with one's leader. 5:20-23; 17:2-3
Carnality. 14:10-12; 15:24; 16:1-3; 17:2-3
Questioning God's care & provision. 14:10-12; 15:24; 16:1-3; 17:2-3
Unbelief. 14:10-12; 15:24; 16:1-3; 17:2-3
Characteristic - Trait. Of carnal, distrust-ful persons. 14:10-12; 15:24; 16:1-3; 17:2-3
Discussed. 15:24
Fact. Is not against God's servants, but against God Himself. 16:4-15
Of Israel.
At Egypt. Against Moses. Because of Pharaoh's reaction against him: more intense oppression. 5:20-23
At Marah. Over bitter water. 15:22-27; 15:24
At Rephidim. Because of no water. 17:1-7
At the Red Sea. Faced with an imposs-ible situation. 14:10-12
At the wilderness of Sin. Because of no food. 16:1-3
One of two great sins of Israel. 16:1-36; 16:1-3
Results. Causes pain, hurt. 14:10-12, see 15; 15:22-27; 15:25; 17:4

CROSS, DAILY - SELF-DENIAL (See **COMMITMENT; DEDICATION; SURRENDER**)

CRY - CRYING (See **PRAYER; SEEK-ING GOD**)

CURIOUS - CURIOSITY
Duty. To stop & seek the meaning of things. 3:1-3, esp. 3

CURSED - CURSED (See **JUDGMENT**)

CUT OFF (See **JUDGMENT**)
Who is to be cut off.
The evil person: is cut off when God wills. 9:14-16, esp. 15
The unbeliever: refuses to cast away all leaven (evil). 12:14-20, esp. 15, 19

DAILY CROSS (See **CROSS, DAILY**)

DAMNED (See **JUDGMENT; WRATH OF GOD**)
Why people are **d**.
Brutality & savage treatment of people. 7:8-11:10; 7:20-22; 10:21-29
Failing to get rid of all leaven (evil). 12:14-20, esp. 15, 19
Greed: love of money, wealth, eco-nomic security. 8:2-4; 10:1-20
Hardness of heart. 7:8-13; 7:14
Idolatry. 7:8-11:10; 7:14-25; 7:20-22; 8:9-11; 8:16-18; 8:19; 8:20-32; 10:21-29

Living an evil life. 9:14-16, esp. 15
Rejection of God & the oppression of people. 7:8-11:10; 7:20-22; 8:1-15; 8:2-4; 8:5-6; 8:16-18; 8:21; 9:2-3; 10:1-20; 10:21-29
Sinful living: indulgence, extravag-ance, luxury, ease. 7:20-22; 9:17-21; 10:1-2; 10:1-20; 10:21-29

DARK - DARKNESS (See **DARKNESS, SPIRITUAL**)
Fact. Was one of the ten plagues. 10:21-29

DARKNESS, SPIRITUAL
Results.
Causes a hard heart. 10:21-29
Causes the judgment of God to fall. 10:21-23

DAY, THE LORD'S (See **SABBATH**)
Duty. To keep every week. 16:16-30

DEATH - DYING
Caused by - Penalty of. Unbelief; rejec-tion of God; sin, evil, & oppression of people. 11:1-10; 12:29
Deliverance from **d**.
By believing in the lamb of God. 12:1-13:16; Chart; 12:1-13; 12:21-28
By the blood of the lamb. 12:1-13:16; Chart; 12:1-13; 12:21-28
Fact. Death of firstborn. Was one of the ten plagues against the evil Egyptians. 11:1-10

DECEIT - DECEIVE - DECEPTION (See **HYPOCRISY; LYING; SELF-DECEPTION**)
Message of **d**. Magic & trickery. Used to secure loyalty. 7:10-13; 8:7-8
Who & what **d**.
Magicians. In Pharaoh's court.
Imitated the miracles of Moses. 7:10-13; 8:7-8
Failed to imitate the miracles of Moses. 8:16-18
Men through history who exalt self to be God. 7:17
Rulers. Making promises to please God & believers. 8:7-8; 8:25-29; 9:27-28; 10:16-17; 10:24-26
Rulers who exalt themselves to be God (Pharaoh). 8:1-15

DECISION (See **CONFESSION; PRO-FESSION, SPIRITUAL or RELI-GIOUS**)
Duty.
Must choose between obedience & chastisement. 4:24-26; 15:26-27
Must choose to accept God's promises. 6:6-9, esp. 9
Responses, Positive.
To obey God's call & serve Him (Moses). 3:11-4:17; see 4:9; 4:18-31
To obey God's call. Several men. 7:10

DEDICATION (See **CEREMONY; COMMITMENT; COMMUNION; CROSS, DAILY; CONSECRATION; SELF-DENIAL; SANCTIFICATION; SURRENDER**)
Duty.
To give one's whole body to God. 13:3-10
To sanctify, set one's child apart to God. 13:1-16
To sanctify, set one's self apart to God. Intro. VII, pt.24
Of the firstborn. (See **FIRSTBORN**, Dedication of)
Stirred by.
God's call to service. 3:1-10
God meeting one's need. 6:1-7:7; see 5:20-23
Victory given by God. 15:1-21; 17:13-16
Victory over impossible trials & obstacles. 14:19-28; 15:1-21
Victory over one's enemies. 14:19-28; 15:1-21; 17:13-16

DEFILE - DEFILEMENT (See **ENVIRONMENT; FILTHINESS; POLLUTION; SIN; UNCLEANNESS**)
Cause of **d**.
Eating leavened bread: partaking of evil. 12:14-20
Partaking of the Passover & not believing. 12:42-51
Results. To be cut off. 12:14-20, esp. 15, 19

DEGRADATION, SPIRITUAL (See **SIN**)
Caused by. Rejection of God; sin, evil, oppression of people. 7:8-11:10; 7:14-25; 7:17; 8:1-15; 8:9-11; 8:20-32; 9:1-7; 9:3-5

DELIVERANCE (See **REDEMPTION; SALVATION**)
Fact.
God delivered & protected Israel from the ten plagues. 8:22-23; 9:6; 10:23; 11:7-8; 12:34-31
Is the theme of the great book of Exodus. Intro.; 1:1-22;
From what.
Bitter experiences. 15:22-27
Enemies—all enemies. 17:8-16
Hunger. 16:1-36; 17:1-7
Judgment. 10:23; 11:7-8; 12:1-13; 12:21-51
Obstacles & problems—impossible obstacles & problems. 14:10-12; 14:13-15
Slavery. 12:30-33
Thirst. 16:1-36
Trials—all trials. 1:1-5
How a person is **d**.
By God.
Always **d**. us through all trials. 1:1-5; 14:1-31; 14:19-28; 15:22-27; 16:1-36; 17:1-7; 17:8-16
Six facts declared about God's great **d**. 15:3-12
Through the Red Sea, through the greatest trials & problems. 14:1-31; 14:19-28
By heeding God's threefold challenge. 14:13-15

Of Israel.
D. from slavery & from God's judgment. 12:21-51
How God **d**. Israel through the Red Sea. 14:19-28
Israel's Great Emancipation; Israel's First Day of Independence. 12:1-13:16
Why God delivered Israel. 12:40-41
Songs of God's great **d**. After crossing the Red Sea. 15:1-21
Why God **d**. believers. Three reasons. 12:40-41

DENY - DENIAL (See **AGNOSTIC; ATHEIST; BACKSLIDING; HUMANISM; REJECTION; UNBELIEF**)
By whom.
Agnostics. 8:1-15
False messiahs. 7:8-11:10 (pt.5); 8:1-15
Followers of the reincarnation philosophy. 8:1-15
Humanists. 9:1-7
Idolaters. 7:8-11:10 (pt.5); 7:14-15; 8:1-15; 8:16-19; 8:20-32; 9:1-7; 9:8-12; 9:13-35; 10:1-2; 10:22-29; 11:1-10; 12:21-51
List of men who **d**. & rejected God. 7:17
Results. Judgment. Ten plagues upon Egypt. 7:8-11:10
Warning against **d**. Will result in chastisement. 15:25-26

DENYING SELF (See **SELF-DENIAL**)

DEPRAVITY (See **MAN**, Depravity)
Proof of. Trials of wilderness wanderings. 13:17-18:27
Source. Heart of man. 13:17-18:27

DESCENDANTS (See **GENEALOGY; GODLY SEED, THE PROMISED; SEED, THE PROMISED**)

DESERT (See **CITIES - AREAS**)
Of Shur. Discussed. 15:22
Of Sin. 16:1

DESERTION (See **BACKSLIDING; DENIAL**)

DESIRE (See **LUST; PASSION**)
Bad & evil **d**.
For pleasures & food of the world. 15:24; 16:1-4; 17:5-6
For slavery & bondage instead of God & the promised land. 14:10-12
For the waters of this world (pleasures, indulgences, kicks, thrills). 15:24; 17:5-6

DESPAIR (See **GRIEF; HELPLESSNESS; HOPELESSNESS; SORROW**)

DESPERATE - DESPERATION (See **HELPLESSNESS; HOPELESSNESS**)
In what.
Facing impossible trials & obstacles. 12:10-12
Facing the crisis of hunger. 16:1-36
Facing the crisis of slavery & savage oppression. 1:11-14; 2:23-25; 5:2-14

Facing the crisis of thirst. 15:22-27; 17:1-7
Facing the judgment of God. 8:7-8; 8:25-29; 9:27-28; 10:16-17; 12:30-33
Facing the savagery of a holocaust. 1:8-22
Facing the threat of murder. 2:1-10
Facing the threat to one's life. 2:11-25

DESPISE - DESPISING - DESPITE (See **BITTER; CONTEMPT; HATRED; MALICE**)

DESPONDENCY (See **DISAPPOINTMENT; DISCOURAGEMENT; GRIEF; HOPELESSNESS; SORROW**)
Caused by.
Complaining, murmuring, grumbling of people. 5:20-23; 14:10-12; 17:2-3
Impossible trials & obstacles. 14:13-15, esp. 15; 15:24; 17:4
Not understanding God's timing. 5:20-23

DESTINY (See **CALL - CALLING; DEATH; ETERNAL LIFE; PURPOSE**)

DESTITUTE - DESTITUTION (See **NEEDY, THE; SIN**)
Caused by. Sin & the judgment of God.
Upon the rulers & nations. Ten plagues upon Egypt. 7:8-11:10

DESTROY - DESTRUCTION
Who or what is **d**.
Economy of a major nation (Egypt). Because of sin, evil, & rejection of God. 8:2-4; 9:2-3; 9:34-35; 10:24-26; 11:1-10; 14:5-9
Firstborn of unbelievers (Egypt). 12:29; 12:30-31
Military of an oppressive nation (Egypt). 14:19-28

DETEST - DETESTABLE
Who is **d**. Shepherds & the Jews (Israelites). 8:25-29, esp. 26-27

DEVIL (See **SATAN**)

DEVOTION - DEVOTIONS (See **CONSECRATION; COMMUNION; PRAYER; QUIET TIME**
Duty. To arise early for prayer & study of God's Word. 16:16-30; 16:31
Example of. List of people who arose early for **d**. 16:16-30

DILIGENCE - DILIGENTLY (See **ENDURANCE; PERSEVERANCE; STEDFASTNESS; ZEAL**)
Example of. Moses. In the daily administration (management) of Israel. 18:13-27

DISAPPOINTMENT (See **DISSATISFACTION; DISCOURAGEMENT; SIN**, Results)
Caused by.
Arguing, unsupportive wife. 4:24-26
Complaining & grumbling people. 15:24; 15:25; 16:1-3; 17:2-3; 17:4
Exposing secret sin. 2:13-15
God not acting quickly enough. 5:20-23
Of God. With Moses. Because of Moses' excuses & objections to God's call. 4:13-17

DISASTER (See **CATASTROPHE; CALAMITIES**)

DISCIPLINE, GODLY (See **CHASTISEMENT**)
Caused by. Disobedience. 16:16-30, esp. 20-21, 27-30

DISCOURAGE - DISCOURAGEMENT (See **DISAPPOINTMENT; HOPELESSNESS; SIN**, Results)

DISCRIMINATION (See **BARRIERS; BIGOTRY; DIVISION; FAVORITISM; PARTIALITY; PREJUDICE**)

DISEASE (See **HEALING; SICKNESS; SUFFERING**)
Caused by.
Disobedience. 4:24-26
Judgment of God. Upon the unrighteous & evil of this earth. Ten plagues. 9:8-12
Examples of. 9:1 (Chart)
Kinds of **d**.
Boils. 9:8-12
Murrain, anthrax. 9:2-3

DISHONESTY (See **HYPOCRISY; LYING; STEALING**)

DISHONOR (See **SHAME**)

DISOBEDIENCE (See **BACKSLIDING; COMPROMISE; DOUBLE-MINDED; FICKLE; HALF-HEARTED; INCONSISTENT; INSTABILITY; LUKEWARM; NEUTRALITY; SIN; UNBELIEF; UNFAITHFUL**)
Caused by.
Unbelief. Not believing in God's care & provision. 14:10-12; 15:24; 16:1-36; 17:1-7
Weakness. Giving in to the fussing & objections of a spouse. 4:24-26
Of Israel.
In gathering manna & hoarding it. Unbelief, distrust of God's provision. 16:16-30
In gathering manna on the Sabbath. 16:16-30
Was one of the two great sins of Israel. 16:1-36; 16:1-3
Results. Chastisement, correction of God. 15:25-26
Source. Heart of man. 13:17-18:27

DISSATISFACTION (See **DISCOURAGEMENT; HOPELESSNESS; SIN**, Results)
Answer - Solution.
The Bread of Life, Jesus Christ. 16:31
The water of life, Jesus Christ. 15:22-23
Caused by.
Spiritual thirst. 15:22-23
Worldliness. 3:8

DISSENSION (See **ARGUMENT; CONTENTION; DIVISION; STRIFE**)

DISTRESS - DISTRESSED (See **AFFLICTIONS; DISAPPOINTMENT; SUFFERING**)

DIVINE (See **GOD; JESUS CHRIST**)

DIVISION (See **ARGUMENT; CONTENTION; DISCRIMINATION; STRIFE**)

DOUBLE-MINDED (See **BACKSLIDING; COMPROMISE; FICKLENESS; HALF-HEARTED; INCONSISTENCY; INSTABILITY**)
Caused by. Greed for power, wealth, fame, image. 8:15; 9:12; 9:34-35; 10:20; 11:1-10

DOUBLE-TONGUED (See **BACKSLIDING; DOUBLE-MINDED; FICKLENESS; INSTABILITY**)

DOUBT - DOUBTING (See **QUESTIONING; UNBELIEF**)
What is questioned & **d**.
God's call & one's ability & qualifications. 3:11-4:17
God's call & one's speaking ability. 4:10-12
God's call & people's acceptance. 3:13-22; 4:1-9
God's care & provision. 5:20-23; 15:24; 16:1-3; 17:2-3
God's leadership, His timing in delivering us. 5:20-23
God's power to save & deliver. 14:10-12

DRAW - DRAWN - DRAW NEAR (See **COMMUNION; DEDICATION; DEVOTION; PRAYER**)

DROWN - DROWNING
Example of. The Egyptian army was **d**. in the Red Sea. 14:19-28, esp. 28

DULL - DULLNESS, SPIRITUAL (See **COMPLACENCY; HARDNESS; HEART, HARD; INSENSITIVITY**)

DUST
Of the ground. Is controlled by God. 8:16-19; 8:19

DWELLING, GOD'S HOLY
Fact. God's redeemed people are being led to God's holy **d**. 15:13-18
Meaning. 15:13-18

DYING TO SELF (See **CROSS, DAILY - SELF-DENIAL**)

EARNEST (See **COMMITMENT; DILIGENCE**)

EARTH (See **CREATION; UNIVERSE**)
Fact. God is the God of all the **e**. 8:22-23; 9:13-35
Fate of. Will be recreated into a perfect **e**. 2:24

EARTH & HEAVEN, NEW (See **HEAVEN; UNIVERSE**)
Discussed. 2:24
Fact. Will be recreated into a perfect **e**. 2:24

EARTHQUAKE
At the Red Sea when it divided for Israel to cross. 14:19-28, esp. 19-20

ECONOMY - ECONOMICS (See **WEALTH**)
Love of wealth, money, **e**. stability. Causes men to oppress & enslave others. 8:2-4; 11:1-10
Of Egypt. Was devastated by the ten plagues. 8:2-4; 9:2-3; 9:34-35; 10:24-26; 11:1-10; 14:5-9

EGYPT - EGYPTIANS (See **PHARAOH**)
Beliefs. In the occult & magic. 9:8-12
Fact.
History of. Discussed. Intro.VI
Economy would have collapsed if freed Israel. 8:2-4; 11:1-10
Idolatry of. List of idols & gods. Chart. 7:8-11:10 (pt.6)
Judgment of. Ten plagues. Discussed. 7:8-11:10
Military army of Egypt. Was large, massive. Destroyed in the Red Sea. 14:1-31
Rulers of. Conquered by Hyksos people. 1:8
Sins of.
Enslaved people of Israel. 1:8-22; 8:2-4
Idolatry, slavery, & rejection of God, the only true & living God. 7:8-11:10; 7:14-25; 7:17; 8:1-15; 8:9-11; 8:16-19; 8:20-32; 9:1-7; 9:3-5; 9:8-12; 9:13-35; 10:1-2; 10:21-29; 11:1-10; 12:21-29; 12:21-51
Indulgence, comfort. 7:20-21
Symbol - Type of. The world & worldliness. 3:7-8; Intro. VII, pt.2

ELDERLY, THE
Fact. Can be called to serve God even when **e**. 7:6-7

ELDERS OF ISRAEL (See **LEADERS**)
Fact.
Were recognized by God to be the representatives of the people. 3:13-22, esp. 16; 17:5
Were the representatives of the people. 3:13-22, esp. 16; 4:27-31, esp. 29-31; 12:21; 17:5

ELEAZAR
Son of Aaron. 6:13-27 (Chart)

ELECT - ELECTION (See **CALL - CALLED; CHOSEN**)

ELEMENTS
Of the universe. Are controlled by God. 8:16-19

ELIEZER
Son of Moses. 18:1-8, esp. 4

ELIM, City or Area of
Discussed. 15:27

ELKANAH
Descendent of Levi. 6:13-27 (Chart)

ELOQUENT (See **MESSENGERS; MINISTER; PREACHER; SPEAK - SPEECH; TONGUE**)
Fact. Moses was not **e**. 4:10-12

ELZAPHAN
Descendent of Levi. Son of Uzziel. 6:13-27 (Chart)

EMANCIPATION (See **FREEDOM**)
Of whom. Israel's Great Emancipation, Great Day of Independence. 12:1-13:16; 12:34-41

EMBARRASSED (See **SHAME**)
Caused by.
Apparent failure & rejection. 14:10-12, see 14:13-15, esp. 15; 15:24; 17:4
Exposure of secret sin. 2:13-15

EMPATHY (See **COMPASSION; MERCY; SYMPATHY**)

EMPLOYMENT (See **LABOR; MANAGERS - MANAGEMENT; SERVICE; WORK**)

EMPTINESS (See **HOPE; LIFE; NEW LIFE; NEW MAN; MEANING; PURPOSE**)

ENCHANTMENT (See **MAGICIANS; SORCERY**)

ENCOURAGE - ENCOURAGEMENT (See **COMFORT - COMFORTED**)
By God. God's great e. to Moses. 6:1-7:7
How God e.
By rebuking & charging us to go forth. 4:13-17; 14:13-15
By speaking to us & assuring us. 6:1-7:7
Needed by. Moses. 6:1-7:7
Who can be e.
The believer who is threatened. 17:4
The crushed, broken, desperate. 6:1-5, esp. 5
The despondent, the hopeless. 5:20-23, see 6:1-7:7; 14:13-15, esp. 15; 15:25
The suffering. 3:7-8; 3:9-10

ENDURANCE (See **PERSEVERANCE, STEDFASTNESS**)
Duty.
To e. against one's enemies. 17:8-16
To e. against the rejection of unbelievers. 5:1-23; see 6:1-7:7
To e. in prevailing prayer. 17:10-12
To e. in proclaiming the message of God: mercy & justice. 7:8-11:10
To e. in the mission of God despite grumblers & threats. 5:20-23; 14:10-12; 15:22-27; 16:1-36; 17:1-7

ENEMIES
Conquered - Victory over.
By courage & trust in God's power. 14:13-15
By God's almighty power. 14:19-28
By prayer, intercessory prayer. 17:8-16

ENSLAVE - ENSLAVEMENT (See **SLAVERY**)
Why people are e. One basic reason. Economic. 8:2-4; 11:1-10

ENSLAVEMENT, SPIRITUAL
By what.
Greed, money, wealth, power, position, fame. 8:2-4; 11:1-10
Sex & material possessions. 3:8
The world, its pleasures, food, & comfort. 14:10-12; 16:1-3; 17:2-3

ENTANGLE - ENTANGLEMENT (See **SNARES; WORLDLINESS**)
Sin of.
Attracted by bright lights & becoming e. with worldliness. 1:1-5
Lusting after the women, men, & possessions of the world. 3:8
Wanting to return to the world, its pleasures, comfort, &possessions. 14:10-12; 16:1-3; 17:2-3

ENTHUSIASM - ENTHUSIASTIC (See **DEVOTION; DILIGENCE; ZEAL**)

ENTICE - ENTICEMENT
Who was or is e. Israel. By the worldliness of the Canaanites. 3:8

ENVIRONMENT (See **DEFILE; POLLUTION**)

EQUALITY OF MAN (See **ONENESS - UNITY**)
Basis of. Creation. By the only living & true God. 11:1-10
Fact. Egyptians did not believe all people were equal. 11:1-10

ESCAPE, NO
From what. Judgment. 7:8-11:10; 10:21-23
Who will not e. Those who are evil & oppress people & reject God. 7:8-11:10

ESTABLISH - ESTABLISHED (See **GROWTH; SPIRITUAL; SECURITY**)

ETERNAL LIFE (See **HEAVEN; LAND, THE PROMISED**)

ETHAM, City or Area of
Discussed. 13:20

EVIL ASSOCIATIONS (See **SEPARATION**)
Results.
Idolatry. 2:23-25; 3:13-22 (pt.1)
Pulls a person down. 3:8

EVIL DESIRE (See **LUST**)

EVIL HEART (See **HEART, HARD**)

EXALT - EXALTATION (See **BOASTING; PRIDE; SELF-EXALTATION**)

EXAMINE - EXAMINATION (See **TEST - TESTING**)

EXCOMMUNICATION
What caused e. according to Israel's laws. Eating leavened bread (evil)during the Feast of Unleavened Bread. 12:14-20, esp. 15, 19

EXCUSES (See **PROCRASTINATION**)
Against God's call. Listed.
Feeling incapable. 3:11-12
Feeling one is not eloquent nor gifted. 4:10-12
Ignorance of God. 3:13-22
Moses' five e. 3:11-4:17
Not wanting to go. Refusing God's call. 4:13-17
Skepticism. 3:13-22
Unbelief of people. 4:1-9

EXHAUSTION (See **BURDENED; PRESSURE; TIRED; YOKE**)
What causes e.
Oppression & enslavement. 1:11-14; 2:11; 5:2-14; 5:20-23
Overwork. 18:13-27

EXHORT - EXHORTATION
Message of e.
Salvation, redemption, deliverance. 6:1-7:7
To fear not, be courageous. 14:13-15

EXODUS (See **FREEDOM**)
Of Israel. From Egypt. 12:1-13:16; 13:34-41
Promised.
To Israel. To encourage. 6:6-9
To Moses. During a great trial. 6:1-5
Theme of. Deliverance, salvation, redemption. 1:1-22

EXPECTATION (See **HOPE**)

EXPOSURE - EXPOSED
Of sin. Moses' secret sin of murder was e. 2:13-15

FAIL - FAILURE (See **POWERLESSNESS**)
Cause of. A carnal spirit. 2:11-12; 2:13-15
Supposed f. Moses felt like he was a f. 5:21-23; 14:13-15, esp. 15; 17:4

FAITH (See **BELIEVE - BELIEF**)
Duty.
To believe in the blood of the sacrificed lamb, the Lamb of God. 12:1-13:16; 12:21-51
To not fear, stand still, & believer God. 14:13-15
Test of. (See **TEST - TESTING**)

FAITHFUL - FAITHFULNESS (See **TRUSTWORTHY**)
Duty.
To be f. despite complaints & grumbling. 14:10-12, see 14:13-15; 15:22-27; 16:1-36; 17:1-7
To be f. despite opposition. 5:20-23; 17:4
Of God.
Fulfills His promises to us. 1:6-7
Gives victory over all our enemies. 17:8-16
Leads us away from trouble. 13:17-18
Leads us by day & by night. 13:20-22
Leads us to the promised land of heaven. 13:19
Provides for us. Meets all our needs. 15:22-27; 16:1-36; 17:1-7

FAITHLESSNESS (See **DOUBT; UNBE-LIEF; UNFAITHFULNESS**)

FALLING AWAY - FALL, SPIRITUAL (See **BACKSLIDING; DENIAL**)
Example of. Pharaoh. 8:15; 8:32

FALSE PROFESSION (See **PROFESSION, FALSE**)

FALSEHOOD (See **DECEPTION; HYPOCRISY; LIE - LIARS - LYING**)

FAME - FAMOUS (See **PRIDE; SELF-EXALTATION**)

FAMILY - FAMILIES (See **CHILDREN; PARENTS**)
Duty.
To dedicate children to God. 13:1-16
To protect one another. 2:1-10
To teach children the meaning of the Passover, of salvation. 12:3-4; 12:21-28, esp. 26-27
To trust God to protect children. 2:3-4
Problems within. Division, separation. Example. Moses. 4:24-26; 18:1-8

FAMILY OF GOD (See **BELIEVERS; CHURCH; CONGREGATION**)

FAMINE (See **HUNGER; STARVATION**)

FATE (See **DEATH; DESTINY; JUDGMENT**)

FATHER (See **CHILDREN; FAMILY**)

FAULT-FINDERS (See **COMPLAINING; CRITICISM; GRUMBLING**)

FAVORITISM (See **DISCRIMINATION; PARTIALITY; PREJUDICE**)

FEAR (See **TERROR**)
Caused by. Sin. Moses killed an Egyptian & had to flee Egypt. 2:11-25
Deliverance from - Overcome by. Heeding God's threefold challenge. 14:13-15
Duty. To never be overcome by **f**. 14:10-12
Results - Causes one to.
Become despondent. 14:13-15, esp. 15
Complain, criticize others. 14:10-12
Make excuses. Fight against God's call. 3:11-4:17

FEARLESS - FEARLESSNESS (See **BOLDNESS; COURAGE**)
How to be **f**. By heeding God's threefold challenge. 14:13-15

FEAST - FEASTS
F. of Tabernacles. Hebrew Calendar. 12:1-2
F. of Unleavened Bread.
Discussed. 12:1-13:16 (pt.7); 12:14-20; Intro. VII, pt.22
Unbelievers not to participate in. 12:14-20, esp. 15, 19

FELLOWSHIP (See **BROTHERHOOD; NEIGHBOR; ONENESS; UNITY**)

FERVENT - FERVENCY (See **DILIGENCE; ENDURANCE; ZEAL**)

FICKLE - FICKLENESS (See **DOUBLE-MINDED; INSTABILITY; WAVERING**)

FIDELITY (See **DEDICATION; FAITHFULNESS**)

FIERCE (See **ANGER; HOSTILITY; VIOLENCE; WRATH**)

FIGHT - FIGHTING (See **ARGUMENT; CONTENTION; STRIFE**)

FILTHY - FILTHINESS (See **DEFILE - DEFILEMENT; ENVIRONMENT; POLLUTION; SIN; UNCLEANNESS**)
Caused by.
Flies covering everything. One of the plagues upon Egypt. 8:21
Frogs. One of the plagues upon Egypt. 8:5-6

FINANCES (See **GREED; MATERIALISM; MONEY; STEWARDSHIP**)

FINGER
Of God. Controls all things. 8:19

FIRE (See **HELL; JUDGMENT; LAKE OF FIRE**)

FIRE, PILLAR OF CLOUD & FIRE (See **CLOUD, PILLAR OF CLOUD & FIRE**)

FIRSTBORN - DEDICATION OF THE FIRSTBORN
Dedication of.
Discussed. 13:1-16; Intro. VII, pt.24
Was closely tied to the Passover. 12:1-13:16 (pt.1)
Inheritance of. listed. 4:20-23
Judgment of. Death of **f**. was one of the ten plagues against Egypt. 11:1-10; 12:21-51
Name - Title. Given to Israel. First time used. 4:20-23
Rights & privileges of. Described. 6:13-27

FLESH - FLESHLY LUSTS (See **CARNAL**)

FLY - FLIES (See **INSECTS**)
Fact. Was one of the plagues cast upon Egypt. 8:20-32
Plague of. Used by God to judge Egypt. 8:20-32

FOLLOW - FOLLOWING GOD (See **COMMITMENT; DEDICATION; GUIDANCE; OBEDIENCE**)

FOOD (See **MANNA; MEAT; NEEDS - NECESSITIES**)
Fact. Is one of the basic needs of man. 16:1-36

FOOD, SPIRITUAL (See **BREAD; BREAD OF LIFE; MANNA**)
Source. God. Provides the bread from heaven for us. 16:1-36; 16:31

FOREBEAR - FORBEARANCE (See **ENDURANCE; PERSEVERANCE; STEDFASTNESS**)

FORBEARANCE OF GOD (See **PATIENCE**, Of God)

FOREKNOWLEDGE OF GOD (See **CHOSEN; ELECTION; PREDESTINATION**)
Fact.
Predicted the deliverance of Israel from slavery. 3:7-8; 6:6-9
Predicted the promised land. 2:24; 3:13-22, esp. 17
Predicted the promised seed. 1:6-7
Remembered His covenant with Israel. 6:1-5

FOREORDAINED (See **CHOSEN; ELECTION; FOREKNOWLEDGE; PRE-DESTINATION**)

FORGETFULNESS, SPIRITUAL
F. of what.
One's commitment to obey God (Pharaoh). 8:7-8, see 8:15; 8:25-29, see 8:32; 9:27-28, see 9:34-35; 10:16-17, see 10:20; 10:24-26, see 10:29
One's commitment to trust & follow God. 14:10-12; 15:24; 16:1-3; 17:2-3

FORGIVENESS, SPIRITUAL (See **BLAMELESS; PARDON; REDEMPTION; REMISSION; SPOTLESS**)
Source. The blood of the sacrificial lamb, the Lord Jesus Christ. 12:1-13:16 (pt.4); 12:1-13; 12:21-28; Intro. VII, pt.18

FORNICATION (See **ADULTERY; IMMORALITY; LUST; SEX**)

FORSAKE - FORSAKING (See **BACKSLIDING; DENIAL; DESERTION; FALLING AWAY; SELF-DENIAL**)
Of God. Example of. Pharaoh. 8:15; 8:32
Of leaders. Israel failed to support Moses. 5:20-23; 14:10-12; 16:1-3; 17:2-3

FOUNDATION, SPIRITUAL
Of life. Is Jesus Christ. He is our Rock. 17:6
Typed - Symbolized - Pictured. By the Rock, the Lord Jesus Christ. 17:6; Intro. VII, pt.31

FOUNTAIN OF LIFE (See **WATER, LIVING; THIRST, SPIRITUAL**)

FREEDOM (See **SLAVERY; ENSLAVEMENT**)
Duty. No person, government, or armed force is to deny **f**. to people. 8:1
Fact.
A God-given right.
Is God's will for man. 6:1-5; 6:6-9; 7:15-16; 8:1; 8:20; 9:13-14
Is God's will for people. 5:1-23; 7:15-16; 8:1; 8:20
Why people are not freed. For economic & financial reasons. Egypt an example. 8:2-4; 11:1-10

FRIENDS - FRIENDSHIP (See **BROTHERHOOD**)

FRIGHT (See **FEAR**)

FROGS
Plague of **f**. Used by God to judge Egypt. 8:1-15

FRUITBEARING (See **ABUNDANCE; BELIEVER; DEDICATION; MINISTRY; REWARDS; SERVICE**)

FRUITFUL (See **ABUNDANCE; FULNESS, SPIRITUAL; FULFILLMENT; HUNGER, SPIRITUAL; SATISFACTION**)

FRUITLESS (See **UNFRUITFUL**)

FULNESS OF TIME
Fulfilled by Christ. 12:6-11

FULNESS, SPIRITUAL (See **ABUNDANCE; HUNGER, SPIRITUAL; SATISFACTION, SPIRITUAL**)

GEOGRAPHICAL LOCATIONS (See **CITIES - AREAS**)

GENEALOGY (See **CHARTS; DESCENDANTS; SEED or DESCENDANTS, GODLY**)
Of Aaron. 6:13-27
Of Jacob. 6:13-27
Of Moses. 6:13-27

GERSHOM (See **STRANGER - STRANGERS**)
Son of Moses. 18:1-8, esp. 3

GERSHON
Grandson of Jacob. Son of Levi. 6:13-27 (Chart)

GIFTS
Fact.
Egyptians gave **g**. to Israelites when they freed them. 3:13-22, esp. 21-22; 12:34-41, esp. 35-36
Principles. To request & accept gifts from oppressors. 3:13-22, esp. 21-22; 12:34-41, esp. 35-36

GIVE - GIVING (See **BENEVOLENCE; MINISTERING; STEWARDSHIP**)

GLORY OF GOD
Appeared to Israel. To rebuke & strike fear in them for sin. 16:4-15, esp. 9-10
Appeared to Moses. In the burning bush. 3:1-3
Discussed. Shekinah glory. 16:10
How God gains **g**. How God is glorified.
By executing justice & judgment. 14:16-18
By rebuking & striking fear in sinners. 16:4-15, esp. 9-10
By revealing Himself & calling men to serve Him. 3:1-10

GLORY, SHEKINAH (See **SHEKINAH GLORY**)

GLORYING IN MAN (See **ARROGANCE; BOASTING; HAUGHTINESS; PRIDE; SELF-SUFFICIENCY**)
Sin of.
Exalting man to be god. 5:2-14; 7:17
Exalting self (man) above God. 5:2-14, esp. 2; 7:17

GNATS (See **INSECTS**)
Was one of the plagues cast upon Egypt. 8:16-19

GOD
Anger of. (See **ANGER**, of God)
Appearance of. To Moses. In the burning bush. 3:1-3; 3:13-22, esp. 16
Faithfulness of. (See **FAITHFULNESS**, Of God)
Glory of. (See **GLORY OF GOD**)
Knowledge - Omniscience of.
Predicted the deliverance of Israel from slavery. 3:7-8; 6:6-9
Predicted the promised land. 2:24; 3:13-22, esp. 17
Predicted the promised seed. 1:6-7
Remembered His covenant with Israel. 6:1-5
Names - Titles - Identity.
Chart of names combined with Jehovah. 3:14-15
Discussed. 3:14-15
I AM. 3:14-15
Jehovah. Eighteen combined names. 3:14-15; 4:10-11
LORD. 4:10-11
LORD. 4:10-11; 6:1-5
The LORD is my Banner (Jehovah-Nissi). 17:15
The LORD who heals (Jehovah-Rophe). 15:26
Yahweh. 3:14-15
Nature - Attributes - What God is Like
Distinctive, unique. Has no equal; no one is like the LORD. 7:14-25; 8:1-15; 8:9-11; 9:14-16
Holy. (See **HOLY - HOLINESS**, Of God)
Is unchangeable. I AM. 3:14-15
Is living. 3:4-6
Is the God of true believers. 11:7-8
Is the Great Savior of mankind. 10:1-20
Is the LORD of mercy. 8:9-11
Is the LORD, the God of Redemption, the only living & true God. 7:14-25
Is the Redeemer in every land, all the world. 8:22-23
Power of - Omnipotence of.
Can stop men from standing before Him. 9:11
Controls all things, even the most minute, basic elements of the universe. 8:16-19
Controls the animal-life of the world. 9:1-7
Demonstrated in dividing the Red Sea. 14:1-31; 14:19-28
Demonstrated in freeing Israel from Egyptian slavery. 12:21-51
Demonstrated in the great Exodus from Egypt. 12:21-51
Described as. Finger of God. 8:16-19
Has power over all the land & every land. 8:22-23
Has power over mankind, over the food supply & all else. 10:1-20
Has power over the earth, its weather & natural disasters. 9:13-35
Has power over the reproduction of life. 8:9-11
Rules over body & health. 9:8-12
Rules over light & darkness. 10:23

Presence of. Promises.
To be with His dear servant. 3:11-12
To guide His dear people by day & by night. 13:20-22
Providence - Sovereignty of.
Chart: the God of History. 7:5
Controls all things, even the minute dust of the ground. 8:19
Controls all things, even the most minute, basic elements of the universe. 8:16-19
Controls the animal-life of the world. 9:1-7
Controls the animals & livestock of the world. 9:3-5
Controls the people, nations, rulers, & governments of the world. 9:14-16
Demonstrated in the ten plagues. 7:8-11:10; 9:14-16
Guided the birth & childhood of Moses. 2:5-8
Has no equal. There is no one like the LORD. 8:1-15
Has power over light & darkness. 10:21-29
Has power over the body & health. 9:11
Is involved in the affairs of men. 7:5
Is the God of every land. 8:22-23
Is the LORD of all power, the LORD who executes justice. 8:9-11
Is the LORD over the earth. 9:13-35
Rules over all things. 9:29-32
Wrath of. (See **JUDGMENT; WRATH**)

GODS, FALSE (See **IDOLATRY**)
Fact.
Are only the notions, ideas, & imaginations of men. 7:14-25
People worship & believe in all kinds of false gods. 7:14-25
List.
Of Egypt's false gods. 7:8-11:10 (pt.6)
Of men throughout history who worshipped themselves or other gods. 7:17
Who or what was thought to be a god.
Pharaoh. 7:17; 8:1-15
Spirit of man (humanism). 7:17; 8:1-15

GODLESS - GODLESSNESS (See **AGNOSTIC; ATHEISM; IDOLATRY; SIN; UNGODLY; UNRIGHTEOUSNESS**)

GODLY - GODLINESS (See **HOLY - HOLINESS; RIGHTEOUSNESS**)

GOOD - GOODNESS (See **GOOD WORKS; MINISTERING; SERVICE**)
Result.
Saved the life of Moses. 3:1-10
Saved the lives of children condemned by the king (Pharaoh). 1:15-21

GOOD WORKS (See **MINISTERING; SERVICE**)
Described as. Helping others. 18:1-27
Example of.
Aaron. Serving with Moses as his spokesman. 4:27-31; 6:28-7:7
Jethro. Helped Moses organize the judgeship of Israel. 18:13-27

354

GOSHEN, LAND OF
Discussed. 8:22

GOSSIP - GOSSIPERS (See **ACCUSATIONS, FALSE; BUSYBODIES; COMPLAINING; SLANDER; TONGUE**)

GOVERNMENT (See **CITIZENSHIP**)
Facing crises. Egyptian **g.** facing economic collapse from the ten plagues.
8:2-4; 9:2-3; 9:34-35; 10:24-26;
11:1-10
Fact. Is under the control of God.
9:14-16
Kinds of.
Evil. What a person is to do about evil **g.** 2:2
Theocratic. Under God's law.
18:13-26
Rebellion - Resistance to. What a person is to do about evil **g.** 2:2
Rulers. Officials of.
Magicians. (See **MAGICIANS**)
Pharaoh. (See **PHARAOH**)

GRACE (See **COMPASSION**, Of God; **MERCY**)

GRATITUDE (See **THANKFUL - THANKSGIVING**)

GREED (See **COVET - COVETOUSNESS**)
Example of. Pharaoh. Enslaving others for wealth & power. 8:2-4; 11:1-10
Results.
Brings the judgment of God upon one.
7:8-11:10
Causes men to oppress others. 1:8-22;
5:2-14; 8:2-4; 11:1-10

GREETING
Example of. Cordial **g.** by godly men.
Moses & Aaron. After 40 years separation. 4:27-32
Moses & Jethro, his father-in-law, after some absence. 18:1-8

GRIEF - GRIEVED (See **DISAPPOINTMENT; SORROW, GODLY**)
Caused by.
Complaining, grumbling. 14:10-12;
15:23; 16:1-3; 17:2-3
False accusations. 14:10-12; 15:23;
16:1-3; 17:2-3
Feeling that one has failed. 5:20-23
Of God. Caused by. Arguing, objecting to His call to service. 4:13-17

GRIPE - GRIPING (See **COMPLAINING; MURMURING; TONGUE**)

GROWTH, SPIRITUAL (See **NOURISHMENT, SPIRITUAL**)
List. Of men who arose early for daily devotions. 16:16-30
Source - How one grows.
By arising early for prayer & study of God's Word. 16:16-30; 16:31
By intercessory prayer. 17:8-16
By learning & teaching the Passover (God's judgment & salvation) to others. 12:21-28, esp. 26-27
By reverencing & humbling oneself before God. 3:1-10

GRUMBLE - GRUMBLING (See **COMPLAINING; MURMURING**)
Caused by.
Being upset with one's leader. 5:20-23; 17:2-3
Carnality. 14:10-12; 15:24; 16:1-3; 17:2-3
Questioning God's care & provision.
14:10-12; 15:24; 16:1-3; 17:2-3
Unbelief. 14:10-12; 15:24; 16:1-3;
17:2-3
Characteristic - Trait. Of carnal, distrustful persons. 14:10-12; 15:24; 16:1-3;
17:2-3
Discussed. 15:22-27; 15:24
Fact. Is not against God's servants, but against God Himself. 16:4-15
Of Israel.
At Egypt. Against Moses. Because of Pharaoh's reaction against him: more intense oppression. 5:20-23
At Marah. Over bitter water. 15:22-27; 15:24
At Rephidim. Because of no water.
17:1-7
At the Red Sea. Faced with an impossible situation. 14:10-12
At the wilderness of Sin. Because of no food. 16:1-3
One of two great sins of Israel. 16:1-36; 16:1-3
Results. Causes pain, hurt. 5:20-23;
14:13-15, esp. 15; 15:22-27; 15:25; 17:4

GUIDANCE
Of God.
Leads believers away from trouble.
13:17-18
Leads believers by day & by night.
13:17-22
Leads believers by His presence.
13:20-22
Led Israel by the pillar of cloud & fire.
13:20-22
Results. Fivefold. 15:13-18, esp. 14-16

GUILT (See **JUDGMENT; SHAME**)
Caused by.
A false profession. 9:27-28
Disobeying God & suffering His judgment. 9:27-28; 12:30-33, esp. 32

HAIL (See **STORMS**)
Was one of the ten plagues cast upon Egypt. 9:13-35

HALF-HEARTED (See **BACKSLIDING; COMPROMISE; DOUBLE-MINDED; FICKLENESS; INCONSISTENT; INDECISIVE; INSTABILITY; NEUTRALITY**)
Caused by. Greed for wealth, position, power, fame. 10:7-11; 10:24-26
Example of. Pharaoh tried to do one half of what God demanded. 10:7-11;
10:24-26

HAND
Meaning. Hebrew meaning. 4:13-17

HAND OF GOD (See **JUDGMENT**)
Controls the animal life of the world.
9:1-7
Meaning. The judgment of God. 3:13-22,
esp. 20; 9:2-3
The power of God. 3:13-22, esp. 20

HANOCH
Grandson of Jacob. Son of Reuben. 6:13-27 (Chart)

HAPPY - HAPPINESS (See **JOY; REJOICING**)
Source - Stirred by.
Deliverance, salvation of God: through the greatest of obstacles (Red Sea).
15:1-21
Reunion of brothers. 4:27-31
Reunion of family. 18:9-12

HARD - HARDENED - HARDNESS OF HEART (See **HEART; REJECTION; UNBELIEF**)
Described. Nature of. Five things. 13:17-18:27
Discussed. Judicial judgment of God.
4:21; 10:1; 10:27-29
Persons who were **h.** Pharaoh. 4:21;
7:14; 8:15; 8:19; 8:32; 9:7; 9:12; 9:17-21; 9:34-35; 10:1; 10:27-29

HATE - HATRED (See **ANGER; HOSTILITY; MALICE; RAGE**)

HAUGHTY - HAUGHTINESS (See **ARROGANCE; BOASTING; PRIDE; SELF-SUFFICIENCY**)

HEAL - HEALING
Source. God.
Has power over the human body.
9:8-12
The LORD (Jehovah Rophe). 15:26

HEALTH
Chart. Of diseases & physical problems.
9:10
Facts.
Not controlled by man, not in the final analysis. 9:8-12
Power over. Controlled by God. 9:8-12

HEAR - HEARING (See **OBEDIENCE**)
Duty.
To believe God's glorious message of deliverance. 4:27-31, esp. 31
To diligently **h.** the commandments of God. 15:26-27
Results. Will be healed by the power of God. 15:26-27

HEART (See **COMPASSION; DEPRAVITY**)
Kind of.
Hard **h.** (See **HARD - HARDENED**)
4:21; 13:17-18:27
Unwilling **h.** 5:2-14, esp. 2

HEAVEN (See **EARTH & HEAVEN, NEW**)
Duty. To journey to **h.** living at peace with others. 13:17-18 (Thgt.2)
Journey to **h.**
Are led by the very presence of God Himself. 13:20-22
Must walk living at peace with others.
13:17-18 (Thgt.2)
Symbolized, pictured by the wilderness wanderings. 13:17-18:27
(pt.B, 2)

Will face all kinds of trials & problems along the journey.
    Bitter water (trials). 15:22-27
    Hunger. 16:1-36
    Overwork. 18:1-27
    Thirst. 17:1-7
    Warfare. 17:8-16
Symbol - Type of. Land of Canaan. 2:24

HEAVEN & EARTH, NEW
Discussed. 2:24
Fact. Will be recreated into a new **h**. 2:24

HEAVENLY BODIES (See **HEAVEN & EARTH, NEW; OUTER SPACE**)

HEAVY - HEAVINESS (See **BURDEN; BROKEN-HEARTED; COMPASSION; SORROW, GODLY**)

HEBREWS (See **ISRAEL**)

HEBRON
Descendent of Jacob. Grandson of Levi. 6:13-27 (Chart)

HELL (See **JUDGMENT; LAKE OF FIRE**)

HELP - HELPING (See **GIVE - GIVING; GOOD WORKS; MINISTERING; SERVICE**)
Described as. Helping others. 18:1-27
Example of.
    Aaron. Serving with Moses as his spokesman. 4:27-31; 6:28-7:7
    Jethro. Helped Moses organize the judgeship of Israel. 18:13-27

HELPLESS - HELPLESSNESS (See **DESPERATION; HOPELESS – HOPELESSNESS**)
Answer - Solution to **h**.
    God's power to deliver through trials. 14:1-31; 15:22-27
    God's power to feed man. 16:1-36
    God's power to give us victory over all enemies. 17:8-16
    God's power to give water. 15:22-27; 17:1-7
    God's power to guide us through life. 13:17-22
    God's power to solve the hunger of life. 16:1-36
    God's power to solve the thirst of life. 15:22-27
Caused by.
    Impossible, hopeless situations, obstacles, trials, & temptations. 14:13-15, esp. 15; 15:24; 17:4
    Not understanding God's timing. 5:20-23

HERBS
Bitter **h**. Eaten at Passover. Symbolized bitter trials of slavery. 12:6-11, esp. 8; Intro. VII, pt.19

HERITAGE, SPIRITUAL (See **INHERITANCE**)

HEZRON
Grandson of Jacob. Son of Reuben. 6:13-27 (Chart)

HIDE - HID (See **SECRET - SECRECY; SIN**, Secret **s.**)
Example. Moses was forced to **h**. from Pharaoh because of murder. 2:11-25
Moses' mother **h**. him as a baby to save his life. 2:1-10

HIGH-MINDED (See **ARROGANCE; BOASTING; PRIDE; SELF-SUFFICIENCY**)

HISTORY
God & **h**. Chart: the God of history. His involvement in **h**. 7:5
Of Egypt. General Survey of. Intro. VI
Of Israel. Was in Egypt for 430 years. 12:40-41

HITTITES
Land of. Promised to Israel. 3:7-8; 3:8

HIVITES
Land of. Promised to Israel. 3:7-8; 3:8

HOARDING
Example of. Israel gathering & **h**. the manna (bread). Distrusting God's daily provision. 16:16-30

HOLD FAST (See **ENDURANCE; PERSEVERANCE; STEDFASTNESS**)

HOLIDAYS
Religious **h**. Duty. To observe. Importance of. 12:15-16

HOLY - HOLINESS
Of God.
    Duty. To reverence & fear God's **h**. 3:4-6
    Meaning. 3:4-6

HONEST - HONESTY (See **TRUSTWORTHY**)

HONOR - HONORED (See **GLORY; PRIDE; RECOGNITION**)

HOPE (See **INHERITANCE; SPIRITUAL; REWARD**)
For what.
    Deliverance from God's judgment. 12:1-13:16
    Deliverance from oppression & slavery. 1:1-22; 1:18-22; 2:23-25; 4:20-23; 5:1-23; 6:1-7:7; 12:1-13:16
    Deliverance through the wilderness of this world to the promised land of heaven. 13:17-18:27
    The promised land (symbol of heaven). 2:24; 4:13-22; 6:1-5; 6:6-9, esp. 8; 13:17-18:27
    The promised seed. 1:6-7

HOPELESS - HOPELESSNESS (See **DESPERATION; DISAPPOINTMENT; HELPLESSNESS**)
Caused by. Unbelief. Failure to trust God's care & provision. 14:10-12; 15:22-27; 16:1-3; 17:1-7
Results. Complaining, grumbling, murmuring. 14:10-12; 15:24; 16:1-3; 17:2-3

HOREB, MOUNT
Discussed. 3:1

HORSE
Use of. In the military. By Egypt. 14:5-9

HOSPITALITY (See **GREETING**)
Example of. Moses. Receiving his father-in-law, Jethro, after a long absence. 18:1-8

HOSTILITY (See **ANGER; VIOLENCE; RAGE; WRATH**)
Caused by.
    A hard heart, the rejection of God. 10:27-29
    Choosing Christ over the world's riches & power. 2:13-15
    Proclaiming the Word of God. 5:1-23
Result.
    Oppression. 1:8-22; 5:1-23
    Persecution of believers. 1:8-22

HUMANISM - HUMANIST
Error of.
    Exalting man to be god. 5:2-14, esp. 2; 7:17; 8:1-15
    Many believe that the combined spirit of man is god. 8:1-15
List of men who worship man. 7:17

HUMILIATE - HUMILIATION (See **ABASED - SHAME**)

HUMILITY (See **MEEKNESS; UNWORTHY**)
Example of. Moses. When God called, Moses felt incapable. 3:11-12

HUNGER & THIRST (See **HUNGER & THIRST, SPIRITUAL**)
Caused by. Wilderness, deserts of this world as the believer journeys to the promised land.
    Bitter water at Marah: bitter experiences made sweet. 15:22-27
    Hunger in the wilderness: God's provision of heavenly bread. 16:1-36
    Thirst in the wilderness: God's provision of water. 17:1-7
Crisis of. Third crisis of Israel in the wilderness. Two great sins of Israel: complaining & unbelief. 16:1-36
Results.
    Leads to complaining, grumbling. 16:1-36
    Lusting after the flesh pots of this world. 16:1-3

HUNGER & THIRST, SPIRITUAL (See **ABUNDANCE; FULNESS, SPIRITUAL; LIFE; SATISFACTION**)
Answer to.
    God's provision. 15:25; 15:27
    Jesus Christ. 17:5-6; 17:6
    Keeping the LORD's day. 16:16-30
    The manna, the bread of God. 16:1-36; 16:16-30; 16:31
Caused by.
    Bitter waters (trials) of this world. 15:22-23
    Lusting after the flesh pots of this world. 16:1-3
    Unbelief & distrust. 15:24; 16:1-3; 17:2-3

HUR
Prevailed in prayer with Moses. 17:10-12

HYKSOS
Nation of people who conquered Egypt. 1:8

HYPOCRISY - HYPOCRITE - HYPO-CRITICAL (See DECEIT; LYING; PROFESSION, FALSE)
Of false messengers. Pharaoh's magicians imitated the miracle performed by Moses. 8:7-8; 8:16-18

HYSSOP
Fact.
Was a small, bushy plant with leaves that absorbed liquid. 12:21-28
Was used at the Passover. To smear the lamb's blood on the door frame. 12:21-28

I AM (See NAME - NAMES)
Discussed. 3:14-15

I WILLS
Of God. Seven "I wills." 6:6-9

IDOLS - IDOLATRY (See GODS, FALSE)
Discussed. The gods of Egypt—in the ten plagues. Chart. 7:8-11:10 (pt.6)
Example of or list of **I.** or false gods.
Of Egypt. 7:8-11:10 (pt.6)
Of men through history who exalted themselves to be God. 7:7
Of rulers who exalted themselves above God (Pharaoh). 7:17; 8:1-15
Fact.
Is despised by God. 9:1-7; 9:8-12
Is universal: people believe in & worship all kinds of things. 7:14-25; 8:1-15; 8:20-32; 9:1-7
Is utterly foolish for people to worship. 7:14-25
Judgment of. God plagued Egypt because of **I.** 8:19; 8:20-32; 9:3-5
Nature of.
Are only false gods created by man's imaginations. 7:14-25
God's power over demonstrated in the ten plagues. 7:8-11:10; 7:20-22; 8:9-11; 8:19; 9:3-5
Of Egypt. Described. 7:17; 8:1-15; 8:9-11; 8:20-32; 9:3-5; 9:8-12
Of Israel. Worshipped the false gods of Egypt. 2:23-25; 3:13-22

IGNORANCE - IGNORANT
About God.
Caused by. Hard heart. 7:22-25; 8:19; 8:32; 9:7; 9:12; 9:34-35; 10:20; 10:27-29; 11:9-10
Caused by. Rejection of God. 5:2-14, esp. 2

IGNORE - IGNORING (See NEGLECT - NEGLECTING)

ILLOGICAL
What is **i.**
Hard heart. 7:22-25; 8:19; 8:32; 9:7; 9:12; 9:34-35; 10:20; 10:27-29; 11:9-10
Rejection of God. 10:27-29

IMAGINATIONS, EVIL
Results. Creates false gods. (See IDOLATRY)

IMMATURITY, SPIRITUAL (See CARNAL)

IMMORALITY (See LUST; SIN; WORLDLY - WORLDLINESS)

IMMORTALITY (See ETERNAL LIFE; HEAVEN; LAND, PROMISED)

IMMUTABLE - IMMUTABILITY (See GOD, Nature)

IMPARTIAL - IMPARTIALITY (See DISCRIMINATION; FAVORITISM; PREJUDICE)

IMPATIENCE
What caused **i.**
A heart hardened against God's Word & God's messenger. 10:27-29
People who reject God time & again. 11:7-8
Unbelief, grumbling, murmuring. 14:10-12; 15:24; 16:1-3; 17:2-3

IMPENITENT - IMPENITENCE (See HARD OF HEART; REBELLION; STUBBORN)

IMPERFECTION (See SIN; UNBELIEF)

IMPURE - IMPURITY (See DEFILEMENT; UNCLEANNESS)

INCONSISTENCY - INCONSISTENT (See COMPROMISE; DOUBLE-MINDED; HALF-HEARTED; WAVERING)
Caused by.
False religion & worship. 3:8
Greed, love of money. 10:7-11; 10:24-26
Lusting for the food & satisfactions of the world. 16:1-36
Lusting for the security of the world instead of the trials of following God. 14:10-12
Lusting for the wells (pleasures, indulgences) of the world. 15:22-27; 17:1-7
Worldliness: lusting after sex, pleasure, & possessions. 3:8
Example of. Israel. 14:10-12; 15:22-27; 16:1-36; 17:1-7

INDECISION - INDECISIVE (See DOUBLE-MINDED; HALF-HEARTED; WAVERING)

INDEPENDENT - INDEPENDENCE (See SELF-SUFFICIENCY)

INDIFFERENCE (See HARDNESS OF HEART; STUBBORN)

INDIGNATION (See ANGER; RAGE; WRATH)

INDULGE - INDULGENCE (See LUST; WORLDLINESS)

INFIDEL (See AGNOSTIC, ATHEIST, UNBELIEVER)

INGRATITUDE
Caused by.
Grumbling, complaining, murmuring. 12:10-12; 15:22-27; 16:1-36; 17:1-7
Unbelief. 12:10-12; 15:22-27; 16:1-36; 17:1-7
Example of. Israel's **i.** to Moses. 12:10-12; 17:2-3

INHERITANCE, EARTHLY
Promised. To Israel. 2:24; 3:7-8; 3:13-22, esp. 17; 6:6-9

INHERITANCE, SPIRITUAL (See HOPE; PROMISES; REWARD)
Promised. To believers. 2:24; 3:7-8; 3:13-22, esp. 17; 6:6-9

INIQUITY (See SIN)

INITIATIVE (See FERVENCY; ZEAL)

INJUSTICE (See DECEPTION; STEALING)

INSANE - INSANITY
Caused by. Hard heart. 10:27-29

INSECT
Kinds.
Flies. 8:21
Lice (or gnats). 8:16-18
Locusts. 10:4-6
Maggots. 16:16-30, esp. 20

INSECURE - INSECURITY (See DOUBLE-MINDEDNESS; FEAR; INCONSISTENCY; WAVERING)

INSENSITIVE - INSENSITIVITY (See COMPLACENT; DULL - DULLNESS, SPIRITUAL; HARD - HARDNESS; HEART, HARD; SLOTHFUL)

INSTABILITY (See BACKSLIDING; COMPROMISE; DOUBLE-MINDED; FICKLENESS; HALF-HEARTED)

INSTRUCT - INSTRUCTION
Duty.
To **i.** that God is the God of salvation & deliverance. 13:1-16
To **i.** the judgment of God to children. 10:1-2
To **i.** the Passover, that Jesus Christ is the Lamb of God. 12:21-28
To **i.** three great lessons. 13:11-16
To see **i.** as a gift from God. 2:2

INSUFFICIENT - INSUFFICIENCY
Feelings of. Moses. 3:11-12

INTEGRITY (See HONEST - HONESTY)

INTELLIGENCE (See KNOWLEDGE; UNDERSTANDING)

INTERCESSION (See PRAYER)
Example of. Nine great Biblical examples of **i.** 8:30-31
Of Moses.
Cried out to God because the people attacked & grumbled against him. 5:20-23; 15:25; 17:4
Cried out to God for water. 15:25

Interceded for the lost souls of Egypt, for God to remove judgment. 8:12-14; 9:33
Interceded for victory in war. 17:8-16
Results. Stops the judgment of God. 8:12-14; 8:30-31; 9:33; 10:18-19

INTOLERANCE (See **BIGOTRY; DIS-CRIMINATION; PREJUDICE**)

INVITATION (See **CALL; DECISION**)

IRRESPONSIBLE - IRRESPONSIBILI-TY (See **INCONSISTENCY; SIN**)

ISRAEL
Chosen by God. New race of people created by God Himself. 1:1-22
Crises of. (See **ISRAEL, Trials - Crises of**)
Deliverance of.
　Deliverance through the Red Sea. 14:1-31
　Song of Praise. After God's great deliverance through the Red Sea. 15:1-21
Enslavement of. By Egypt.
　Discussed. Three major persecutions. 1:8-22
　Groaned & cried for deliverance. 2:23-24
Exodus of. Took Joseph's bones with them. 13:19
Failure - Sins of.
　Attacked, grumbled against Moses. 5:20-23; 14:10-12; 15:24; 16:1-3; 17:2-3
　Compromised with the Canaanites, their immorality & worldliness. 3:8
　Ignorance about God. 3:13-22
　Tested God: questioned Him; demanded He prove Himself. 17:2-3
　Worshipped the false gods of Egypt. 2:23-25; 3:13-22
Faith of Israel.
　Believed & obeyed God by fleeing Egypt (the world) just as God instructed. 12:21-28; 12:34-41; 12:50
　Believed & obeyed God by hiding behind the blood of the lamb. 12:21-28
　Believed the promised, the covenant of God. 13:19
　Repented & cried out to God. 2:23-25
History of.
　Delivered through the Red Sea. 14:1-31
　Freed from Egyptian slavery. Numbered over two million people. 12:34-41
　Freed from Egyptian slavery. Requested silver, gold, & clothing from the Egyptians. 12:34-41
　Greatest event was the deliverance from Egyptian slavery. 12:1-13:16
　How Israel escaped the judgment of God. 12:34-41
　In Egypt for 430 years. 12:40-41
　Israel's First Great Emancipation; First Day of Independence. 12:21-51
　Israel's great freedom march. 12:34-41
In Egypt.
　A holocaust, an attempt to decrease the population. 1:8-22
　Enslaved & oppressed by Egypt. 1:8-22

Enslaved. Suffered brutality & savage oppression. 1:8-22; 7:8-11:10
King who enslaved Israel. 1:8
Was in Egypt 430 years. 1:1-5
Were ignorant of God & idolatrous. 3:13-22
Why God led Israel into Egypt. 1:1-5
Judgment of. Reasons for j. Idolatry. Israel worshipped the false gods of Egypt. 2:23-25; 3:13-22
Military of. Commander-in-chief. Joshua appointed by Moses. 17:8-9
Names - Titles. God's Son, His firstborn. First time used in Scripture. 4:20-23
Needs met. By God.
　Gave food. 16:1-36
　Gave water. 15:25; 17:1-7
Persecution - Oppression of. By Egypt. Brutal, savage oppression. 1:8-22; 2:23-25; 5:2-14; 7:15-16
Population of. Great growth of. 1:6-7
Purpose of. Fivefold purpose. 1:1-22; 9:1
Test - testing of. (See **TEST - TEST-ING, Of Israel**)
Trials - Crises of.
　1st crisis in the wilderness wanderings: Crossing the Red Sea. God's Great Deliverance. 14:1-31
　2nd crisis in the wilderness wanderings: Bitter Water at Marah. Bitter experience made sweet. 15:22-27
　3rd crisis in the wilderness wanderings: Hunger. The two great sins of Israel. 16:1-36
　4th crisis in the wilderness wanderings: Thirst. God's Provision. 17:1-7
　5th crisis in the wilderness wanderings: War - warfare. Victory through prevailing prayer. 17:8-16
　6th crisis in the wilderness wanderings: Separation & overwork. Helping others. 18:1-27

ITHAMAR
Son of Aaron. 6:13-27 (Chart)

IZHAR
Descendent of Jacob. Grandson of Levi. 6:13-27 (Chart)

JACHIN
Grandson of Jacob. Son of Simeon. 6:13-27 (Chart)

JAMIN
Grandson of Jacob. Son of Simeon. 6:13-27 (Chart)

JEHOVAH (See **NAME - NAMES**)
Chart. Of names combined with Jehovah. 3:14-15
Discussed. 3:14-15; 4:10-11
I AM. 3:14-15

JEMUEL
Grandson of Jacob. Son of Simeon. 6:13-27 (Chart)

JESUS CHRIST
Blood of. (See **JESUS CHRIST**, Death)
　Is necessary to stay behind or under His blood. 12:21-28
　Pictured (typed, symbolized) in the Passover Lamb. Discussed. 12:1-13:16

Results. Delivers from judgment. 12:1-13:16; 12:1-13; 12:21-51; Intro. VII, pt.18
Death.
　Pictured (typed, symbolized) in the Passover Lamb. Discussed. 12:1-13:16
　Results.
　　Delivers from judgment. 12:1-13:16; 12:1-13; 12:21-51; Intro. VII, pt.15
　　Symbolized. Makes the bitter experiences of life sweet. 15:25, Thgt.2
Resurrection. Pictured in the Hebrew Calendar. 12:1-2
Return of. Pictured in the Hebrew Calendar. 12:1-2
Typed - Symbolized - Pictured.
　As the Bread of Life. 16:1-36; 16:31; Intro. VII, pt.30
　As the Lamb of God. 12:5; Intro. VII, pt.16
　As the living water. 17:5-6; Intro. VII, pt.31
　As the Rock, the Stone. 17:6; Intro. VII, pt.31

JETHRO OR REUEL
Moses' father-in-law. Gave Moses fatherly counsel about organization & delegation of responsibility. 18:13-27

JEWS (See **HEBREWS; ISRAEL**)

JOSEPH
Fact. Bones were taken to the promised land. Great faith. 13:19

JOSHUA
Leader of Israel.
　Appointed commander of Israel's military. By Moses. 17:8-9
　Defeated the Amalekites. 17:8-16

JOY (See **HAPPINESS; REJOICING**)
Source of - Stirred by.
　Deliverance.
　　God's glorious deliverance of a people, a nation. 14:1-31
　　Praising God for His great deliverance from an impossible situation (Red Sea). 15:1-21
　Reunion: with family after years of separation. 18:1-8

JUDGING OTHERS (See **BLAME - BLAMING; CRITICISM; DIVISION; SLANDER**)

JUDGMENT (See **DAMNED; HELL; JUDICIAL JUDGMENT OF GOD; JUSTICE; WRATH OF GOD**)
How to escape j.
　By prayer, intercession. 8:12-14
　By teaching the j. of God to children. 10:1-2
　By the LORD, His mercy & grace. 10:1-2
　Demonstrated by Israel. 12:34-44
　Illustrated in the Passover. 12:21-28
Example of. Egypt (See **PLAGUES, TEN**)
Fact. Ten plagues stand as a picture of God's j. for all generations. 10:1-2

Purpose of.
Discussed. 9:14-16; 10:1-2; 11:9-10
How God gains glory by executing **j**.
14:16-18
Seen in the ten plagues cast upon
Egypt. 7:4-11:10
Severalfold. 11:9-10
Threefold. 10:1-2
Twofold. 9:11; 9:14-16
Reasons for **j**. - Why God **j**.
Brutality & savage treatment of
people. 7:8-11:10; 7:20-22; 10:21-
29
Failing to get rid of all leaven (evil).
12:14-20, esp. 15, 19
Greed: love of money, wealth, eco-
nomic security. 8:2-4; 10:1-20
Hardness of heart. 7:8-13; 7:14
Idolatry. 7:8-11:10; 7:14-25; 7:20-22;
8:9-11; 8:16-18; 8:19; 8:20-32;
10:21-29
Living an evil life. 9:14-16, esp. 15
Rejection of God & the oppression of
people. 7:8-11:10; 7:20-22; 8:1-15;
8:2-4; 8:5-6; 8:16-18; 8:21; 9:2-3;
10:1-20; 10:21-29
Sinful living: indulgence, extravagance,
luxury, ease. 7:20-22; 9:17-21;
10:1-2; 10:1-20; 10:21-29
Surety of.
Against those who reject God. 7:17-
19; 7:20-22; 8:5-6; 8:16-18; 8:24;
9:2-3; 9:3-5; 9:22-26; 10:1-2; 10:4-6;
10:12-15; 11:1-3; 11:4-6; 12:29
Demonstrated by Israel. 12:30-33

JUDGMENT, JUDICIAL (See **JUST -
JUSTICE**)
Caused by. Hard hearts. 4:21; 10:1
Purpose. To rectify all the wrongs done
to people. 10:1-20
Upon whom. Egypt. Plagues, The Ten.
Chart. 7:8-11:10
A catastrophic hail & thunderstorm.
9:13-15
Boils afflicted man & animal. 9:8-12
Darkness covered the land. 10:21-29
Death of the firstborn. 11:1-10;
12:21-51
Disease & death of livestock. 9:1-7
Flies swarmed over the land. 8:20-32
Frogs everywhere. 8:1-15
Lice or gnats infested the land.
8:16-19
Locust swarmed over the land.
10:1-20
Water turned to blood. 7:14-25

JUST - JUSTICE (See **JUDGMENT,
JUDICIAL**)
Fact. God executes **j**. 10:1-3
Of God.
How God gains glory by executing **j**.
14:16-18
Proven by His execution of **j**. upon
Egypt. 10:1-3; 12:21-51; 14:16-18;
14:19-28
Was executed upon the Egyptians.
12:21-51

JUSTIFIED - JUSTIFICATION (See
PERFECTION; RIGHTEOUSNESS)
Source - How a person is **j**.
Believing the promises of God. 12:5
The blood of Christ. 12:5

KEEP - KEEPING (See **OBEDIENCE**)
Duty.
To **k**. believing & trusting God.
15:24; 16:1-3; 17:2-3
To **k**. God's commandments. 15:25-26
To **k**. the Sabbath Day. 16:16-30

KEPT - KEEPING POWER OF GOD
(See **ASSURANCE; PREDESTINA-
TION; SECURITY**)

KILL - KILLING (See **MURDER**)

KIND - KINDNESS (See **CARE - CAR-
ING; COMPASSION; GRACE; MER-
CY; MINISTERING**)

KING (See **PHARAOH**)
Of Egypt. (See **EGYPT; PHARAOH**)

KINGDOM OF GOD
Fact. Pictured. In the Hebrew Calendar.
12:1-2

KINSHIP (See **BROTHERHOOD; FAMI-
LY**)

KNOW - KNOWING - KNOWLEDGE
(See **INSIGHT; SPIRITUAL SIGHT;
UNDERSTANDING**)
How to **k**. God.
By praying & studying His Word.
12:14; 16:16-30
By the blood of the Lamb (Jesus
Christ). 12:1-13:16; 12:1-13
By walking in newness of life. 12:17-19
Knowledge of God. Lack of.
List of men who did not **k**. God. 7:17
Lack of. Not **k**. God. (See **IGNOR-
ANCE**, About God)

KOHATH
Grandson of Jacob. Son of Levi. 6:13-27
(Chart)

KORAH
Descendent of Jacob & Levi. Grandson
of Kohath. 6:13-27 (Chart)

LABOR - LABORERS (See **WORK, SEC-
ULAR; EMPLOYEES - EMPLOYERS**)
Dangers of. Overwork. 18:13-27
Duty.
To be diligent in all **l**. 18:13-27
To guard against overwork. 18:13-27
Kinds of.
Enslaved **l**. 1:11-14; 3:7-8; 3:9-10;
6:6-9, esp. 6
Hard, exhaustive **l**. 1:11-14; 18:13-27

LAMB
Discussed. Passover Lamb. 12:1-13:16;
12:21-28; Intro. VII, pt.16
Sacrificial **l**. Symbol - Type - Picture of.
Jesus Christ. 12:1-13:16; 12:21-28; In-
tro. VII, pt.16
Symbol - Type - Picture of. Jesus Christ.
12:1-13:16; 12:21-28; Intro. VII, pt.16

LAMB OF GOD
Christ is the Lamb of God.
Discussed. 12:1-13:16; 12:21-28; In-
tro. VII, pt.16
Symbolized - Typed - Pictured by.
Passover lamb. 12:1-13:16; 12:21-
28; Intro. VII, pt.16

LAMB, PASSOVER
Discussed. 12:1-13:16; 12:21-28; Intro.
VII, pt.16

LAND (See **CITIES - AREAS**)
Fact. God is the God of every **l**. 8:22-23

LAND, PROMISED
Believed in. By Moses. 2:15-22, esp. 22
Described. As spacious & flowing with
milk & honey. 3:7-8
Discussed. 2:24
Remembered. By God. 2:23-25
Symbol - Type - Picture of. Promised
land of heaven. 2:24; 3:7-8; 12:21-28,
esp.25

LAW - LAWS (See **COMMANDMENT;
LAW, CIVIL**)
Breaking the **l**. Example. Moses. Killed
an Egyptian. 2:11-12
Evil **l**.
Of Egypt. A murderous law to kill all
newborn Israelite boys. 1:15-21
What a person is to do about evil **l**.
2:2

LAYMEN (See **BELIEVERS**)

LEAD - LEADER (See **GUIDANCE;
STAFF**)
Called by God.
Aaron. 4:13-17; 4:27-31; 6:13-27, esp.
13; 7:1-7
Moses. Saved by his mother's faith &
courage. 2:1-10
Fact. God Himself was the **l**. of Israel.
13:17-22
Heart of.
Must have a heart of service, diligent,
exhaustive service. 18:13-27
Needs heart of a shepherd. Example
of. Moses. 3:1-3

LEAD, THE HEAVY METAL
Use of. To symbolize the drowning of the
Egyptian army. 15:3-12, esp. 10

LEADING ASTRAY (See **BACKSLID-
ING**)

LEAVEN
Symbol - Type - Picture of. Evil. 12:14;
12:15-16; 12:17-19; 12:19; Intro. VII,
pt.21
Was not allowed in the Passover. 12:14-
20; 12:34-41, esp. 39

LEGACY (See **HERITAGE; ROOTS;
GENEALOGY; HISTORY**)

LEPROSY
Discussed. 4:6-7; 9:8-12 (Chart)
Symbol - Type. Of Sin. 4:6-7

LETHARGY (See **LABOR - LABOR-
ERS; SLOTHFUL**)

LEVI
Genealogy. Chart of. 6:13-27
Son of Jacob. 6:13-27 (Chart)

LEVITES
Division of. Divided into three families.
6:13-27

LIBERATOR (See **FREEDOM; LIB-ERTY**)
Who was a l.
God. 12:1-13:16; 12:21-51; 13:17-18:17
Moses. 12:1-13:16; 12:21-51; 13:17-18:17

LIBERTY (See **FREEDOM**)
Duty. No person, government, or armed force is to deny f. to people. 8:1
Fact. A God-given right.
Is God's will for man. 6:1-5; 6:6-9; 7:15-16; 8:1; 8:20; 9:13-14
Is God's will for people. 5:1-23; 7:15-16; 8:1; 8:20
Why people are not freed. For economic & financial reasons. Egypt an example. 8:2-4

LIBINI
Descendent of Jacob. Grandson of Levi. 6:13-27 (Chart)

LICE (See **INSECTS**)
Fact. Was one of the ten plagues cast upon Egypt. 8:16-19

LIE - LYING - LIARS
Example of Pharaoh. Promised to free the enslaved Israelites, then changed time & again. 8:7-8; 8:25-29; 9:27-28; 10:16-17; 10:24-26

LIFE (See **REDEEM - REDEMPTION; SALVATION**)
Nature.
Is a pilgrimage of faith. 13:17-18:27 (pt.A, 3); Intro. VII, pt.25
Is a walk through the *wilderness wanderings* of the world. 13:17-18:27; Intro. VII, pt.25
New l. (See **NEW LIFE**)
Value of. Is of little value to societies of history. 1:22

LIFE, ETERNAL (See **ETERNAL LIFE; HEAVEN; LAND, THE PROMISED**)

LINE or DESCENDANTS, THE PROMISED (See **SEED, THE PROMISED; SEED, THE GODLY**)

LIPS UNCIRCUMCISED
Symbolized. Unworthiness. 6:10-12, esp. 12; 6:28-7:5, esp. 6:30

LISTEN - LISTENING (See **HEAR - HEARING; OBEDIENCE**)

LIVESTOCK
Fact. Death of. Was one of the ten plagues of Egypt. 9:1-7

LIVING WATER (See **WATER, LIVING; THIRST, SPIRITUAL**)

LOCUST
Fact. Was one of the ten plagues cast upon Egypt. 10:1-20

LONELY - LONELINESS (See **BELIEVERS; BROTHERHOOD; CHURCH; FELLOWSHIP; FRIENDSHIP; HOPE**)

LONGSUFFERING (See **ENDURANCE; PATIENCE**)
Of God.
In dealing with Israel in the wilderness wanderings. 17:5-6
Is l., giving chance after chance to repent. 10:4-6; 10:21-29
Over the rejection of rulers & nations. Over the idolatry, evil, & brutal enslavement of people, & the rejection of God. 7:8-11:10; 7:14-25; 7:17; 8:1-15; 8:9-11; 8:16-19; 8:20-32; 9:1-7; 9:3-5; 9:8-12; 9:13-35; 10:1-2; 10:21-29; 11:1-10; 12:21-29; 12:21-51

LOOKED
Meaning. 2:11, pt.3

LORD'S DAY, THE
Duty. To keep every week. 16:16-30

LORD, ANGEL OF
Appearances of.
To Israel. In the pillar of cloud & fire. 13:20-22
To Moses. In the burning bush. 3:1-3
Identity. Discussed. 3:1-3
Work of.
To call believers to service. 3:1-3
To guide & lead God's people. 13:20-22

LORD, THE (See **NAME - NAMES**)
Discussed. 3:14-15; 4:10-11
Meaning. Basic meaning. 6:1-5

LOST, THE (See **UNBELIEVER; UNGODLY; UNRIGHTEOUS; UNSAVED**)

LOVE (See **BROTHERHOOD**)

LOW - LOWLINESS - LOWLINESS OF MIND (See **HUMILITY; MEEKNESS**)

LOYAL - LOYALTY (See **COMMITMENT; DEDICATION**)

LUKEWARM (See **BACKSLIDING; COMPROMISE; DOUBLE-MINDED; DISOBEDIENT; FICKLE; HALF-HEARTED; INCONSISTENT; INSTABILITY; NEUTRALITY; UNFAITHFULNESS**)

LUST (See **DESIRE; PASSION**)
Results.
Craves after men & women: sex. 1:1-5; 3:8
Craves after the food, the fleshpots of the world. 16:1-3; 17:2-3
Craves after the security of the world instead of God. 14:10-12
Craves after worldliness. 1:1-5; 3:8
Sin of.
Accumulates (gathers) & hoards. 16:16-30, esp. 19-20
Craves after men & women: sex. 1:1-5; 3:8
Disobeys God. 16:16-30, esp. 19-20

MAGICIANS (See **OCCULT**)
Described. Used trickery & occult to deceive Pharaoh. 7:10-13; 8:7-8
Failure of. Failure to imitate miracles. 8:16-18
Methods of. Imitate miracles.
Caused frogs to seek higher ground. 8:7-8
Seemingly turned rods into snakes. 7:10-13
Seemingly turned water to blood. 7:22-25

MAHALI
Descendent of Jacob. Grandson of Levi. 6:13-27 (Chart)

MAJESTY (See **GLORY OF GOD; GOD**, Nature - Attributes)

MALICE - MALICIOUSNESS (See **ANGER; HATE; RAGE; WRATH**)
Trials - Characteristic of. Evil rulers.
Enslaving & brutalizing people. 1:8-22; 2:11-12; 3:7-8; 3:13-22, esp. 17; 5:1-23; 6:1-5, esp. 5
Launching a holocaust against people. 1:8-22; 2:11-12; 5:1-23
Seeking to control the population by murder. 1:8-22; 1:22; 2:1-10

MAN
Depravity of. (See **DEPRAVITY; SIN**)
Errors - Misconceptions of.
Exalts self to be god. 8:1-15; 7:17
Humanistic philosophy. 8:1-15; 7:17
Fact. Is not a god: does not determine his fate. 8:1-15; 8:20-32; 9:8-12; 9:14-16
Nature.
Is to blame others. 5:20-23; 14:10-12; 15:24; 16:1-4; 17:2-3
Is to complain, grumble, murmur. 5:20-23; 14:10-12; 15:24; 16:1-4; 17:2-3
Is to question, blame God (Moses). 5:20-23; 14:13-15
Needs of. (See **NEEDS - NECESSITIES**)

MANAGERS - MANAGEMENT (See **ECONOMY; LABOR; WORK**)
Duty.
Not to overwork. 18:13-27
To delegate authority. Example of. Moses. 18:13-27
Wise management.
Delegation of authority. Example of. Moses. 18:13-27
Representative organization. 3:13-22, esp. 16; 4:27-31, esp. 29-31; 12:21; 17:5

MANIFEST - MANIFESTATION (See **REVELATION**)
Of God.
His glory in the pillar of cloud. To rebuke sin. 16:4-15, esp. 9-10
His glory. To guide His people. 13:20-22
His name, His most basic name. 3:13-22, esp. 13-15; 3:14-15
His presence, glory, & holiness. To Moses. 3:1-10
His Shekinah glory. 16:10

MANKIND (See **MAN**)

MANNA
Discussed. 16:31
Kept in the Ark of the Covenant.
16:31-35
Promised by God. 16:4-15; 16:16-30;
16:31
Provision of. First provision. 16:4-15
Type - Symbol - Picture.
Daily devotion. Spiritual nourishment.
16:16-30; 16:31
God's provision. 16:1-36; Intro. VII,
pt.30
Jesus Christ. 16:31

MARAH, City or Area of
Bitter water of Marah. Site of Israel's
first crisis in the wilderness. 15:22-27
Discussed. 15:23

MARRIAGE - MARRIED
Fact. Moses separated from his wife, but
was later reconciled. 4:24-26; 18:1-8
Problems - Dangers to.
Arguing & bitterly opposing a
spouse's obeying God. 4:24-26;
18:1-8, esp. 2
Refusing to obey God. 4:24-26;
18:1-8, esp. 2

MASSACRE (See MURDER)

**MATERIALISM (See GREED;
WEALTH; WORLDLINESS)**
Example of. Pharaoh. Enslaving others
for wealth & power. 7:20-21; 8:2-4;
11:1-10
Results.
Brings the judgment of God upon one.
7:8-11:10
Causes men to oppress others. 1:8-22;
5:2-13; 8:2-4; 11:1-10

**MATURITY (See GROWTH, SPIRI-
TUAL)**

**MEANING - MEANINGFUL (See ABUN-
DANCE; FRUITFUL; FULFILLMENT;
FULNESS, SPIRITUAL; HUNGER,
SPIRITUAL; PURPOSE; SATISFAC-
TION)**

**MEANINGLESS (See EMPTINESS;
HOPE; LIFE; NEW LIFE; NEW MAN)**

MEAT
Dangers of. Lusting after the fleshpots of
the world. 16:1-3

**MEDITATE - MEDITATION (See
QUIET TIME)**
Duty. To m. early morning with the
LORD. 16:16-30; 16:31
Example of. List of people who m. early
morning—daily. 16:16-30

**MEEK - MEEKNESS (See HUMILITY;
UNWORTHY)**

**MEMORIAL - MEMORIALIZE – MEM-
ORIALIZED (See ALTARS; CONSE-
CRATION; DEDICATION)**
What was or is to be m. or remembered.
Dedication of Firstborn. 13:1-2
Feast of Unleavened Bread. 12:14
Passover. 12:1-2

Rephidim.
Place where Israel grumbled for
lack of water. 17:7
Place where the altar was built to
honor God's power to give victory
over all enemies. 17:13-16

MERARI
Grandson of Jacob. Son of Levi. 6:13-27
(Chart)

**MERCY - MERCIFUL (See COMPAS-
SION)**
Of God.
Is merciful despite man's hard heart.
9:29-32; 10:21-29
Is seen in meeting the needs of man
despite disobedience. 13:17-22;
14:10-12; 15:22-27; 16:1-36; 17:1-7
Is seen in not accepting "no" to His
call, not allowing Moses to reject
God's call. 4:13-17

MESSAGE
Duty. Must obey God & proclaim the m.
regardless of difficulty. 6:10-12

**MESSENGER (See MINISTER; WIT-
NESS - WITNESSING)**
Call - Called. Aaron. To be the spokesman of God for Moses. 4:13-17; 4:27-
31; 5:13-27, esp. 13; 7:1-7
Duty. To go & proclaim God's Word regardless of ability. 6:10-12

**MESSIAH - MESSIAHSHIP OF JESUS
CHRIST (See SEED, THE PROMISED)**

MIDIAN, LAND OF
Discussed. 2:15-22

MIDWIVES
Fact. Refused to obey Pharaoh's orders to
kill all newborn Hebrew boys. 1:15-21

MIGDOL, City of
Discussed. 14:2

MIGHT (See POWER)

MILITARY
Of Amalekites.
Defeated by Israel. Led by Joshua.
17:8-16
Total destruction predicted by God.
17:13-16
Of Egypt. Was massive. Destroyed at
Red Sea. 14:1-31

**MINISTER (See AMBASSADOR; MES-
SENGER; SERVANT OF GOD)**
Accusations - Criticism against. Mis-
treatment of. (See ACCUSATIONS,
FALSE)
Call of. (See CALL - CALLED)
Are never too old to serve God. 6:28-7:7
Credentials of. True credentials. 7:8-13
Duty.
Must not allow handicaps to keep one
from serving. 3:11-12; 4:10-12;
6:10-12
To go & proclaim God's Word regard-
less of ability. 6:10-12
Needs of. The LORD's very special pres-
ence & assurance in times of need.
6:1-5

**MINISTRY - MINISTERING (See
HELP - HELPING; SERVICE)**
Excuses against. Five excuses against.
3:11-4:17
Fact. Are never too old to serve God.
6:28-7:5; 7:6-7

MIRACLES
Burning bush. 3:1-4
Manna (bread) provided. 16:1-36
Moses' hand made leprous. 4:1-9, esp.
6-7
Moses' rod turned to serpent. 4:1-9, esp.
3-4; 7:8-13
Pillar of cloud & fire. 13:20-22
Red Sea crossed. 14:1-31
Ten plagues. 7:8-11:10
Boils affected man & animal. 9:8-12
Catastrophic hail & thunderstorm.
9:13-35
Darkness covered the land. 10:21-29
Death of firstborn son. 11:1-10; 12:29
Disease struck the livestock. 9:1-7
Flies swarmed over the land. 8:20-32
Frogs everywhere. 8:1-15
Lice or gnats infested the land.
8:16-19
Locusts swarmed over the land.
10:1-20
Water turned to blood. 7:14-25
Victory given over enemies (Amalekites).
17:8-16
Water provided. 17:1-7
Water purified - bitter waters sweetened.
15:22-27

MIRIAM
Sister of Moses. 2:2
Song of. Sung after crossing the Red Sea.
15:19-21

MISERY - MISERABLE (See AGONY)
Caused by.
Chastisement of God. 8:2-4; 8:16-18;
8:21; 8:24; 10:21-23; 12:30
Darkness. 10:21-23
Death. 11:4-6; 12:30
Flies. 8:20-32
Frogs. 8:2-4
Lice, gnats. 8:16-18

MISHAEL
Descendent of Levi & son of Uzziel.
6:13-27 (Chart)
Uncle of Moses & Aaron. Brother of
Moses' father, Amram. 6:13-27 (Chart)

**MISSIONARIES (See WITNESS - WIT-
NESSING)**
Fact. Israel was called to be the m. force
to the world. 1:1-22 (pt.2)

MISSIONS
Call to. Israel. Was called to be God's
missionary force to the world. 1:1-22

MOB (See RIOTS)
Example of.
Threatened to stone Moses. 17:4
Were ready to attack Moses. 5:20-23;
16:1-3

MONEY (See GREED; WEALTH)
Love of. Causes men to oppress & enslave people. 8:2-4; 11:1-10

MORALS - MORALITY (See **PURITY; SPOTLESS; UNDEFILED; VIRTUE**)

MOSES
Birth of. Picture of a believing, courageous mother. 2:1-10
Call of.
A study of God's call to service. 3:1-10
Argued against. Five excuses. 3:11-4:17
By God to deliver Israel from slavery to Egypt. 2:1-7:7
Was given repeatedly. 3:1-10; 4:13-17; 6:13-27, esp. 13; 7:1-7
Carnal, fleshly nature. Killed an Egyptian. 2:11-12
Character of.
Growth of. 2:15-22
Kind of man Moses was. 3:1-3
Chastisement of. Because he failed to obey God. 4:24-26
Compassion. For his people in their slavery. 2:11
Faith of.
Gave up the riches of Egypt. 2:13-15
Identified with Israel. 2:11; 2:13-15
In promised land. 2:15-22
Refused the throne of Egypt. 2:13-15
Family of.
Brother & sister. 2:2
Mother of. Believing, courageous woman. 2:1-10
Genealogy. Chart of. 6:13-27
Justice of. Stood up for the oppressed. 2:11; 2:11-12; 2:13-15; 2:15-22
Life of.
A prince of Egypt. 2:3-4; 2:5-8; 2:9-10; 2:11; 2:11-12; 2:13-15
Almost died because of disobedience to God. 4:24-26
Flight from Egypt to Midian. 2:15-22
Murdered an Egyptian. 2:11-12
Nothing known about Moses from birth to age forty. 2:11-25
Preparation for ministry. In Midian. 2:15-22
Was 80 years old when called to serve God. 7:6-7
Problems - Discouragements.
Blamed for the oppression launched by Pharaoh. 5:20-23
Blamed for trials, problems faced by the Israelites. 14:10-12; 14:13-15, esp. 15; 15:24; 16:1-3; 17:2-3
Crushed, broken. 6:1-7:7
Over the grumbling accusations of the Israelites. 14:10-12; 14:13-15, esp. 15; 15:25; 17:4
Over the rejection of his message & by the Israelites. 5:20-23
Early events that changed his life. 2:11-25
Symbolized - Typed - Pictured. Christ. Intro. VII, pt.7

MOTHER - MOTHERS
Of godly men. Of Moses. A believing, courageous m. 2:1-10

MOURN (See **GRIEF; SORROW, GODLY**)

MOUTH (See **SPEECH; TONGUE**)

MURDER
Committed by. Moses. 2:11-12
Who **m**. Societies of all generations. Murder the defenseless, aged, handicapped, & weak. 1:22
Who was **m**. Babies. Egyptian law passed by Pharaoh to kill all newborn Israelite boys. 1:15-21

MURMUR - MURMURING (See **ACCUSATION, FALSE; COMPLAINING; CRITICISM; GRUMBLING**)
Caused by.
Being upset with one's leader. 5:20-23; 17:2-3
Carnality. 14:10-12; 15:24; 16:1-3; 17:2-3
Questioning God's care & provision. 14:10-12; 15:24; 16:1-3; 17:2-3
Unbelief. 14:10-12; 15:24; 16:1-3; 17:2-3
Characteristic - Trait. Of carnal, distrustful persons. 14:10-12; 15:24; 16:1-3; 17:2-3
Discussed. 15:24
Fact. Is not against God's servants, but against God Himself. 16:4-15
Of Israel.
At Egypt. Against Moses. Because of Pharaoh's reaction against him: more intense oppression. 5:20-23
At Marah. Over bitter water. 15:22-27; 15:24
At Rephidim. Because of no water. 17:1-7
At the Red Sea. Faced with an impossible situation. 14:10-12
At the wilderness of Sin. Because of no food. 16:1-3
One of two great sins of Israel. 16:1-36; 16:1-3
Results. Causes pain, hurt. 5:20-23; 14:10-12; 14:13-15, esp. 15; 15:22-27; 15:25; 17:4

MURRAIN
A disease that attacks livestock. 9:2-3
Was one of the ten plagues cast upon Egypt. 9:2-3

MUSHI
Descendent of Jacob. Grandson of Levi. 6:13-27 (Chart)

NAASHON
Aaron's brother-in-law. 6:13-27, esp. 23

NADAB
Son of Aaron. 6:13-27 (Chart)

NAME - NAMES
Basic name of God: I AM (Jehovah, Yahweh). 3:13-22; 3:14-15
Duty. To declare God's **n**. to people. 3:13-22
The name of God. (See **GOD**, Names - Titles)

NATIONS (See **CITIES - AREAS; CITIZENSHIP; CIVIL AUTHORITIES; GOVERNMENT; WORLD**)
Discussed.
Canaanites. 3:8
Egypt. 1:8; Intro. VI
Israel. 1:1-7
Midian. 2:15-22
Fact.
Are under the control of God. 9:14-16
God is the God of every **n**. 8:22-23

NATURAL CATASTROPHES (See **PLAGUES, THE TEN**)

NATURAL MAN (See **CARNAL; FLESH; MAN; WORLDLY - WORLDLINESS**)

NATURE (See **EARTH; WORLD**)
God's power over.
Controls all things, even the most minute particles. 8:16-19
Controls body & health. 8:1-15; 9:8-12
Controls light & darkness. 10:21-29
Controls the animal life of the world. 8:1-15; 9:1-7
Controls the weather. 9:13-35
Controls the whole earth. 9:13-35
Has power over the insects. 8:16-19; 8:20-32; 10:1-20
Has power over the water. 7:14-25
Has power over the seas (Red Sea). 14:19-28
Has power to provide food. 16:1-36
Has power to provide water. 17:1-7
Has power to purify water. 15:22-27

NATURE, DIVINE (See **NEW BIRTH; NEW LIFE; NEW MAN; SALVATION**)
Source. Blood of Jesus Christ.
Righteousness: getting rid of all leaven (evil); eating only unleavened bread (righteousness). 12:1-13:16 (pt.7); 12:6-11 (pt.6); 12:14-20; Intro. VII, pt.2
Turning away from the *old life* & beginning the *new life* of righteousness. 12:1-13:16 (pt.7); 12:6-11 (pt.6); 12:14-20; Intro. VII, pt.22

NEEDS - NECESSITIES
Basic - Essential **n**.
Food. 16:1-36
Water. 17:1-7
N. of men - of life.
Deliverance. (See **DELIVERANCE; SALVATION; VICTORY**)
Food. One of the basic **n**. of man. 16:1-36
Guidance. (See **GUIDANCE**)
LORD's encouragement & presence. In time of desperation. 5:20-23, see 6:1-5
Water.
Bitter water purified by God for His people. 15:22-27
One of the basic **n**. of man. 17:1-7
What is needed. LORD's presence. In times of desperation. 6:1-5

NEEDY, THE (See **DESTITUTE - DESTITUTION**)
Care for. By God.
For His people when oppressed. 3:7-8; 3:13-22, esp. 16-17
For His people when overworked. 18:13-27
For His people when under armed attack. 14:1-31; 17:8-16
For His people when without basic essentials. 15:22-27; 16:1-36; 17:1-7

NEGLECT - NEGLECTED (See IG-NORE - IGNORING)
Danger of **n**. God. 5:2-14, esp. 2
What is **n**. Devotions. Feasting upon the Bread of Life. 16:16-30; 16:31
What is **n**. Prayer. 14:10-12; 15:24; 16:1-3; 17:2-3
What is **n**. Remembering God's former help & deliverance. 14:10-12; 15:24; 16:1-3; 17:2-3

NEGOTIATE
Example of. Pharaoh tried to **n**. with God. 10:7-11; 10:24-26

NEIGHBOR (See BROTHERHOOD; LOVE)

NEPHEG
Descendent of Jacob & Levi. Grandson of Kohath. 6:13-27 (Chart).

NEUTRALITY (See COMPROMISE; DOUBLE-MINDED; FICKLENESS; HALF-HEARTED; INCONSISTENCY; INDECISION)

NEW BIRTH (See NEW CREATION; NEW LIFE; NEW MAN; REGENER-ATION; SALVATION)
Symbolized - Typed - Pictured.
By the Feast of Unleavened Bread. 12:1-13:16 (pt.7); 12:14-20; 12:34-41, esp. 39; Intro. VII, pt.22
By the Passover Feast. Blood of Christ. 12:1-13:16; 12:1-13; Intro. VII, pt.15

NEW CREATION (See BORN AGAIN; CONVERSION; NEW BIRTH; NEW LIFE; NEW MAN; SALVATION)
Symbolized - Typed - Pictured. By the Feast of Unleavened Bread. 12:1-13:16 (pt.7); 12:14-20; 12:34-41, esp. 39; Intro. VII, pt.22

NEW LIFE (See BORN AGAIN; NEW BIRTH; NEW CREATION; NEW MAN; OLD MAN; SALVATION)
Symbolized - Typed - Pictured.
By Israel's deliverance from slavery & beginning a *new life* marching to the promised land. 12:1-13:16 (pt.7); 12:14-20
By the Feast of Unleavened Bread. 12:1-13:16 (pt.7); 12:14-20; 12:34-41, esp. 39; Intro. VII, pt.22
By the Passover. 12:1-2; 12:6-11

NEW MAN (See CONVERSION; NEW BIRTH; NEW CREATION; NEW LIFE; OLD MAN; SALVATION)
Duty.
To be ready to flee one's old life & pursue one's new life. 12:1-3:6 (pt.7); 12:14-20; 12:34-41, esp. 39
To be ready to put off the old man & put on the new man. 12:1-3:6 (pt.7); 12:14-20; 12:34-41, esp. 39
Symbolized - Typed - Pictured. By the Feast of Unleavened Bread. 12:1-13:16 (pt.7); 12:14-20; 12:34-41, esp. 39; Intro. VII, pt.22

NILE RIVER
Fact. Was turned to blood by God as a plague. 7:14-25; 7:17-19; 7:20-22

NOURISHMENT, SPIRITUAL (See GROWTH, SPIRITUAL)
Duty. To arise early & seek spiritual nourishment. 16:16-30; 16:31
Example of. List of people who arose early. 16:16-30; 16:31

OATH - OATHS (See COVENANT; PROMISES)

OBEY - OBEDIENCE (See COMMIT-MENT; DEDICATION; DISOBE-DIENCE; ENDURANCE; FAITHFUL-NESS)
Duty.
To accept God's call without making excuses. 3:11-4:17
To obey God. 15:25-26; 16:4-15, esp. 4; 16:16-30
To obey God despite discouragement. 14:13-15; 15:25; 17:4
To obey God despite opposition. 5:20-21, see 6:1-7:7
To obey God despite spouse's lack of support. 4:24-26
To obey the *covenant of o*. 15:25-26
Example of. Several men. 7:10
Importance of. Is a covenant of **o**. Demanded by God. 15:25-26
Results.
Four fruits, results. 4:18-31
Will make one healthier. 15:25-26

OBJECTIONS
Against God's call.
Because of apparent failure. 5:20-23
Five **o**. (Moses). 3:11-4:17

OBSTINATE - OBSTINACY (See HARD - HARDNESS OF HEART; RE-JECTION; STUBBORN UNBELIEF)

OCCULT (See MAGICIANS; SOR-CERY; ZODIAC)
Fact. **O**. was practiced in the cabinet of Pharaoh. 9:8-12

OFFEND - OFFENDING (See STUM-BLINGBLOCK)
How we **o**. people.
By oppression. 1:8-22; 2:23-25; 5:2-24
By sin. 2:13-14

OFFERING - OFFERINGS (See GIVE - GIVING; SACRIFICES - SACRIFI-CIAL SYSTEM; STEWARDSHIP; TITHING)
Kinds of **o**. Passover Lamb. 12:1-13:16; 12:1-13; 12:21-28
Purpose of **o**.
To offer, dedicate one's firstborn, one's children to God. 13:1-16
To worship & celebrate God's great deliverance. 18:9-12
Symbolized - Typed - Pictured. By Feast of Unleavened Bread. 12:1-13:16 (pt.7); 12:14-20; 12:34-41, esp. 39; Intro. VII, pt.22

OLD AGE (See ELDERLY, THE)

OLD TESTAMENT (See BIBLE; WORD OF GOD)
Purpose of.
Sevenfold purpose for the record of the wilderness wanderings. 13:17-18:27
To teach us how to march through the wilderness (trials) of this world. 13:17-18:27 (pt.B)

OMISSION (See NEGLECT - NEG-LECTING)
Sins of.
Devotions. Failing to feast upon the Bread of Life. 16:16-30; 16:31
Failing to obey God. Because of wife's objections. 4:24-26
Prayerlessness. 14:10-14; 15:24; 16:1-3; 17:2-3

OMNIPOTENCE (See GOD, Power of; JESUS CHRIST, Power of)

OMNISCIENCE (See GOD, Knowledge; JESUS CHRIST, Knowledge – Omni-science)

ONENESS (See BROTHERHOOD; FELLOWSHIP; UNITY)

OPPORTUNITY (See SECOND CHANCE)
Fact. Even the most evil are given oppor-tunity after opportunity to repent. 10:4-6; 10:21-29

OPPOSE - OPPOSITION (See CON-FLICT; DISSENSION; DIVISION; STRIFE)
Caused by.
Not knowing God. 5:2-14, esp. 2
Not waiting on God's timing; reacting to apparent failure. 5:20-23
Not trusting God's care & provision; unbelief. 5:20-23; 14:10-12; 15:24; 16:1-3; 17:2-3

OPPRESSED - OPPRESSION (See PER-SECUTION)
Causes of. Three causes. 1:8-10
Who was or is **o**. Israel. By Egypt. 1:8-22; 2:23-25; 5:2-14; 7:8-11:10
Why people are **o**. For greed: financial & economic reasons. 8:2-4; 11:1-10

OPTIMISM - OPTIMISTIC (See FAITH; HOPE)

ORDER - ORDERLINESS (See ORGAN-IZATION; PLAN - PLANNING)

ORDINANCE (See BAPTISM; CERE-MONY; LORD'S SUPPER; MEM-ORIAL; RITUAL)
Discussed.
Dedication of Firstborn. 13:1-6
Feast of Unleavened Bread. 12:14-20; 12:34-41, esp. 39
Passover. 12:1-13:16; 12:1-13

ORDINANCE, RELIGIOUS
Duty. To observe. Importance of. 12:15-16

ORGANIZE - ORGANIZATION (See **MANAGEMENT; PLAN - PLANNING**)
Errors - Danger of.
Lack of **o**. 18:13-27
Not delegating responsibility. 18:13-27
Overwork. 18:13-27
Structure of.
Israel's judges. 18:13-27
Israel's people. Their march from Egypt was in military formation. 13:17-18; 14:19-28

OUTCAST (See **CUT OFF; DISCRIMINATION; DIVISION; JUDGMENT; PREJUDICE**)
Who is **o**. The evil person—when God wills. 9:14-16, esp. 15
Who is **o**. The unbeliever: the person who failed to cast away all of the leaven (evil). 12:14-20, esp. 15, 19

OUTER DARKNESS (See **JUDGMENT**)

OUTREACH (See **COMMISSION; EVANGELISM; MISSION; WITNESSING**)

OVER-CONFIDENCE (See **SELF-SUFFICIENCY**)

OVERCOME - OVERCOMERS (See **CONQUEST; TRIUMPH; VICTORY**)

OVERSEERS (See **LEADER**)
Failure of. Not waiting on God's timing; reacting to apparent failure. 5:20-23

OVERWORK
Caused by.
An attempt to control the population. 1:8-22; 5:1-23
Reaction to appeals for mercy & compassion. 5:1-23
Slavery. 1:8-22
Duty. To guard against. Example. Moses. 18:13-27
Example of. Moses **o**. 18:1-27

PALLU
Grandson of Jacob. Son of Reuben. 6:13-27 (Chart)

PARDON (See **BLAMELESS; FORGIVENESS; SPOTLESS**)

PARENTS
Duty of parents.
To dedicate children to God. 13:1-16
To protect one another. 2:1-10
To teach children the meaning of the Passover, of salvation. 12:21-28, esp. 26-27
To trust God to protect children. 2:3-4
Duty toward parents. To obey, even in threatening situations. Miriam watched over Moses. 2:1-10, esp. 4, 7-8
Faith of.
Irresponsible or evil. 4:24-26
Sins & failures of. Not obeying God in circumcising (dedicating, baptizing) a child. 4:24-26

Problems within.
Division, separation. Example. Moses. 4:24-26; 18:1-8
Irresponsible or evil . 4:24-26

PARTAKE - PARTAKER
What believers are not to **p**. of. Leaven, symbolizes sin & evil. 12:14-21; 12:34-41, esp. 39
What believers are to **p**. of.
The bread from heaven, the bread of life, Jesus Christ Himself. 16:31
The Lamb of God, Christ's sacrifice. 16:6-11, pt.3
The manna, the bread of God. To **p**. every day. 16:16-30

PARTIALITY (See **BIGOTRY; DISCRIMINATION; FAVORITISM; PREJUDICE**)

PASSION - PASSIONS (See **DESIRE; LUST**)

PASSOVER - PASSOVER FEAST
Discussed. 12:1-13:16; 12:21-51
Fact. Included three major celebrations. 12:1-13:16 (pt.8)
Meaning. 12:1-13:16; 12:1-13
Preparation of. 12:1-13; 12:21-28
Symbolized - Typed - Pictured. The death of Christ. 12:1-13; 12:21-28; Intro. VII, pt.15

PASTOR (See **MESSENGERS; MINISTERS**)
Heart of. Needs the heart of a shepherd. Example of. Moses. 3:1-3

PATIENCE (See **ENDURANCE; LONG-SUFFERING**, Of God; **PERSEVERANCE**)
Example of. Moses. Was **p**. with the unbelief, complaining, & grumbling of Israel. 14:10-12; 15:24; 16:1-3; 16:2-3
Of God. (See **LONGSUFFERING**, Of God)
Does end. Example of. With Egypt. 11:1-10
Example of. Was very **p**. with Pharaoh, giving chance after chance to repent. 10:21-29; 10:4-6

PEACE (See **FORGIVENESS; PEACE, RECONCILIATION; SOCIAL - WORLD PEACE**)
Duty. To seek peace between two people fighting. 2:13-14
Lack of. Caused by.
Anger, arguing, & fist-fighting. 2:13-14
Carnal nature. Uncontrolled reaction. 2:11-12
Feeling threatened. 17:8

PEACE, SOCIAL - WORLD PEACE (See **CONFLICT; WAR**)
Duty. To seek peace between two people fighting. 2:13-14
Lack of. Caused by.
Anger, arguing, & fist-fighting. 2:13-14
Carnal nature. Uncontrolled reaction. 2:11-12
Feeling threatened. 17:8
Source - How one secures **p**. Preserving prayer. 17:8-16

PEACEMAKERS
Example of. Moses.
Seeking peace between Pharaoh & God and between Egypt & Israel. 7:15-16; 8:1; 8:20; 9:1; 9:13-14; 10:3
Seeking peace between two men fighting. 2:13-14

PENALTY (See **SIN**, Results)

PENITENCE (See **CONFESSION; FORGIVENESS; REPENTANCE**)

PEOPLE (See **MAN; WORLD**)

PERDITION (See **DESTROY - DESTRUCTION; JUDGMENT**)

PERFECT - PERFECTION (See **JUSTIFICATION; RIGHTEOUSNESS**)
Source - How one is **p**.
Believing the promise of God. 12:5
Hiding behind the blood of Christ. 12:5

PERISH - PERISHING (See **DEATH; DESTRUCTION; JUDGMENT**)

PERIZZITES
Land of. Promised to Israel. 3:7-8; 3:8

PERJURY (See **WITNESS OF MAN; LYING**)

PERMISSIVE - PERMISSIVENESS (See **IMMORALITY; PARENTS**)

PERSECUTION - PERSECUTORS (See **OPPRESSION**)
Causes of.
Five reasons why people **p**. God's people. 5:2-14
Three causes. 1:8-10

Judgment of persecutors. (See **JUDGMENT**)
Example of. Ten plagues upon Egypt. 7:8-11:10
Overcoming. How God's people overcome **p**. 1:8-22

PERSEVERE - PERSEVERANCE - PERSISTENCE (See **ENDURANCE; STEDFASTNESS**)
Duty.
To **p**. against one's enemies. 17:8-16
To **p**. against the rejection of unbelievers. 5:1-23; see 6:1-7:7
To **p**. in prevailing prayer. 17:10-12
To **p**. in proclaiming the message of God: mercy & justice. 7:8-11:10
To **p**. in the mission of God despite grumblers & threats. 5:20-23; 14:10-12; 15:22-27; 16:1-36; 17:1-7

PERSUADE - PERSUASION
Evil **p**. (See **STUMBLINGBLOCK**)

PESTILENCE (See **INSECT**)

PHARAOH (See **EGYPT; KING**)
Character. Discussed. 5:2-14
Discussed.
　First confrontation with Moses.
　　5:1-23
　Who the Pharaoh was who enslaved
　　Israel. 1:8
Fact. Was raised up by God to demon-
　strate that God has power over the
　rulers of the earth. 9:14-16
Heart of.
　Was hard, rock-hard. 4:21; 7:10-13;
　　7:14; 7:22-25; 8:15; 8:19; 8:32; 9:7;
　　9:17-21; 9:34-35
　Was wicked. Passed a murderous law
　　to kill all Israelite boys. 1:15-21
Officials of. Three groups of officials.
　7:10-13
Symbol - Type of. Satan. 1:11-14; Intro.
　VII, pt.3

PHILISTINES
God led Israel to bypass Philistine when
　fleeing Egypt. 13:17-18

PHILOSOPHY - PHILOSOPHERS
Reaction to the gospel. List. Men who re-
　jected God through history. 7:17

PHINEHAS
Grandson of Aaron. 6:13-27 (Chart)

PHYSICAL FOOD (See **GOOD; FOOD,
SPIRITUAL**)

PHYSICAL WORLD & DIMENSION
(See **CORRUPTION; WORLD**)
Is corruptible, wasting away. (See **COR-
RUPTION; MAN**)

PI HAHIROTH, City or area of
Discussed. 14:2

PILGRIM (See **BELIEVER; SOJOURN-
ER**)
Described as. Believer upon earth. Home
　is heaven. 2:15-22, esp. 22; 18:1-8, esp.
　3-4
Discussed. Trials.
　Bitter, polluted water: bitter expe-
　　riences made sweet. 15:22-27
　Hemmed in on all sides (Red Sea):
　　God's great deliverance. 14:1-31
　Hunger: God's provision of the heav-
　　enly bread. 16:1-36
　The wilderness wanderings (journey).
　　13:17-18:17; Intro. VII, pt.25
　Thirst: God's provision of water.
　　17:1-7
　Warfare: victory through prevailing
　　prayer. 17:8-16

PILLAR OF CLOUD & FIRE
Discussed. 13:20-22

PITHOM, City of
Discussed. 1:11

PITY (See **COMPASSION**)

PLACES (See **CITIES - AREAS**)

PLAGUES, THE TEN
Caused by - Reasons for. A hard heart.
　7:14-25; 8:1-15; 8:19; 8:20-32; 8:21;
　9:1-7; 9:3-5; 9:11; 9:14-16; 9:29-32;
　10:1-20; 10:1-2; 10:21-29; 11:1-10;
　11:9-10
Listed.
　Darkness. 10:21-29
　Death of the firstborn. 11:1-10;
　　12:21-51
　Festering boils. 9:8-12
　Flies. 8:20-32
　Frogs. 8:1-15
　Hail & lightning. 9:13-35
　Lice, gnats. 8:16-19
　Livestock disease. 9:1-7
　Locusts. 10:1-20
　Water of Nile turned to blood.
　　7:14-25
Discussed. 7:8-11:10
Purpose. Discussed. 7:8-11:10
Stand as a picture of God's judgment for
　all generations. 10:1-2

PLAN - PLANNING (See **CONSTRUC-
TION; ORGANIZATION**)

PLANT LIFE (See **HYSSOP; TREE**)

PLEASURE - PLEASURE-SEEKERS
(See **LUST; WORLDLY - WORLDLI-
NESS**)

POLLUTION (See **DEFILEMENT; EN-
VIRONMENT; FILTHINESS; SIN;
UNCLEANNESS**)

POOR - POVERTY (See **NEED - NE-
CESSITIES; NEEDY, THE**)
Example. Israel.
　As slaves were p., paid little if any
　　wages. 11:1-3; 12:34-41
　As slaves. Most possessions & valua-
　　bles had been confiscated. 11:1-3;
　　12:34-41

**POOR IN SPIRIT - POVERTY, SPIRI-
TUAL** (See **HUMILITY; MEEKNESS;
LOWLINESS OF MIND**)

POPULATION
P. of Israel.
　Attempts to control or destroy. By
　　Egypt. 1:8-22
　Grew by leaps & bounds during Egyp-
　　tian slavery. 1:1-7

POSITION (See **AMBITION; ASPIRA-
TION**)

POSSESSIONS (See **COVET - COVE-
TOUSNESS; GREED; MATERIAL-
ISM; WEALTH; WORLDLINESS**)
Example of. Pharaoh. Enslaving others
　for wealth & power. 7:20-21; 8:2-4;
　11:1-10
Results.
　Brings the judgment of God upon one.
　　7:8-11:10
　Causes men to oppress others. 1:8-22;
　　5:2-13; 8:2-4; 11:1-10

POWER - POWERFUL (See **POWER
OF GOD**)
Sin of.
　Using p. to enslave people. 1:8-22;
　　5:2-14; 7:14-25; 8:1-15; 9:1-7; 9:1;
　　9:13-14; 10:1-20; 10:21-29; 11:1-10
　Using p. to exalt oneself above others.
　　1:8-22; 5:2-14; 7:17; 8:1-15; 9:14-16;
　　9:17-21; 10:1-20; 10:21-29; 11:1-10
　Using p. to force labor. 1:8-22; 5:2-14
　Using p. to kill innocent people. 1:15-
　　21; 1:22

POWER OF DARKNESS
Conquered by - Victory over. The cross
　of Jesus Christ. Intro. VII, pt.28

POWER OF GOD (See **GOD**, Power of)
Power of - Omnipotence of.
　Can stop men from standing before
　　Him. 9:11
　Controls & sustains all things. Most
　　minute particles of universe. 8:19
　Controls all things, even the most
　　minute, basic elements of the uni-
　　verse. 8:16-19
　Controls the animal-life of the world.
　　9:1-7
　Demonstrated in dividing the Red Sea.
　　14:1-31; 14:19-28
　Demonstrated in freeing Israel from
　　Egyptian slavery. 12:21-51
　Demonstrated in His judgment. Cast
　　ten plagues upon Egypt. (See
　　PLAGUES, THE TEN)
　Demonstrated in the great Exodus of
　　Israel. 12:21-51
　Described as. Finger of God. 8:19
　Has power over all the land & every
　　land. 8:22-23
　Has power over mankind, over the
　　food supply & all else. 10:1-20
　Has power over the earth, its weather
　　& natural disasters. 9:13-35
　Has power over the reproduction of
　　life. 8:9-11
　Proven.
　　By launching the ten plagues upon
　　　Egypt. 7:8-11:10
　　By turning Moses' rod into a snake.
　　　4:1-9; 7:8-11:10; 7:10-13
　Rules over body & health. 9:8-12
　Rules over light & darkness. 10:23

POWERLESSNESS (See **FAIL - FAIL-
URE**)
Caused by.
　Carnality. Reactionary spirit. Why
　　Moses was p. to help his people.
　　2:11-25, esp. 11-15
　Despair because of criticism & grum-
　　blings of people. 14:10-12, see 15;
　　15:24, see 25; 16:1-3; 17:2-3, see 4
　Facing impossible obstacles & prob-
　　lems. 14:1-31, esp. 10-14
　Not understanding God's timetable.
　　5:20-23

PRAISE - PRAISED (See **PRAYER;
THANKSGIVING; WORSHIP**)
Songs of.
　Miriam. Sung after crossing the Red
　　Sea. 15:19-21
　Moses. Great song of praise for
　　deliverance through the Red Sea.
　　15:1-21

PRAY - PRAYER - PRAYING (See **IN-TERCESSION**)
Answers to.
Deliverance. 14:1-31, esp. 15
Encouragement. 6:1-7:7, see 5:20-23
Food. 16:4-15
Nine different people heard by God. 8:30-31
Victory in battle. 17:8-16
Victory over bitter trials. 15:25
Water. 17:4, see 1-7
Kinds of. Prevailing prayer. Victory through prevailing **p**. 17:8-16
Results.
God's assurance. 6:1-7:7, see 5:20-23
Victory over enemies. 17:8-16
When needed.
When enemies attack. 17:8-16
When facing desperate needs. 14:1-31, esp. 15; 15:22-27; 16:1-36, esp. 4; 17:1-7; 17:8-16
When people falsely accuse. 5:20-23

PRAYERLESSNESS
Caused by.
Critical, complaining, grumbling spirit. 14:10-12; 15:4; 16:1-3; 17:2-3
Unbelief. 14:10-12; 15:4; 16:1-3; 17:2-3

PREACH - PREACHING (See **MINISTER; WITNESSING**)
Call to.
Arguments against. 3:11-4:17
Excuses against. 3:11-4:17
Reluctant to **p**. Moses. 3:11-4:17
Excuses against. Feeling one is not eloquent, not a good speaker. 4:10-12

PREDESTINATION (See **CHOSEN; ELECTION; FOREKNOWLEDGE; FOREORDAINED**)

PREJUDICE (See **BARRIERS; BIGOTRY; DISCRIMINATION; FAVORITISM; PARTIALITY**)
Example of. Egyptians were **p**. against both shepherds & the Jews. 8:25-29, esp. 26-27

PREPARE - PREPARATION (See **COMMITMENT; CROSS - SELF-DENIAL; DEDICATION; DEVOTION; READY - READINESS**)

PRESENCE OF GOD (See **GLORY OF GOD**)

PRESSURE (See **ANXIETY**)

PRETEND - PRETENDING - PRETENSION (See **DECEIT; PROFESSION, FALSE; HYPOCRISY; LYING**)

PRIDE (See **ARROGANCE; BOASTING; GLORYING IN MAN; HAUGHTINESS; SELF-SUFFICIENCY**)
Results.
Exalting man to be god. 5:2-14, esp. 2; 7:17; 8:1-15
Exalting self (man) above God. 5:2-14, esp. 2; 7:17; 8:1-15
Using power to exalt oneself above others. 1:8-22; 5:2-14; 7:17; 8:1-15; 9:14-16; 9:17-21; 10:1-20; 10:21-29; 11:1-10

PRIEST - PRIESTS (See **HIGH PRIEST**)
Genealogy. Family of Aaron's priesthood. 6:13-27
Name of some priests. Jethro. Moses' father-in-law. **P**. of Midian. 2:14-22

PRIESTHOOD
P. of Aaron. Genealogy, family tree of. 6:13-27

PRINCIPALITIES (See **ANGELS; EVIL SPIRITS; GOVERNMENT; SATAN**)
Conquered - Victory over. By the cross of Jesus Christ. Intro. VII, pt.9, 28

PRIVILEGE (See **BELIEVERS; BLESSINGS; REWARDS**)

PROBLEMS (See **AFFLICTIONS; TRIALS - TRIBULATION; SUFFERINGS**)

PROCRASTINATION (See **EXCUSES; SLOTHFULNESS**)

PROFESSION, FALSE - PROFESSION ONLY (See **CONFESSION, FALSE; DECEIT; HYPOCRISY; LYING; UNBELIEF**)
Example of. Pharaoh. 8:15; 8:32
Fact. Sincerity is not enough. 8:32; 10:16-17

PROFESSION, SPIRITUAL OR RELIGIOUS (See **CONFESSION; PROFESSION, FALSE**)

PROMISES (See **INHERITANCE, SPIRITUAL; REWARD**)
Fulfilled.
To Abraham. 1:1-22; 1:6-7; 2:23-25; 3:4-6
To Abraham & his seed. 1:1-22; 1:6-7
To Abraham, Isaac, & Jacob. 1:1-22; 1:6-7; 2:23-25
To believers: are always fulfilled. 3:4-6
Surety of.
God always fulfills His **p**. to believers. 1:6-7
What the promises are.
Four great **p**. of God. 1:6-7
God's presence.
To be with His dear servant. 3:11-12
To guide His dear people by day & by night. 13:20-22
Seven "I wills" of God. 6:6-9
The promised land. 2:24
The promised seed. 1:6-7
To Abraham & his seed. 1:1-22; 1:6-7
To Abraham, Isaac, & Jacob. Fulfilled. 1:1-22; 1:6-7; 2:23-25
To Abraham. Fulfilled. 1:1-22; 1:6-7; 2:23-25; 3:4-6

PROMISED LAND (See **LAND, THE PROMISED**)

PROPHECY
P. concerning Israel.
To be freed from slavery. 3:7-8; 3:13-22, esp. 17; 6:6-9
To be given the promised land. 2:24; 3:7-8
To be given the promised seed. 1:6-7; 6:1-6

PROPHET
Call of.
Arguments against. 3:11-4:17
Excuses against. 3:11-4:17
Reluctant **p**. Moses. 3:11-4:17
Who were **p**. Aaron. 6:28-7:5, esp. 7:1

PROPHETESS
Example of. Miriam. 15:20-21

PROPITIATION (See **JESUS CHRIST**, Blood of)

PROSELYTE
Qualifications.
Must be circumcised. 12:42-51
Must obey the law. 12:42-51

PROTECT - PROTECTION
How to be protected from God's judgment. (See **JUDGMENT**, Duty - How to escape)
Of God.
Protected Israel from the plagues. 8:22-23; 9:6; 10:23; 11:7-8; 12:34-41
Protects His people from judgment. 9:7

PROUD (See **PRIDE**)

PROVE - PROVED (See **TEST - TESTING**)

PROVIDENCE (See **GOD**, Sovereignty of)

PROVISION, DIVINE (See **CARE; PROMISES**)

PROVISION, GOD'S (See **BLESSINGS; PROMISES**)
What God provides.
Deliverance. (See **DELIVERANCE**)
Food. Quail & manna. Given to Israel in the wilderness. 16:4-15
Guidance. By day & by night. Guided Israel. 13:17-22
Manna. Bread from heaven. 16:4-15; 16:31
Victory over enemies. 14:1-31; 17:8-16
Water. Given to Israel. 15:22-27; 17:1-7

PROVOKED (See **ANGER; RAGE; WRATH**)

PUFFED UP (See **ARROGANCE; HAUGHTINESS; PRIDE; SELF-EXALTATION**)

PUNISHMENT (See **FIRE; HELL; JUDGMENT; LAKE OF FIRE**)

PURE - PURITY (See **CLEAN - CLEANLINESS; FORGIVENESS; MORALS - MORALITY; VIRTUE**)
How to be made pure.
By Jesus Christ. 3:7-8
By the blood of the Passover lamb, Christ Himself. 12:1-13:16 (pt.4); 12:1-13; 12:21-28

PURPOSE
Of Israel. Fivefold **p**. 1:1-22

PURPOSELESS (See EMPTINESS; HOPE; LIFE; MEANING; NEW LIFE; NEW MAN)

PUTIEL
Father-in-law to Eleazar. 6:13-27, esp. 25

QUARREL (See ARGUE - ARGUMENTS; CONFLICT; DIVISION; STRIFE)

QUENCH - QUENCHING
Duty. Not to **q.** God's call. 3:11-4:17

QUESTION - QUESTIONING
What is **q.**
God's call. 3:11-4:17; 5:20-23
God's care & provision. 5:20-23; 14:10-12; 15:24; 16:1-3; 17:2-3
God's existence & right to demand obedience. 5:2-14, esp. 2
God's timing: letting one apparently fail. 5:20-23

QUIET - QUIETNESS (See MEDITATION; QUIET TIME)

QUIET TIME (See DEVOTIONS; MEDITATION)
Duty. To arise early to spend time with the LORD. 16:16-30; 16:31
Example of. List of people who arose early for quiet time. 16:16-30

RACE, NEW
Identity of.
God's people. 1:1-22
Israel. 1:1-22

RAGE (See ANGER; CONTENTION; WRATH)
Caused by.
Disappointment in leadership. 5:20-23; 17:4
Hard heart. 10:27-29
Loss of wealth, power, position, honor, fame, rule. 14:5-9
Rejection of God. 11:7-8
Unbelief & rebellion against God. 17:2-3, see 17:4

RAILING - RAILER (See ARGUING; MOCKERY; SCOLDING)

RAMESES, City of (See CITIES - AREAS)
Discussed. 1:11

RANSOM (See REDEEM; REDEMPTION)
Meaning. 13:13

RASHNESS (See RECKLESS - RECKLESSNESS)
Result. Murder. 2:11-12

RATIONALISM - RATIONALISTS (See PHILOSOPHY - PHILOSOPHERS; REASON; UNBELIEF; WISDOM, of Men)

READY - READINESS
Duty.
To be **r.** to flee the world. 12:14-20; 12:34-41, esp. 39
To be **r.** to put all leaven out of one's life, all sin & evil. 12:14-20; 12:34-41, esp. 39

REAP - REAPING (See JUDGMENT; WITNESSING)
Facts.
The reaping of judgment. A hardened heart reaps ruin. 8:15; 8:19; 8:32; 9:7; 9:13; 9:34-35, esp. 35; 10:20; 10:27-29; 11:9-10, esp. 10
The reaping of sin.
A carnal heart **r.** broken relationships & the life of a fugitive. 2:11-25
A disobedient non-supportive wife **r.** marital separation. 4:24-26
A disobedient servant **r.** chastisement. 4:24-26

REASON - REASONING (See PHILOSOPHY)
Errors - Failures of.
Is used to argue against God's call. 3:1-4:17
Is used to deny & reject God. List of men. 7:17
Essential
In management & organization. 18:13-27
In work. 18:13-27

REBELLION (See REJECTION; SEDITIONS; UNBELIEF)
Against God.
By believers. 14:10-12, esp. 11-12; 15:24; 16:1-3; 17:2-4, esp. 2-3
By rulers (Pharaoh). 5:2-24, esp. 2; 7:11-13, esp. 13; 7:22-25, esp. 22-23; 8:12-15, esp. 15; 8:19; 9:7; 9:12; 9:34-35; 10:7-11; 10:24-26; 10:27-29; 11:9-10; 14:1-4; 14:5-9; 14:10-12, esp. 10; 14:16-18

REBUKE - REBUKED (See SCOLD - SCOLDING)
Reasons for **r.**
Deceit. 8:25-29, esp. 29
Disobedience. 4:24-26, esp. 24
Fighting between brothers. 2:13-14
Lack of faith in God. 14:13-15, esp. 13-14
Poor stewardship. 18:13-27, esp. 17-23
Rejecting God's call. 4:13-17, esp. 14
Taking advantage of the weak. 2:15-22, esp. 17

RECEIVE - RECEIVED (See OBEDIENCE)
Duty.
To **r.** the instructions of God.
About how to escape death. 12:1-13
About how to **r.** the counsel of others. 18:13-27, esp. 17-23
To **r.** the promises of God.
The covenant of God. 2:23-25; 6:1-5
The promise of health. 13:11-26, esp. 11; 15:13-18
The promised land. 3:7-8, esp. 8; 3:13-22, esp. 17; 6:6-9, esp. 8-9
To **r.**, obey the call of God. 3:11-4:17, esp. 13; see 3:1-10; 4:18-31

RECEPTIVE - RECEPTIVITY (See CONFESSION; DECISION)

RECKLESS - RECKLESSNESS (See RASHNESS)
In relation to God.
Disobeying the commandments of God. 4:24-26
Rejecting the warning of God. 7:17-19; 8:2-4; 8:16-19; 8:21; 9:2-3; 9:8-12; 9:17-21; 10:4-6; 10:21-29; 11:4-6

RECOGNITION (See HONOR; PRIDE; SELF-RIGHTEOUSNESS; SELF-SEEKING)

RECOMPENSE (See RETALIATION; REVENGE)

RECONCILE - RECONCILIATION (See JESUS CHRIST, Death; JUSTIFICATION; PROPITIATION; REDEMPTION)
Duty. To be **r.** to one's wife (Moses). 4:24-26; 12:1-13; 18:1-8
How one is **r.** By the blood of the sacrifice. 12:1-13:16

RED SEA (See CITIES - AREAS)
Crossing of.
By Israel. God's great deliverance. 14:1-3
How God delivered Israel through the Red Sea. 14:19-28
Why God divided the Red Sea. Three reasons. 14:16-18
Discussed. 14:16-18

REDEEM - REDEMPTION (See DELIVERANCE; PROPITIATION; RANSOM; RECONCILIATION; SALVATION)
Discussed. 13:13
Fact.
Is the theme of the great book of Exodus. 1:1-22
Two significant facts about **r.** 3:7-8
Meaning. 13:13
Purpose - Results.
To cause the judgment of God to pass over man. 12:1-13:16 (pt.2); 12:1-13; 12:21-51
To cleanse & forgive man for his sins. 12:1-13:16 (pt.4); 12:1-13; 12:21-28
To deliver man from slavery. 12:1-13:16 (pt.3); 12:1-13; 12:21-51
To **r.** & save man. 12:1-13:16; 12:1-13; 12:21-51
Source. The blood of the sacrificial Lamb, the Lamb of God, Jesus Christ. 12:1-13:16; 12:1-13; 12:21-51

REDEEMED, THE
Fact. Are being led to God's holy dwelling (the promised land of heaven). 15:13-18

REDEEMER
Fact.
God is the great Redeemer in every land or nation. 8:22-23
God is the great Redeemer of mankind. 10:1-20

REFORM - REFORMATION (See CONFESSION, FALSE; PROFESSION, FALSE)

REFORM - REFORMATION

Attempts to r. Sincerity is not enough. 8:32; 9:27-28; 10:16-17

What stirs a person to attempt r. Judgment. 8:1-15, esp. 7-8; 8:20-32, esp. 25-29; 9:13-35, esp. 27-28; 10:1-20, esp. 16-17

REFUSE - REFUSING (See **DENIAL; REJECT - REJECTION; UNBELIEF**)

By whom.

Agnostics. 8:1-15

False messiahs. 7:8-11:10 (pt.5); 8:1-15

Followers of the reincarnation philosophy. 8:1-15

Humanists. 9:1-7

Idolaters. 7:8-11:10 (pt.5); 7:14-15; 8:1-15; 8:16-19; 8:20-32; 9:1-7; 9:8-12; 9:13-35; 10:1-2; 10:22-29; 11:1-10; 12:21-51

Results. Judgment. Ten plagues upon Egypt. 7:8-11:10

Warning against r. Will result in chastisement. 15:25-26

REGENERATION (See **BORN AGAIN; CONVERSION; NEW BIRTH; QUICKENING; SALVATION**)

REINCARNATION

Belief in. By many people. 8:1-15

REJECT - REJECTED - REJECTION (See **AGNOSTICISM; ATHEISM; DENIAL; HARD - HARDNESS; REBELLION; STUBBORN; UNBELIEF**)

Of God.

Caused by. Ignorance of God. 7:17

List. Of men who r. God & worshipped themselves or other gods. 7:17

Why men reject.

Disobedience. 3:11-4:17, esp. 4:13

Fear of God. 1:15-21

Ignorance of their times. 1:8-10, esp. 8

Lack of faith in God. 17:2-3

REJOICE - REJOICING (See **HAPPINESS; JOY; PRAISE; WORSHIP**)

RELATIONSHIP WITH GOD

Personal r. The LORD is "my strength," "my song"—five r. are given. 15:1-2

RELATIONSHIPS (See **BROTHERHOOD**)

Destruction, collapsing of r.

Between a husband & wife. 4:24-26

Between a murderer & his victim. 2:11-12

Between a nation & its rulers. 1:8-22

Between a ruler & his servants. Wx.10:7-11, esp. 7

Between a spiritual leader & his people. 14:10-12; 15:24; 16:1-3; 17:2-3

Between brothers. 2:13-14

RELIGION (See **CEREMONY; RELIGIONISTS; RITUAL; TEACHING, FALSE**)

Chart. Of Egyptian gods. 7:8-11:10, Div. Overview

False approaches to r.

By Canaanites. 3:8

By Egyptians. 7:10-13, esp. 11; 7:22-25, esp. 22; 8:7-8, esp. 7; 8:16-18; 9:11

RELIGION, FALSE (See **HUMANISM; OCCULT; REINCARNATION; TEACHING, FALSE**)

Of Canaanites. 3:8

RELUCTANCE - RELUCTANT

What a person is r. to do. Obey God's call. 3:11-4:17, esp. 4:13

REMEMBER - REMEMBERING - REMEMBRANCE

Essential - Importance of. God r. His promises, His covenant with His people. 2:23-25, esp. 24; 3:7-8; 3:13-22, esp. 17; 6:1-5, esp. 4

REMISSION OF SINS (See **FORGIVENESS, SPIRITUAL; PARDON; REDEMPTION**)

Symbolized - Typed - Pictured. By the sacrificial lamb: the Lamb of God, the Lord Jesus Christ. 12:1-13:16 (pt.4); 12:1-13; 12:21-28; Intro. VII, pt.18

REMORSE (See **BROKEN-HEARTED; CONFESSION; CONTRITION; SORROW, GODLY; REPENTANCE**)

RENEW - RENEWAL (See **COMMITMENT; CONVERSION; DEDICATION; SALVATION**)

RENEW - RENEWED

How to be r. By prayer. 5:20-23, see 6:1-7:7

REPENT - REPENTANCE (See **CONVERSION; SALVATION**)

Warning against false r.

Hardens the heart more & more. 8:15; 8:19; 8:32; 9:7; 9:13; 9:34-35, esp. 35; 10:20; 10:27-29; 11:9-10, esp. 10

Leads to more judgment. 9:27-28

REPHIDIM, City of (See **CITIES - AREAS**)

Discussed. 17:1

REPROACH - REPROACHING (See **REBUKE; REPROOF**)

REPROBATE (See **APOSTASY; BACKSLIDING; DENIAL**)

REPROOF - REPROVE (See **REBUKE; REPROACH**)

REPUTATION (See **FAME; RECOGNITION; TESTIMONY**)

Duty. To know the r. of godly men. 1:8-11, esp. 8

RESIST - RESISTANCE

Danger - Warning.

Must not r. God's call. 3:11-4:17, see 3:1-10

Must not r. the Word of God. 5:2-14, esp. 2; 7:14; 7:22-25, esp. 22-23; 8:15; 8:19; 8:32; 9:7; 9:12; 9:34-35; 10:20; 10:27-29

Duty. To r. ungodly instructions. 1:15-21

RESOURCES (See **PROMISES**)

Described - Listed.

Food. 16:4-15

God's name. "I am that I am." 3:13-22, esp. 14

God's name. "I am the LORD." 6:1-5

God's name. "The LORD our Banner." 17:13-16, esp. 15

God's name. "The LORD our Healer." 15:26-27, esp. 26

Godly counsel. 18:13-27, esp. 24-26

Guidance. 13:20-22

Prayer. 17:10-12

Protection from judgment. 12:1-13:16

The world's treasures. 12:34-41, esp. 35-36

Water. 15:25; 17:5-6

RESPECTER OF PERSONS (See **DISCRIMINATION; FAVORITISM; PARTIALITY; PREJUDICE**)

RESPONSIBILITY (See **BELIEVERS; MINISTERS**)

Duty.

To be courageous parents. 2:1-10

To be faithful in work. 3:1-3, esp. 1; 18:13-27

To God & not to men. 1:15-21, esp. 17

To lead others out of bondage. 2:23-25

To obey God. (See **OBEDIENCE**)

To serve God without hesitation. 3:11-4:17

Error - Danger of.

Not delegating r. 18:13-27

Overwork. 18:13-27

REST, HEAVENLY (See **LAND, THE PROMISED; ETERNAL LIFE; HEAVEN**)

REST, SPIRITUAL & ETERNAL (See **LAND, THE PROMISED; ETERNAL LIFE; HEAVEN**)

Discussed. 2:24

God. The promise of the promised land. 2:24 (pt.3)

RESTITUTION (See **RICH - RICHES**)

Duty. To pay r. to freed slaves. 11:1-3

Made by Egypt. Gave all their treasures to God's people. 3:13-22, esp. 21-22; 11:1-31, esp. 2-3; 12:34-41, esp. 35-36

RESTLESS - RESTLESSNESS (See **ANXIETY; IMPATIENCE; PRESSURE; STRESS; TENSION; UNEASINESS**)

Caused by.

A crisis humanly impossible to solve. 15:22-27; 16:1-3; 17:2-3

Distrust, unbelief. Not trusting the care & provision of God. 15:22-27; 16:1-3; 17:2-3

Fear. A hopeless, impossible situation & problem. 14:13-15

RESTORATION (See **CONFESSION; FORGIVENESS, SPIRITUAL; REPENTANCE; SALVATION**)

Of God's people. R. to the promised land. 3:7-8, esp. 8; 3:13-22, esp. 17; 6:1-5, esp. 4; 6:6-9, esp. 8; 13:3-10, esp. 5, see 13:11; 15:13-18, esp. 15-17

Warning. Do not lose hope in God's promise of r. 14:10-12, esp. 11-12

RESTRAINT - RESTRAIN (See **GOD, POWER OF**)

RESURRECTION
Described as. Firstfruits. Hebrew Calendar. 12:1-2

RETALIATION - RESISTANCE (See **HATE; RAGE; REVENGE; VENGEANCE**)

RETRIBUTION (See **JUDGMENT**)

RETURN OF JESUS CHRIST (See **JESUS CHRIST**, Return)
Described as. Feast of Trumpets. Hebrew Calendar. 12:1-2

REUBEN
Son of Jacob. 6:13-27 (Chart)

REUEL or JETHRO (See **JETHRO**)

REVEALED - REVELATION (See **MANIFEST - MANIFESTATION**)
The revelation of several things.
God's glory. In the pillar of cloud. 13:20-22; 16:4-15, esp. 9-10
God's name, His most basic name. 3:13-22, esp. 13-15; 3:14-15
God's presence, glory & holiness. To Moses. 3:1-10
The importance of the sacrificial lamb, the Lamb of God, the Lord Jesus Christ. 12:1-13:16; 12:1-13; 12:21-51
The Shekinah glory. 16:10
The way to escape the judgment of God. 12:1-13:16; 12:1-13; 12:21-51

REVENGE - REVENGEFUL (See **ANGER; RAGE; RETALIATION; VENGEANCE**)
Caused by. Reacting against the godly. 1:8-22; 2:13-15, esp. 15; 5:2-24, see 15-19; 10:22-29; 14:5-9

REVERENCE (See **HONOR**, of God; **WORSHIP**)
Duty. To approach God in r. 3:4-6
For God. Stirred by.
A word from God. 4:27-31, esp. 31
Deliverance by God. 14:29-31, esp. 31
Fear of God. 1:15-21, esp. 17
God's call to man. 3:1-10, esp. 3, 5
Lack of r. Due to unbelief, ignorance of God. 5:2-14, esp. 2

REVILE - REVILER (See **ACCUSATIONS, FALSE; CONFLICT; REPROACH; STRIFE**)

REVIVE - REVIVAL (See **QUICKEN - QUICKENING; RENEW - RENEWAL; REPENTANCE**)

REWARD (See **HOPE; INHERITANCE; PROMISES; SPIRITUAL**)

REWARD OF UNBELIEVERS (See **JUDGMENT**)

RICH - RICHES (See **MATERIALISM; MONEY; RESTITUTION; TREASURE, SPIRITUAL; WEALTH**)
Warning about r. Must not be secured by stealing & slave-labor. 3:13-22, esp. 21-22; 11:1-3, esp. 2-3; 12:34-41, esp. 35-36

RIDICULE (See **MOCKERY**)
Why the godly are r. 5:15-19, esp. 17-18

RIGHTEOUS - RIGHTEOUSNESS (See **GODLY - GODLINESS; JUSTICE; JUSTIFICATION; PERFECTION**)
Described as. The Passover lamb: without any blemish or defect. 12:5
Symbolized - Typed - Pictured in. The Passover lamb: its purity & perfection. 12:5; Intro. VII, pt.16

RIOT - RIOTING (See **MOB**)
Against whom. Moses.
Israelites were about to stone him. 17:4
Israelites were ready to attack him. 5:20-23; 16:1-3

RISE - RISEN (See **JESUS CHRIST**, Resurrection)

RITUAL (See **CEREMONY; RELIGION**)

ROB - ROBBERY (See **STEALING**)

ROCK, THE
Type - Symbol - Picture of. Jesus Christ. 17:6; Intro. VII, pt.31

ROD, OF MOSES
Uses of. Turned into a snake. 4:1-9; 7:10-13; Intro. VII, pt.9

ROOTS, FAMILY
Chart of.
Aaron. 6:13-27
Jacob. 6:13-27
Moses. 6:13-27

RUDE - RUDENESS (See **DISHONOR; MOCKERY; REPROACH; REVILE; RIDICULE**)

RULERS
Fact. Are under the control of God. 9:14-16

SABBATH
Duty. To keep the Sabbath every week. 16:16-30

SACRIFICE (See **COMMITMENT; CROSS - SELF-DENIAL; DEDICATION**)
Duty.
To s. all we are & have. 2:13-15, see Heb.11:24-26
To s., dedicate the firstborn, giving our best to God. 13:11-16

SACRIFICES - SACRIFICIAL SYSTEM
Duty.
To believe, trust the sacrificial lamb & escape judgment. 12:1-13:16; 12:1-13; 12:21-28
To offer s. to God, even when the world does not understand. 3:13-22, esp. 18-19; 5:2-14, esp. 3; 5:15-19, esp. 17

SADNESS (See **DISAPPOINTMENT**)
Caused by. Bondage. 1:8-22; 2:23-25; 5:20-23

SAFETY (See **SECURITY**)

SAINTS (See **BELIEVERS**)

SALVATION - SAVED (See **DELIVERANCE; JUSTIFICATION; REDEMPTION; Related Subjects**)
Duty. To remember the day of our s. Pictured in the Dedication of the Firstborn. 13:1-2
Fact.
Is the theme of the great book of *Exodus*. 1:1-22
Two significant facts about s. 3:7-8
How one is s. - Conditions - Source. God. He Himself takes the initiative to s. 2:23-25; 3:7-8, see 3:9-10; 3:13-22, esp. 17; 4:20-23; 6:1-7:7, esp. 6:1-13; 12:1-13; 12:42-51; 14:29-31
Purpose - Results.
To cause the judgment of God to pass over man. 12:1-13:16 (pt.2); 12:1-13; 12:21-51
To cleanse & forgive man for his sins. 12:1-13:16 (pt.4); 12:1-13; 12:21-28
To deliver man from slavery. 12:1-13:16 (pt.3); 12:1-13; 12:21-51
To save & redeem man. 12:1-13:16; 12:1-13; 12:21-51
Source.
God. He always saves His people—through all. 1:1-7
God's grace. Not by works. Proof is Israel. 1:1-22
God's Son. The blood of the sacrificial Lamb, the Lamb of God, the Lord Jesus Christ. 12:1-13:16; 12:1-13; 12:21-51
Symbol - Type - Picture of.
The ark. 2:3-4; Intro. VII, pt.5
The Passover. 12:1-13; Intro. VII, pt.15

SANCTIFY - SANCTIFICATION (See **SEPARATE - SEPARATION**)
Duty.
To live a holy, s. life from the world. 12:14-20; 12:34-41, esp. 39
To s. your self: purge all leaven (evil) from your life. 12:14-20
To s., give the firstborn—your best—to God always. 13:1-2
To s., give your children to God. 13:1-2
Symbolized - Typed - Pictured. By the Dedication of the Firstborn. Setting apart a life for God. Intro. VII, pt.24

SANITY (See **INSANITY**)

SARCASM (See **MOCKERY; REPROACH; RIDICULE; SCOFFING**)
Caused by.
A hard heart. 5:15-19, esp. 17, 18
A lack of compassion & mercy. 5:15-19, esp. 17, 18

SATAN

Type of. Pharaoh. 1:11-14; 3:7-8; Intro. VII, pt.3

Work - Strategy of.

Arouses believers to enter the depths of sin. 2:11-12

Arouses men & nations to oppress & persecute God's people. 1:8-22; 5:2-14

Arouses men to murder. 1:8-22; 2:11-12

Arouses men to react, to act. 5:2-14, esp. 14

Arouses rulers & nations to war. 14:5-9; 17:8-16

Causes believers to fear. 2:13-14, esp. 14; 14:13-15

Imitates God's power. 7:11-13; 7:22-25, esp. 22; 8:16-18, esp. 18, see 8:19

Promotes the false worship of other gods. 3:8; 7:8-11:10 (pt.6)

Tempts & arouses men to destroy the plan & work of God. 1:8-22; 2:11-25

SATISFACTION, SELF (See **COMPLA-CENT; SLEEP, SPIRITUAL; SLOTH-FUL**)

SATISFACTION, SPIRITUAL (See **ABUNDANCE; BLESS - BLESSINGS; FULNESS, SPIRITUAL; GROWTH, SPIRITUAL; HUNGER, SPIRITUAL; LIFE; NEEDS - NECESSITIES; IN-TRODUCTION, Type Chart**)

Source.

Devotions, daily. 16:16-30

God. Drawing near God. 16:4-15, esp. 9-10

Prayer, meditation. 16:4-15

Receiving the Bread of Life, the Lord Jesus Christ. 16:31

The Bread of Heaven, a picture of Jesus Christ. 16:4

Symbolized - Typed - Pictured. Manna - God's provision: the bread from heaven. Intro. VII, pt.30

SAVAGE - SAVAGERY (See **ABUSE; MURDER; OPPRESSION; PERSE-CUTION; RAGE**)

Caused by.

Anger & hatred. 1:8-22

Seeking revenge. 14:5-9

SAVIOR (See **JESUS CHRIST; SALVA-TION**)

Fact. God is the Savior in every land & nation. 8:22-23

Source - Origin. Was sent by God through Israel to the world. 1:1-22

SCANDAL - SCANDALOUS SINS (See **IMMORTALITY; MURDER; SIN; Related Subjects**)

Discussed.

Accusing falsely. 17:2-3, esp. 3, see 17:4

Complaining, grumbling, murmuring. 15:24

Grumbling & disobedience (unbelief). 16:1-3

Trusting in man instead of God. 17:2-3

SCATTERED

Results. Families torn apart when s. 5:2-14, esp. 12

SCHEME - SCHEMING (See **DECEP-TION; LYING**)

SCIENCE (See **TECHNOLOGY**)

SCOFF - SCOFFERS - SCOFFING - SCORN (See **MOCKERY; RE-PROACH; RIDICULE; SARCASM**)

Characteristic - Trait of. Bitter & vengeful people. 5:2-19, esp. 2

SCOLD - SCOLDING (See **REBUKE**)

SCRIPTURE (See **BIBLE, WORD OF GOD**)

SEA - SEAS (See **CITIES - AREAS**)

Red Sea. Discussed. 14:16-18

SEASONS

Discussed. Hebrew calendar. Agricultural s. 12:1-2

SECOND CHANCE (See **OPPORTUNI-TY**)

Fact. God gives opportunity after opportunity. 10:4-6; 10:21-29

Given to whom.

Moses. Given a second call. 6:28-7:5

Pharaoh, more than once. 5:1-23, esp. 2; 7:11-13, esp. 13; 7:22-25, esp. 22; 8:15; 8:19; 8:32; 9:7; 9:12; 9:34-35; 10:20; 10:27-29, esp. 27

SECOND COMING (See **JESUS CHRIST**, Return)

SECRET - SECRECY (See **EXPOSE - EXPOSURE**)

Secret sins. Impossible to hide. 2:11-12, esp. 2:13-15

SECULAR - SECULARISM (See **HU-MANISM; MATERIALISM; POSSES-SIONS; WORLDLY - WORLDLI-NESS**)

SECULAR WORK (See **BUSINESS; EMPLOYMENT; LABOR; WORK, SECULAR**)

SECURITY (See **ASSURANCE; CON-FIDENCE**)

Comes by - Source.

God.

His Word, His encouragement. 5:20-23, see 6:1-7:17

In protecting His people from judgment. 8:22-23; 9:6; 10:23; 11:7-8; 12:34-41

Obedience. Perfect obedience to God. 12:1-13:16

Persevering prayer. 15:25; 17:8-16

The blood of the sacrificed lamb, the Lord Jesus Christ. 12:1-13:16; 12:1-13; 12:21-51

The LORD, His fighting our enemies for us. 12:13-15

SEDITIONS (See **APOSTASY; DENIAL; REBELLION; REJECTION; UNBE-LIEF**)

SEDUCE - SEDUCTION (See **DECEIVE - DECEPTION; RAPE**)

Of false teaching. The false teaching of the world's idols. 7:8-11:10 (pt.6)

SEE - SEEING (See **HEAR - HEARING; OBEDIENCE; SPIRITUAL SIGHT - UNDERSTANDING**)

SEED or DESCENDENT, THE GODLY (See **SEED, THE PROMISED; GENE-ALOGY, CHARTS**)

SEED, THE PROMISED (See **LINE, THE PROMISED; GRACE, OF GOD**)

Discussed. 1:6-7

Surety of. Fulfilled by God Himself. 1:1-22; 1:6-7

Why God gave the great promise to the world. Five major reasons. 1:1-22

SEEK - SEEKING (See **PERSEVER-ANCE**)

How man seeks God. By prayer. (See **PRAYER**)

Man seeks the things of the world.

Fleshpots of the world. 16:1-3; 17:23

Security of the world. 1:8-10; 14:10-12

Selfish things. Forcing others to serve him. 14:5-12, esp. 5

Wealth & power. 1:8-10; 7:20-21; 8:2-4; 11:1-10

Worldliness, sex, pleasure. 1:1-5; 3:8

SEGREGATION (See **BIGOTRY; DIS-CRIMINATION; PREJUDICE**)

SELF - SELFISH - SELFISHNESS (See **GREED; SELF-SUFFICIENCY**)

SELF-CENTERED (See **ARROGANCE; GLORYING IN MAN; PRIDE; SEL-FISHNESS**)

SELF-CONFIDENCE (See **SELF-SUFFICIENCY**)

Lack of. Moses lacked self-confidence, greatly so. Felt inadequate. 3:11-4:17; 5:20-23

SELF-CONTROL (See **COMMITMENT; DEDICATION; DISCIPLINE; MIND; TEMPERANCE**)

Lack of - Losing self-control.

Because of bitterness against God's messenger. 10:27-29

Because of fear. 14:13-15

Because of seeing someone oppressed. 2:11-12

SELF-DECEPTION (See **DECEIVE - DECEPTION; HYPOCRISY; LYING**)

SELF-DENIAL (See **COMMITMENT; CROSS, DAILY; CROSS - SELF-DENIAL; DEDICATION; DISCI-PLINE; SACRIFICE; SELF-CONTROL; UNSELFISHNESS**)

SELF-DEPENDENCE (See **SELF-SUFFICIENCY**)

SELF-EXALTATION - SELF-IMPORTANCE (See **BOASTING; GLORYING IN MAN; PRIDE**)
Example of.
List of men through history who exalted self above God. 7:17
Ruler who exalted self above God (Pharaoh). 5:2-14, esp. 2; 7:17; 8:1-15
Judgment of God. 7:8-11:10, see 5:2
Results.
Exalting man to be god. 5:2-14, esp. 2; 7:17; 8:1-15
Exalting self (man) above God. 5:2-14, esp. 2; 7:17; 8:1-15
Using power to exalt oneself above others.

SELF-GLORYING (See **BOASTING; GLORYING IN MAN; PRIDE; SELF-EXALTATION; SELF-SUFFICIENCY**)

SELF-INDULGENCE (See **INDULGENCE; LUST; SELFISHNESS; WORLDLINESS**)

SELF-RIGHTEOUS - SELF-RIGHTEOUSNESS (See **HYPOCRISY; RELIGIONISTS**)
Example of. List of men through history who exalted self above God. 7:17
Ruler who exalted self above God (Pharaoh). 5:2-14, esp. 2; 7:17; 8:1-15

SELF-SUFFICIENCY - SELF-SUFFICIENT (See **BOASTING; GLORYING IN MAN; PRIDE**)
Errors of - Misconceptions of.
Blinds one to the truth. 5:2-14, esp. 2
Feeling that one can handle matters by oneself without God (Moses). 2:11-12
Sensing no need for God. 5:2-14, esp. 2; 7:17
Thinking one does not have to obey God. 4:24-26
Results.
Abuse & cruel treatment of people. 5:2-14, esp. 2
Carnal, fleshly behavior, leading to a ruined life. 2:13-15
Chastisement of God. 4:24-26
Exalts self to be god (Pharaoh). 7:17; 8:1-15
Judgment. The hand of God's judgment falling upon one (Pharaoh & the evil Egyptians). 7:8-11:10

SELF-WILL (See **HARD - HARDNESS OF HEART; STUBBORN**)
Results. Ignores the will of God. 5:2-14, esp. 2; 8:15; 8:19; 8:32; 9:7; 9:13; 9:34-35, esp. 35; 10:20; 10:27-29; 11:9-10, esp. 10

SELFISHNESS (See **SELF - SELFISHNESS**)

SENSATIONALISM - SPECTACULAR (See **SIGNS**)

SENSUALITY (See **ADULTERY; CARNAL; FLESH; FORNICATION; IMMORALITY; LUST**, Related Subjects)

SENT (See **AMBASSADOR; CALL - CALLED; COMMISSION; MESSENGER; WITNESSING**)

SEPARATE - SEPARATION (See **DEDICATION; SANCTIFICATION; WORLDLINESS**)
Duty.
To live a holy, **s.** life from the world, a new life. 12:14-20; 12:21-28 (pt.1); 12:34-41, esp. 39
To not allow unbelievers to participate in Feasts. 12:14-20, esp. 15, 19
To put all evil out of one's presence. 12:15-16
Essential. To hide oneself behind the blood of the sacrificed lamb. 12:1-13; 12:21-51; Intro. VII, pt.15, 17, 18
Illustration of. Israel's failure to live a life of **s.** 1:1-5; 3:8

SEPARATION, MARITAL
Fact. Moses apparently separated from his wife, but was later reconciled. 4:24-26; 18:1-8

SERPENT
Fact: Moses' rod was turned into a **s.** 4:1-9; 7:10-13
Symbol - Type - Picture.
Of God's power. His supreme power. 7:8-13
Of Pharaoh's power. 4:1-9 (pt.2); 7:10-13

SERVANT - SLAVES - SLAVERY
Duty. Must **s.** either God or the world. Cannot serve two masters. 8:1; 8:20; 9:1; 9:13; 10:7-11, esp. 7-8

SERVANT, OF GOD (See **AMBASSADOR; MESSENGER; MINISTER**)
Credentials - Qualifications. Three credentials. 7:8-9

SERVE - SERVICE - SERVING (See **HELP - HELPING; MINISTERING; WORKS, GOOD**)
Arguments against. Five arguments against. 3:11-4:17
Call to. (See **CALL - CALLED**)
Are never too old to serve God. 6:28-7:5; 7:6-7
Excuses against. Five excuses against. 3:11-4:17

SEX (See **ADULTERY; FORNICATION; IMMORALITY; LUST**; Related Subjects)

SHAME - SHAMEFUL (See **GUILT**)
Caused by.
A false profession. 9:27-28
Disobeying God & suffering His judgment. 9:27-28; 12:30-33, esp. 32

SHAUL
Grandson of Jacob. Son of Simeon. 6:13-27 (Chart)

SHEEP (See **LAMB**)
Symbol - Type - Picture of.
Jesus Christ. 12:1-13:16; 12:1-13; 12:21-51; Intro. VII, pt.15, 16, 17, 18, 20
Passover Lamb. Sacrifice of. 12:1-13:16; 12:1-13; 12:21-51; Intro. VII, pt.15, 16, 17, 18, 20
Protection from judgment. 12:1-13:16; 12:1-13; 12:21-51; Intro. VII, pt.15, 16, 17, 18, 20

SHEKINAH GLORY (See **GLORY OF GOD**)
Discussed. 16:10
Fact.
Appeared to Moses in the burning bush. 3:1-3
Rebuked Israel for sin of unbelief & grumbling. 16:4-15, esp. 10

SHEPHERD
Fact. Were despised by the Egyptians. 8:25-29
Traits - Characteristics of.
Faithful care of the flock. 3:1-3
Minister. 3:1-3
Who was a **s.** Moses. 3:1-3
Work of. Fivefold work. 3:1-3

SHIMI
Descendent of Jacob. Grandson of Levi. 6:13-27 (Chart)

SHOES
Symbol of. Preparation to enter God's holy presence. 3:4-6, esp. 5

SHUR, DESERT OF (See **CITIES - AREAS**)
Discussed. 15:22

SICK - SICKNESS (See **HEAL - HEALING; SUFFERINGS**)
Caused by. Sin.
Disobedience to God's clear command. 4:24-26
Not keeping God's commandments. 15:25-27
Healed by. God's mercy. 15:26
Purpose. Deliverance from. By God.
If obey Him. 15:25-27
If repent of disobedience. 4:24-26

SIGN - SIGNS
Discussed. 4:8
Fact. Was duplicated by magicians of Egypt. 7:10-13
Given to. Moses. To prove that he was sent by God. 4:1-9
Listed.
Moses' hand. 4:1-2, esp. 6-8
Moses' staff. 4:1-9, esp. 2-5
Water from the Nile. 4:1-9, esp. 9
Purpose.
To confirm the messenger of God. 4:27-31, esp. 30-31
To rebuke sin. 16:4-15, esp. 10

SIMEON
Son of Jacob. 6:13-27 (Chart)

SIN - SINS (See **DEPRAVITY; SINNER; TEMPTATION**)
Acts of sin.
Sins of behavior.
Criticism. 15:24
Grumbling & complaining. 15:24; 16:1-3
Murder. 2:11-14
Sins toward God, Christ, or the Holy Spirit.
Idolatry. 7:8-11:10; Div. Overview
Ignorance of God. 5:2-14, esp. 2
Reluctant obedience. 3:11-4:17
Sorcery. 7:11-13

371

Sins toward others.
  Enslaving people. 1:8-22
  Feeling superior because of race or
    genes. 11:1-10
  Prejudice, feeling superior. 11:1-10
Secret **s.**
  Results. Threefold results. 2:13-15
  Who tried to hide **s.** Moses. 2:13-15

SIN, DESERT OF (See **CITIES -**
AREAS)
  Discussed. 16:1

SINAI, MOUNT (See **CITIES - AREAS**)
  Discussed. 3:1

SINCERE - SINCERITY
  Fact. Is not enough to get us to heaven.
    10:16-17

SING - SINGING
  Occasions for. After a great victory.
    15:1-21

SINNER - SINNERS (See **DEPRAVITY;**
MAN; SIN)

SKEPTIC - SKEPTICISM (See **AG-**
NOSTIC; ATHEIST; DENIAL; HU-
MANISM; REJECTION; UNBELIEF)

SLANDER - SLANDERING (See **ACCU-**
SATION; BLAME; CRITICISM; JE-
SUS CHRIST, Accusations Against;
JUDGING OTHERS; MINISTER; Ac-
cusations against; **TONGUE**)
  Who is it that **s.** People who are unhappy
    with their leader & their God. 17:2-3

SLAVERY - ENSLAVEMENT - SER-
VANT
  Attitude of God to **s.**
    Hates. Despises. Hates oppression,
      abuse, brutality, & savagery. 7:8-
      11:10; 8:20; 9:1-7; 9:1; 11:1-10
    Wills for no people to be enslaved.
      7:15-16
  Duty. To free & pay restitution. 11:1-3
  Sin of.
    Mistreatment, oppression, brutality,
      abuse, savagery. 1:8-22; 5:1-23; 7:8-
      11:10
    Murder. 1:8-22
    Population control. 1:8-22
  Who was **e.** Israel. To Egypt. 1:8-22;
    5:1-23; 7:8-11:10
  Why people are **e.**
    Economic & financial reasons (Egypt).
      1:8-10; 5:2-14; 8:2-4; 11:1-10
    Five reasons. 5:2-14
    Free labor. 1:8-22; 8:2-4; 11:1-10
    Greed. To fill one's pockets. 1:8-10;
      5:2-14; 8:2-4; 11:1-10
    Three reasons. 1:8-10

SLEEP, SPIRITUAL (See **COMPLA-**
CENT; DULLNESS, SPIRITUAL;
HARD - HARDNESS; SLOTHFUL)

SLEEPINESS (See **DULLNESS, SPIRI-**
TUAL; SLEEP, SPIRITUAL; SLOTH-
FUL)

SLOTHFUL - SLOTHFULNESS (See
COMPLACENCY; DULLNESS, SPIR-
ITUAL; INSENSITIVE; HALF-
HEARTED; SLEEP, SPIRITUAL)

SLUGGARD (See **SLOTHFULNESS**)

SLUMBER - SLUMBERED (See **COM-**
PLACENCY; DULLNESS, SPIRI-
TUAL; SLEEP, SPIRITUAL; SLOTH-
FULNESS)

SNAKE (See **SERPENT**)

SNARE - SNARES (See **ENTANGLE;**
WORLDLINESS)

SOCIETY (See **CITIZENSHIP; GOV-**
ERNMENT; WORLD)

SOJOURN - SOJOURNER (See **BE-**
LIEVER; PILGRIM)

SOLDIER (See **MILITARY**)
  Strength of. The arsenal of the world's
    mightiest army. 14:5-9

SON OF GOD (See **JESUS CHRIST**)

SONG (See **PRAISE; SINGING**)
  Of Miriam. Sung after crossing the Red
    Sea. 15:19-21
  Of Moses. Moses' great Son of Praise,
    praising God for His deliverance
    through the Red Sea. 15:1-21

SORCERER - SORCERY (See **AS-**
TROLOGY; MAGICIANS; OCCULT;
SUPERSTITION)
  Described. 7:10-13
  Error of. Men fear & respect supernatural
    forces other than God. 7:10-13; 7:22-25;
    8:7-8; 8:16-18

SORROW - SORROWFUL (See **DISAP-**
POINTMENT; GRIEF; HEAVY -
HEAVINESS; HOPELESSNESS;
SORROW, GODLY)
  Caused by.
    Carnal reaction. 2:11-25
    Judgment of God. 12:29-30
    Unbelief & complaining. 5:20-23;
      14:10-12; 15:24; 16:1-3; 17:2-3

SORROW, GODLY (See **BROKEN-**
HEARTED; COMPASSION; CON-
TRITION; HUMILITY; REPEN-
TANCE)
  Caused by.
    Rejection. By one's own people. Mos-
      es an example. 5:20-23; 15:25; 17:4
    The burdens & sufferings of people.
      2:11
    The sins, complaining, & unbelief of
      people. 15:25; 17:4

SOUL-WINNING (See **PREACHING;**
WITNESSING)

SOUNDNESS—MADE WHOLE (See
BODY, HUMAN; HEALING)

SOVEREIGNTY
  Of God.
    Facts.
      Can stop men from standing before
        Him. 9:11
      Controls all things, even the minute
        dust of the ground. 8:19
      Controls the animals & livestock of
        the world. 9:3-5
      Controls the people, nations, rulers,
        & governments ofthe world.
        9:14-16
      God has no equal. There is no one
        like the LORD. 8:1-15
      Has no equal. No one is like God in
        all the earth. 9:14-16
      Has no equal. No one is like the
        LORD our God. 7:14-25; 8:9-11
      Has power over light & darkness.
        10:21-29
      Has power over the body & health.
        9:11
      Is living. 3:4-6
      Is the God of every land. 8:22-23
      Is the God of true believers. 11:7-8
      Is the Great Savior of mankind.
        10:1-20
      Is the LORD of all power, the LORD
        who executes justice. 8:9-11
      Is the LORD of mercy. 8:9-11
      Is the LORD over the earth.
        9:13-35
      Is the LORD, the God of Redemp-
        tion, the only living & true God.
        7:14-25
      Is the Redeemer in every land, all
        the world. 8:22-23
    Has power over the rulers & nations of
      the world. 9:14-16

SOW - SOWING (See **REAPING; WIT-**
NESSING)

SPACE, OUTER (See **HEAVENLY**
BODIES; HEAVEN & EARTH, NEW)

SPEAK - SPEECH (See **ELOQUENT;**
MESSENGER; MINISTER;
PREACHER; TONGUE)
  Inadequacies of. Feeling one is not elo-
    quent. 4:10-11

SPECTACULAR, THE (See **MIR-**
ACLES; SENSATIONALISM; SIGNS)

SPECULATIONS (See **PHILOSOPHY;**
RATIONALISM; REASONING;
TEACHERS, FALSE)

SPIRIT (See **MAN; SALVATION**)

SPIRITISM (See **ASTROLOGY; MA-**
GICIANS; SORCERY; SUPERSTI-
TION)

SPIRITS, EVIL (See **EVIL SPIRITS;**
SATAN)

SPIRITUAL ABANDONMENT (See
JUDGMENT)

SPIRITUAL BLESSINGS (See **BLESS-**
INGS)

SPIRITUAL BLINDNESS (See **DENIAL; DULLNESS, SPIRITUAL; UNBELIEF**)

SPIRITUAL BONDAGE (See **BONDAGE, SPIRITUAL; ENSLAVEMENT, SPIRITUAL**)

SPIRITUAL DEATH (See **DEATH, SPIRITUAL**)

SPIRITUAL EXPERIENCE (See **BELIEVER; GLORY**)
God knows exactly what spiritual experiences a believer needs. 3:1-10

SPIRITUAL FOUNDATION (See **FOUNDATION, SPIRITUAL; ROCK**)

SPIRITUAL GROWTH - MATURITY (See **GROWTH, SPIRITUAL; MATURITY**)

SPIRITUAL HUNGER (See **HUNGER & THIRST, SPIRITUAL**)

SPIRITUAL IMMATURITY (See **CARNAL; IMMATURITY, SPIRITUAL**)

SPIRITUAL INHERITANCE (See **INHERITANCE; REWARD**)

SPIRITUAL INSENSITIVITY (See **COMPLACENT; SPIRITUAL BLINDNESS; DULLNESS, SPIRITUAL; HARD - HARDNESS**)

SPIRITUAL INSIGHT (See **KNOWLEDGE; SPIRITUAL SIGHT; UNDERSTANDING**)

SPIRITUAL REBIRTH (See **BORN AGAIN; NEW BIRTH; NEW CREATION; NEW MAN; REGENERATION; SALVATION**)

SPIRITUAL SATISFACTION (See **ABUNDANCE; BLESSINGS; FULLNESS, SPIRITUAL; HUNGER & THIRST, SPIRITUAL; SATISFACTION, SPIRITUAL**)

SPIRITUAL SIGHT - SPIRITUAL UNDERSTANDING (See **KNOWLEDGE; UNDERSTANDING**)
Into what. The holiness of God. 3:1-10

SPIRITUAL STRUGGLE - WARFARE
Caused by.
Feeling incapable, sensing one's inability. 3:11-4:17
The enemies of the believer. 17:8-16
Unbelief. 5:20-23; 14:10-12; 15:24; 16:1-3; 17:2-3
Duty.
To discipline & control & fight with all one's might. 7:10-12
To pray. 5:20-23; 15:25; 17:4; 17:10-12
To stand still & watch God's mighty deliverance (before God). 14:13-15
Fact. Believer faces a daily struggle against several things. 3:8

SPIRITUAL THIRST (See **HUNGER & THIRST, SPIRITUAL; SATISFACTION, SPIRITUAL**)

SPIRITUAL WORLD - SPIRITUAL DIMENSION (See **ETERNAL LIFE; HEAVEN**)

SPITE (See **ANGER; BITTER; CONTEMPT; DESPISE; HATRED; MALICE**)

SPOT - SPOTLESS (See **BLAMELESS; CLEAN - CLEANLINESS; FORGIVENESS; PURE - PURITY**)
Symbol - Type - Picture. The Passover Lamb - purity & perfection. 12:5; Intro. VII, pt.16

STABLISH - STABILITY (See **FAITHFULNESS; FOUNDATION; SECURITY**)

STAFF - STAFFING (See **LEADER**)

STAND FAST
Duty.
To s. & watch as the LORD delivers one. 14:13-15
To s. against one's enemies. 17:8-16
To s. in exhaustive work. 18:13-27
To s. in prayer. 17:8-16
To s. in proclaiming God's message: mercy & judgment. 7:8-11:10
To s. in the mission of God despite grumblers & threats. 5:20-23; 14:10-12; 15:22-27; 16:1-36; 17:1-7

STAND FAST - STAND FIRM (See **ENDURANCE; PERSEVERANCE; STEDFASTNESS**)
Duty. To stand firm in the LORD. 14:13-15, esp. 13-14

STATE (See **CITIZENSHIP; GOVERNMENT; NATION**)

STARVATION (See **FAMINE; HUNGER**)
Crisis of. Faced by Israel in the wilderness. 16:1-36

STEALING
Example of. Egyptian stole possessions from Israelites when enslaved them. 3:13-22, esp. 21-22; 12:34-41, esp. 35-36

STEWARDSHIP (See **BENEVOLENCE; GIVING; MINISTERING; TITHE**)
Duty.
To give one's children to God. 13:1-16
To give the first of everything to God. 13:1-2
Lack of. Organization. Wasting time, energy, & people. 18:13-27

STILLNESS (See **QUIETNESS**)
Duty. To be still & watch God's glorious deliverance. 14:13-15

STONE, THE (See **ROCK, THE**)
Type - Symbol - Picture of.
Of Jesus Christ. 17:6
Of living water. 17:5-6; 17:6
Of rest & support. 17:10-12; Intro. VII, pt.34

STORMS (See **CALAMITIES; CATASTROPHE; DISASTER; HAIL; THUNDER-STORM**)
Evidence of - Proof of. Proof that the earth is the LORD's. 9:13-35
Use of. By God. To divide the Red Sea. 14:19-28; 14:29-31

STRANGER - STRANGERS (See **PILGRIMS**)
Described as. Believer. In the promised land. 18:1-8 (pt.3)
Fact. Moses named his son Gershom, meaning "a stranger" in a strange land. 18:1-8 (pt.3)

STRENGTH - STRENGTHEN (See **POWER**)
Source of s.
God's Word, His encouragement. 6:1-5, see 5:20-23
Prevailing prayer. 17:8-16
Standing still. Watching the power of God's deliverance. 14:13-15
The LORD. To conquer the enemies that attack believers. 17:8-16
The LORD. To walk through the impossible obstacles. 14:13-15

STRESS (See **ANXIETY; IMPATIENCE; PRESSURE; TENSION; UNEASINESS**)

STRIFE (See **ARGUMENT; CONFLICT; DIVISION**)
Source - What causes s.
Abuse, mistreatment, misunderstanding, feeling wronged. 5:20-23
Agnosticism, atheism. 7:17
Denial of God. Not knowing God. 5:2-14, esp. 2; 7:17
False accusations & criticism. 5:20-23; 14:10-12, see 14:15; 15:25; 16:1-3; 17:4
Fear. 14:10-12; 17:8-16
Greed, wealth, power. 1:8-22; 5:2-14; 8:2-4; 11:1-10
Unsupportive spouse. 4:24-26

STRIVE - STRIVING (See **DEDICATION; DILIGENCE; ZEAL**)

STRONG (See **POWER; STRENGTH**)

STUBBORN (See **HARD - HARDNESS; REJECTION; SELF-WILL; UNBELIEF**)

STUDY (See **DEVOTION; MEDITATION; WORD OF GOD**)

SUBSTITUTION
Symbolized - Typed - Pictured.
The death of Christ. 12:1-13
The lamb. Died as a s. for the believer. 12:1-13; Intro. VII, pt.15, 17

SUCCOTH, City of (See **CITIES - AREAS**)
Discussed. 13:20

SUFFERING (See **DISEASE; PERSE-CUTION; SICKNESS; TRIALS - TRIBULATIONS**)
Caused by.
 Evil rulers & oppressors. 1:8-22; 5:2-14; 7:8-11:10
 Judgment. Of sin, evil, brutal oppression, & rejection of God. 7:8-11:10
 Sin. Disobedience to God. 4:24-26
Deliverance from **s**.
 By prayer. 5:20-23
 By repenting & obeying God. 4:24-26
Duty. Not to distrust God when **s**. 14:10-12; 15:24; 16:1-3; 17:2-3

SUPERNATURAL (See **MIRACLES**)

SUPERSTITION (See **ASTROLOGY; MAGICIANS; SOOTHSAYERS; SORCERY**)

SUPPLICATION (See **INTERCESSION; PRAYER**)

SUPPLY (See **NEEDS - NECESSITIES; SATISFACTION, SPIRITUAL**)

SUPPLY, DIVINE (See **BLESSINGS; FULNESS, SPIRITUAL; NEEDS; SATISFACTION, SPIRITUAL**)
What God **s**.
 Bread. 16:1-36
 Deliverance through the greatest of trials: the Red Sea. 14:1-31
 Food. 16:1-36
 His presence, guidance by day & by night. 13:17-22
 Necessities of life. 15:22-27; 16:1-36; 17:1-7
 Victory over enemies—all trials. 17:8-16
 Water. 15:22-27; 17:1-7

SURETY (See **ASSURANCE; CONFIDENCE; SECURITY**)

SURRENDER (See **COMMITMENT; CONSECRATION; CROSS, DAILY; DEDICATION; DEDICATION; HEART; SELF-DENIAL**)
Duty.
 To be so surrendered that one becomes an instrument in the LORD's hands. 3:1-10, see 3:11-4:17; see 4:18-31
 To give one's whole body to God. 13:3-10
To God. Moses **s**. to God's call. 4:18-31

SWAYING (See **BACKSLIDING; DOUBLE-MINDED; FICKLE; HALF-HEARTED**)

SYMBOL - SYMBOLS (See **TYPES**)

SYMPATHY - EMPATHY (See **CARE; COMPASSION; LOVE**)

TABERNACLES, FEAST OF (See **FEASTS**)
Date when celebrated. Hebrew Calendar. 12:1-2

TABLES (See **CHARTS**)

TALENT - TALENTS (See **ABILITY**)

TEACH - TEACHER - TEACHING (See **INSTRUCT - INSTRUCTION**)
Duty. To teach children. (See **CHILDREN**, Duty toward)

TEACHERS, FALSE (See **APOSTASY; DECEIVE; RELIGIONISTS**)
List of men through history who questioned or denied. 7:17

TEACHING, FALSE (See **APOSTASY; TEACHERS, FALSE**)
Error of. Deceives. 7:8-11:10 (pt.6); 7:10-13; 7:22-25; 8:7-8; 8:16-18
Message - Teaching of.
 Exalts the spirit of man to be god. 8:1-15
 Humanism. 8:1-15
 Reincarnation. 8:1-15

TECHNOLOGY (See **SERVICE**)
Purpose. To build the most advanced war machines possible. 14:5-9

TEMPERANCE - TEMPERATE (See **DISCIPLINE; SELF-CONTROL**)

TEMPORAL (See **CORRUPTION; MATERIALISM**)

TEMPTATION
Described as. A wilderness experience. 13:17-18:27
Duty.
 Must not complain, grumble, murmur, or disobey. 15:24; 16:1-3; 17:2-3
 Must not give in to discouragement. 5:20-23; 14:13-15, esp. 15; 17:4
 Must not yield to unbelief. 5:20-23; 14:10-12; 15:22-27; 16:1-3; 17:2-3

TEN COMMANDMENTS (See **COMMANDMENTS**)

TENDER - TENDERNESS - TENDER-HEARTED (See **COMPASSION; MERCY; MINISTERING; SYMPATHY**)
Of God.
 For the crushed, broken, desperate. 6:1-5, esp. 5
 Stirred by the sufferings of His people. 3:7-8; 3:9-10
Results.
 Can change our lives. 2:11
 Meets the needs of the world. 2:11

TENSION (See **ANXIETY; PRESSURE; STRESS; UNEASINESS**)
Caused by.
 Being falsely accused & criticized. 5:20-23; 14:10-12, see 15; 15:25; 16:1-3; 17:4
 Divided family; unsupportive spouse. 4:24-26; 18:1-8
 Facing impossible trials, problems, & obstacles. 5:20-23; 14:10-12, see 15; 15:25; 16:1-3; 17:4
 Murder. 2:13-14
 Overwork. 18:13-27
 Unbelief, not trusting God's care & provision. 5:20-23; 14:10-12, see 15; 15:25; 16:1-3; 17:4

TERROR (See **FEAR; FRIGHT**)
Caused by.
 Judgment of God. 9:22-26, see 9:27-28
 Life-threatening trial & situation. 12:29-33; 14:19-27, esp. 25
 Sin. Moses killed an Egyptian & had to flee for his life. 2:11-25

TEST - TESTING
Man **t**. God. Israel questioned God's goodness & demanded He prove Himself. 17:2-3
Of Israel.
 God **t**. their faith, trust. 16:4-15
 Why God **t**. Israel. Several reasons. 15:25
Purpose of **t**.
 Seven purposes. 15:25
 Three reasons. 17:1
 To **t**. their faith, trust. 16:4-15; 17:10-12

TESTAMENT, OLD (See **BIBLE; COVENANT, OLD; WORD OF GOD**)

TESTIMONY (See **WITNESS - WITNESSING**)
Duty - Essential.
 For believers to have a good **t**. (Moses). 2:13-15
 For believers to have a strong **t**. of prayer. 5:20-23; 15:25; 16:4-15, esp. 4-5, 11-12; 17:4; 17:8-16

THANKFUL - THANKFULNESS - THANKSGIVING (See **GRATITUDE; PRAISE; REJOICING; WORSHIP**)
Duty.
 To give **t**. publicly after God delivers & saves. 15:1-21
 To thank God for always giving us victory through Christ. 17:8-16
 To thank God for answered prayer. 4:27-31, esp. 31

THIEVES - THEFTS (See **STEALING**)

THIRST
Crisis of.
 Second crisis of Israel in the wilderness at Marah. Bitter Waters Made Sweet. 15:22-27
 Fourth crisis of Israel in the wilderness at Rephidim: God's Provision. 17:1-7
Fact.
 Cannot be satisfied with bitter water. 15:22-27
 Water is one of the basic needs of man. 15:1-7

THIRST, SPIRITUAL (See **FOOD, SPIRITUAL; HUNGER, SPIRITUAL; WATER, LIVING**)
Source of satisfaction.
 Living water, the Lord Jesus Christ. 17:1-7; Intro. VII, pt.31
 Not found in the wells of this earth, but in Jesus Christ. 15:22-23; 15:25; 17:1-7; 17:6
 Pure water, the Lord Jesus Christ. 15:22-27; Intro. VII, pt.29

Symbol - Type - Picture.
God's healing, His sweetening or purifying of the bitter trials of life. 15:22-27; 15:26; Intro. VII, pt.29
God's provision of water, living water. 17:1-7; 17:6; Intro. VII, pt.31

THOUGHT - THOUGHTS (See **MIND; THINKING, POSITIVE; WISDOM**)
Evil thoughts.
Caused by - Source. The heart. 1:8-22; 7:11-13, esp. 13; 7:22-25, esp. 22-23; 8:15; 8:19; 8:32; 9:7; 9:34-35; 10:20; 10:27-29, esp. 27
Creates false gods. 7:8-11:10 (pt.6)

THUNDERSTORM (See **STORMS**)
Fact. Was one of the ten plagues cast upon Egypt. 9:13-35

TIME
Facts. God knows the exact & the best time to act. 2:23-25; 3:7-8; 3:13-22, esp. 16-17; 6:6-9
Fullness of. God sent His Son to earth in the fullness of **t**. 12:6-11 (pt.1)

TIME, FULNESS OF (See **FULNESS OF TIME**)

TIRED - TIREDNESS (See **BURDENED; PRESSURE; WEARY - WEARINESS; YOKE**)
Caused by.
Poor organization. 18:13-27
Prevailing in prayer to the point of exhaustion. 17:10-12
Solution to.
Delegation of responsibility. 18:13-27
Friends who will share advice & counsel. 18:13-27
People who will help. 17:10-12
Reorganization. 18:13-27
The Rock of rest & support, the Lord Jesus Christ. 17:10-12 (pt.4); 17:6; Types Intro. VII, pt.34

TITHE - TITHING (See **STEWARDSHIP**)

TONGUE (See **BOASTING; COMPLAINING; SPEAKING EVIL; WORDS**)
Duty. To pray, not complain, grumble, & murmur. 14:10-12; 15:24; 16:1-3; 17:2-3
Sins of.
Complaining, grumbling, & murmuring. 5:20-23; 14:10-12; 15:24; 16:1-3; 17:2-3
Threatening others. 17:4

TORMENT (See **FIRE, EVERLASTING; HELL; JUDGMENT; LAKE OF FIRE**)

TRADITION (See **CEREMONY; RELIGION; RELIGION, FALSE; RITUAL; TEACHING, FALSE**)

TRAINING (See **DISCIPLES**, Training of; **TEACHERS - TEACHING**)

TRAITORS (See **APOSTASY; DENY - DENIAL; REJECTION; UNBELIEF**)

TRANSFORM - TRANSFORMED - TRANSFORMATION (See **CONVERSION; NEW CREATION; NEW LIFE; RENEW - RENEWAL; REPENTANCE**)

TRANSGRESSION (See **SIN; TRESPASS; Specific Sin of Interest**)

TREASURE, SPIRITUAL (See **BLESSINGS; FULNESS, SPIRITUAL; RICHES**)

TREE
Fact. God used a **t**. to purify the waters of Marah for His people. 15:25

TREE, FAMILY
Chart of.
Aaron. 6:13-27
Jacob. 6:13-27
Moses. 6:13-27

TRESPASS (See **TRANSGRESSION; SIN; Specific Sin of Interest**)

TRIALS - TRIBULATIONS (See **LIFE**, Storms of; **SUFFERING; TEMPTATION**)
Attitude toward. Complaining or trusting God. 15:22-23
Caused by.
Man himself. Brings **t**. upon himself. How? Several ways. 17:1
Sin & rebellion against God. 7:8-13; 7:14-25; 8:1-15; 8:16-19; 8:20-32; 9:1-7; 9:8-12; 9:13-35; 10:1-20; 10:21-29; 11:1-10; 14:1-4
Unbelief. 6:6-9
Deliverance through **t**. - How to conquer.
By God.
His faithfulness. 1:1-7
Leads away from all **t**. 13:17-18
By heeding the message of God. Threefold challenge. 14:13-15
Of Israel. (See **ISRAEL**, Trials - Crises of)
Purpose of.
Seven purposes. 15:25
To test & prove us. 15:25; 16:4-15, esp. 4; 17:7; 17:10-12

TRIUMPH (See **CONQUER; OVERCOMERS; VICTORY - VICTORIOUS LIVING**)
Described as. A glorious **t**. 15:1-2

TROUBLEMAKER (See **ARGUMENTS; COMPLAINING; GRUMBLING; JUDGING OTHERS; SLANDER**)

TRUCEBREAKERS
Example of. Pharaoh broke his agreement to free Israel. 8:15; 8:32; 9:34-35; 10:20

TRUMPETS, FEAST OF
A somber assembly before the Day of Atonement. 12:1-2

TRUST - TRUSTED (See **BELIEVE - BELIEVING; FAITH; OBEDIENCE**)
Duty.
Not to put trust in man but in God. 17:2-3
To **t**. God day by day, to **t**. Him every day. 16:16-27
To **t**. God to take care of one's needs, not to complain. 15:24; 16:1-3; 17:2-3
To **t**. one's soul to God, not to complain. 14:10-12

TRUSTS, FALSE
Error - Mistake of. Trusting man not God. 17:2-3

TRUSTWORTHY (See **FAITH - FAITHFULNESS**)
Example of. Moses.
Served despite false accusations & grumbling & attacks of his own people. 14:10-12; 15:24; 16:1-3; 17:2-3
Served despite facing impossible obstacles. 14:5-9
Served despite opposition. 14:10-12; 15:24; 16:1-3; 17:2-3
Served until he was totally exhausted. 18:13-27

TRUTH - TRUTHFULNESS
Source of. Bible. Exposes the **t**. of God's people, their sins. Intro. V, Special Features
Those who reject the **t**. Deny God's existence. 2:17; 5:2-24, esp. 2

TURNING BACK
Who turned back. Pharaoh turned back from God. 8:15; 8:32; 9:34-35; 10:20
Who wanted to turn back. Israel. 14:10-12; 16:1-3; 17:2-3

TYPES - SYMBOLS - PICTURES (See **Introduction VII, Type Chart**)
Discussed.
Aaron: a picture of a spokesman or ambassador. 4:13-17; 4:27-31; 6:13-7:7; Intro. VII, pt.11
Bitter herbs: the bitter days of Israel's slavery to sin. 12:6-11; Intro. VII, pt.19
Bitter waters at Marah: bitter trials of life. 15:22-27; 15:26; Intro. VII, pt.29
Blood from the lamb: the forgiveness of sin. 12:1-13:16; 12:6-11; 12:12-13; Intro. VII, pt.18
Burning bush: a picture of the glory, presence, & holiness of God. 3:1-10; Intro. VII, pt.8
Children of Israel: the people of God. 1:1-7; 1:6-7; Intro. VII, pt.1
Circumcision: a sign of God's covenant with man. 4:24-26; Intro. VII, pt.12
Dedication of the firstborn: sanctification, setting apart. 13:1-16; Intro. VII, pt.243; Intro. VII, pt.24
Egypt: a picture of the world. 1:8-22; Intro. VII, pt.2
Egyptian magicians: a picture of false messengers. 7:10-13; Intro. VII, pt.14

Eliezer, Moses' youngest son: God is my Helper. 18:1-8 (pt.3) ; Intro. VII, pt.36

Gershom, Moses' eldest son: a stranger in a strange land. 2:15-22 (pt.5) ; Intro. VII, pt.6

Jehovah Nissi: God's name is the banner of the believer. 17:13-16; 17:15; Intro. VII, pt.35

Leaven: evil. 12:1-13:16 (pt.7); 12:14-20; 12:34-41 (pt.4) ; Intro. VII, pt.21

Manna: God's provision, the Bread from heaven. 16:1-36; 16:31; Intro. VII, pt.30

Massah: testing. 17:7; Intro. VII, pt.33

Meribah: argument, contention, & strife. 17:7; Intro. VII, pt.32

Moses' basket (ark): salvation, safety, & security. 2:3-4; 2:3; Intro. VII, pt.5

Moses' leprous hand: God's power over health, disease, life, sin, & death. 4:1-9 (pt2); 4:6-7; Intro. VII, pt.10

Moses' staff: God's power over Pharaoh & over Egypt. 4:1-9; Intro. VII, pt.9

Moses: a comparison with Christ. 3:1f; Intro. VII, pt.7

No broken bones on the lamb: a picture of unity. 12:42-51 (pt.1) ; Intro. VII, pt.23

Passover Feast: salvation, deliverance from God's judgment. 12:1-13:16; 12:1-13; 12:21-28; Intro. VII, pt.15

Passover Lamb: purity & perfection. 12:5; Intro. VII, pt.16

Pharaoh's defeat: a picture of God's complete & total victory over enemies. 14:1-31; Intro. VII, pt.28

Pharaoh: a picture of Satan. 1:11-14; Intro. VII, pt.3

Red Sea: a picture of deliverance through the greatest trials & obstacles. 14:1-31; 14:16-18; Intro. VII, pt.27

Roasting & eating of the Passover lamb: identifying with the lamb's death. 12:6-11; Intro. VII, pt.20

Rock at Rephidim: God's provision of water. 17:5-6; 17:6; Intro. VII, pt.31

Slaughter of the lamb: substitutionary atonement. 12:1-13:16; 12:6-11; 12:12-13; Intro. VII, pt.17

Taskmasters: a picture of evil men persecuting God's people. 1:11-14; Intro. VII, pt.4

Ten plagues: a picture of God's judgment upon all who reject Him & oppress people. 7:8-11:10; Intro. VII, pt.13

The pillar of cloud & fire: a picture of God's awesome presence & guidance. 13:20-22; 16:10; Intro. VII, pt.26

The stone that Moses sat upon: a picture of support & salvation. 17:10-12 (pt.4) ; Intro. VII, pt.34

Unleavened Bread: a picture of urgency, of the believer's new life of righteousness. 12:1-13:16 (pt.7); 12:14-20; 12:34-41 (pt.4) ; Intro. VII, pt.22

Wilderness wanderings (journey): the pilgrimage of the believer. 13:17-18:27; Intro. VII, pt.25

UNBELIEF (See **AGNOSTICISM; ATHEISM; DENIAL; HARDNESS; LOST, THE; MAN; REJECTION**)

Caused by.
  Greed. 1:8-22; 5:2-14; 8:2-4; 11:1-10
  Hard heart. 7:14; 8:15; 8:19; 8:32; 9:7; 9:12; 9:17-21; 9:34-35; 10:1; 10:27-29
  Ignorance of God. 5:2-14, esp. 2
Example of. List. Of men throughout history who rejected God. 7:17
In what. God.
  His care & provision. 15:24; 16:1-3; 17:2-3
  His power to deliver from one's enemies. 14:10-13
List of unbelievers. List of men throughout history who rejected God. 7:17
Of Israel. Was one of two great sins of Israel. 16:1-36; 16:16-30
Source. Heart of man. 13:17-18:27

UNBELIEVERS

Nature - Who unbelievers are.
  A person who comes to God some way other than Christ's blood. 12:6-11 (pt.4)
  A person who does not believe in the blood of the lamb. 12:6-11 (pt.2); 12:12-13
  A person who does not hide behind the blood of Christ. 12:21-28 (pt.1)
  A person who does not separate—set his life apart—to God. 12:42-51
  A person who roams out in the world. 12:21-28 (pt.1)
  Double-minded. A ruler (Pharaoh) who repented but turned back time & again. 8:15; 8:32; 9:34-35; 10:20

UNBLAMABLE (See **BLAMELESS; CLEANLINESS; FORGIVENESS; PERFECTION; RIGHTEOUSNESS; SPOTLESS**)

UNBLEMISHED (See **BLAMELESS; CLEANSED; PERFECTION; RIGHTEOUSNESS; SPOT - SPOTLESS**)

Symbolized - Typed - Pictured. By the Passover Lamb - purity & perfection. 12:5; Intro. VII, pt.16

UNCERTAIN - UNCERTAINTY (See **ASSURANCE; INSECURITY; INSTABILITY; SECURITY**)

Answers to - Deliverance from **u**.
  By placing the anchor of one's hope in God. 14:13-15
  By prayer—intercessory prayer. 5:20-23; 17:8-16

UNCHANGEABLE - UNCHANGEABLENESS (See **GOD**, Nature; **JESUS CHRIST**, Nature)

UNCLEAN - UNCLEANNESS (See **DEFILE - DEFILEMENT; FILTHY - FILTHINESS; POLLUTION; SIN**, Results; **UNCLEANNESS**)

UNDEFILED (See **CLEANSED; MORALITY; PERFECTION; PURITY; RIGHTEOUSNESS; SPOTLESS**)

UNDERSTANDING (See **INSIGHT; KNOWLEDGE; SPIRITUAL SIGHT; WISDOM**)

Lack of.
  Not **u**. severe crises & problems. 15:25; 17:4
  Not **u**. why God's mission seemingly failed (Moses). 5:20-23
  Not **u**. why one faces an impossible obstacle. 14:13-15, esp. 15

UNEASY - UNEASINESS (See **ANXIETY; IMPATIENCE; PRESSURE**)

UNEQUALLY YOKED

Caused by. Disobedient, unsupportive wife. 4:24-26; 18:1-2 (pt.2)

UNFAITHFUL - UNFAITHFULNESS (See **BACKSLIDING; COMPROMISE; DISOBEDIENCE; FAITHFULNESS; LUKEWARM; NEUTRALITY; UNBELIEF**)

UNFRUITFUL - UNFRUITFULNESS (See **BACKSLIDING; COMPROMISE; DISOBEDIENCE; HALF-HEARTED; LUKEWARM**)

UNGODLY - UNGODLINESS (See **DEPRAVITY; EVIL; GODLESS; LOST, THE; SIN; UNBELIEVERS; UNGODLINESS; UNRIGHTEOUSNESS**)

Judgment of. (See **JUDGMENT**)

UNHOLY (See **DEFILED; FILTHY; SIN; UNCLEAN**)

UNITY (See **BROTHERHOOD; DIVISION; FELLOWSHIP; NEIGHBOR; ONENESS**)

Result. Will protect us against our enemies. 13:17-18
Source - Comes by. Jointly partaking of Christ. 12:42-51, esp. 46
Symbolized - Typed - Pictured.
  By Jesus Christ. Having no broken bones. 12:42-51; Intro. VII, pt.23
  By the sacrificed lamb. Having no broken bones. 12:42-51; Intro. VII, pt.23

UNIVERSE (See **HEAVEN & EARTH, NEW**

New **u**. Will be recreated into a new **u**. 2:24

UNJUST, THE (See **LOST, THE; UNBELIEVERS; UNGODLY, THE**)

UNLEAVENED BREAD, FEAST OF (See **FEASTS**)

Discussed. 12:14-20; Intro. VII, pt.22
Fact. Is closely tied to the Passover. 12:1-13:16
Symbol - Type - Picture.
  Righteousness. 12:14; Intro. VII, pt.22
  The need to rush away from evil toward the promised land. 12:14-20; 12:17-19; Intro. VII, pt.22

UNMERCIFUL (See **HATE; MALICE; WRATH**)
Caused by.
Greed & power, economic & financial reasons. 1:8-10; 5:2-14; 8:2-4; 11:1-10
Mean & ruthless spirit. 5:2-14
Population control. 1:8-22; 5:1-23

UNREST (See **ANXIETY; IMPATIENCE, RESTLESS; STRESS; TENSION; UNEASINESS**)

UNRIGHTEOUSNESS - UNRIGHTEOUS, THE (See **DEPRAVITY; SIN; UNGODLY; UNBELIEVER; WICKEDNESS**)

UNSAVED (See **LOST, THE; UNBELIEVERS; UNGODLY, THE**)

UNSELFISH - UNSELFISHNESS (See **CROSS, DAILY; SELF-DENIAL; HUMILITY**)
Example of. Aaron. Served in second place to Moses. 4:13-17; 4:27-31; 5:1; 6:13-27; 6:28-7:7

UNWILLING - UNWILLINGNESS
Result. Makes excuses against God's call. 3:11-4:17
Result. Rejects the plea for compassion & mercy (Pharaoh). 5:2-14, esp. 2; 7:14-16; 8:20; 9:1; 9:13-14; 10:3-4

UNWORLDLINESS (See **SPIRITUAL; WORLDLY - WORLDLINESS**, Deliverance from)

UNWORTHY - UNWORTHINESS (See **HUMILITY; MEEKNESS**)

URGENT - URGENCY (See **OPPORTUNITY; READINESS; TIME**)
Duty.
To repent: rush away from evil while still time. 12:1-13:16 (pt.7); 12:14-20; Intro. VII, pt.22
To turn away from the old life & begin the new life while still time. 12:1-13:16 (pt.7); 12:14-20; Intro. VII, pt.22

UTOPIA (See **HEAVEN; HEAVEN & EARTH, NEW; HOPE; PROMISES**)

UZZIEL
Descendent of Jacob. Grandson of Levi. 6:13-27 (Chart)

VAIN (See **EMPTY; PURPOSELESS**)

VARIANCE (See **ARGUMENT; DIVISION; STRIFE**)

VAUNT - VAUNTING OF SELF (See **ARROGANCE; BOASTING; GLORYING IN MAN; HAUGHTINESS; PRIDE; SELF-SUFFICIENCY**)

VENGEANCE (See **RETALIATION; REVENGE**)
Warning.
God will take v. 12:29; 14:16-18; 14:19-28
To those who oppress His people. 6:28-7:7; 17:13-16

VICTORY
How to achieve v.
By heeding God's threefold challenge. 14:13-15
By prayer, intercessory prayer. 17:8-16
By trusting God's care, provision, & power. 14:1-31; 15:1-21; 15:22-27; 16:1-36; 17:1-7; 17:8-16
What does man need v. over.
Bitter trials & experiences. 15:22-27
Complainers, grumblers, murmurers. 15:24; 16:1-3; 17:2-3
Despair. 14:13-15, esp. 15; 17:4
Emptiness: spiritual hunger & thirst. 16:1-36; 17:1-7
Enemies. 14:1-31; 17:8-16
Evil men. 1:8-22; 5:2-14; 7:8-11:10
Fear. 14:13-15; 17:4
Impossible trials, obstacles & problems. 14:1-31
Loneliness: spiritual emptiness, hunger, & thirst. 16:1-36; 17:1-7
Oppression, persecution. 1:8-22; 5:2-14; 7:8-11:10
Purposelessness: lack of fulfillment & satisfaction. 16:1-36
Sense of inability, lack of talent. 3:11-4:17
Unbelief; distrust. 5:20-23; 14:10-12; 15:24; 16:1-36; 17:2-3

VIGILANT - VIGILANCE (See **DILIGENCE; ENDURANCE; PERSEVERANCE; READINESS; STEDFASTNESS; WATCHFULNESS**)

VINDICTIVE (See **RETALIATION; REVENGE; VENGEANCE**)

VIOLENCE (See **ABUSE; MURDER; OPPRESSION; PERSECUTION**)

VIRTUE (See **MORALITY; PURITY; SPOTLESS; TRUTH; UNDEFILED**)

VISION, WORLDWIDE
Of God. Called Israel to be His missionary force to the world. 1:1-22 (pt.2)

VOCATION (See **CALL - CALLED; EMPLOYMENT; LABOR; WORK**)

VOW - VOWS (See **COMMITMENT; DEDICATION; PROMISE**)

WAGES (See **EMPLOYEE; EMPLOYER; EMPLOYMENT; LABOR; WORK, SECULAR**)
Fact. Egyptians paid Israelites for goods & w. stolen during enslavement years. 3:13-22, esp. 21-22; 12:34-41, esp. 35-36

WAGES OF SIN
Warning.
Moses reaped the loss of everything because of murder. 2:11-25
Pharaoh & his people reaped the ten plagues of judgment & a devastated economy & nation. 7:8-11:10

WAITING UPON THE LORD (See **PRAYER**)

WAKEFULNESS, SPIRITUAL (See **WATCH - WATCHFULNESS**)

WALK, BELIEVER'S (See **BELIEVER, Life - Walk; WILDERNESS WANDERINGS**)

WANDERERS (See **APOSTASY; BACKSLIDING; DENIAL; TURNING BACK**)

WANDERINGS, WILDERNESS (See **WILDERNESS WANDERINGS**)

WANT (See **NEEDS - NECESSITIES**)

WAR - WARFARE
Victory over.
Amalekites: through prevailing prayer. 17:8-16
Egyptian military: by God's great deliverance. 14:1-31
Victory through prayer. Helping others. 18:1-27

WARFARE, SPIRITUAL (See **SPIRITUAL STRUGGLE - WARFARE**)
Power of. Prevailing prayer. 17:13-16

WARN - WARNING
Against unbelief - against hardening one's heart. 5:2-14, esp. 2; 7:11-13; 7:14; 8:15; 8:19; 8:32; 9:7; 9:12; 9:34-35; 10:1-2; 10:20; 10:27-29; 11:9-10

WASHED - WASHING, SPIRITUAL (See **CLEANSED; FORGIVENESS; PURE - PURITY**)

WATCH - WATCHED - WATCHFULNESS
Duty.
To stand still & w. the salvation of the LORD when facing trials. 14:13-15
To w. in prayer. 17:8-16
Meaning. 2:11, pt.3

WATER (See **THIRST; THIRST, SPIRITUAL; WATER, LIVING**)
Fact. Was turned into blood in Egypt by God as a plague. 7:14-25
How to secure. By prayer. 15:25; 17:4
Plague upon. Turned to blood by God to judge Egypt. 7:14-25
Type - Symbol - Picture of.
Bitter water: the bitter trials & experiences of life. 15:22-27; Intro. VII, pt.29
Jesus Christ. 17:5-6; 17:6; Intro. VII, pt.31
Man's spiritual thirst. 17:1-7
What w. does. Quenches thirst. 15:22-27; 17:1-7

WATER, LIVING
Source. Not the wells of this earth but Jesus Christ. 15:22-23; 17:5-6
Type - Symbol - Picture of.
Jesus Christ. 15:22-27; 17:5-6; 17:6; Intro. VII, pt.31
Spiritual thirst. 17:1-7; Intro. VII, pt.31

WAVER - WAVERING (See **BACK-SLIDING; COMPROMISE; DOUBLE-MINDED; FICKLENESS; HALF-HEARTED; INCONSISTENT; IN-STABILITY**)

WEALTH (See **MATERIALISM; RICHES**)
  Love of. Causes men to oppress & enslave others. 1:8-22; 5:2-14; 8:2-4; 11:1-10

WEARY - WEARINESS (See **BURDENED; LABOR; OVERWORK; PRESSURE; TIRED; YOKE**)

WEEPING (See **BROKEN-HEARTED; CRYING; REMORSE; SORROW, GODLY**)

WELCOME - WELCOMING (See **GREETING; HOSPITALITY**)

WHISPERING - WHISPERERS (See **BUSYBODIES; COMPLAINING; GOSSIP; GRUMBLING; MURMUR-ING; SLANDER**)

WICKED - WICKEDNESS (See **DE-PRAVITY; EVIL; GODLESS; SIN; UNGODLINESS; UNRIGHTEOUS-NESS**)
  Source of. The heart. 7:11-13; 7:14; 8:15; 8:19; 9:7; 9:12; 9:34-35; 10:20; 10:27-29; 11:9-10

WIFE - WIVES (See **FAMILY; PAR-ENTS; WOMEN**)
  Of whom. Moses. Discussed. 2:15-22, esp. 21; 4:20-26; 18:1-8

WILDERNESS
  Described. 13:17-18:27

WILDERNESS WANDERINGS (See **BELIEVER**, Life - Walk; **PILGRIM; SOJOURNING; STRANGER**)
  Discussed. 13:17-18:27; Intro. VII, pt.25
  Reveals depravity, sinfulness of the human heart. 13:17-18:27
  Why God led Israel through the wilderness wanderings. Seven reasons. 13:17-18:27
  Where Israel stopped in Egypt.
    Etham. 13:20
    Pi Hahiroth. 14:2
    Succoth. 13:20
  Where Israel stopped in the wilderness.
    Elim: abundant provision. 15:27
    Desert of Sin. Third Crisis. Hunger: God's provision of food. 16:1-36
    Marah. Second crisis. Bitter water: bitter experiences made sweet. 15:22-27
    Red Sea. First crisis. Crossing the Red Sea: God's great deliverance. 14:1-31
    Rephidim:
      Fourth crisis. God's provision of water. 17:1-7
      Fifth crisis. Warfare: victory through prevailing prayer. 17:8-16
      Sixth crisis. Marital separation & overwork. 18:1-27

WILL OF GOD (See **GOD**, Nature of; Sovereignty of)

WISDOM (See **INSIGHT; KNOWL-EDGE; UNDERSTANDING**)
  Of men. (See **DENIAL; IDOLATRY; PHILOSOPHY; REASON - REA-SONING; UNBELIEF**)

WISE MEN
  Described. 7:10-13

WITCHCRAFT (See **ASTROLOGY; SOOTHSAYER; SORCERY; SU-PERSTITION**)

WITNESS - WITNESSING (See **MES-SENGER**)
  Call to w. Israel was chosen by God to be His w. to the world. 1:1-22

WITNESSING TO GOD & CHRIST (See **MESSAGE; MESSENGER; MISSION-ARIES; PREACHING; TEACHING; TESTIMONY**)
  Call to. (See **CALL - CALLED**)
  Duty.
    To proclaim God's message of deliverance to God's people. 4:27-31
    To proclaim God's message of deliverance to rulers. 5:1; 7:8-11:10
  Problems confronting w.
    Denial of God. 7:7
    Hard hearts. (See **HARD – HARD-ENED**)
    Ignorance of God. 5:2-14, esp. 2
    Unwilling heart. 5:2-14, esp. 2

WONDERS (See **MIRACLES**)

WORD OF GOD (See **BIBLE; NEW TESTAMENT; OLD TESTAMENT; SCRIPTURE; TRUTH**)
  Source. Given to the world by God through Israel. 1:1-22

WORDS (See **TONGUE**)

WORK, PHYSICAL or SECULAR (See **EMPLOYMENT; LABOR**)
  Dangers of. Overwork (Moses). 18:13-27
  Duty.
    To be diligent in all w. (Moses). 18:13-27
    To guard against overwork. 18:13-27
  Fact. Sin has caused oppressive, enslaved w., a struggle for survival. 1:8-22; 5:2-14

WORKS, GOOD (See **HELP - HELP-ING; MINISTERING; SERVICE**)

WORLD (See **CITIZENSHIP; GOV-ERNMENT; NATIONS; UNIVERSE**)
  Fact.
    God is the God of all the w. 8:22-23
    To be recreated in a new w. 2:24
  Symbol - Type of. Egypt. 1:8-22; 3:7-8; 7:8-11:10; 12:1-13:16; 14:1-31

WORLD HISTORY (See **HISTORY**)

WORLD, SPIRITUAL (See **ETERNAL LIFE; HEAVEN; SPIRITUAL WORLD**)

WORLDLY - WORLDLINESS (See **COMPROMISE; SEPARATION**)
  Deliverance from.
    By choosing God instead of the pleasures of sin. 12:14-20
    By separating from the world. 12:34-41
  Judgment of. 12:1-13:16
  Illustration of. Israel compromised with the world of the Canaanites. 1:5; 3:8
  Sin of. Wanting to return to the w., its pleasures. 16:1-3; 17:2-3
  Symbol - Type - Picture. Egypt. 1:8-22; 3:7-8; 7:8-11:10; 12:1-13:16; 14:1-31

WORRY (See **ANXIETY; INSECURI-TY**)

WORSHIP (See **CHURCH; PRAISE; PRAYER; REVERENCE; THANKSGIVING**)
  Duty. To worship God daily. To have daily devotions. 16:16-30; 16:31
  Of idols. (See **IDOLATRY**)
  Stirred by.
    Proclaiming God's great promise of deliverance. 4:27-31
    Victory over enemies. 15:1-21; 15:13-16

WORSHIP, FALSE (See **GOD'S, FALSE; IDOLATRY**)
  Of Egypt. Were following a false w. 12:12-13
  Of many gods (polytheism). A common practice by many people. 7:14-25

WRATH (See **ANGER; HOSTILITY; VIOLENCE**)

WRATH OF GOD (See **ANGER**, of God; **HOSTILITY; JUDGMENT**)
  Caused by - Reason. Hard & unrepentant hearts. 7:11-13; 7:14; 8:15; 9:19; 9:7; 9:12; 9:34-35; 10:20; 10:27-29; 11:9-10; 14:1-31
  Deliverance from. By the blood of the Lamb. 12:1-13:16; 12:1-13; 12:21-51

WRATH OF MAN (See **ANGER; HOS-TILITY; VIOLENCE**)
  Results. Brutal & savage oppression & enslavement of people. 5:1-23

YAHWEH (See **NAME - NAMES**)
  Discussed. 3:14-15; 4:10-11
  Meaning. 3:14-15; 4:10-11
    Basic meaning of name. 6:1-5

YIELD (See **CONSECRATION; CROSS, DAILY; DEDICATION; SELF-DENIAL; SURRENDER**)
  Duty.
    To be so yielded that one becomes an instrument in the LORD's hands. 3:1-10, see 3:11-4:17; see 4:18-31
    To give one's whole body to God. 13:3-10
    To God. Moses y. to God's call. 4:18-31

YOKE (See **BONDAGE; SLAVERY**)

YOUTH - YOUNG PEOPLE (See **CHILDREN**)

ZEAL - ZEALOUS (See **DEDICATION; DILIGENCE; ENDURANCE; ENTHUSIASM; PERSEVERANCE; STEDFASTNESS**)

Example of. Moses. In his daily work. 18:13-27

ZICHRI

Descendent of Jacob & Levi. Grandson of Kohath. 6:13-27 (Chart)

ZITHRI

Descendent of Levi. Son of Uzziel. 6:13-27 (Chart)

ZODIAC (See **OCCULT**)

Fact. People worship the z.; believe the stars determine their fate, destiny. 7:14-25

ZOHAR

Grandson of Jacob. Son of Simeon. 6:13-27 (Chart)

LEADERSHIP MINISTRIES WORLDWIDE

PURPOSE STATEMENT

LEADERSHIP MINISTRIES WORLDWIDE exists to equip ministers, teachers, and laypersons in their understanding, preaching, and teaching of God's Word by publishing and distributing worldwide *The Preacher's Outline & Sermon Bible*® and derivative works to reach & disciple all people for Jesus Christ.

MISSION STATEMENT

1. To make the Bible so understandable – its truth so clear and plain – that men and women everywhere, whether teacher or student, preacher or hearer, can grasp its message and receive Jesus Christ as Savior, and…

2. To place the Bible in the hands of all who will preach and teach God's Holy Word, verse by verse, precept by precept, regardless of the individual's ability to purchase it.

The Preacher's Outline & Sermon Bible and derivative works have been given to LMW as LMW Resources for printing and distribution worldwide at/below cost, by those who remain anonymous. One fact, however, is as true today as it was in the time of Christ:

THE GOSPEL IS FREE, BUT THE COST OF TAKING IT IS NOT

LMW depends on the generous gifts of believers with a heart for Him and a love for the lost. They help pay for the printing, translating, and distributing of LMW Resources into the hands of God's servants worldwide, who will present the Gospel message with clarity, authority, and understanding beyond their own.

LMW was incorporated in the state of Tennessee in July 1992 and received IRS 501 (c)(3) non-profit status in March 1994. LMW is an international, nondenominational mission organization. All proceeds from USA sales, along with donations from donor partners, go directly to underwrite translation and distribution projects of LMW Resources to preachers, church and lay leaders, and Bible students around the world.

LMW RESOURCES

This material, like similar works, has come from imperfect man and is thus susceptible to human error. We are nevertheless grateful to God for both calling us and empowering us through His Holy Spirit to undertake this task. Because of His goodness and grace, ***The Preacher's Outline & Sermon Bible***® New Testament and the Old Testament volumes have been completed.

LMW Resources include *The Minister's Personal Handbook, The Believer's Personal Handbook,* and other helpful resources available in printed form as well as electronically on various digital platforms.

God has given the strength and stamina to bring us this far. Our confidence is that as we keep our eyes on Him and remain grounded in the undeniable truths of the Word, we will continue to produce other helpful resources for God's dear servants to use in their Bible study and discipleship.

We offer this material, first, to Him in whose name we labor and serve and for whose glory it has been produced and, second, to everyone everywhere who studies, preaches, and teaches the Word.

Our daily prayer is that each volume will lead thousands, millions, yes even billions, into a better understanding of the Holy Scriptures and a fuller knowledge of Jesus Christ the Incarnate Word, of whom the Scriptures so faithfully testify.

You will be pleased to know that Leadership Ministries Worldwide partners with Christian organizations, printers, and mission groups around the world to make LMW Resources available and affordable in many countries and foreign languages. It is our goal that *every* leader around the world, both clergy and lay, will be able to understand God's holy Word and present God's message with more clarity, authority, and understanding—all beyond his or her own power.

LEADERSHIP MINISTRIES WORLDWIDE
1928 Central Avenue • Chattanooga, TN 37408
1(800) 987-8790
Email: info@lmw.org
lmw.org

11/22

Product Listing

THE PREACHER'S OUTLINE & SERMON BIBLE® (POSB)   *Available in KJV (44 vols) & NIV (40 vols)*

OLD TESTAMENT

- Genesis I: Chs. 1–11
- Genesis II: Chs. 12–50
- Exodus I: Chs. 1–18
- Exodus II: Chs. 19–40
- Leviticus
- Numbers
- Deuteronomy
- Joshua
- Judges, Ruth
- 1 Samuel
- 2 Samuel
- 1 Kings
- 2 Kings
- 1 Chronicles
- 2 Chronicles
- Ezra, Nehemiah, Esther
- Job
- Psalms I: Chs. 1-41
- Psalms II: Chs. 42-106
- Psalms III: Chs. 107-150
- Proverbs
- Ecclesiastes, Song of Solomon
- Isaiah I: Chs. 1-35
- Isaiah II: Chs. 36-66
- Jeremiah I: Chs. 1-29
- Jeremiah II: Chs. 30-52, Lamentations
- Ezekiel
- Daniel, Hosea Joel, Amos, Obadiah, Jonah, Micah, Nahum
- Habakkuk, Zephaniah, Haggai, Zechariah, Malachi

NEW TESTAMENT

- Matthew I: Chs. 1–15
- Matthew II: Chs. 16–28
- Mark
- Luke
- John
- Acts
- Romans
- 1 & 2 Corinthians
- Galatians, Ephesians, Philippians, Colossians
- 1 & 2 Thessalonians, 1 & 2 Timothy, Titus, Philemon
- Hebrews, James
- 1 & 2 Peter, 1, 2, & 3 John, Jude
- Revelation
- Master Outline & Subject Index

Handbooks

- **What the Bible Says to the Believer** — The Believer's Personal Handbook
  11 Chapters. – Over 500 Subjects, 300 Promises, & 400 Verses Expounded - Gift leatherette or paperback options

- **What the Bible Says to the Minister** — The Minister's Personal Handbook
  12 Chapters. - 127 Subjects - 400 Verses Expounded - Gift leatherette or paperback options

- **What the Bible Says to the Business Leader**—The Business Leader's Personal Handbook
  12 Chapters – Over 100 topics plus hundreds of scriptural values for conducting business in a 21st-century world — Paperback

- **What the Bible Says About Series** — Various Subjects

everyWORD

Scripture, Outline, Commentary of the Gospels with ESV Scripture

- everyWORD: Matthew 1–16:12

- everyWORD: Matthew 16:13–28:20

- everyWORD: Mark

- everyWORD: Luke 1–13:21

- everyWORD: Luke 13:22–24:53

- everyWORD: John

- **The Teacher's Outline & Study Bible™** - Various New Testament Books
  Complete 30 - 45 minute lessons – with illustrations and discussion questions
- *Practical Illustrations — Companion to the POSB Arranged by topic and Scripture reference*
- *LMW Resources on various digital platforms Learn more on our website at lmw.org*
- *Contact for resources in other languages*

Contact Us

LEADERSHIP MINISTRIES WORLDWIDE
1928 Central Avenue • Chattanooga, TN 37408
1(800) 987-8790 • E-mail - info@lmw.org
Order online at lmw.org